FOR
STUDENTS

Over the past four years we have spent time in classrooms across Canada, speaking to students just like you.

We've asked what you want to see in a textbook, how you learn, how many hours a week you spend online, and what you find most valuable when preparing for a test. Based on your feedback, we've developed a new hybrid learning solution—**LOOK**. Your textbook, the Chapter Review cards, and the online resources found at **www.icanlookinout.com** present a new, exciting, and fresh approach to learning. Check out the website for great tools like

- Interactive quizzing
- Interactive e-book
- Flashcards
- Games
- PowerPoint slides
- Videos
- **And more!**

NELSON / EDUCATION

LOOK, Canadian Edition

by Ronald B. Adler, Judith A. Rolls, and Russell F. Proctor II

Vice President, Editorial Director:
Evelyn Veitch

Editor-in-Chief, Higher Education:
Anne Williams

Executive Editor:
Laura Macleod

Senior Marketing Manager:
Amanda Henry

Senior Developmental Editor:
Linda Sparks

Photo Researcher:
Nicola Winstanley

Permissions Coordinator:
Nicola Winstanley

Content Production Manager:
Jennifer Hare

Production Service:
Bill Smith Group

Copy Editor:
Sheila Wawanash

Proofreader:
Jennifer Hwo

Indexer:
Anesi Indexing

Senior Production Coordinator:
Ferial Suleman

Design Director:
Ken Phipps

Managing Designer:
Franca Amore

Interior Design:
Greg Devitt

Cover Design:
Johanna Liburd (front cover) and Sharon Lucas

Cover Images:
© Heide Benser/Corbis (male with video phone); Yuri_Arcurs/iStockphoto (female with headset)

Compositor:
Bill Smith Group

Printer:
RR Donnelley

Library and Archives Canada Cataloguing in Publication Data

Main entry under title:

Adler, Ronald B. (Ronald Brian), 1946-
LOOK/Ronald B. Adler, Judith A. Rolls, Russell F. Proctor II. — Canadian ed.

Includes bibliographical references and index.
ISBN: 978-0-17-650410-6

1. Interpersonal communication—Textbooks. I. Rolls, Judith A. (Judith Ann) II. Proctor, Russell F. III. Title.

BF637.C45A335 2011
158.2   C2010-907368-1

ISBN 13: 978-0-17-650410-6
ISBN 10: 0-17-650410-9

Looking Out, Looking In
Brief Contents

James Lauritz/CORBIS

Andy Cox/Stone/Getty Images

© Masterfile Corporation (Royalty-free Division)

Looking Out, Looking In
Contents

Kevin Winter/Getty Images

Image Source

chsher bakova yuliya/Shutterstock

© iStockphoto.com/sjlocke

Looking Out, Looking In

Contents

Dmitriy Shironosov/Shutterstock

Philip Date/Shutterstock

© iStockphoto.com/Jodi Matthews

Looking Out, Looking In

Contents

© iStockphoto.com/Cliff Parnell

20th Century Fox/The Kobal Collection

CHAPTER 1

A FIRST LOOK AT INTER-PERSONAL COMMUNICATION

Learning Outcomes

LO¹ Assess the needs (physical, identity, social, and practical) that communicators are attempting to satisfy in a given situation or relationship.

LO² Apply the transactional communication model to a specific situation.

LO³ Describe how the communication principles on pages 9–10 and misconceptions on pages 10–11 are evident in a specific situation.

LO⁴ Describe the degree to which communication is qualitatively impersonal or interpersonal, as well as the consequences of this level of interaction.

LO⁵ Diagnose the effectiveness of various communication channels in a specific situation.

LO⁶ Use the criteria on pages 17–20 to determine the level of communication competence in a specific instance or a relationship.

LO¹
Why We Communicate

As human beings, we are clearly wired for interaction and most of us wouldn't opt to live in isolation. In fact, isolation is so painful it is used as a punishment in penal systems. Bob Kull studied the effects of isolation by secluding himself on an island off the coast of Chile while he was gathering data for his Ph.D. dissertation at the University of British Columbia. He concluded that while there were moments of bliss, it was hard to escape the spiritual and emotional darkness to which he was subjected.[1] This perspective is in keeping with that of W. Carl Jackson, an adventurer who sailed around the Atlantic Ocean in 21 days and wrote that "I found life without people had no meaning."[2] Further, when former news correspondent Terry Anderson reflected on his seven years as a hostage in Lebanon, he said flatly, "I would rather have had the worst companion than no companion at all."[3]

It appears that what human beings really want is communication and relationships. This need for connection and interaction seems even more pronounced today. People are in constant touch with friends, family, and colleagues through the various miracles of technology. They feel cut off from the world without their electronic devices. In fact, many students can barely get through an entire class without them. Overall, we communicate to fulfil our physical, identity, and social needs and to attain practical goals.

Mandy Godbehear/Shutterstock

Physical Needs

It's hard to believe that communication affects our physical health and can even be a matter of life or death. Frederick II, emperor of Germany from 1196 to 1250, may inadvertently have been the first person to prove this point:

> He bade foster mothers and nurses to suckle the children, to bathe and wash them, but in no way to prattle with them, for he wanted to learn whether they would speak the Hebrew language, which was the oldest, or Greek, or Latin, or Arabic, or perhaps the language of their parents, of whom they had been born. But he laboured in vain because all the children died. For they could not live without the petting and joyful faces and loving words of their foster mothers.[4]

We now know that a lack of social relationships negatively affects our health, and medical researchers have provided considerable evidence of this. For example, socially isolated people are four times more susceptible to the common cold[5] and three times more likely to die prematurely. The type of relationship doesn't seem to matter: Marriage, friendship, religious, and community ties all seem to increase longevity.[6] Compared to their married counterparts, divorced men and women have higher cancer rates.[7] Further, the death of a close relative increases the likelihood of your own death.[8] Even living in an unhappy marriage can increase illness rates by 35 percent and reduce life span by an average of four years.[9]

By contrast, a life that includes positive relationships leads to better health. Socializing for 10 minutes a day, for example, improves memory and boosts intellectual function,[10] and stress hormones decline the more often people hear expressions of affection.[11] This might account for why the Canadian Health Network's definition of wellness is broad-based and recognizes the importance of social support and close personal relationships.[12] This stance is acknowledged elsewhere, as well. A hospital in Ireland opened a pub on its premises to help short- and long-term residents meet their social needs. Because much of Irish life centres on the pub, the facility affords an opportunity for seniors to interact with the other daily patrons. The pub provides a more inviting atmosphere than sitting in a residents' lounge, with nothing to see or do.[13]

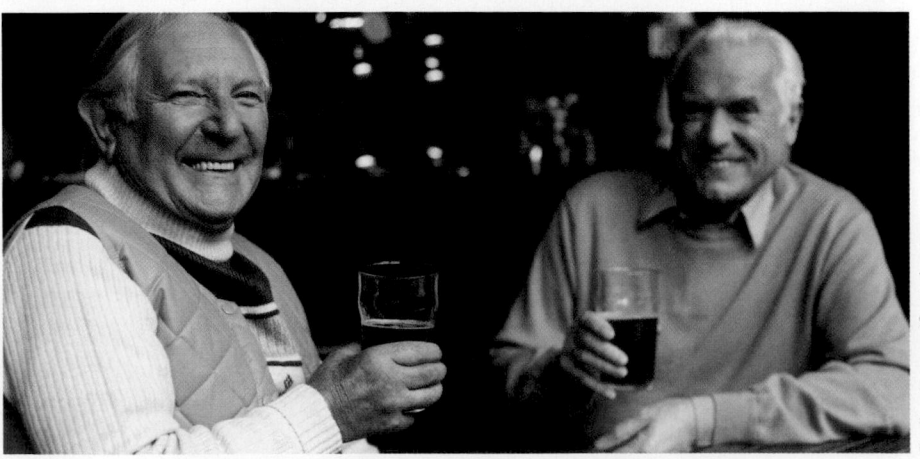
Radius Images/Getty Images

Identity Needs

In addition to helping us survive, communication is the only way we learn who we are; our sense of identity comes from our interactions with others. Learning if we're smart, creative, skilled, or inept does not come from looking in the mirror but from seeing how others react to us.

Deprived of communication, we would have no sense of ourselves. Communication scholar John Stewart dramatically illustrates this in *Bridges Not Walls*, where he cites the famous "Wild Boy of Aveyron" case. The boy was discovered in France, digging for vegetables in a village garden. Spending his childhood without contact, he showed no human social behaviours—he couldn't speak and uttered only weird cries. More significant was his lack of any identity as a human being. As author Roger Shattuck put it, "The boy had no human sense of being in the world. He had no sense of himself as a person related to other persons."[14] Only with the influence of a loving "mother" did the boy begin to behave—and, we can imagine, think of himself—as a human. Like the boy of Aveyron, each of us enters the world with little or no sense of identity and we learn who we are through others.

The film *Cast Away* captures the pain of being isolated from communication with others.

> You're tattooed on my skin
> Don't know where you end
> and I begin
> You're tattooed on my soul
> Are you the part that makes
> me whole
>
> —Damhnait Doyle and Christopher Ward,
> "Tattooed"

Social Needs

Besides helping to define who we are, communication also satisfies a whole range of social needs that include pleasure, affection, companionship, escape, relaxation, and control.[15]

Research suggests a strong link between effective interpersonal communication and happiness. In a study of over 200 college students, the happiest 10 percent described themselves as having a rich social life.[16] In another study, women reported that "socializing" was more satisfying than virtually any other activity.[17] Married couples who are effective communicators are reported to be happier than less skilful couples.[18]

In spite of knowing that communication is vital to social satisfaction, many people aren't very successful at managing their interpersonal relationships. One study revealed that 25 percent of the 4,000-plus adults surveyed knew more about their dogs than about their neighbours' backgrounds.[19]

Research also suggests that the number of close friendships we have is in decline. A 1985

Invitation TO INSIGHT

The Marathon

After Tanya Brann-Barrett, a communication professor at Cape Breton University, ran her first Boston Marathon, she said that she could never have done it without the help of so many others. She expressed her gratitude to all those who clapped, yelled, and reached out with their hands and hearts; to the little boys who jumped with glee as their fingers touched hers; to the women of Wellesley College for their screams, energy, and enthusiasm; to the lone man who held a Nova Scotia flag; to the woman from Vancouver who shared her Canadian pride; to the man who shouted, "Only 200 yards to the cut of the hill and it's all downhill after that"; to the people of Boston, whose resounding cheers came from every window in every building to help her through the last mile; to her special friend for having faith that she could realize her dream; to her running sisters, who supported her through months of training and monitored her race from home; to her parents for their unconditional love; and to her husband and two sons, who screamed her name as she ran the last few yards. As she said, "While some may imagine that a marathon is a solitary journey, for me, nothing could be further from the truth."

In what ways did communication help Tanya to satisfy her physical, social, identity, and practical needs?

T. Brann-Barrett, "Thank You," unpublished document, May 2004.

study reported that North Americans had an average of 2.94 close friends, but 20 years later, that number had dropped to 2.08.[20] It's also worth noting that educated individuals had larger and more diverse networks than those with less education. Because positive relationships with others are so vital, some theorists argue that they may be our single most important source of satisfaction and emotional wellbeing, and that this holds across cultures.[21]

> Most people have a sense of belonging with someone. Everyone wants to belong.
>
> —Dr. David Kuhl,
> *What Dying People Want: Practical Wisdom for the End of Life*

Practical Goals

Finally, communication is used most often to satisfy our **instrumental goals**: getting others to do what we want. Some instrumental goals are quite basic. For example, communication is the tool that lets you tell the hairstylist to take just a little off the sides or makes it possible to negotiate household duties. Other instrumental goals are more important. Career success is a prime example. One study showed that the ability to speak and listen effectively were the top factors that helped university graduates find jobs.[22] On-the-job communication is just as important. The Conference Board of Canada, in its *Employability Skills 2000+* pamphlet, identified a set of characteristics required "to enter, stay in, and progress in the world of work." Of these, basic communication skills such as speaking, listening, reading and writing, problem solving, demonstrating positive attitudes and behaviours toward others, adaptability, and teamwork all fall within the rubric of good interpersonal communication.[23]

Psychologist Abraham Maslow suggested that the physical, identity, social, and practical needs we have been discussing fall into five hierarchical categories, each of which must be satisfied before moving on to the next.[24] The most basic of these needs are *physical*: air, water, food, rest, and the ability to reproduce. The second level is *safety*: protection from threats to our well-being. Beyond physical and safety needs are the *social* needs we have mentioned already. The third level

has to do with *self-esteem*: the desire to believe that we are worthwhile, valuable people. The final category described by Maslow is *self-actualization*: the desire to develop our potential to the maximum, to become the best person we can be. As you read on, think about the many ways in which communication is necessary to satisfy these needs.

FIGURE 1.1
Maslow's Hierarchy of Needs

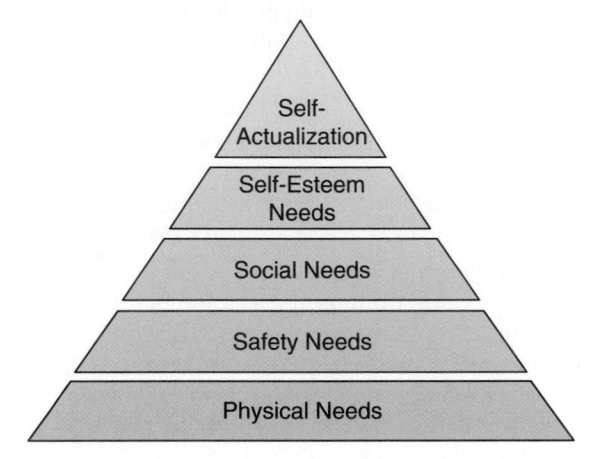

LO²
The Process of Communication

We've been discussing *communication* as though the meaning of this word were perfectly clear. Before going further, we need to explain systematically what happens when people exchange messages. This will introduce a working vocabulary that will be used throughout the text.

A Linear View

In the early days of studying communication as a social science, researchers thought of communication as something that a sender "does" to a receiver, and this resulted in a **linear communication model**.

FIGURE 1.2
Linear Communication Model

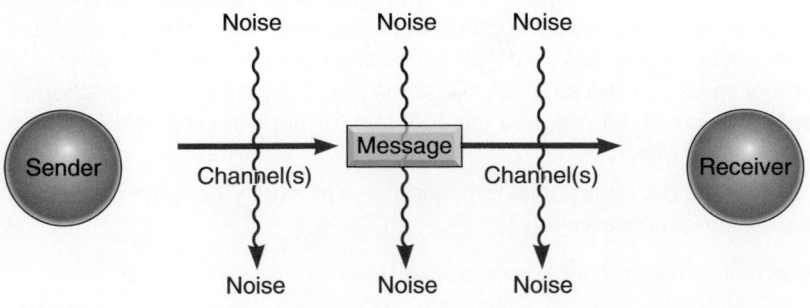

Instrumental goals
Goals aimed at getting others to behave in desired ways.

Linear communication model
A characterization of communication as a one-way event in which a message flows from sender to receiver.

According to the linear model in Figure 1.2 (p. 6),

a **sender** (the person creating the message)

encodes (puts thoughts into symbols, usually words) a

message (the information being transmitted), sending it through a

channel (the medium through which the message passes) to a

receiver (the person attending to the message) who

decodes (makes sense of the message), while contending with

noise (distractions that disrupt transmission).

Notice how the vocabulary in Figure 1.2 sounds like the language of electronic media. There is a linear, machinelike quality to familiar phrases such as "We're having a communication breakdown" and "I don't think I'm getting through to you." But these familiar phrases—and the thinking they represent—obscure important features of human communication, and hence the model doesn't really represent what occurs in interpersonal interaction. That is why more advanced models have been developed. Of particular interest is the transactional model of communication.

A Transactional View

The **transactional communication model** (Figure 1.3) expands the linear model to better capture communication as a uniquely human process. Some concepts and terms from the linear model are retained in the transactional model, while others are enhanced, added, or eliminated.

The transactional model uses the word *communicator* instead of *sender* and *receiver*, thus reflecting the simultan-

eous nature of communication. Consider, for example, what might occur when you and a housemate negotiate chores. As soon as you begin to hear (receive) the words sent by your partner, "I want to talk about cleaning the kitchen..." you grimace and clench your jaw (sending a nonverbal message of your own while receiving the verbal one). This reaction leads your housemate to interrupt herself defensively, sending a new message: "Now wait a minute..."

A transactional model also shows that communicators often occupy different **environments**—fields of experience that affect how they understand others' behaviour. In communication terminology, *environment* refers not only to a physical location but also to the personal experiences and cultural background that participants bring to a conversation.

Consider some factors that might contribute to different environments:

- Person A might belong to one ethnic group and person B to another.
- A might be rich and B poor.
- A might have lived a long, eventful life and B might be young and inexperienced.
- A might be passionate about a subject and B indifferent to it.

Sender
The creator of a message.

Encode
The process of putting thoughts into symbols, most commonly words.

Message
Information sent from a sender to a receiver.

Channel
The medium through which a message passes from sender to receiver.

Receiver
One who notices and attends to a message.

Decode
The process in which a receiver attaches meaning to a message. Synonymous with interpretation.

Noise
External, physiological, or psychological distractions that interfere with the accurate transmission and reception of a message.

Environments are not always obvious. Notice how the model in Figure 1.3 shows that the environments of A and B overlap. This area represents the background that the communicators have in common. As the shared environment becomes smaller, communication becomes more difficult. For example:

- Bosses who have trouble understanding the perspective of their employees are less effective managers, and workers who do not appreciate the challenges of being a boss are more likely to be uncooperative.

FIGURE 1.3

Transactional Communication Model

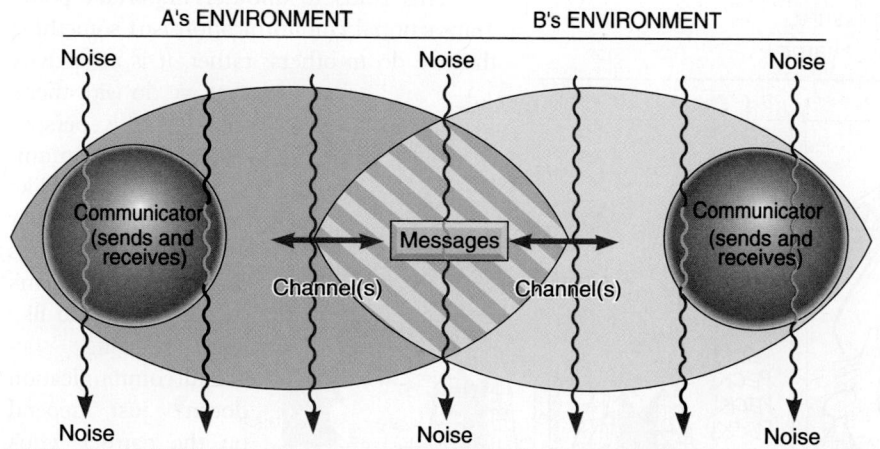

- Parents who have trouble recalling their youth are likely to clash with their children, who have no idea that parenting is such a huge responsibility.
- Members of a dominant culture who have never been part of a minority may not appreciate the concerns of people from non-dominant cultures, whose own perspectives make it hard to understand the cultural blindness of the majority.

Communication channels retain a significant role in the transactional model, and their importance can be seen in the following example: Should you say "I love you" in person? Over the phone? By renting space on a billboard? Via e-mail? In a voice mail? In a text message? Channel selection matters even more when sending breakup messages. A recent study of 1000 cellphone users found that 45 percent had used their phones to end a relationship—usually by text![25]

The transactional model also retains the concept of noise but broadens its focus. In the linear model, the focus is on noise in the channel—what is known as *external noise*—such as loud music or too much cigarette smoke in a crowded room. But in the transactional model, noise also resides *within* communicators. This includes *physiological noise*—biological factors that interfere with accurate reception, such as illness, fatigue, hearing loss,

and so on—and *psychological noise*: forces within that interfere with the ability to understand a message accurately. For instance, a student might become so upset that he failed a test that he is unable (or unwilling) to understand where he went wrong. Psychological noise can cause many communication problems.

> **It's not surprising that communication between human beings is so difficult, considering that so much of what each of us feels most deeply can't help but seem the merest trivia to almost everyone else.**
>
> —Alden Nowlan,
> *Various Persons Named Kevin O'Brien*

For all the insights they offer, models can't capture some important features of interpersonal communication. A model is a "snapshot," but communication more closely resembles a "motion picture." In real life it's difficult to isolate a single discrete "act" of communication from the events that precede and follow it.[26] Consider the *Zits* cartoon on this page. If you read only the final frame, Jeremy appears to be the victim of his mother's nagging. If you then read the first three frames, you might conclude that if Jeremy were more responsive to his mother, she might not need to be so persistent. And if you watched the two of them interact over the days and weeks preceding the incident in this cartoon, you would have a larger (but still incomplete) picture of the relational history that contributed to this event. In other words, the communication pattern that Jeremy and his mother have created together contributes to the quality of their relationship.

This leads to another important point: Transactional communication isn't something that we do *to* others; rather, it is an activity that we do *with* them. In this sense, person-to-person communication is rather like dancing with a partner in that it depends on another person's involvement. And like good dancing, successful communication doesn't just depend on the partner who's

TABLE 1.1

Examples of Noise

External Noise
Sounds, running motors, talking, music, smoke, temperature, perfumes, smells, visual distractions, clothing, lighting, language, nonverbal communication, culturally diverse mannerisms

Physiological Noise
Pain, hunger, fatigue, visual problems, pounding heart, body temperature, thirst, itch, twitching, hearing loss, numbness, dizziness

Psychological Noise
Embarrassment, anger, disappointment, confusion, nervousness, inadequacies, fear, joy, pressure, boredom, pessimism, optimism, apathy, shame

leading. Both partners must coordinate their movements. Likewise, the way you communicate almost certainly varies from one partner to another.

Now the definition of *communication* can be summarized. **Interpersonal communication** is a continuous transactional process involving participants who occupy different but overlapping environments and create relationships through the exchange of messages, many of which are affected by external, physiological, and psychological noise.

LO³
Communication Principles and Misconceptions

Before we look at the qualities of interpersonal communication, it's important to define what communication is, what it isn't, what it does, and what it can't accomplish.

Communication Principles

Based on what you've learned so far, it's possible to draw several important conclusions about interpersonal communication.

Communication Can Be Intentional or Unintentional

Some communication is clearly intentional: You plan your words carefully before asking for a big favour or offering criticism. Some scholars argue that only intentional messages like these qualify as communication, but others hold that even unintentional behaviour is communicative. Suppose, for instance, that a friend overhears you muttering complaints to yourself. Even though you didn't intend for him to hear your remarks, they certainly carried a message.

In addition, we unintentionally send many nonverbal messages. You might not be aware of your sour expression or sigh of boredom, but others see and hear them nonetheless. The debate continues about whether unintentional behaviour should be considered communication, and it's unlikely that the issue will ever be settled in the near future.[27] In *Looking Out/Looking In*, we will look at the communicative value of both intentional and unintentional behaviour.

Communication Is Irreversible

At times, we've all said something we immediately regretted and wished that the words could have been erased. But, alas, that's impossible. While an apology can mollify hurt feelings or further explanation can clear up a misunderstanding, the impression you've created cannot be erased. It is no more possible to "unreceive" a message than to "unsqueeze" a tube of toothpaste. Words said and deeds done are irretrievable.

It's Impossible Not to Communicate

Many theorists agree that it is impossible not to communicate because whatever you do—whether you speak or

Andresr/Shutterstock

"We can pause, Stu—we can even try fast-forwarding—but we can never rewind."

© Michael Maslin/The New Yorker Collection/www.cartoonbank.com

remain silent, confront or avoid—you provide others with information about your thoughts and feelings. In this sense, we are like transmitters that can't be shut off. We constantly send messages.

Of course, the people who decode your message may not be accurate. For example, they might take your kidding seriously or underestimate your feelings. Sometimes the intended message doesn't even resemble the one that others infer from your actions. Thus, when we talk about "a communication breakdown" or "miscommunication," we rarely mean that communication has ended. Instead we mean that it is inaccurate, ineffective, or unsatisfying.[28]

This explains why the best way to enhance understanding is to discuss your intentions and your interpretations of the other person's behaviour until you have negotiated a shared meaning.

Communication Is Unrepeatable

Because communication is an ongoing process, it is impossible to repeat an event. A certain smile that worked well when you met a stranger last week might not work with one you encounter tomorrow: It might feel stale or be inappropriate for a different person or occasion. Even with the same person, you can't recreate an event. Why? Because neither of you is the same person. You've both lived longer and the behaviour isn't original. Your feelings about each other may have changed. You need not constantly invent new ways to act around familiar people, but realize that the "same" words and behaviours are different each time they are spoken or performed.

Communication Has a Content and a Relational Dimension

Practically all exchanges operate on two levels: the content level and the relational level. The **content dimension** involves the information being explicitly discussed. The content of "Turn left at the next corner" or "You can buy that for less online" is obvious. The **relational dimension** expresses how the parties feel toward one another.[29] Imagine, for example, two ways of saying, "It's your turn to do the dishes": one that is demanding and another that is matter-of-fact. The different tones of voice can send very different relational messages.

Content message
A message that communicates information about the subject being discussed.

Relational message
A message that expresses the social relationship between two or more individuals.

Sometimes the content dimension of a message is all that matters. For example, you probably aren't concerned about the service rep's feelings about you as long as you get your car fixed. At other times, the relational dimension message is important. This explains why arguments can develop over

Drawing by Gail Machlis, *Quality Time*, July 21, 1994. *Quality Time* © 1994 Gail Machlis. Reprinted with permission of the artist. All rights reserved.

apparently trivial subjects like whose turn it is to wash the dishes or how to spend the weekend.

Communication Misconceptions

Along with understanding the communication principles, avoiding the following misconceptions can save a good deal of interpersonal trouble.[30]

More Communication Is Always Better

Whereas not communicating enough can cause problems, there are also situations when *too much* communication is a mistake. Sometimes excessive communication is unproductive, like when two people "talk a problem to death" without making progress. As one book puts it, "More and more negative communication merely leads to more and more negative results."[31] Even too much noncritical communication can backfire. Pestering a prospective employer or texting too many "call me" messages to a friend can generate a negative reaction.

Meanings Are in Words

It's a big mistake to assume that saying something is the same thing as communicating it. The words that make perfect sense to you can be interpreted in entirely different ways by others.

Successful Communication Always Involves Shared Understanding

There are times when success in communication comes from not completely understanding one another. For example, we are often deliberately vague about something. Perhaps you find a friend's new tattoo grotesque, but when asked how you like it, you say, "Wow, that's really unusual." In such cases, clarification is sacrificed for the sake of kindness and relational maintenance.

Some research shows that satisfying relationships depend in part on flawed understanding. Couples who *think* their partners understand them are more satisfied with each other than those who *actually* understand what the other person says and means.[32]

"My wife understands me."

© Mike Twohy/The New Yorker Collection/www.cartoonbank.com

A Single Person or Event Causes Another's Reaction

Another common misconception is thinking that any single thing we say or do causes a particular outcome when, in fact, many factors affect how others will react to your communication. If you lose your temper and say something to a friend that you immediately regret, your friend's reaction depends on a host of events besides your unjustified remark. These include her frame of mind at the moment (uptight or mellow), elements of her personality (judgmental or forgiving), your relational history (supportive or hostile), and so forth. Because communication is a transactional, ongoing, collaborative process, it's usually a mistake to think that any event occurs in a vacuum.

Communication Can Solve All Problems

Sometimes even the best-planned, best-timed communication won't solve a problem. Imagine asking an instructor to explain why you received a poor grade on a project that you believe deserved top marks. The instructor outlines the reasons for your low grade and sticks to that position after listening to you carefully. Has communication solved the problem? Hardly.

Sometimes clear communication can even *cause* problems. Suppose, for example, that a friend asks you for an honest opinion of the $400 outfit he just bought. Your clear and sincere answer, "I think it makes you look weird," might do more harm than good. Deciding when and how to self-disclose isn't always easy.

LO[4]
The Nature of Interpersonal Communication

Now that you have an understanding of the communication process, it's time to look at what makes some types uniquely interpersonal.

Two Views of Interpersonal Communication

Communication scholars define interpersonal communication in two ways: quantitatively and qualitatively.[33] A **quantitative** definition focuses on the number of people involved and includes *any* interaction between two people, usually face to face. Two people interacting is referred to as a **dyad**, and this type of interaction is called *dyadic* communication. So, in a quantitative sense, the terms *dyadic communication* and *interpersonal communication* are interchangeable. Using a quantitative definition, a sales clerk talking to a customer or a police officer issuing a ticket are interpersonal acts because they involve two people and are probably **impersonal** in nature. For instance, a clerk might tell you to have a nice day without even looking at you.

Some scholars argue, however, that it's not quantity that distinguishes interpersonal communication, it is *quality*.[34] Using a qualitative definition, interpersonal communication occurs when people treat one another as unique individuals, regardless of the context or the number of people involved. Several features distinguish qualitative interpersonal communication from less personal communication. These features include uniqueness, irreplaceability, interdependence, disclosure, and intrinsic rewards.[35]

> **Quantitative definition of interpersonal communication**
> Impersonal communication, usually face to face, between two individuals.
>
> **Dyad**
> Two people interacting.
>
> **Impersonal communication**
> Behaviour that treats others as objects rather than as individuals.

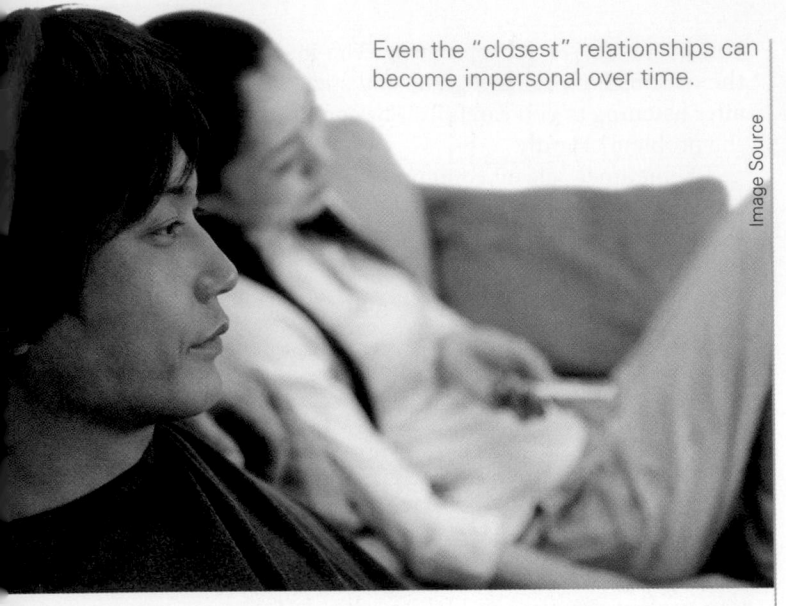

Even the "closest" relationships can become impersonal over time.

Image Source

The first feature is *uniqueness*. **Qualitative** interpersonal relationships are characterized by the development of unique rules and roles, and, therefore, every relationship is different. For example, in one relationship you might exchange good-natured insults, whereas in another you are rather formal. Likewise, you might handle conflicts as they arise with one friend and withhold resentments until they build up and explode with another. One communication scholar coined the term *relational culture* to describe people in close relationships who create their own unique ways of interacting.[36]

A second feature of qualitatively interpersonal relationships is *irreplaceability*. Because interpersonal relationships are unique, they can't be replaced. This explains why we usually feel so sad when a relative dies or a love affair cools down. No matter how many other relationships we have, that particular one can't ever be replaced.

Interdependence is a third feature of qualitatively interpersonal relationships. This simply means that in a qualitative interpersonal relationship, the other's experiences affect you as well. While this can bring pleasure, at other times it may be a burden. But interdependence goes beyond the level of joined fates—our very identity depends on the nature of our interaction with others. As Kenneth Gergen explains, "One cannot be 'attractive' without others who are attracted, a 'leader' without others willing to follow, or a 'loving person' without others to affirm with appreciation."[37]

A fourth feature is *disclosure* of personal information. While we don't typically reveal much about ourselves in impersonal relationships, we tend to disclose private thoughts and feelings when we're in a qualitative interpersonal relationship.

The final feature of interpersonal communication is *intrinsic rewards*. In impersonal communication, payoffs have little to do with the people involved. You talk to potential buyers of your used car not to develop a relationship but

> **Qualitative definition of interpersonal communication**
> Communication in which the parties consider one another as unique individuals rather than as objects. Such communication is characterized by minimal use of stereotyped labels; by unique, idiosyncratic rules; and by a high degree of information exchange.

Invitation TO INSIGHT

How Personal Are Your Relationships?

Use the characteristics of qualitatively interpersonal communication described on pages 11–12 to think about your own relationships.

1. Make a list of several people who are close to you—family members, people you live with, friends, co-workers, and so on.

2. Use the scales that follow to rate each relationship. To distinguish the relationships from one another, use a different color of ink for each one.

3. Consider comparing your results with those of classmates or friends.

After completing the exercise, ask yourself the important question: How satisfied are you with the answers you have found?

Uniqueness

1	2	3	4	5

Standardized, habitual ———————————— Unique

Replaceability

1	2	3	4	5

Replaceable ———————————— Irreplaceable

Dependence

1	2	3	4	5

Independent ———————————— Interdependent

Disclosure

1	2	3	4	5

Low disclosure ———————————— High disclosure

Intrinsic rewards

1	2	3	4	5

Unrewarding ———————————— Rewarding

rather to sell the vehicle. By contrast, you spend time in qualitatively interpersonal relationships with friends, lovers, and others because you find the time personally rewarding.

Because relationships that are unique, irreplaceable, interdependent, disclosing, and intrinsically rewarding are rare, qualitatively interpersonal communication is relatively scarce. Considering the number of people with whom you communicate daily (classmates, neighbours, etc.) or the amount of time engaged in online bantering, personal relationships are by far in the minority.

Communicators who strive to acquire a large number of "friends" on social networking websites like Facebook and Twitter are engaging in superficial, impersonal relationships. As one critic put it, "The idea . . . is to attain as many of these not-really-friends as possible . . . Like cheap wine, 'friends' provide a high that can only be sustained by acquiring more and more of them. Quantity trumps quality."[38]

Personal and Impersonal Communication: A Matter of Balance

Most relationships aren't *either* interpersonal or impersonal. Rather, they fall somewhere on a continuum between these two extremes. You might appreciate the unique sense of humour of a grocery clerk or connect on a personal level with the person cutting your hair. Or a demanding, by-the-book boss might show an occasional flash of humanity.

Just as there's a personal element in many impersonal settings, we also communicate in impersonal ways with the people we care most about. When we're distracted, tired, busy, or just not interested, we don't want to be personal. In fact, interpersonal communication is rather like rich food—it's fine in moderation, but too much can make you uncomfortable.

The personal–impersonal balance in relationships also changes over time. New lovers talk excessively about their feelings, but as time passes, their communication becomes more routine. The percentage of time communicating about personal, relational issues drops as conversation about less intimate topics increases. While interpersonal communication can make life worth living, it isn't possible or desirable all the time. The challenge is to balance the two types.

LO[5]
Mediated Interpersonal Communication

Clearly, face-to-face conversation isn't the only way people create and maintain personal relationships. Along with the telephone and old-fashioned correspondence, **mediated communication** channels provide many other

"Richard, we need to talk. I'll e-mail you."

© Aaron Bacall/The New Yorker Collection/www.cartoonbank.com

ways to interact. Instant messaging, e-mailing, blogging, tweeting, and social networking websites like Facebook and MySpace are some of the many options. In fact, research suggests that the difference between face-to-face and virtual relationships is eroding.[39]

Benefits of Mediated Communication

A growing body of research reveals that mediated communication isn't the threat to relationships that some critics once feared. Most Internet users report that the amount of time spent online doesn't affect the amount of time they spend with their family or friends, and three-quarters said they didn't feel ignored when household members spent time online.[40] In fact, the majority of Internet users said that IMing, e-mail, websites, and chat rooms had a "modestly positive impact" on their ability to communicate with family members and to make new friends. Over half of those surveyed said they had more personal relationships since they started to use the Internet.[41] Families that use mediated communication—particularly cellphones— stay in touch more regularly.[42]

More recent studies suggest that the role that mediated communication plays in people's relationships and decision making is a positive one.[43] They show that mediated communication enriches social networks and that this is true across generations. For example,

- Internet users have more social networks than non-users.

> **Mediated communication**
> The use of computer-based tools (e-mail, instant messaging, social networking sites, testing, etc.) for the purpose of human interaction.

- Mediated communication is "glocalized," connecting people who live next door as well as those across the globe.
- Computer-based communication encourages offline interaction and can keep relationships alive and active.
- Text-only format can bring people closer by minimizing the perception of differences due to gender, social class, ethnicity, and age.
- Text-only messages can stimulate both self-disclosure and direct questioning between strangers, resulting in greater interpersonal attraction.[44]

Pitroviz/Shutterstock

Social Networking, Survival, and Healing

James Gritz/Photodisc/Getty Images

If you dig enough, you'll find little bits and pieces of my life scattered across the Net. For many people, this sort of transparency is unnerving. For me, it's always been a source of comfort in the storm that has been my life. Throughout 20 years of drinking and drugs, I've always had cyberfriends who, for reasons I can't explain, have stayed up late and saved me more times than I can count.

When I made the decision—or more accurately, when the decision smashed down upon me—to get sober, I was terrified, embarrassed, and angry. I certainly didn't think I needed anyone to help me.

Sometime near the end of the third month, the last bits of my sanity were gone. I couldn't function any longer. That's when I turned to the Web. I began to post what I've been told was an ever-increasing series of erratic blurbs—some directly to FriendFeed and others on Twitter, Facebook, and MySpace.

Those messages started a dialogue that took on a life of its own. I began to get e-mails, phone calls, text messages, tweets, and other digital notes from people around the world. Some offered kind words. Some offered support. Many people shared their own stories of addiction. In my darkest times, these notes would come. And always, without question, they pulled me back from the brink.

Many of these messages were from people I have known for years. Another handful came from childhood friends and people I'd grown up with. Some I had known well; many I had not. Others came from complete strangers. I have no idea how they found me.

The moment when I knew I'd be okay came one night during a cross-country drive. The phone rang as I blew through Tennessee, but I didn't recognize the number so I let it go to voice mail. When I pulled into a gas station, I listened to the message. The woman on the phone didn't leave her name, and to this day I have no idea who she was. She told me about her father and his drinking. She told me that she was proud of me for getting sober and that she wanted me to keep trying. Already tenuous with my emotions, I sat on the side of the road crying. I listened to that message dozens of times, over and over.

The encouragement kept coming: strangers leaving messages about their lives, encouraging me to keep going. Throughout the next few months, my life became a 24-hour shower of love. There wasn't one free moment that wasn't taken up by someone making sure that my dumb ass wasn't back at the bar, that I wasn't looking for ways to die, and that I was doing the right thing. I still couldn't bring myself to leave the house. I rarely left my couch. I couldn't communicate with most people. But I was never alone.

AA keeps me sane. But social media got me there. Without that far-reaching network of people—friends and strangers alike—I wouldn't be here today.

Brad K.

Reprinted with permission from Brad King.

It's important to note that mediated communication isn't a replacement for face-to-face interaction. College students who frequently use instant messaging found face-to-face communication better "in terms of satisfying individuals' communication, information, and social needs."[45] However, mediated communication can promote and reinforce relationships in that if you regularly communicate with friends and family online, you're likely to call and see them more often.[46]

Mediated interaction can increase both the quantity and quality of interpersonal communication for several reasons. First, it is easier to maintain relationships.[47] Busy schedules can make it tough for people separated by long distances and multiple time zones to connect. However, the *asynchronous* nature of e-mail provides a way to share information in a way that otherwise would be impossible. Communicators don't have to connect in real time. Instant messaging is another way to keep in touch: Discovering that a friend or relative is online is "like walking down the street and sometimes running into a friend," says Laura Balsam, a New York computer consultant.[48] Even when face-to-face communication is convenient, some people find it easier to share personal information via mediated channels. Sociolinguist Deborah Tannen describes how e-mail can transform the quality of relationships when individuals begin connecting online.[49] Experiences like these explain why Steve Jobs, the co-founder of Apple, suggested

that personal computers be renamed "*inter*personal computers."[50] Although mediated communication can enhance relationships, Barry Wellman from the University of Toronto notes that most people typically incorporated all the avenues of communication.[51]

Challenges of Mediated Communication

Despite its benefits, mediated communication presents several challenges, as is explained below.

Leaner Messages

Face-to-face communication is rich because it abounds with nonverbal cues that help clarify the meanings of one another's words and offer hints about each person's feelings.[52] By comparison, most mediated communication is a much leaner channel for conveying information. For instance, imagine you haven't heard from a friend in several weeks and you decide to ask, "Is anything wrong?" Your friend replies, "No, I'm fine." If you received this message as a face-to-face response, it would contain a rich array of cues to interpret the message: Facial expressions, vocal tone, and so on. Compare that response to a text message that contains only words. At least a phone message would give you a few vocal cues.

Because most mediated messages are leaner than the face-to-face variety, they can be harder to interpret. Irony and attempts at humour can easily be misunderstood. As a receiver, it's important to clarify your interpretations before jumping to conclusions. And as a sender, think

Somos/Veer/Getty Images

about how to send unambiguous messages so they are not misunderstood.

The leanness of mediated messages presents another challenge: The absence of nonverbal cues allows cybercommunicators to carefully manage their identities. Further, Joseph Walther identifies a phenomenon that he calls "hyperpersonal" communication—accelerating the discussion of personal topics and relational development beyond what normally happens in face-to-face interaction.[53] This may explain why some communicators who meet online "rush" into marriage. Others have difficulty shifting to a face-to-face relationship.[54]

Disinhibition

The tendency to transmit messages without considering their consequences can be especially great in online communication, where we don't see, hear, or sometimes even know the target of our remarks. This is referred to as **disinhibition** and it can take two forms.

The first is volunteering personal information you may not want some receivers to see. A quick scan of home pages on Facebook, MySpace, or Friendster reveals images and texts that could prove embarrassing in some contexts: "Here I am just before my DUI arrest." This may not be the kind of thing you want prospective employers or certain family members to see.

In addition to offering personal information about their life, individuals on mediated communication are more direct—often in a critical way—than they would be in in face-to-face interaction.[55] Sometimes communicators take disinhibition to the extreme by *flaming*—blasting off angry, even vicious, e-mails, text messages, and website postings.

Disinhibition
The tendency to transmit messages without considering their consequences.

Communication competence
The ability to accomplish one's personal goals in a manner that maintains or enhances the relationship in which it occurs.

Permanence

Nothing really goes away on the Internet. A regrettable text message, e-mail, or web posting can be archived virtually forever. Even worse, it can be retrieved and forwarded in ways that can only be imagined in your worst dreams. The best advice is to take the same approach with mediated messages that you take in person: Think twice before saying something you may later regret.

LO⁶
What Makes an Effective Communicator?

It's easy to recognize good communicators and even easier to spot poor ones. But what are the characteristics of effective communication? Answering this question has been a leading challenge for communication scholars, and they have identified some important and useful information about communication competence.[56]

Communication Competence Defined

Communication competence involves achieving one's goals in a manner that, ideally, maintains or enhances the relationship in which it occurs.[57] This definition may seem vague and wordy, but it is guided by several important characteristics described below.

There Is No "Ideal" Way to Communicate

Just as there are many kinds of beautiful music or art, so are there many kinds of competent communication. Some very successful communicators are serious whereas others use humour, some are gregarious whereas others are quieter, and some are more straightforward whereas others hint diplomatically. One way to learn new, effective

When it comes to communication competence, TV character Dr. Gregory House (played by Hugh Laurie) clearly lacks interpersonal communication skills. He does, however, demonstrate professional competencies.

ways of communicating is by observing models, but don't try to copy others, as it won't reflect your own style or values.

Competence Is Situational

Communication that is competent in one setting might be a colossal blunder in another. The insulting jokes you trade with friends might be offensive to family members, or last Saturday night's romantic approach would be labelled harassment in the workplace.

Because competent communication behaviour varies so much from one situation and person to another, it's more accurate to talk about *degrees* or *areas* of competence.[58] For example, you might deal quite skilfully with peers but feel clumsy interacting with people who are much older, wealthier, or more educated than you are. Even your competence level with one person may vary from situation to situation. So, rather than think that you are a terrible communicator in general, it's more accurate to say that you handle some situations better than others.

Competence Is Relational

Because communication is transactional—something we do with others rather than to others—behaviour that is appropriate in one relationship isn't necessarily effective in others. One important measure of competence is whether the people with whom you are communicating view your approach as effective.[59] For example, researchers have discovered that people

deal with jealousy by keeping closer tabs on the partner, acting indifferent, decreasing affection, talking the matter over, and acting angry.[60] The researchers concluded that approaches that work in some relationships would be harmful to others. These findings demonstrate that competence comes from finding ways to interact that work for you and for the other people involved.[61]

Competence Can Be Learned

To some degree, biology is destiny when it comes to communication style.[62] Studies of identical and fraternal twins suggest that traits including sociability, anger, and relaxation seem to be a partial function of our genetic makeup. However, biology isn't the only factor that shapes how we communicate. Because communication involves a set of skills that anyone can learn, skill training has been found to help people overcome speech anxiety.[63] Training can also make people better at detecting when others are lying.[64] Further, college students typically become more competent communicators over the course of their studies.[65] This all means that your level of competence can improve through education and training.[66] Reading this book and taking this course can help you become more competent.

> You did the best that you knew how. Now that you know better, you'll do better.
>
> —Maya Angelou

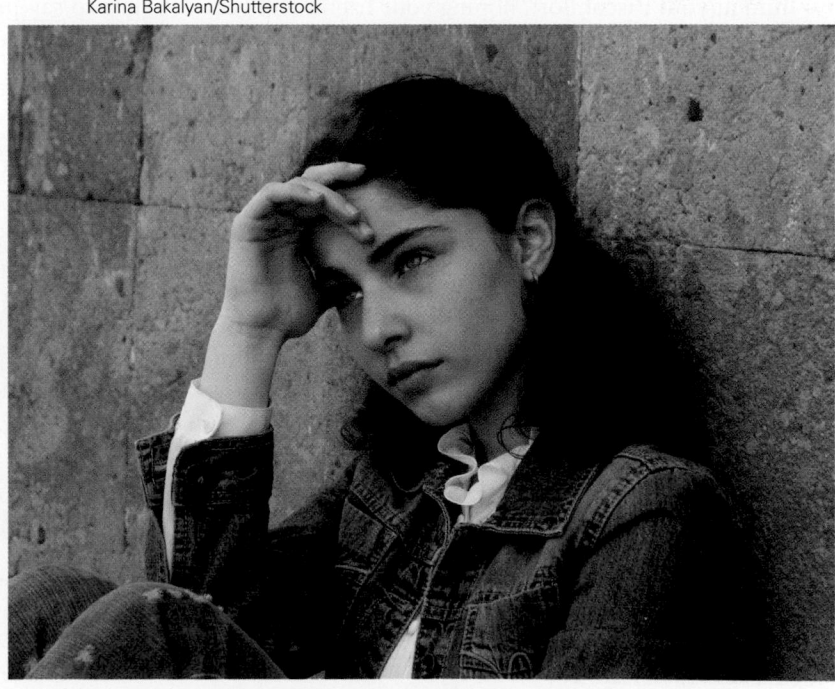

CHAPTER 1 A First Look at Interpersonal Communication

Dilbert © Scott Adams/Dist. by United Feature Syndicate, Inc.

Characteristics of Competent Communicators

Even though competent communication varies from one situation to another, scholars have identified several common denominators that characterize effective communication.

A Wide Range of Behaviours

Effective communicators possess a wide range of behaviours.[67] To understand the importance of having a large communication repertoire, imagine that someone you know repeatedly tells jokes—perhaps racist, sexist, or ageist ones—that you find offensive. You could respond in a number of ways. You could

- say nothing, figuring that the risks of bringing the subject up would be greater than the benefits.
- ask a third party to say something to the jokester about the offensiveness of the stories.
- hint at your discomfort, hoping your friend will get the point.
- joke about your friend's insensitivity, counting on humour to soften the blow of your criticism.
- express your discomfort in a straightforward way, asking your friend to stop telling the offensive jokes, at least around you.
- demand that your friend stop.

With this choice of responses, you could pick the one that has the best chance of success. But if you were able to use only one or two of these responses, say always keeping quiet or always hinting, your chances of success would be greatly reduced. Poor communicators are easy to spot because of their limited range of responses. Some are chronic jokers, others are always belligerent, and still others are quiet in almost every situation. Like a chef who can prepare only a few dishes, these people are forced to rely on a small range of responses again and again, whether or not they are successful.

Having a repertoire of options available to manage unwanted offers of help is something many people with disabilities have learned.[68] Some options include performing a task quickly, before anyone has the chance to intervene; pretending not to hear the offer; accepting in order not to seem rude or ungrateful; using humour to deflect the person; declining the offer with thanks; and assertively refusing help from those who won't take no for an answer.

Ability to Choose the Most Appropriate Behaviour

Simply possessing a large range of communication skills is no guarantee of success. You have to know which skills work best in a particular situation. Although it's impossible to say precisely how to act in every situation, three factors can help guide your decision: context, goal, and knowledge of the person.

Lauren Cohen/Apeture/Getstock.com

1. The communication *context*—time and place—will almost always influence how you act. For example, the sombre, low-key communication style one finds at a funeral would be out of place at a graduation party.

2. Your *goal* will also shape the approach you take. Inviting a new neighbour over for a cup of tea or coffee would be the right approach if you want to encourage a friendship. If you want to maintain your privacy, it would be wiser to be polite but cool.

3. Your *knowledge of the other person* should shape your approach. If, for instance, a person was very sensitive or insecure, your response might be supportive and cautious. With an old, trusted friend, you could be blunt. The social niche of the other party can also influence your communication. You would probably act differently around the president of your institution than you would toward a classmate, even in identical circumstances.

Skill at Performing Behaviours

There is a big difference between knowing *about* a skill and being able to put it into practice. It is necessary to perform the required skill effectively.[69] Like any other skills—playing a musical instrument or learning a sport, for example—you will pass through four stages on your road to communication competence.[70] See the skill builder on this page.

Cognitive Complexity

Social scientists use the term **cognitive complexity** to describe the ability to construct a variety of frameworks for viewing an issue.[71] To understand how cognitive complexity can increase competence, imagine that a longtime friend seems angry with you. One possible explanation is that your friend is offended by something you've done. Another possibility is that something upsetting has happened to your friend. Or perhaps

Cognitive complexity
The ability to construct a variety of frameworks for viewing an issue.

SKILL BUILDER

Stages in Learning Communication Skills

Learning any new skill requires moving through several levels of competence.

1. Beginning Awareness

The first step is becoming aware of a new and better way of behaving. Just as a tennis player learns a new serve that can improve power and accuracy, so should reading bring you new information about *communication competence*.

2. Awkwardness

Just as you were awkward when you first tried to ride a bicycle or drive a car, so may your initial attempts at communicating in new ways also be awkward. As the saying goes, "You have to be willing to look bad if you want to get good."

3. Skilfulness

If you keep working at your new skill, you'll reach a point where you can do it but it won't be natural to you. You'll still need to think about what you're doing. As an interpersonal communicator, you can expect this stage of skilfulness to be marked by a great deal of thinking and planning. But you'll find that you're getting increasingly good results.

4. Integration

Integration occurs when you're able to perform well without thinking about it. The behaviour becomes automatic, a part of your repertoire.

FIGURE 1.4

Stages in Learning Communication Skills

123render/iStockphoto

nothing is wrong; you're just being overly sensitive. Considering the issue from several angles might prevent you from overreacting or misunderstanding the situation and thus increase the odds of resolving the problem constructively.

Empathy

Empathy involves feeling and experiencing another person's situation almost as they do. This ability is so important that some researchers have labelled empathy the most important aspect of communication competence.[72] Getting a feel for how others view the world is a useful and important way to become a more effective communicator.

Self-Monitoring

Whereas increased cognitive complexity and empathy help you understand others better, **self-monitoring** is one way to understand *yourself*. Self-monitoring describes the process of paying close attention to your own behaviour and using these observations to shape the way you behave. Self-monitors can separate a part of their consciousness and observe their behaviours from a detached viewpoint, making observations such as:

> "I'm making a fool of myself."
> "I'd better speak up now."
> "This approach is working well. I'll keep it up."

Although too much self-monitoring can be problematic, communicators who are aware of their behaviour and the impression it makes are more skilful communicators.[73] They are more accurate in judging others' emotional states, better at remembering information about others, less shy, and more assertive. By contrast, low self-monitors don't even recognize their incompetence. They are blissfully ignorant of their shortcomings and more likely to overestimate their skills.[74] For example, experimental subjects who scored in the lowest quartile on joke-telling skills were more likely than their funnier counterparts to grossly overestimate their sense of humour.

Empathy
The ability to project oneself into another person's point of view, so as to experience the other's thoughts and feelings.

Self-monitoring
The process of attending to your own behaviour and using these observations to shape the way you behave.

Commitment

One feature that distinguishes effective communication—at least in qualitatively interpersonal relationships—is commitment. People who care about relationships communicate better than those who don't.[75] This concern shows up in at least two ways. The first is *commitment*

to the other person, which is revealed in a variety of ways: spending time with a person instead of rushing, listening carefully instead of doing all the talking, using language that makes sense to the other person, and being open to change after hearing the other person's ideas. Effective communicators also care about *the message*. They are sincere, know what they are talking about, and demonstrate verbally and nonverbally that they care about what they say.

So how do you measure up? Competence isn't a trait that people possess or lack, but rather it's a state that we achieve more or less frequently. The goal is not to become perfect but to boost the percentage of time when you communicate in ways outlined in this section.

John Bradley/Getty Images

Competence in Intercultural Communication

As our world becomes more multicultural, the likelihood of interacting with people from different backgrounds is greater than ever. As a result, it's important to understand that competent behaviour in one culture might be considered completely inept, or even offensive, in another.[76] Customs like belching after a meal or appearing nude in public that might be appropriate in some parts of the world would be considered outrageous in others. Other differences are more subtle. For example, self-disclosing and speaking clearly, which is valued among North Americans, may be considered aggressive and insensitive by many people in Asian countries, who think of subtlety and indirectness as appropriate.[77]

Even within a single society, co-cultures may have different notions of appropriate behaviour. For instance, students from the Mi'kmaq nation have said in class that avoiding eye contact when speaking with their elders demonstrates respect. However, when this same behaviour is directed toward non-Aboriginal authority figures such as university professors, deans, or judges, it may be perceived as insolence rather than the courtesy it is meant to convey. Competent communicators are able to adapt their style to suit the individual and cultural preferences of others.[78]

In addition to the characteristics of competent communication, communicating with people from different cultural backgrounds calls for several additional ingredients.[79] First, it helps to know the rules of a specific culture. For example, the kind of self-deprecating humour that North Americans find amusing is likely to fall flat among Arabs from the Middle East.[80] But beyond the basics, there's also attitudes and skills called "culture-general" that help communicators build relationships with people from other backgrounds.[81] For example, imagine you've just been hired to work in a Japanese-owned company in Canada that has manufacturing operations in Mexico and customers around the world. You'll be surrounded by co-workers, supervisors, and clients from cultures and co-cultures different from

SKILL BUILDER

Check Your Competence

Other people are often the best judges of your competence as a communicator. They can also offer useful information about how to improve your communication. Find out for yourself by following these steps:

1. Choose a person with whom you have an important relationship.

2. In cooperation with this person, identify several contexts in which you communicate. For example, you might choose different situations, such as handling conflicts, lending support to friends, or expressing feelings.

3. For each situation, have your friend rate your competence by answering the following questions:
   a. Do you have a wide repertoire of response styles in this situation, or do you always respond in the same way?
   b. Are you able to choose the most effective way of behaving for the situation at hand?
   c. Are you skilful at performing behaviours? (Note that knowing how you want to behave isn't the same as being able to behave that way.)
   d. Do you communicate in a way that leaves others satisfied?

4. After reviewing your partner's answers, identify the situations in which your communication is most competent.

5. Choose a situation in which you would like to communicate more competently, and with the help of your partner
   a. Determine whether your repertoire of behaviours needs to be expanded.
   b. Identify the ways in which you need to communicate more skilfully.
   c. Develop ways to monitor your behaviour in the key situation to get feedback on your effectiveness.

123render/iStockphoto

yours. To communicate effectively on your occasional business trips abroad, you'll need to possess the following attributes.

Motivation

The desire to communicate successfully with strangers is an important start. People high in willingness to communicate with people from other cultures report a greater number of "intercultural" friends than those who are less willing to reach out.[82] Motivation is particularly important in intercultural interactions because they can be quite challenging at times.

Back at your multinational company, motivation will play a major role during visits to Japan. You might first be pleased and then exhausted to discover that parties and banquets, typically with much alcohol, are part of the business scene. Even if you're a seasoned partygoer, you may need to draw on a deep well of motivation to spend yet another evening toasting strangers when you'd rather be recovering from jet lag.

Tolerance for Ambiguity

A tolerance for ambiguity will make it possible to accept equivocal and sometimes incomprehensible messages that characterize intercultural communication. In Asian cultures, for instance, reticence is valued. However, you might interpret an unwillingness to talk as a lack of friendliness. In cross-cultural situations like this, ambiguity is a fact of life, and a challenge.

Open-Mindedness

It's one thing to tolerate ambiguity, but it's another to become open-minded about cultural differences. When communication styles don't match those of our own culture, we have a tendency to think of them as "wrong." For example, in some situations you may be aghast at the casual tolerance of poverty beyond anything at home, or with a practice of kickbacks and bribery that doesn't jibe with our notions of what is ethical. In these situations, principled communicators don't usually compromise deeply held beliefs about what is right. At the same time, competence requires you to recognize that people who behave differently are following different rules.

Knowledge and Skill

The rules and customs of one group might be quite different from another's. When travelling in Latin America, for example, you'll find that meetings don't begin or end at their scheduled time and that it takes participants quite a while to "get down to business." Rather than seeing this as irresponsible and unproductive, you'll want to recognize that the meaning of time is different in that culture. Likewise, the gestures others make, the distance they stand from you, and the eye contact they maintain have ambiguous meanings that you'll need to learn and adopt.

At your new job, you'll want to engage in *mindfulness*—awareness of your own behaviour and that of others.[83] Communicators who lack this quality blunder through intercultural encounters *mindlessly*, oblivious of how their own behaviour may confuse or offend others and of how behaviour they consider weird may be simply different. In a mindful state, you can use three strategies to move toward a more competent style of intercultural communication.[84] *Passive observation* involves noticing the behaviours used by members of a different culture and then using these insights to communicate in ways that are most effective. *Active strategies* include reading, watching films, and asking experts or members of the other culture how to behave, as well as taking intercultural communication courses.[85] The third strategy, *self-disclosure*, involves volunteering personal information to people from the other culture with whom you want to communicate. One type of self-disclosure is to confess your cultural ignorance: "This is very new to me. What's the right thing to do in this situation?" This approach can be risky, given that some cultures may not value candour and self-disclosure as much as others. Nevertheless, most people are pleased when strangers attempt to learn the practices of their culture, and they are usually more than willing to offer information and assistance.

Communication in the Workplace

Interpersonal communication is also important in our professional lives. Organizational communication theory tells us that communication activities create patterns that affect organizational life and that organizational cultures are created through communication processes.[86] Employers know that communication affects employee satisfaction and general productivity. One study of 2500 Canadian workers reported that the strongest correlate of a healthy work environment was communication.[87] A study of the IT sector revealed that interpersonal communication is the most important factor in terms of promotion to management positions.[88]

On-the-job communication skills can even make the difference between life and death. One police department cited "bad communication" among the most common reasons for shooting errors by its officers.[89] Communication skills are just as essential for doctors, nurses, and other

medical practitioners.[98] Researchers discovered that "poor communication" was the root of over 60 percent of reported medical errors—including death, serious physical injury, and psychological trauma.[99] Other research revealed a significant difference between the communication skills of physicians who had no malpractice claims against them and doctors with claims.[100]

In addition, today's workplace is managing four generations of workers: veterans (born before 1945), baby boomers (born 1946 to 1966), Generation X (born 1967 to 1979), and Generation Y (born 1980 to 1995). According to Paula Allan of Toronto's FGIWorld, a firm that helps organizations address their mental, physical, and social health issues, each group has its "own set of values, view of authority, work and communication style, and expectation of leadership and work environment."[101] Veterans are used to top-down management and take pride in their work. Baby boomers also tend to appreciate hierarchy, favour diplomacy, prefer to work independently, and are willing to work hard and put in long hours. In contrast, tech-savvy Generation Xers dislike hierarchy, prefer teamwork, are loyal to their own careers, and are candid in conversations. Generation Ys are also tech-savvy and value teamwork. They want to balance work and family life, believe in informality, and are better educated and more ethnically diverse.[102] It's easy to understand how clashes could arise based on generational placement, and this presents a challenge in today's work world. No matter what the field, research confirms what experienced workers already know—that communication skills are crucial in finding and succeeding in a job. See the box on the left.

(On the Job)

Communication and Career Success

Communication skills often make the difference between being hired and being rejected. In one widely followed annual survey, employers list the skills and qualities for their ideal candidate. Communication skills always top the list, ranking ahead of technical skills, initiative, analytical ability, and computer skills.[90] In another survey, 1000 managers rated the abilities to speak and listen effectively as the two most important factors in helping college graduates find jobs in a competitive workplace—more important than technical competence, work experience, and specific degree earned.[91] When 170 well-known business and industrial firms were asked to list the most common reasons for *not* offering jobs to applicants, the most frequent replies were "inability to communicate" and "poor communication skills."[92]

Once you've been hired, the need for communication skills is important in virtually every career.[93] Engineers spend the bulk of their working lives speaking and listening, mostly in one-to-one and small-group settings.[94] Accounting professionals spend 80 percent of their time on the job communicating with others, individually and in groups.[95] One executive at computer giant Sun Microsystems made the point forcefully: "If there's one skill that's required for success in this industry, it's communication skills."[96] Writing in *The Scientist*, a commentator echoed this sentiment: "If I give any advice, it is that you can never do enough training around your overall communication skills."[97]

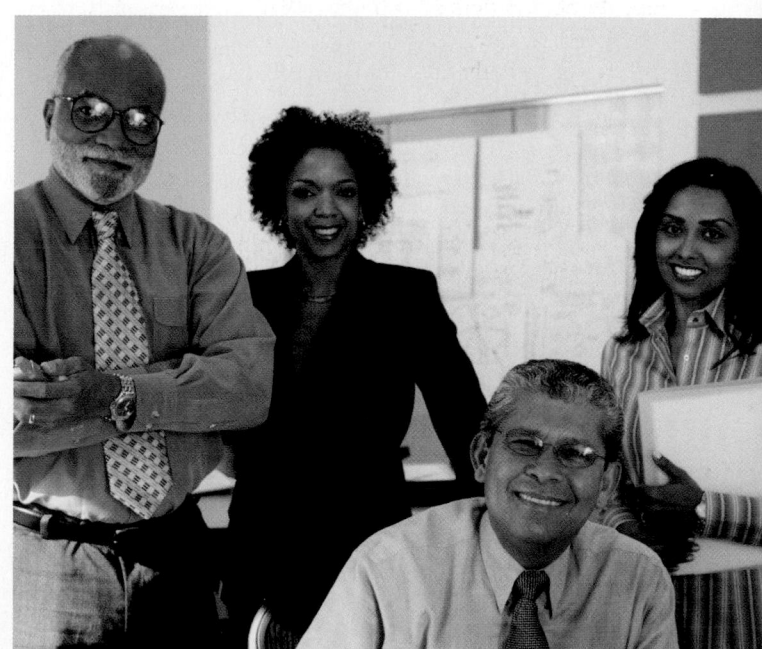

Jon Feingersh Photography Inc./Blend Images/Getty Images

Endnotes

1. Interview with Vicki Gabereau, CTV Canadian Television, March 19, 2003; and B. Kull (2004). "My Year Alone in the Wilderness." *Canadian Geographic*, 124, 2–12. The interview and article, plus more about Bob Kull's experience, are available at www.bobkull.org. Accessed Aug.1, 2007. Also see R. Kull (2008). *Solitude: Seeking Wisdom in Extremes*. Novato, CA: New World Library.

2. VPI (Sept. 7, 1978). *Wisconsin State Journal*.

3. A. Gawande (March 30, 2009). "Hellhole." *The New Yorker*, 36–45.

4. J. B. Ross and M. M. McLaughlin (Eds). (1949). *A Portable Medieval Reader*. New York: Viking.

5. S. Cohen, W. J. Doyle, D. P. Skoner, B. S. Rabin, & J. M. Gwaltney (1997). "Social Ties and Susceptibility to the Common Cold." *Journal of the American Medical Association, 277*, 1940–1944.

6. C. H. Kroenke, L. D. Kubzansky, E. S. Schernhammer, M. D. Holmes, & I. Kawachi (2006). "Social Networks, Social Support, and Survival After Breast Cancer Diagnosis." *Journal of Clinical Oncology*, 24, 1105–1111; H. Litwin & S. Shiovitz-Ezra (2006). "Network Type and Mortality Risk in Later Life." *Gerontologist*, 46, 735–743; and C. F. Mendes de Leon (2005). "Why Do Friendships Matter For Survival?" *Journal of Epidemiology and Community Health, 59*, 538–539.

7. J. Lynch (1977). *The Broken Heart: The Medical Consequences of Loneliness* (pp. 239–242). New York: Basic Books.

8. W. D. Rees and S. G. Lutkins (1967). "Mortality of Bereavement." *British Medical Journal*, 4, 13.

9. Public Health Agency of Canada (October 1, 2002). "Our Relationships Influence our Physical Health." Canadian Health Network, www.canadian-health-network.ca/servlet/ContentServer?cid=1039795127660&pagename=CHN-RCS%2FCHNResource%2FCHNResourcePageTemplate&c=CHNResource&lang=En. Accessed July 12, 2006.

10. O. Ybarra, O. E. Burnstein, P. Winkielman, M .C. Keller, M. Manis, E. Chan, & J. Rodriguez (2008). "Mental Exercising Through Simple Socializing: Social Interaction Promotes General Cognitive Functioning." *Personality and Social Psychology Bulletin*, 34, 248–259.

11. K. Floyd & S. Riforgiate (2006). "Human Affection Exchange: XII. Affectionate Communication Is Related to Diurnal Variation in Salivary Free Cortisol." *Western Journal of Communication, 75*, 351–368.

12. Ibid.

13. K. Ritchie (November 15, 2005). "A Nursing Home with a Twist." Australian Broadcasting Corporation, www.abc.net.au/am/content/2005/s1506885.htm. Accessed July 12, 2006.

14. R. Shattuck (1980). *The Forbidden Experiment: The Story of the Wild Boy of Aveyron* (p. 37). New York: Farrar, Straus & Giroux.

15. R. B. Rubin, E. M. Perse, & C. A. Barbato (1988). "Conceptualization and Measurement of Interpersonal Communication Motives." *Human Communication Research, 14*, 602–628.

16. E. Diener & M. E. P. Seligman (2002). "Very Happy People." *Psychological Science, 13*, 81–84.

17. D. Kahneman, A. B. Krueger, D. A. Schkade, N. Schwartz, & A. A. Stone (n.d.). "A Daily Measure." *Science, 306*, 1645.

18. U.S. Rehman & A. Holtzworth-Munroe (2007). "A Cross-Cultural Examination of the Relation of Marital Communication Behaviour to Marital Satisfaction." *Journal of Family Psychology, 21*, 759–763.

19. J. Rochmis (n.d.). "Study: Humans Do Many Things." *Wired magazine* online, www.wired.com/culture/lifestyle/news/2000/02/34387. Accessed July 13, 2010.

20. M. McPherson, L. Smith-Lovin, & M. E. Brashears (2006). "Social Isolation in America: Changes in Core Discussion Networks over Two Decades." *American Sociological Review*, 71, 353–375. See also M. McPherson, L. Smith-Lovin, and M. E. Brashears (2008). "The Ties That Bind Are Fraying." *Contexts*, 7, 32–36.

21. H. T. Reis & S. L. Gable (2003). "Toward a Positive Psychology of Relationships." In C. L. Keyes & J. Haidt (Eds.). *Flourishing: The Positive Person and the Good Life* (pp. 129–159). Washington, DC: American Psychological Association.

22. D. B. Curtis, J. L. Winsor, & R.D. Stephens (1989). "National Preferences in Business and Communication Education." *Communication Education, 38*, 6–14. See also M. S. Peterson, "Personnel Interviewers' Perceptions of the Importance and Adequacy of Applicants' Communication Skills," *Communication Education* 46 (1997): 287–291.

23. Conference Board of Canada (2000). Employability Skills 2000+. www.conferenceboard.ca/education/learning-tools/employability-skills.htm. Accessed July 12, 2006.

24. A. H. Maslow (1968). *Toward a Psychology of Being*. New York: Van Nostrand Reinhold.

25. P. Mychalcewycz (February 12, 2009). "Breaking Up Via Text Message Becoming Commonplace, Poll Finds." www.switched.com. Accessed May 30, 2010.

26. See, for example, R. K. Shelly (1997). "Sequences and Cycles in Social Interaction." *Small Group Research, 28*, 333–356.

27. See R. Buck & C. A. VanLear (2002). "Verbal and Nonverbal Communication: Distinguishing Symbolic, Spontaneous, and Pseudo-Spontaneous Nonverbal Behaviour." *Journal of Communication* 52, 522–541; and T. Clevenger Jr. (1991). "Can One Not Communicate? A Conflict of Models." *Communication Studies* 42, 340–353. For a detailed rationale of the position argued in this section, see G. H. Stamp & M. L. Knapp (1990). "The Construct of Intent in Interpersonal Communication." *Quarterly Journal of Speech* 76, 282–299.

28. For a thorough discussion of communication difficulties, see N. Coupland, H. Giles, & J. M. Wiemann (Eds.) (1991). *Miscommunication and Problematic Talk*. Newbury Park, CA: Sage.

29. J. P. Dillard, D. H. Solomon, & M. T. Palmer (1999). "Structuring the Concept of Relational Communication." *Communication Monographs*, 66, 49–65; and P. Watzlawick, J. Beavin, & D. Jackson (1967). *Pragmatics of Human Communication*. New York: Norton.

30. For a similar list of characteristics, see J. C. McCroskey & V. P. Richmond (1996). *Fundamentals of Human Communication: An Interpersonal Perspective*. Prospect Heights, IL: Waveland.

31. A. Sillars (1998). "(Mis)Understanding." In B. H. Spitzberg and W. R. Cupach (Eds.). *The Dark Side of Close Relationships*. Mahwah, NJ: Erlbaum.

32. J. C. McCroskey & L. Wheeless (1976). *Introduction to Human Communication* (p. 5). Boston: Allyn and Bacon. See also D. H. Cloven & M. E. Roloff (1991). "Sense-Making Activities and Interpersonal Conflict: Communicative Cures for the Mulling Blues." *Western Journal of Speech Communication*, 55, 134–158. See also D. Stiebel (1997). *When Talking Makes Things Worse! Resolving Problems When Communication Fails*. Kansas City, MO: Andrews and McMeel.

33. M. V. Redmond (1995). "Interpersonal Communication: Definitions and Conceptual Approaches." In M. V. Redmond (Ed.). *Interpersonal Communication: Readings in Theory and Research* (pp. 4–11). Fort Worth, TX: Harcourt Brace.

34. See, for example, G. R. Miller & M. Steinberg (1975). *Between People: A New Analysis of Interpersonal Communication*. Chicago: SRA; and J. Stewart & C. Logan (1998). *Together: Communicating Interpersonally*, 5th ed. New York: McGraw-Hill.

35. For further discussion of the characteristics of impersonal and interpersonal communications, see Arthur P. Bochner (1984). "The Functions of Human Communication in Interpersonal Bonding." In C. C. Arnold and J. W. Bowers (Eds.). *Handbook of Rhetorical and Communication Theory* (p. 550). Boston: Allyn and Bacon; S. Trenholm & A. Jensen (1992). *Interpersonal Communication*, 2nd ed. (pp. 27–33). Belmont, CA: Wadsworth; and J. Stewart & G. D'Angelo (1998). *Together: Communicating Interpersonally*, 5th ed. (p. 5). New York: McGraw-Hill.

36. J. Wood (1997). *Relational Communication*, 2nd ed. Belmont, CA: Wadsworth.

37. K. J. Gergen (1991). *The Saturated Self: Dilemmas of Identity in Contemporary Life* (p. 158). New York: Basic Books.

38. M. Daum (March 7, 2009). "The Age of Friendaholism." *Los Angeles Times*, B 13.

39. L. Rainie and J. Anderson (2008). *The Future of the Internet III: How Experts See It*. Washington, DC: Pew Internet & American Life Project.

40. UCLA Internet Report (2000). "Surveying the Digital Future." UCLA Center for Communication Policy.

41. "Surveying the Digital Future: Year Four," op. cit.

42. B. Wellman, A. Smith, A. Wells, & T. Kennedy (2008). *Networked Families*. Washington, DC: Pew Internet & American Life Project.

43. See, for example, J. Boase, J. B. Horrigan, B. Wellman, & L. Rainie (January 2006). *The Strength of Internet Ties*. Washington, DC: Pew Internet & American Life Project; A. Lenhart, M. Madden, & P. Hitlin (July 2005). *Teens and Technology: Youth are Leading the Transition to a Fully Wired and Mobile Nation*. Washington, DC: Pew Internet & American Life Project; and J. Boase & B. Wellman (2006). "Personal Relationships: On and Off the Internet." In D. Perlman & A.L. Vangelisti (Eds.). *The Cambridge Handbook of Personal Relationships*. New York: Cambridge University Press.

44. L. M. Atheunis, P. M. Valkenburg, & J. Peter (2007). "Computer-Mediated Communication and Interpersonal Attraction: An Experimental Test of Two Explanatory Hypotheses." *CyberPsychology & Behaviour, 10*, 831–835.

45. A. J. Flanagin (2005). "IM Online: Instant Messaging Use Among College Students." *Communication Research Reports*, 22, 175–187.

46. J. Boase, J. B. Horrigan, B. Wellman, & L. Rainie (January 2006). *The Strength of Internet Ties*. Washington, DC: Pew Internet & American Life Project.

47. M. Dainton & B. Aylor (2002). "Patterns of Communication Channel Use in the Maintenance of Long-Distance Relationships." *Communication Research Reports, 19*, 118–129.

48. M. Marriott (1998). "The Blossoming of Internet Chat." *New York Times* online.

49. D. Tannen (May 16, 1994). "Gender Gap in Cyberspace." *Newsweek*, 52–53.

50. D. Kirkpatrick (March 23, 1992). "Here Comes the Payoff from PCs." *Fortune*, 93–102.

51. B. Wellman (2004). "Three Ages of Internet Studies: Ten, Five and Zero Years Ago." *New Media and Society, 6*, 123–129.

52. K. S. Surinder & R. B. Cooper (2003). "Exploring the Core Concepts of Media Richness Theory: The Impact of Cue Multiplicity and Feedback Immediacy on Decision Quality. *Journal of Management Information Systems, 20*, 263–299.

53. J. Walther & A. Ramirez (2010). "New Technologies and New Directions in Online Relating." In S. W. Smith and S. R. Wilson (Eds.). *New Directions in Interpersonal Communication Research* (pp. 264–284). Los Angeles: Sage.

54. A. Ramirez & S. Zhang (2007). "When Online Meets Offline: The Effect of Modality Switching on Relational Communication." *Communication Monographs*, 74, 287–310.

55. S. A. Watts (2007). "Evaluative Feedback: Perspectives on Media Effects." *Journal of Computer-Mediated Communication, 12*, http://jcmc.indiana.edu/vol12/issue2/watts.html. Accessed June 1, 2009.

56. For a thorough review of this topic, see B. H. Spitzberg & W. R. Cupach (1989). *Handbook of Interpersonal Competence Research*. New York: Springer-Verlag.

57. For a thorough discussion of the nature of communication competence, see B. H. Spitzberg & W. R. Cupach (2002). "Interpersonal Skills." In M. L. Knapp & J. A. Daly (Eds.). *Handbook of Interpersonal* Communication, 3rd

ed. Thousand Oaks, CA: Sage.; and S. R. Wilson & C. M. Sabee (2003). "Explicating Communicative Competence as a Theoretical Term." In J. O. Greene & B. R. Burleson (Eds.). *Handbook of Communication and Social Interaction Skills*. Mahwah, NJ: Erlbaum.

58. B. H. Spitzberg (1991). "An Examination of Trait Measures of Interpersonal Competence." *Communication Reports, 4,* 22–29.

59. B. H. Spitzberg (2000). "What Is Good Communication?" *Journal of the Association for Communication Administration, 29,* 103–119.

60. L. K. Guerrero, P. A. Andersen, P. F. Jorgensen, B. H. Spitzberg, & S. V. Eloy (1995). "Coping with the Green-Eyed Monster: Conceptualizing and Measuring Communicative Responses to Romantic Jealousy." *Western Journal of Communication, 59,* 270–304.

61. See B. J. O'Keefe (1988). "The Logic of Message Design: Individual Differences in Reasoning about Communication." *Communication Monographs, 55,* 80–103.

62. See, for example, A. D. Heisel, J. C. McCroskey, & V. P. Richmond (1999). "Testing Theoretical Relationships and Non-Relationships of Genetically-Based Predictors: Getting Started with Communibiology." *Communication Research Reports, 16,* 1–9; and J. C. McCroskey & M. J. Beatty (2000). "The Communibiological Perspective: Implications for Communication in Instruction." *Communication Education, 49,* 1–6.

63. J. Ayres & T. Hopf (1993). *Coping with Speech Anxiety.* Norwood, NJ: Ablex. See also M. Allen, J. Bourhis, T. Emmers-Sommer, & E. Sahlstein (1998). "Reducing Dating Anxiety: A Meta-Analysis." *Communication Reports, 11,* 49–55.

64. M. A. deTurck & G. R. Miller (1990). "Training Observers to Detect Deception: Effects of Self-Monitoring and Rehearsal." *Human Communication Research, 16,* 603–620.

65. R. B. Rubin, E. M. Perse, & C. A. Barbato (1988). "Conceptualization and Measurement of Interpersonal Communication Motives." *Human Communication Research, 14,* 602–628.

66. S. P.Morreale & J. C. Pearson (2008). "Why Communication Education is Important: The Centrality of the Discipline in the 21st century." *Communication Education, 57(2),* 224–240.

67. D. Hemple (in press). "Invitational Capacity." In F. van Emeren & P. Houtlosser. *The Practice of Argumentation. Amsterdam:* John Benjamins.

68. D. O. Braithwaite & N. Eckstein (2003). "Reconceptualizing Supportive Interactions: How Persons with Disabilities Communicatively Manage Assistance."*Journal of Applied Communication Research, 31,* 1–26.

69. B. R. Burleson (2007). "Constructivism: A General Theory of Communication Skill." In B. B. Whaley & W. Samter (Eds) *Explaining Communication: Contemporary Theories and Exemplars* (pp. 105–128). Mahwah, NJ: Erlbaum.

70. D. B. Wackman, S. Miller, & E. W. Nunnally (1976). *Student Workbook: Increasing Awareness and Communication Skills* (p. 6). Minneapolis, MN: Interpersonal Communication Programs.

71. B.R. Burleson and S.E. Caplan. (1998). "Cognitive Complexity." In J. C. McCroskey, J. A. Daly, M. M. Martin, & M. J. Beatty (Eds.). *Communication and Personality: Trait Perspectives* (pp. 233–286). Creskill, NJ: Hampton Press.

72. J. M. Wiemann & P. M. Backlund (1980). "Current Theory and Research in Communication Competence." *Review of Educational Research, 50,* 185–199; and S. G. Lakey & D. J. Canary (2002). "Actor Goal Achievement and Sensitivity to Partner as Critical Factors in Understanding Interpersonal Communication Competence and Conflict Strategies." *Communication Monographs, 69,* 217–235. See also M. V. Redmond (December 1985). "The Relationship between Perceived Communication Competence and Perceived Empathy." *Communication Monographs, 52,* 377–382; and M. V. Redmond (1989). "The Functions of Empathy (Decentering) in Human Relations." *Human Relations, 42,* 593–605.

73. Research summarized in D. E. Hamachek (1987). *Encounters with the Self,* 2nd ed. (p. 8.). Fort Worth, TX: Holt, Rinehart and Winston. See also J. A. Daly, A. L. Vangelisti, & S. M. Daughton (1995). "The Nature and Correlates of Conversational Sensitivity." In M. V. Redmond (Ed.). *Interpersonal Communication: Readings in Theory and Research.* Fort Worth, TX: Harcourt Brace.

74. D. A. Dunning & J. Kruger (December 1999). "Unskilled and Unaware of It: How Difficulties in Recognizing One's Own Incompetence Lead to Inflated Self-Assessments." *Journal of Personality and Social Psychology, 77,* 1121–1134.

75. Adapted from the work of R. P. Hart as reported by M. L. Knapp (1984) in *Interpersonal Communication and Human Relationships* (pp. 342–344). Boston: Allyn and Bacon. See also R. P. Hart & D. M. Burks (1972). "Rhetorical Sensitivity and Social Interaction." Speech Monographs 39, 75–91; and R. P. Hart, R. E. Carlson, & W. F. Eadie (1980). "Attitudes toward Communication and the Assessment of Rhetorical Sensitivity." *Communication Monographs, 47,* 1–22.

76. See Y. Y. Kim (1991). "Intercultural Communication Competence: A Systems-Theoretic View." In S. Ting-Toomey & F. Korzenny (Eds.). *Cross-Cultural Interpersonal Communication.* Newbury Park, CA: Sage; and G. M. Chen & W. J. Sarosta (1996). "Intercultural Communication Competence: A Synthesis." In B. R. Burleson & A. W. Kunkel (Eds.). *Communication Yearbook 19.* Thousand Oaks, CA: Sage.

77. J. K. Burgoon & N. E. Dunbar (2000). "An Interactionist Perspective on Dominance-Submission: Interpersonal Dominance as a Dynamic, Situationally Contingent Social Skill." *Communication Monographs, 67,* 96–121.

78. L. Chen (1997). "Verbal Adaptive Strategies in U.S. American Dyadic Interactions with U.S. American or East-Asian Partners." *Communication Monographs, 64,* 302–323.

79. See, for example, C. Hajek & H. Giles (2003). "New Directions in Intercultural Communication Competence: The Process Model." In B. R. Burleson & J. O. Greene

(Eds.). *Handbook of Communication and Social Interaction Skills*. Mahwah, NJ: Erlbaum; and S. Ting-Toomey & L.C. Chung (2005). *Understanding Intercultural Communication*. Los Angeles: Roxbury.

80. M. Kalliny, K. Cruthirds, & M. Minor (2006). "Differences between American, Egyptian and Lebanese Humour Styles: Implications for International Management." *International Journal of Cross-Cultural Management, 6*, 121–134.

81. L. A. Samovar & R. E. Porter (2004). *Communication Between Cultures*, 5th ed. Belmont, CA: Wadsworth.

82. J. W. Kassing (1997). "Development of the Intercultural Willingness to Communicate Scale." *Communication Research Reports, 14*, 399–407.

83. J. K. Burgoon, C. R. Berger, & V. R. Waldron (2000). "Mindfulness and Interpersonal Communication." *Journal of Social Issues, 56*, 105–128.

84. C. R. Berger (1979). "Beyond Initial Interactions: Uncertainty, Understanding, and the Development of Interpersonal Relationships." In H. Giles & R. St. Clair (Eds.). *Language and Social Psychology* (pp. 122–144). Oxford: Blackwell.

85. L. J. Carrell (1997). "Diversity in the Communication Curriculum: Impact on Student Empathy." *Communication Education, 46*, 234–244.

86. S. W. Littlejohn & K. Foss (2005). *Theories of Human Communication*, 8th ed., pp. 266–268. Belmont, CA: Thomson Wadsworth.

87. G. S. Lowe, G. Schellenberg, & H. S. Shannon (2003). "Correlates of Employees' Perceptions of a Healthy Work Environment." *American Journal of Health Promotion, 17*, 390–399.

88. H. Solomon (1999). "Soft Skills Key to IT Success, Execs Say." *Computing Canada, 25*, 1.

89. "Harper's Index" (December, 1994). *Harper's*, 13.

90. *Job Outlook 2010* (2009). Bethlehem, PA: National Association of Colleges and Employers.

91. J. L. Winsor, D. B. Curtis, & R. D. Stephens (1997). "National Preferences in Business and Communication Education: An Update." *Journal of the Association for Communication Administration, 3*, 170–179. See also M. S. Peterson (1997). "Personnel Interviewers' Perceptions of the Importance and Adequacy of Applicants' Communication Skills." *Communication Education, 46*, 287–91.

92. F. S. Endicott (1979). *The Endicott Report: Trends in the Employment of College and University Graduates in Business and Industry*. Evanston, IL: Placement Center, Northwestern University.

93. See, for example, N.M. Hindi, D.S., Miller, & S.E. Catt (2004). "Communication and Miscommunication in Corporate America: Evidence from Fortune 200 Firms." *Journal of Organizational Culture, 8*, 13–26.

94. See, for example, A. L. Darling & D. P. Dannels (2003). "Practicing Engineers Talk about the Importance of Talk: A Report on the Role of Oral Communication in the Workplace," *Communication Education, 52*, 1–16.

95. D. A. Nellermoe, T. R. Weirich, & A. Reinsteinv (1999). "Using Practitioners' Viewpoints to Improve Accounting Students' Communications Skills." *Business Communication Quarterly, 62*, 41–60.

96. August 22, 1999. *Santa Barbara News-Press*, J1

97. J. Richman (September 2, 2002). "The News Journal of the Life Scientist." *The Scientist, 16*, 42.

98. L. B. Mauksch, D. C. Dugdale, S. Dodson, & R. Epstein (2007). "Relationship, Communication, and Efficiency in the Medical Encounter." *Archives of Internal Medicine, 168*, 1387–1395; and F. Holmes (2007). "If You Listen, the Patient Will Tell You the Diagnosis." *International Journal of Listening, 21*, 156–161.

99. *Sentinel Event Statistics* (2008). Oakbrook Terrace, IL: Joint Commission on Accreditation of Healthcare.

100. W. Levinson, D. Roter, & J. P. Mullooly (1997). "Physician-Patient Communication: The Relationship with Malpractice Claims Among Primary Care Physicians and Surgeons." *Journal of American Medical Association, 277*, 553–59. See also H. P. Rodriguez, A. C. Rodday, R. E. Marshall, K. L. Nelson, W. H. Rogers, and D. G. Safran (2008). "Relation of Patients' Experiences with Individual Physicians to Malpractice Risk." *International Journal for Quality in Health Care, 20*, 5–12.

101. P. Allen (September, 2004). "Welcoming Y." *Benefits Canada*, 51–53.

102. A. J. DuBrin & T. Geerinck (2004). *Human Relations for Career and Personal Success, Third Canadian Edition*. Toronto: Pearson Education Canada, p. 33. Also see P. Allen (September, 2004). "Welcoming Y." *Benefits Canada*, 51–53.

CHAPTER **2**

COMMUNICATION AND IDENTITY:

Creating and Presenting the Self

LEARNING OUTCOMES

LO¹ Describe the relationship between self-concept, self-esteem, and communication.

LO² Explain how self-fulfilling prophecies shape the self-concept and influence communication.

LO³ Demonstrate how the principles on pages 44–45 can be used to change the self-concept, and hence, communication.

LO⁴ Compare and contrast the perceived self and the presenting self as they relate to identity management.

LO⁵ Describe the role that identity management plays in both face-to-face and mediated relationships.

Who are you? Take a moment to make a list of all the characteristics that describe you by referring to the outline below. You'll need your list as you read the rest of this chapter, so be sure to complete it now.

> Your moods or feelings (e.g., happy, angry, excited)
> Your appearance (e.g., attractive, short)
> Your social traits (e.g., friendly, shy)
> Talents you have or do not have (e.g., musical, nonathletic)
> Your intellectual capacity (e.g., smart, visual-learner)
> Your strong beliefs (e.g., religious, environmentalist)
> Your social roles (e.g., parent, girlfriend)
> Your physical condition (e.g., healthy, overweight)

Now look at what you've written. How did you define yourself? As a student? A man or woman? By your appearance? Your beliefs? Your social roles? There are many ways of identifying yourself. But the words you've chosen probably represent your most important characteristics. In other words, this would be a description of the "real you."

LO¹
Communication and the Self

So how does this self-analysis relate to interpersonal communication? The short answer is that who you are both reflects and affects your communication with others. The long answer involves everything from biology to socialization to culture to gender. But, first, let's look at two terms that are basic to the relationship between the self and communication: self-concept and self-esteem.

Self-Concept and Self-Esteem

There's a good likelihood that the list you created included emotional descriptions such as happy or sad, confident or nervous. Such characteristics show that how you *feel* about yourself is a big part of who you think you are. What we think and feel about ourselves are important components of the self and we'll examine these now.

Self-Concept

Who you think you are can be described as your **self-concept**: the relatively stable set of perceptions you hold about yourself. If a mirror could reflect not only your physical features but other aspects of yourself—emotional states, talents, likes, dislikes, values, roles, and so on—the reflection you'd see would be your self-concept.

You probably recognize that the self-concept list you recorded earlier is only a partial one. To complete the description, you'd have to add items until your list ran into hundreds of words.

Self-concept
The relatively stable set of perceptions individuals hold about themselves.

Take a moment to respond to the question "Who am I?" over and over again. Now add these responses to the list. Of course, not every item on your self-concept list is equally important. For example, the most significant part of one person's self-concept might consist of social roles, and for another it might be physical appearance, health, friendships, accomplishments, or skills.

You can discover how much you value each part of your self-concept by rank-ordering the items on your list. Try it now: Place a 1 next to the most fundamental item about you, a 2 next to the second-most fundamental item, and continue in this manner until you've completed your list.

This self-concept you've just described is extremely important. To see just how important it is, try the "Take Away" exercise on the left.

For most people, this exercise dramatically illustrates just how fundamental the concept of self is. Even when the item being abandoned is an unpleasant one, it's often hard to surrender. When asked to let go of their most central feelings or thoughts, most people balk. "I wouldn't be *me* without that," they insist. Of course, this proves our point: The concept of self is perhaps our most fundamental possession, for without a self-concept it would be impossible to relate to the world.

Invitation TO INSIGHT

Take Away

1. Find a comfortable spot where you can think without being interrupted. This exercise can be done in a group with the leader giving instructions, or you can do it alone by reading the directions yourself when necessary.

2. Close your eyes and get a mental picture of yourself. Besides visualizing your appearance, include in your image less observable features—your disposition, your hopes, your concerns—including all the items you described in the first exercise.

3. Keep this picture in mind, but now imagine what would happen if the last item on your list disappeared from your makeup. How would you be different? Does giving up that item leave you feeling better or worse? How hard was it to let go of that item?

4. Now, without taking back at the item you just abandoned, give up the next-least-important item on your list and see what difference this makes to you. After pausing to experience your thoughts and feelings, give up each succeeding item on your list one by one.

5. After you've abandoned the number one feature of who you are, take a few minutes to add back the parts of yourself you abandoned, then read on.

"Oh, thank you. I only wish I felt as good as I look."

© Bernard Schoenbaum/The New Yorker Collection/www.cartoonbank.com

Self-Esteem

While self-concept describes who you think you are, **self-esteem** involves evaluations of self-worth. A hypothetical communicator's self-concept might include being quiet, argumentative, or self-controlled. His or her self-esteem would be determined by the value she or he places on these qualities. Consider the following:

Quiet "I'm a coward for not speaking up" *versus* "I enjoy listening more than talking."

Argumentative "I'm pushy, and that's obnoxious" *versus* "I stand up for my beliefs."

Self-controlled "I'm too cautious" *versus* "I think carefully before I say or do things."

Table 2.1 summarizes some important differences between communicators with high and low self-esteem. Such differences make sense when you realize that people who dislike themselves are likely to believe that others won't like them either. They imagine that others view them critically, then accept these imagined or real criticisms as proof that they are unlikable people. Sometimes this low self-esteem is manifested in hostility toward others; they think that the only way to look good is to put others down.

Having high self-esteem has obvious benefits, but it doesn't guarantee interpersonal success.[1] While people with exaggerated self-esteem may *think* they make better impressions on others or have better friendships and romantic lives, neither impartial observers nor objective tests verify these beliefs. Instead, people with an inflated sense of self-worth may irritate others by coming

Self-esteem
The part of the self-concept that involves evaluations of self-worth.

TABLE 2.1

Differences between Communicators with High and Low Self-Esteem

People with High Self-Esteem

1. Likely to think well of others.
2. Expect to be accepted by others.
3. Evaluate their own performance more favourably than people with low self-esteem.
4. Perform well when being watched: are not afraid of others' reactions.
5. Work harder for people who demand high standards of performance.
6. Inclined to feel comfortable with others they view as superior in some way.
7. Able to defend themselves against negative comments of others.

People with Low Self-Esteem

1. Likely to disapprove of others.
2. Expect to be rejected by others.
3. Evaluate their own performance less favourably than people with high self-esteem.
4. Perform poorly when being watched: are sensitive to possible negative reaction.
5. Work harder for undemanding, less critical people.
6. Feel threatened by people they view as superior in some way.
7. Have difficulty defending themselves against others' negative comments: are more easily influenced.

Summarized by Don E. Hamachek. *Encounters with the Self,* 2nd ed. (New York: Holt, Rinehart, and Winston, 1982), pp. 3–5.

FIGURE 2.1

The Relationship between Self-Esteem and Communication Behaviour

across as condescending know-it-alls, especially when their self-worth is challenged.[2]

Biological and Social Roots of the Self

How did you become the kind of communicator you are? Were you born that way or were you a product of your environment? As you'll now see, both play a major role in determining the way you are.

Biology and the Self

Take another look at the "Who am I?" list you developed, and you will almost certainly find some terms that describe your **personality**—characteristic

> **Personality**
> Characteristic ways that you think and behave across a variety of situations.

ways that you think and behave across a variety of situations. Your personality tends to be stable throughout your life, and often it grows more pronounced over time.[3] Research suggests that personality is actually part of our genetic makeup.[4] For example, people who were judged shy as children still show a distinctive reaction in their brains as adults when they encounter new situations.[5] In fact, we now know that biology accounts for personality traits such as extroversion,[6] shyness,[7] assertiveness,[8] verbal aggression,[9] and overall willingness to communicate.[10] To some degree, therefore, we're "programmed" to communicate in characteristic ways.

Social scientists have grouped personality traits into five primary categories, and these categories are recognized in cultures as diverse as German and Chinese.[11] Take a look at Table 2.2[12] and identify the terms that best describe your personality. While labels like "neurotic" and

TABLE 2.2

The "Big Five" Personality Traits

Extroverted	Introverted	Agreeable	Antagonistic
Sociable	Reserved	Courteous	Rude
Fun-loving	Sober	Selfless	Selfish
Talkative	Quiet	Trusting	Suspicious
Spontaneous	Self-controlled	Cooperative	Uncooperative
Open	**Not Open**	**Neurotic**	**Stable**
Imaginative	Unimaginative	Worried	Calm
Independent	Conforming	Vulnerable	Hardy
Curious	Incurious	Self-pitying	Self-satisfied
Broad interests	Narrow interests	Impatient	Patient
Conscientious	**Undirected**		
Careful	Careless		
Reliable	Undependable		
Persevering	Lax		
Ambitious	Aimless		

© Leo Callum/The New Yorker Collection/www.cartoonbank.com

It's more likely that your personality fits somewhere along a continuum for each trait. You may be somewhat shy, a little argumentative, or moderately self-controlled.

Further, while you may have a disposition toward traits like shyness or aggressiveness, you can still control how you actually communicate. More and more research suggests that personality is flexible, dynamic, and shaped by experiences.[13] For example, shy people can learn how to reach out to others, and those with aggressive tendencies can learn to communicate in more sociable ways. As one author put it, "Experiences can silence genes or activate them. Even shyness is like Silly Putty once life gets hold of it."[14]

Socialization and the Self-Concept

Other people play a major role in shaping our self-concept. If, for example, you grew up on a deserted island, you would have no way of knowing if you were smart, attractive, short, tall, mean, skinny, fat, and so forth. Even if you could view your reflection in a mirror, you still wouldn't know how to evaluate your appearance without appraisals from others or people with whom to compare yourself. In fact, people play a major role in shaping how we regard ourselves. This process of shaping occurs in two ways: reflected appraisal and social comparison. To gain insight into this notion, try the exercise on the left.

"antagonistic" can be hard to acknowledge, the descriptors underneath them may be more typical of you. You will notice that several dimensions of these personality types relate to communication.

Keep in mind that these traits are not an either-or matter but rather a matter of degree. You are not shy *or* sociable, argumentative *or* agreeable, self-controlled *or* spontaneous.

Invitation TO INSIGHT

"Ego Boosters" and "Ego Busters"

This exercise should help you identify how others have shaped your self-concept and how you shape the self-concept of others.

1. Recall someone you know, or once knew, who was an "ego booster"—someone who helped enhance your self-esteem by acting in a way that made you feel accepted, competent, worthwhile, important, appreciated, or loved. This person needn't have played a crucial role in your life as long as the role was positive. A family member with whom you've spent most of your life can be an "ego booster," but so can the stranger on the street who spontaneously offers an unexpected compliment.

2. Now recall an "ego buster" from your life—someone who acted in a large or small way to reduce your self-esteem.

3. This time, recall instances when you were an ego booster to someone else—when you intentionally or unintentionally boosted another's self-esteem. Think of times when your actions left another person feeling valued, loved, needed, and so on.

4. Finally, recall instances when you were an ego buster. What did you do to diminish another's self-esteem? Were you aware of the effect of your behaviour at the time? Your answer might show that some events we intend as boosters have the effects of busters.

> **Some people have so much respect for their superiors they have none left for themselves.**
>
> —Peter McArthur

Reflected Appraisal

Sociologist Charles Cooley used the metaphor of a mirror to identify the process of **reflected appraisal** in that each of us develops a self-concept that reflects the way we believe others see us.[15] In other words, we are likely to feel less valuable, lovable, and capable to the degree that others have communicated ego-busting signals, and we will probably feel good about ourselves to the degree that others affirm our value.[16] The self-concept that you

> **Reflected appraisal**
> The theory that a person's self-concept matches the way the person believes others regard him or her.

These same principles continue later in life, especially when messages come from **significant others**—people whose opinions we especially value. A look at the ego boosters and ego busters you described in the previous exercise will show that the evaluations of a few especially important people can be powerful. Family members are the most obvious type of significant other, and their ego busters can be particularly hurtful as a result.[17] Others can have an equal impact: a special friend, a professor, or perhaps an acquaintance whose opinion you value. The importance of significant others becomes clearer when you ask yourself how you feel about yourself as a student, as a person attractive to others, as a competent worker. You'll find that your self-evaluations were probably influenced by the way others regarded you.

> **It is thus with most of us; we are what other people say we are. We know ourselves chiefly by hearsay.**
>
> —Eric Hoffer

The impact of significant others is especially strong during adolescence. Whether or not teenagers are included in or excluded from peer groups is a crucial factor in their self-concept development.[18] Fortunately, parents who understand this notion can help them develop a strong self-concept.[19] After the age of 30, however, most people are not as influenced by significant others and their self-concepts don't change radically, at least not without a conscious effort.[20]

Social Comparison

While the messages of others shape our self-concept, so too does **social comparison**: evaluating ourselves in terms of how we compare with others.

Feelings of *superiority* or *inferiority* depend on whom we are comparing ourselves with,[21] particularly in today's media-saturated world. For instance, research shows that young women who regularly compare themselves with ultra-thin models develop negative appraisals of their own bodies.[22] In one study, young women's perceptions of their bodies changed for the worse after watching just 30 minutes of televised images of the "ideal" female form.[23] Men who compare themselves to media-idealized male physiques also evaluate their bodies negatively.[24] Even popular TV makeover shows—with their underlying message of "you must improve your appearance"—can lead viewers

Significant other
A person whose opinion is important enough to affect one's self-concept strongly.

Social comparison
Evaluation of oneself in terms of or by comparison to others.

described in the list at the beginning of this chapter is a product of the messages you have received throughout your life.

Reflected appraisal begins early in life and children learn to judge themselves by the messages they receive. Some of these are positive: "You're so cute!" "I love you." "What a big girl." Other messages are negative: "What's the matter with you? Can't you do anything right?" "You're a bad boy." "Leave me alone. You're driving me crazy!" Because children are trusting souls, they have no other way of viewing themselves and they accept these evaluations at face value.

"Now look what you've done!"

to feel worse about themselves.[25] It's not likely that any of us will be as beautiful as a Hollywood star, as agile as a professional athlete, or as wealthy as a millionaire. Nonetheless, many people judge themselves against such unreasonable standards and suffer accordingly.[26] These distorted self-images can lead to serious behavioural disorders such as depression, anorexia nervosa, and bulimia.[27]

Social comparison also allows us to decide if we are *similar to* or *different from* others. A child who is interested in acting but lives in a setting where drama is regarded as weird will accept this label unless there is support from others. Likewise, adults who want to improve the quality of their relationships but are surrounded by friends and family who don't recognize or acknowledge the importance of these matters may think of themselves as oddballs. Thus, it's easy to recognize that the **reference groups** against which we compare ourselves play another important role in shaping our self-concepts. However, not every part of one's self-concept is shaped by others. If, for instance, you visited a Thai restaurant and then cooked a similar meal at home that had the same authentic taste and texture, you might consider yourself an adept chef.

While some features of the self are immediately apparent, the *significance* we attach to them depends greatly on the opinions of others. For example, we once heard a woman in her 80s describing her youth. "When I was a girl, we didn't worry about weight. Some people were skinny and others were plump, and we pretty much accepted the bodies God gave us." In those days it was unlikely that weight would have found its way onto the self-concept list you constructed because it wasn't considered significant. This is not the case today: The popular media continually promote the latest diet fads and television ads are filled with scenes of slender, happy people. No wonder everyone wants to "lose a few pounds." While this campaign may stem from the need to be fit and healthy, we generally see slimness as desirable because others tell us it is. In societies where obesity is the ideal, extremely heavy people regarded themselves as beautiful. In the same way, the fact that

G. Napolitano/Film Magic/Getty Images

The namesake of the TV series *Ugly Betty* was smart, kind, and diligent. But she wasn't as thin or beautiful as her co-workers at the high-fashion magazine where she worked. Social comparison led to Betty's ongoing struggle with shyness and low self-esteem.

one is single or married, solitary or sociable, aggressive or passive takes on meaning depending on the interpretation that society attaches to those traits.

By now you might be thinking, "I'm shy or lack confidence because of the way others have treated me. I can't help being what I am." To an extent, you are a product of your environment, but having a poor self-concept in the past is no reason for continuing to do so in the future. You *can* change your attitudes and behaviours, as you'll soon read.

Characteristics of the Self-Concept

Now that we know more about where the self-concept comes from, let's look at some of its characteristics.

Image Source/Getty Images

> **Reference groups**
> Groups against which we compare ourselves, thereby influencing our self-concept and self-esteem.

Cipher in the Snow

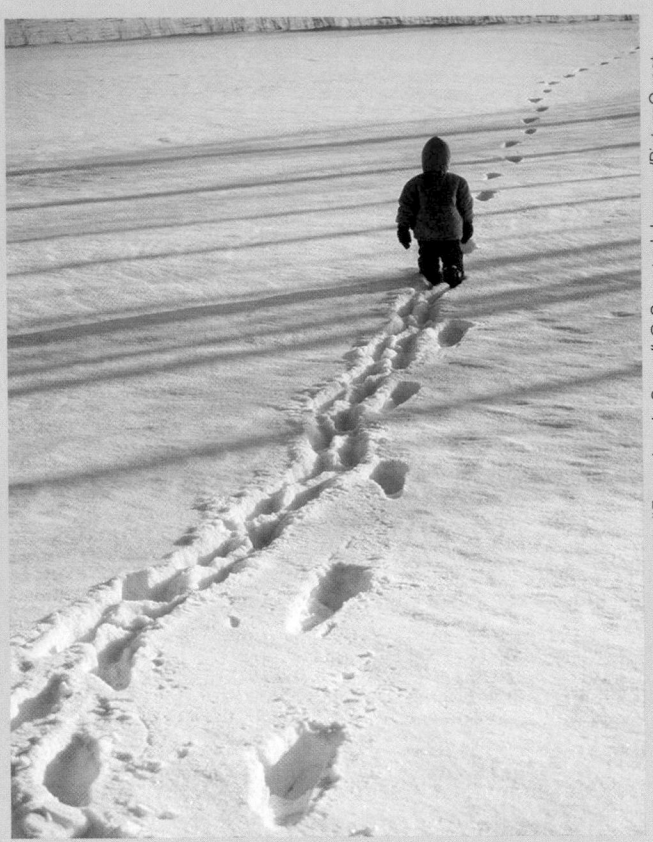

"Footprints in Snow" © Comstock Images/PictureQuest

It started with tragedy on a biting cold February morning. I was driving behind the Milford Corners bus as I did most snowy mornings on my way to school. It veered and stopped short at the hotel, which it had no business doing, and I was annoyed as I had to come to an unexpected stop. A boy lurched out of the bus, reeled, stumbled, and collapsed on the snow bank at the curb. The bus driver and I reached him at the same moment. His thin, hollow face was white even against the snow.

"He's dead," the driver whispered.

It didn't register for a minute. I glanced quickly at the scared young faces staring down at us from the school bus. "A doctor! Quick! I'll phone from the hotel . . ."

"No use, I tell you, he's dead." The driver looked down at the boy's still form. "He never even said he felt bad," he muttered. "Just tapped me on the shoulder and said, real quiet, 'I'm sorry. I have to get off at the hotel.' That's all. Polite and apologizing like."

At school, the giggling, shuffling morning noise quieted as the news went down the halls. I passed a huddle of girls. "Who was it? Who dropped dead on the way to school?" I heard one of them half-whisper.

"Don't know his name; some kid from Milford Corners" was the reply.

It was like that in the faculty room and the principal's office. "I'd appreciate your going out to tell the parents," the principal told me. "They haven't a phone and, anyway, somebody from school should go there in person. I'll cover your classes."

"Why me?" I asked. "Wouldn't it be better if you did it?"

"I didn't know the boy," the principal admitted levelly. "And in last year's sophomore personalities column I note that you were listed as his favourite teacher."

I drove through the snow and cold down the bad canyon road to the Evans place and thought about the boy, Cliff Evans. His favourite teacher! I thought. He hasn't spoken two words to me in two years! I could see him in my mind's eye all right, sitting back there in the last seat in my afternoon literature class. He came in the room by himself and left by himself. "Cliff Evans," I muttered to myself, "a boy who never talked." I thought a minute. "A boy who never smiled. I never saw him smile once."

The big ranch kitchen was clean and warm. I blurted out my news somehow. Mrs. Evans reached blindly toward a chair. "He never said anything about bein' ailing."

His stepfather snorted. "He ain't said nothin' about anything since I moved in here."

Mrs. Evans pushed a pan to the back of the stove and began to untie her apron. "Now hold on," her husband snapped. "I got to have breakfast before I go to town. Nothin' we can do now anyway. If Cliff hadn't been so dumb, he'd have told us he didn't feel good."

After school I sat in the office and stared blankly at the records spread out before me. I was to close the file and write the obituary for the school paper. The almost bare sheets mocked the effort. Cliff Evans, white, never legally adopted by stepfather, five young half-brothers and sisters. These meager strands of information and the list of D grades were all the records had to offer.

Cliff Evans had silently come in the school door in the mornings and gone out the school door in the evenings, and that was all. He had never belonged to a club. He had never played on a team. He had never held an office. As far as I could tell he had never done one happy, noisy kid thing. He had never been anybody at all.

How do you go about making a boy into a zero? The grade school records showed me. The first and second grade teachers' annotations read "sweet, shy child," "timid but eager." Then the third grade note had opened the attack. Some teacher had written in a good, firm hand, "Cliff won't talk. Uncooperative. Slow learner." The other academic sheep had followed with "dull"; "slow-witted"; "low IQ." They became correct. The boy's IQ score in the ninth grade was listed as 83. But his IQ in the third grade had been 106. The score didn't go under 100 until the seventh grade. Even shy, timid, sweet children have resilience. It takes time to break them.

I stomped to the typewriter and wrote a savage report pointing out what education had done to Cliff Evans. I slapped a copy on the principal's desk and another in the sad, dog-eared file. I banged the typewriter and slammed the file and crashed the door shut, but I didn't feel much better. A little boy kept walking after me, a little boy with a peaked, pale face, a skinny body in faded jeans, and big eyes that had looked and searched for a long time and then had become veiled.

I could guess how many times he'd been chosen last to play sides in a game, how many whispered child conversations had excluded him, how many times he hadn't been asked. I could see and hear the faces and voices that said over and over, "You're a nothing, Cliff Evans."

A child is a believing creature. Cliff undoubtedly believed them. Suddenly it seemed clear to me: When finally there was nothing left at all for Cliff Evans, he collapsed on a snowbank and went away. The doctor might list "heart failure" as the cause of death, but that wouldn't change my mind.

We couldn't find 10 students in the school who had known Cliff well enough to attend the funeral as his friends. So the student body officers and a committee from the junior class went as a group to the church,

being politely sad. I attended the services with them, and sat through it with a lump of cold lead in my chest and a big resolve growing through me.

I've never forgotten Cliff Evans nor that resolve. He has been my challenge year after year, class after class. I look for veiled eyes or bodies scrouged into a seat in an alien world. "Look, kids," I say silently, "I may not do anything else for you this year, but not one of you is going to come out of here a nobody. I'll work or fight to the bitter end doing battle with society and the school board, but I won't have one of you coming out of here thinking himself a zero."

Most of the time—not always, but most of the time—I've succeeded.

Jean Mizer

Discussion Starters

How do you think Cliff Evans would respond to the question "Who are you?" How would he describe his moods or feelings, appearance, social traits, talents, intellectual capacity, beliefs, social roles, and physical condition? What types of verbal and nonverbal messages do you think he received from his mother, stepfather, siblings, teachers, and peers? Could there be a Cliff Evans in your life, and if so, would you respond differently to that individual after reading this story? Have *you* ever felt like Cliff Evans?

The Self-Concept Is Subjective

The first characteristic of the self-concept is that it is subjective. Although we tend to believe that our self-concept is accurate, it may well be distorted. For example, researchers found that there is no relationship between the way college students rate their ability as interpersonal communicators, public speakers, or listeners and their true effectiveness.[28] In all cases, they rated their communication skills higher than their actual performance warranted. In another study, men ranked themselves on their ability to get along with others,[29] and defying mathematical laws, all subjects put themselves in the top half of the population; 60 percent rated themselves in the top 10 percent of the population; and an amazing 25 percent in the top 1 percent. The men also had lofty appraisals of their leadership and athletic abilities. Other research shows that perceptions of superiority tend to increase over time![30] The same holds for Internet daters. They too often have a "foggy mirror"—and see themselves more positively than others do.[31]

Not all distortion of the self-concept is positive. Many people view themselves more harshly than the objective facts warrant. We all experience temporary cases of the "uglies," convinced that we look much worse than we actually do. But people are more critical of themselves

when they experience negative moods than when they feel more positive.[32] Although we all suffer occasional bouts of self-doubt, some people suffer from long-term or even permanent states of excessive self-doubt and criticism.[33] Such a chronic condition can influence how they approach and respond to others.

There are several reasons for distorted evaluations. One is *obsolete information*. We cling to past failures even though they don't predict failure in the future. Likewise, your past successes don't guarantee future success. Perhaps your jokes were once well received or your work was superior, but now the facts have changed.

Distorted feedback can also create a self-image that is worse or better than the facts warrant. Overly critical parents can foster a negative self-image. Or the remarks of cruel friends, uncaring teachers, excessively demanding employers, or even memorable strangers can have a lasting effect. Other distorted messages are unrealistically positive. Bosses may think they are excellent managers when assistants shower them with false praise in order to keep their jobs or get promoted. Likewise, a child's inflated ego may be based on the praise of doting parents.

Another cause of a negative self-concept is based on *perfection*. For example, children's stories and advertisements imply that the way to be a hero, the way to be liked and admired, is to show no flaws. Parents perpetuate this myth by refusing to admit that they are ever wrong or unfair. Children quickly learn that a "well-adjusted, successful" person has no faults. Naively believing that other people are perfect contributes greatly to a negative self-concept.

> Today in Canada, black people still contend with racism at every level of society. And yet, the way my children will define themselves, and be defined by others, remains up for grabs. Racial identity is about how you see yourself, about how you construct a sense of belonging, community, awareness, and allegiance.
>
> —Lawrence Hill

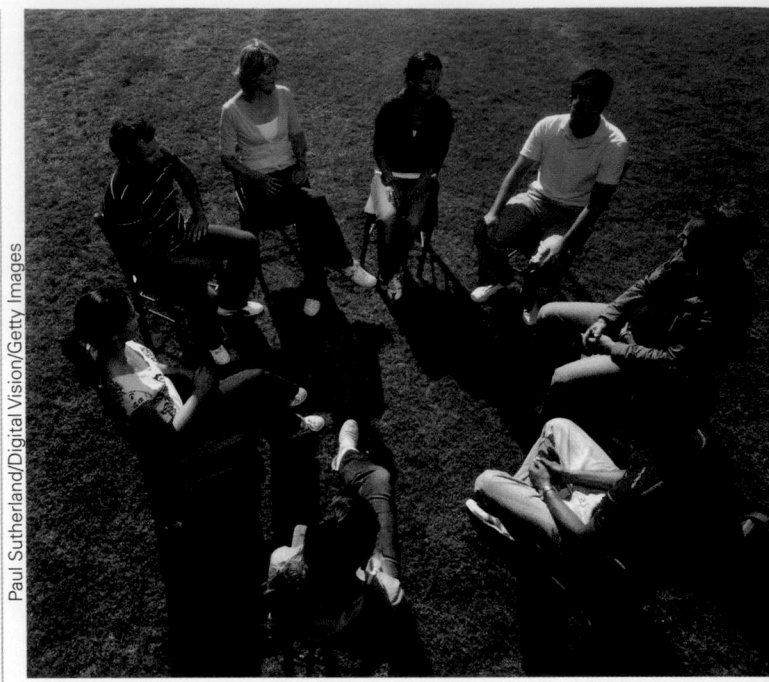

Because perfection doesn't exist, expecting to achieve it is a sure ticket to an unnecessarily poor self-concept. For example, one study out of McMaster University and the University of Montreal found that women who exercised in front of mirrors expressed greater anxiety about their physical appearance than women who didn't. The authors concluded that standing in front of a mirror enhances self-awareness, and when the self is not quite up to the ideal, negative self-evaluations occur.[34]

A final reason why people sell themselves short is connected to *social expectations*. Canadians are, for the most part, modest people who consider talking about their strengths to be bragging, confusing this with the people who boast about achievements they haven't accomplished.[35] This convention leads us to focus on shortcomings rather than accomplishments. It's acceptable to proclaim that you failed to achieve a goal, but to express your pride at a job well done is considered boastful. Eventually, we begin to believe our disparaging remarks and see ourselves as much worse than we actually are. To avoid falling into the trap of becoming overly critical, try to recognize your strengths. Give the exercise on the left a try.

Invitation TO INSIGHT

Recognizing Your Strengths

1. In groups of three to five people, share three personal strengths or accomplishments. These needn't be momentous feats—it's perfectly acceptable to talk about some part of yourself that leaves you feeling pleased or proud. You might say that instead of procrastinating, you completed an assignment before the due date, that you spoke up in class even though you were afraid of disapproval, or that you bake a fantastic chocolate cake.

2. To help you get started, consider the following:
   a. How have you grown in the past year? How are you more skilled or wise, or a better person than you previously were?
   b. What features do you possess that make your friends and family members appreciate you?

3. Did you have a hard time thinking of things to share? Would it have been easier to list the things that are *wrong* with you? If so, was this because you are a wretched person or because you tend to stress your defects and ignore your strengths? Consider how such a habit can affect your self-concept. Then ask yourself why it would be better to express your strengths more often.

The Self-Concept Resists Change

Although we all change, there is a tendency to cling to an existing self-concept, even when evidence shows that it is outdated. Seeking and attending to information that conforms to an existing self-concept has been labelled **cognitive conservatism**.

> **Cognitive conservatism**
> The tendency to seek and attend to information that conforms to an existing self-concept.

Cognitive conservatism leads us to seek out individuals who support our self-concept. For example, both college students and married couples with high self-esteem seek out partners who view them favourably and those with negative self-esteem seek out people who view them unfavourably.[36] It appears that we are less concerned with learning the "truth" about ourselves than with reinforcing a familiar self-concept.

We're often reluctant to revise a previously favourable self-concept because we honestly believe that the old truth still holds, in spite of the facts to the contrary. A student who did well in earlier years but now has failed to study might be unwilling to admit that the label "good scholar" no longer applies. Or a worker might resent a supervisor's mentioning increased absences and low productivity. These people aren't *lying;* they just don't get it.

Courtesy of Ellison Robertson

The tendency to cling to an outmoded self-perception even holds when the new image is more favourable. One former student with physical features attractive enough to appear in any glamour magazine characterized herself as "ordinary" and "unattractive"—even when classmates noted her beauty. When questioned, she described how she had to wear thick glasses and braces on her teeth from childhood into her late teens and how she had been teased constantly. Even though the braces were gone and she wore contacts, she still saw herself as ugly and brushed aside our compliments. She insisted that we were just being nice but she knew how she *really* looked. This student exemplifies how we deny ourselves a much happier life when we resist change by clinging to obsolete pictures of ourselves.

A second problem arising from an obsolete self-concept is self-delusion and lack of growth. If you hold an unrealistically favourable picture of yourself, you won't see the real need for change and the opportunity to learn new skills, change a relationship, or improve your physical condition. You'll stay with the familiar and comfortable delusion that everything is all right. As time goes by, this delusion will be harder to maintain, which will lead to a third type of problem: defensiveness. In fact, the problem of defensiveness is so great that it is examined in detail in a later chapter.

Influences on Identity

How we view ourselves and others is also influenced by diversity, culture, and gender.

Diversity

The challenges and opportunities that come from diversity are becoming more apparent in our increasingly diverse society. Unlike Americans, who attempt to shed their ethnicity, Canadians celebrate differences. In fact, Canada's groundbreaking Multiculturalism Act, passed in 1988, acknowledges the value of cultural pluralism to Canadian identity. Immigrants coming to Canada retain their language, customs, and religion and thus add to the richness of our land. Researchers Jacqueline Oxman-Martinez and Jill Hanley reported that in 2001, two-thirds of Canada's population growth consisted of immigrants. They predict that, according to Statistics Canada, "one in five Canadians will belong to a visible minority" by 2017. Canada's "self-concept" is changing. As these authors write, "These changes demand a revision of our national image, our sense of what is Canadian, to fully reflect this racial and ethnic diversity."[37]

Language is another feature of diversity that affects self-concept. This is particularly evident in Canada, an officially bilingual country. However, in an attempt to maintain the distinct Québécois culture, the controversial Bill 101 made French the official language in Quebec. Francophones clearly recognize that to lose your language is to lose your sense of self. If your primary language is not the majority one, or when it lacks prestige, the sense of being a member of what social scientists call the "out-group" is strong. At

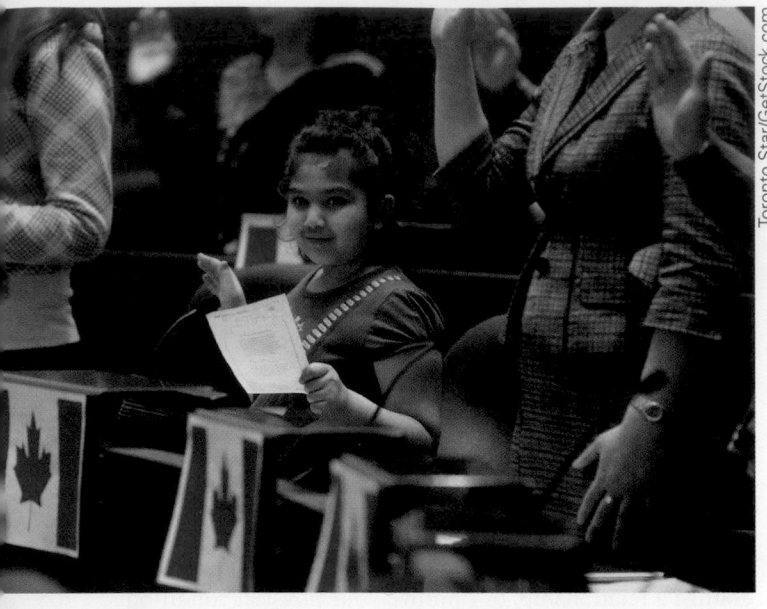

Toronto Star/GetStock.com

this point, the speaker of a non-dominant tongue can react in one of two ways: either to feel pressured to assimilate by speaking the "better" language or to refuse to accommodate to the majority language and maintain loyalty to the ethnic tongue.[38] In either case, the self-concept is affected. On one hand, the feeling is likely to be, "I'm not as good as speakers of the native language," and on the other, the belief is, "There's something unique and worth preserving in my language." This experience is exemplified by Canada's First Nations people, who during the 1950s and 1960s were forced to speak English in residential schools. This resulted in the loss of their language and related cultural norms. It is only in recent years that Canada's Aboriginal peoples are reclaiming their identity.

> Canada is the only country I know of in which, throughout my lifetime, to be pro-Canadian has been interpreted in terms of a negative attitude towards other countries.
>
> —Norman Ward,
> in J.H. Bedekop, ed.,
> *The Star-Spangled Beaver*

Culture

Our self-concept is also shaped by the culture in which we have been reared.[39] Most Western cultures are highly individualistic, whereas Asian ones tend to be collectivistic. When asked to identify themselves, Canadians, Americans, Australians, and Europeans would probably respond by giving their first name, surname, street, town, and country. Many Asians do it the other way around.[40] If you ask Hindus for their identity, they will provide their caste as well as their name and village. The Sanskrit formula for identifying oneself begins with lineage and goes on to state family and house, and ends with one's personal name.[41] If you asked members from collectivistic cultures to make a "Who am I?" list, there would be far more group references than those from individualistic cultures.[42]

These naming conventions aren't just cultural curiosities; they reflect a way of viewing oneself. In collective cultures, people gain identity through group associations. Feelings of pride and self-worth are not shaped solely by what an individual does, but also by behaviours of other members of the community. This linkage explains the traditional Asian denial of self-importance—a strong contrast to the self-promotion that is common in individualistic Western cultures.[43] In Chinese written language, for example, the pronoun *I* looks very similar to the word for "selfish."[44] Table 2.3 (p. 41) summarizes some differences between individualistic cultures and more collective ones.

Dmitry Shironosov/Shutterstock

TABLE 2.3

The Self in Individualistic and Collectivistic Cultures

Individualistic Cultures

- Self is separate, unique individual; should be independent, self-sufficient.
- Individual should take care of him- or herself and immediate family.
- Many flexible group memberships; friends based on shared interests and activities.
- Individual achievement and initiative rewarded; individual decisions encouraged; individual credit and blame assigned.
- High value placed on autonomy, change, youth, individual security, equality.

Collectivistic Cultures

- People belong to extended families or in-groups; "we," or group, orientation.
- Person should take care of extended family before self.
- Emphasize belonging to a very few permanent in-groups that have a strong influence over the person.
- Contributing to group goals and well-being rewarded; cooperation with in-group members prioritized; group decisions valued; credit and blame shared.
- High value placed on duty, order, tradition, age, group security, status, and hierarchy.

Adapted from the NEBRASKA SYMPOSIUM ON MOTIVATION, volume 37, by permission of the University of Nebraska Press. Copyright © 1989 by the University of Nebraska Press.

Such cultural differences can affect the level of comfort or anxiety that people feel when communicating. In collective societies, there is a higher degree of communication apprehension. For example, as a group, residents of China, South Korea, and Japan exhibit a significantly higher degree of anxiety about speaking out than do members of individualistic cultures.[45] But the high level of communication apprehension isn't a problem—just the opposite, in fact. In collectivistic societies, reticence is valued. The goal is to *avoid* calling attention yourself. So while a self-concept that includes assertiveness might make a Westerner feel proud, it would more likely cause shame in Asian countries.

The difference between individualism and collectivism shows up in everyday interaction. Communication researcher Stella Ting-Toomey has developed a theory that explains cultural differences in terms of honesty and directness.[46] She suggests that in individualistic Western cultures, where there is a strong "I" orientation, the norm of speaking directly is honoured; whereas in collectivistic cultures, where the desire is to build connections, then indirect approaches that maintain harmony are more desirable. While "I gotta be me" represents Western culture, "If I hurt you, I hurt myself" is more in keeping with the Asian approach.

Gender

Imagine that you were born as a member of the opposite sex. Would you express your emotions, deal with conflict, or relate to friends and strangers in the same way? The answer is almost certainly no.

Right from the beginning, being male or female shapes the way others communicate with us, and thus how we shape our sense of self. For example, people want to know the sex of a child as soon as, or even before, it is born. As the *Cathy* cartoon on page 42 shows, only then do people know how to behave.[47] Comments about boys focus on size, strength, and activity; comments about girls address beauty, sweetness, and facial responsiveness. The underlying message is that some behaviours are masculine and others feminine. Little girls are often praised for acting "sweet." The same principle operates in adulthood: Men

Seiya Kawamoto/Getty Images

In her hit song "If I Were a Boy," pop star Beyoncé expresses her belief that male gender role expectations are more liberating than those imposed on women.

who stand up for their beliefs are considered "tough" or "persistent," whereas women who do so are called "nags" or "bitches."[48] It's not hard to see how gender roles and labels like these can have a profound effect on how women and men view themselves and on how they communicate.

Gender differences are also associated with self-esteem. One study of 550 Canadian secondary school students showed that male adolescents have higher self-esteem than their female counterparts.[49] Researchers from the Department of Sociology at the University of Western Ontario found that women, across ages, had lower levels of self-esteem than men did.[50] These results may be linked to gender expectations in that competitiveness is valued more in men than in women. It isn't surprising that the self-esteem of adolescent young men is closely related to having abilities that are superior in some way to those of their peers,

Kevin Winter/Getty Images

Self-fulfilling prophecy
A prediction or expectation of an event that makes the outcome more likely to occur than would otherwise have been the case.

whereas teenage women's self-worth is tied more closely to the success of their social relationships and verbal skills.[51]

LO²
The Self-Fulfilling Prophecy and Communication

The self-concept not only determines how you see yourself in the present but it can actually influence your future behaviour and that of others. This is known as the **self-fulfilling prophecy**. It refers to the notion of making predictions about future behaviours and feelings and then acting according to these predictions.

The self-fulfilling prophecy has four stages:

1. Holding an expectation (for yourself or for others)
2. Behaving in accordance with that expectation
3. The expectation coming to pass
4. Reinforcing the original expectation

To see how this process operates, imagine that you're scheduled for a job interview. You're nervous about how you'll do and aren't sure that you're really qualified for the position. You share your concerns with a professor who knows you well and a friend who works for the company. Both assure you that you're perfect for the job. Based on these comments, you arrive at the interview feeling good about yourself. You speak with authority and sell yourself with confidence. The employers are impressed and you receive the job offer. Your conclusion: "I can and will do this well."

Thanks to the assurances of your professor and friend, your expectations about the interview were upbeat (stage 1). Because of your optimistic attitude, you communicated

cathy®   **by Cathy Guisewite**

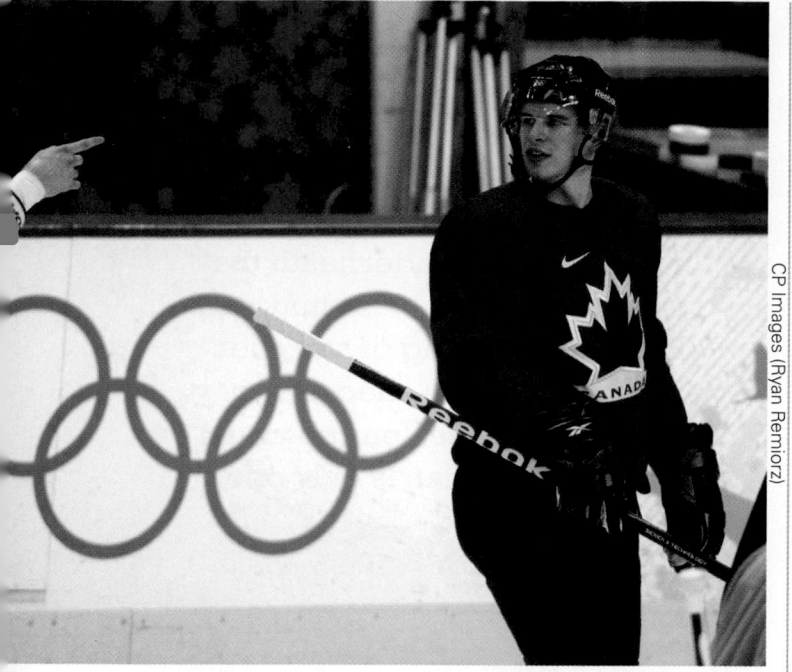
CP Images (Ryan Remiorz)

Self-imposed prophecies operate in many ways that affect everyday communication. Say you wake up in a sour mood and think to yourself, "This is going to be a bad day." After this declaration, you act in ways that make it come true. On the other hand, if you approached the same day thinking it can only get better, this expectation will probably be met. Researchers have found that putting a smile on your face, even if you're not happy, can lead to a more positive disposition.[57]

Other-Imposed Prophecies

The second category of self-fulfilling prophecies is **other-imposed prophecies**, where your actions are governed by the expectations that others have of you. The classic example was demonstrated by Robert Rosenthal and Lenore Jacobson in a study they described in their book *Pygmalion in the Classroom*.[58] The experimenters told teachers that 20 percent of the children in a certain elementary school showed unusual potential for intellectual growth. The names of these 20 percent were randomly selected, and eight months later these "magic" children showed significantly greater gains in IQ than did the other children. What led to the actual change in the intellectual performance of these allegedly "special" students was a change in the teachers' expectations regarding their intellectual performance. Although the children were no more intelligent than their classmates, they had learned that their teachers—significant others—believed that they were and they performed accordingly.

> **Self-imposed prophecy**
> Occurs when your own expectations influence your behaviour.
>
> **Other-imposed prophecy**
> Occurs when your actions may be governed by the expectations that others have of you.

Clearly, teachers affect students' self-concepts. When a teacher communicates to a child the message "I think you're bright," the child accepts that evaluation and changes her self-concept to include it. Unfortunately, the same principle holds for students whose teachers send the message "I think you're stupid."

This type of self-fulfilling prophecy is also a powerful force for shaping the self-concept and thus the behaviour of people outside schools.[59] In psychotherapy, patients who believe they will benefit from treatment often do so regardless of the type of treatment they receive. In the same vein, when doctors believe that patients will improve, they often do so because of this expectation. If doctors think there is little hope, patients often fail to recover.[60] Apparently the patient's self-concept as sick or well—as shaped by the doctor—plays an important role in determining the actual state of health.

confidently in the interview (stage 2). Your confident behaviour—along with your qualifications—led to a job offer (stage 3). Finally, the positive results reinforced your positive self-assessment and you'll be an excellent employee (stage 4).

Self-fulfilling prophecies have a tremendous influence in our lives and, to a great extent, we become what we believe. In this sense, we and those around us constantly create and recreate our self-concepts. There are two types of self-fulfilling prophecies: self-imposed and other-imposed.

Self-Imposed Prophecies

Self-imposed prophecies occur when your own expectations influence your behaviour. For instance, perhaps you've faced an audience at one time or another when you were fearful and forgotten your remarks, not because you were unprepared but because you said to yourself, "I know I'll blow it."

We have to watch our self-imposed prophecies.[52] Communicators who believe they are incompetent are less likely to pursue rewarding relationships and more likely to sabotage their existing relationships.[53] On the other hand, students who perceive themselves as capable do better academically.[54] In another study, subjects who were sensitive to social rejection tended to expect rejection, perceived it where it didn't exist, and overreacted in ways that jeopardized the quality of their relationships.[55] Finally, communicators who feel anxious about giving speeches seem to create self-fulfilling prophecies about doing poorly that cause them to perform less effectively.[56]

"YOU'RE A VERY FINE FELLOW!"

Drawing by Gahan Wilson. © Gahan Wilson. Reprinted by permission.

It's important to note that you must do more than believe something about a person to shape his or her expectations; you must communicate that belief. If parents have faith in their children but the kids aren't aware of that confidence, they won't be affected by their parents' expectations. Therefore, self-fulfilling prophecies are both a communication and a psychological event.

LO^3
Changing Your Self-Concept

If you're not happy with parts of your self-concept, take comfort in the fact that we have the power to change a great deal of our communication-related traits.[61] While there's no quick method for becoming the person you'd like to be, we can offer several suggestions that will help you move closer to your goals.

Have a Realistic Perception of Yourself

Unrealistic perceptions sometimes come from giving yourself more credit than you deserve or from being overly self-critical. An unrealistically poor self-concept can also arise from the inaccurate feedback of others. Perhaps you receive an excessive number of prickly messages and not enough fuzzy, warm messages. Workers with overly critical supervisors, children with cruel "friends," and students with unsupportive teachers are all prone to low self-concepts owing to excessively negative feedback. If you fall into this category, it's important to seek out more supportive people who will acknowledge your assets as well as your liabilities. Doing so is often a quick and sure boost.

"There is more to you than mere money-lust, Duddy, but I'm afraid for you. You're two people, that's why. The scheming little bastard I saw so easily and the fine, intelligent boy underneath that your grandfather, bless him, saw. But you're coming of age soon and you'll have to choose. A boy can be two, three, four potential people, but a man is only one."

—Mordecai Richler,
The Apprenticeship of Duddy Kravitz

Elena Elisseeva/Shutterstock

Have Realistic Expectations

It's important to determine if some of your dissatisfaction might come from expecting too much of yourself. Expecting to communicate perfectly, handle every conflict productively, be totally relaxed and skillful in conversations, or be 100 percent helpful when others have problems is unrealistic. Nobody can do that. Expecting perfection is to doom yourself to unhappiness.

Sometimes it's easy to be hard on yourself because everyone around you seems to be handling themselves better than you. But what may seem like confidence and skill in others could be a front to hide uncertainty. Perhaps they too are imposing demands of perfection on themselves.

In situations where others seem more competent than you, try to judge yourself against your own growth and not against their behaviours. Rather than feel miserable, realize that you are probably a better, wiser, or more skilled person than you used to be. Thinking like this can be very satisfying.

Have the Will to Change

We often say that we want to change, but we're not really willing to work at it. Sometimes we maintain an unrealistic self-concept by claiming that we "can't" be the person we'd like to be when in fact we're simply not willing to do what's required. Check out the Skill Builder titled "Reevaluating Your Can'ts" to see how many of your can'ts are actually won'ts. You can change if you make an effort.

Have the Skill to Change

Often trying isn't enough. In some instances you're not sure how to change. To remedy this, you can seek advice—from books, from the Internet, and from instructors, counsellors, other experts, and, of course, friends. While not all of the advice will be useful, you're sure to find some that is helpful. A second method is to observe models—people who handle themselves in the ways you would like to master. Watch what people you admire do and say, not to copy them

Columbia/The Kobal Collection/Rosenthan, Zade

In *The Pursuit of Happyness*, Christopher Gardner (Will Smith) uses persuasive communication skills and determination to overcome poverty and build a better life for himself and his son. In Gardner's words, "If you want somethin', go get it. Period."

but rather to adapt their behaviours to fit your personal style. At this point, you might think it is impossible to change how you think about yourself, but it is possible if you are serious. You don't need to be perfect, but you can change your self-concept and raise your self-esteem if you choose.

SKILL BUILDER

Reevaluating Your "Can'ts"

1. Choose a partner and take turns making and listing statements that begin with "I can't . . ." Try to focus your statements on your relationships with family, friends, co-workers, students, and even strangers—anyone with whom you have a hard time communicating. Sample statements:
   "I can't be myself with strangers I'd like to get to know at parties."
   "I can't stay off Facebook for more than a few hours."
   "I can't bring myself to ask my supervisor for the raise I think I deserve."
   "I can't ask questions in class."

2. Notice your feelings (self-pity, regret, concern) as you make and reveal each statement to your partner.

3. Now repeat aloud each statement you've just made, except this time change each "can't" to a "won't." After each sentence, tell your partner whatever thoughts you have about what you've just said.

4. After you've finished, decide whether "can't" or "won't" is more appropriate for each item and explain your choice to your partner.

5. Are there any instances of the self-fulfilling prophecy in your list—times when your decision that you "can't" do something was the only force keeping you from doing it?

123render/iStockphoto

"Hah! This is the Old King Cole nobody ever sees."

© Dana Fradon/The New Yorker Collection/www.cartoonbank.com

LO⁴
Presenting the Self: Communication as Identity Management

So far we have described how communication shapes the way communicators view themselves. In the remainder of this chapter we will turn the tables and focus on the topic of **identity management**—the communication strategies that people use to influence how others view them.

Public and Private Selves

Until now, we have referred to the "self" as if each of us had only one identity. In truth, however, each of us has several different selves, some private and others public.

The **perceived self** is a reflection of the self-concept. Your perceived self is the person you believe yourself to be in moments of honest self-examination. We can call the perceived self "private"

Identity management
The communication strategies people use to influence how others view them.

Perceived self
The person you believe yourself to be in moments of honest self-examination. It may be identical with or different from the presenting and ideal selves.

Presenting self
The image a person presents to others. It may be identical with or different from the perceived and ideal selves.

because you are unlikely to reveal all of it to another person. You might, for example, be reluctant to share some feelings about your intelligence ("I'm not as smart as I wish I were"), your goals ("The most important thing to me is becoming rich"), your motives ("I care more about myself than about others"), or a host of other things.

The **presenting self** is a public image—the way we want others to view us. Typically, the presenting self that we seek to create is a socially approved image: diligent student, loving partner, conscientious worker, loyal friend, and so on. Social norms often create a gap between the perceived and presenting selves.

You can recognize the difference between public and private behaviours by recalling a time when you observed a driver, alone in the car, behaving in ways that would never be acceptable in public. We've all done things when we were alone that we would never do in public.

Characteristics of Identity Management

Now that you have a sense of what identity management is, we can look at some of its characteristics.

We Strive to Construct Multiple Identities

Most of us have more than one identity. In the course of a day, most people play a variety of roles: respectful student,

Jann Arden is known as a performer whose humour and honesty allow you to gain some insight into who she is really is as a person.

Rick Madonik/GetStock.com

joking friend, friendly neighbour, and helpful worker, to suggest just a few. The ability to construct multiple identities is one element of communication competence, and changing the language we use or our speaking style is one way to do this. A style of speaking, or even the language itself, can reflect a choice about how to construct one's identity. For example, a scholarly female biology professor plays on the faculty/staff hockey team against a student group. When asked how she manages her communication style, she responded that in the classroom she is dogmatic and authoritarian but also lively and enthusiastic. When delivering scientific papers, she minimizes the human element to appear serious and informative. On the ice, however, changes in her communication style have less to do with her verbal alterations. To be accepted as an equal in that context, she shows she means business by checking and light sticking.

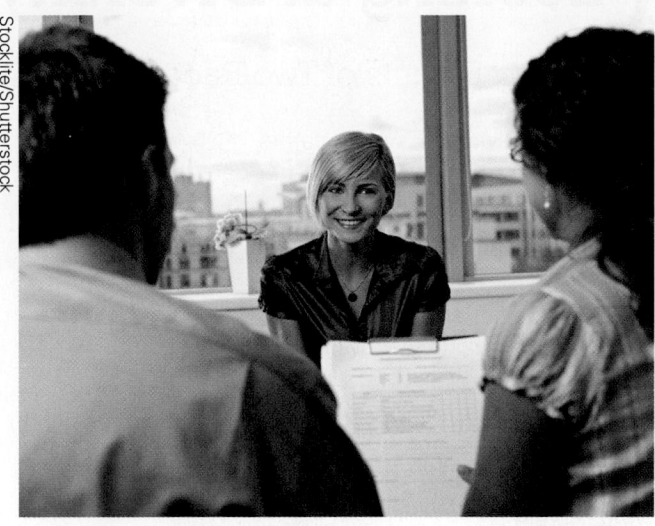

Stocklite/Shutterstock

We even strive to construct different identities with the same person. Think of the different roles you play in your family—from helpless child to dedicated family member, from young rebel to responsible adult. Likewise, in romantic relationships, we switch from friend to lover to business partner to critic and so forth, depending on the context.

Identity Management Is Collaborative

Sociologist Erving Goffman used a drama metaphor to describe identity management, suggesting that each of us is a kind of playwright creating our own role in terms of how we want others to see us.[62] This identity-related communication can be viewed as a kind of theatre process where we collaborate with other actors to improvise scenes in which our characters mesh.

Identity Management Can Be Deliberate or Unconscious

Sometimes we are highly aware of managing impressions, such as during an employment interview, but in other cases we unconsciously act in ways that are really small public performances.[63] For example, experimental subjects expressed facial disgust in reaction to eating sandwiches laced with a supersaturated saltwater solution only when someone else was present. When they were alone, they made no faces while eating the same sandwiches.[64] Another study showed that communicators engage in facial mimicry, such as smiling or looking sympathetic in response to another's message, in face-to-face settings only when their expressions can be seen by the other person. However, when they speak on the phone and their reactions cannot be seen, they do not make the same expressions.[65]

These studies suggest that most of our behaviour is aimed at sending messages to others—in other words, identity management. But the experimental subjects didn't consciously think, "Somebody is watching and I better act accordingly." Instead, their actions were instantaneous and outside of their conscious awareness. Therefore, it seems like an exaggeration to suggest that *all* behaviour is aimed at making impressions. However, most people consciously or unconsciously communicate in ways that help construct desired identities for themselves and others.

Identity Management Varies by Situation

The degree to which we consciously manage our identities varies from one situation to another. For instance, most of us work harder at creating a desired impression in the early stages of a relationship—especially when we're seeking the approval of people whose opinion we value. Again, think of how carefully you present yourself to a potential boss during the interview process.[66] The same principle operates in courtship situations. University men changed their self-presentation more when they were talking to women they found attractive than they did when talking to less attractive women.[67] In another study, researchers found

(Looking at Diversity)

Having Parents of Two Races

Jennifer Mather, whose father is Chinese and mother British, relates how her heritage and culture affected her sense of self.

The first time I realized I was any different from other kids was on the first day of Grade 1 (I didn't go to kindergarten). The only girl who would talk to me was another little Asian girl named Mikki. She was Japanese, I think. I went to a private Catholic school in North Vancouver because my father believed we would get a better education. I was one of the few non-whites, and I looked much more Asian when I was younger. (Nowadays, most people think I'm Italian.) I was devastated when Mikki left the next year. In school pictures, I stick out like a sore thumb: dark hair, dark eyes, in a sea of fair-haired lightness and Canadian mousey-brownness. Only a few times did the nasty older boys call me "Chink," but it still made my face burn with shame, and made me feel as ugly as the word sounds.

My dad made my older sister and I go to Chinese school on Saturdays. My father was in the restaurant business, so we ate a lot of traditional Chinese meals. Not the stuff North Americans call Chinese food, like electric-yellow lemon chicken, but real food that was in and out of a wok in what seemed like seconds, filling the kitchen with fragrant smells of ginger, garlic, and exotic spices. And rice. Lots and lots of rice.

Both my parents worked hard to maintain our Asian roots—in fact, we celebrated the Chinese holidays much more than the traditional North American ones. Christmas and birthdays came and went, but Chinese New Year was at least a week's worth of celebration and ritual: must clean house from top to bottom on New Year's Eve to get rid of all the bad luck; must not shower on New Year's Day for fear of washing away all the good spirits for the coming year; mustn't use scissors or anything sharp on New Year's Day in case you "cut away" all the luck.

I think the cultural differences were especially hard on my mom. My father is the oldest of 10, and it was his job to go west and bring the rest of the family over from China. At one point my grandparents and all of my nine aunts and uncles lived in our basement. They initially weren't that keen on my mom, in light of the fact that (a) she wasn't Chinese and (b) she produced two daughters. But after my brother was born, he helped smooth the waters. It was like living with the Last Emperor.

I am proud of my heritage and culture, although I must say I am now more Western than Eastern. In some ways, I think being half-Chinese in Vancouver is more difficult than being 100 percent Asian—only because I've been privy to many a conversation where people complain about the so-called Asian invasion of our fair city, or how Orientals are such bad drivers. It floors them when I eventually tell them I'm half-Chinese, and sometimes I take a perverse pleasure in seeing their faces redden.

---

that people are less concerned with identity management among familiar people of the same sex than with less familiar people of the same sex or people of the opposite sex, regardless of how well we know them.[68]

People Differ in Their Degree of Identity Management

Some people are much more aware of their identity management behaviour than others. High self-monitors pay attention to their own behaviour and others' reactions and adjust their communication to create the desired impression. By contrast, low self-monitors express what they think and feel without paying attention to the impression their behaviour creates.[69] Complete the "Self-Monitoring Inventory" on page 49 to gauge your self-monitoring behaviours.

High self-monitors have clear communication advantages.[70] They can usually create the identity they want, acting interested when bored or friendly when

they really feel quite the opposite. This allows them to handle social situations smoothly, often putting others at ease. They are also good "people readers" who can adjust their behaviour to get the desired reaction from others. But there are some disadvantages to being an extremely high self-monitor. Sometimes they don't experience events completely because a portion of their attention will always be viewing the situation from a detached position. One study found that high self-monitors often feel less intimacy, satisfaction, and commitment in their romantic relationships, in part because they hide what they really think and feel.[71]

Low self-monitors have a simpler, more focused idea of who they are and typically act the same way regardless of the situation, and therefore they are easy to read—what you see is what you get. Although this lack of flexibility may make their social interaction less smooth in many situations, low self-monitors can be counted on to be straightforward communicators.

Neither extremely high nor low self-monitoring is the ideal. There are many situations when paying attention to yourself and adapting your behaviour can be useful and others when reacting without considering the effects is a better approach. This need for a range of behaviours demonstrates the notion of communicative competence. Flexibility is the key to successful relationships.

LO⁵
Why Manage Identities?

Social scientists have identified several overlapping reasons for why we shape our identities.[72]

To Start and Manage Relationships

Have you ever consciously and carefully managed your approach when meeting someone you wanted to know better? Did you try to be charming and witty—or perhaps

"I do not want to be perfect.
I want to appear to be perfect."

© William Haefeli/The New Yorker Collection/www.cartoonbank.com

cool and suave? If so, you were trying to manage your identity to initiate a relationship. Once it was up and running, you probably still managed your identity, although not as much.

To Gain the Compliance of Others

Sometimes we manage our identity to get others to do what we want. You might dress up for a visit to traffic court in the hope that your image (responsible citizen) will convince the judge to treat you sympathetically. You might chat sociably with neighbours you don't find especially interesting so they'll lend you tools and garden equipment.

To Save Others' Face

We often modify ourselves to support the way other people want to be seen. For example, able-bodied people often mask their discomfort upon encountering someone with a disability by acting nonchalant or stressing the similarities they share.[73] Young children who haven't learned about the importance of face-saving often embarrass their parents by behaving inappropriately ("Mommy, why is that man so fat?"). By the time they enter school, what was once excusable or even amusing just isn't acceptable.

Invitation TO INSIGHT

Self-Monitoring Inventory

These statements concern personal reactions to a number of situations. No two statements are exactly alike, so consider each statement carefully before answering. If a statement is true or mostly true as applied to you, circle the T. If a statement is false or not usually true as applied to you, circle the F.

1. I find it hard to imitate the behaviour of other people. T F
2. I guess I put on a show to impress or entertain people. T F
3. I would probably make a good actor. T F
4. I sometimes appear to others to be experiencing deeper emotions than I actually am. T F
5. In a group of people, I am rarely the center of attention. T F
6. In different situations and with different people, I often act like very different persons. T F
7. I can argue only for ideas I already believe. T F
8. To get along and be liked, I tend to be what people expect me to be rather than anything else. T F
9. I may deceive people by being friendly when I really dislike them. T F
10. I'm not always the person I appear to be. T F

Scoring: Give yourself 1 point for each of questions 1, 5, and 7 that you answered F. Give yourself 1 point for each of the remaining questions that you answered T. Add up your points. If you are a good judge of yourself and scored 7 or above, you are probably a high self-monitoring individual; 3 or below, you are probably a low self-monitoring individual.

Mark Snyder, "The Many Me's of the Self-Monitor," *Psychology Today* (March 1983): 34. Reprinted with permission.

Alter Egos in a Virtual World

Time was that the word *avatar* meant the earthly manifestation of a god. You might have also used it to describe an archetype. But in the earliest days of the Internet—back in the 1980s, when no one was looking—an avatar became one's digital self.

If this is news to you, consider yourself extravagantly late to the costume party that is online role playing. Let's get you up to speed. Introducing 27-year-old wife and mother Becky Glasure, who complains of never being taken seriously.

Becky Glasure and Stygion Physic, her avatar in the online role-playing game *City of Heroes*.

"Maybe I just exude it, I don't know. But I feel like I'm this short person with this squeaky little Filipino voice and nobody wants to pay attention." Glasure's first online game was *Everquest* and her avatar was female. But all anyone noticed were her pixel breasts, and this despite her considerable gaming expertise.

Fed up, she switched digital identities. "And I picked the biggest guy I could find," she says. She called him Stygion Physic—Stygion from the River Styx, Physic for healing. That's the closest she could get to Bad Medicine in the game *City of Heroes*.

And with her change of avatar, her pleasure in the game changed. "When I play this big guy, everybody listens to me," she says. "Nobody argues with me. If there's a group of people standing around, I say, 'OK, everybody follow me!' And they do. No questions asked."

Cue the cyberanalysts and virtual ethnographers, including Tracy Spaight, who's been inquiring into human gaming behaviour for as long as there have been online games. "In the virtual world you can be anything you want to be . . . construct a persona that is wildly different from your real-world self."

Spaight's own fascination with role playing, avatars, and gaming has been realized in the book and travelling exhibit Alter Ego: Avatars and Their Creators. Cooper and

Spaight travelled to China, Japan, South Korea, parts of Europe, and the United States to photograph and interview gamers, whittling down some 3000 applicants to the several dozen people featured in their book.

There is ample repetition. For one, quite a number of avatars are just younger, thinner, and prettier versions of their creators. For another, just as many avatars are polar opposites of their people.

Cooper's portrait of Jason Rowe, for instance, stops you dead. He stares straight at you out of startled blue eyes. But what takes you aback is his frail body, his clenched hands, and the ominous ventilator strapped to his face.

Jason Rowe and his avatar, Rurouni Kenshin, who rides Imperial speeder bikes in *Star Wars Galaxies*.

"My condition is called Duchenne muscular dystrophy," Rowe told Spaight. "It pretty much affects all the muscles in the body. They don't function." His avatar is a steely, robot-like character who rides Imperial speeder bikes and fights monsters, his head helmeted, his face unseen. "My character in the game is a lot different from what you see here in real life," Rowe says. "[It] pretty much gave me a window to the world."

In the four years since he created his avatar, this frail 32-year-old has had an unprecedented life experience: Online, he is treated as an equal among his peers. "Not disabled," he says. "Not in a wheelchair. In virtual worlds, everyone is on common ground."

Rowe didn't set out to overcome people's prejudice. And Glasure, whose male avatar became a leader, doesn't mean to lose patience when friends and family don't fall in line. But stay in costume long enough—whether a general in a Civil War reenactment or a wench at a Renaissance fair—and the lines may blur between who you are and who you're pretending to be.

Ketzel Levine

Alter Ego: Avatars and Their Creators by Robbie Cooper, London: Chris Boot Ltd., 2007. Reprinted with permission.

To Explore New "Selves"

Sometimes we try on a new identity to see if it changes how others view us and how we view and feel about ourselves. Trying on new selves can also be a means to self-improvement. For example, teens who experimented with new identities online reached out more to people of different ages and cultural backgrounds than they did in their face-to-face lives. As a result, they actually increased their social competence.[74]

How Do We Manage Identities?

Now that we've examined why we might shape our identities, in this section we look at how we manage identities.

Face-to-Face Impression Management

Communicators manage their identity in three ways: manner, setting, and appearance.[75] *Manner* consists of a communicator's words and nonverbal actions. For example, some physicians are friendly and conversational, whereas others adopt a curt and impersonal approach. (Think of the TV show *Grey's Anatomy*, and the difference between brusque Dr. Yang and the caring Izzy Stevens.) Much of a communicator's manner comes from what he or she says. A doctor who remembers details about your interests or hobbies is quite different from one who sticks to clinical questions. One who explains a medical procedure creates a different impression than one who reveals little to the patient.

Nonverbal behaviours also play a big role in creating impressions. A doctor who greets you with a smile and a handshake comes across differently than one who gives nothing more than a nod. Manner also varies widely in other professions and settings—professors, salespeople, hairstylists, and so on—and the impressions they create shape how others view them.

A second dimension of identity management is *appearance*—the personal items that people use to shape an image. Sometimes appearance is part of creating a professional image. A physician's white lab coat, a tailored suit, and a rumpled outfit create very different impressions. Off the job, clothing selection sends messages about whether a person is trendy or traditional. Some people dress in ways that accent their sexuality; others hide it. Clothing can say, "I'm an athlete," "I'm wealthy," or "I'm an environmentalist." Makeup and hairstyle also send messages.

Tattoos also make a statement, and the design or the words chosen say even more. One fascinating study explored the communicative function of tattoos worn by some people to announce they were HIV-positive.[76] Beyond being a practical announcement, these tattoos can also be a vehicle for identity management. One wearer explained that his tattoo conveyed the refusal to internalize shame, a commitment to safer sex practices, a challenge to stereotypes about weak "AIDS victims," and an educational tool that generates discussion by making the condition visible.

> Before flying to London
> I must visit
> Some downtown Fredericton
> hardware store
> and invest
> in a couple of modest but
> distinguishable nylon
> Canadian flags to sew upon
> my baggage
> and shoulders
> Without them
> Europeans will feel
> that I have to be
> American
> And that just isn't close enough
>
> —Joseph Sherman,
> "The Colours"

A final way to manage identities is through the choice of *setting*—physical items used to influence how others view us. The automobile is a major example, and this explains why many people lust after far more expensive and powerful cars than they need. A sporty convertible doesn't just get drivers from one place to another, it also makes statements about the kind of people they are. Vanity plates offer another opportunity for identity management. Owners typically display names and topics related to their work, hobbies, and interests. In most provinces, requests for vanity plates are scrutinized for cultural, religious,

Hill Street Studios/Blend Images/Getty Images

prejudicial, or sexual connotations. Family names such as Too Long Dong and Giver, for example, are rejected.

Physical settings also influence our identities. The physical setting we choose and the way we arrange it are another important way to manage identities. While the colours, artwork, and music you choose for your apartment or room reflect your tastes, they also create an environment that presents a desired front to others.

"On the Internet, nobody knows you're a dog."

Impression Management in Mediated Communication

Identity management occurs in other ways as well. Consider the care you take when drafting a résumé or writing a letter to a lover. In addition to the message, you probably make strategic decisions about its appearance. Will you use plain white paper or something more distinctive, and will you print out your words or write them in longhand? People think carefully about considerations like these because they instinctively know that the *way* a message is presented conveys as much as the words it contains.

Communicators also manage their identity in the media. When it comes to placing personal ads for romantic partners, younger people emphasize physical appearance and are more likely to play up sexuality. By contrast, people over age 50 are more likely to focus on personality features.

You might think that instant messages, texting, and e-mail messages limit the potential for impression management because they lack nonverbal messages (tone of

voice, postures, gestures, or facial expressions). However, this may actually be an *advantage* for communicators who want to manage the impressions they make.[77] Communicating through mediated channels such as e-mail, blogs, and web pages allow you to edit your messages until your create just the desired impression.[78] With e-mail, and to a lesser degree with text messaging and IMing, you can compose difficult messages without forcing the receiver to respond immediately, and you can ignore others' messages rather than give an unpleasant response.

Perhaps most important, when communicating via text-based technology you don't have to worry about stammering or blushing, what you're wearing, or what you look like. In mediated communication, strangers can change their age, history, personality, appearance, and other matters that would be impossible to hide in person.[79] Among teens, a quarter have pretended to be a different person online and a third confess to having given false information about themselves while e-mailing and instant messaging. A survey of one online dating site's participants found that 86 percent felt others misrepresented their physical appearance in their posted descriptions.[80]

Like the one-to-one and small-group channels of e-mail and instant messaging, "broadcasting" on the media is also a tool for managing one's identity. Blogs, personal web pages, and profiles on social networking websites like MySpace, Facebook, and Friendster all provide opportunities for communicators to construct an identity.[81] Even the simple choice of a screen name (lovemyporsche, fun2bewith, footballdude) says something about you and is likely to lead others to create impressions of you.[82] It may also be wise to look at your personal sites through the eyes of potential employers. What kind of impression are you making from their perspective? The words, images, and sounds that self-publishers choose make a statement about how they want others to regard them. Interestingly, people are more likely to prefer mediated channels when their own self-presentation is threatened.[83]

> You're not fooling anyone when you become
> Somebody else
> Round everyone else
>
> —Avril Lavigne,
> "Complicated"

Identity Management and Honesty

Some readers might think of identity management as an academic label for phoniness, and there certainly are situations where identity management is dishonest. Manipulative dates who pretend to be affectionate to gain sexual favours, job applicants who lie about their academic records to get hired, or salespeople who pretend to be dedicated to customer service when their real goal is to make a quick buck are all being dishonest.

Dreamworks/THE KOBAL COLLECTION/Cooper, Andrew

But managing impressions doesn't make you a liar. In fact, it is almost impossible to imagine how we could communicate effectively without making decisions about which front to present in one situation or another. Each of us has a repertoire of faces—a cast of characters—and part of being a competent communicator is choosing the best face for the situation. Consider a few examples:

- You offer to teach a friend a new skill: playing the guitar, operating a computer program, or sharpening up a tennis backhand. Your friend is making slow progress with the skill, and you find yourself growing impatient.
- At work you face a belligerent customer. You don't believe anyone has the right to treat you this way.
- A friend or family member makes a joke about your appearance that hurts your feelings. You aren't sure whether to make an issue of the joke or to pretend that it doesn't bother you.

In each of these situations, you have a choice about how to act, and it's an oversimplification to say that there's only one honest way to behave. Identity management involves deciding which part of you to reveal. When teaching a new skill, for example, you choose to be "patient" instead of "impatient." At work you have the option of acting defensive or nondefensive in difficult situations. Deciding which face to show to others is an important decision because you are sharing a real part of yourself.

Communication in the Workplace

Constructing multiple identities and selecting the appropriate one for the context are particularly relevant to the workplace. Andrew DuBrin and Terri Geerinck, two human resources specialists, note that we often want to create good impressions on our superiors. To do this, they recommend that you have a strong work ethic, demonstrate emotional intelligence, appreciate your manager's strengths, show an interest in the organization's products, and create a strong presence.[84]

The authors also recommend that you be dependable, honest, and ethical. However, this may not always be easy to achieve, especially when asked by an unethical superior to do something less than upstanding. Deciding how to behave and manage your identity in such a situation isn't easy. Further, self-fulfilling prophecy can also influence your communication at work. Check out "Self-Fulfilling Prophecies in the Workplace" to get an understanding of how this can work.

(On the Job)

Self-Fulfilling Prophecies in the Workplace

An abundance of research shows how self-fulfilling prophecies can affect job performance. For example,

- A group of clerks was told they were expected to punch about 550 cards per day. They were also told that processing more cards might cause stress. A second group was not given any limits or warnings; they were told to punch as many cards as they could. The first group averaged 550 cards and indeed reported stress when they tried to do more. The second group averaged almost 2000 cards a day with no signs of stress.[85]
- Military personnel who were randomly labelled as having high potential performed up to the expectations of their superiors. They were also more likely to volunteer for dangerous special duty.[86]
- A group of welders with relatively equal aptitudes began training. Everyone, including the trainer, was told that five of the welders had higher scores on an aptitude test—even though they'd been chosen randomly. All five finished at the top of the class. They had fewer absences and significantly higher final test scores. Most impressively, they learned the skills of their trade twice as quickly as those who weren't identified as being so talented.[87]

Many more studies of self-fulfilling prophecies show how managers can help employees become more productive by communicating high expectations.[88]

While this is valuable information for supervisors, self-fulfilling prophecies can assist those in non-managerial positions as well. Having positive expectations and communicating them confidently is an asset in any field or position. The salesperson who approaches a client or customer with high expectations ("I can succeed here") and then behaves accordingly is more likely to be successful than those with lower hopes. It may sound simple, but research confirms that positive expectations can lead to positive communication, which can lead to positive results.

Endnotes

1. R. F. Baumeister (2005). *The Cultural Animal: Human Nature, Meaning, and Social Life.* New York: Oxford University Press; and R. F. Baumeister, J. D. Campbell, J. I. Krueger, & K. D. Vohs (2003). "Does High Self-Esteem Cause Better Performance, Interpersonal Success, Happiness, or Healthier Lifestyles?" *Psychological Science in the Public Interest, 4,* 1–44.

2. K. D. Vohs & T. F. Heatherton (2004). "Ego Threats Elicit Different Social Comparison Process Among High and Low Self-Esteem People: Implications for Interpersonal Perceptions." *Social Cognition, 22,* 168–191.

3. W. Soldz & G. E. Vaillant (1999). "The Big Five Personality Traits and the Life Course: A 45-Year Longitudinal Study." *Journal of Research in Personality, 33,* 208–232.

4. For a summary of research on heritability of personality, see W. Wright (1998). *Born That Way: Genes, Behaviour, Personality.* New York: Knopf.

5. C. E. Schwartz, C. I. Wright, L. M. Shin, J. Kagan, & S. L. Rauch (June 20, 2003). "Inhibited and Uninhibited Infants 'Grown Up': Adult Amygdalar Response to Novelty." *Science,* 1952–1953.

6. J. G. Cole & J. C. McCroskey (2000). "Temperament and Socio-Communicative Orientation." *Communication Research Reports, 17,* 105–114.

7. A. D. Heisel, J. C. McCroskey, & V. P. Richmond (1999). "Testing Theoretical Relationships and Non-Relationships of Genetically-Based Predictors: Getting Started with Communibiology," *Communication Research Reports, 16,* 1–9.

8. Cole & McCroskey, op. cit.

9. C. J. Wigley (1998). "Vergal Aggressiveness." In J. C. McCroskey, J. A. Daly, M. M. Martin, & M. J. Beatty (Eds.). *Personality and Communication: Trait Perspectives.* New York: Hampton.

10. J. C. McCroskey, A.D. Heisel, & V. P. Richmond (2001). "Eysenck's Big Three and Communication Traits: Three Correlational Studies." *Communication Monographs, 68,* 360–366.

11. R. R. McCrae & P. T. Costa Jr. (1987). "Validation of the Five-Factor Model of Personality across Instruments and Observers," *Journal of Personality and Social Psychology, 52,* 81–90.

12. R. R. McCrae & P. T Costa. Jr. (1997). "Personality Trait Structure as a Human Universal." *American Psychologist, 52,* 509–516.

13. C. Dweck (2008). "Can Personality Be Changed? The Role of Beliefs in Personality and Change." Current Directions in Psychological Science, 6, 391–394.

14. S. Begney (2008, December 1). "When DNA Is Not Destiny." *Newsweek, 152,* 14.

15. C. H. Cooley (1912). *Human Nature and the Social Order.* New York: Scribner's.

16. C. Jaret, D. Reitzes, & N. Shapkina (2005). "Reflected Appraisals and Self-Esteem." *Sociological Perspectives, 48,* 403–419.

17. S. Salimi, S. Mirzamani, & M. Shahiri-Tabarestani (2005). "Association of Parental Self-Esteem and Expectations

with Adolescents' Anxiety about Career and Education." *Psychological Reports, 96*, 569–578; and A. L. Vangelisti & L. P. Crumley (1998). "Reactions to Messages that Hurt: The Influence of Relational Contexts." *Communication Monographs, 65*, 173–196.

18. L. Leets & Sunwolf (2004). "Being Left Out: Rejecting Outsiders and Communicating Group Boundaries in Childhood and Adolescent Peer Groups." *Journal of Applied Communication Research, 32*, 195–223.

19. A. Sillars, A. Koerner, & M.A. Fitzpatrick (2005). "Communication and Understanding in Parent-Adolescent Relationships." *Human Communication Research, 31*, 107–128.

20. T. Adler (October 1992). "Personality, Like Plaster, Is Pretty Stable over Time." *APA Monitor*, 18.

21. J. D. Brown, N. J. Novick, K. A. Lord, & J. M. Richards (1992). "When Gulliver Travels: Social Context, Psychological Closeness, and Self-Appraisals." *Journal of Personality and Social Psychology, 62*, 717–734.

22. M. Krcmar, S. Giles, & D. Helme (2008). "Understanding the Process: How Mediated and Peer Norms Affect Young Women's Body Esteem." *Communication Quarterly, 56*, 111–130.

23. P. N. Myers & F. A. Biocca (1992). "The Elastic Body Image: The Effect of Television Advertising and Programming on Body Image Distortions in Young Women." *Journal of Communication, 42*, 108–134.

24. C. M. Strong (2005). "The Role of Exposure to Media Idealized Male Physiques on Men's Body Image." *Dissertation Abstracts International, 65*, 4306.

25. K. N. Kubric & R. M. Chory (2007). "Exposure to Television Makeover Programs and Perceptions of Self." *Communication Research Reports, 24*, 283-291.

26. D. Grodin & T. R. Lindlof (1995). *Constructing the Self in a Mediated World*. Newbury Park, CA: Sage.

27. M. Han (2003). "Body Image Dissatisfaction and Eating Disturbance among Korean College Female Students: Relationships to Media Exposure, Upward Comparison, and Perceived Reality." *Communication Studies, 34*, 65–78; and K. Harrison & J. Cantor (1997). "The Relationship Between Media Consumption and Eating Disorders." *Journal of Communication, 47*, 40–67.

28. L. J. Carrell & S. C. Willmington (1996). "A Comparison of Self-Report and Performance Data in Assessing Speaking and Listening Competence." *Communication Reports, 9*, 185–191.

29. D. Meyers (May 1980). "The Inflated Self." *Psychology Today, 14*, 16.

30. A. B. Canton & K. H. Teigen. "Better Than Average and Better With Time: Relative Evaluations of Self and Others in the Past, Present, and Future." *European Journal of Social Psychology, 38*, 343–353.

31. N. Ellison, R. Heino, & J. Gibbs (2006). "Managing Impressions Online: Self-Presentation Processes in the Online Dating Environment." *Journal of Computer-Mediated Communication, 11*, http://jcmc.indiana.edu/vol11/issue2/ellison.html, article 2. Accessed September 11, 2006.

32. E. D. Sturman & M. Mongrain (2008). "The Role of Personality in Defeat: A Revised Social Rank Model." *European Journal of Personality, 22*, 55–79; and J. D. Brown & T. A. Mankowski (1993). "Self-Esteem, Mood, and Self-Evaluation: Changes in Mood and the Way You See You." *Journal of Personality and Social Psychology, 64*, 421–430.

33. M. A. Gara, R. L. Woolfolk, B. D. Cohen, & R. B. Goldston (1993). "Perception of Self and Other in Major Depression." *Journal of Abnormal Psychology, 102*, 93–100.

34. K. A. Martin Ginis, M. E. Jong, & L. Gauvin (2003). "To See or Not to See: The Effects of Exercising in Mirrored Environments on Sedentary Women's Feeling States and Self-Efficacy," *Health Psychology, 22*, 354–361.

35. L. C. Miller, L. L. Cooke, J. Tsang, & F. Morgan (1992). "Should I Brag? Nature and Impact of Positive and Boastful Disclosures for Women and Men." *Human Communication Research, 18*, 364–399.

36. B. Bower (August 15, 1992). "Truth Aches: People Who View Themselves Poorly May Seek the 'Truth' and Find Despair." *Science News*, 110–111; and W. B. Swann (2005). "The Self and Identity Negotiation." *Interaction Studies, 6*, 69–83.

37. J. Oxman-Martinez & J. Handley (2005). "Health and Social Services for Canada's Multicultural Population: Challenges for Equity." Canadian Heritage, www.pch.gc.ca/mutli/canada2017/4_e.cfm. Accessed Dec. 8, 2005.

38. H. Giles & P. Johnson (1987). "Ethnolinguistic Identity Theory: A Social Psychological Approach to Language Maintenance," *International Journal of Sociology of Languages, 68*, 69–99.

39. W. W. Wilmot (1995). *Relational Communication*. New York: McGraw-Hill, pp. 35–54.

40. J. Servaes (1989). "Cultural Identity and Modes of Communication." In J. A. Anderson (Ed.). *Communication Yearbook 12* (p. 396). Newbury Park, CA: Sage.

41. A. Bharti (1985). "The Self in Hindu Thought and Action." In A. J. Marsella, G. DeVos, & F. L. K. Hsu (Eds.). *Culture and Self: Asian and Western Perspectives* (pp. 185–320). New York: Tavistock.

42. S. Bochner (1994). "Cross-Cultural Differences in the Self Concept: A Test of Hofstede's Individualism/Collectivism Distinction." *Journal of Cross-Cultural Psychology, 25*, 273–283.

43. W. B. Gudykunst & S. Ting-Toomey 1988. *Culture and Interpersonal Communication*. Newbury Park, CA: Sage.

44. L. A. Samovar & R. E. Porter (1991). *Communication between Cultures*. Belmont, CA: Wadsworth, p. 91.

45. D. Klopf (1984). "Cross-Cultural Apprehension Research: A Summary of Pacific Basin Studies." In J. Daly & J. McCroskey (Eds.). *Avoiding Communication: Shyness, Reticence, and Communication Apprehension*. Beverly Hills, CA: Sage.

46. S. Ting-Toomey (1988). "A Face-Negotiation Theory." In Y. Kim & W. Gudykunst (Eds.). *Theory in Interpersonal Communication*[. Newbury Park, CA: Sage.

47. L. C. Lederman (1993). "Gender and the Self." In L. P. Arliss & D. J. Borisoff (Eds.). *Women and Men Communicating: Challenges and Changes* (pp. 41–42). Fort Worth, TX: Harcourt Brace.

48. For more examples of gender-related labels, see A. Wittels (1978). *I Wonder . . . A Satirical Study of Sexist Semantics.* Los Angeles: Price Stern Sloan.

49. N. Khanlou (2004). "Influences on Adolescent Self-Esteem in Multicultural Canadian Secondary Schools," *Public Health Nursing, 21,* 404–411.

50. J. A. MacMullin and J. Cairney (2004). "Self-Esteem and the Intersection of Age, Class, and Gender." *Journal of Aging Studies, 18,* 75–90.

51. M. Knox, J. Funk, R. Elliott, & E. G. Bush (2000). "Gender Differences in Adolescents' Possible Selves." *Youth and Society, 31,* 287–309.

52. Dweck, C. S. (2006). *Mindset: The New Psychology of Success.* New York: Random House.

53. J. Kolligan Jr. (1990). "Perceived Fraudulence as a Dimension of Perceived Incompetence." In R. J. Sternberg & J. Kolligen Jr. (Eds.). *Competence Considered.* New Haven, CT: Yale University Press. See also A. L. Vangelisti, S. D. Corbin, A. E. Lucchetti, & R. J. Sprague (1999). "Couples' Concurrent Cognitions: The Influence of Relational Satisfaction on the Thoughts Couples Have as They Converse." *Human Communication Research, 25,* 370–398.

54. B. Zimmerman, A. Bandura, & M. Martinez-Pons (1992). "Self-Motivation for Academic Attainment: The Role of Self-Efficacy Beliefs and Personal Goal Setting." *American Educational Research Journal, 29,* 663–676.

55. G. Downey & S. I. Feldman (1996). "Implications of Rejection Sensitivity for Intimate Relationships." *Journal of Personality and Social Psychology, 70,* 1327–1343.

56. P. D. MacIntyre & K. A Thivierge (1995). "The Effects of Speaker Personality on Anticipated Reactions to Public Speaking." *Communication Research Reports, 12,* 125–133.

57. C. L. Kleinke, T. R. Peterson, & T. R. Rutledge (1998). "Effects of Self-Generated Facial Expressions on Mood." *Journal of Personality and Social Psychology, 74,* 272–279.

58. R. Rosenthal & L. Jacobson (1968). *Pygmalion in the Classroom.* New York: Holt, Rinehart and Winston.

59. P. D. Blank (Ed.) (1993). *Interpersonal Expectations: Theory, Research, and Applications* Cambridge: Cambridge University Press.

60. R. M. Perloff, B. Bonder, G. B. Ray, E. B. Ray, & L. A. Siminoff (2006). "Doctor-Patient Communication, Cultural Competence, and Minority Health." *American Behavioral Scientist, 49,* 835–852.

61. For a thorough discussion of this subject, see M. E. P. Seligman (1993). *What You Can Change and What You Can't.* New York: Knopf.

62. E. Goffman (1959). *The Presentation of Self in Everyday Life.* Garden City, NY: Doubleday; and (1971) *Relations in Public.* New York: Basic Books.

63. M. R. Leary & R. M. Kowalski (1990). "Impression Management: A Literature Review and Two-Component Model." *Psychological Bulletin, 107,* 34–47.

64. V. Brightman, A. Segal, P. Werther, & J. Steiner (1975). "Ethological Study of Facial Expression in Response to Taste Stimuli." *Journal of Dental Research, 54,* 141.

65. N. Chovil (1991). "Social Determinants of Facial Displays." *Journal of Nonverbal Behaviour, 15,* 141–154.

66. See, for example, R. A. Giacalone & P. Rosenfeld (Eds.) (1991). *Applied Impression Management: How Image-Making Affects Managerial Decisions.* Newbury Park, CA: Sage.

67. D. Morier & C. Seroy (1994). "The Effect of Interpersonal Expectancies on Men's Self-Presentation of Gender Role Attitudes to Women." *Sex Roles, 31,* 493–504.

68. M. Leary, J. B. Nezlek, D. Downs, et al. (1994). "Self-Presentation in Everyday Interactions: Effects of Target Familiarity and Gender Composition." *Journal of Personality and Social Psychology 67,* 664–673.

69. M. Snyder (1987). *Public Appearances, Private Realities: The Psychology of Self-Monitoring.* New York: W. H. Freeman.

70. The following discussion is based on material in D. E. Hamachek (1992). *Encounters with the Self,* 3rd ed. Fort Worth, TX: Harcourt, pp. 24–26.

71. C. N. Wright, A. Holloway, & M. E. Roloff (2007). "The Dark Side of Self-Monitoring: How High Self-Monitors View Their Romantic Relationships." *Communication Reports, 20,* 101–114.

72. For a more detailed discussion of identity-related goals, see S. Metts & E. Grohskopf (2003). "Impression Management: Goals, Strategies, and Skills." In J. O. Greene and B. R. Burleson (Eds.). *Handbook of Communication and Social Skills.* Mahwah, NJ: Erlbaum.

73. L. M. Coleman & B. M. DePaulo (1991). "Uncovering the Human Spirit: Moving beyond Disability and 'Missed' Communications." In N. Coupland, H. Giles, & J. M. Wiemann (Eds.), *"Miscommunication" and Problematic Talk* (pp. 61–84). Newbury Park, CA: Sage.

74. P.M. Valkenburg & J. Peter (2008). "Adolescents' Identity Experiments on the Internet: Consequences for Social Competence and Self-Concept Unity." Communication Research, 35, 208–231.

75. J. W. Vander Zanden (1984). Social Psychology, 3rd ed. New York: Random House, pp. 235–237.

76. D. Brouwer (1998). "The Precarious Visibility Politics of Self-Stigmatization: The Case of HIV/AIDS Tattoos." *Text and Performance Quarterly, 18,* 114–136.

77. P. B. O'Sullivan (2000). "What You Don't Know Won't Hurt Me: Impression Management Functions of Communication Channels in Relationships." *Communication Monographs, 26,* 403–432. See also S. B. Barnes (2003). *Computer-Mediated Communication: Human-to-Human Communication across the Internet.* Boston: Allyn and Bacon, pp. 136–162.

78. J. Sanderson (2008). "The Blog is Serving Its Purpose: Self-Presentation Strategies on 38Pitches.com." *Journal of Computer-Mediated Communication, 13,* 912–936.

79. J. R. Suler (2002). "Identity Management in Cyberspace." *Journal of Applied Psychoanalytic Studies 4,* 455–459.

80. J. L. Gibbs, N. B. Ellison, & R. D. Heino (2006). "Self-Presentation in Online Personals: The Role of Anticipated Future Interaction, Self-Disclosure, and Perceived Success in Internet Dating." *Communication Research, 33,* 1–26.

81. See, for example, D. Chandler (n.d.). "Personal Home Pages and the Construction of Identities on the Web," www.aber.ac.uk/ ~dgc/webident.html. Accessed May 8, 2006.

82. R. Bennett (April 4, 2008). "Revealed: Secrets of Choosing on Online Dating Name." *Times Online.*

83. O' Sullivan, op. cit.

84. A. J. DuBrin and T. Geerinck (2004).*Human Relations for Career and Personal Success, Third Canadian Edition.* Toronto: Pearson Education Canada, pp. 259–261.

85. P. D. Blank (Ed.) (1993). *Interpersonal Expectations: Theory, Research, and Applications.* Cambridge: Cambridge University Press.

86. C. E. Johnson (2006). *Ethics in the Workplace: Tools and Tactics for Organizational Transformation.* Thousand Oaks, CA: Sage.

87. Turk, W. (2009). "Let's Go For Self-Fulfilling Prophecies." *Defense AT&L, 38,* 56–59.

88. Eden, D. (1990). *Pygmalion in Management: Productivity as a Self-Fulfilling Prophecy.* New York: Simon & Schuster; and Eden, D. (1990). "Pygmalion Without Interpersonal Contrast Effects: Whole Groups Gain From Raising Manager Expectations." *Journal of Applied Psychology, 75,* 394–98.

CHAPTER **3**

PERCEPTION:

WHAT YOU SEE IS WHAT YOU GET

LEARNING OUTCOMES

LO¹   Describe how the processes of
selection, organization, interpretation, and negotiation shape communication in a given situation.

LO²   Explain how the influences on
perception affect communication
in a specific situation.

LO³   Analyze how the common tendencies in perception distort your
perceptions of another person,
and hence your communication.
Use this information to present
a more accurate alternative set
of perceptions.

LO⁴   Demonstrate how you might use
the skill of perception checking in a
significant relationship.

LO⁵   Enhance your cognitive complexity
by applying the "pillow method" in
a significant disagreement. Explain
how your expanded view of this
situation might affect your communication with the other(s) involved.

Study M. C. Escher's drawing titled *Relativity*. It pictures
a strange universe where inhabitants of each world exist
at right angles, using the same staircase but oblivious to
one another's existence. Each has his or her own concep-
tion of up and down, right and left. From our perspective, the characters defy the rules of gravity.

This surreal vision provides a useful metaphor for
challenges we encounter every day. Each of us experiences reality differently, and failing to understand other
people's point of view can lead to practical and relational
problems. But perceptual differences can also enhance our
relationships. By seeing the world through others' eyes we
can gain insights that are different from—and often more
valuable than—those arising out of our own experiences.

LO¹
The Perception Process

Perception can be described as the process whereby we assign meaning to the world around us. However, everybody tunes in to the world differently. Perhaps you've seen photos of sights invisible to the unaided eye— maybe an infrared photo of a familiar area or the vastly enlarged image of a minute object taken by an electron microscope—or you've noticed how animals can hear sounds and smell odours that are not apparent to humans. Experiences like these remind us that there is much more going on in the world than we are able to experience with our limited senses. Our idea of reality is only a partial one. On a personal level, for example, we've all failed to notice something unusual about a friend—perhaps a new hairstyle or a sad expression—until it's called to our attention.

We notice some events and fail to recognize others because we simply can't be aware of everything that's going on around us, no matter how attentive we are. As William James said, "To the infant the world is just a big blooming, buzzing confusion." But as we grow, we learn to manage these data and make sense of the world. Perception is very important, because how we interpret events influences how we communicate with others. There are four steps in the perception process: selection, organization, interpretation, and negotiation.

Selection

Because we're exposed to more input than we can possibly manage, the first step in perception is **selection** of the data to which we will attend. Several factors make some messages more noticeable than others.

Stimuli that are *intense* attract our attention. Something that is louder, larger, or brighter, although not always in a positive way, will stand out. Think of those loud infomercials. *Repetitious stimuli* also attract attention.[1] Just as a quiet but steadily dripping faucet can come to dominate our awareness, so do people to whom we're frequently exposed become noticeable. *Contrast* or *change* also invite attention. Put differently, unchanging people or things become less noticeable, and this may account for why we take wonderful people for granted. It's only when they go away or stop being so wonderful that we appreciate them.

Motives also influence what is selected from our environment. If you're late for an appointment, you'll notice whatever clocks may be around you, and if you're hungry, you'll spot any restaurants or billboards advertising food. Motives also determine how we perceive people. For example, people looking for romantic adventures will be aware of attractive potential partners. In emergency situations, however, police or medical personnel would be more important and potential partners are overlooked.

Selection also involves ignoring cues. If, for example, you think someone is a terrific person, you'll overlook their serious flaws. Or if you are focused on examples of unfair male bosses, you might not recognize unfair female supervisors.

> It doubles your perception, to write from the point of view of someone you're not.
>
> —Michael Ondaatje

Organization

Once we select information, we must arrange it in some meaningful way. You can see how the principle of **organization** works by looking at Figure 3.1 (p. 61). The picture can be viewed as either a face or as the word *Liar,* depending on whether you focus on the light or the dark areas. We make sense of stimuli by noticing data that stand out as a *figure* against a less striking *ground*. The drawing is interesting because it allows us to choose between two sets of figure–ground relationships.

This principle of figure–ground organization operates in nonvisual ways as well. Recall how certain speech can suddenly stand out from a babble of voices. Sometimes the words are noticeable because they include your name, whereas at other times they might be spoken by a familiar voice.

Manchan/Photodisc/Getty Images

FIGURE 3.1

We also use **perceptual schemata**—cognitive frameworks that allow us to organize the raw data we have selected—to make sense of information about others. *Physical constructs* allow us to classify people according to their appearance: male or female, attractive or sloppy, big or small, young or old. *Role constructs* use social position—student, lawyer, husband—as a means of organization. *Interaction constructs* focus on social behaviour: friendly, intense, helpful, or sarcastic. The fourth organizing schema uses *psychological constructs* to organize people according to their apparent personalities, such as curious, nervous, insecure, and so on. Finally, *membership constructs* help us identify others according to the group or groups they belong to: union rep, Liberal, etc.

The perceptual schemata we use shape the way we think about and communicate with others. If you've classified a professor, for example, as "friendly," you'll handle questions or problems one way. If you've put the professor in the "pompous" category, your behaviour will probably be quite different. What constructs do you use

Perceptual schemata
Cognitive frameworks that allow individuals to organize perceptual data that they have selected from the environment. These include physical, role, interaction, psychological, and membership constructs.

AT THE MOVIES

Crash (2004), Rated R

You might like to see the movie *Crash* to see the effects of inaccurate stereotyping. Over 36 hours in Los Angeles, the lives of several strangers collide. Because they come from such different backgrounds, this diverse group of people rely on stereotypes—usually relating to race—to form snap judgments of each other. Unfortunately, their judgments are almost always wrong.

Again and again, the characters' assumptions keep them from understanding the human beings they are encountering. Matt Dillon plays an angry cop who goes out of his way to humiliate a black citizen. An upper-class housewife (Sandra Bullock) believes a Mexican-American locksmith (Michael Pena) is a gangbanger who plans to burgle her home, even though he is actually a gentle man struggling to build a safe life for his family. An Iranian businessman (Shaun Toub) keeps being misidentified as an Arab. Two clean-cut young black men (Larenz Tate and Ludacris) bemoan the fact that they are regarded with fear by whites in an upscale neighbourhood.

Since childhood, most of us have been reminded not to judge a book by its cover. *Crash* provides a dramatic example of the problems that can result from ignoring this maxim.

Invitation TO INSIGHT

Your Perceptual Filters

1. Identify the perceptual schemata described in the preceding section that you would use to classify people in each of the following contexts:
   a. spending time with new acquaintances at a party
   b. socializing with fellow workers on the job
   c. choosing teammates for an important class project
   d. offering help to a stranded motorist

   Describe both the general type of organizing scheme (for example, "physical," "membership") and the specific category within each type (such as "attractive," "roughly the same age as me").

2. Consider
   a. other schemata you might use in each context
   b. the different consequences of using the schemata you originally chose and the alternative you identified in the preceding step
   c. how your relationships might change if you used different constructs

THE INVESTIGATION

HE WAS A REAL TALL GUY DRESSED NORMALLY, WITH LIGHT, DRY HAIR.

HE WAS A HEALTHY, GOOD LOOKING YOUNG KID... BUT DRESSED RATHER SHABBILY.

HE WAS REAL BIG AND REAL OLD.

HE WAS A WELL-DRESSED SORT, A LITTLE OVERWEIGHT AND WITH A LOT OF HAIR.

I REMEMBER HE HAD A LARGE HEAD AND HE SMELLED FUNNY.

HE WAS SURELY A WESTERNER.

HE WAS A SCRAWNY LITTLE SHORT-HAIRED TWERP FROM BACK EAST.

HE HAD DARK HAIR AND A CUTE NOSE. A REAL DOLL.

HE WAS A ROUGH, FURRY GUY WITH LITTLE BEADY EYES. PROBABLY INEDIBLE.

Courtesy John Jonik

to classify the people? Consider how your relationship might change if you used different schemata.

Stereotyping

Once we select an organizing scheme to classify people, we use that scheme to make generalizations and predictions about members of the groups who fit the categories

we use. For example, if you were especially aware of gender, you might be alert to the differences between the way women and men behave or the way they are treated. If sports play an important part in your life, you might think of athletes differently than others. If ethnicity is important, you'll notice differences between members of various ethnic groups.

There's nothing wrong with generalizations as long as they are accurate. In fact, it's impossible to get through life without them. But when generalizations lose touch with reality, they lead to **stereotyping**—categorizing individuals according to a set of characteristics assumed to belong to all members of a group.[2] Stereotypes may be based on a kernel of truth, but they go beyond the facts at hand and make claims that usually have no valid basis.

> **Stereotyping**
> Categorizing individuals according to a set of characteristics assumed to belong to all members of a group.

You can begin to get a sense of your tendency to make generalizations and to stereotype by completing the following sentences:

1. Women are _____
2. Men are _____
3. Inuit people are _____
4. Vegetarians are _____
5. Wrestlers are _____
6. Older people are _____

You probably completed each sentence without much hesitation. Does this mean you were stereotyping? You can answer this question by deciding whether your generalizations fit the three characteristics of stereotypes (we'll use "older people" as an example):

- *You often categorize people on the basis of an easily recognized characteristic.* Age is relatively simple to identify, so you might categorize someone who appears to be in her 80s as "elderly."
- *You ascribe a set of characteristics to most or all members of a category.* Based on your (limited) experiences with some senior relatives, you conclude that older people don't hear well and they're not mentally alert.
- *You apply the set of characteristics to any member of the group.* When you meet a senior citizen, you talk very loudly and slowly… which can be extremely annoying to fit, healthy older people who don't fit your stereotype.

Once we buy into stereotypes, we often seek out isolated behaviours that support our inaccurate beliefs. But such stereotypes can have devastating effects for those being stereotyped. Canadian Muslims and Arabs are often targets of racial profiling. Rasha Mourtada writes of the obstacles Muslims face when attempting to fly out of Canada for business purposes. To combat these difficulties, companies are offering equivalent positions that do not require international travel and are working on regulations to have frequent-flier employees bypass discriminating procedures.[3] But racial profiling also occurs on Canadian streets. University of Toronto sociologists Scott Wortley and Julian Tanner note a Toronto survey that found that "black youth are much more likely to be stopped and searched by the police than youth from other racial backgrounds."[4] These examples demonstrate the negative effects of stereotyping.

Stereotyping doesn't always arise from bad intentions, and careless generalizations can grow from good intentions. For example, knowing that people raised in collectivistic cultures tend to conform to group norms may lead you to mistakenly think that anyone from that background will be a selfless team player. But not all members of a group are equally collectivistic, or individualistic, for that matter. A close look at North Americans of European and Latin descent showed differences within each group.[5] Some Latinos were more independent than some Euro-Americans and vice versa. Moreover, teens in Japan, a traditionally collectivist culture, feel torn between individualism and collectivism; that is, between time-honoured traditions and contemporary trends.[6] As our "global village" becomes more connected, generalizations about specific cultures are likely to become less accurate.

Stereotypes don't always lead to communication problems. If a person fits the pattern in your mind, there may be no difficulties. But if your mental image and the person's characteristics don't match, problems can arise. This was illustrated in the following experiment.[7] In one phase of the experiment, white and black students were presented with stories in which a prejudicial act may or may not have taken place. For example, a man who has been promised a hotel room over the phone is later denied

Troy Aossey/Taxi/Getty Images

the room when he shows up in person. Four race combinations were used for each story: white perpetrator/black victim, white perpetrator/white victim, black perpetrator/white victim, and black perpetrator/black victim. In almost all instances, participants were more likely to label the combination of white perpetrator and black victim as prejudice than any other combination. Further, females were more likely than males, and blacks were more likely than whites, to label an action as prejudiced. These results suggest that a prototypic, or "model," stereotype exists about racism (whites oppress blacks, men oppress women, and not the reverse) and that "participants who belong to traditionally oppressed groups (blacks, women) may be more sensitive to potential prejudice." In other words, we select, organize, and interpret behaviour in ways that fit our existing notions about others' motives.

(Looking at Diversity)

Christa Kilvington: Socioeconomic Stereotyping

© Cengage Learning

What comes to mind when you hear the description "straight A student"? How about when you hear "single mom on social assistance"? Most likely you get two very different mental pictures. Did you think of both individuals as complete opposites? And yet, I am both: a college student with straight-A grades who is also a single mother on social assistance.

To some people, the combination doesn't fit. They figure that anyone smart enough to earn straight As shouldn't have ended up on social assistance, or that anybody on social assistance is probably too lazy to be a top student.

The stereotypes people use to classify me shape the way they communicate. People who only know me from school have no idea of my economic situation. They see me as intelligent and ambitious—an academic standout. They speak to me formally and respectfully. Those who know me only by my income level (caseworkers, health care workers) communicate in a very different way. When I go to the social assistance office, I am often treated as unintelligent, lazy, and dishonest. People speak to me in condescending and disrespectful tones.

Why do some people equate income level with intelligence or treat me and others differently because of our economic status? Why is it all right to treat people disrespectfully because they're poor? Stereotypes exist for a reason, but it's important to go beyond them to find out each person's unique story. When you open your mind to the possibility that there is more to a person than meets the eye, that is when you grow as a person yourself.

Punctuation

Punctuation
The process of determining the causal order of events.

Interpretation
The process of attaching meaning to sense data; synonymous with *decode*.

The process of organizing goes beyond our generalized perceptions of people. We can also organize our interactions in terms of what communication theorists call **punctuation**: the tendency to determine the causal order of events.[8] In other words, how actions are interpreted depends on when the interpreter thinks they occurred. For example, visualize a running quarrel between a husband and wife. The husband accuses the wife of being critical, whereas she complains that he is withdrawing from her. Notice that the order in which each partner punctuates this cycle is different and that affects how the quarrel looks. The husband begins by blaming the wife: "I withdraw because you're so critical." The wife organizes the situation differently, starting with the husband: "I criticize because you withdraw." After the cycle gets rolling, it is impossible to say which accusation is accurate. Figure 3.2 illustrates how this process operates.

Anyone who has seen two children scrap over "who started it" understands that haggling over causes and effects won't solve a conflict. Rather than argue about whose punctuation of an event is correct, it's more productive to move on and figure out how to make things better.

> **We don't see things as they are. We see things as we are.**
>
> —Anaïs Nin

Interpretation

Once information has been selected and organized, it must be interpreted. **Interpretation**, the process of attaching meaning to sense data, plays a role in virtually every interpersonal act. Is the person who smiles at you across

FIGURE 3.2

The Same Event Can Be Punctuated in More than One Way

Punctuation #1

Criticizing ⟶ Withdrawing ⟶ Criticizing ⟶ Withdrawing

Punctuation #2

Withdrawing ⟶ Criticizing ⟶ Withdrawing ⟶ Criticizing

a crowded room interested in romance or simply being polite? Is a friend's kidding a sign of affection or irritation? Should you take an invitation to "drop by any time" literally or not? How you interpret these events depends on several factors.

Degree of involvement with the other person. We sometimes view people with whom we have or seek a relationship more favourably than others.[9] For example, male subjects were asked to critique presentations by women who allegedly owned restaurants. Half of these presentations were designed to be competent and half to be incompetent. The men who were told they would be having a casual date with the female speakers judged their presentations— whether competent or not—more highly than those who didn't expect any involvement with the speakers.[10]

Personal experience. What meaning have similar events held? If, for example, you've been gouged by landlords in the past, you might be skeptical when a new landlord insists that careful housekeeping will ensure that your cleaning deposit will be refunded.

Assumptions about human behaviour. Believing that people do as little work as possible to get by, or that most do the best they can, shapes the way we interpret their actions.

SKILL BUILDER

Punctuation Practice

You can appreciate how different punctuation patterns can influence attitudes and behaviour by following these directions.

1. Use the format pictured in Figure 3.2 to diagram the following situations:
   a. A father and daughter are growing more and more distant. The daughter withdraws because she interprets her father's coolness as rejection. The father views his daughter's aloofness as a rebuff and withdraws further.
   b. The relationship between two friends is becoming strained. One jokes to lighten up the tension, and the other becomes more tense.
   c. A dating couple is on the verge of breaking up. One partner frequently asks the other to show more affection. The other withdraws physical contact.

2. Identify two punctuating schemes for each of the situations described in step 1. Consider how the differing schemes would affect the way the two people in each situation respond to one another.

   Now identify a difficult communication issue in your own life. Punctuate it in two ways: how you would punctuate it and how the other person might punctuate it. Discuss how seeing the issue from the other person's point of view might change the way you communicate as you discuss the issue.

123render/iStockphoto

Attitudes. Our attitudes shape the way we make sense of others' behaviours. For example, what would you think if you overheard one man say, "I love you," to another? In one study, people with a high degree of homophobia—the fear of or discrimination against homosexuals—assumed that the speaker was gay. Those with lower levels of homophobia regarded the affectionate statement as platonic rather than romantic.[11]

Expectations. Anticipation shapes interpretations. If you were told in advance that the instructor was terrific, would it affect how you perceived the teacher? According to one study, it would. Students who read positive comments about instructors on a website viewed those teachers as more credible and attractive than students who did not read them.[12] Clearly, our expectations influence our perceptions.

Knowledge. If you know that a friend has just been jilted by a lover or laid off from a job, you'll

S. GROSS

"I don't care if she is a tape dispenser. I love her."

interpret his aloof behaviour differently than you would if you didn't know what had happened. If you know that an instructor speaks sarcastically to all students, you won't be as likely to take such remarks personally.

Self-concept. The world seems very different when you're feeling insecure. For example, when a person is being teased, the recipient's self-concept is the single greatest factor in determining whether the teaser's motives will be interpreted as friendly or hostile, and hence the recipient will respond with comfort or defensiveness.[13] The same goes for happiness and sadness or any other opposing emotions. The way we feel about ourselves strongly influences how we interpret others' behaviour.

Relational satisfaction. A behaviour that seems positive when you're happy with a partner might seem completely different when you're not. Couples in unsatisfying relationships tend to blame one another when things go wrong.[14] They also tend to believe that their partners are selfish and have negative intentions. Unhappy spouses are more likely than happy ones to negatively interpret their mate's behaviour.

Although we have talked about selection, organization, and interpretation separately, they can occur in differing sequences. For example, a parent or babysitter's past interpretations (such as "Jason is a troublemaker") can influence future selections (his behaviour becomes especially noticeable) and the organization of events (when there's a fight, the assumption is that Jason started it). Like all communication, perception is an ongoing process and it's hard to pin down beginnings and endings.

Negotiation

Thus far, perception has been discussed in terms of what occurs in each individual's mind. But perception isn't just a solitary activity: A big part of it occurs between and among people as they influence one another's perceptions and try to achieve a shared perspective. This process is known as **negotiation**.

Think of negotiation as an exchange of stories. Scholars call the stories we use to describe our personal worlds **narratives**.[15] Virtually every interpersonal situation can be described by more than one narrative, and they often differ. You see this in courtrooms; they're filled with opponents who tell very different narratives about who is the "villain" and who is the "hero." Even happy families have stories that place members in particular roles—the scatterbrain, the smart one, the athlete, and so on. In best-case scenarios, family storytelling enhances perspective taking and leads to family satisfaction and functioning.[16]

When our narratives clash, we can either hang on to our own point of view or negotiate a shared narrative that creates some common ground. Shared narratives make for smoother communication. For example, romantic partners who celebrate their successful struggles against relational obstacles are happier than those who don't have this shared appreciation.[17] Likewise, couples that agree on important turning points in their relationships are more satisfied than those who have different views of what incidents were most important.[18]

Shared narratives don't have to be accurate to be powerful. Couples who have been happily married for more than 50 years seem to collude in a relational narrative that doesn't jibe with the facts.[19] While they say they rarely have conflict, objective analysis says otherwise. Without overtly agreeing to do so, they blame outside forces for their problems instead of each other. They offer the most charitable interpretations of each other's behaviours, believing that their spouse acts with good intentions when things don't go well. They seem willing to forgive and forget. Communication researcher Judy Pearson evaluates these findings thus:

> Should we conclude that happy couples have a poor grip on reality? Perhaps they do, but is the reality of one's marriage better known by outside onlookers than by the players themselves? The conclusion is evident. One key to a long happy marriage is to tell yourself and others that you have one and then to behave as though you do![20]

LO²
Influences on Perception

How we select, organize, interpret, and negotiate information is influenced by several factors.

Physiological Influences

Within the wide range of human similarities, each of us perceives the world differently because of physiological factors. Consider the long list of physiological factors that shapes our views of the world.

The Senses

Differences in how each of us sees, hears, tastes, touches, and smells stimuli can affect interpersonal relationships. Consider the following everyday situations:

> "Turn down that radio! It's going to make me go deaf."

> "It's not too loud. If I turn it down, it will be impossible to hear it."

Negotiation
What occurs between and among people as they influence one another's perceptions and try to achieve a shared perspective.

Narratives
The stories we use to describe our personal worlds.

SALLY FORTH

by Greg Howard

SALLY FORTH © KING FEATURES SYNDICATE

"It's freezing in here."

"Are you kidding? We'll suffocate if you turn up the heat!"

Differences in vision and hearing are the easiest to recognize, but there is also evidence that identical foods taste differently to different individuals.[21] Odours can please or repel. Temperature variations that leave some of us uncomfortable are inconsequential to others. Recognizing these differences won't eliminate them, but it will help you remember that other people's preferences aren't crazy, just different.

Age

Older people often view the world differently than younger ones because of greater scope and number of experiences. Developmental differences also shape perceptions. Swiss psychologist Jean Piaget described a series of stages that children pass through on their way to adulthood.[22] For example, younger children are incapable of performing mental feats that are natural to the rest of us. Until the age of seven, they aren't able to take another person's point of view. This fact helps explain why children often seem egocentric, selfish, and uncooperative. A parent's exasperated plea, "Can't you see I'm too tired to play?" just won't make sense to an energetic four-year-old who imagines that everyone feels the same way.

> Sometimes very young children can look at the old, and a look passes between them, conspiratorial, sly, and knowing. It's because neither are human to the middling ones.
>
> —Margaret Laurence,
> *The Stone Angel*

Health and Fatigue

We've all had a cold, flu, or some other ailment that left us feeling tired, less sociable, or just not able to think straight. This affected how we related to others. Keep in mind how

Monkey Business Images/Shutterstock

Trying on Old Age

Andersen Ross/Getty Images

How would you like to travel through time? That is, how would you like a glimpse into your golden years? That's the opportunity students are getting in psychologist Randall Wright's class on aging and human development.

Wright asked students to put together a costume that would make them look like senior citizens to casual observers. To create the illusion of age, Wright suggested wearing earplugs to reduce hearing, wrapping joints with elastic bandages to create stiffness, and using or discarding glasses to impair eyesight.

The students put in five hours of role playing as older versions of themselves. They also submitted descriptions and ratings of the exercise, as well as photographs of how they looked before and after donning their costumes.

Most of the students gained valuable insights during their sojourn in old age. Even such mundane activities as walking across the street took on new meanings, as one student observed: "With our legs wrapped, we walked considerably slower than most people. Inevitably, cars had to wait for us … not only do you feel a bother to other people, you worry about your life."

One student described how it felt to be ignored, while another was accosted by a group of boys in a passing car who screamed insults and demanded money.

Not all the experiences were frightening, however. One student was asked when he had last eaten and was offered $10 as he pretended to rummage in a garbage can for food. Another male student said that "the highlight of my experiment came when a little old lady on the opposite bench winked at me."

Being old for a few hours was an eye-opening exercise, the students overwhelmingly agreed. "Most felt that the simulation increased their knowledge and understanding of the elderly," says Wright. "In this case, living the lesson was better than learning it from a textbook."

Holly Hall

Discussion Starter
In what ways has this reading heightened your awareness of how senior citizens experience life?

---

illness might affect the communication of others and don't be afraid to let others know when you feel ill. And just as being ill can affect your relationships, so can being overly tired. It's best not to deal with important issues at such times.

Hunger

People often get grumpy when they don't eat and sleepy after stuffing themselves. Sadly, teenagers whose families do not get enough food were almost three times as likely to be suspended from school, twice as likely to have difficulty getting along with others, and four times as likely to have no friends.[23]

Biological Cycles

Most of us can identify ourselves as early birds or night owls. This is because we all have a daily cycle wherein body temperature, sexual drive, alertness, tolerance to stress, and mood continually change.[24] These changes are mostly due to hormonal cycles. For instance, adrenal hormones, which affect feelings of stress, are secreted at higher rates during some hours. In the same manner, the male and female sex hormones enter our systems at variable rates. We often aren't conscious of these changes, but they surely influence the way we relate to one another. Once we are aware of how these cycles govern our own and others' feelings and behaviours, we can deal with important issues at the most effective times.

Psychological Challenges

Some perceptual differences are rooted in neurology. People with ADHD (attention deficit hyperactivity disorder) are easily distracted and have difficulty delaying gratification. Those with ADHD might find a long lecture boring and tedious, while other audience members are fascinated by the same lecture. People with bipolar disorder experience significant mood swings that dramatically affect their perceptions of events, friends, and even family members. Therefore, when others see and respond to the world differently, there may be causes beyond what we immediately recognize.

Cultural Differences

Another perceptual gap that often blocks communication is culture. Every culture has its own way of looking

Andersen Ross/Getty Images

at the world. But sometimes problems arise out of poor translation from one language to another. Here are some examples.

- General Motors was baffled when its Chevrolet Nova model did not sell well in Latin American countries. In Spanish, *no va* means "does not go."
- One airline lost customers when it promoted the "rendezvous lounges" on its planes flying Brazilian routes. In Portuguese, *rendezvous* is a place to have sex.
- McDonald's Corporation was chagrined to learn that in French Canadian slang, "big macs" are large breasts.[25]

Nonverbal behaviours also have different meanings in different cultures. In many cultures, the OK sign, made by touching the thumb and forefinger, is an obscene gesture representing the female genitalia. To a woman, it's a

(Looking at Diversity)

Attention Deficit Disorder and Communication by Jason Rothman.

Attention Deficit Disorder and Communication

Jason Rothman explains how attention deficit disorder (ADD) affected his communication and how others perceived him.

I've had attention deficit disorder (ADD) my whole life. One website describes ADD's symptoms as "inattention, distractibility, impulsivity, and in some cases, hyperactivity." This is the way I behaved, especially before my ADD was diagnosed and treated.

When I was a young child, my parents quickly realized that I was having a hard time sitting still. They also realized that I was easily distracted, hyperactive, and impulsive to the point where I said and did anything that came into my mind. At first they didn't know what to do. Eventually we found a therapist who diagnosed my condition and helped me find medication that worked.

Beginning in my earliest years of school, my teachers would single me out for not paying attention. They thought I was misbehaving, but actually I was so overstimulated by what was going on around me that I couldn't sort out school tasks from everything else. Almost anything would capture my attention—a noise outside the room, music, other kids' movements, or even when somebody dropped a pencil on the ground by mistake. And because ADD limits impulse control, sometimes I would speak out during class at the wrong times. The problem

continued into high school. I acquired a reputation as a discipline problem because I couldn't keep focused on school business. It's not that I was deliberately causing trouble; it's just that I was so stimulated and distracted that sitting still and focusing on classwork was almost impossible.

ADD complicated my social life, too. In conversations with friends, my mind would wander and I would tune out. At other times, I would interrupt. This made people think that I was rude or that I didn't care about what they were saying. Just like in school, it wasn't that I didn't care about other people but that I didn't have the control that other people take for granted.

Getting my ADD diagnosed was the beginning of gaining more control over my communication. Medication was a real help, although I've found ways to cope without needing it so much. I've found ways of focusing my attention and tuning out background distractions. I'm doing much better in school and my social life is running much more smoothly.

If you ever know someone who seems inattentive and impulsive, you might ask whether they have ADD or some other neurological processing problem. If so, you can help a lot by asking them to explain their situation to you and trying to find ways of communicating that work for you and them. Talking one to one in a place without distractions can be a big help. Above all, don't take their behaviour personally and don't embarrass them about something they can't control.

proposition for sex, and to a man, it suggests he's gay.[26] Imagine the problems that could result from just one innocent gesture.

In Middle Eastern countries, personal odours play an important role in interpersonal relationships. Arabs consistently breathe on people when they talk. As anthropologist Edward Hall explains:

> To smell one's friend is not only nice, but desirable, for to deny him your breath is to act ashamed. [North] Americans, on the other hand, trained as they are not to breathe in people's faces, automatically communicate shame in trying to be polite. Who would expect that when our highest diplomats are putting on their best manners they are also communicating shame? Yet this is what occurs constantly, because diplomacy is not only "eyeball to eyeball" but breath to breath.[27]

Even beliefs about the value of talk differ from one culture to another.[28] Western cultures view talk as desirable and silence is considered negative in that it suggests a lack of interest, unwillingness to communicate, hostility, anxiety, shyness, or a sign of interpersonal incompatibility. Westerners find silence embarrassing and awkward. In Asian cultures, expression of thoughts and feelings is discouraged and silence is valued. As Taoist sayings indicate, "In much talk there is great weariness," or "One who speaks does not know; one who knows does not speak." Unlike Westerners, Japanese and Chinese believe that remaining quiet is proper when there's nothing to say. To Asians, a talkative person is often considered a show-off or an insincere person.

Obviously, this intercultural feature can lead to communication problems. The talkative Westerner and the

Photo courtesy of Chris Greene.

silent Asian are behaving in "proper" ways, yet each views the other with disapproval. This may require them to recognize and deal with their **ethnocentrism**—the attitude that one's own culture is superior to others. Ethnocentric people believe that anyone who does not belong to his or her in-group is somehow strange, wrong, or even inferior.

Ethnocentrism
The attitude that one's own culture is superior to others.

We see this in our own country. Take the notion of time, for instance. Aboriginal time is experiential in nature; that is, there is no particular time, only what is occurring at the moment. Non-Aboriginal Canadians—perceived as immigrants by Aboriginal peoples—think of time as event-driven, moving in a linear fashion. Because of these perceptual differences, Aboriginal students arriving late for class may be pigeonholed as apathetic, undependable, or irresponsible when in fact a momentary matter may have consumed their attention. One Native student related that if he was leaving for the university and his son wanted to play, that was more important than getting to a scheduled class. Failure to recognize such perceptual differences can lead to unfortunate and unnecessary misunderstandings.

The way we communicate with strangers also reflects ethnocentric thinking. Author Anne Fadiman explains why Hmong immigrants from the mountains of Laos prefer their traditional shamanistic healers, called *txiv neeb*, to Western doctors. You'll see in the excerpt below that while both perspectives make sense, neither group can get beyond its familiar set of perceptions

Invitation TO INSIGHT

New Body, New Perspective
You can get a clearer idea of how physiology influences perception by trying the following exercise.

1. Choose one of the following situations:
   an evening in a singles bar
   a volleyball game
   a doctor's physical examination

2. How would the event you chose seem different if:
   your eyesight was much worse (or better)
   you had a hearing loss
   you were 8 inches taller (or shorter)
   you were coming down with a serious cold
   you were a member of the opposite sex
   you were 10 years older (or younger)
   you had ADHD

to see the other culture's point of view:

> A *txiv neeb* might spend as much as eight hours in a sick person's home; doctors forced their patients, no matter how weak they were, to come to the hospital, and then might spend only 20 minutes at their bedsides. *Txiv neebs* were polite and never needed to ask questions; doctors asked about their sexual and excretory habits. *Txiv neebs* could render an immediate diagnosis; doctors often demanded samples of blood (or even urine or feces, which they liked to keep in little bottles), took X-rays, and waited for days for the results to come back from the laboratory—and then, after all that, sometimes they were unable to identify the cause of the problem. *Txiv neebs* never undressed their patients; doctors asked patients to take off all their clothes, and sometimes dared to put their fingers inside women's vaginas. *Txiv neebs* knew that to treat the body without treating the soul was an act of patent folly; doctors never even mentioned the soul.[29]

Geography also influences perceptions. Sixty percent of Canadians define themselves according to the region they live in.[30] Our distinct climates, histories, and economics influence how we think about ourselves and others, and any one event might be viewed differently by individuals from the Prairies, downtown Toronto, or the North.

Social Roles

Social roles can also cause communication breakdowns. From the time we're born, we're indirectly taught a set of roles we're expected to play. Prescribed roles help society function smoothly and help us know what's expected of us. But narrowly defined roles can lead to wide gaps in understanding. When roles become unquestioned and rigid, people tend to see the world from their own viewpoint, having no experiences that show

© iStockphoto.com/sjlocke

them how other people see it. Naturally, communication suffers in such situations.

Gender Roles

Although people use the terms *sex* and *gender* interchangeably, they have two distinct meanings. *Sex* refers to biological characteristics of a male or female, whereas *gender* refers to the social and psychological dimensions of masculine and feminine behaviour. Research shows that males and females do perceive the world differently, for reasons ranging from genes to neurology to hormones.[31] However, even researchers who focus on biological differences between females and males acknowledge that societal gender roles and stereotypes affect perception dramatically.[32]

Gender roles are socially approved ways that men and women are expected to behave. Children learn sex-typed behaviour by watching other people, being exposed to media, and being reinforced for appropriate behaviours.[33] Once they learn these customary roles, violations are regarded as unusual and undesirable.

Some theorists suggest that stereotypical masculine and feminine behaviours are not opposite poles of a single continuum, but rather two separate sets of behaviours.[34] From this perspective, an individual can act in a masculine

TABLE 3.1
Gender Roles

	Male	Female
Masculine	Masculine males	Masculine females
Feminine	Feminine males	Feminine females
Androgynous	Androgynous males	Androgynous females
Undifferentiated	Undifferentiated males	Undifferentiated females

or feminine manner, or exhibit both types of characteristics. The male–female dichotomy, then, is replaced with four psychological sex types: masculine, feminine, **androgynous** (combining masculine and feminine traits), and undifferentiated (neither masculine nor feminine).

Combining the four psychological sex types with the traditional physiological sex types produces the eight categories listed in Table 3.1.

Androgynous
Possessing both feminine and masculine traits.

Androgynous individuals behave in a variety of ways, depending on the nature and context of the relationship.

THE FAMILY CIRCUS

OH, NO! THAT SIREN MEANS SOMEBODY'S IN TROUBLE!

AH, YES! THAT SIREN MEANS SOMEBODY IS GETTING HELP!

FAMILY CIRCUS © Bill Keene, Inc. KING FEATURES SYNDICATE

> The primary area in which there remain dramatic differences between the values of men and women is in the orientation toward violence. Men are significantly more likely than women to believe that violence is an unavoidable fact of everyday life, and an acceptable way of resolving disputes; men are also much more likely than women to be entertained by violent sports, movies, or television. Women, on the other hand, are much less likely to accept violence as normative, and much more likely to worry about being violently attacked or victimized.
>
> —Michael Adams,
> *Sex in the Snow*

For example, an androgynous woman would feel comfortable fixing motorcycles or going hunting as well as playing the traditional mother and wife roles. An androgynous male might be happy decorating the home, caring for the children, and working as a professional wrestler. You can see how an androgynous individual would have a greater repertoire of behaviours than would a sex-typed person.

Occupational Roles

Even our jobs can influence our perception. For example, five people walk through a park—a botanist, a zoologist, a meteorologist, a communicologist, and a pickpocket. The botanist is fascinated by the trees and other plants. The zoologist looks for interesting animals. The meteorologist notices changes in the sky. The communicologist concentrates on the interactions among the people in the park. And, of course, the pickpocket takes advantage of the others' absorption to help himself.

Frederick Bass/Getty Images

OPERATION EMPATHY: PREPARATION FOR THE CHANGING POLICE ROLE

We are all aware that it is extremely difficult to immerse the average police officer into situations that will reveal the feelings of the down-and-outer, the social outcast, the have-nots, and show us their perspective of normal law-enforcement procedures. Obviously the officer, in his or her police role, would not fit into such a context. But suppose he or she was a person with a great deal of courage, willing for the sake of experimentation to become a bum, a skid row habitant.

A group of police officers who were willing to become skid row habitants were carefully selected and conditioned for the role they were about to play. Each was given three dollars with which to purchase a complete outfit of pawn shop clothing. Among other props were such items as a shopping bag filled with collected junk, and a wine bottle camouflaged with a brown paper sack.

Conditioned and ready, our officers, assigned in pairs, moved into an urban skid row district. They soon discovered that when they tried to leave the area, walking a few blocks into the legitimate retail sections, they were told, "Go back where you belong!" Our officers knew in reality they were not "bums," but they found that other citizens quickly categorized them and treated them accordingly.

During the skid row experiment, our officers ate in soup kitchens and shelters like the other outcasts and derelicts. They roamed the streets and the alleys, and discovered many levelling experiences. Some were anticipated, others were not. Perhaps the most meaningful experience of the skid row exercise occurred to Tom Courtney, a young juvenile officer with five years' police service.

It was dusk, and Tom and his partner were sauntering back to a prearranged gathering place. Feeling a little sporty, the pair decided to "polish off" the bottle of wine. They paused in a convenient parking lot, and Tom tipped the bottle up. As if from nowhere, two uniformed police officers materialized before the surprised pair. Tom and his partner were spread-eagled against a building and searched. Forgetting the admonishment not to reveal identities and purpose unless absolutely necessary, Tom panicked and identified himself.

Later, Tom found it difficult to explain why he was so quick in his revelation. "You wouldn't understand," he told me; then blurted he thought he "might get shot."

I found it difficult to receive this as a rational explanation, especially since Tom stated that the officers, while firm, were courteous at all times. With some additional prodding, Tom admitted that as he was being searched, he suddenly thought of every negative thing he had ever heard about the police. He even perceived a mental flash of a newspaper headline: "Police Officer Erroneously Shot While on Field Experiment."

"I know better now," Tom continued, "but when you feel that way about yourself, you believe—you believe."

I attempted to rationalize with Tom his reason for fear. I asked if he was certain that the officers were courteous. He replied in the affirmative, but added, "They didn't smile, or tell me what they were going to do next." Tom had discovered a new emotional reaction within his own personal makeup, and it left a telling impression.

Today, Tom Courtney is still telling our department personnel, "For God's sake, smile when you can. And above all, tell the man or woman you're shaking down what you are going to do. Take the personal threat out of the encounter, if you can."

Equally important as Tom's experience, I believe, is the lesson we learned about personal judgments. Our men in the "Operation Empathy" experiment found they were judged by the so-called normal population as "being like" all the other inmates of skid row, simply because their appearance was representative.

Perhaps we would all do well to heed the lesson, for now, more than at any other time in our history, police officers and the RCMP must guard against the natural tendency to lump people into categories simply because they look alike.

R. Fred Ferguson

From "Field Experiment: Preparation for the Changing Police Role" by Fred Ferguson. Used by courtesy of the author.

(On the Job)

Roles and Perceptions

Perhaps the most dramatic illustration of perception and occupational roles came from a psychology experiment conducted by Philip Zimbardo.[35] Zimbardo recruited a group of middle-class, well-educated young men and randomly chose 11 to serve as "guards" and 10 to be "prisoners" in a mock prison set. Guards were issued uniforms, handcuffs, whistles, and billy clubs; prisoners were placed in rooms with metal bars, bucket toilets, and cots. The guards established their own rules for the experiment: no talking during meals, rest periods, and after lights out. Head counts at 2:30 a.m. Short rations for troublemakers.

Faced with these conditions, the prisoners resisted. Some barricaded their doors with beds. Others went on hunger strikes. Several ripped off their identifying number tags. The guards clamped down hard on protesters. Some turned sadistic and abusive, while others threw prisoners into solitary confinement. One group forced prisoners to call each other names and clean out toilets with their bare hands.

Within a short time, the experiment became reality for both prisoners and guards. Several inmates had stomach cramps and lapsed into uncontrollable weeping. Others got headaches, and one broke out in a head-to-toe rash after his request for early "parole" was denied.

Scheduled to go on for two weeks, Zimbardo had to call off the experiment in six days. The simulation had become too intense. "I knew by then that they were thinking like prisoners and not like people," he said. "If we were able to demonstrate that pathological behaviour could be produced in so short a time, think of what damage is being done in 'real' prisons."

In this dramatic exercise, 21 well-educated, middle-class citizens turned, almost overnight, into sadistic bullies or demoralized victims. Clearly, it shows us that *what* we are is determined largely by society's designation of *who* we are.

Rhetorician Kenneth Burke and others have called the tendency to view the world through the lens of one's job an "occupational psychosis."[36] The best antidote to occupational psychosis is to step outside one's role and regard others as you would independent of your job. Or try the role reversal exercise described in "Invitation to Insight" on page 71.

© iStockphoto.com/Bonnie Schupp

Relational Roles

Think back to the "Who am I?" list you made in Chapter 2. It's likely that your list included roles you play in relation to others: daughter, roommate, husband, friend, etc. These roles not only define you, they also affect your perception.

Take, for example, the role of parent. New mothers and fathers will attest that having a child alters how they see the world. They might perceive their baby's crying as a need for comfort, while nearby strangers have a less charitable appraisal. As the child grows, parents become more aware of the messages in the child's environment. One father said he never noticed how much football fans swore until he took his six-year-old to a game. In other words, his father role affected what he heard and how he interpreted it.

Your romantic roles—partner, spouse, boyfriend/girlfriend, sweetheart, etc.—also affect your perception. For example, you may see your sweetheart as more attractive than other people do, and perhaps you overlook some noticeable faults.[37] Your romantic role can also change the way you view others. One study found that people in love view other romantic candidates as less attractive than they normally would.[38] But when the "love goggles" come off and partners break up, they often ask, "What did I ever *see* in that person?" The answer—in part—is what your relational role led you to see.

Inspirestock/JupiterImages

LO³
Common Tendencies in Perception

Social scientists use the term **attribution** to describe the process of attaching meaning to behaviour. We attribute meaning both to our own actions and to the actions of others, but we often use different yardsticks. Research has uncovered several perceptual tendencies that can lead to attribution errors.[39]

We Judge Ourselves More Charitably than Others

In an attempt to convince ourselves and others that the positive face we show to the world is accurate, we judge ourselves more generously, and this tendency is called the **self-serving bias**.[40] When others suffer, we somehow think it's their fault, but when we're the victims, there are always extenuating circumstances. Consider the following: When *others* botch a job, we think they weren't listening well or trying hard enough; when *we* botch a job, it was unclear directions or not enough time that caused the problem. When *friends* get caught speeding, we say they should have been more careful; when *we* get the ticket, we deny that we were driving too fast.[41]

We Cling to First Impressions

We label people according to our first impressions in order to make some interpretations about them: "She seems cheerful." "He seems sincere." "They sound awfully conceited."

When first impressions are accurate, labels help us decide how to respond to them in the future. When labels are inaccurate, however, we tend to hang onto them, making

conflicting information fit our opinion.

This tendency to form an overall positive impression on the basis of one positive characteristic is called the **halo effect**. Typically, positive impressions stem from physical attractiveness and leads people to attribute other virtues to the good-looking person.[42] For example, employment interviewers rate mediocre but attractive job applicants higher than their less attractive candidates.[43] When employers form positive impressions, they then ask questions that confirm their image.[44] Attractive applicants who moved from one job to another are thought to be industrious, go-getters, or ambitious. Less attractive candidates who made a negative impression and moved from job to job might be thought of as unreliable, and it may be impossible for them to dispel a phenomenon sometimes referred to as "the devil effect."[45]

The power of first impressions is also important in personal relationships. College roommates who had positive initial impressions of each other were likely to have positive subsequent interactions, manage their conflicts constructively, and continue living together.[46] Roommates who got off to a bad start tended to spiral negatively.

We Assume that Others Are Similar to Us

We tend to think that others' views are similar to our own, and this applies in a wide range of situations:

- You've heard a slightly raunchy joke that you think is pretty funny. You assume that it won't offend a somewhat straitlaced friend. It does.

- An instructor has a tendency to get off the subject during lectures. If you were a professor, you'd want to know if anything you were doing was creating problems for your students. You decide your instructor will probably be grateful for some constructive criticism—you're wrong.

Examples like these show that others don't always think or feel the way we do and that assuming that similarities exist can lead to problems.[47] One way to find out the other person's real position is to engage in perception checking, which will be discussed shortly.

"The truth is, Cauldwell, we never see ourselves as others see us."

Drawing by Lorenz. Reprinted with permission from the *Saturday Evening Post.*

We Are Influenced by the Obvious

Being influenced by the obvious is understandable. The problem, however, is that the most obvious factor is not necessarily the only one—or the most significant one for an event. What we need to do is look beyond the obvious to what else might be going on. For example:

- When two children (or adults, for that matter) fight, it may be a mistake to blame the one who lashes out first. Perhaps the other was equally responsible by teasing or refusing to cooperate.
- You might complain about an acquaintance whose malicious gossip or arguing has become a bother, forgetting that by putting up with such behaviour in the past you have been at least partially responsible.
- You might blame an unhappy working situation on the boss, overlooking other factors beyond her control, such as a change in the economy, the policy of higher management, or the demands of customers or other workers.

"Of course I care about how you imagined I thought you perceived I wanted you to feel."

LO⁴
Perception Checking

Serious problems can arise when people treat interpretations as if they were true. Like most people, you probably resent others jumping to conclusions about your behaviour.

> **Perception checking**
>
> A three-part method for verifying the accuracy of interpretations, including a description of the behaviour, two possible interpretations, and a request for clarification of the interpretation.

The skill of **perception checking** provides a better way to handle your interpretations.[48] Perception checking is a tool to help you understand others accurately instead of assuming that your first interpretation is correct.

Elements of Perception Checking

A complete perception check has three parts:

1. A description of the behaviour you noticed
2. At least two possible interpretations of the behaviour
3. A request for clarification about how to interpret the behaviour

For example:

> "When you rushed out of the room and slammed the door," (*behaviour*) "I wasn't sure whether you were mad at me" (*first interpretation*) "or just in a hurry." (*second interpretation*) "How *did* you feel?" (*request for clarification*)

> "You haven't laughed much in the last couple of days." (*behaviour*) "It makes me wonder whether something's bothering you" (*first interpretation*) "or whether you're just feeling quiet." (*second interpretation*) "What's up?" (*request for clarification*)

> "You said you really liked the job I did." (*behaviour*) "On the other hand, there was something about your voice that made me think you may not like it." (*first interpretation*) "Maybe it's just my imagination, though." (*second interpretation*) "How do you really feel?" (*request for clarification*)

Because the goal of perception checking is mutual understanding, it is a cooperative approach to communication. Besides more accurate perceptions, it minimizes defensiveness. Instead of saying, in effect, "I know what you're thinking …" it takes the more respectful approach that implies, "I know I'm not qualified to judge you without some help."

Perception Checking Considerations

Like all communication skills, perception checking isn't a mechanical formula that works in every situation. The following factors must be considered when deciding when and how to use this approach.

Completeness

Sometimes a perception check won't need all the parts listed earlier to be effective:

> "You haven't dropped by lately. Is anything the matter?" (single interpretation combined with request for clarification)

"I can't tell whether you're kidding me about being cheap or if you're serious." (*behaviour combined with interpretations*) "Are you mad at me?"

Sometimes even the most skimpy perception check—a simple question like "What's going on?"—will do the job. You might also rely on other people to help you make sense of confusing behaviour: "Rachelle has been awfully quiet lately. Do you know what's up?" A complete perception check is most necessary when the risk of sounding judgmental is highest.

Nonverbal Congruency

A perception check can succeed only if your nonverbal behaviour reflects the open-mindedness of your words. An accusing tone of voice or a hostile glare contradicts a sincerely worded request for clarification and suggests that you've already made up your mind about the other person's intentions.

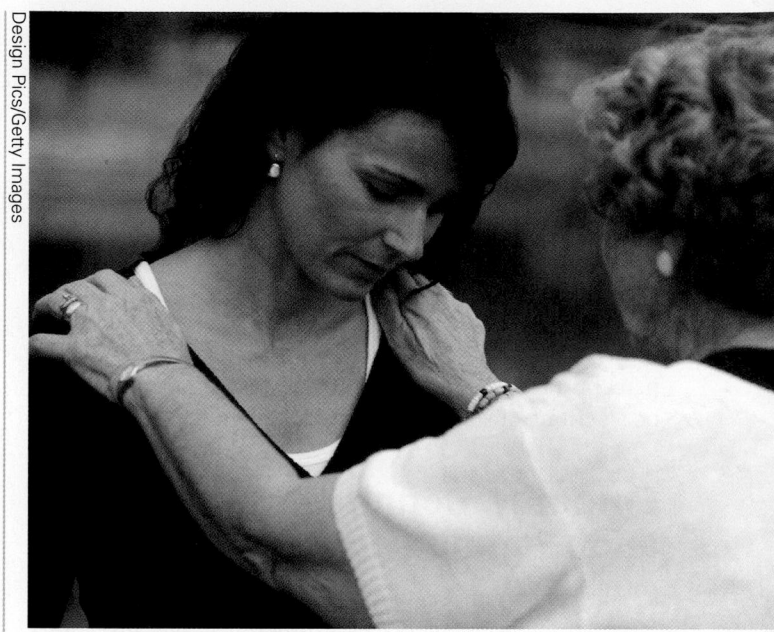

(**In Real Life**) Perception Checking in Everyday Life

Perception checking only works if it is sincere and fits your personal style. The following examples show how perception checking sounds in everyday life and may help you find ways to use it when you are faced with ambiguous messages.

My Boss's Jokes

I get confused by my boss's sense of humour. Sometimes he jokes just to be funny, but other times he uses humour to make a point without coming right out and saying what's on his mind. Last week he was talking about the upcoming work schedule and he said with a laugh, "I own you all weekend!" I have a life besides work, so his comment left me worried.

I used a perception check to figure out what he meant: "Brad, when you told me, 'I own you all weekend,' I wasn't sure whether you were kidding or whether you really expect me to work Saturday and Sunday. Were you serious?"

He kind of smiled and said, "No, I was just kidding. You only have to work Saturday and Sunday."

I still couldn't be sure whether or not he was serious, so I checked again: "You're kidding, right?"

My boss replied, "Well, I do need you at least one day, and two would be better." Once I figured out what he really meant, we worked out a schedule that had me work Friday evening and Saturday morning, which gave me the time off I needed.

If I hadn't used the perception check, I would have wound up worrying about being tied up all weekend and getting mad at my boss for no good reason. I'm glad I spoke up.

My Dad's Affection

My father and I have a great relationship. A while back I picked him up at the airport after a week-long business trip and a long cross-country flight. On the way home, he was quiet—not his usual self. He said he was exhausted, which I understood. When we got home, he brightened up and started joking and playing with my younger brother. I thought to myself, "Why is he so happy to see my brother when he hardly said a word to me?" I didn't say anything at the time. The next day I felt resentful toward my dad, and it showed. He said, "What's up with you?" But I was too embarrassed to say anything.

After learning this approach in class, I tried a perception check. I said, "Dad—when you were quiet on the way home after your business trip and then you perked up when you got home and saw Jaime, I wasn't sure what was up. I thought maybe you were happier to see him than me, or that maybe I'm imagining things. How come you said you were tired with me and then you perked up with Jaime?"

My dad felt awful. He said he was tired in the car, but once he got back to the house he was glad to be home and felt like a new man. I was too wrapped up in my mind to consider this alternative.

Cultural Rules

The straightforward approach of perception checking works best in *low-context cultures* such as North America and Western Europe, where language is used as clearly and logically as possible. These groups appreciate the kind of straight talking that perception checking embodies. Members of *high-context cultures* (common in Latin America and Asia) value social harmony over clarity. They are likely to regard perception checking as potentially embarrassing, preferring less direct ways of understanding one another. Thus, a "let's get this straight" perception check that might work in our country would be a serious mistake in Mexico or Asia.

Empathy, Cognitive Complexity, and Communication

While perception checking is a valuable tool for clarifying ambiguous messages, sometimes we just don't understand where people are coming from. This is where empathy can help.

Empathy

Empathy is the ability to recreate another person's perspective, and while it's impossible to completely understand a person's viewpoint, we can learn how the world appears to him or her. Used here, *empathy* involves three dimensions.[49] On one level, empathy involves *perspective taking*—an attempt to understand the viewpoint of another person. To do this, you must set aside your own opinions. Empathy also has an *emotional* dimension that helps us get closer and gain a sense of the other person's fear, joy, sadness, and so on. A third dimension of empathy is a genuine *concern* for the welfare of the other person. When we empathize, we go beyond just thinking and feeling as others do and genuinely care about their well-being.

> **Empathy**
> The ability to project oneself into another person's point of view so as to experience the other's thoughts and feelings.

Humans are "hardwired" to empathize with others—it's built into our brains.[50] Bestselling author Daniel Goleman believes that cultivating this tendency is the essence of "social intelligence."[51] The ability to empathize exists in even the youngest children. Virtually from birth, infants become visibly upset when they hear another baby crying, and if one child hurts its finger, another baby might put its own finger into its mouth as if in pain. When children see their parents cry, they wipe their own eyes even though they're not crying.

Although children have a basic capacity to empathize, studies with twins suggest that the degree to which we are born with the ability to sense how others

SKILL BUILDER

Perception Checking Practice

Practise your perception checking ability by developing three-part verifications for the following situations:

1. You made what you thought was an excellent suggestion to an instructor. The professor looked uninterested but said she would check on the matter right away. Three weeks have passed, and nothing has changed.

2. A neighbour and good friend has not responded to your "Good morning" for three days in a row. This person is usually friendly.

3. You haven't received the usual daily phone call from the folks back home in over a week. The last time you spoke, you had an argument about where to spend the holidays.

4. An old friend with whom you have shared the problems in your love life for years has recently changed. The formerly casual hugs and kisses have become longer and stronger, and the occasions where you "accidentally" brush up against each other have become more frequent.

123render/iStockphoto

are feeling seems to vary according to genetic factors.[52] Further, environment also plays a role. Specifically, how parents communicate with their children affects their ability to understand others' emotional states.[53] When parents indicate to children how their misbehaviour makes others feel ("Look how sad Jessica is because you took her toy. Wouldn't you be sad if someone took away your toys?"), those children are more likely to learn that their acts have emotional consequences than when parents simply label behaviours as inappropriate ("That was a mean thing to do!"). Studies also show that allowing children to experience and manage frustrating events can help increase their empathic concern for others later in life.[54]

"How would you feel if the mouse did that to you?"

© William Steig/The New Yorker Collection/www.cartoonbank.com

of satisfying communication in various contexts, including marriage,[56] helping others who are feeling distressed,[57] persuading others,[58] and advancing your career.[59]

There is also a connection between cognitive complexity and empathy.[60] The more ways you have to understand others and interpret their behaviours, the greater the likelihood that you'll see the world from their perspective. Cognitive complexity can also help people describe situations more thoroughly and less simplistically.[61] Further, cognitively complex people are better at identifying and understanding sarcasm—an abstract form of communication that is sometimes lost on those with less mental acumen.[62] Fortunately, our cognitive complexity skills can be enhanced through training.[63]

Culture also influences our ability to empathize. For example, people raised in individualist cultures, which value independence, are often less adept at perspective taking than those from collectivist cultures, which value interdependence.[55] In one study, Chinese and American subjects played a communication game that required participants to take on the perspective of their partners. In all measures, the collectivist Chinese participants had greater success than did their American counterparts. This suggests that culture shapes the way we perceive, understand, and empathize with others.

Many people confuse empathy with **sympathy**, but they differ in a couple of ways. First, sympathy means that you feel compassion for another person's predicament, whereas empathy means you have a personal sense of what the predicament is like. Consider the difference between sympathizing and empathizing with a homeless person. When you sympathize, it's the other person's confusion, joy, or pain. When you empathize, the experience becomes your own, at least for the moment. It's one thing to feel bad (or good) *for* someone—sympathy—but it's more profound to feel bad (or good) *with* someone—empathy.

Cognitive Complexity

Given how important empathy is in relationships, how can we become more empathetic? Understanding the notion of cognitive complexity can help.

Cognitive Complexity and Communication

Cognitive complexity is the ability to construct a variety of frameworks for viewing an issue. Research shows that it can increase the chances

LO⁵
Increasing Your Cognitive Complexity: The Pillow Method

Some issues are too complex and serious to be handled with perception checking. To enhance your empathy, writer Paul Reps describes a tool that will help you get insight into another's position—the **pillow method**.[64]

Developed by a group of Japanese schoolchildren, it gets its name from the fact that problems have four sides and a middle, just like a pillow (Figure 3.3). As the example on page 81 shows, viewing an issue from

Sympathy
Compassion for another's situation.

Pillow method
A way of understanding an issue from several perspectives, rather than with an egocentric "I'm right and you're wrong" attitude.

FIGURE 3.3
The Pillow Method

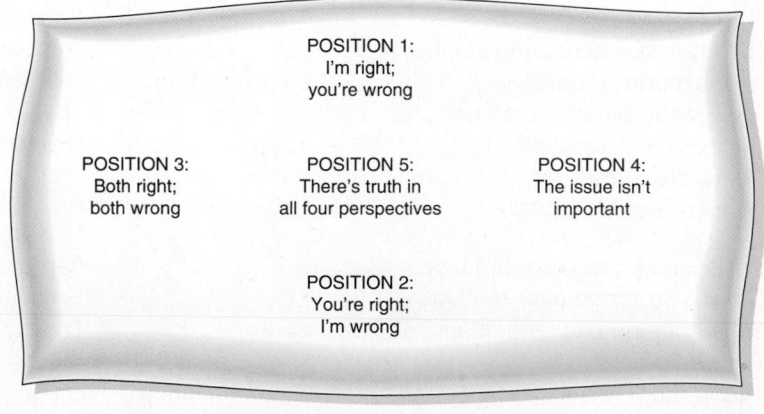

POSITION 1:
I'm right;
you're wrong

POSITION 3:
Both right;
both wrong

POSITION 5:
There's truth in
all four perspectives

POSITION 4:
The issue isn't
important

POSITION 2:
You're right;
I'm wrong

each of these perspectives leads to valuable insights—and in so doing enhances cognitive complexity.

Position 1: I'm Right, You're Wrong

This is the perspective we usually take when viewing an issue. We immediately see the virtues in our position and find fault with those who disagree with us. Detailing this position takes little effort and provides little new information.

Position 2: You're Right, I'm Wrong

At this point you switch perspectives and build the strongest possible arguments to explain how another person can view the issue differently from you. Besides identifying the strengths in the other's position, this is the time to play the devil's advocate and find flaws in your own.

Finding flaws in your position and trying to support the other's position requires discipline and a certain amount of courage, even though this is only an exercise and you will soon be able to retreat to position 1 if you choose. But most people learn that switching perspectives reveals there is some merit to the other person's perspective.

There are some issues-, such as criminal behaviour, deceit, and disloyalty, where it seems impossible to call the other position "right." However, you might be able to arrive at position 2 by realizing that the other person's behaviour is understandable. For example, without approving, you may be able to understand how someone would resort to violence, tell lies, or cheat. Whatever the particulars, the goal of position 2 is to find some way of comprehending how anyone could behave in a way that you originally found impossible to defend.

It was six men of Indostan
To learning much inclined,
Who went to see the elephant
Though all of them were blind
That each by observation
Might satisfy his mind.

The first approached the elephant
And, happening to fall
Against the broad and sturdy side,
At once began to bawl:
"Why, bless me! But the elephant
Is very much like a wall!"

The second, feeling of the tusk,
Cried: "Ho! What have we here
So very round and smooth and sharp?
To me, 'tis very clear,
This wonder of an elephant
Is very like a spear!"

The third approached the animal,
And, happening to take
The squirming trunk within his hands
Thus boldly up he spake:
"I see," quoth he, "the elephant
Is very like a snake!"

The fourth reached out his hand
And felt about the knee:
"What most this wondrous beast is like
Is very plain," quoth he:
"Tis clear enough the elephant
Is very like a tree!"

The fifth, who chanced to touch the ear,
Said: "E'en the blindest man
Can tell what this resembles most—
Deny the fact who can:
This marvel of an elephant
Is very like a fan!"

The sixth no sooner had begun
About the beast to grope
Than, seizing on the swinging tail
That fell within his scope,
"I see," quoth he, "the elephant
Is very like a rope!"

And so these men of Indostan
Disputed loud and long,
Each in his own opinion
Exceeding stiff and strong;
Though each was partly in the right,
And all were in the wrong.

John G. Saxe

John G. Saxe

David J. Green - lifestyle themes/GetStock.com

Example: My Mother and Facebook

Background

My mother recently opened a Facebook account and sent me an invitation to become her friend. I ignored her request for a couple of weeks, until she finally asked why I hadn't responded. The talk turned into an argument. She couldn't understand why I didn't want her as a Facebook friend. I couldn't understand why she wanted to butt into my personal life.

Position 1: I'm Right, She's Wrong

Facebook was created for college students, not middle-aged parents. The fact that my mom wants access to my personal world feels like an invasion of privacy—like reading my diary or rummaging through my belongings. If she wants to keep up with her friends on Facebook, that's her business—but leave me out of it.

Position 2: She's Right, I'm Wrong

When I objected to my mom snooping, she said she'd stop looking at my page if it makes her uncomfortable. So she's right in saying that I don't need to worry about her judgments. When I told her I'd be embarrassed to have her commenting on my life, she promised not to write on my wall, tag embarrassing pictures of me, or do anything else visible.

Position 3: Both of Us Are Right and Both Are Wrong

I'm justified to be concerned about my mom being freaked out by some things on my Facebook page. She's justified in wanting to know more about my life and how my generation communicates. I'm probably overreacting when I worry about her reactions or demand that she keep her nose out of my business. She's wrong not to appreciate my desire for privacy.

Position 4: The Issue Isn't Important

I don't think anything I or my friends post on my Facebook page would change my relationship with my mom. Turning this into a major issue is probably not worth the hurt feelings that have resulted from this mini-crisis.

Conclusion

Viewing this issue from several angles calmed me down and made it easier for my mother and I to have a good talk. We decided that I would friend her for a trial period. If I decide her looking at my page has become a problem, she agreed to willingly remove herself from my friends list.

> ### There are three sides to every argument. Yours. The other guy's. And the right side.
>
> —Mordecai Richler,
> *Son of a Smaller Hero*

Position 3: Both Right, Both Wrong

From this position you acknowledge the strengths and weaknesses of each person's arguments. If you've done a good job with position 2, it should be clear that there is some merit and some flaws in both points of view. Taking a more even-handed look at the issue can lead you to be less critical and more understanding of another's point of view.

Position 3 can also help you find the commonalities between your position and the other's. Perhaps you've both been right to care so much about the issue, but both wrong in failing to recognize the other person's concerns. Perhaps there are underlying values that you both share and similar mistakes that you've both made. In any case, the perspective of position 3 should help you see that the issue isn't as much a matter of complete right and wrong as it first appeared to be.

Position 4: The Issue Isn't as Important as It Seems

This perspective helps you realize that the controversy isn't as critical as you thought. Although it is hard to think of some issues as unimportant, most concerns are less important than we make them out to be. The impact of even the most traumatic events—the death of a loved one or the breakup of a relationship, for example—usually lessens over time. The effects may not disappear, but we learn to accept them and get on with life. The importance of a dispute can also fade when you realize that you've let it overshadow other equally important parts of your relationship to the point that it made you forget about the other ways in which you are close to the other person.

Conclusion: There Is Truth in All Four Perspectives

The final step is recognizing that each position has some merit. This fifth stage is very different from the "I'm right and you're wrong" attitude that most people bring to an issue. While it seems impossible for a position to be both right and wrong or important and unimportant, your own experience will show how there can be some truth in each position.

After you have looked at an issue from these five perspectives, it is almost certain that you will gain new insights. These insights may not cause you to change your mind or even solve the problem at hand. Nonetheless, understanding can increase your tolerance for the other person's position and thus improve the communication climate.

Perception in the Workplace

Perception also plays a major role in the workplace, beginning with first impressions. Today, not only will you be scrutinized by your qualifications, the content and design of your résumé, and how you do in the interview, but potential employers will also be checking your social networking sites. You might want to consider the types of impressions you may be creating.

Once hired, there is a correlation between job satisfaction and the quality of communication and social support. Canadians who see their workplace as healthy have more workplace satisfaction, less absenteeism, higher morale, and lower levels of intentions to quit.[65] However, perceptual differences will always exist. A common example is introducing new procedures whose costs and benefits are often perceived differently by managers and workers.

Another source of perceptual differences is diversity. Leaders in global virtual teams noted that cultural diversity greatly enriched their teams but also created challenges in the areas of language, cultural values, and management styles.[66] Some of these challenges might be dispelled through perception checking or the pillow method.

Finally, empathy plays a role in the workplace with both colleagues and clients. For example, counsellors and people working in health care need to remain cognizant of the fact that what may be routine procedures for them may be quite traumatic to clients.

SKILL BUILDER

Pillow Talk

Try using the pillow method in your life. It isn't easy, but once you begin to understand it, the payoff in increased understanding is huge.

1. Choose a person or viewpoint with whom or with which you strongly disagree. If you've chosen a person, it's best to have him or her there with you, but if that's not possible, you can do it alone.

2. What disagreement should you choose? No doubt there are many in your life:

   Parent–child   Friend–friend
   Teacher–student   Nation–nation
   Employer–employee   Co-worker–Co-worker
   Brother–sister

3. For each disagreement you choose, really place yourself in each position on the pillow as you encounter it:
   a. Your position is correct and your opponent's is wrong.
   b. Your opponent's position is correct and yours is wrong.
   c. Both your positions are correct and both are wrong.
   d. It isn't important which position is right or wrong.
   e. Finally, affirm the fact that there is truth in all four positions.

4. The more important the disagreement is to you, the harder it will be to accept positions 2 through 5 as valid. But the exercise will work only if you can suspend your present position and imagine how it would feel to hold the other ones.

5. How can you tell if you've been successful with the pillow method? The answer is simple: If, after going over all the steps, you can understand—not necessarily accept, but just understand—the other person's position, you've done it. After you've reached this understanding, do you notice any change in how you feel about the other person?

123render/iStockphoto

Endnotes

1. The graphic demonstrations of factors influencing perception in this and the following paragraph are borrowed from D. Coon & J. Mitterer (2010). *Introduction to Psychology*, 12th ed. Belmont, CA: Wadsworth/Cengage.

2. G. W. Allport (1958). *The Nature of Prejudice*. New York: Doubleday Anchor, p. 85.

3. R. Mourtada (2004). "A Climate of Fear." *Canadian Business, 77*, 24–25.

4. See S. Wortley & J. Tanner (2005). "Inflammatory Rhetoric? Baseless Accusations? A Response to Gabor's Critique of Racial Profiling Research in Canada." *Canadian Journal of Criminology and Criminal Justice, 47*, 581–609; and S. Wortley & J. Tanner (2003). "Data, Denials, and Confusion: The Racial Profiling Debate in Toronto." *Canadian Journal of Criminology and Criminal Justice, 45*, 367–389.

5. J. Oetzel (1998). "The Effects of Self-Construals and Ethnicity on Self-Reported Conflict Styles." *Communication Reports, 11*, 133–144.

6. N. Nishizawa (2004). "The 'Self' of Japanese Teenagers: Growing Up in the Flux of a Changing Culture and Society." *Dissertation Abstracts International, 65*, 2642.

7. M. L. Inman & R. S. Baron (1996). "Influence of Prototypes on Perceptions of Prejudice." *Journal of Personality and Social Psychology, 70*, 727–739.

8. P. Watzlawick, J. Beavin, & D. D. Jackson (1967). *Pragmatics of Human Communication*. New York: Norton, p. 65.

9. V. Manusov (1993). "It Depends on Your Perspective: Effects of Stance and Beliefs about Intent on Person Perception." *Western Journal of Communication, 57*, 27–41.

10. T. Adler (June 1992). "Enter Romance, Exit Objectivity." *APA Monitor*, 18.

11. K. Floyd & M. T. Morman (2000). "Reacting to the Verbal Expression of Affection in Same-Sex Interaction." *Southern Communication Journal, 65*, 287–299.

12. C. Edwards, A. Edwards, Q. Quingmei, & S. T. Wall (2007). "The Influence of Computer-Mediated Word-of-Mouth Communication on Student Perceptions of Instructors and Attitudes toward Learning Course Content." *Communication Education, 56*, 255–277.

13. J. K. Alberts, U. Kellar-Guenther, & S. R. Corman (1996). "That's Not Funny: Understanding Recipients' Responses to Teasing." *Western Journal of Communication, 60*, 337–357. See also R. Edwards, R. Bello, F. Brandau-Brown, & D. Hollems (2001). "The Effects of Loneliness and Verbal Aggressiveness on Message Interpretation." *Southern Communication Journal, 66*, 139–150.

14. See T. N. Bradbury & F. D. Fincham (1990). "Attributions in Marriage: Review and Critique." *Psychological Bulletin, 107*, 3–33; and V. Manusov (1990). "An Application of Attribution Principles to Nonverbal Behaviour in Romantic Dyads." *Communication Monographs, 57*, 104–118.

15. C. L. M. Shaw (1997). "Personal Narrative: Revealing Self and Reflecting Other." *Human Communication Research, 24*, 302–319.

16. J. K. Kellas (2005). "Family Ties: Communicating Identity through Jointly Told Family Stories." *Communication Monographs, 72*, 365–389.

17. J. Flora & C. Segrin (2000). "Relationship Development in Dating Couples: Implications for Relational Satisfaction and Loneliness." *Journal of Social and Personal Relationships, 17*, 811–825.

18. L. A. Baxter & G. Pittman (2001). "Communicatively Remembering Turning Points of Relational Development in Heterosexual Romantic Relationships." *Communication Reports, 14*, 1–17.

19. S. L. Murray, J. G. Holmes, & D. W. Griffin (2004). "The Benefits of Positive Illusions: Idealization and the Construction of Satisfaction in Close Relationships." In *Close Relationships: Key Readings* (pp. 317–338). Philadelphia: Taylor & Francis. See also J. M. Martz, J. Verette, X. B. Arriaga, L. F. Slovik, C. L. Cox, & C. E. Rosbult (1998). "Positive Illusion in Close Relationships." *Personal Relationships, 5*, 159–181.

20. J. C. Pearson (1996). "Positive Distortion: 'The Most Beautiful Woman in the World.'" In K. M. Galvin and P. Cooper (Eds.). *Making Connections: Readings in Interpersonal Communication* (p. 177). Beverly Hills, CA: Roxbury.

21. For a detailed description of how the senses affect perception, see N. Ackerman (1990). *A Natural History of the Senses*. New York: Random House.

22. J. Piaget (1952). *The Origins of Intelligence in Children*. New York: International Universities Press.

23. K. Alaimo, C. M. Olson, & E. A. Frongillo (2001). "Food Insufficiency and American School-Aged Children's Cognitive, Academic, and Psychosocial Development." *Pediatrics, 108*, 44–53.

24. M. Maguire (2005). "Biological Cycles and Cognitive Performance." In A. Esgate et al., *An Introduction to Applied Cognitive Psychology* (pp. 137–161). New York: Psychology Press. See also C. Cooper & C. McConville (1990). "Interpreting Mood Scores: Clinical Implications of Individual Differences in Mood Variability." *British Journal of Medical Psychology, 63*, 215–225.

25. R. Armao (Jan. 1981). "Worst Blunders: Firms Laugh through Tears." *American Business*, 11.

26. R. Harrison (1972). "Nonverbal Behaviour: An Approach to Human Communication." In R. Budd and B. Ruben (Eds.). *Approaches to Human Communication*. New York: Spartan Books.

27. E. T. Hall (1969). *The Hidden Dimension*. New York: Doubleday Anchor, p. 160.

28. H. Giles, N. Coupland, & J. M. Wiemann (1992). "Talk Is Cheap… But 'My Word Is My Bond': Beliefs about Talk." In K. Bolton & H. Kwok (Eds.). *Sociolinguistics Today: International Perspectives*. London: Routledge & Kegan Paul.

29. A. Fadiman (1997). *The Spirit Catches You and You Fall Down*. New York: Farrar, Straus, and Giroux, p. 33.

30. H. Hiller, *Canadian Society: A Macro Analysis.* Scarborough, ON: Prentice-Hall, 1991, p. 36.

31. J. B. Becker, K. J. Berkley, N. Geary, E. Hampson, J. P. Herman, & E. Young (2007). *Sex Differences in the Brain: From Genes to Behaviour.* New York: Oxford University Press.

32. D. F. Halpern (2000). *Sex Differences in Cognitive Abilities,* 3rd ed. Mahwah, NJ: Erlbaum.

33. See S. A. Rathus (1993). *Psychology,* 5th ed. Fort Worth, TX: Harcourt Brace Jovanovich, pp. 640–643; and C. Wade & C. Tavris (1987). *Psychology.* New York: Harper & Row, pp. 488–490.

34. S. L. Bem (1985). "Androgyny and Gender Schema Theory: A Conceptual and Empirical Integration." In T. B. Sonderegger (Ed.). *Nebraska Symposium on Motivation: Psychology and Gender.* Lincoln: University of Nebraska Press.

35. P. G. Zimbardo, C. Haney, & W. C. Banks (April 8, 1973). "A Pirandellian Prison." *New York Times Magazine.*

36. K. Burke, *Permanence and Change.* Berkeley: University of California Press, 1984, p. 38.

37. V. Swami & A. Furnham (2008). "Is Love Really So Blind?" *The Psychologist, 21,* 108–111.

38. G. C. Gonzaga, M. G. Haselton, J. Smurda, M. Davies, & J. C. Poore (2008). "Love, Desire, and the Suppression of Thoughts of Romantic Alternatives." *Evolution and Human Behaviour, 29,* 119–126.

39. D. Hamachek (1992). *Encounters with the Self,* 3rd ed. Fort Worth, TX: Harcourt Brace Jovanovich.

40. For a review of these perceptual biases, see Hamachek, *Encounters with the Self.* See also Bradbury & Fincham, op. cit. For an example of the self-serving bias in action, see R. Buttny (1997). "Reported Speech in Talking Race on Campus." *Human Communication Research, 23,* 477–506.

41. S. L. Young (2004). "What the _____ Is Your Problem?: Attribution Theory and Perceived Reasons for Profanity Usage During Conflict." *Communication Research Reports, 21,* 338–347.

42. K. Dion, E. Berscheid, & E. Walster (1972). "What Is Beautiful Is Good." *Journal of Personality and Social Psychology, 24,* 285–290.

43. L. Watkins & L. Johnston (2000). "Screening Job Applicants: The Impact of Physical Attractiveness and Application Quality." *International Journal of Selection and Assessment, 8,* 76–84.

44. T. Dougherty, D. Turban, & J. Collander (1994). "Conforming First Impressions in the Employment Interview." *Journal of Applied Psychology, 79,* 659–665.

45. G. I. Cook, R. L. Marsh, & J. L. Hicks (2003). "Halo and Devil Effects Demonstrate Valenced-Based Influences on Source-Mentoring Decisions." *Consciousness and Cognition, 12,* 257–278.

46. C. I. Marek, M. B. Wanzer, & J. L. Knapp (2004). "An Exploratory Investigation of the Relationship between Roommates' First Impressions and Subsequent Communication Patterns." *Communication Research Reports, 21,* 210–220.

47. B. Keysar (2007). "Communication and Miscommunication: The Role of Egocentric Processes." *Intercultural Pragmatics, 4,* 71–84.

48. See, for example, A. Sillars, W. Shellen, A. McIntosh, & M. Pomegranate (1997). "Relational Characteristics of Language: Elaboration and Differentiation in Marital Conversations." *Western Journal of Communication, 61,* 403–422.

49. J. B. Stiff, J. P. Dillard, L. Somera, H. Kim, & C. Sleight (1988). "Empathy, Communication, and Prosocial Behaviour." *Communication Monographs, 55,* 198–213.

50. This research is described by D. Goleman (2006) in *Social Intelligence.* New York: Bantam. See also J. Decety, K. Michalska, & Y. Aktsuki (2008) "Who Caused the Pain? An fMRI Investigation of Empathy and Intentionality in Children." *Neuropsychologia, 46,* 2607–2614.

51. Goleman, op cit.

52. M. Davis (1994). "The Heritability of Characteristics Associated with Dispositional Empathy." *Journal of Personality, 62,* 369–391.

53. B. Burleson, J. Delia, & J. Applegate (1995). "The Socialization of Person-Centered Communication: Parental Contributions to the Social-Cognitive and Communication Skills of Their Children." In M. A. Fitzpatrick & A. Vangelisti (Eds.). *Perspectives in Family Communication.* Thousand Oaks, CA: Sage.

54. D. M. Tucker, P. Luu, & D. Derryberry (2005). "Love Hurts: The Evolution of Empathic Concern through the Encephalization of Nociceptive Capacity." *Development and Psychopathology, 17,* 699–713.

55. S. Wu & B. Keysar (2007). "Cultural Effects on Perspective Taking." *Psychological Science, 18,* 600–606.

56. R. Martin (1992). "Relational Cognition Complexity and Relational Communication in Personal Relationships." *Communication Monographs, 59,* 150–163. See also B. R. Burleson & S. E. Caplan (1998). "Cognitive Complexity." In J. C. McCroskey, J. A. Daly, M. M. Martin, and M. J. Beatty (Eds.). *Communication and Personality: Trait Perspectives* (pp. 233–286). Creskill, NY: Hampton Press.

57. Burleson & Caplan, op. cit., p. 22.

58. B. R. Burleson (1989). "The Constructivist Approach to Person-Centered Communication: Analysis of a Research Exemplar." In B. Dervin, L. Grossberg, B. J. O'Keefe, & E. Wartella (Eds.). *Rethinking Communication: Paradigm Exemplars* (pp. 33–72). Newbury Park, CA: Sage.

59. B. D. Sypher & T. Zorn (1986). "Communication-Related Abilities and Upward Mobility: A Longitudinal Investigation." *Human Communication Research, 12,* 420–431.

60. Joireman, J. (2004). "Relationships Between Attributional Complexity and Empathy." *Individual Differences Research, 2,* 197–202.

61. Medvene, L., Grosch, K., & Swink, N. (2006). "Interpersonal Complexity: A Cognitive Component of Person-Centered Care." *The Gerontologist, 46,* 220–226.

62. Rockwell, P. (2007). "The Effects of Cognitive Complexity and Communication Apprehension on the Expression and Recognition of Sarcasm." In A. M. Columbus (Ed.). *Advances in Psychology Research, 49,* 185–196. Hauppauge, NY: Nova Science Publishers.

63. C. Little, J. Packman, M. H. Smaby, & C. D. Maddux (2005). "The Skilled Counselor Training Model: Skills Acquisition, Self-Assessment, and Cognitive Complexity." *Counselor Education & Supervision, 44,* 189–200.

64. P. Reps (1967). "Pillow Education in Rural Japan." In *Square Sun, Square Moon.* New York: Tuttle.

65. G. S. Lowe, G. Schellenberg, & H.S. Shannon (2003). "Correlates of Employees' Perceptions of a Healthy Work Environment." *American Journal of Health Promotion, 17,* 390–399.

66. L. Dubé & G. Paré (2001). "Global Virtual Teams," *Communications of the ACM, 44,* 71–75.

Emotions:
Feeling, Thinking, and Communicating

LEARNING OUTCOMES

LO¹ Describe how the four components listed on pages 88–89 affect your emotions, and hence your communication.

LO² Describe how the influences on emotional expression listed on pages 90–94 have affected your communication in an important relationship.

LO³ Apply the guidelines for effectively communicating emotions (pages 95–100) in an important situation.

LO⁴ Identify and dispute the fallacies (pages 100–108) that are creating debilitative emotions in an important situation. Explain how more rational thinking can lead to more constructive communication.

The role of emotions in human affairs is apparent to social scientists and lay people alike. Daniel Goleman coined the term **emotional intelligence** to describe the ability to understand and manage one's own emotions and be sensitive to others' feelings.[1] Emotional intelligence is positively linked to self-esteem, life satisfaction, and self-acceptance,[2] as well as with healthy relationships and conflict management.[3] Clearly, emotional intelligence is vital to both personal and interpersonal success. Because emotions play such an important role in virtually all types of relationships, this chapter is devoted to the topic.

> **Emotional intelligence**
> The ability to understand and manage one's own emotions and be sensitive to others' feelings.

© NBC/Everett Collection

Consider how emotional intelligence is—and is not—exhibited by the characters in the TV show *The Office*.

CHAPTER 4 Emotions: Feeling, Thinking, and Communicating

LO[1]
What are Emotions?

Suppose an extraterrestrial visitor asked you to explain emotions. How would you answer? According to social scientists, there are several components to what we label as feelings.[4]

Physiological Factors

Strong emotions are generally accompanied by physiological changes. For example, fear increases heart rate, blood pressure, adrenaline secretions, and blood sugar level but slows digestion and pupil dilation.[5] Marriage researcher John Gottman notes that similar symptoms also occur when couples are in intense conflicts.[6] He calls the condition "flooding" and has found that it impedes effective problem solving.

Some physiological changes (a churning stomach or tense jaw) are recognizable to the person having them, and these internal cues can offer a significant clue to your emotions.

Nonverbal Reactions

While some physical changes that accompany emotions are external, observable ones such as blushing, sweating, or shaking, others involve behaviour: a distinctive facial expression, posture, or gestures; modification in vocal tone or rate; and so on. Although it's reasonably easy to tell when someone is feeling a strong emotion, the ambiguity of nonverbal behaviour makes it difficult to know exactly what emotion that might be. A slumped posture and sigh could signify sadness or fatigue. Likewise, trembling hands might indicate excitement or fear. Therefore, it's dangerous to assume we can "read" a person's emotions with great accuracy.

Nonverbal behaviour can also induce emotional states. In one study, experimental subjects were able to create various emotional states by altering their facial expressions.[7] When subjects were coached to move their facial muscles to look afraid, angry, disgusted, amused, sad, surprised, and contemptuous, the subjects' bodies responded as if they were actually having these feelings. In another experiment, subjects who were coached to smile actually reported feeling better, and when they altered their expressions to look unhappy, they felt worse than before.[8]

Cognitive Interpretations

While there can be a direct connection between physical behaviour and emotional states, the mind and our self-talk play a major role in how we feel. For instance, it's interesting to note that the physiological components of fear—racing heart, perspiration, tense muscles, and

"Emo" artists like Alexisonfire have both fans and critics of the emotionally expressive music. Clearly, however, *all* music and lyrics offer a means for expressing feelings.

elevated blood pressure—are similar to the physical changes that accompany excitement, joy, and other emotions. If we were to measure a person's physical condition during a strong emotion, we wouldn't know if the person was trembling with fear or quivering with excitement. The label an individual applies to these physical symptoms determines whether symptoms will be experienced or interpreted as fright, joy, or anger.[9]

Psychologist Philip Zimbardo offers an interesting example of this principle:

I notice I'm perspiring while lecturing. From that I infer I am nervous. If it occurs often, I might even label myself a "nervous person." Once I have the label, the next question I must answer is, "Why am I nervous?" Then I start to search for an appropriate explanation. I might notice some students leaving the room, or being inattentive. I am nervous because I'm not giving a good lecture. That makes me nervous. How do I know it's not good? Because I'm boring my audience. I am nervous because I am a boring lecturer and I want to be a good lecturer. I feel inadequate. Maybe I should open a delicatessen instead. Just then a student says, "It's hot in here, I'm perspiring, and it makes it tough to concentrate on your lecture." Instantly, I'm no longer "nervous" or "boring."[10]

Zimbardo found that changing his self-talk, or interpretation, of the event affected the way he felt about it. Social scientists refer to this process as **reappraisal**—rethinking the meaning of emotionally charged events in ways that alter their emotional impact.[11] Research shows that reappraisal is vastly superior to suppressing one's feelings: It often leads to lower stress, higher self-esteem, and increased productivity.[12] Here are two examples:

> **Reappraisal**
> Rethinking the meaning of emotionally charged events in ways that alter their emotional impact.

- You lost your job, while some less ambitious co-workers were not fired; hence your self-esteem is shattered. You lack confidence as you look for new employment. You could reappraise the event and interpret it as an opportunity to find a better position where hard work and contributions to the firm are appreciated.
- A friend says malicious things about you behind your back. Even though you are hurt, you interpret her actions as statements about *her* character, not yours. You demonstrate your character by not speaking poorly about her to others.

Reappraisal is not about denying your feelings. Recognizing and acknowledging positive (happiness, relief, love) and negative (hurt, anger, grief) emotions is vital to psychological and relational health.

chsher bakova yuliya/Shutterstock

Verbal Expression

While nonverbal actions are generally better at conveying emotions, sometimes it takes words to identify them. For example, whether your friend's uncharacteristically short temper is a sign of anger at you or something less personal, or if a lover's unenthusiastic response is a sign of boredom or the result of a long workday can be determined most accurately through verbal expression. In fact, perception checking would be useful in cases such as these.

Primary and Mixed Emotions

Some researchers believe there are several "basic," or **primary emotions**.[13] However, there isn't much agreement about what those emotions are or about what makes them "basic."[14] Further, primary emotions in one culture may not be primary in others, and some emotions have no direct equivalent in other cultures.[15] For example, shame is a central emotion in the Chinese experience, while it's much less relevant in Western cultures.[16] However, most

FIGURE 4.1

Intensity of Emotions

Annoyed	**Angry**	
Pensive	**Sad**	**Grieving**
Content	**Happy**	**Ecstatic**
Anxious	**Afraid**	**Terrified**
Liking	**Loving**	**Adoring**

scholars acknowledge that *anger, joy, fear,* and *sadness* are common human emotions.

Sometimes we experience conflicting primary emotions at the same time. These are referred to as **mixed emotions**. For instance, you expect your friend from another city to arrive around 6, give or take the traffic. When he waltzes in at 11:30 with a flippant, "Oh, I got a late start," you're angry that he didn't get in touch but relieved and happy that he's safe.

Primary emotions
Basic emotions such as anger, joy, fear, and sadness.

Mixed emotions
Feeling two or more conflicting emotions at the same time.

Intense and Mild Emotions

We also experience emotions with different degrees of intensity, as Figure 4.1 illustrates. Some people understate

"What the hell was that? Something just swept over me—like contentment or something."

© Robert Weber/The New Yorker Collection/www.cartoonbank.com

their emotions, failing to let others know how strongly they feel. Saying that you're "annoyed" when a friend breaks an important promise would probably be an understatement. In other cases, people chronically overstate the strength of their feelings. To them, everything is "wonderful" or "terrible." The problem with this sort of exaggeration is that there are no words left to describe a truly intense emotion. If chocolate chip cookies are "fabulous," how does it feel to fall in love?

Intensity of Emotions

When people aren't able to talk about their emotions constructively, it can result in social isolation, unsatisfying relationships, anxiety and depression, and misdirected aggression.[17] How parents talk to children about emotions also affects their development.[18] Two distinct parenting styles have been identified: emotion coaching, which gives children skills to communicate their emotions, and emotion dismissing, which does not. Unfortunately, children who grow up in families where parents dismiss emotions are at higher risk for behaviour problems than those who are raised in families that practise emotion coaching.[19] Clearly, emotions are very complex, and guidelines for communicating them are provided later in the chapter.

Invitation TO INSIGHT

Recognizing Your Emotions

Keep a three-day record of your feelings by taking a few minutes each evening to recall and record the emotions you felt during the day, the people involved, and the circumstances in which the emotion occurred.

At the end of the three-day period, you can understand the role that emotions play in your communication by answering the following questions:

1. How did you recognize the emotions you felt: through physiological stimuli, nonverbal behaviours, or cognitive processes?

2. Did you have any difficulty deciding which emotions you were feeling?

3. What emotions do you have most often? Are they mild or intense?

4. In what circumstances do you or do you not show your feelings? What factors influence your decision to show or not show your feelings? The type of feeling? The person or persons involved? The situation (time, place)? The subject that the feeling involves (money, sex, and so on)?

5. What are the consequences of the type of communicating you just described in step 4? Are you satisfied with these consequences? If not, what can you do to become more satisfied?

LO^2
Influences on Emotional Expression

While most people are comfortable stating facts or expressing opinions, they rarely disclose how they feel. There are several reasons for this.

Personality

There is an increasingly clear relationship between personality and the way we experience and communicate emotions.[20] Extroverted people, for example, who tend to be upbeat, optimistic, and enjoy social contact, report more positive emotions than do less extraverted individuals.[21] Likewise, people with neurotic personalities, who tend to worry, feel anxious, or apprehensive, report more negative emotions.

These personality traits are at least partially biological in nature in that there's a relationship between personality type

"I'm not an emotional person myself. Fortunately, Georgina feels things for both of us."

© Robert Weber/The New Yorker Collection/www.cartoonbank.com

and brain activity.[22] People who test high on measures of extroversion have greater brain reactivity to positive stimuli than do less extroverted people. Those who score high on the neuroticism measures have more brain reactions to negative stimuli. Such research confirms the familiar belief that some people do see the cup as half full while others see it as half empty.

But personality doesn't have to govern your communication satisfaction. Introverted people find ways to reach out to others. For example, chat rooms, instant messaging, e-mail, and computer dating services all provide low-threat ways for reticent communicators to approach others and get acquainted.[23]

Culture

While people from different cultures generally experience the same emotions, similar events can generate different feelings.[24] Eating snails might bring a smile of delight to many Quebec residents, while other Canadians might grimace in disgust. Research has shown that fear of strangers and of risky situations is more likely to frighten North Americans and Europeans than those living in Japan. Japanese individuals are more apprehensive about relational communication.[25] Further, Asian Americans and Hong Kong Chinese value calmness, whereas European Americans tend to value excitement.[26]

There are also differences in the degree to which people in various cultures display their feelings. For example, people from warmer climates have been found to be more emotionally expressive than those who live in cooler climates.[27] Even people from the southern part of their countries were more emotionally expressive than were northerners!

Whether a culture is individualistic or collectivistic is another factor that influences emotional expression. Collectivistic cultures such as Japan's and India's prize harmony among members of their "in-group" and discourage expression of any negative emotions that might upset relationships among people who belong to it. Members of highly individualistic cultures like Canada's are comfortable revealing their feelings to people they trust.[28] However, whereas collectivists are frank about expressing negative emotions toward outsiders, individualists are more likely to hide such emotions as dislike.[29] It's easy to see how these differences could lead to communication problems. For example, individualistic North Americans might view collectivistic Asians as less than candid, while people raised in Asia could easily regard North Americans as overly demonstrative.[30]

The phrase "I love you" offers another interesting example. North Americans say "I love you" more frequently (and to more people) than do members of most other cultures.[31] Further, there are significant cultural differences about when, where, how often, and with whom the phrase should be used. Middle Easterners believe that "I love you" should only be expressed between spouses. North American men using the phrase cavalierly with Middle Eastern women might find that they're making a marriage proposal. People in Eastern Europe, India, and Korea hold that the phrase be used sparingly so it won't lose its power and meaning. Interestingly, across cultures, women tend to say "I love you" more often than men.

"I'm not in one of my moods. I'm in one of your moods."

© Victoria Roberts/The New Yorker Collection/www.cartoonbank.com

Gender

Even within a culture, biological sex and gender roles shape how women and men experience and express their emotions.[32] In fact, biological sex is the best predictor of

CHAPTER 4 Emotions: Feeling, Thinking, and Communicating

Making the Big Move

Alejandra Sanchez made a decision to move to Canada that provides good examples of the mixed emotions most people might feel when they immigrate.

Immigrating to another country isn't easy. While many new Canadians leave their native land because of unstable governments, lack of opportunities, and a host of other reasons, they also leave behind their families, customs, languages, and professions. Thus, newly arrived immigrants experience a myriad of mixed emotions.

Alejandra Sanchez emigrated from Mexico with her husband and four children in 2004. While she was excited about living in Canada, it was difficult to leave her extended family. She had no idea what the future would bring, and that had to be balanced against leaving successful professional careers and all that went with them.

Alejandra worried about her children's initial loneliness but was soon reassured as they made their way and developed new friendships. So too was Alejandra's loneliness somewhat relieved by new friends with whom she was able to share her Mexican food, culture, and music. Then there was the language barrier. Alejandra felt insecure speaking English, and she was concerned for her Spanish-speaking children. But this was replaced by amazement at how, in just a few short months, they could speak English! She actually feared they might lose some of their Spanish language.

Coming to Canada was a huge decision, but was it the right one? Alejandra says, "You never know the meaning of immigrating until you face the fact that you are here, now, in a new country. Of course, there is positive learning, but I believe it is too soon to know if it was the 'best' decision for everyone in the family . . . I still do not know . . . and perhaps I will never know."

Maybe part of the answer is in Alejandra's response to her first half marathon on Canadian soil. Excited about the race, she also felt fear, nostalgia, and pride as the Canadian anthem opened the ceremonies. When she crossed that finish line, however, she realized that her sense of accomplishment was in many ways analogous to her first year in Canada—a journey that is really just beginning.

---

the ability to detect and interpret emotional expressions—better than academic background, amount of foreign travel, cultural similarity, or ethnicity.[33] For example, women are more attuned to emotions than men,[34] both within and across cultures.[35] Further, females were 10 to 15 percent more accurate than men when it came to remembering emotional images and their reactions to these emotion-producing stimuli. Further, women's reactions were significantly more intense than men's.

Research on emotional expression suggests that there is at least some truth in the stereotypical unexpressive male and the more expressive female.[36] Overall, women are more likely to express positive emotions (love, liking, joy, and contentment) and feelings of vulnerability (including fear, sadness, loneliness, and embarrassment). Men are more likely than women to reveal their strengths.[37] On the Internet, women were more likely than men to use emoticons (such as the smiley face symbol) and to express their feelings.[38]

Gender isn't the only factor that affects emotional sensitivity. A second factor is whether the other person is of the same or a different sex. Men are more likely to express feelings, especially positive ones, to a woman than to a man.[39]

A third factor is the person or people with whom we are communicating. Dating and married couples are better at recognizing each other's emotional cues than are strangers, just as people from the same culture seem to be

William Whitehurst/CORBIS

Emoticons, from the words *emotion* and *icons,* are a way to express and clarify feelings in mediated messages.

better at interpreting each other's emotions.[40] Not surprisingly, people in close relationships are likely to experience and express more emotions than those in less close relationships, and those emotions, both positive and negative, are stronger.[41] Therefore, the potential for feeling hurt and neglected is stronger in romantic relationships than in other types of relationships.[42]

Finally, power is a factor in that people who are less powerful learn to read the more powerful person's signals. One experiment revealed that "women's intuition" should be relabelled "subordinate's intuition." In male–female twosomes, the person with less control—regardless of sex—was better at interpreting the leader's nonverbal signals than vice versa.[43]

Social Conventions

While expressions of emotion is rare in our society,[44] those that are shared are usually positive. Communicators are often reluctant to send messages that embarrass or threaten the "face" of others,[45] especially in the early stages of a new relationship.[46] They also attempt to suppress unpleasant emotions in contexts such as child rearing, the workplace, and personal relationships. One study of married couples revealed that partners often shared complimentary feelings ("I love you") or face-saving ones ("I'm sorry I yelled at you"). They also willingly disclosed both positive and negative feelings about absent third parties ("I like Jonathan," "I'm uncomfortable around Sarah"). On the other hand, the husbands and wives rarely verbalized face-threatening feelings ("I'm disappointed in you") or hostility ("I'm mad at you").[47]

Surprisingly, social rules even discourage too much expression of positive feelings.[48] While a hug and kiss for Mother is all right, a young man is more likely to shake hands with Dad. Canadians witnessed this when the media caught Prime Minister Stephen Harper dropping his children at school. Instead of kissing them goodbye, he shook their hands. *The Globe and Mail* received more than 40 letters responding to the formal sendoff—more than for any other event it reported that day.[49]

"I've been thinking—it might be good for Andrew if he could see you cry once in a while."

© Robert Weber/The New Yorker Collection/www.cartoonbank.com

Expression of emotions is also shaped by the requirements of many social roles. Researchers use the term **emotion labour** to describe situations in which managing and even suppressing emotions is both appropriate and necessary.

Fear of Self-Disclosure

In a society that discourages emotional expression, to do so seems risky.[50] Someone who maintains an image of confidence and certainty may find it frightening to say, "I'm sorry. I was wrong." Someone who has never relied on others might have a hard time saying, "I'm lonesome. I want your friendship."

When people do muster up the courage to share feelings, they run the risk of being misunderstood. For instance, an expression of affection might be construed as a romantic invitation,[51] or a confession of uncertainty might look like a sign of weakness. Such expressions might make others feel uncomfortable or be used against you. Little wonder many people are reluctant to express their emotions.

Emotional Contagion

Our emotions are also influenced by the feelings of those around us through **emotional contagion**: the process by which emotions are transferred from person to person.[52] As one commentator observed, "We

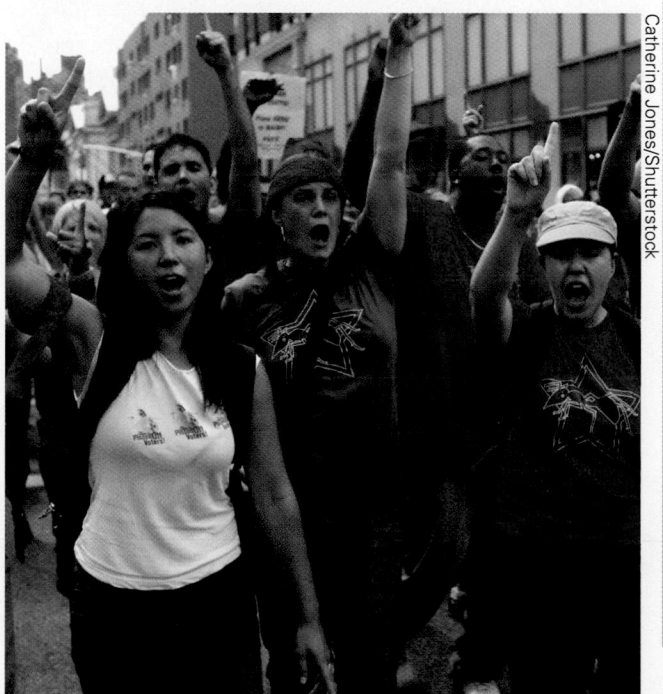

Catherine Jones/Shutterstock

> **Emotion labour**
> The notion that managing and even suppressing emotions is both appropriate and necessary
>
> **Emotional contagion**
> The process by which emotions are transferred from one person to another.

catch feelings from one another as though they were some kind of social virus."[53] There is evidence that students "catch" the mood of their teachers[54] and that husbands and wives directly influence each other's emotions.[55] In fact, our happiness (or unhappiness) can actually be affected by neighbours, friends of friends, and even total strangers.[56]

Most of us recognize the degree to which emotions are "infectious." A calm person can leave us feeling peaceful and a grouch can ruin our sunny mood. This process occurs quickly and with very little apparent verbal communication.[57] In one study, two volunteers completed a survey that identified their moods. Then they sat quietly, facing each other, for a two-minute period, supposedly waiting for the researcher to return. Then they completed another emotional survey which indicated that the brief exposure resulted in the less expressive partner's moods coming to resemble the moods of the more expressive one. If an expressive communicator can shape another person's emotions with so little input in such a short time, it's easy to understand how "infectious" emotions can be with prolonged contact. For example, the emotional responses of dating couples and college roommates become dramatically similar in just a few minutes.[58]

My First Flame

© Getty Images

To flame, according to *Que's Computer User's Dictionary*, is "to lose one's self-control and write a message that uses derogatory, obscene, or inappropriate language."

My flame arrived on a windy Friday morning. I got to work at 9, removed my coat, plugged in my PowerBook, and, as usual, could not resist immediately checking my e-mail. I saw I had a message from a technology writer who does a column about personal computers for a major newspaper, and whom I knew by name only. I had recently published a piece about Bill Gates, the [former] chair of Microsoft, and as I opened his e-mail it was with the pleasant expectation of getting feedback from a colleague. Instead, I got:

Crave this, a**hole: Listen, you toadying dips**t scumbag . . . remove your head from your rectum long enough to look around and notice that real reporters don't fawn over their subjects, pretend that their subjects are making some sort of special contact with them, or, worse, curry favour by telling their subjects how great the a**-licking profile is going to turn out and then brag in print about doing it.

I felt cold. People whose bodies have been badly burned begin to shiver, and the flame seemed to put a chill in the center of my chest which I could feel spreading slowly outward. The insults, being premeditated, were more forceful than insults spoken in the heat of the moment.

No one had ever said something like this to me before. In any other medium, these words would be, literally, unspeakable. The guy couldn't have said this to me on the phone, because I would have hung up and not answered if the phone rang again, and he couldn't have said it to my face, because I wouldn't have let him finish. If this had happened to me in the street, I could have used my status as a physically large male to threaten the person, but in the online world my size didn't matter. I suppose the guy could have written me a nasty letter. He probably wouldn't have used the word *rectum*, though, and he probably wouldn't have mailed the letter; he would have thought twice while he was addressing the envelope. But the nature of e-mail is that you don't think twice. You write and send.

What would Emily Post advise me to do? Flame the dips**t scumbag right back? I did spend most of that Friday in front of the screen composing the mostly vile insults I could dream up—words I have never spoken to another human being, and would never speak in any other medium, but which I found easy to type into the computer. I managed to restrain myself from sending my reply until I got home and asked my wife to look at it. She had the good sense to be horrified.

I asked [computer expert John Norstad] to look at it. He said, "My 13-year-old daughter is a Pearl Jam fan, and the other night she asked me if there might be some Pearl Jam stuff on the net. So we logged on and looked around, and we were able to download some Pearl Jam posters, some music, some song lyrics—really neat stuff. But then we came to the Pearl Jam newsgroup, and there was a really terrible flame war going on in there. People were saying really awful things to each other, things I was embarrassed to be sitting next to my daughter reading . . . Terrible things. After a while, my daughter looked over at me and asked, 'Daddy, do these people have a life?' And I said, 'No, darling, most of them don't have a life.'"

John Seabrook

LO^3
Guidelines for Expressing Emotions

People who know how to express their emotions are healthier, and underexpression of feelings can lead to serious health risks such as cancer, asthma, and heart disease.[59] However, *overly* expressive people also suffer physiologically. When people lash out verbally, their blood pressure jumps between 20 and 100 points.[60] The key to health, then, is to learn how to express emotions *constructively*.

Expressing emotions effectively can also improve relationships.[61] On the job, managers and organizational researchers suggest that constructively expressing emotions can lead to career success as well as help workers feel better.[62] Of course, the rules for expressing emotions in the workplace are usually more strict than those in personal relationships, so handle with care.[63]

"Honey, let's play 'emoting.' It will give you an edge in business."

© J.P. Rini/The New Yorker Collection/www.cartoonbank.com

TABLE 4.1
Some Differences between High and Low Affection Communicators

Compared to low affection communicators, high affection communicators are
1. Happier
2. More self-assured
3. More comfortable with interpersonal closeness
4. Less likely to be depressed
5. Less stressed
6. In better mental health
7. More likely to engage in regular social activity
8. Less likely to experience social isolation
9. More likely to receive affection from others
10. More likely to be in satisfying romantic relationships

"Human Affection Exchange: V. Attributes of the Highly Affectionate," *Communication Quarterly.* 50(2):135–152. Taylor & Francis Ltd. Reprinted by permission of the publisher (Taylor & Francis Lts. http//www.informaworld.com).

While showing every feeling of boredom, fear, anger, or frustration could get you into trouble, withholding emotions can be personally frustrating and can keep relationships from growing and prospering. The following suggestions can help you decide when and how to express your emotions.

Recognize Your Feelings

Some people are acutely aware of their emotional states and use the knowledge when making important decisions.[64] By contrast, people with a low affective orientation are usually unaware of their emotional states and tend to regard feelings as useless or unimportant information.

Beyond being *aware* of one's feelings, it's valuable to be able to *identify* them. College students who can pinpoint negative emotions such as nervousness, anger, sadness, shame, and guilt are better able to manage them.[65] This explains why the ability to distinguish and label emotions is a vital component of emotional intelligence.[66] You can tune in to your feelings by recognizing any physiological changes you may experience and monitoring your nonverbal behaviours, your thoughts, and the verbal messages you send to others. It's not far from the verbal statement "I hate this!" to the realization that you're angry (or bored, nervous, or embarrassed).

Recognize the Difference between Feeling, Talking, and Acting

Just because you feel a certain way doesn't mean you must always talk about it, and talking about a feeling doesn't mean you must act on it. In fact, people who act out angry feelings actually feel worse than those who experience anger without lashing out.[67]

Understanding the difference between having feelings and acting them out can help you express yourself

© Leo Callum/The New Yorker Collection/www.cartoonbank.com

TABLE 4.2

Common Human Emotions

afraid	concerned	exhausted	hurried	nervous	sexy
aggravated	confident	fearful	hurt	numb	shaky
amazed	confused	Fed	hysterical	optimistic	shocked
ambivalent	content	fidgety	impatient	paranoid	shy
angry	crazy	flattered	impressed	passionate	sorry
annoyed	defeated	foolish	inhibited	peaceful	strong
anxious	defensive	forlorn	insecure	pessimistic	subdued
apathetic	delighted	free	interested	playful	surprised
ashamed	depressed	friendly	intimidated	pleased	suspicious
bashful	detached	frustrated	irritable	possessive	tender
bewildered	devastated	furious	jealous	pressured	tense
bitchy	disappointed	glad	joyful	protective	terrified
bitter	disgusted	glum	lazy	puzzled	tired
bored	disturbed	grateful	lonely	refreshed	trapped
brave	ecstatic	happy	loving	regretful	ugly
calm	edgy	harassed	lukewarm	relieved	uneasy
cantankerous	elated	helpless	mad	resentful	up
carefree	embarrassed	high	mean	restless	vulnerable
cheerful	empty	hopeful	miserable	ridiculous	warm
cocky	enthusiastic	horrible	mixed	romantic	weak
cold	envious	hostile	mortified	sad	wonderful
comfortable	excited	humiliated	neglected	sentimental	worried

constructively in tough situations. If you recognize that you are upset with a friend, it's possible to explore why you feel so upset. Expressing your feeling ("Sometimes I get so mad at you that I could scream") might open the door to resolving whatever is bothering you. Pretending that nothing is the matter is unlikely to diminish your resentful feelings, which can then go on to contaminate the relationship.

> **An emotion without social rules of containment and expression is like an egg without a shell: a gooey mess.**
>
> —Carol Tavris

Expand Your Emotional Vocabulary

Most people suffer from impoverished emotional vocabularies and think they're expressing feelings when in fact their statements are counterfeits of emotion. For example, it sounds emotionally revealing to say, "I feel like going to a show," or "I feel we've been seeing too much of each other." But neither statement has any emotional content. In the first sentence, the word *feel* really stands for an intention: "I *want* to go to a show." In the second sentence, the "feeling" is really a thought: "I *think* we've been seeing too much of each other." You can recognize the absence of emotion in each case by adding a genuine word of feeling to it. For instance, "I'm *bored* and I want to go to a show," or "I think we've been seeing too much of each other and I feel *confined*."

Relying on a small vocabulary is as limiting as using only a few terms to describe colours. To say that the ocean in all its moods and the sky with its daily variations are both "blue" tells only a fraction of the story. Likewise, it's

overly broad to use a term like *good* or *great* to describe how you feel in situations as different as earning a high grade, finishing a marathon, and hearing the words "I love you" from a special person.

There are several ways to express a feeling verbally:[68]

- By using *single words*: "I'm angry" (or "excited," "depressed," "curious," and so on)
- By describing what's happening to you: "My stomach is tied in knots," "I'm on top of the world"
- By describing what you'd like *to do*: "I want to run away," "I'd like to give you a hug," "I feel like giving up"

Sometimes communicators inaccurately minimize the strength of their feelings—"I'm a *little* unhappy," or "I'm *pretty* excited." Not all feelings are strong ones—we feel degrees of sadness and joy—but some people tend to discount almost every feeling. Do you?

"It's not a word I can put into feelings."

In other cases, communicators express feelings in a coded manner. You'll see this when the sender is uncomfortable about revealing a feeling and just hints at the message. For example, an indirect way to say, "I'm lonesome," might be, "I guess there isn't much happening this weekend, so if you're not busy, why don't you drop by?" This message is so indirect that any feeling may not be recognized. This is why people who send coded messages stand less chance of having their feelings understood and their needs met.

When expressing your feelings, make sure that both you and your partner understand that your feeling is centred on a specific set of circumstances, not the whole relationship. Instead of saying, "I resent you," say, "I resent it when you don't keep your promises." Rather than, "I'm bored with you," say, "I'm bored when you talk about your money."

CHAPTER 4 Emotions: Feeling, Thinking, and Communicating

Express Multiple Feelings

Many times, the feeling you express isn't the only one you're experiencing. For example, you might express anger but overlook the confusion, disappointment, frustration, or embarrassment that preceded it. Recall the example earlier in the chapter where an out-of-town friend was supposed to arrive at a particular time but didn't show up until much later. Most of us would feel relieved to see the friend arrive safe and sound but be angry at him or her for not getting in touch sooner. Thus, we would experience mixed emotions.

Despite the commonness of mixed emotions, we often communicate only one feeling—usually the most negative one. This leaves the other person with little idea of the full range of your feelings. Consider the different reaction you would get by showing all your emotions in, for instance, the example above.

Consider When and Where to Express Your Feelings

Often the first flush of a strong feeling isn't the best time to speak out. If a noisy neighbour wakes you, storming over to complain could result in saying things you'll regret later. It's probably wiser to wait until you have thought through exactly what you want to say and how you want to say it. "Imagining interactions" in advance of actual conversations enhances relationships by allowing communicators to rehearse the message and consider how others might respond.[69] Being rushed, tired, or distracted by another matter are good reasons to postpone the visit. Dealing with your emotions can sometimes take a great amount of time and effort, and fatigue or distraction will make it difficult to follow through in the manner you've stated. Further, it's important to ensure that the recipient of your message is ready to hear you out before you begin.

> Speak when you are angry, and you will make the best speech you will ever regret.
>
> —Ambrose Bierce

> Anyone can become angry. That is easy. But to be angry with the right person to the right degree, at the right time for the right purpose, and in the right way: This is not easy.
>
> —Aristotle

SKILL BUILDER

Feelings and Phrases

Think about how you would communicate your feelings to the different people in the situations below. Then, in small groups, discuss the similarities and differences among your approaches.

1. You receive a terse text message cancelling a date or appointment. It's the third time the other person has cancelled at the last minute.
   a. An instructor
   b. A family member
   c. A classmate you don't know well
   d. Your best friend

2. The other person posts an inappropriate comment on your Facebook wall.
   a. An instructor
   b. A family member
   c. A classmate you don't know well
   d. Your best friend

3. The other person compliments you on your appearance, then says, "I hope I haven't embarrassed you."
   a. An instructor
   b. A family member
   c. A classmate you don't know well
   d. Your best friend

4. The other person gives you a hug and says, "It's good to see you."
   a. An instructor
   b. A family member
   c. A classmate you don't know well
   d. Your best friend

After a long and frustrating search, Logan thought he had found the ideal job. The interview went well. As Logan was leaving, the interviewer said he was "very well qualified" and said, "You'll be hearing from us soon." That conversation took place almost two weeks ago, and Logan hasn't heard a word from the company.

The transcripts below reflect two very different ways of responding to this difficult situation. The first one ignores, and the second one follows, the "Guidelines for Expressing Emotions" described on pages 95–98. In each, Logan begins by ruminating (p. 100) about the employer's failure to get in touch as promised.

Ignoring Guidelines for Emotional Expression

Logan doesn't explicitly recognize a single emotion he is experiencing (p. 98), let alone any mixed emotions (p. 98). Rather than accepting responsibility for his own feelings, he blames the employer for "driving me crazy" (p. 99) "I can't believe those inconsiderate idiots! Who do they think they are, promising to call soon and then doing nothing? They're driving me crazy."

Logan jumps to the conclusion that a job offer isn't forthcoming and lashes out without considering any alternatives. "I give up. Since they aren't going to hire me, I'm going to call that interviewer and let her know what a screwed-up company they're running. I'll probably get her voice mail, but that's even better: That way I can say what's on my mind without getting nervous or being interrupted. They have no right to jerk me around like this, and I'm going to tell them just that." (Angrily dials phone.)

Following Guidelines for Emotional Expression

Logan identifies his mixture of feelings as a starting point for deciding what to do (p. 98). "I'm mad at the company for not keeping in touch like they

promised. I'm also confused about whether I'm as qualified as I thought I was, and I'm starting to worry that maybe I didn't do as well in the interview as I thought. I'm also sorry I didn't ask her for a more specific time than 'soon.' And I'm really unsure about whether to give up, wait for them to call me, or reach out to the company and ask what's going on."

He recognizes the difference between what he would like to do (chew out the interviewer) and what is more appropriate and effective (p. 96–97). "If I'm not going to get the job, I'd like to chew out that interviewer for promising to call. But that would probably be a bad idea—burning my bridges, as my family would say."

Logan uses a perception check (pp. 76–78), sharing his feelings with the employer in a non-blaming way. He deliberately considers when and how to express himself (p. 98), choosing e-mail as the best channel to achieve his goals (p. 99). "Maybe I'll call her and say something like, 'I'm confused. You said at the interview that I'd hear from you soon, but it's been almost two weeks now with no word.' I could ask whether I misunderstood, although I doubt that, or whether they need some more information from me. Let me think about that overnight. If the idea still sounds good in the morning, I'll call them."

Having decided to e-mail the employer, Logan could use the "constructive conflict skills" described in Chapter 10 (pp. 285–288) to compose his e-message. He could begin by speaking positively about his continued interest in the company, then raise his concern about not having heard from them, and then close by saying that he's looking forward to hearing back from them. "Actually, an e-mail would be better: I could edit my words until they're just right, and an e-mail wouldn't put the interviewer on the spot like a phone call."

There are also cases where you may choose not to express your feelings verbally. In such cases, writing out your thoughts and feelings can have mental, physical, and emotional benefits.[70] One study found that writing about feelings of affection can actually reduce the writer's cholesterol level.[71]

Accept Responsibility for Your Feelings

It's important to ensure that your language reflects that you are responsible for your feelings.[72] Instead of saying,

"You make me angry," say, "I'm getting angry." Instead of saying, "You hurt my feelings," say, "I feel hurt when you do that." People don't make us like or dislike them, and believing that they do denies the responsibility that we have for our own emotions.

Be Mindful of the Communication Channel

The different channels we use to communicate make a difference in how others interpret our messages, especially when it comes to expressing emotions.

Given the number of communication channels available today, deciding when to use mediated channels—such as e-mail, instant messaging, cell-phones, social media sites, PDAs, and blogging—calls for a level of analysis that wasn't required in the past.[73] For instance, is voice mail an appropriate way to end a relationship? Is it acceptable to use CAPITAL LETTERS in an instant message to express displeasure? If you're excited about some good news, should you tell your family and friends in person before putting it in your blog?

Most people recognize that channel selection depends in part on the kind of message they're sending. However, in one survey, students said they would have little trouble expressing positive messages in person but preferred mediated channels for negative messages.[74] So much for the face-to-face breakup.

"Flaming" is an extreme example of how computer-mediated channels lend themselves to expressing negative emotions. The kind of civility that most people accept as appropriate in other communication channels doesn't seem to hold on the Internet. Before saying something you may later regret, it's worth remembering the principle that communication is irreversible. Once you hit the Send button, you cannot retract an emotional outburst.

Difficult emotions can spoil the quality of a relationship.

Blend Images/Superstock

LO⁴
Managing Difficult Emotions

Although feeling and expressing many emotions adds to the quality of interpersonal relationships, not all feelings are beneficial.

Facilitative and Debilitative Emotions

There are two types of emotions: **facilitative emotions**, which contribute to effective functioning, and **debilitative emotions**, which keep us from functioning and relating effectively.

One difference between the two types is their *intensity*. For instance, a certain amount of anger or irritation can be constructive and provide that extra "oomph" to improve unsatisfying conditions. Rage, on the other hand, usually make matters worse, as in the case of "road rage."[75] The same holds true for fear. A little nervousness before an important athletic contest or job interview energizes you and improves your performance (mellow athletes or prospective employees usually don't do well).[76] But total terror is something else. And even a little suspicion can make people more effective communicators.

One study revealed that couples that doubted that their relational partners were telling the truth were better at detecting deception than were trusting mates.[77] Of course, an extreme case of paranoia would have the opposite and debilitative effect, reducing the ability to interpret the partner's behaviour accurately.

Not surprisingly, debilitative emotions like communication apprehension can lead to a variety of problems in personal, business, educational, and even medical settings.[78] When people become anxious, they often speak less, and when they do manage to speak up, they're not as effective as their more confident counterparts.[79]

A second characteristic that distinguishes debilitative feelings from facilitative ones is *duration*. Feeling depressed after a relationship breakup or the loss of a job is natural, but spending the rest of your life grieving your loss accomplishes nothing. In the same way, staying angry at someone for a long time is just as punishing to you as it is to the wrongdoer. Social scientists call this **rumination**: dwelling persistently on negative thoughts that, in turn, intensify negative feelings. Rumination can increase feelings of sadness, anxiety, and depression,[80] and "ruminaters" are more likely to lash out with displaced aggression at innocent bystanders.[81]

Many debilitative emotions involve communication. Here are a few examples, offered by readers of *LOOK*.

Facilitative emotions
Emotions that contribute to effective functioning.

Debilitative emotions
Emotions that prevent a person from functioning effectively.

Rumination
Dwelling persistently on negative thoughts that, in turn, intensify negative feelings.

When I first came to college, I had to leave my boyfriend. I was living with three girls, and for most of the first semester I was so lonesome and unhappy that I was a pretty terrible roommate.

I got so frustrated with my overly critical boss that I lost my temper and quit one day. I told him what a horrible manager he was and walked off the job right then and there. Now I'm afraid to list my former boss as a reference, and I'm afraid my temper tantrum will make it harder for me to get a new job.

I've had ongoing problems with my family, and sometimes I get so upset that I can't concentrate on my work or school, or even sleep well at night.

In the following pages you will learn a method for dealing with debilitative feelings like these in a way that will improve your effectiveness as a communicator.

> There's nothing good or bad but thinking makes it so.
>
> —Shakespeare,
> *Hamlet*

Sources of Debilitative Emotions

For most people, feelings seem to have a life of their own. You wish you could feel calm when approaching strangers, yet your voice quivers. You try to appear confident when asking for a raise, yet your eye twitches nervously. Where do feelings and indications of feelings like these come from?

While feelings may come from our genetic makeup or from emotional memories, much of what we feel is connected to how we think about things—the **self-talk** that goes into how we label events and situations.

For example, it's common to say that strangers or your boss make you feel nervous, in the same way you would say that a bee sting makes you feel pain. The apparent similarities between physical and emotional discomfort become clear if you look at them in the following way:

Event	Feeling
Bee sting	physical pain
Meeting strangers	nervous feelings

However, this apparent similarity between physical pain and emotional discomfort (or pleasure) isn't as great as it seems to be. Cognitive psychologists argue that it is not *events* that cause people to feel bad, but rather the *beliefs they hold* about these events. As discussed earlier in the chapter, *reappraisal* involves changing our thoughts to help manage our emotions.

Albert Ellis, who developed an approach to reappraisal called *rational emotive therapy,* provides an example. If you were walking by a friend's house and that person stuck his head out the window and called you a string of vile names, you would probably feel hurt and upset. But if your friend was living in a mental health facility and did the same thing, your reactions or feelings would be different. Perhaps you would be sad for your friend. The difference in your feelings has to do with your thinking. In the first instance, you might think that your friend is very angry with you or that you had done something terribly wrong. In the second case, you would probably assume that your friend was having a psychotic episode and you would be more apt to feel sympathetic.

> **Self-talk**
> The process of thinking. On some level, self-talk occurs as a person interprets another's behaviour.

ZITS © ZITS PARTNERSHIP, KING FEATURES SYNDICATE

This example illustrates that the way people *interpret* events during the process of self-talk determines their feelings.[82] Thus, the model for emotions looks like this:

Event	Thought (Self-talk)	Feeling
Being called names	"I've done something wrong."	hurt, upset
Being called names	"My friend must be sick."	concern, sympathy

The same principle applies in more common situations. The words "I love you" can be interpreted as a genuine expression of deep affection, or they might be decoded in a variety of other ways: for example, as an attempt at manipulation, a sincere but mistaken declaration uttered in a moment of passion, or a way to make the recipient feel better. One study revealed that women are more likely than men to regard expressions of love as genuine statements.[83] It's easy to imagine how different interpretations of a statement like "I love you" can lead to different emotional reactions:

Event	Thought (Self-talk)	Feeling
Hearing "I love you"	"This is a genuine statement."	delight (perhaps)
Hearing "I love you"	"S/he's just saying this to manipulate me."	anger

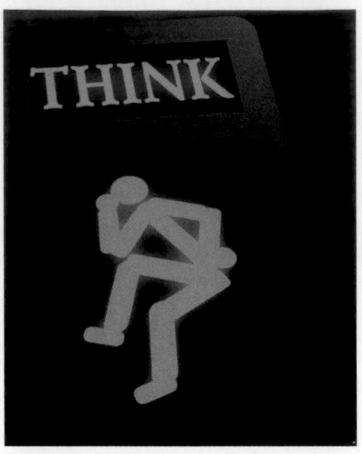

Carol and Mike Werner/Photolibrary/Getty Images

Most emotions come from the way we think. When thoughts are irrational, unwelcome emotions can interfere with effective communication.

Irrational Thinking and Debilitative Emotions

We can understand debilitative emotions by examining our self-talk. Debilitative feelings that come from accepting irrational thoughts are called **fallacies**. These lead to illogical conclusions and in turn to debilitating feelings. They are so powerful because we are usually unaware of such thoughts.[84]

1. The Fallacy of Perfection

The **fallacy of perfection** is the irrational belief that worthwhile communicators should be able to handle every situation with complete confidence and skill.

If you accept this belief, you'll probably assume that people won't appreciate you unless you are perfect. Admitting mistakes, saying, "I don't know," and expressing feelings of uncertainty may seem like social defects, and therefore you may be tempted to try to *appear* perfect. But the costs of such deception are high. Such performances use so much psychological energy that the approval is less enjoyable.

> **Fallacies**
> Debilitative feelings that come from accepting irrational thoughts.
>
> **Fallacy of perfection**
> The irrational belief that a worthwhile communicator should be able to handle every situation with complete confidence and skill.

> The mind is its own place, and in itself can make a Heav'n of Hell, a Hell of Heav'n.
>
> —John Milton,
> *Paradise Lost*

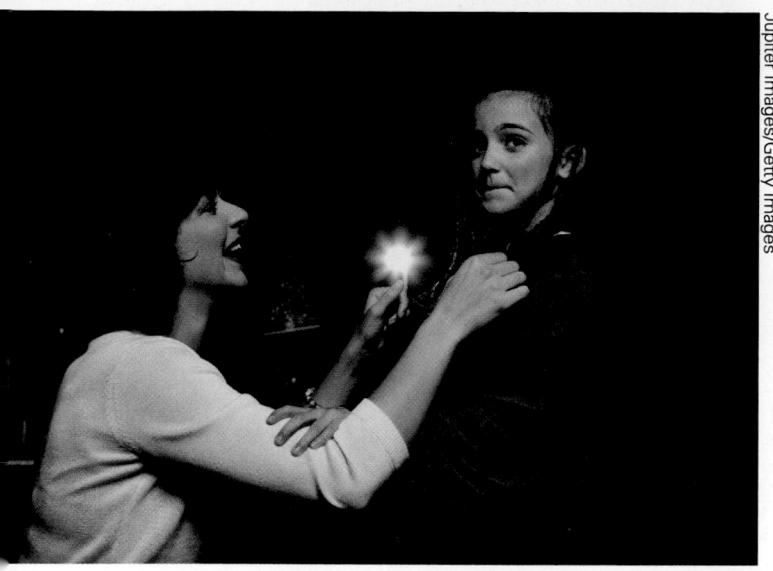

Subscribing to the myth of perfection diminishes self-esteem. How can you act like yourself when you don't measure up to the way you ought to be? Accepting the idea that you don't have to be perfect is very liberating. Then you can acknowledge that

Like everyone else, you sometimes have a hard time expressing yourself.
Like everyone else, you make mistakes from time to time, and there is no reason to hide this.
You are honestly doing the best you can to realize your potential, to become the best person you can be.

2. The Fallacy of Approval

The **fallacy of approval** is based on the notion that it is vital to get the approval of virtually everyone. People who accept this belief go to incredible lengths to seek acceptance, even when they have to sacrifice their own principles and happiness to do so. This can lead to some ludicrous situations:

Feeling nervous because people you really don't like seem to disapprove of you.
Feeling apologetic when others are at fault.
Feeling embarrassed after behaving unnaturally to gain another's approval.

Besides denying your principles and needs, the fallacy of approval implies that others will only respect you if you go out of your way to please them, which simply isn't true. It's difficult to respect people who have compromised important values to gain acceptance or to think highly of people who repeatedly deny their own needs. Striving for universal approval is irrational because it's simply not possible and the price of abandoning your own needs and principles is too high.

Fallacy of approval
The irrational belief that it is vital to win the approval of virtually every person a communicator deals with.

Fallacy of shoulds
The inability to distinguish between what is and what should be.

> The juggler comes closest to our hearts when he misses the ball.
>
> —Richard J. Needham, columnist
> *"A Friend in Needham"*

3. The Fallacy of Shoulds

The **fallacy of shoulds** is the inability to distinguish between what is and what should be. You can see the difference by imagining a person who is full of complaints about the world:

That I Would Be Good

that I would be good even if I did nothing
that I would be good even if I got the thumbs down
that I would be good if I got and stayed sick
that I would be good even if I gained ten pounds

that I would be fine even if I went bankrupt
that I would be good if I lost my hair and my youth
that I would be great if I was no longer queen
that I would be grand if I was not all knowing

that I would be loved even when I numb myself
that I would be good even when I am overwhelmed
that I would be loved even when I was fuming
that I would be good even if I was clingy

that I would be good even if I lost sanity
that I would be good
whether with or without you

Alanis Morissette

"There shouldn't be rain on weekends."
"People ought to live forever."
"Money should grow on trees."

Insisting that the unchangeable be changed won't affect reality one bit, but many people engage in this sort of irrational thinking. They confuse *is* with *should*.

"My friend should be more understanding."
"They should be more friendly."
"You should work harder."

The message in each of these cases is that you would *prefer* people to behave differently. However, it's unreasonable to *insist* that the world operate the way you want it to or to feel cheated when things aren't ideal.

Imposing the fallacy of shoulds on yourself leads to misery. Aaron Beck points out some unrealistic self-imposed "shoulds":[85]

"I should be able to find a quick solution to every problem."
"I should never feel hurt; I should always be happy and serene."

In the film *Yes Man*, Jim Carrey's character discovers the problems that arise from trying to please everybody.

Warner Bros/The Kobal Collection

"I should always demonstrate the utmost generosity, considerateness, dignity, courage, unselfishness."

Becoming obsessed with "shoulds" results in three consequences. First, such people are seldom satisfied with what they have or who they are. Second, complaining without acting does nothing to change unsatisfying conditions. Third, complaining can build a defensiveness in others, who resent being nagged. For example, it's more effective to say, "I wish you'd be more punctual," instead of "You should be on time."

4. The Fallacy of Overgeneralization

The **fallacy of overgeneralization** consists of two types. The first occurs when we base a belief on a limited amount of evidence. For instance,

"I'm so stupid! I can't even figure out how to download music on my iPod."
"Some friend I am! I forgot my best friend's birthday."

In such cases, we focus on a small shortcoming as if it represented the entire situation and we ignore any positive attributes.

A second type of overgeneralization occurs when we *exaggerate* shortcomings:

"You *never* listen to me."
"You're *always* late."

Absolute statements like these are almost always false and lead to discouragement or anger. It's better to replace overgeneralizations with more accurate messages:

"You often don't listen to me."
"You've been late three times this week."

5. The Fallacy of Causation

The **fallacy of causation** is based on the irrational belief

> **Fallacy of overgeneralization**
> Irrational beliefs in which conclusions (usually negative) are based on limited evidence or communicators exaggerate their shortcomings.
>
> **Fallacy of causation**
> The irrational belief that emotions are caused by others and not by the person who experiences them.

AT THE MOVIES

Yes Man (2008), Rated 13+

Carl Allen (Jim Carrey) is a man of many emotions—most of them negative. He's been depressed and lonely since a recent divorce, and he regularly rejects his friends' attempts to get him out of the house. His pattern is to say no to every invitation that comes his way—until he attends a motivational seminar that convinces him he needs to say yes. To everything.

Allen's new approach leads to a host of counterintuitive choices, many of which are risky and dangerous (and of course amusing). The adventures that follow help him experience feelings of happiness, contentment, and love that otherwise might have escaped him.

But feeling obliged to say yes comes with a price. Allen wrestles with some of the debilitative emotions described in this chapter as he subscribes to the fallacies of approval, shoulds, and helplessness. Ultimately, Allen realizes there's a time for yes and a time for no. He also learns that sound choices based on rational thinking are the best route to happiness.

that emotions are caused by others rather than by our own self-talk.

This fallacy causes trouble in two ways. The first is when people become overly cautious about communicating because they don't want to "cause" pain or inconvenience for others. For example,

> Visiting friends or family out of a sense of obligation rather than a genuine desire to see them.
> Keeping quiet when another person's behaviour is bothering you.
> Pretending to be interested in a speaker when you're late for an appointment.

There's certainly no excuse for intentionally saying things to hurt someone, and sometimes you'll choose to inconvenience yourself to make life easier for someone. However, it's an overstatement to say that you cause others' feelings. More accurately, they *respond* to your behaviour with their own feelings. For example, you wouldn't say that you make others fall in love with you. But you could say that you act in a way that someone might fall in love with you. In the same way, it's incorrect to say that you *make* others angry, upset—or happy, for that matter. It's more fitting to say that others create their own responses to your behaviour.

The fallacy of causation also operates when we believe that others cause *our* emotions. While it can seem as if they do, the same actions that can make you happy or unhappy on one day have little effect at other times. The insult that affected your mood strongly yesterday leaves you unaffected today. Why? Because in the latter case you attached less importance to either. It's your reaction, not their actions, that determines how you feel.

6. The Fallacy of Helplessness

The **fallacy of helplessness** suggests that satisfaction in life is determined by forces beyond your control. People who see themselves as victims make statements like

> "I was born with a shy personality. There's nothing I can do about that."
> "I can't tell my boss that she's putting too many demands on me. I might lose my job."

These statements are mistaken in that there are many things you can do if you really want to. Most "can't" statements can be rephrased as "won't" statements ("I can't tell her what I think" becomes "I won't be honest with her") or as "don't know how" statements ("I can't have an interesting conversation" becomes "I don't know what to say"). Once these inaccurate "can'ts" are rephrased, it becomes clear that they're either a matter of choice or something that calls for your action, and thus different from saying you're helpless.

The self-fulfilling prophecy is also at work with such an attitude. Believing that there is only one way to look at something will be followed by consistent behaviours. On the other hand, acknowledging that there is a way to change puts the responsibility for your predicament on *your* shoulders. Don't sell yourself short.

Fallacy of helplessness The irrational belief that satisfaction in life is determined by forces beyond one's control.

Fallacy of catastrophic expectations The irrational belief that the worst possible outcome will probably occur.

7. The Fallacy of Catastrophic Expectations

Communicators who subscribe to the **fallacy of catastrophic expectations** assume that if something bad can possibly happen, it will. Typical catastrophic expectations include

> "If I invite them to the party, they probably won't want to come."

Hans Neleman/CORBIS

Imagining the worst possible outcome can create unnecessary debilitative feelings.

"If I speak up to try to resolve a conflict, things will probably get worse."

"If I apply for the job I want, I probably won't be hired."

After you start expecting catastrophic consequences, the self-fulfilling prophecy begins to build. One study revealed that people who believed that their romantic partners would not change for the better were more likely to behave in ways that contributed to the breakup.[86]

While it's naive to assume that all your interactions with others will meet with success, it's just as naive to assume that they won't. To escape the fallacy of catastrophic expectations, think about the consequences if you don't communicate successfully. It's not as bad as you think. So what if you don't get the response you want? Are these matters really *that* serious?

> ## FOR SALE—
> ## ONE HOME-MADE COFFIN.
> ## Never been used. Fit 6'2".
> ## Reason for Selling:
> ## Improved Health.
> ## Phone 97937.
>
> Classified advertisement,
> *Saskatoon Star-Phoenix*

Finally, it's important to realize that thinking rationally won't completely eliminate debilitative emotions.

Some debilitative emotions are very rational, such as grief over someone's death or euphoria over a new job. But thinking rationally can eliminate many debilitative emotions from your life.

Minimizing Debilitative Emotions

Social scientists and therapists have developed a simple yet effective approach that can be used to help you cut down on the self-defeating thinking that leads to debilitative emotions.[87]

> ## Telling it in plain words
> ## Makes me see how I feared
> ## the wrong thing.
>
> —Margaret Avison,
> *'The Agnes Cleves Papers'*

1. **Monitor your emotional reactions.** The first step is to recognize your debilitative emotions. One way to recognize emotions is through your physiological stimuli: butterflies in the stomach, racing heart, etc. Although such stimuli might signify food poisoning, more likely they are symptoms of a strong emotion. Also look for behaviours that might suggest your feelings: stomping instead of walking normally, speaking in a sarcastic tone of voice, or just being unusually quiet, for example.

   While it may seem strange to look for emotions, we often suffer from debilitative emotions without even noticing them. For example, after a trying day, you might find yourself frowning and realize that you've been wearing that mask without realizing it.

2. **Note the activating event.** Once you're aware of how you're feeling, the next step is to figure out what triggered your response. Sometimes it is obvious, like being accused unfairly (or fairly) of foolish behaviour or being rejected by someone. In other cases, however, the activating event isn't so apparent. Sometimes it's a series of incidents that triggers a debilitative emotion. The best way to identify activating events is to notice the circumstances in which you have debilitative feelings. You may find that they occur when you're around *specific* people or certain *types of individuals* or in certain *settings*.

Invitation TO INSIGHT

How Irrational Are You?

1. Return to the situations described in the exercise "Talking to Yourself" on page 102. Examine each one to see whether your self-talk contains any irrational thoughts.

2. Keep a two- or three-day record of your debilitative emotions. Are any of them based on irrational thinking? Examine your conclusions and see if you repeatedly use any of the fallacies described in the preceding section.

3. Take a class poll to see which fallacies are most "popular." Also discuss what subjects seem to stimulate most of this irrational thinking (e.g., schoolwork, dating, jobs, family).

3. **Record your self-talk.** This is the point at which you link the activating event to your feeling. To eliminate debilitative emotions, it's important to write down your self-talk. Putting your thoughts on paper helps you to see whether they actually make any sense.

While monitoring your self-talk might be difficult at first, you'll soon find that you will be able to identify the thoughts that lead to your debilitative emotions. Once you get in the habit of recognizing your internal monologue, you'll be able to identify your thoughts quickly and easily.

4. **Reappraise your irrational beliefs.** Reappraising your irrational beliefs is the key to success in the rational-emotive approach. Use the list of irrational fallacies discussed earlier to discover which of your internal statements are based on mistaken thinking.

Replacing self-defeating self-talk with more constructive thinking improves self-confidence and relational communication.[88] Nonetheless, this approach triggers objections from some readers.

"The rational emotive approach sounds like nothing more than trying to talk yourself out of feeling bad." This accusation is totally correct. If we talk ourselves into feeling bad, why not talk ourselves out of feeling bad, especially when such feelings are based on irrational thoughts?

"The kind of reappraising we just read sounds phony and unnatural. I don't talk to myself in sentences and paragraphs." There's no need to dispute your irrational beliefs in any special literary

SKILL BUILDER

Rational Thinking

1. Return to the diary of irrational thoughts you recorded on page 106. Examine the self-talk in each case and write a more rational interpretation of the event.

2. Now try out your ability to think rationally on the spot. You can do this by acting out the scenes listed in step 4 below. You'll need three players for each one: a subject, the subject's "little voice"—his or her thoughts—and a second party.

3. Play out each scene by having the subject and second party interact while the "little voice" stands just behind the subject and says what the subject is probably thinking. For example, in a scene where the subject is asking an instructor to reconsider a low grade, the little voice might say, "I hope I haven't made things worse by bringing this up. Maybe he'll lower the grade after rereading the test. I'm such an idiot! Why didn't I keep quiet?"

4. Whenever the little voice expresses an irrational thought, the observers who are watching the skit should call out, "Foul." At this point the action should stop while the group discusses the irrational thought and suggests a more rational line of self-talk. The players should then replay the scene with the little voice speaking in a more rational way.

   Here are some scenes. Of course, you can invent others as well.
   a. Two people are just beginning their first date.
   b. A potential employee has just begun a job interview.
   c. A teacher or boss is criticizing the subject for showing up late.
   d. A student and instructor run across each other in the market.

123render/iStockphoto

style. The important thing is to understand what thoughts led you into your debilitative emotions so you can reappraise them clearly.

"This approach is too cold and impersonal. It seems to aim at turning people into cold-blooded, calculating, emotionless machines." This is simply not true. Rational thinkers can still dream, hope, and love—there's nothing necessarily irrational about feelings like these. Even basically rational people indulge in a bit of irrational thinking once in a while. But they usually know what they're doing.

"This technique promises too much. There's no chance I could rid myself of all unpleasant feelings, however nice that might be." We can answer this by assuring you that rational emotive thinking probably won't totally solve your emotional problems. However, it can reduce their number, intensity, and duration. This method is not the answer to all your problems, but it can make a significant difference—which is not a bad accomplishment.

Finally, you may wish to talk to others about certain situations and emotions you encounter. Often the experience of "telling someone your story" or attempting to

© iStockphoto.com/Stuart Freeman

explain how and why you feel a certain way can actually give you insight into what is happening to you. Further, a trusted listener may also provide another perspective as well as some sound advice.

Communication in the Workplace

More than ever, today's employers are looking to hire individuals with emotional intelligence. Recruiters are quick to state that emotional intelligence skills are just as if not more important than job-related skills.[89] Employers assume that interviewees have the requisite job-related skills, but it's the team players with good social skills, an understanding of themselves, and the ability to deal effectively in emotionally charged situations who will be hired.

Further, employers are less willing to put up with bullying, which according to the Canada Safety Council (CSC) is more prevalent than harassment.[90] In fact, the Canadian Human Rights Commission (CHRC) ensures that everyone "has an equal opportunity to work and live without being hindered by discriminatory practices."[91] The CSC is encouraging employers to identify bullying as an unacceptable behaviour.[92] Nor are employees

"So the prince and the princess lowered their expectations and lived reasonably contentedly forever after."

Drawing by Steve Delmonte © 1998 Used by permission.

taking kindly to emotional outbursts at work. While such behaviour rarely leads to job loss, it can certainly stall advancement.[93] Many people recommend that when you encounter someone who has lost his or her cool, politely excuse yourself and leave. There's no need to put up with unprofessional, impolite behaviours, and to do so only reinforces the acceptance of such emotional displays.

But emotions play out in other ways as well, as the examples below demonstrate.

- If firefighters don't mask their emotions of fear, disgust, and stress, it will impede their ability to help the people whose lives they are trying to save. Emotion management training is therefore vital for new firefighters.[94]
- Correctional officers at two minimum-security prisons described the tension of needing to be "warm, nurturing, and respectful" to inmates while also being "suspicious, strong, and tough." The officers acknowledged that it's taxing to manage competing emotions and juggle conflicting demands.[95]

It's not always easy to manage emotions, especially when you're feeling fearful, stressed, angry, or defensive. Nevertheless, it's vital for success on the job.

(In Real Life) Rational Thinking in Action

The following scenarios demonstrate how the rational thinking method applies in everyday challenges. Notice that thinking rationally doesn't eliminate debilitative emotions. Instead, it helps keep them in control, making effective communication more possible.

Situation 1: Dealing with Annoying Customers

Activating Event

I work in a shopping mall that swarms with tourists and locals. Our company's reputation is based on service, but lately I've been losing my patience with the customers. The store is busy from the second we open until we close. Many of the customers are rude, pushy, and demanding. Others expect me to be a tour guide, restaurant reviewer, medical consultant, and even a babysitter. I feel like I'm ready to explode.

Beliefs and Self-Talk

1. I'm sick of working with the public. People are really obnoxious!
2. The customers should be more patient and polite instead of treating me like a servant.
3. This work is driving me crazy! If I keep working here, I'm going to become as rude as the customers.
4. I can't quit. I could never find another job that pays this well.

Reappraising Irrational Beliefs

1. It's an overgeneralization to say that *all* people are obnoxious. Actually, most of the customers are fine. Some are even very nice. About 10 percent of them cause most of the trouble. Recognizing that most people are OK leaves me feeling less bitter.

2. It's true that obnoxious customers *should* be more polite, but it's unrealistic to expect that everybody will behave the way they ought to. After all, it's not a perfect world.

3. By saying that the customers are driving me crazy, I suggest that I have no control over the situation. I'm an adult, and I am able to keep a grip on myself. I may not like the way some people behave, but it's my choice how to respond to them.

4. I'm not helpless. If the job is too unpleasant, I can quit. I probably wouldn't find another job that pays as well as this one, so I have to choose which is more important: money or peace of mind. It's my choice.

Situation 2: Meeting My Girlfriend's Family

Activating Event

Tracy and I are talking about marriage—maybe not soon, but eventually. Her family is very close, and they want to meet me. I'm sure I'll like them, but I'm not sure what they will think about me. I was married once before, at a young age. It was a big mistake, and it didn't last. Furthermore, I was laid off two months ago, and I'm between jobs. The family is coming to town next week, and I am very nervous about what they will think of me.

Beliefs and Self-Talk

1. They've *got* to like me! This is a close family, and I'm doomed if they think I'm not right for Tracy.

2. No matter how sensibly I act, all they'll think about is my divorce and unemployment.

3. Maybe the family is right. Tracy deserves the best, and I'm certainly not that!

Reappraising Irrational Beliefs

1. The family's approval is definitely important. Still, my relationship with Tracy doesn't depend on it. She's already said that she's committed to me, no matter what they think. The sensible approach is to say I *want* their approval, but I don't *need* it.

2. I'm expecting the absolute worst if I think that I'm doomed no matter what happens when we meet. There is a chance that they will dislike me, but there's also a chance that things will work out fine. There's no point in dwelling on catastrophes.

3. Just because I've had an imperfect past doesn't mean I'm wrong for Tracy. I've learned from my past mistakes, and I am committed to living a good life. I know I can be the kind of husband she deserves, even though I'm not perfect.

Endnotes

1. D. Goleman (1995). Emotional Intelligence: Why It Can Matter More Than I.Q. New York: Bantam. See also D. Goleman (2006). Social Intelligence: The New Science of Human Relationships. New York: Bantam.

2. A. Carmeli, M. Yitzhak-Halevy, & J. Weisberg (2009). "The Relationship Between Emotional Intelligence and Psychological Wellbeing." *Journal of Managerial Psychology, 24,* 66–78.

3. L. Smith, P. C. Heaven, & J. Ciarrochi (2008). "Trait Emotional Intelligence, Conflict Communication Patterns, and Relationship Satisfaction." Personality and Individual Differences, 44, 1314–1325.

4. S. Planalp, J. Fitness, & B. Fehr (2006). "Emotion in Theories of Close Relationships." In A. L. Vangelisti & D. Perlman (Eds.). The Cambridge Handbook of Personal Relationships (pp. 369–384). New York: Cambridge University Press; and R. F. Baumeister (2005). *The Human Animal.* New York: Oxford University Press.

5. G. M. Rochman & G. M. Diamond (2008). "From Unresolved Anger to Sadness: Identifying Physiological Correlates." Journal of Counseling Psychology, 55, 96–105.

6. J. M. Gottman & N. Silver (1999). The Seven Principles for Making Marriages Work. New York: Three Rivers Press.

7. P. Ekman, R. W. Levenson, & W. V. Friesen (September 16, 1983). "Autonomic Nervous System Activity Distinguishes among Emotions." Science, 221, 1208–1210.

8. C. L. Kleinke, T. R. Peterson, & T. R. Rutledge (1998). "Effects of Self-Generated Facial Expressions on Mood." Journal of Personality and Social Psychology, 74, 272–279.

9. S. Valins (1966). "Cognitive Effects of False Heart-Rate Feedback." Journal of Personality and Social Psychology, 4, 400–408.

10. P. Zimbardo (1977). Shyness: What It Is, What to Do about It. Reading, MA: Addison-Wesley, p. 53.

11. K. N. Ochsner & J. J. Gross (2008). "Cognitive Emotion Regulation: Insights From Social Cognitive and Affective Neuroscience." *Current Directions in Psychological Science,* 17, 153–158.

12. J. C. Wallace, B. D. Edwards, A. Shull, & D. M. Finch (2009). "Examining the Consequences in the Tendency to Suppress and Reappraise Emotions on Task-Related Job Performance." *Human Performance,* 22, 23–43; S. A. Moore,

L. A. Zoellner, & N. Mollenholt (2008). "Are Expressive Suppression and Cognitive Reappraisal Associated with Stress-Related Symptoms?" *Behaviour Research and Therapy, 46,* 993–1000; and J. B. Nezlek & B. Kuppens (2008). "Regulating Positive and Negative Emotions in Daily Life." *Journal of Personality, 76,* 561–580.

13. R. Plutchik (1980). Emotion: A Psychoevolutionary Synthesis. New York: Harper & Row; and P. R. Shaver, S. Wu, & J. C. Schwartz (1992). "Cross-Cultural Similarities and Differences in Emotion and its Representation: A Prototype Approach." In M. S. Clark (Ed.). Emotion (pp. 175–212). Newbury Park, CA: Sage.

14. P. Ekman (1999). "Basic Emotions." In T. Dalgleish & T. Power (Eds.). The Handbook of Cognition and Emotion (pp. 45–60). Sussex, UK: John Wiley & Sons; and A. Ortony & T. J. Turner (1990). "What's Basic about Basic Emotions?" Psychological Review, 97, 315–331.

15. M. Ferrari & E. Koyama (2002). "Meta-Emotions about Anger and Amae: A Cross-Cultural Comparison." Consciousness and Emotion, 3, 197–211.

16. Shaver et al., op. cit.

17. Goleman, op. cit.

18. J. M. Gottman, L. F. Katz, & C. Hooven (1997). Meta-Emotion: How Families Communicate Emotionally. Mahwah, NJ: Erlbaum.

19. E. S. Lunkenheimer, A. M. Shields, & K. S. Kortina (2007). "Parental Emotion Coaching and Dismissing in Family Interaction." Social Development, 16, 232–248.

20. J. C. McCroskey, V. P. Richmond, A. D. Heisel, & J. L Hayhurst (2004). "Eysenck's Big Three and Communication Traits: Communication Traits as Manifestations of Temperament." Communication Research Reports, 21, 404–410; and J. J. Gross, S. K. Sutton, & T. V. Ketelaar (1998). "Relations between Affect and Personality: Support for the Affect-Level and Affective-Reactivity Views." Personality and Social Psychology Bulletin, 24, 279–288.

21. P. T. Costa & R. R. McCrae (1980). "Influence of Extraversion and Neuroticism on Subjective Well-Being: Happy and Unhappy People." Journal of Personality and Social Psychology, 38, 668–678.

22. T. Canli, Z. Zhao, J. E. Desmond, E. Kang, J. Gross, & J. D. E. Gabrieli (2001). "An MRI Study of Personality Influences on Brain Reactivity to Emotional Stimuli." Behavioural Neuroscience, 115, 33–42.

23. L. Kelly, R. L. Duran, & J. J. Zolten (2001). "The Effect of Reticence on College Students' Use of Electronic Mail to Communicate with Faculty." Communication Education, 50, 170–176. See also B. W. Scharlott & W. G. Christ (2001). "Overcoming Relationship-Initiation Barriers: The Impact of a Computer-Dating System on Sex Role, Shyness, and Appearance Inhibitions." Computers in Human Behaviour, 11, 191–204.

24. C. Goddard (2002). "Explicating Emotions across Languages and Cultures: A Semantic Approach." In S. R. Fussell (Ed.). The Verbal Communication of Emotions. Mahwah, NJ: Erlbaum.

25. S. Ting-Toomey (1991). "Intimacy Expressions in Three Cultures: France, Japan, and the United States." International Journal of Intercultural Relations, 15, 29–46. See also C. Gallois (1993). "The Language and Communication of Emotion: Universal, Interpersonal, or Intergroup?" American Behavioural Scientist, 36, 309–338.

26. J. L. Tsai, B. Knutson, & H. H. Fung (2006). "Cultural Variation in Affect Valuation." Journal of Personality and Social Psychology, 90, 288–307.

27. J. W. Pennebaker, B. Rime, & V. E. Blankenship (1996). "Stereotypes of Emotional Expressiveness of Northerners and Southerners: A Cross-Cultural Test of Montesquieu's Hypotheses." Journal of Personality and Social Psychology, 70, 372–380.

28. Ibid., p. 176. See also Gallois, op. cit.

29. H. C. Triandis (1994). Culture and Social Behaviour. New York: McGraw-Hill, p. 169. See also F. M. Moghaddam, D. M. Taylor, & S. C. Wright (1993). Social Psychology in Cross-Cultural Perspective. New York: Freeman.

30. S. T. Mortenson (2009). "Interpersonal Trust and Social Skill in Seeking Social Support Among Chinese and Americans." *Communication Research, 36,* 32–53.

31. R. Wilkins & E. Gareis (2006). "Emotion Expression and the Locution 'I Love You': A Cross-Cultural Study." International Journal of Intercultural Relations, 30, 51–75.

32. L. K. Guerrero, S. M. Jones, & R. R. Boburka (2006). "Sex Differences in Emotional Communication." In K. Dindia & D. J. Canary (Eds.). Sex Differences and Similarities in Communication, 2nd ed. Mahweh, NJ: Erlbaum; and S. R. Wester, D. L. Vogel, P. K. Pressly, & M. Heesacker (2002). "Sex Differences in Emotion: A Critical Review of the Literature and Implications for Counseling Psychology." Counseling Psychologist, 30, 630–652.

33. J. Swenson & F. L. Casmir (1998). "The Impact of Culture-Sameness, Gender, Foreign Travel, and Academic Background on the Ability to Interpret Facial Expression of Emotion in Others." Communication Quarterly, 46, 214–230.

34. T. Canli, J. E. Desmond, Z. Zhao, & J. D. E. Gabrieli (2002). "Sex Differences in the Neural Basis of Emotional Memories." Proceedings of the National Academy of Sciences, 10, 10,789–10,794.

35. J. Merten (2005). "Culture, Gender and the Recognition of the Basic Emotions." Psychologia: An International Journal of Psychology in the Orient, 48, 306–316.

36. See, for example, A. W. Kunkel & B. R. Burleson (1999). "Assessing Explanations for Sex Differences in Emotional Support: A Test of the Different Cultures and Skill Specialization Accounts." Human Communication Research, 25, 307–340.

37. D. J. Goldsmith & P. A. Fulfs (1999). "'You Just Don't Have the Evidence': An Analysis of Claims and Evidence in Deborah Tannen's You Just Don't Understand." In M. E. Roloff (Ed.). Communication Yearbook 22 (pp. 1–49). Thousand Oaks, CA: Sage.

38. D. F. Witmer & S. L. Katzman (1999). "On-Line Smiles: Does Gender Make a Difference in the Use of Graphic

Accents?" Journal of Computer-Mediated Communication, 2, online. Domain name expired.

39. K. Floyd (1997). "Communication Affection in Dyadic Relationships: An Assessment of Behaviour and Expectancies." Communication Quarterly, 45, 68–80.

40. Ibid.

41. M. S. Clark & E. J. Finkel (2005). "Willingness to Express Emotion: The Impact of Relationship Type, Communal Orientation, and Their Interaction." Personal Relationships, 12, 169–180.

42. J. A. Feeney (2005). "Hurt Feelings in Couple Relationships: Exploring the Role of Attachment and Perceptions of Personal Injury." Personal Relationships, 12, 253–271.

43. S. E. Snodgrass (1985). "Women's Intuition: The Effect of Subordinate Role on Interpersonal Sensitivity." Journal of Personality and Social Psychology, 49, 146–155.

44. S. B. Shimanoff (1984). "Commonly Named Emotions in Everyday Conversations." Perceptual and Motor Skills, 58, 514. See also J. M. Gottman (1982). "Emotional Responsiveness in Marital Conversations." Journal of Communication, 32, 108–120.

45. J. G. Haybe & S. Metts (2008). "Managing the Expression of Emotion." *Western Journal of Communication*, 72, 374–396; and S. B. Shimanoff (1988). "Degree of Emotional Expressiveness as a Function of Face-Needs, Gender, and Interpersonal Relationship." Communication Reports, 1, 43–53.

46. C. E. Waugh & B. L. Fredericson (2006). "Nice to Know You: Positive Emotions, Self-Other Overlap, and Complex Understanding in the Formation of a New Relationship." *The Journal of Positive Psychology*, 1, 93–106.

47. S. B. Shimanoff (1985). "Rules Governing the Verbal Expression of Emotions between Married Couples." Western Journal of Speech Communication, 49, 149–165.

48. S. Duck (1992). "Social Emotions: Showing Our Feelings about Other People." Human Relationships. Newbury Park, CA: Sage. See also S. B. Shimanoff (1985). "Expressing Emotions in Words: Verbal Patterns of Interaction." Journal of Communication, 35, 16–31.

49. G. Galloway (January 28, 2006). "Smile Mr. Harper, You're Now on Candid Camera." The Globe and Mail, A8.

50. L. B. Rosenfeld (1979). "Self-Disclosure Avoidance: Why I Am Afraid To Tell You Who I Am." Communication Monographs, 46, 63–74.

51. L. A. Erbert & K. Floyd (2004). "Affectionate Expressions as Face-Threatening Act: Receiver Assessments." Journal of Social and Personal Relationships, 17, 230–246.

52. E. Hatfield, J. T. Cacioppo, R. L. Rapson, & K. Oatley (1984). Emotional Contagion. Cambridge: Cambridge University Press. See also S. Colino (May 30, 2006). "That Look—It's Catching." Washington Post, HE01.

53. Goleman, op. cit., p. 115.

54. A. B. Bakker (2005). "Flow Among Music Teachers and Their Students: The Crossover of Peak Experiences." Journal of Vocational Behaviour, 66, 822–833.

55. C. R. Goodman & R. A. Shippy (2002). "Is it Contagious? Affect Similarity Among Spouses." Aging and Mental Health, 6, 266–274.

56. P. Belluck (December 5, 2008). "Strangers May Cheer You Up, Study Says." New York Times, A12.

57. E. S. Sullins (1991). "Emotional Contagion Revisited: Effects of Social Comparison and Expressive Style on Mood Convergence." Personality and Social Psychology Bulletin, 17, 166–174.

58. C. Anderson, D. Keltner, & O. P. John (May 2003). "Emotional Convergence between People over Time." Journal of Personality and Social Psychology, 84, 1054–1068.

59. T. DeAngelis (1992). "Illness Linked with Repressive Style of Coping." APA Monitor, 23(12), 14–15.

60. A. W. Seigman & T. W. Smith (1994). Anger, Hostility, and the Heart. Hillsdale, NJ: Erlbaum.

61. S. Graham, J. Y. Huang, M. S. Clark, & V. S. Helgeson (2008). "The Positives of Negative Emotions: Willingness to Express Negative Emotions Promotes Relationships." Personality and Social Psychology Bulletin, 34, 394–406; and E. Kennedy-Moore & J. C. Watson (1999). Expressing Emotion: Myths, Realities, and Therapeutic Strategies. New York: Guilford.

62. S. Nelton (Feb. 1996). "Emotions in the Workplace." Nation's Business, 25–30.

63. M. W. Kramer & J. A. Hess (2002). "Communication Rules for the Display of Emotions in Organizational Settings." Management Communication Quarterly, 16, 66–80.

64. M. Booth-Butterfield & S. Booth-Butterfield (1998). "Emotionality and Affective Orientation." In J. C. McCroskey, J. A. Daly, M. M. Martin, & M. J. Beatty (Eds.). Communication and Personality: Trait Perspectives. Creskill, NY: Hampton.

65. L. F. Barrett, J. Gross, T. Christensen, & M. Benvenuto (2001). "Knowing What You're Feeling and Knowing What to Do About It: Mapping the Relation Between Emotion Differentiation and Emotion Regulation." Cognition and Emotion, 15, 713–724.

66. D. Grewal & P. Salovey (2005). "Feeling Smart: The Science of Emotional Intelligence." American Scientist, 93, 330–339; and S. H. Yoo, D. Matsumoto, & J. LeRoux (2006). "The Influence of Emotion Recognition and Emotion Regulation on Intercultural Adjustment." International Journal of Intercultural Relations, 30, 345–363.

67. B. J. Bushman, R. F. Baumeister, & A. D. Stack (1999). "Catharsis, Aggression, and Persuasive Influence: Self-Fulfilling or Self-Defeating Prophecies?" Journal of Personality and Social Psychology, 76, 367–376.

68. For an extensive discussion of ways to express emotions, see S. R. Fussell (2002). The Verbal Communication of Emotions. Mahwah, NJ: Erlbaum.

69. J. M. Honeycutt (2003). Imagined Interactions: Daydreaming About Communication. Cresskill, NJ: Hampton Press; and J. M. Honeycutt & S. G. Ford (2001). "Mental Imagery and Intrapersonal Communication: A Review of Research on Imagined Interactions (IIs) and

Current Developments." Communication Yearbook, 25, 315–338.

70. J. Pennebaker (2004). Writing to Heal: A Guided Journal for Recovering from Trauma and Emotional Upheaval. Oakland, CA: Harbinger.

71. K. Floyd, A. C. Mikkelson, C. Hesse, & P. M. Pauley (2007). "Affectionate Writing Reduces Total Cholesterol: Two Randomized, Controlled Studies." Human Communication Research, 33, 119–142.

72. S. Metts & B. Wood (2008). "Interpersonal Emotional Competence." In M. T. Motley (Ed.). Studies in Applied Interpersonal Communication (pp. 267–285). Thousand Oaks, CA: Sage.

73. B. H. Spitzberg (2006). "Preliminary Development of a Model and Measure of Computer-Mediated Communication (CMC) Competence." Journal of Computer-Mediated Communcation, 11, article 12, http://jcmc.indiana.edu/vol11/issue2/ spitzberg.html. Accessed September 11, 2006.

74. P. B. O'Sullivan (2000). "What You Don't Know Won't Hurt Me: Impression Management Functions of Communication Channels in Relationships." Human Communication Research, 26, 403–431.

75. T. E. Galovski, L. S. Malta, & E. B. Blanchard (2005). Road Rage: Assessment and Treatment of the Angry, Aggressive Driver. Washington, DC: American Psychological Association.

76. S. D. Mallalieu, S. Hanton, & G. Jones (2003). "Emotional Labeling and Competitive Anxiety in Preparation and Competition." Sports Psychologist, 17, 157–174.

77. S. A. McCornack & T. R. Levine (1990). "When Lovers Become Leery: The Relationship between Suspicion and Accuracy in Detecting Deception." Communication Monographs, 57, 219–230.

78. J. Bourhis & M. Allen (1992). "Meta-Analysis of the Relationship between Communication Apprehension and Cognitive Performance." Communication Education, 41, 68–76.

79. M. L. Patterson & V. Ritts (1997). "Social and Communicative Anxiety: A Review and Meta-Analysis." In B. R. Burleson (Ed.). Communication Yearbook 20. Thousand Oaks, CA: Sage.

80. C. L. Rusting & S. Nolen-Hoeksema (1998). "Regulating Responses to Anger." Journal of Personality and Social Psychology, 74, 790–803.

81. B. J. Bushman, A. M. Bonacci, W. C. Pedersen, E. A. Vasquez, & N. Miller (2005). "Chewing on It Can Chew You Up: Effects of Rumination on Triggered Displaced Aggression." Journal of Personality and Social Psychology, 88, 969–983.

82. D. R. Vocate (1994). "Self-Talk and Inner Speech." In D. R. Vocate (Ed.). Intrapersonal Communication: Different Voices, Different Minds. Hillsdale, NJ: Erlbaum.

83. M. Booth-Butterfield & M. R. Trotta (1994). "Attributional Patterns for Expressions of Love." Communication Reports, 7, 119–129.

84. J. A. Bargh (1988). "Automatic Information Processing: Implications for Communication and Affect." In H. E. Sypher & E. T. Higgins (Eds.). Communication, Social Cognition, and Affect. Hillsdale, NJ: Erlbaum.

85. A. Beck (1976). Cognitive Therapy and the Emotional Disorders. New York: International Universities Press.

86. S. Metts & W. R. Cupach (1990). "The Influence of Relationship Beliefs and Problem-Solving Relationships on Satisfaction in Romantic Relationships." Human Communication Research, 17, 170–185.

87. A. Meichenbaum (1977). Cognitive Behaviour Modification. New York: Plenum. See also A. Ellis & R. Greiger (1977). Handbook for Rational-Emotive Therapy. New York: Springer; and M. Wirga & M. DeBernardi (March 2002). "The ABCs of Cognition, Emotion, and Action." Archives of Psychiatry and Psychotherapy, 1, 5–16.

88. A. Chatham-Carpenter & V. DeFrancisco (1997). "Pulling Yourself Up Again: Women's Choices and Strategies for Recovering and Maintaining Self-Esteem." Western Journal of Communication, 61, 164–187.

89. J.J. Liptak (2005). "Using Emotional Intelligence to Help College Students Succeed in the Workplace," Journal of Employment Counseling, 42, 171–187.

90. Canada Safety Council. "Bullying in the Workplace," www.safety-council.org/info/OSH/bullies.html. Accessed Feb. 21, 2006.

91. Canadian Human Rights Commission. "Discrimination and Harrassment," www.chrc-ccdp.ca/discrimination/ default-en.asp. Accessed Feb. 21, 2006.

92. Canada Safety Council. "Bullying in the Workplace."

93. T. Shawn Taylor (Feb. 2006). "Office Outbursts." Reprinted from the Chicago Tribune in Reader's Digest, 176.

94. C. Scott & K. K. Myers (2005). "The Socialization of Emotion: Learning Emotion Management at the Fire Station." Journal of Applied Communication Research, 33, 67–92.

95. K. I. Miller & J. Koesten (2008). "Financial Feeling: An Investigation of Emotion and Communication in the Workplace." Journal of Applied Communication Research, 36, 8–32.

CHAPTER

LANGUAGE:

BARRIER *AND*
BRIDGE

LEARNING OUTCOMES

LO¹ Analyze a real or potential misunderstanding in terms of semantic or pragmatic rules.

LO² Describe how principles in the section titled "The Impact of Language" operate in your life.

LO³ Rephrase disruptive statements in less inflammatory terms.

LO⁴ Recast "if" statements, "but" statements, and "you" statements into statements that reflect your responsibility for the message.

LO⁵ Analyze how gender and/or cultural differences may affect the quality of interaction.

Language Is Symbolic

Communication is an amazing tool that allows us to exchange ideas or abstract thoughts, talk about the past, or just play with one another. Sometimes, however, even simple messages that are clear to you can prove confusing to others. You ask the hairstylist to "take a little off the sides," only to find that her definition of "a little" was equivalent to your description of "a lot." Or you and a friend argue the merits of "feminism" without realizing that you're both working from entirely different definitions. Misunderstandings like these remind us that meanings come from people, not words.

These aspects of communication occur because language is *symbolic*—words stand for things, events, etc. The problem lies in the fact that the connection between words and what they represent is arbitrary. For example, there is nothing particularly "fivelike" about the word *five*. It represents the number of fingers on your hand only because English speakers agree that it does. French speakers use *cinq*, German speakers use *fünf*, and computer programmers use 00110101 to represent the same concept.

Even sign language, the nonverbal system used by individuals with hearing loss, is symbolic and not the pantomime it might seem. There are actually hundreds of different sign languages:[1] American Sign Language, British Sign Language, French Sign Language, Danish Sign Language, Chinese Sign Language—even Australian Aboriginal and Mayan sign languages.

Calvin and Hobbes

by Bill Watterson

Semantic rules
Rules that govern the meaning of language, as opposed to its structure.

We get into trouble with words, or symbols, when we and our conversational partners have different connotations for them. If that were not true, the hairstylist would know exactly what you mean.

> "I don't know what you mean by 'glory,'" Alice said.
> Humpty Dumpty smiled contemptuously. "Of course you don't—till I tell you. I meant 'there's a nice knock-down argument for you!'"
> "But 'glory' doesn't mean 'a nice knock-down argument,'" Alice objected.
> "When I use a word," Humpty Dumpty said, in a rather scornful tone, "it means just what I choose it to mean—neither more nor less."
> "The question is," said Alice, "whether you can make words mean so many different things."
> "The question is," said Humpty Dumpty, "which is to be master—that's all."
>
> —Lewis Carroll, *Through the Looking Glass*

LO¹
Understandings and Misunderstandings

Most people vastly overestimate how well others understand them and how well they understand others.[2] Therefore, we'll begin by looking at the rules we use to understand—and misunderstand—one another's speech.

Understanding Words: Semantic Rules

Semantic rules govern the meaning that is assigned to words. They make it possible for us to agree that bikes are for riding and books are for reading, and help us know

"Let me get this straight now. Is what you want to build a jean factory or a gene factory?"

> Language ... came from our desire to transcend our isolation and have some sort of connection with one another ... When we communicate with one another and we feel that we have connected and we think that we're understood, we have a feeling of almost spiritual communion. And that feeling might be transient, but it's what we live for.
>
> —From the film *Waking Life*

whom we will or won't encounter when we enter a restroom. Without semantic rules, communication would be impossible because everyone would use symbols in unique ways and there would be no shared meaning.

Semantic misunderstandings arise when people assign different meanings to the same words. In the next few pages, we will look at some of the most common misunderstandings.

"What part of oil lamp next to double squiggle over ox don't you understand?"

© Eric Lewis/The New Yorker Collection/www.cartoonbank.com

Equivocation

Equivocal language consists of words, word orders, phrases, or expressions that have more than one commonly accepted definition, as the following newspaper headlines illustrate:

> Family Catches Fire Just in Time
> Man Stuck on Toilet; Stool Suspected
> 20-Year Friendship Ends at the Altar

Some equivocal misunderstandings can be embarrassing. One woman recalled that when she was in Grade 4, the teacher asked the class what a period was. She shared everything she had learned about girls getting their period! Of course, the teacher was talking about the dot at the end of sentences.[3]

Other examples of equivocal statements are more serious. A nurse gave a client a scare when she told him that he "wouldn't be needing" his robe, books, and shaving materials anymore. The patient became exceptionally quiet, and when she inquired about his behaviour, she discovered that the poor man thought he was going to die. Instead, the nurse meant he was going home.

The seemingly simple phrase of "I love you" illustrates the various ways in which three simple words can be interpreted. Imagine the troubles that can—and do—arise when people express their love to one another without really knowing what their notion of *love* means.

Because it's difficult to catch and clarify every equivocal statement while speaking, the responsibility for interpreting statements accurately rests in large part with the receiver.

Relative Language

Relative words gain their meaning through comparison. For example, whether or not you attend a large or small institution depends on what the others are like. Alongside a campus like the University of British Columbia with over 30,000 students, your university or college may seem small. But compared with even smaller institutions, it could be quite large. Relative words such as *fast, slow, smart, stupid, short,* or *long* can only be defined through comparison.

Some relative terms are so common that we mistakenly assume they have a clear meaning. But if you try to turn them into something measurable, they become clearer. Health care practitioners have learned that patients often use vague descriptions to describe their pain: "It hurts a little," or "I'm pretty sore." Using a numeric pain scale can give a more precise response—and lead to a better diagnosis.[4] When patients rank their pain from 1 to 10, with 10 being the most severe pain they've ever experienced, the number 7 becomes more concrete and specific than "It aches a bit." This technique can be used to rate anything from the movies to job satisfaction.

When factual and inferential statements are set side by side like this, the difference between them is clear. In everyday conversation,

Equivocal language
Words, word orders, phrases, or expressions that have more than one commonly accepted definition.

Relative words
Words that gain their meaning through comparison.

however, we often present our inferences as if they were facts, and in doing so we invite an unnecessary argument.

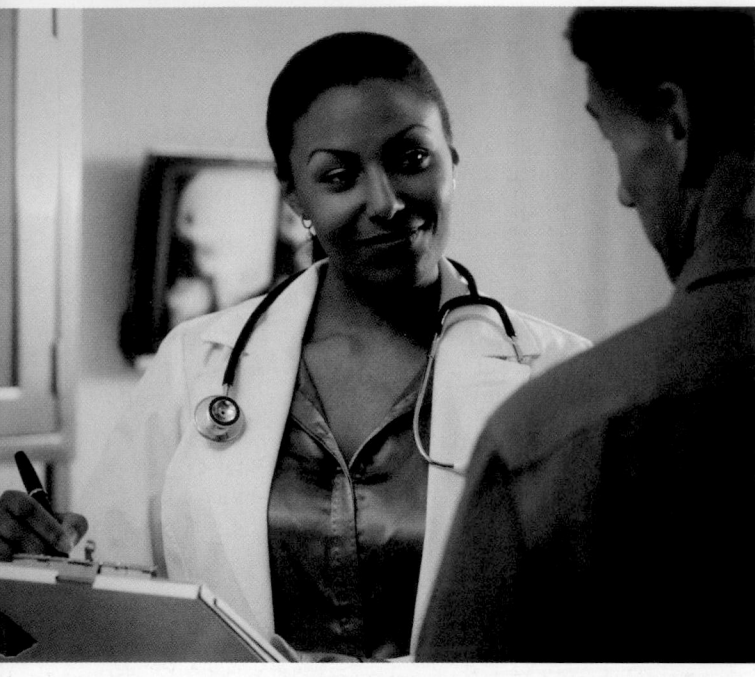

© iStockphoto.com/Steve Cole

> **Conversation has more vitality, more fun and more drama than writing. What I say is being used as a probe and it's not a package. I'm probing around without making special pronouncements. Most people say things as the result of thinking, but I use it to probe.**
>
> —Marshall McLuhan, quoted in *Weekend Magazine*

Static Evaluation

"Matt is a nervous guy." "Grace is short-tempered." "You can always count on Jonathan." Statements that contain or imply the word *is* lead to the mistaken assumption that people are consistent and unchanging—an incorrect belief known as **static evaluation**. Instead of labelling Matt as permanently nervous, it's more accurate to indicate the situations in which he behaves nervously. The same goes

A Philosopher's View of Love

Mike Flippo/Shutterstock.com

Shakespeare famously said that "love is a many splendored thing." It is also a many 'meaning-ed' thing because we don't always know what someone means when they say they love something. We say we love all sorts of things—ice cream, a car, a favorite singer, God, siblings, parents, or a romantic partner, but do these expressions of love have anything in common?

Plato suggested that they do. They all express a desire for something we don't possess but are moved to do so. Therefore, whether it's a shirt or a person you love, you want them to be yours, or to continue possessing them if they're already yours.

But what makes you love someone or something and hence desire to possess it? Here, we find a wide variety of answers. Some scholars say that your love of something is based on the object's qualities (we love a house because of its location or a person because of his or her looks). Others say that this is shallow love, only applicable to things. We don't, after all, trade in our partners whenever a newer, more striking version comes along. Some argue that love is more like a gift, modeled after God's love of humans—He loves us in spite of, not because of our qualities. This position also misses something because we fall in love with people because of their qualities. Perhaps both views should be combined. We start by falling in love with the person's qualities but that love transcends those qualities so, e.g., it's her particular sense of humor we love, and not humor in general.

While all uses of the word *love* have something in common, our love of things and people differ substantially. Perhaps we don't recognize this because we don't attend to the various meanings of love.

Robert Scott Stewart
Cape Breton University

Courtesy of Scott Stewart

for Grace, Jonathan, and the rest of us: We are much more changeable than static.

Abstraction

When it comes to describing problems, goals, appreciation, and requests, we can choose vague, unclear **abstract language** or **behavioural language** that refers specifically to things that people do or say, or language somewhere in between. Figure 5.1 illustrates how an event or situation can be described at various levels of specificity and abstraction along an **abstraction ladder**. The ladder's bottom-rung description is concrete and behavioural, and thus is probably clearer than the top-rung's abstract injunction to develop a "better attitude."

We often use higher-level abstractions as verbal shorthand. For instance, we say, "Thanks for cleaning up," instead of using more specific language, such as, "Thanks

FIGURE 5.1

Abstraction Ladder

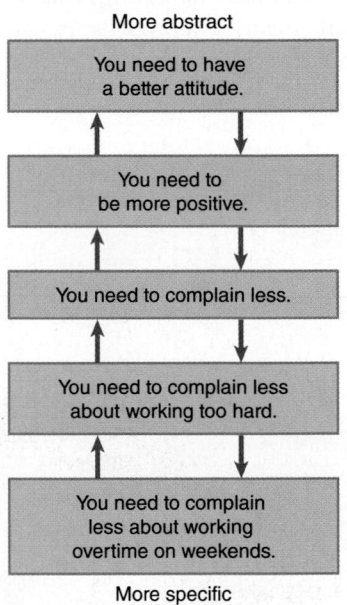

More abstract

You need to have a better attitude.

You need to be more positive.

You need to complain less.

You need to complain less about working too hard.

You need to complain less about working overtime on weekends.

More specific

"Be honest with me, Roger. By 'mid-course correction' you mean divorce, don't you."

for washing the dishes, vacuuming the rug, and making the bed." Sometimes politicians use high-level abstraction so they can make speeches without making any specific commitments that may be held against them later.

Although such verbal shorthand can be useful, highly abstract language can also lead to blanket judgments and stereotyping: "Marriage counsellors are worthless," "Mounties are rude," or "Skateboarders are delinquents." Overly abstract expressions like these can cause people to *think* in generalities, ignoring uniqueness. Such stereotyping can injure interpersonal relationships by categorizing and evaluating people in ways that may not be accurate.

To ensure clarity on your part, try to begin with a general statement and follow it with specific examples—in other words, work from high- to low-level abstraction. A boss might say to employees, "While I was away, you did a

Abstract language
Language that is vague and unclear.

Behavioural language
Language that refers to specific things that people do or say.

Abstraction ladder
A range of more to less abstract terms describing an event or object.

cathy

by Cathy Guisewite

Excerpt from "Method for Calling Up Ghosts" by Al Purdy, *Beyond Remembering: The Collected Poems of Al Purdy*, edited and selected by Al Purdy and Sam Solecki; Harbour Publishing, 2000.

And something I've thought
of every now and then:
how everything we do or say
has an effect somewhere,
passes outward from itself
in widening circles,
a sort of human magic by
which a word moves outside
the nature of a word
as side effect of itself
the nature of a word being
that when it's been said
it will always be said
— a recording exists in
the main deep of sound.

—Al Purdy,
"Method for Calling Up Ghosts"

great job. You dealt with some difficult customers, you got the orders out on time, and you got the interns lined up with their mentors."

Understanding Structure: Syntactic Rules

Syntactic rules
Rules that govern the way symbols can be arranged, as opposed to the meanings of those symbols.

Syntactic rules govern the grammar of a language. You can appreciate how syntax contributes to the meaning of a statement by considering two versions of a letter:

Version 1
Dear John:

I want a man who knows what love is all about. You are generous, kind, thoughtful. People who are not like you admit to being useless and inferior. You have ruined me for other men. I yearn for you. I have no feelings whatsoever when we're apart. I can be forever happy—will you let me be yours?

Mary

SKILL BUILDER

Down-to-Earth Language

You can appreciate the value of non-abstract language by translating the following into behavioural terms.

In each case, describe the person or persons involved, the circumstances in which the behaviour occurs, and the precise behaviours involved. What differences can you expect when you use behavioural descriptions like the ones you have created here?

1. An abstract goal for improving your interpersonal communication (for example, be more assertive or stop being so sarcastic)

2. A complaint you have about another person (for example, that he or she is "selfish" or "insensitive")

3. A request for someone to change (for example, "I wish you'd be more punctual," or "Try to be more positive")

4. An appreciation you could share with another person (for example, "Thanks for being so helpful," or "I appreciate your patience")

123render/iStockphoto

Version 2

Dear John:

I want a man who knows what love is. All about you are generous, kind, thoughtful people, who are not like you. Admit to being useless and inferior. You have ruined me. For other men, I yearn. For you, I have no feelings whatsoever. When we're apart, I can be forever happy. Will you let me be?

Yours,

Mary

Semantic rules don't explain why these letters send virtually opposite messages; the different meanings come from the syntax.

Although most of us aren't able to describe the syntactic rules that govern our language, we recognize when they are violated. A humorous example is the way the character Yoda speaks in the *Star Wars* movies. Phrases such as "the dark side are they" or "your father he is" often elicit a chuckle because they bend syntactical norms. Sometimes, however, apparently ungrammatical speech is simply following a different set of syntactic rules, reflecting regional or co-cultural dialects. Linguists believe it is crucial to view such dialects as *different* rather than *deficient* forms of English.[5]

Understanding Context: Pragmatic Rules

Semantic and syntactic problems don't account for all misunderstandings.[6] To appreciate a different type of communication challenge, imagine a young female's response to her older male boss's statement "You look nice today." She would understand the meaning of the words, and the syntax is clear. The message, however, could have several interpretations: a simple compliment, a come-on, or a suggestion that she didn't normally look nice. If the boss

"I never said 'I love you.' I said 'I love ya.' Big difference."

© Leo Callum/The New Yorker Collection/www.cartoonbank.com

and employee share the same interpretation, their communication would be smooth. If they interpret the statement differently, potential problems and tensions could arise. This example might also be explained by using the terms *denotative meaning* and *connotative meaning*. Denotative refers to the dictionary meaning of a word; connotative refers to what a particular word or phrase means to you. While the dictionary meaning of the word *nice* might be *pleasant, pleasing, and agreeable,* in the context described here, you can see how the young woman is trying to determine what her boss's connotative meaning is.

In situations like this, we rely on **pragmatic rules** to decide how to interpret messages in a given context. Pragmatic rules govern the way speech operates in

> **Pragmatic rules**
> Linguistic rules that help communicators understand how messages may be used and interpreted in a given context.

When Syntactic Rules Are Broken

Sometimes, seemingly ungrammatical speech is simply following a different set of syntactic rules. The English spoken by some members of the black community— a form of speech recently termed by some as Ebonics— treats forms of the verb *to be* differently than does standard English.[1] An ungrammatical expression like "I be angry" is perfectly correct in Ebonics and means "I've been angry for a while." Ebonics might loosely be referred to as pidgin, a speech variety that blends two or more languages in a simplified syntactic structure.

In southeast New Brunswick, many francophones speak a linguistic variation called *chiac*, a combination of French and English. *Chiac* speakers, however, "experience disparaging remarks concerning their vernacular, and many experience significant hardships in learning

'standard' French in school."[2] Cooperative education placement officers note that *chiac*-speaking students have difficulty securing employment in private and government offices where standard English and/or French is the norm.

1. M. L. Hecht, M.J. Collier, & S.A. Ribeau (1993). *African American Communication: Ethnic Identity and Cultural Interpretation.* Newbury Park, CA: Sage, pp. 84–89.
2. R. Allard & R. Landry (1998). "French in New Brunswick." In J. Edwards (Ed.). *Language in Canada.* Cambridge: Cambridge University Press, pp. 202–225.

Double Double, Please: The Language of Tim Hortons

Imagine landing in Canada and going to Tim Hortons for the first time. Upon arriving at "Tim's," "Timmy's," or "Horton's," you notice a peculiar ordering ritual. You hear words like "medium double double," "large triple single," "small French vanilla," "large with milk," "double cup it," "medium tea with milk, bag in," etc. It's almost as if you have to learn a new language just to order a coffee! Here's a quick lesson in this precise, built-for-speed Hortons dialogue.

If you want a large coffee with two creams and two sugars, plus a Boston cream doughnut, you say, "Large double double and a Boston cream." You don't say "coffee," "cappuccino," or "doughnut," just the size and type will do. Note that the cream always comes first, the sugar second. If you want milk, however, you must state that outright, and this holds for Sugar Twin as well. So if you want a small coffee with two milks and one Sugar Twin, you will order "small double single with milk and twin."

It's expected that patrons know how to order in Tim Hortonese, and employees can become frustrated with customers who don't know the language. So don't make any mistakes. For instance, do not order a "medium regular with one cream and one sugar" because a "medium regular" is a coffee with one cream and one sugar. All you need to say is, "medium regular."

A typical order from a patron may be: a large cup of coffee with milk, a large cup of French vanilla cappuccino, and two sour cream–glazed doughnuts. With the Tim Hortons "no muss, no fuss, that's us" language style, all the customer has to say is, "a large with milk, a large French vanilla, and two sour cream–glazed," and they're on their way!

Dawn White

---

everyday interaction, and there are no pragmatic rules in any dictionary. They're typically unstated, but they're just as important as semantic and syntactic rules when trying to make sense of others' messages.

To appreciate how pragmatic rules operate, think of communication as a kind of cooperative game where success depends on everyone understanding and following the same rules. This is why communication scholars use the term *coordination* to describe the way conversation operates when everyone involved uses the same set of pragmatic rules.[7] For example, if someone says to you, "What's up?" you wouldn't look upwards to see. You know that the phrase is a way of asking what was new. You'd also know not to give a lengthy response, so you might say, "Not too much. How's it going with you?" As English speakers, we understand the unspoken pragmatic rules. However, a person with a limited knowledge of English might be confused by the question "What's up?"

Interestingly, people in individual relationships also create their own sets of pragmatic rules. Consider the use of humour. The teasing and joking you exchange with one friend might be considered tasteless or offensive in another relationship.[8] For instance, imagine an e-mail message typed in CAPITAL LETTERS and filled with CURSE WORDS, INSULTS, NAME-CALLING, and EXCLAMATION MARKS!!! How would you interpret such a message? An observer may consider this an example of "flaming" and be appalled, when in fact the message might be a fun-loving case of "verbal jousting" between buddies.[9]

If you have a good friend you call by a less-than-tasteful nickname as a term of endearment, then you understand the concept. However, those who aren't privy to your relationship's pragmatic rules are likely to misunderstand you, so you'll want to be wise about when and where to use these "personal codes."

Invitation TO INSIGHT

Your Linguistic Rules

To what extent do linguistic rules affect your understanding of and relationships with others? Explore this question by following these steps:

1. Recall a time when you encountered someone whose speech violated the syntactic rules that you're used to. What was your impression of this person? To what degree was this impression influenced by her or his failure to follow familiar linguistic rules? Consider whether this impression was or was not valid.

2. Recall at least one misunderstanding that arose when you and another person followed different semantic rules. Use hindsight to consider whether this misunderstanding (and others like it) could be avoided. If semantic misunderstandings can be minimized, explain what approaches might be useful.

3. Identify at least two pragmatic rules that govern the use of language in one of your relationships. Share these rules with other students. Do they use language in the same way as you and your relational partner?

LO² The Impact of Language

In addition to helping communicators understand one another, language also shapes our perceptions and reflects the attitudes we hold toward one another.

Naming and Identity

"What's in a name?" Juliet asked rhetorically. If Romeo had been a social scientist, he would have answered, "A great deal."

Research has demonstrated that names shape the way others think of us, the way we view ourselves, and the way we act. Early studies of the impact of naming claimed that people with unusual names suffered everything from psychological and emotional disturbance to failure in college.[10] This may account for why international students anglicize their names—Yingqi becomes Christy and Quin becomes Becky. More recent studies show that people even have negative appraisals of unusual name spellings.[11] This is interesting, given that BabyCenter (see below) indicated that Canadian parents tend to give popular names different spellings. For instance, they found the popular name Kaitlyn was spelled at least nine different ways: Kaitlyn, Kaitlin, Katelynn, Katelyn, Caitlyn, Caitlin, Caitlynn, Katelyn, and Kaitlyn.[12]

Of course, what makes a name (and its spelling) unusual changes with time. In 1900, Bertha, Mildred, and Ethel were among the most popular baby names. In 2009, names like Madison, Ava, and Chloe, which would have been unusual a century ago, were the most popular names for Canadian baby girls and boys names included Aiden, Ethan, and Lucas.[13]

> I also have to thank my wife, Mrs. Hank Snow.
>
> —Hank Snow, born in Nova Scotia, accepting a country-and-western music award in the fall of 1979

Recognizing how names affect one's identity, many women wonder how they should label themselves after marriage. Should they take their husband's last name, hyphenate their own and their husband's name, or keep their birth name? One study found that women who took their husband's names placed the most importance on relationships and issues of self were the least important. Women keeping their names put their personal concerns ahead of the relationship and social expectations. Women who hyphenated their names fell somewhere between the groups, valuing self and relationships equally.[14]

Then there's the question of how to address women. Men are always addressed as Mr., whereas women may be called Ms., Miss, or Mrs. The form of address can influence others' perceptions of them, as well as their own self-concept and behaviour. Most people know what Miss or Mrs. signifies, but many people erroneously believe that Ms. signifies a divorced woman. However, Ms. is simply the equivalent of Mr., which doesn't identify a person's marital status. Therefore, Ms. White could be married, single, divorced, separated, or otherwise.

The power of naming extends beyond individuals. The terms used to label groups affects the way they regard themselves and the way others view them. For instance, people with disabilities prefer to be called just

Canada's Top Baby Names

You can generally tell someone's approximate age by their names, because certain names tend to be popular at certain times. BabyCenter has compiled its annual list of popular Canadian baby names for 2009. Take a look below.

BabyCenter Canada's Top 15 Girls' Names

1.	Kaitlyn	9.	Sophie
2.	Sophia	10.	Danica
3.	Olivia	11.	Madison
4.	Emma	12.	Chloe
5.	Ava	13.	Abigail
6.	Isabella	14.	Peyton
7.	Mikayla	15.	Brooklyn
8.	Emily		

BabyCenter Canada's Top 15 Boys' Names

1.	Aiden	9.	Logan
2.	Ethan	10.	Cayden
3.	Lucas	11.	Jackson
4.	Liam	12.	Alexander
5.	Noah	13.	Evan
6.	Jacob	14.	Nathan
7.	Jayden	15.	William
8.	Jack		

Republished with permission from babycentre.ca

that, people with disabilities, rather than disabled.[15] If you stop and think for a moment, referring to individuals as disabled automatically excludes other possibilities and reduces their personhood to that of disability. Referring instead to a person with a disability suggests that the disability is simply one attribute of many that the individual possesses.

Affiliation

How we speak can also build and demonstrate solidarity with others. For instance, communicators are attracted to others whose style of speaking is similar to theirs.[16] Likewise, communicators who want to affiliate with someone adapt their speech by altering their vocabulary choice, rate, number and placement of pauses, and level of politeness.[17] Adolescents who all adopt the same vocabulary of slang words and speech mannerisms illustrate the principle of linguistic solidarity. The same process works among members of street gangs or military personnel. One study even showed that adopting the swearing patterns of bosses and co-workers can help people feel connected on the job.[18] Communication researchers call the process of adapting one's speech style to match that of others **convergence.** We also see convergence in cyberspace. Members of online communities develop a shared language or conversational style, and their affiliation is evident through the use of the word *we*.[19] On a larger scale, IM and e-mail users use shortcuts that mark them as Internet-savvy. If you know what ROTFL, IMHO, and JK mean, you're probably part of that group. (For the uninitiated, those acronyms mean "Rolling on the floor laughing," "In my humble opinion," and "Just kidding.") Interestingly, IMers may find that their cyberlanguage creeps into everyday conversations.[20] It's not uncommon for people to say "LOL" instead of "laughing out loud."

Communicators also adapt their speech to gain acceptance. For instance, immigrants strive to master the host language in hopes of gaining material success. And employees seeking advancement speak more like their superiors.

But the principle of speech accommodation also works in reverse. Communicators who want to distance themselves from others adopt the strategy of **divergence**—speaking in a way that emphasizes their differences. For example, a lawyer or physician who wants to establish credibility with a client might use more professional jargon to demonstrate their knowledge and show how different they are. You also see this with teens who adopt the slang of particular subcultures to show divergence with adults and convergence with their peers.[21]

Of course, it's important to recognize when and when not to use convergence or divergence. Using ethnic or racial epithets when you're not a member of that in-group can be inappropriate and even offensive. One of the pragmatic goals of divergence is the creation of norms about who has the "right" to use certain words and who does not.

Power

There are also language patterns that add to or detract from a speaker's power to influence others. Notice the difference between these two statements:

> "Excuse me, Professor. I hate to say this, but I . . . uh . . . I guess I won't be able to turn in the assignment on time. I had a personal emergency, and . . . well . . . it was just impossible to finish it by today. I'll have it on your desk on Monday, OK?"

> "I won't be able to turn in the assignment on time. I had a personal emergency, and it was impossible to finish it by today. I'll have it on your desk Monday."

AT THE MOVIES

Mean Girls (2004), Rated 13+

To see linguistic convergence in action, you might want to watch *Mean Girls*. Cady Heron (Lindsay Lohan) was raised in African bush country by her zoologist parents and has her first formal schooling experience at North Shore High in the US. She soon learns that social life there is as vicious as anything she witnessed in the wild.

At the urging of her unpopular friends, Cady infiltrates the popular Plastics clique, and part of fitting in is learning their slang, which includes terms like "fetch" (cool), "word vomit" (babbling), and the self-explanatory "fugly." But the more Cady uses the Plastics slang, the more her values and behaviours become like theirs. By movie's end, she makes some important decisions about herself and her friends.

Convergence
The process of adapting one's speech style to match that of others with whom the communicator wants to identify.

Divergence
Speech mannerisms that emphasize a communicator's differences from others.

Angela Hampton/GetStock.com

Powerful speech is one way—but not the only way—to get what you want.

identifies several language markers that are illustrated in the statements you just read. This speaking style is referred to as powerless language, ingratiating language, or **deferential language**[22] where the speaker includes hedges, hesitations, intensifiers, polite forms, tag questions, and disclaimers in their message. Speakers whose talk is free of these mannerisms are rated as more competent, dynamic, and attractive than speakers who defer to the listener.[23] Nondeferential language (the absence of the markers noted above) can help candidates in job interviews in that applicants using a nondeferential style are thought to be more competent and employable than candidates who speak less forcefully.[24] Even using a single type of powerlessness marker can make you appear less authoritative or socially attractive.[25]

While deferential language gets results in North American, it's not so successful elsewhere. In Japan, where saving face for others is important,[26] communicators tend to speak in ambiguous terms and use hedge words and qualifiers. In Mexico, to prevent others from feeling ill at ease, people use the deferential markers described here, and in Korea, indirect language (e.g., "perhaps," "could be") is preferred over "direct" speech.

Even in cultures that value assertiveness, language that is *too* powerful may intimidate or annoy others. Consider these two different approaches to handling a common situation:

> "Excuse me. My baby is having a little trouble getting to sleep. Would you mind turning down the music just a little?"

Whether or not the professor finds the excuse acceptable, it's clear that the second one sounds more confident, whereas the first is apologetic and uncertain. Table 5.1

TABLE 5.1

Examples of Deferential Language

Hedges	"I'm *kinda* disappointed . . ." "I *think* we should . . ." "I *guess* I'd like to . . ."
Hesitations	"*Uh,* can I have a minute of your time?" "*Well,* we could try this idea . . ." "I wish you would—*er*—try to be on time."
Intensifiers	"I'm *really* glad to see you." "I'm not *very* hungry."
Polite forms	"Excuse me, *sir* . . ."
Tag questions	"It's about time we got started, *isn't it?*" "*Don't you think* we should give it another try?"
Disclaimers	"*I probably shouldn't say this, but . . .*" "*I'm not really sure, but . . .*"
Rising inflections	(See the reading on page 162 in Chapter 6)

"My baby can't sleep because your music is too loud. Please turn it down."

The more polite, if less powerful, approach would probably produce better results. If you come across as too powerful, you may get what you're seeking in the short term but make your relationship more difficult in the long term. Furthermore, statements that are too powerful can convey disrespect and superiority and are likely to antagonize rather than gain compliance.

In some situations, polite, deferential language can even enhance a speaker's effectiveness.[27] For example, an administrator might say to an assistant, "Would you mind redoing these figures?" In truth, both know that this is an order, not a request, but the questioning form is more considerate and leaves the assistant feeling better about the boss.[28] The importance of achieving both content and relational goals helps explain why a mixture of powerful speech and polite speech is usually most effective.[29]

LO[3]
Disruptive Language

Sometimes people understand one another perfectly and still wind up in a conflict. While not all disagreements can or should be avoided, you can minimize the kinds of clashes that don't need to happen by being aware of the following linguistic habits.

Fact–Opinion Confusion

Fact–inference confusion occurs when inferences are presented as facts. Factual statements can be verified as true or false. By contrast, **inferences** are conclusions based on a speaker's beliefs. See the examples below:

Fact	Opinion
You forgot my birthday.	You don't care about me.
You keep interrupting me.	You're a control freak.
It rains more in Vancouver than it does in Kamloops.	The climate is better in Kamloops than in Vancouver.

When factual and opinion statements are set side by side, the difference between them is clear. In everyday conversation, however, we often present opinions as if they were facts, and this can invite unnecessary argument. For example:

"Spending that much on a pair of shoes is a waste of money!"
"*Canadian Idol* is the best show on TV."

It would be less antagonistic if you were to say things like "I believe . . . ," "In my opinion . . . ," or "It seems to me . . ."

Problems also arise when we confuse factual statements with inferential statements. The following shows how arguments can arise when we label our inferences as facts:

A: Why are you mad at me?
B: I'm not mad at you. Why have you been so insecure lately?
A: I'm not insecure. It's just that you've been so critical.
B: What do you mean, "critical"? I haven't been critical . . .

Rather than argue with someone, a better approach is to use perception checking. Recall from Chapter 3 that you identify the observable behaviours (facts), offer two possible interpretations, and then ask the person to comment on what you've said.

"You've been asking me whether I still love you a lot lately (*fact*), and that makes me think you're feeling insecure (*1st inference*). Or maybe I'm behaving differently (*2nd inference*). What's on your mind?" (*question*)

Emotive Language

Emotive language appears to describe something but really announces the speaker's positive or negative attitude toward it. If you approve of a friend's roundabout

Philip Date/Shutterstock

SKILL BUILDER

FACT–INFERENCE CONFUSION

In small groups or alone, read the following story and then indicate whether the statements are true, false, or questionable.

A couple decided to go boating on a sunny summer day. He packed the fishing rods in the speedboat, then asked his wife if the petrol tank was full. She said, "Yes, the petrol tank is full." They drove down to the jetty, launched the boat, and sped out to sea. After about 10 minutes, the boat's motor spluttered, then stopped. They arrived back at the shore several hours later.

Statements about the Story

1. The couple went boating.
   ❏ T ❏ F ❏ ?

2. The couple intended to go fishing.
   ❏ T ❏ F ❏ ?

3. They didn't catch any fish because the motor stopped.
   ❏ T ❏ F ❏ ?

4. The motor stopped because they ran out of petrol.
   ❏ T ❏ F ❏ ?

5. They couldn't have run out of petrol because the wife had looked in the tank and had seen that it was full.
   ❏ T ❏ F ❏ ?

6. She said that the petrol tank was full.
   ❏ T ❏ F ❏ ?

7. He believed that what she said about the petrol was true.
   ❏ T ❏ F ❏ ?

8. The boat's motor stopped after 10 minutes.
   ❏ T ❏ F ❏ ?

9. The boat sped out to sea on a sunny summer day.
   ❏ T ❏ F ❏ ?

10. Because the motor broke down, they had to row back to shore.
    ❏ T ❏ F ❏ ?

11. The car they used to tow the boat had a full tank of petrol.
    ❏ T ❏ F ❏ ?

12. The water was calm.
    ❏ T ❏ F ❏ ?

For further explanation of these results, go to http://www.dh.id.au/ InfTest1.htm.

Answers: 1.T 2.? 3.? 4.? 5.? 6.T 7.? 8.? 9.F 10.? 11.? 12.?

approach to difficult subjects, you'll call her "tactful"; if you disapprove, you'll accuse her of "beating around the bush." You can appreciate how emotive words can be editorial statements when you consider these examples:

If you approve, you say	If you disapprove, you say
thrifty	cheap
traditional	old-fashioned
extrovert	loudmouth
cautious	cowardly
progressive	radical
information	propaganda
eccentric	crazy

© Marian Henley/The New Yorker Collection/www.cartoonbank.com

To avoid arguments involving emotive words, it's better to describe the person, thing, or idea in neutral terms and to label your opinions as such. Instead of saying, "Quit making sexist remarks," say, "I really don't like it when you call us girls instead of women." Not only is this more accurate, but it will be better received by others.

Emotive labels can also result in ugly consequences, as Canadian researcher Colleen Reid's work shows. She found that women living in poverty were often referred to as "welfare cases," "welfare bums," "lazy," and "bad mothers."[30]

LO[4]
The Language of Responsibility

It is through language that we can learn if speakers are willing to take responsibility for their beliefs and feelings. Such a responsibility says a great deal about a person and can shape the tone of a relationship. To see how, read on.

"It" Statements

Notice the difference between the sentences in each set:

"It bothers me when you're late."
"I'm worried when you're late."

Bitching It Out (Out with Bitching)

Different words hold different taboos for different people. I personally don't care when people swear or reference things I've only read about on Urban Dictionary. I don't feel much remorse when I use the word *lame* when referring to that Friday night I spent watching *High School Musical* by myself. But I abhor "the B word." Let me explain why.

Some say that *bitch* is an insult for both genders. That's actually what makes the word so chauvinist. The most frequently used version of *bitch* directed at women makes us think of a boss who is abrasive or a girl who always gets what she wants. The term takes on new meaning when it's used to describe men. While a woman who is a bitch is generally at the top of some social or economic hierarchy, the same term applied to a man means he is weak or subordinate (i.e., "a little bitch"). Even the height of power for a woman is a low place for men. At least, that's what the word implies.

The word *bitch* has attached itself to empowered women. If you disagree, think of the biggest, well, bitch you know. Consider describing her to someone else. What other term could you use? The word automatically comes with a superficial gender-biased archetype of power. To phase out its usage would be to help phase out the idea that women in power have different leadership capabilities than men.

Of course, *bitch* is used in other ways. For example, one can bitch about something. I find that the verb tags along with the noun's oppressive meaning. Bitching is nagging. For women it's expected; for men it shows weakness. Again, the word reinforces the gender divide. It's also a popularized term—especially visible in hip-hop and rap music—for women in general. To say that this slang definition is harmless is ridiculous. I like to think my sex is composed of more than "hoes and tricks." But that's another discussion.

The only usage I don't find fault with seems to be *bitchin'*, as in cool. That doesn't refer to any one sex. If we all try to make a conscious effort to let go of such troublesome vocabulary choices, we can make an impact in escaping their disappointing societal implications. And that's pretty bitchin'.

Alice Stanley

"Bitching It Out (Out with Bitching)" by Alice Stanley. Copyright © 2009, Alice Stanley. This article originally appeared in *The Bygone Bureau*, http://bygonebureau.com. Reprinted by permission of the author.

"It's nice to see you."
"I'm glad to see you."

"It's a boring class."
"I'm bored in the class."

As their name implies, **"it" statements** replace the personal pronoun *I* with the less immediate word *it*. By contrast, **"I" language** clearly identifies the speaker as the source of a message. Communicators who use "it" statements attribute ownership to some unidentified source. This habit isn't just imprecise, it's an unconscious way to avoid taking a position.

"But" Statements

"But" statements cancel out the thought that precedes it:

"You're really a great person, but I think we ought to stop seeing each other."
"You've done good work for us, but we're going to have to let you go."
"This paper has some good ideas, but because it's late, it gets a D."

This approach can be a face-saving strategy but when the goal is to be absolutely clear, it's better just to state the central idea without the distraction of the "but" statement.

HERMAN®

8-29 © 1986 Jim Unger

"Four blocks north. If it's not there, eight blocks south."

HERMAN © Jim Unger/Dist. by Newspaper Enterprise Association, Inc.

© iStockphoto.com/Rich Legg

Invitation TO INSIGHT

Conjugating "Irregular Verbs"

To demonstrate emotive language, try this simple technique. Take an action or personality trait and show how it can be viewed either favourably or unfavourably, according to the label it's given. For example:

I'm casual.
You're a little careless.
He's a slob.
Or try this one:
I'm thrifty.
You're money conscious.
She's a tightwad.

1. Try a few conjugations yourself, using the following statements:
   a. I'm tactful.
   b. I'm conservative.
   c. I'm quiet.
   d. I'm relaxed.
   e. My child is high-spirited.
   f. I have high self-esteem.

2. Now recall at least two situations in which you used emotive language as if it was a description of fact and not an opinion. A good way to recall these situations is to think of a recent disagreement and imagine how the other people involved might have described it differently than you.

Questions

Some questions are sincere requests for information, while others are just a way to avoid making a declaration. "How many textbooks are assigned in that class?" may hide the statement "I'm afraid to get into a class with too much reading." Or "Are you doing anything tonight?" can be a less risky way of saying, "I want to go out with you tonight."

Sometimes being indirect can be a tactful way to approach a difficult topic, but when used unnecessarily, it can be a way to avoid saying what you mean.

"I" and "You" Language

Although there's a tendency to think that using *I* is egotistical ("I did this" and "I did that," etc.), it's also a way to take responsibility for what you say. For example, the statement "Doug did a good job" makes it sound as if it is a fact. But the job may not seem good to others, only to that individual. A more responsible statement would be, "*I think* Doug did a good job," or "*In my view*, Doug did a good job and we should hire him again." "I" language can also have a disarming effect on others and enables them to be vulnerable, if need be.

Jason Stitt/Shutterstock

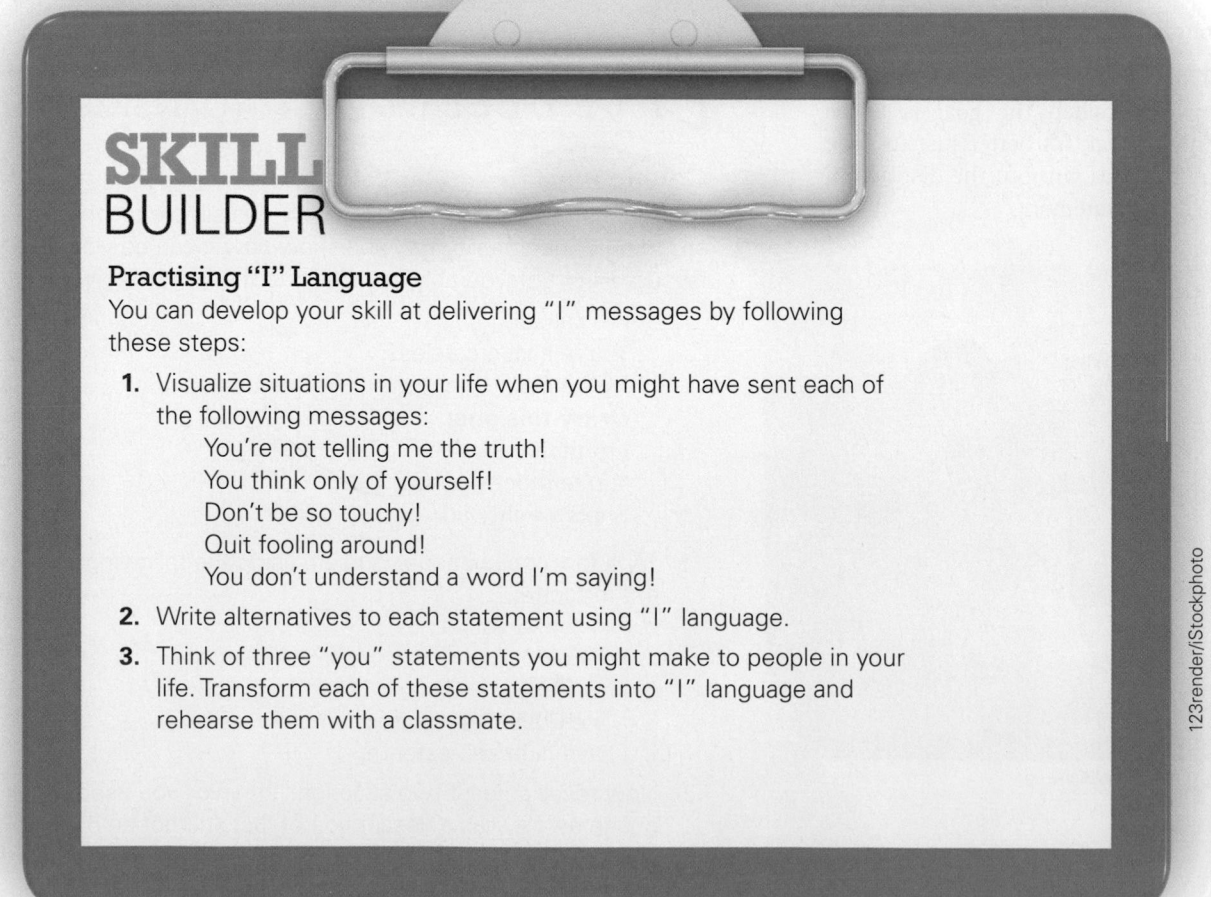

SKILL BUILDER

Practising "I" Language

You can develop your skill at delivering "I" messages by following these steps:

1. Visualize situations in your life when you might have sent each of the following messages:

   You're not telling me the truth!
   You think only of yourself!
   Don't be so touchy!
   Quit fooling around!
   You don't understand a word I'm saying!

2. Write alternatives to each statement using "I" language.

3. Think of three "you" statements you might make to people in your life. Transform each of these statements into "I" language and rehearse them with a classmate.

123render/iStockphoto

"You" language is quite different in that it judges the other person. Notice how the following statements imply that the subject of the complaint is doing something wrong:

"You left this place a mess!"
"You didn't keep your promise!"
"You're really crude sometimes!"

Other forms of "you" language don't even contain the pronoun *you*, but it is implied rather than stated outright:

"That was a stupid joke!" ["Your jokes are stupid."]
"Don't be so critical!" ["You're too negative."]
"Mind your own business!" ["You're too nosy."]

Whether stated outright or implied, "you" language arouses defensiveness in others. A less provocative and more accurate way to express a complaint is with "I" language.[31] "I" language shows that speakers take responsibility for the gripe by describing their reaction to a behaviour rather than making any judgments about its worth.

To make a complete "I" statement, you must have four parts, and they can appear in any order. They describe:

1. The other person's behaviour
2. Your interpretation
3. Your feelings
4. The consequences the other's behaviour has for you

The following examples illustrate how they sound in everyday conversation:

"I get embarrassed [*feeling*] when you talk about my bad grades in front of our friends [*behaviour*]. I'm afraid they'll think I'm stupid [*interpretation*]. That's why I got so worked up last night [*consequence*]."

Zokara/Shutterstock

"When you didn't pick me up on time this morning [*behaviour*], I was late for class, and I wound up getting chewed out by the professor [*consequence*]. It seemed to me that my being on time didn't seem important [*interpretation*]. That's why I got so mad [*feeling*]."

"I haven't been very affectionate [*consequence*] because you've hardly spent any time with me in the past few weeks [*behaviour*]. I'm not sure if you're avoiding me or if you're just busy [*interpretation*]. I'm confused [*feeling*] about how you feel about me."

For "I" statements to work, however, they must be delivered with the right tone of voice, facial expressions, and posture to be accepted. Otherwise, the listener is likely to become defensive. To make your actions match your words, remind yourself before speaking that your goal is to explain how the other's behaviour affects you, not to act like a judge and jury.

Despite its obvious advantages, even the best-constructed and delivered "I" messages won't always succeed. As author Thomas Gordon points out, "I" statements can leave the recipient feeling "hurt, sorry, surprised, embarrassed, defensive, argumentative, or even tearful."[32] Furthermore, "I" language in large doses can sound egotistical. Research shows that self-absorbed people, also known as "conversational narcissists," are identified by their constant use of *I*.[33] For this reason, "I" language works best in moderation.

"We" Language

One way to avoid overuse of "I" language is to consider the pronoun *we*. **"We" statements** imply that the issue is a concern for both parties. Consider a few examples:

"We need to figure out a budget that doesn't bankrupt us."

"I think we have a problem. We can't seem to talk about money without fighting."

"We aren't doing a very good job of keeping the place clean, are we?"

"We" language builds a constructive climate, a kind of "we're in this together" orientation that reflects the transactional nature of communication. It also signals closeness, commonality, and cohesiveness with others.[34]

But "we" statements aren't always appropriate. Some listeners will think that you're quite presumptuous to be speaking for them. You could get a response like, "We have a problem! Maybe *you* have a problem, but don't tell me *I* do!"

(In Real Life) "I" and "You" Language on the Job

Rebecca is frustrated by Tom's absences from work. She's kept quiet because she likes Tom and doesn't want to sound like a complainer. However, today was the final straw. Rebecca confronted him with "you" language.

Jason Harris © Cengage Learning

Rebecca Where have you been? You're almost an hour late!

Tom (*Surprised by Rebecca's angry tone*) I had a few errands to run. What's the problem?

Rebecca We all have errands to run, but you shouldn't do them on company time.

Tom (*Feeling defensive*) Why are you worried? The boss hasn't complained.

Rebecca That's because we all cover for you—making excuses when you're late or leave early.

Tom (*Now too defensive to consider Rebecca's concerns*) I thought we all covered for each other. I worked late for a week last year so you could go to a wedding.

Rebecca Nobody was lying then. We have to make up stories all the time about where you are. You're putting me in a difficult spot, Tom, and I can't keep covering for you.

Tom (*Feeling too guilty and angry from Rebecca's judgments to acknowledge his mistakes*) Fine. Sorry to put you out.

Now let's look at this same scenario using "I" language to describe the problem.

Rebecca Tom, I need to talk to you about a problem. (*Rebecca identifies the problem as hers instead of attacking Tom.*)

Tom What's up?

Rebecca You know how you come to work late or take long lunch hours?

Tom (*Sensing trouble ahead*) Yeah?

Rebecca Well, it's putting me in a tight spot. (*Rebecca describes the problem in behavioural terms and then express her feeling.*) When the boss asks where you are, I make excuses or even lie for you. But he's starting to get suspicious and I'm worried about that.

Tom (*Feeling defensive because he knows he's guilty but also sympathetic to Rebecca's position*) I don't want to get you in trouble. It's just that I've got a lot of personal stuff going on.

Rebecca I know. I just want you to understand that it's getting impossible to cover for you any longer.

Tom Yeah, OK. I appreciate what you've done. Thanks.

The "I" language helped Rebecca confront Tom without blaming or attacking him. Even if Tom doesn't change, Rebecca's got the problem off her chest, and she did so in a respectful way.

TABLE 5.2

Pronoun Use and Its Effects

	Advantages	Disadvantages	Tips
"I" language	Takes responsibility for personal thoughts, feelings, and wants. Less defence-provoking than evaluative "you" language.	Can be perceived as egotistical, narcissistic, and self-absorbed.	Use "I" messages when other person doesn't perceive a problem. Combine "I" with "we" language.
"We" language	Signals inclusion, immediacy, cohesiveness, and commitment.	Can speak improperly for others.	Combine with "I" language. Use in group settings to enhance unity. Avoid when expressing personal thoughts, feelings, and wants.
"You" language	Signals other-orientation, particularly when the topic is positive.	Can sound evaluative and judgmental, particularly during confrontations.	Use "I" language during confrontations. Use "you" language when praising or including others.

Because too much of any pronoun comes across as inappropriate, combining pronouns is a good idea. Researchers have found that I/we combinations (e.g., "I think that we . . ." or "I would like to see us . . .") have a good chance of being received favourably.[35] Table 5.2 (p. 132) summarizes the advantages and disadvantages of each type of language and offers suggestions for approaches that have a good chance of success.

LO[5]
Gender and Language

Do women and men communicate differently? Some researchers believe that their styles are so dramatically different it's as if they're from different cultures.[36] Others suggest that differences are minimal and insignificant.[37] After reading this section, you'll be able to judge for yourself.

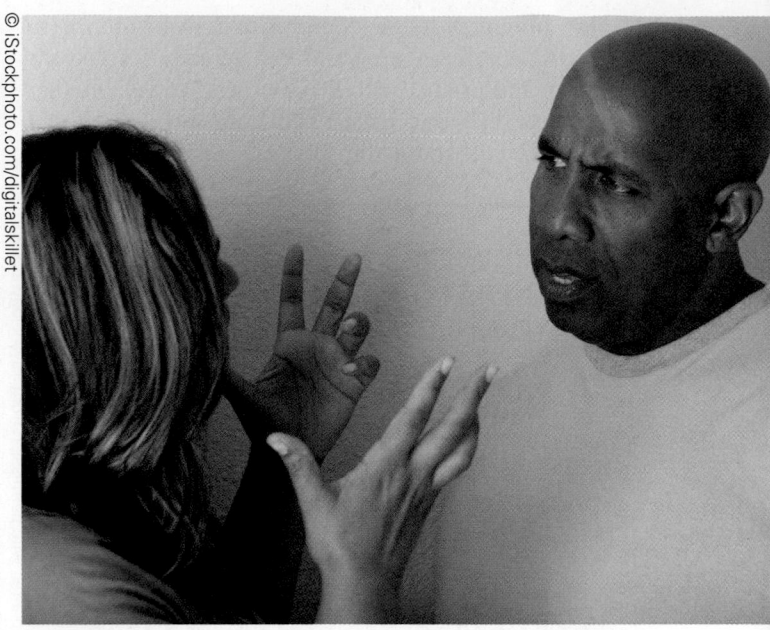

Content

Despite the changes in gender roles in the last two generations, research suggests that the content of women's and men's speech remains consistent.[38] Women and men both talk about work, movies, and television, but they reserve discussion of sex and sexuality for members of the same sex. Female friends discuss personal and domestic subjects, relationship problems, family, health and reproductive matters, weight, food and clothing, men, and other women. Men are more likely to discuss music, current events, sports, business, and other men. Both men and women were equally likely to discuss personal appearance, sex, and dating in same-sex conversations. When they gossip, women talk more about family and close friends, while men gossip about sports figures and media personalities. The gossip of neither sex was more derogatory than that of the other.

However, researchers report that men and women think that the gossip of the opposite sex is "trivial." "I want to talk about important things," a woman might say, "like how we're getting along. All he wants to talk about is the news or what we'll do this weekend." Likewise, some men complain that women ask for and offer more details than necessary and focus too often on feelings and emotions.

"Talk to me, Alice. I speak woman."

The content of women's and men conversation is so diverse that computer programs can actually scan words and syntax and predict with 80 percent accuracy whether the author is male or female.[39] The results indicated that male authors talk about things and female authors focus on feelings. The women used more pronouns (*I, you, she, their, myself*), while men used more nouns.

Reasons for Communicating

Regardless of their sex, most people communicate to maintain social relationships, and they do so by being friendly, showing interest, and talking about topics that interest the other person.[40] But *how* men and women accomplish this is often different. For instance, men are more likely to make conversations fun by including jokes and good-natured teasing. By contrast, women's discussions commonly involve feelings, relationships, and personal problems.[41] In fact, communication researcher Julia Wood flatly states that "for women, talk *is* the essence of relationships."[42] They gain a sense of satisfaction and empathy by talking with their friends in that they "know they're not alone" in their feelings and perceptions.[43] In other words, while men *like* same-sex conversations, women *need* them. For example, wives spend more time than husbands communicating in ways that help maintain their relationship.[44]

Conversational Style

While women and men behave differently in conversations, the differences aren't as dramatic as you might imagine.[45] For instance, who do you think talks more, men or women? Researchers have found that they both speak about the same number of words per day.[46] But in mixed-sex conversations, women ask more questions, while men interrupt more and are more likely to use judgmental adjectives ("Reading can be a drag"), directives ("Think of some more"), and "I" references ("I have a lot to do").[47] Women are more likely to use intensive adverbs ("He's *really* interested"), emotional references ("If he really cared about you . . ."), uncertainty verbs

> Consider the marriage of a man who has had most of his conversations with other men, to a woman who has had most of hers with other women . . . He is used to fast-paced conversations that typically stay on the surface with respect to emotions, that often enable him to get practical tips or offer them to others, and that are usually pragmatic or fun. She is used to conversations that, while practical and fun, too, are also a major source of emotional support, self-understanding, and the understanding of others. Becoming intimate with a man, the woman may finally start expressing her concerns to him as she might to a close friend. But she may find, to her dismay, that his responses are all wrong. Instead of making her feel better, he makes her feel worse. The problem is that he tends to be direct and practical, whereas what she wants more than anything else is an empathetic listener. Used to years of such responses from close friends, a woman is likely to be surprised and angered by her husband's immediate "Here's what ya do . . ."
>
> —Mark Sherman and Adelaide Haas, "Man to Man, Woman to Woman," *Psychology Today*

("It seems to me . . ."), tag questions ("It's a great day, isn't it?"), and contradictions ("It's cold, but that's OK"). Such differences make men's speech more direct, succinct, and task-oriented, whereas women's deferential speech is more indirect, elaborate, and focused on relationships.

Women are also more likely to show support, demonstrate equality, and make an effort to keep the conversation going.[48] In all, it's not surprising that female speech often contains statements of sympathy and empathy: "I've felt like that myself." Women are also inclined to invite the other person to share information: "How did you feel about that?" Because of its focus on nurturing relationships, female speech is often somewhat tentative. Saying "This is just my opinion . . ." is less likely to put off a conversational partner than a more definite "Here's what I think . . ." This deferential, accommodating style can actually make women more persuasive than men who use a more powerful language style.[49] But the style can be less effective when persuading women. Overall, women who are willing and able to be flexible in their approach can persuade both other women and men.

Women's historical role in society may at least in part account for why they tend to use a less powerful language style. If this is the case, there should be fewer differences as women gain equality. Given their concern for developing harmonious relationships, women may also use a deferential style to build rapport.[50]

A final explanation has to do with gender roles. Gender roles can influence a communicator's style more than his or her biological sex. For example, one study revealed that masculine subjects used significantly more dominance language than did either feminine or androgynous subjects.[51] Feminine subjects expressed slightly more submissive behaviours and more equivalence behaviours than did the androgynous subjects, and their submissiveness and equivalence were much greater than those of the masculine subjects, regardless of their biological sex. In gay and lesbian relationships, conversational styles reflect power differences in the relationship more than the biological sex of the communicators.[52]

Nongender Variables

But the link between gender and language use isn't as clear-cut as it might seem. Several researchers have found that men and women's communication styles are much more similar than different. For example, male

and female supervisors in similar positions behave the same way and are equally effective.

Research has revealed that factors other than gender also influence language use.[53] For example, social philosophy plays a role. Feminist wives talk longer than their partners, whereas non-feminist wives speak less than their partners. In addition, cooperative or competitive orientations of speakers have more influence on speaking style than gender.[54] So does occupation: for example, male daycare teachers' speech to their students resembles the language of female teachers more closely than it resembles the language of fathers at home.

Culture and Language

Translating ideas from one language to another isn't always easy,[55] and the sometimes bungled results can be amusing. For example, an American firm unknowingly introduced its product, Pet milk, to French-speaking markets without realizing that the word *pet* in French means "to break wind."[56] Likewise, the English-speaking representative of a soft drink manufacturer naively drew laughs from Mexican customers when she offered free samples of Fresca. In Mexican slang, the word *fresca* means "lesbian."

> Language is a steed that carries one into a far country.
>
> —Arab proverb

Invitation TO INSIGHT

O CANADA, OUR DAH DAH DAH DAH DUM

In 2002, in a movement to make the lyrics of our national anthem gender-inclusive, one Canadian senator argued that the line "all thy sons command" should be changed. Some people agreed; others did not. Then in 2010 it came up again. But given the climate when Parliament reconvened after the controversial prorogation, the issue was considered a diversion from several other controversial issues. So for the second time the move to include gender-inclusive lyrics in Canada's national anthem was dropped.

What do you think? Based on your understanding of language and communication, debate your position with someone in the class who opposes you.

Adapted from C. Cosh, "O Canada, Our Dah Dah Dah Dah Dum," *Report/Newsmagazine (Alberta Edition)*, March 18, 2002, p. 3.

Difficult as it may be, translation is only a small part of the problem. For example, Japanese insurance companies warn their policyholders who are visiting North America to avoid saying "I'm sorry" if they are involved in a traffic accident.[57] While interpreted in Japan as a sign of good will, it is perceived as an admission of guilt in North American, particularly in the US.

Differences in the way language is used can make communicating across cultures a challenging task. We see this in our own country. In Newfoundland, many people speak Newfoundland English—a dialect consisting of words and lexical items unique to Newfoundland or to specific areas of the island. For instance, *drite* refers to dryness in the air, *dwall* to a short, light sleep, *joog* to a drop of liquid, and *quoit* to skipping flat stones over the water. If you accept an offer for a bung-your-eye, you'll get a strong alcoholic beverage. The mercantile class in St. John's is referred to as the *fishocracy*. You may also hear individuals use certain past-time constructions, such as "How many times am I after telling you?" as opposed to "How many times have I told you?" These and other phonological features might be very confusing to someone who is unfamiliar with the culture and the language.[58]

Of course, the issue of language and culture is particularly salient here in Canada with its two national languages—English and French. Interestingly, both the anglophone and francophone shares of the population are actually on the decline. While Canada's population still consists mainly of English and French speakers, the number of allophones—those having a mother tongue other than French or English—has been increasingly on the rise. Allophones had made up 12.5 percent since 1996,[59] but that percentage had increased to 20.1 by 2006.[60] The 2006 census also reaffirmed that one of the Chinese languages is ranked the third-most-spoken mother tongue.[61]

Paula Solloway/ GetStock.com

People often ask me whether Canadian English is getting more Americanized—if it's going to be swallowed up by American English. Working on the dictionary, we found that, in spite of living next to this behemoth for over 200 years, we've managed to maintain our own linguistic identity and continue to invent new Canadianisms every year. "Toonie" was a good example a few years ago, and just this year we've noted a new form of floor hockey called "schlockey." At the University of Guelph, they've just developed a new kind of genetically engineered pig that they've called the "Enviropig." Who knows, maybe "Enviropig" will become as much a part of our common vocabulary as "canola" and "triticale" are now.

—Katherine Barber, editor-in-chief,
Canadian Oxford Dictionary

Courtesy of Katherine Barber

Verbal Communication Styles

When a communicator tries to use the verbal style from one culture in a different one, problems are likely to arise.[62] These can include matters related to formality and informality, precision or vagueness, and brevity or detail, and directness.

In terms of *directness*, anthropologist Edward Hall identified two distinct cultural ways of using language.[63] **Low-context cultures** use language to express thoughts, feelings, and ideas as clearly and logically as possible. Low-context communicators look for the meaning of a statement in the words spoken. By contrast, **high-context cultures** use language to maintain social harmony. Rather than upset others by speaking clearly, high-context communicators learn to discover meaning from the context in which a message is delivered: the speaker's nonverbal behaviours, the relationship's history, and the general social rules that govern the interaction. Table 5.3 summarizes some key language differences in low- and high-context cultures.

Canada and the US are low-context cultures, and we value straight talk and grow impatient with "beating around the bush." Most Asian and Middle Eastern cultures fit the high-context patterns that focus on harmony. Communicators avoid speaking clearly so as not to threaten another person's "face." They are less likely to offer a clear no to an undesirable request. Instead, they will probably use roundabout expressions like "I agree with you in principle, but . . ." or "I sympathize with you . . ." For example, Dr. Dejun Liu, a former Chinese colleague, explained that when he is at home, he speaks Chinese. He focuses on the listener and says things in an unclear fashion on purpose. He explained that one doesn't always want to be clear because understanding would emerge from the context. At the university, however, Dr. Liu's speech style was more direct and succinct. He also noted that cultural differences don't fade when we speak another language. He told the story of an Asian colleague who wasn't being promoted. She, in the Asian tradition, was waiting for her superior to tell her to apply. In Canadian universities this is not the custom, and she quickly adapted her ways.

Linguistic relativism
The notion that the world-view of a culture is shaped and reflected by the language its members speak.

Language styles also vary in terms of *elaboration* and *succinctness*. Arabic speakers, for instance, have a much richer and more expressive style than English-speaking communicators. Strong assertions and exaggerations that would sound ridiculous in English are common in Arabic. This contrast can lead to misunderstandings.

As one observer put it, first, an Arab feels compelled to overassert in almost all types of communication because others expect him [or her] to. If an Arab says exactly what he [or she] means without the expected assertion, other Arabs may still think that he [or she] means the opposite. For example, a simple no by a guest to the host's requests to eat more or drink more will not suffice. To convey the meaning that he [or she] is actually full, the guest must keep repeating no several times, coupling it with an oath such as "By God" or "I swear to God." Second, an Arab often fails to realize that others, particularly foreigners, may mean exactly what they say even though their language is simple. To the Arabs, a simple no may mean the indirectly expressed consent and encouragement of a coquettish woman. On the other hand, a simple consent may mean the rejection of a hypocritical politician.[64]

TABLE 5.3
Low- and High-Context Communication Styles

Low Context	High Context
Majority of information carried in explicit verbal messages, with less focus on the situational context.	Important information carried in contextual cues (time, place, relationship). Less reliance on explicit verbal messages.
Self-expression valued. Communicators state opinions and desires directly and strive to persuade others to accept their own viewpoint.	Relational harmony valued and maintained by indirect expression of opinions. Communicators abstain from saying no directly.
Clear, eloquent speech considered praiseworthy. Verbal fluency admired.	Communicators talk "around" the point, allowing the other to fill in the missing pieces. Ambiguity and use of silence admired.

Succinctness is most extreme in cultures where silence is valued. In many First Nations cultures, for example, the favoured way to handle ambiguous social situations is to remain quiet.[65] Contrasting this silent style to the talkativeness in mainstream North American cultures when people first meet, it's easy to imagine how the first encounter between an Inuktitut speaker and an English speaker might feel uncomfortable to both people.

Languages also differ in terms of their *formality* and *informality*. When one of the authors was studying conversational French, she had to gain a sense of when to use *vous*, the formal form of the word *you*, and *tu*, the more familiar usage, which was not only acceptable but expected. In Asia and Africa, formality isn't so much a matter of using correct grammar as of defining social position. The Korean language reflects the Confucian system of relational hierarchies[66] and has special vocabularies for each sex, for different levels of social status, for different degrees of intimacy, and for different types of social occasions. There are different degrees of formality for speaking with old friends, non-acquaintances whose background one knows, and complete strangers. A sign of a learned person is using language that recognizes these relational distinctions.

Language and Worldview

For almost 150 years, theorists have put forth the notion of **linguistic relativism**: that the worldview of a culture is

Language and Heritage

Jose Luis Pelaez/CORBIS

"Mi'ja, it's me. Call me when you wake up." It was a message left on my phone machine from a friend. But when I heard that word *mi'ja,* a pain squeezed my heart. My father was the only one who ever called me this. Because his death is so recent, the word overwhelmed me and filled me with grief.

Mi'ja (MEE-ha), from *mi hija* (me ee-HA). The words translate as "my daughter." Daughter, my daughter,

daughter of mine: They're all stiff and clumsy, and have nothing of the intimacy and warmth of the word *mi'ja*—"daughter of my heart," maybe. Perhaps a more accurate translation of *mi'ja* is "I love you." Sometimes a word can be translated into more than a meaning. In it is the translation of a worldview, a way of looking at things, and, yes, even a way of accepting what others might not perceive as beautiful. *Urraca*, for example, instead of "grackle." Two ways of looking at a black bird. One sings; the other cackles. Or *tocayola*, your name-twin and therefore your friend. Or the beautiful *estrenar*, which means to wear something for the first time. There is no word in English for the thrill and pride of wearing something new.

Spanish gives me a way of looking at myself and the world in a new way. For those of us living between worlds, our job in the universe is to help others see with more than their eyes during this period of chaotic transition.

Sandra Cisneros

shaped and reflected by the language its members speak.[67] A well-known example refers to the notion that the Inuit have many different words, somewhere between 17 to 100, for snow and for various snow conditions. Basic survival in the Arctic led the Inuit to make distinctions that would be unimportant to residents of warmer environments. And once these distinctions were made, speakers are more likely to see the world in ways that match the broader vocabulary.

Even though there is some doubt as to whether there really are so many words for snow,[68] other examples support this the principle.[69] For instance, bilingual speakers seem to think differently when they change languages. When French speakers were asked to interpret a series of pictures, their descriptions were more romantic and emotional than when they described the pictures in English. Likewise, when students in Hong Kong completed a values test, they expressed more traditional Chinese values when they answered in Cantonese than when they answered in English. Such examples demonstrate how powerful language is in shaping cultural identity.

The best-known declaration of linguistic relativism is the **Sapir–Whorf hypothesis**, formulated by Edward Sapir and Benjamin Whorf.[70] This hypothesis suggests that the language we speak affects how we interact with the world around us. Whorf observed that the language spoken by Hopi Native Americans represents a view of reality that is dramatically different from more familiar tongues. The Hopi

> **Sapir–Whorf hypothesis**
> This hypothesis suggests that the language we speak affects how we interact with the world around us.

"The Eskimos have eighty-seven words for snow and not one for malpractice."

© Leo Callum/The New Yorker Collection/www.cartoonbank.com

language makes no distinction between nouns and verbs! Therefore, people speaking Hopi see the entire world as a constant process. In English, nouns characterize people or objects as being fixed or constant, while Hopi view people and objects as constantly changing. You might say that English represents the world like a snapshot, whereas Hopi represents it more like a motion picture.

Another way in which we see linguistic relativism is that fact that some languages contain terms that have no English equivalents.[71] Here are a few examples:

nemawashi (Japanese): The process of informally feeling out all the people involved with an issue before making a decision

lagniappe (French/Creole): An extra gift given in a transaction that wasn't expected by the terms of a contract

lao (Mandarin): A respectful term used for older people, showing their importance in the family and in society

dharma (Sanskrit): Each person's unique, ideal path in life and knowledge of how to find it

koyaanisquatsi (Hopi): Nature out of balance; a way of life so crazy it calls for a new way of living

Once words like these exist, then the ideas that they represent are easier to recognize. But even without such words, each of the ideas just listed is still possible to imagine. Thus, speakers of a language that includes the notion of *lao* would probably treat its older members respectfully, and those who are familiar with *lagniappe* might be more generous.

Although language may shape thoughts and behaviour, it doesn't dominate them absolutely.

Language in the Workplace

One aspect of language that has received particular attention in the workplace is nonsexist, inclusive language—language that reflects both females and males. Researchers and practitioners alike hold that "the elimination of sexist language can improve the quality of work life and heighten employee satisfaction within the workplace."[72] Two gender researchers, Dianna Ivy and Phil Backlund, argue that using nonsexist language demonstrates sensitivity, reflects nonsexist attitudes, and strengthens expression, and is now the contemporary, accepted form of workplace communication.[73] You can do several things to eliminate sexist language practices.

Avoid the generic pronoun. Rather than use the generic pronoun *he* to describe both males and females, use *he or she* or *they*. The latter involves speaking in the plural, which is easier. Say, "Good employees get their projects completed on time," instead of "A good employee gets her or his projects completed on time."

Avoid man-linked terminology. Man-linked language refers only to men. Examples include *mailman, chairman, fireman,* and a host of others. This language maintains sex bias and perpetuates the myth that these positions are more appropriate for men than for women. Words like *man-made* and *mankind* also exclude women, and these can easily be replaced by more inclusive language. In

CHAPTER 5 Language: Barrier and Bridge

Language Sensitivity

Language to Avoid

Sexist Language

Avoid man-linked language such as *chairman, weatherman,* etc., the generic *he* to refer to a male or female, and terms like *lady doctor.* Instead, use *chairperson, meteorologist, they,* or *doctor.*

Heterosexist Language

Avoid the derogatory terms used to describe gays and lesbians and labelling someone by their sexual orientation.

Race, Ethnicity, and National Origin

Avoid referring to individuals by their race, ethnicity, or origin. Ask individuals how they wish to be named.

Disabilities

Avoid saying someone is *disabled, handicapped,* or *crippled.* Instead, use the term *person with a disability.* Don't say that someone is a *polio victim,* for instance; instead, say the person *has [or had] polio.*

Age

Don't refer to people as *old, elderly,* or *geriatric.* Instead, call them *seniors* or *senior citizens.*

---

the last number of years, names of government agencies, organizations, and businesses have been changed to reflect inclusive language. For example, Workman's Compensation is now Workers' Compensation.

Try to use inclusive language. Here are a few examples to get you started:

Sexist, Exclusive Terms	Nonsexist, Inclusive Terms
anchorman	anchor/newscaster
businessman	businessperson
chairman	chair/chairperson
fireman	firefighter
mailman	letter carrier
mankind	humanity
man-made	synthetic
ombudsman	ombudsperson
salesman	salesperson/clerk
spokesman	spokesperson/speaker

Avoid outdated word associations. In the English language, maleness is set up as the standard. For example, one of the authors of this book saw a promo for a television show titled *Women Explorers.* As the title implied, the program featured women who were or had been explorers. If male explorers had been highlighted, the title would just have been *Explorers,* not *Men Explorers.*[74] Instead of using terms like *lady lawyer, female doctor, woman minister,* or *male nurse,* just use *lawyer, doctor, minister,* or *nurse* to refer to both sexes.

Endnotes

1. O. W. Sacks (1989). *Seeing Voices: A Journey into the World of the Deaf.* Berkeley: University of California Press, p. 17.

2. B. Keysar & A. S. Henly (2002). "Speakers' Overestimation of Their Effectiveness." *Psychological Science, 13,* 207–212. See also R. S. Wyer & R. Adava (2003). "Message Reception Skills in Social Communication." In J. O. Greene & B. R. Burleson (Eds.). *Handbook of Communication and Social Interaction Skills* (pp. 291–355). Mahwah, NJ: Erlbaum.

3. T. L. Scott (Nov. 27, 2000). "Teens before Their Time." *Time,* 22.

4. W. E. Prentice (2005). *Therapeutic Modalities in Rehabilitation.* New York: McGraw-Hill.

5. W. Wolfram and N. Schilling-Estes (2005). *American English: Dialects and Variation,* 2nd ed. Malden, MA: Blackwell.

6. N. Coupland, J. M. Wiemann, & H. Giles (1991). "Talk as 'Problem' and Communication as 'Miscommunication': An Integrative Analysis." In N. Coupland, J. M. Wiemann, & H. Giles (Eds.). *"Miscommunication" and Problematic Talk.* Newbury Park, CA: Sage.

7. W. B. Pearce & V. Cronen (1980). *Communication, Action, and Meaning.* New York: Praeger. See also V. Cronen, V. Chen, & W. B. Pearce (1988). "Coordinated Management of Meaning: A Critical Theory." In Y. Y. Kim & W. B. Gudykunst (Eds.). *Theories in Intercultural Communication.* Newbury Park, CA: Sage.

8. E. K. E. Graham, M. Papa, & G. P. Brooks (1992). "Functions of Humour in Conversation: Conceptualization and Measurement." *Western Journal of Communication, 56,* 161–183.

9. P. B. O'Sullivan & A. Flanagin (2003). "Reconceptualizing 'Flaming' and Other Problematic Communication.," *New Media and Society, 5,* 67–93.

10. N. Christenfeld and B. Larsen, B. (2008). "The Name Game." *The Psychologist, 21,* 210–213.

11. A. Mehrabian, A. (2001). "Characteristics Attributed to Individuals on the Basis of Their First Names." *Genetic, Social, and General Psychology Monographs, 127,* 59–88.

12. BabyCenter. (2010). "Canada's Top Baby Names for 2009," www.babycenter.ca/pregnancy/naming/top2009. Accessed March 14, 2010.

13. Ibid.

14. K. Foss & B. Edson (1989). "What's in a Name? Accounts of Married Women's Name Choices," *Western Journal of Speech Communication, 53,* 356–373.

15. Interview with Marie Westhaver by Judith A. Rolls (January, 25, 2003).

16. See, for example, R. K. Aune & Toshiyuki Kikuchi (1993). "Effects of Language Intensity Similarity on Perceptions of Credibility, Relational Attributions, and Persuasion." *Journal of Language and Social Psychology, 12,* 224–238.

17. H. Giles, J. Coupland, & N. Coupland (Eds.) (1991). *Contexts of Accommodation: Developments in Applied Sociolinguistics.* Cambridge: Cambridge University Press.

18. Y. Baruch & S. Jenkins (2006). "Swearing at Work and Permissive Leadership Culture: When Anti-Social Becomes Social and Incivility Is Acceptable." *Leadership & Organization Development Journal, 28,* 492–507.

19. J. Cassell & D. Tversky (2005). "The Language of Online Intercultural Community Formation.," *Journal of Computer-Mediated Communication, 10,* article 2.

20. *NPR Weekend Edition* (February 18, 2006). "OMG: IM Slang is Invading Everyday English," www.npr.org/templates/story/ story.php?storyId=5221618. Accessed September 11, 2006.

21. A. Reyes (2005). "Appropriation of African American Slang by Asian American Youth." *Journal of Sociolinguistics, 9,* 509–532.

22. J. A. Rolls (1998). "The Influence of Language Style and Gender on Leadership Potential: A Review of Relevant Literature." US Educational Resources Information Centre (ERIC Document) Ed 352–686.

23. S. H. Ng & J. J. Bradac (1993). *Power in Language: Verbal Communication and Social Influence.* Newbury Park, CA: Sage, p. 27. See also A. El-Alayli, C. J. Myers, T. L. Petersen, & A. L. Lystad (2008). "I Don't Mean to Sound Arrogant, But . . .": The Effects of Using Disclaimers on Person Perception." *Personality and Social Psychology Bulletin, 34,* 130–143.

24. S. Parton, S. A. Siltanen, L. A. Hosman, & J. Langenderfer (2002). "Employment Interview Outcomes and Speech Style Effects." *Journal of Language and Social Psychology, 21,* 144–161.

25. L. A. Hosman (1989). "The Evaluative Consequences of Hedges, Hesitations, and Intensifiers: Powerful and Powerless Speech Styles." *Human Communication Research, 15,* 383–406.

26. L. A. Samovar & R. E. Porter (2001). *Communication between Cultures,* 4th ed. Belmont, CA: Wadsworth, pp. 58–59.

27. J. Bradac & A. Mulac (1984). "Attributional Consequences of Powerful and Powerless Speech Styles in a Crisis-Intervention Context." *Journal of Language and Social Psychology, 3,* 1–19.

28. J. J. Bradac (1983). "The Language of Lovers, Flovers [sic], and Friends: Communicating in Social and Personal Relationships." *Journal of Language and Social Psychology, 2,* 141–162.

29. D. Geddes (1992). "Sex Roles in Management: The Impact of Varying Power and Speech Style on Union Members' Perception of Satisfaction and Effectiveness." *Journal of Psychology, 126,* 589–607.

30. C. Reid (2004). *The Woulds of Exclusion: Poverty, Women's Health, and Social Justice.* Edmonton, AB: Qual Institute Press.

31. E. S. Kubany, D. C. Richard, G. B. Bauer, & M. Y. Muraoka (1992). "Impact of Assertive and Accusatory Communication of Distress and Anger: A Verbal Component Analysis." *Aggressive Behaviour, 18,* 337–347.

32. T. Gordon. (1974). *T.E.T.: Teacher Effectiveness Training.* New York: Wyden, p. 74.

33. R. Raskin & R. Shaw (1988). "Narcissism and the Use of Personal Pronouns." *Journal of Personality, 56,* 393–404; and A. L. Vangelisti, M. L. Knapp, & J. A. Daly (1990). "Conversational Narcissism." *Communication Monographs, 57,* 251–274.

34. A. S. Dreyer, C. A. Dreyer, & J. E. Davis (1987). "Individuality and Mutuality in the Language of Families of Field-Dependent and Field-Independent Children." *Journal of Genetic Psychology, 148,* 105–117.

35. R. F. Proctor & J. R. Wilcox (1993). "An Exploratory Analysis of Responses to Owned Messages in Interpersonal Communication." *ETC: A Review of General Semantics, 50,* 201–220; and Vangelisti et al., *Conversational Narcissism,* op. cit.

36. See, for example D. Tannen (1990). *You Just Don't Understand: Women and Men in Conversation.* New York: William Morrow; and J. Gray (1992). *Men Are from Mars; Women Are from Venus.* New York: HarperCollins.

37. K. Dindia (2006). "Men are From North Dakota, Women are From South Dakota." In K. Dindia and D. J. Canary (Eds.). *Sex Differences and Similarities in Communication: Critical Essays and Empirical Investigations of Sex and Gender in Interaction,* 2nd ed. Mahwah, NJ: Erlbaum; and D. J. Goldsmith & P. A. Fulfs (1999). "'You Just Don't Have the Evidence': An Analysis of Claims and Evidence in Deborah Tannen's *You Just Don't Understand.*" In M. E. Roloff (Ed.). *Communication Yearbook* 22. Thousand Oaks, CA: Sage.

38. See, for example, A. Haas & M. A. Sherman (1982). "Conversational Topic as a Function of Role and Gender." *Psychological Reports, 51,* 453–454; and B. Fehr (1996). *Friendship Processes.* Thousand Oaks, CA: Sage.

39. S. Argamon, M. Koppel, J. W. Pennebaker, & J. Schler (2009). "Automatically Profiling the Author of an Anonymous Text." *Communications of the ACM, 52,* 119–123.

40. R. A. Clark (1998). "A Comparison of Topics and Objectives in a Cross Section of Young Men's and Women's Everyday Conversations." In D. J. Canary & K. Dindia, (Eds.). *Sex Differences and Similarities in*

Communication: Critical Essays and Empirical Investigations of Sex and Gender in Interaction. Mahwah, NJ: Erlbaum.

41. A. DeCapua, D. Berkowitz, & D. Boxer (2006). "Women Talk Revisited: Personal Disclosures and Alignment Development." *Multilingua, 25,* 393–412.

42. J. T. Wood (1994). *Gendered Lives: Communication, Gender, and Culture.* Belmont, CA: Wadsworth, p. 141.

43. M. A. Sherman & A. Haas (June 1984). "Man to Man, Woman to Woman." *Psychology Today, 17,* 72–73.

44. J. D. Ragsdale (1996). "Gender, Satisfaction Level, and the Use of Relational Maintenance Strategies in Marriage." *Communication Monographs 63,* 354–371.

45. For a summary of research on differences between male and female conversational behaviors, see H. Giles & R. L. Street Jr. (1985). "Communication Characteristics and Behavior." In M. L. Knapp & G. R. Miller (Eds.). *Handbook of Interpersonal Communication* (pp. 205–261). Beverly Hills, CA: Sage; and A. Kohn (February 1988). "Girl Talk, Guy Talk." *Psychology Today, 22,* 65–66.

46. M.R. Mehl, S. Vazire, N. Ramírez-Esparza, R. B. Slatcher, & J. W. Pennebaker (2007). "Are Women Really More Talkative Than Men?" *Science, 317,* 82.

47. A. Mulac (2006). "The Gender-Linked Language Effect: Do Language Differences Really Make a Difference?" In K. Dindia & D. J. Canary (Eds.). *Sex Differences and Similarities in Communication: Critical Essays and Empirical Investigations of Sex and Gender in Interaction,* 2nd ed. Mahwah, NJ: Erlbaum.

48. Clark, op. cit.

49. L. L. Carli (1990). "Gender, Language, and Influence." *Journal of Personality and Social Psychology, 59,* 941–951.

50. See, for example, D. Tannen (1994). *Talking from 9 to 5: Women and Men in the Workplace: Language, Sex and Power.* New York: William Morrow; and Wood, op. cit.

51. D. G. Ellis & L. McCallister (1980). "Relational Control Sequences in Sex-Typed and Androgynous Groups." *Western Journal of Speech Communication, 44,* 35–49.

52. S. Steen & P. Schwarz (1995). "Communication, Gender, and Power: Homosexual Couples as a Case Study." In M. A. Fitzpatrick & A. L. Vangelisti (Eds.). *Explaining Family Interactions* (pp. 310–343). Thousand Oaks, CA: Sage.

53. C. J. Zahn (1989). "The Bases for Differing Evaluations of Male and Female Speech: Evidence from Ratings of Transcribed Conversation." *Communication Monographs, 56,* 59–74.

54. B. A. Fisher (1983). "Differential Effects of Sexual Composition and Interactional Content on Interaction Patterns in Dyads." *Human Communication Research, 9,* 225–238.

55. For a thorough discussion of the challenges involved in translation from one language to another, see L. A. Samovar & R. E. Porter (1991). *Communication between Cultures.* Dubuque, IA: W. C. Brown, pp. 165–169.

56. The examples in this paragraph are taken from D. Ricks (1983). *Big Business Blunders: Mistakes in International Marketing.* Homewood, IL: Dow Jones-Irwin, p. 41.

57. N. Sugimoto (March 1991) *"Excuse Me" and "I'm Sorry": Apologetic Behaviours of Americans and Japanese.* Paper presented at the Conference on Communication in Japan and the United States, California State University, Fullerton, CA.

58. For a thorough discussion, see W. O'Grady & M. Dobrovolsky (1996). *Contemporary Linguistic Analysis: An Introduction,* 3rd ed. (pp. 427–528). Toronto: Copp Clark,.

59. The Daily Online, Statistics Canada (Dec. 2002). "Census of Population: Language, Mobility and Migration," www.statcan.ca/Daily/English/02210/do21210a.htm. Accessed July 12, 2006.

60. The Daily Online, Statistics Canada (Dec. 2007). "2006 Census: Immigration, Citizenship, Language, Mobility and Migration," www.statcan.gc.ca/daily-quotidien/071204/dq071204a-eng.htm. Accessed March 21, 2010.

61. Statistics Canada (2007), op. cit.

62. A summary of how verbal style varies across cultures can be found in Chapter 5 of W. B. Gudykunst & S. Ting-Toomey (1988). *Culture and Interpersonal Communication.* Newbury Park, CA: Sage.

63. E. Hall (1959). *Beyond Culture.* New York: Doubleday, 1959.

64. A. Almaney & A. Alwan (1982). *Communicating with the Arabs.* Prospect Heights, IL: Waveland.

65. K. Basso (1970). "To Give Up on Words: Silence in Western Apache Culture." *Southern Journal of Anthropology, 26,* 213–230.

66. J. Yum (1987). "The Practice of Uye-ri in Interpersonal Relationships in Korea." In D. Kincaid (Ed.). *Communication Theory from Eastern and Western Perspectives.* New York: Academic Press.

67. T. Seinfatt (1989). "Linguistic Relativity: Toward a Broader View." In S. Ting-Toomey and F. Korzenny (Eds.). *Language, Communication, and Culture: Current Directions.* Newbury Park, CA: Sage.

68. L. Martin & G. Pullum (1991). *The Great Eskimo Vocabulary Hoax.* Chicago: University of Chicago Press.

69. H. Giles & A. Franklyn-Stokes (1989). "Communicator Characteristics." In M. K. Asante & W. B. Gudykunst (Eds.). *Handbook of International and Intercultural Communication.* Newbury Park, CA: Sage.

70. B. Whorf (1956). "The Relation of Habitual Thought and Behaviour to Language." In J. B. Carrol (Ed.). *Language, Thought, and Reality.* Cambridge, MA: MIT Press.

71. H. Rheingold (1988). *They Have a Word for It.* Los Angeles: Jeremy P. Tarcher.

72. B. Daily & M. Finch (1993). "Benefiting From Nonsexist Language in the Workplace" *Business Horizons, 36,* 30–34.

73. D. K. Ivy & P. Backlund (2008). *Gender Speak: Personal Effectiveness in Gender Communication.* Boston: McGraw-Hill, p. 147–152.

74. J. A. Rolls (2004). *Public Speaking Made Easy,* 2nd ed. Toronto: Thomson Nelson.

71% The percentage of students who go online to study for a class.

LOG IN!

LOOK was designed for students just like you—busy people who want choices, flexibility, and multiple learning options.

LOOK delivers concise, electronic resources such as discipline-specific activities, flashcards, test yourself questions, crossword puzzles, and more!

At **www.icanlookinout.com**, you'll find electronic resources such as **printable interactive flashcards, downloadable study aids, games, and quizzes** to test your knowledge of key concepts. These resources will help supplement your understanding of core **Interpersonal Communications** concepts in a format that fits your busy lifestyle.

"I really like how you use student's opinions on how to study and made a website that encompasses everything we find useful. Seeing this website makes me excited to study!"

—Abby Boston, Fanshawe College

Visit **www.icanlookinout.com** to find the resources you need today!

CHAPTER

6

Nonverbal
COM-
MUNICATION:

Messages beyond Words

What do you
THINK?
Nonverbal communication isn't as effective as verbal.

1 2 3 4 5 6 7

strongly agree   strongly disagree

LEARNING OUTCOMES

LO¹ Explain the defining characteristics of nonverbal communication as described on pages 146–156.

LO² List and offer examples of each type of nonverbal message introduced in this chapter.

LO³ Recognize how individual factors such as voice, touch, and physical attractiveness are related to nonverbal communication.

LO⁴ Become more aware of how external factors such as distance, environment, and time are related to nonverbal communication.

LO⁵ Improve your nonverbal communication in the workplace.

What's going on in the photo below? You don't have to be a mind reader to recognize that there are several unspoken messages being expressed here. Some social scientists argue that 93 percent of the emotional impact of a message comes from nonverbal sources, while others suggest a more conservative estimate of 65 percent.[1] Regardless of the precise figure, nonverbal communication plays a vital role in human interaction.

Nonverbal communication is defined as messages expressed by other than linguistic means and includes messages transmitted by vocal cues that don't involve language—sighs, laughs, and other assorted noises— and the nonlinguistic dimensions of the spoken word, such as volume, rate, pitch, and so on. Of course,

> **Nonverbal communication**
> Messages expressed by other than linguistic means.

it also includes the features most people think of when they consider nonverbal communication: body language, gestures, facial expressions, and others. Most communication scholars wouldn't define sign languages as nonverbal, however, because they are symbolic in nature, like words. (See Table 6.1.)

TABLE 6.1
The Intersection Between Verbal and Nonverbal Communication

	Verbal	Nonverbal
Vocal	spoken language	signs, snorts, grunts, laughter tone, pitch, rate, laughter
Nonvocal	sign language, emblems	Illustrators, adaptors, facial expressions body orientation

> **What you are speaks so loudly I cannot hear what you say.**
>
> —Ralph Waldo Emerson

LO[1]
Characteristics of Nonverbal Communication

In the following pages, we'll look at characteristics that are true in all the forms and functions of nonverbal communication.

Nonverbal Skills Are Vital

It's hard to overemphasize the importance of effective nonverbal communication and the ability to read and respond to others' nonverbal behaviour.[2] Some people even think that nonverbal communication is more important than verbal communication. Nonverbal encoding and decoding skills are a strong predictor of popularity, attractiveness, and socioemotional well-being.[3] Good nonverbal communicators are more persuasive and have greater success in settings ranging from careers to playing poker to romance. Sensitivity to nonverbal communication is a major part of "emotional intel-

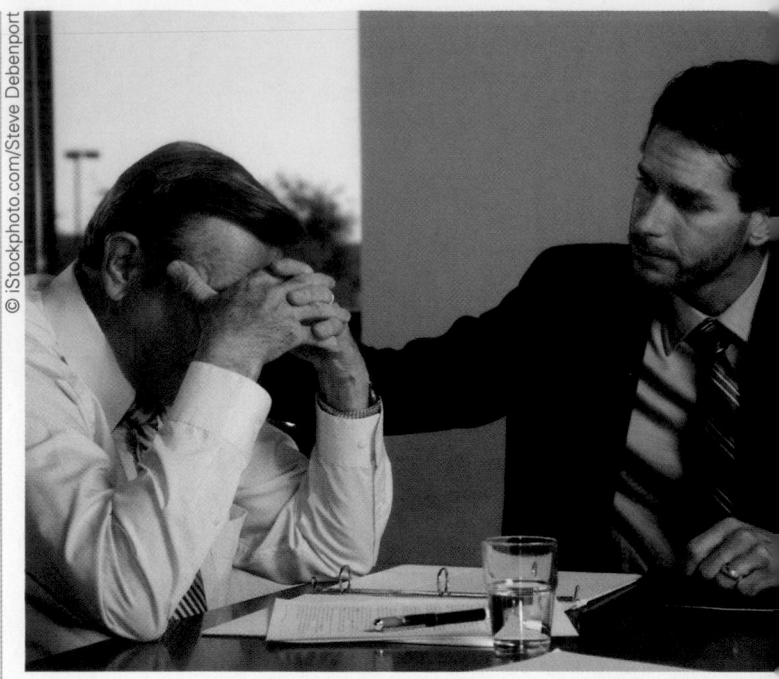

© iStockphoto.com/Steve Debenport

ligence," and researchers recognize that it's impossible to study spoken language without paying attention to its nonverbal dimensions.[4]

All Behaviour Has Communicative Value

In reality, we cannot stop communicating. The impossibility of not communicating is extremely important to understand because it means that each of us is a kind of transmitter that can't be shut off.[5] No matter what we do, we give off information about ourselves through our posture, clothing, facial expressions, eyes, and so forth.[6] Of course, we don't always intend to send nonverbal messages. Unintentional nonverbal behaviours differ from deliberate ones.[7] For example, we stammer, blush, frown, and sweat without meaning to do so. But whether or not our nonverbal behaviour is intentional, others recognize it and make interpretations about us.

Some theorists argue that unintentional behaviours provide information but it shouldn't count as communication.[8] We believe, however, that even unconscious and unintentional behaviours convey messages and are thus worth studying.

> **I could hear every word that he wasn't saying.**
>
> —Jo-Anne Rolls
> "Every Word"

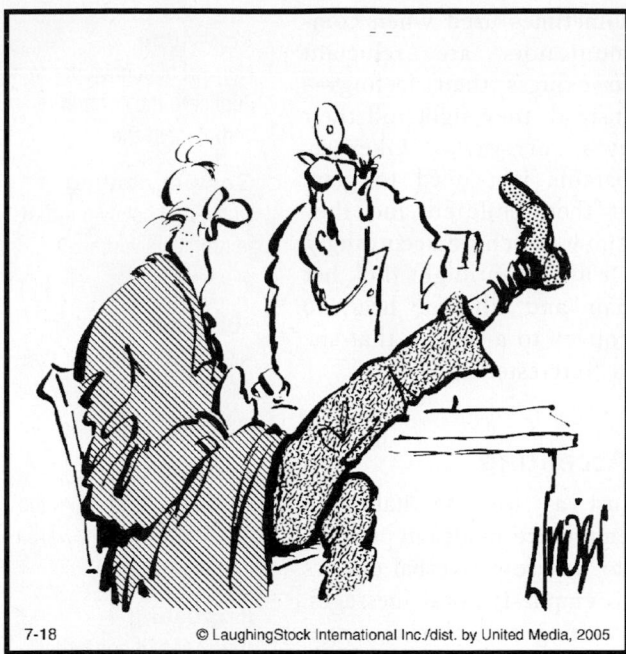

7-18   © LaughingStock International Inc./dist. by United Media, 2005

"Is your leg still stiff?"

HERMAN © Jim Unger/Dist. by Newspaper Enterprise Association, Inc.

Nonverbal Communication Is Primarily Relational

While some nonverbal messages serve utilitarian functions (police officers direct the traffic or surveyors uses hand motions to coordinate their work), nonverbal communication more commonly expresses relational and identity messages.[9]

Take identity management, for example. What do you do when you attend a party and meet new people who you'd like to get to know better? Instead of going up to someone and saying, "Hi! I'm attractive, friendly, and easygoing," you behave in ways that present your identity through nonverbal means.[10] You might smile and try to look relaxed. There's also a good likelihood that you dressed carefully—even if the image you've chosen looks as though you hadn't given a lot of attention to your appearance.

Along with identity management, nonverbal communication defines the kind of relationships we have with others. Whether you greet another person with a wave, a handshake, a nod, a smile, a clap on the back, or a hug, they each send messages about the nature of your relationship with that person.

Nonverbal communication performs a third valuable social function: conveying emotions that we may be unwilling or unable to express—or we aren't even aware of. In fact, nonverbal communication is much better suited to expressing attitudes and feelings (you're tired or you're attracted to a person in the group). It is much more limited when used to express simple facts (the book was written in 2011), past or future tenses (I was stressed yesterday), an imaginary idea (what if . . .), or conditional statements (If you don't get the job, we'll have to find a smaller place).

As technology develops, an increasing number of Internet and phone messages will include both visual and vocal dimensions, making communication richer and enhancing understanding.[11] Until that time, however, we are forced to rely on a few emoticons to relay emotional expression.[12] While such symbols are helpful, they cannot possibly substitute for the rich mixture of nonverbal messages that flow in face-to-face and telephone exchanges. This fact explains why the International Academy of Digital Arts and Sciences in the US offered a $10,000 grant to the person or group that devises "a viable way to infuse digital communication with the same individuality and unspoken cues common in face-to-face interactions."[13]

COMMUNICATION
COMPETENCE

Nonverbal Communication in Everyday Life *Seinfeld* (TV series, 1989–1998, available on DVD)

In this popular television series, familiar characters Jerry, George, Elaine, and Kramer regularly monitor, discuss, and poke fun at people's nonverbal communication traits. Fans of the show remember the "Close Talker," who infringes on others' personal and intimate space, the "Low Talker," who whispers everything she says, the "High Talker," whose vocal pitch is far higher than normal for a man, and the woman with the "man hands." Other antics occur over George's unintentional winking, the size of Elaine's head, Jerry's puffy shirt, and Kramer's body tan. The writers of the show clearly understood that people pay a great deal of attention to nonverbal communication cues.

Nonverbal Communication Serves Many Functions

Don't get the idea that words and actions are unrelated. Nonverbal behaviours can operate in tandem with verbal ones, as you'll see below. For examples, see Table 6.2 (p. 148).

> I was at a stop light, behind a car with a bumper sticker that said, "Honk if you love Jesus." I honked. The driver leaned out his window, flipped me the bird, and yelled, "Can't you see the light is still red, you moron?"
>
> —Dilbert Newsletter

Repeating

If someone asked for directions to the nearest drugstore, you might say, "North of here about two blocks," **repeating** your instructions nonverbally by pointing north. This sort of repetition isn't just decorative: People remember comments accompanied by gestures more than those made with words alone.[14]

Complementing

Even when it doesn't repeat language, nonverbal behaviour reinforces what's been said. **Complementing** nonverbal behaviours match the thoughts and emotions that the communicator is expressing verbally. For example, imagine the difference between saying "thank you" with a sincere facial expression and tone of voice, and saying the same words in a deadpan manner.

Substituting

When a friend asks, "What's up?" you might shrug your shoulders or make a face instead of answering in words. It's easy to recognize expressions that function like verbal interjections and say, "Gosh," "Really?" "Oh, please!" and so on.[15] Nonverbal **substituting** is sometimes used when communicators are reluctant to express their feelings—instead, they sigh, roll their eyes, or yawn. Likewise, parents just need to glare at their children and they know to behave accordingly. Or a woman might flick her hair and tilt her head to convey to a person that she is "interested."

Accenting

Just as we use italics to emphasize an idea in print, so do we use nonverbal devices to emphasize oral messages. Pointing an accusing finger adds emphasis to criticism. **Accenting** certain words with the voice ("It was *your* idea!") is another example.

Regulating

Nonverbal behaviours can serve to **regulate** the flow of verbal communication.[16] For example, parties in a conversation unconsciously send and receive turn-taking cues through their voice.[17] When you are ready to yield the floor, you create a rising vocal intonation pattern, then a falling one, or you draw out the final syllable at the end of your statement. Then you stop speaking. If you want to maintain your turn when another speaker is trying to cut you off, you take an audible breath, use a sustained intonation pattern (because rising and falling patterns suggest the end of a statement), and avoid any pauses in your speech.

Repeating
Nonverbal behaviours that duplicate the content of a verbal message.

Complementing
Nonverbal behaviour that reinforces a verbal message.

Substituting
Nonverbal behaviour that takes the place of a verbal message.

Accenting
Nonverbal behaviours that emphasize part of a verbal message.

Regulating
A function of nonverbal communication in which nonverbal cues control the flow of verbal communication between and among individuals.

TABLE 6.2

Some Differences between Verbal and Nonverbal Communication

	Verbal Communication	Nonverbal Communication
Complexity	One dimension (words only)	Multiple dimensions (voice, posture, gestures, distance, etc.)
Flow	Intermittent (speaking and silence alternate)	Continuous (it's impossible to not communicate nonverbally)
Clarity	Less subject to misinterpretation	More ambiguous
Impact	Has less impact when verbal and nonverbal cues are contradictory	Has stronger impact when verbal and nonverbal cues are contradictory
Intentionality	Usually deliberate	Often unintentional

Dilbert Newsletter

© iStockphoto.com/Kyu Oh

conversation). Of course, such nonverbal signals don't guarantee that the other party will pay attention, interpret, or respond in the ways we hope.

> **Beware of the man whose belly does not move when he laughs.**
>
> —Chinese proverb

Contradicting

People often simultaneously express different and even **contradicting** messages in their verbal and nonverbal behaviours. A common example of this sort of **mixed message** is the experience we've all had of hearing someone with a red face and bulging veins yelling, "Angry? No, I'm not angry!" In situations like these, we tend to believe the nonverbal message instead of the words.[18]

Even subtle mixed messages have a strong impact, and as we grow older, we become better at interpreting these contradictory messages. Children between the ages of 6 and 12 use words to make sense of a message, but adults rely on nonverbal cues to form impressions. Audiences

Contradicting
Nonverbal behaviour that is inconsistent with a verbal message.

Mixed message
Situations in which a person's words are incongruent with his or her nonverbal behaviour.

Conversations are also regulated by nodding ("I understand" or "keep going"), looking away (lack of attention), or moving toward the door (ending the

Universal/THE KOBAL COLLECTION

CHAPTER 6 Nonverbal Communication: Messages beyond Words use nonverbal cues to decide whether speakers are honest[19] as well as to judge if they are competent and composed. Further, differences in nonverbal behaviours influence how persuasive a speaker is.[20] Even the slightest contradiction in verbal and nonverbal messages may suggest that a speaker is lying.

Nonverbal Communication Offers Deception Clues

Signals of deception (lying), often called **leakage**, come through a variety of nonverbal channels, some of which are more revealing than others. While facial expressions offer important information,[21] deceivers are more likely to monitor these **deception cues** and maintain a "poker face." More reliable indicators of lying are pupil dilation[22] and vocal cues.[23] In one experiment, subjects who tried to be deceitful made more speech errors, spoke for shorter periods of time, and had a lower speech rate. Another experiment revealed that liars' voices were more high-pitched than those of truth tellers. See Table 6.3 to learn some of the conditions under which leakage is more likely.

While self-help books and seminars claim that liars can be easily identified, the scientific research doesn't support that notion. Communication scholars Judee Burgoon and Tim Levine, who have studied deception detection for years, have found three consistent results:[24]

- We are accurate in detecting deception only slightly more than half the time—in other words, only a shade better than leaving it to chance.

"I knew the suspect was lying because of certain telltale discrepancies between his voice and nonverbal gestures. Also his pants were on fire."

- We overestimate our abilities to detect others' lies—in other words, we're not as good at catching deception as we think we are.
- We have a strong tendency to judge others' messages as truthful—in other words, we want to believe people wouldn't lie to us, which biases our ability to detect deceit.

As one writer put it, "There is no unique telltale signal for a fib. Pinocchio's nose just doesn't exist, and that makes liars difficult to spot."[25] Furthermore, many prescriptions about liars' nonverbal behaviours are inaccurate. For example, people erroneously believe that liars don't make eye contact and fidget. In reality, liars often sustain *more* eye contact and fidget *less*, in part because they believe that to do otherwise might look deceitful.[26] Popular characterizations of "scientific" lie detection aren't helpful either. One experiment found that viewers who watched the television show *Lie to Me* were actually *worse* at detecting lies than non-viewers, in part because the show focused on nonverbal cues and ignored important verbal content.[27] Therefore, caution should be exercised in making evaluations of others' truth-telling based on limited and ambiguous nonverbal cues.

Nonverbal Communication Is Ambiguous

Nonverbal messages are even more ambiguous than verbal ones. Even something as simple as a wink can be interpreted by college students, for instance, as an

Leakage
Nonverbal behaviours that reveal information a communicator does not disclose verbally.

Deception cues
Nonverbal behaviours that signal the untruthfulness of a verbal message.

TABLE 6.3

Leakage of Nonverbal Cues to Deception

Deception Cues Are More Likely When the Deceiver
Wants to hide emotions being felt at the moment
Feels strongly about the information being hidden
Feels apprehensive or guilty about the deception
Gets little enjoyment from being deceptive
Has not had time to rehearse the lie in advance
Knows there are severe punishments for being caught

Based on P. Ekman (2001). *Telling Lies*. New York: Norton.

Detecting Deception *Lie to Me* (TV series, 2009–)

Dr. Cal Lightman (Tim Roth) is a deception detection expert who studies facial expressions and involuntary body language to determine if someone is lying. His ability to spot and analyze deceivers is amazing—in fact, he seems to know more about the liars than they know about themselves.

Many of Lightman's conclusions are based on the studies of renowned social scientist Paul Ekman, who serves as a consultant for the show. Ekman's years of research offer compelling evidence that liars do indeed sometimes send unconscious nonverbal cues that "leak" how they really think and feel.

But some words of caution are in order for fans of the show. For starters, most of Lightman's conclusions come from analyzing slow-motion recordings—something few people have access to in their daily conversations. Second, many nonverbal cues have multiple meanings and are not necessarily indicators of deceit (just because liars often rub their eyes doesn't mean that an eye rubber is telling a fib). Finally, Lightman (and Ekman) have far more training at analyzing nonverbal communication than the normal person. Their ability to detect deception is clearly the exception, not the norm.

Lie to Me should best be seen as an entertaining look at how social science gives experts some insights into detecting deceit. It would be unwise, however, to use it as a layperson's guide for analyzing and judging the nonverbal behaviour of friends and family. If you accuse someone of lying based on a few nonverbal cues, your chances of being right are only about 50 percent—and those aren't good odds when it could jeopardize a relationship.

Note: The website www.truthaboutdeception.com offers a thorough, current, scholarly, and easy-to-read review of issues related to deception and its detection.

The stars of the TV show *Lie to Me* detect deception by monitoring unconscious nonverbal cues. But is it really that simple?

expression of thanks, a sign of friendliness, a measure of insecurity, a sexual come-on, or an eye problem.[28]

The ambiguous nature of nonverbal behaviours becomes clear in the area of courtship and sexuality. Does a kiss mean "I like you a lot" or "I want to have sex"? Does playing with hair or jewellery mean that you're a little stressed about something or does it mean you're attracted to a person? A group of Safeway workers in the US was asked to smile and make eye contact with their customers. But the group had to file a grievance because their nonverbal gestures were continually interpreted as flirting.[29]

Because of the ambiguous nature of nonverbal communication, it is important not to read, or interpret, one cue but to look at the whole picture. Further, you must consider context, culture, and the nature of the relationship

"That was unkind, darling. When their mouths turn up at the corners they want to be friends."

Drawing by Michael ffolkes. Used by permission of the estate of Michael ffolkes.

Invitation TO INSIGHT

Reading "Body Language"

This exercise will both increase your skill in observing nonverbal behaviour and show you the dangers of being too sure of yourself as an interpreter. You can try the exercise either in or out of class, and the period over which you do it is flexible, from a single class period to several days. In any case, begin by choosing a partner and then follow these directions:

1. For the first period, however long you decide to make it, observe and record each other's behaviours: Notice movements, mannerisms, postures, style of dress, and so on. If you do this exercise out of class over an extended time period, there's no need to let your observations interfere with whatever you'd normally be doing. All you have to do is compile a list of your partner's behaviours. *Do not to interpret* your partner's actions at this stage.

2. At the end of the allotted time, tell each other what you've seen— just the behaviours, not your interpretations.

3. For the next period, your job is not only to observe your partner's behaviour but also to *interpret* it. This time, as you confer, tell your partner what you thought the behaviours revealed. For example, does careless dressing suggest oversleeping, loss of interest in appearance, or the desire to feel more comfortable? If you noticed frequent yawning, did you think this meant boredom, fatigue after a late night, or sleepiness after a big meal? Don't feel bad if your guesses weren't all correct. Remember that nonverbal clues tend to be ambiguous. You may be surprised how checking out the nonverbal clues you observe can help build a relationship with another person.

you have with the person. Keeping an open mind and not jumping to conclusions is essential.

It's more difficult for some people to decode nonverbal signals than it is for others. Young boys often miss nonverbal emotional messages like when teachers express displeasure through arched eyebrows.[30] People with nonverbal learning disorder (NVLD) find it dramatically more difficult to read facial expressions, tone of voice, and other cues.[31] Humour or sarcasm can be especially hard to understand. Thus, they are unable to examine nonverbal cues to ensure that what is said is what is intended.

Influences on Nonverbal Communication

The way we communicate nonverbally is influenced to a certain degree by gender and culture.

Gender

There are a lot of gender differences when it comes to nonverbal communication. For example, women are more expressive and better at recognizing

Culture

Cultures have different nonverbal languages as well as verbal ones.[35] In a Canadian study, for example, anglophones and francophones were asked to rate the gestures of bilingual speakers who each spoke one language and then the other. The results support the stereotype that francophones speak with their hands. Francophones, regardless of which language they spoke, gestured more than anglophones.[36] Some anglophones actually gesture more when they speak French. One English speaker related that when she spoke French, her whole body spoke.

> **Sometimes he'd like to slip his blackness on a white man and say, walk around a while like this, see how it really feels ...**
>
> —Raymond Souster,
> "Jazzman"

others' nonverbal behaviour.[32] More specifically, compared to men, women:

- Smile more
- Use more facial expressions
- Use more head, hand, and arm gestures (but less expansive gestures)
- Touch others more
- Stand closer to others
- Are more vocally expressive
- Make more eye contact[33]

Men's and women's nonverbal communication differs in other ways, too.[34] Women make are more vocally expressive. Men are more likely to lean forward in conversations, and they require and are given more personal space. Women face conversational partners head on, while men typically stand at an angle.

Some nonverbal behaviours have different meanings across cultures. Former Canadian prime minister Pierre Trudeau was noted for using a simple Gallic "shrug" when speaking French, although the gesture is considered inappropriate for an English speaker.[37] The OK gesture, made by joining the tips of thumb and forefinger to form a circle, is a cheery affirmation to most Canadians but means "You're worth zero" in Belgium and France. In Greece and Turkey, the same gesture is a vulgar, insulting, sexual invitation[38] Moving your head back and forth in Turkey to indicate no will be interpreted as "I don't understand," and showing the sole of your shoe to someone in Egypt is a grave insult.[39] Given this sort of cross-cultural ambiguity, you can see how an exchange student or innocent tourist can generate nonverbal misunderstandings.

Other differences can damage relationships without the parties ever recognizing exactly what has gone wrong. According to Edward Hall, North Americans conduct business at a distance of roughly 1.2 metres; people from the Middle East stand much closer.[40] You can visualize the awkward advance-and-retreat pattern that might occur when people from these cultures meet. One author experienced this at a party. While talking to a Middle Eastern man, she noticed that he kept moving closer to her. Feeling that her personal space was being invaded, she kept moving backward. She later learned, however, that he couldn't understand why she was being so rude.

Eye contact patterns also vary around the world.[41] A direct gaze is considered appropriate for speakers seeking power in Latin America, the Arab world, and southern Europe. On the other hand, Asians, Indians, Pakistanis, and northern Europeans gaze at a listener peripherally or not at all.[42] In either case, deviations from the norm are likely to make a listener uncomfortable.

The use of time also depends greatly on culture.[43] North Americans, Germans, and the Swiss tend to be *monochronic* in that they emphasize punctuality, schedules, and completing one task at a time. In South America and in Mediterranean cultures, they are more *polychronic*, with flexible schedules and multitasking.[44] For example, a psychologist teaching at a university in

"When you hold me like this, you make me feel I can do *anything*."

Brazil found that some students arrived halfway through a two-hour class but stayed put asking questions when the class was scheduled to end.[45] This flexibility is very different from what occurs in our Canadian classrooms. As Table 6.4 shows, differences in cultural rules can lead to misunderstandings.

TABLE 6.4

Cultural Differences in Nonverbal Communication Can Lead to Misunderstandings

Behaviours that have one meaning for members of the same culture or co-culture can be interpreted differently by members of other groups.

Behaviour	Probable In-Group Perception	Possible Out-Group Perception
Avoidance of direct eye contact (First Nations)	Used to communicate attentiveness or respect	A sign of inattentiveness; direct eye contact is preferred
Aggressively challenging a point with which one disagrees (African Canadian)	Acceptable means of dialogue; not regarded as verbal abuse or a precursor to violence	Arguments are viewed as inappropriate and a sign of potential imminent violence
Use of finger gestures to beckon others (Asian)	Appropriate if used by adults for children, but highly offensive if directed at adults	Appropriate gesture to use with both children and adults
Silence (First Nations)	Sign of respect, thoughtfulness, and/or uncertainty/ambiguity	Interpreted as boredom, disagreement, or refusal to participate
Touch (Spanish, Italian)	Normal and appropriate for interpersonal interactions	Deemed appropriate for some intimate or friendly interactions; otherwise perceived as a violation of personal space
Public display of intense emotions (African Canadian)	Accepted and valued as measure of expressiveness; appropriate in most settings	Violates expectations for self-controlled public behaviours; inappropriate in most public settings
Touching or holding hands of same-sex friends (Asian)	Acceptable in behaviour that signifies closeness in platonic relationships	Perceived as a sign of homosexuality when displayed by two men.

From M. P. Orbe and T. M. Harris (2001). *Interracial Communication Theory into Practice* (with InfoTrac College Edition), 1st ed. Reprinted with permission from the author.

Despite differences like these, some nonverbal behaviours are universal. Smiles and laughter are signals of positive emotions, for example, while sour expressions convey displeasure in every culture.[46] Charles Darwin believed that expressions like these are the result of evolution, functioning as survival mechanisms that allowed early humans to convey emotional states before the development of language. The innateness of some facial expressions becomes even clearer when we examine the behaviour of children born with impaired heading and sight.[47] They display a broad range of expression—smiling, laughing, and crying in ways virtually identical to seeing and hearing children.

LO² Types of Nonverbal Communication

Knowing the different types of nonverbal communication can enhance your sensitivity to nonverbal messages you send and receive.

Observing What You See

As a grad student, I often had my morning tea and bagel between classes at the student union cafeteria and entertained myself by watching the goings-on. As most people-watchers do, I selected a table with a good view that included the cash register, where most of the "action" occurred. From my carefully selected position, I watched and made inferences about people.

On several occasions, I happened to notice an attractive, dark-haired male student who appeared to be in his junior or senior year. He had strong white teeth that contrasted with his tanned complexion. About six feet tall, he had a trendy haircut and wore blue jeans and hiking boots. Under what looked like a ski jacket (I believe I saw a lift tag), he wore a light-coloured turtleneck and a wool sweater. He had a strong but not overpowering body, and it was clear that he exercised regularly. In fact, he looked like he had just walked out of an L.L. Bean or Eddie Bauer catalogue.

One day he greeted a tall, well-dressed woman in her 50s with a polite hug. They looked surprised but not unhappy to see one another and they chatted. Their relationship seemed to fall somewhere between professional and informal—as though they had known each other at one time. After three or four minutes, both smiled, said goodbye to one another, and looked for seats in different parts of the cafeteria.

I had observed this student's behaviour for a week and a half when our eyes met. Because I was a married woman and seven years his senior, I quickly looked away, not wanting to communicate interest. But shortly after this encounter, we met at a university function. When introduced, we both acknowledged having seen each other in the cafeteria. He noted that when he smiled at me, I hadn't returned it, and as a result, he concluded that I wasn't very friendly. This surprised me—I had no idea my nonverbal response relayed such aloofness.

However, his comments gave me an opportunity to offer my interpretation of him. Based on my observations, I told him that I guessed that he was from an upper-middle-class background—his parents might be doctors or lawyers. He conceded that his father was a doctor, his mother a lawyer, and was quite amazed that I should have guessed this. It was a guess, but based on his appearance—expensive clothing, expensive teeth, and a refined manner. Clearly, he wanted for nothing. I continued by saying that he was probably in the sciences (he was an engineering student), that he skied (he did), and that he lived in a fraternity house (right again). I was correct on all three counts. Again, my predictions were educated guesses, although the lift tag helped a lot. I probably guessed he was in engineering because I thought I had seen him one day with an engineering friend of mine. Regarding the fraternity, most of the guys on campus who looked like him lived in frat houses.

By now, he was becoming uncomfortable. The final straw came when I mentioned his recent interaction with the older woman. I told him that, based on his friendly but polite and distant interaction style, the woman was probably not a professor but rather the mother of a friend. It looked like she had asked how he was, how his courses were going, and he had responded in kind. I took another guess and suggested that perhaps she was the mother of a former girlfriend.

Correct. He was dumbfounded!

Am I a witch with special powers? No, but I do possess the power of observation. And you will have this same power once you hone your sensitivity to nonverbal messages and look beyond what you see. It's easier than you think.

Now, I wonder if anyone was observing me as I enjoyed my tea and bagel.

Judith A. Rolls

Body Movement

The first type of nonverbal communication to be discussed is **kinesics**, the study of body position and motion. This includes **body orientation**, posture, gestures, facial expressions, and eye movements.

Body Orientation

We'll start with body **orientation**—the degree to which we face toward or away from someone with our body, feet, and head. Facing someone directly generally signals your interest and facing away signals a desire to avoid involvement. When two friends are in deep conversation with one another, they face toward one another. Should a third party attempt to join them at this inappropriate time, the friends will likely turn their bodies slightly away from the intruder, thus making it known that they do not wish to be interrupted.

Dmitriy Shironosov/Shutterstock

Fie, fie upon her!
There's language in her eyes,
her cheek, her lip.
Nay, her foot speaks; her wanton
spirits look out
At every joint and motive in
her body.

—William Shakespeare,
Troilus and Cressida

Posture

Another way we communicate nonverbally is through our **posture**. The importance of posture is demonstrated in the number of expressions we have that link emotional states to body postures:

> I won't take this lying down! (Nor will I stand for it!)

I feel the weight of the world on my shoulders.

He can stand on his own two feet.

She's been sitting on that project for weeks.

Posture may be the least ambiguous type of nonverbal behaviour. In one study, observers were asked to assign emotions to 176 computer-generated mannequin figures. The raters had over 90 percent success with postures related to anger, sadness, and happiness.[48] Disgust, on the other hand, was the hardest to identify from body posture, and some raters thought that surprise and happiness had similar postural configurations.

Tension and relaxation also offer clues about feelings. We assume relaxed postures in nonthreatening situations and tighten up in threatening situations.[49] Based on this observation, we can learn how others feel simply by watching how tense or loose they seem to be. Tenseness also denotes status: The lower-status person is generally the more rigid, tense-appearing one, whereas the higher-status person is more relaxed.

Gestures

Gestures—movements of the hands and arms—are an important type of nonverbal communication. In fact, they are so fundamental that people who are sight-impaired from birth use them.[50] Some social scientists claim that a language of gestures was the first form of human communication, preceding speech by tens of thousands of years.[51] Canadian parents seem to agree in that many are teaching their wee

Kinesics
The study of body position and motion.

Body orientation
The degree to which we face toward or away from someone with our body, feet, and head.

Gestures
Motions of the body, usually hands or arms, that have communicative value.

children, as young as five months old, how to use sign language.[52]

The most common forms of gestures are what social scientists call **illustrators**—movements that accompany speech but don't stand on their own.[53] For instance, if someone asked you how to get to a restaurant across town, you might offer street names and addresses, but as you do so, you'll also point your fingers and gesture with your hands to illustrate how to get there. Remove the words from your directions and it's unlikely that the person would find the restaurant. Think also of people who like to "talk with their hands," even when they're on the phone and can't be seen by the other party. North Americans tend to use illustrators more often when they are emotionally aroused—trying to explain difficult ideas when they are furious, horrified, agitated, distressed, or excited.[54] Studies also show that it is easier to comprehend and learn a second language when it is accompanied by illustrators and other nonverbal cues.[55]

> Showing that the right hand was holding no weapon was probably one origin of our habit of waving; another is said to have been the polite raising of the right arm to make room when passing others in narrow lanes. Pushing back visors and hoods to facilitate recognition of one's face may have led to hat-tipping as well as waving and saluting, and the ancient praying gesture, fist to forehead, looks like another forerunner of the salute.
>
> —Margaret Visser,
> *The Way We Are*

A second type of gestures is **emblems**—deliberate nonverbal behaviours that have a precise meaning, known to virtually everyone within a cultural group. Unlike illustrators, emblems can stand on their own and often function as replacements for words. For example, we all know that a head nod means yes, a head shake means no, a wave means hello or goodbye, and a hand to the ear means "I can't hear you." And almost everyone over the age of five knows the meaning of a raised middle finger. But while the thumbs up sign means "good" to us, it is considered an obscene gesture in Iraq and several other countries.[56]

A third type of gestures is **adaptors**, also known as **manipulators**, consist of unconscious bodily movements in response to the environment. These would include fiddling with your hands, clicking a pen, or even shivering. But not *all* fidgeting signals uneasiness.[57] People are also likely to engage in self-touching when relaxed. When they let down their guard, either alone or with friends, they will be more likely to fiddle with an earlobe, twirl a strand of hair, or play with their jewellery. But these same gestures could also be considered *preening gestures* or *courtship behaviours* that suggest an "interest" in someone. Clearly, it's important not to jump to conclusions about the meaning of adaptors.

Actually, *too few* gestures may be as significant an indicator of mixed messages as *too many*.[58] Lack of gesturing may signal a lack of interest, sadness, boredom, or low enthusiasm. Illustrators also decrease whenever someone

Illustrators
Nonverbal behaviours that accompany and support verbal messages.

Emblems
Deliberate nonverbal behaviours with precise meanings known to virtually all members of a cultural group.

Adaptors
Movements in which one part of the body grooms, massages, rubs, holds, fidgets, pinches, picks, or otherwise manipulates another part. Also known as *manipulators*.

The Look of a Victim

Little Red Riding Hood set herself up to be mugged. Her first mistake was skipping through the forest to grandma's house. Her second mistake was stopping to pick flowers. At this point, as you might remember in the story, the mean, heavy wolf comes along and begins to check her out. He observes, quite perceptively, that she is happy, outgoing, and basically unaware of any dangers in her surrounding environment. The big bad wolf catches these nonverbal clues and splits to grandma's house. He knows that Red is an easy mark. From this point we all know what happens.

Body movements and gestures reveal a lot of information about a person. Like Little Red Riding Hood, pedestrians may signal to criminals that they are easy targets for mugging by the way they walk. When was the last time you assessed your "muggability rating"? In a recent study two psychologists set out to identify those body movements that characterized easy victims. They assembled "muggability ratings" of 60 New York pedestrians from the people who may have been the most qualified to judge—prison inmates who had been convicted of assault.

The researchers unobtrusively videotaped pedestrians on weekdays between 10 a.m. and 12 p.m. Each pedestrian was taped for six to eight seconds, the approximate time it takes for a mugger to size up an approaching person. The judges (prison inmates) rated the "assault potential" of the 60 pedestrians on a 10-point scale. A rating of 1 indicated someone was "a very easy rip-off," of 2, "an easy dude to corner." Toward the other end of the scale, 9 meant a person "would be heavy; would give you a hard time," and 10 indicated that the mugger "would avoid it, too big a situation, too heavy." The results revealed several body movements that characterized easy victims: "Their strides were either very long or very short; they moved awkwardly, raising their left legs with their left arms (instead of alternating them); on each step they tended to lift their whole foot up and then place it down (less muggable sorts took steps in which their feet rocked from heel to toe). Overall, the people rated most muggable walked as if they were in conflict with themselves; they seemed to make each move in the most difficult way possible."

Loretta Malandro and Larry Barker

Excerpt from "The Look of a Victim" from *Introduction to Nonverbal Communication* by Loretta Malandro and Larry L. Barker © 1982 by Random House, Inc. Used courtesy of the publisher.

is cautious about speaking. For these reasons, a careful observer will look for either an increase or a decrease in the usual level of gestures.

Face and Eyes

While the face and eyes are the most noticed parts of the body, their nonverbal messages are not the easiest to read. The face is a tremendously complicated channel of expression for several reasons. First, there are at least eight distinguishable positions of the eyebrows and forehead, eight of the eyes and lids, and ten for the lower face.[59] When you multiply this complexity by the number of emotions we feel, you can see why it's almost impossible to compile a dictionary of facial expressions and their corresponding emotions.

Second, there's the speed at which facial expressions can change. For example, slow-motion films show **microexpressions**, those brief expressions that flit across a subject's face in as short a time as it takes to blink an eye.[60] Further, different emotions show most clearly in different parts of the face: happiness and surprise in the eyes and lower face; anger in the lower face, brows, and forehead; fear and sadness in the eyes; and disgust in the lower face.

In spite of the complex way in which the face shows emotions, you can still pick up clues by watching it carefully. Look for expressions that seem exaggerated. When people try to fool themselves or others, they tend to exaggerate the point, while genuine facial expressions usually last no longer than five seconds. After that, we start to doubt they are real.[61] You can also watch people when they aren't thinking about their appearance, because they're more likely to express emotions that they wouldn't show in more guarded moments.

The eyes themselves can send several kinds of messages. Meeting someone's glance with your eyes is usually a sign of involvement, whereas looking away is often a sign of a desire to avoid contact. This principle has a practical application in commerce: Customers leave larger tips when their servers, whether male or female, maintain eye

Microexpression
Brief facial expression.

(Looking at Diversity)

Annie Donnellon: Blindness and Nonverbal Cues

I have been blind since birth, so I've never had access to many of the nonverbal cues that sighted people use. In fact, I think that "sightlings" (a pet name for my friends who are sighted) take for granted how much of their meaning comes through nonverbal channels. When I recently took an interpersonal communication course, the material on nonverbal communication was in some ways a foreign language to me.

For instance, I felt a bit left out when the class discussed things like body movement, eye contact, and facial expressions. I understand how these cues work, but I haven't experienced many of them myself. I have never "stared someone down" or "shot a look" at anyone (at least not intentionally!). While I know that some people "talk with their hands," that's something I've never witnessed and rarely do.

When the subject turned to paralanguage, I was back on familiar territory. I listen very carefully to the way people speak to figure out what they're thinking and feeling. My family and friends tell me I'm more tuned in to these issues than most sightlings are. It's typical for me to ask, "Are you okay today?" when friends send messages that seem mixed. They may say everything's fine, but their voice often tells a different story.

I'm a singer and performer, and some of my biggest frustrations have come from well-meaning teachers who coach me on my nonverbals. I remember one acting instructor asking me, "How do you think your character would express herself nonverbally in this scene?" and I thought to myself, "I have no idea." People who are sighted may think that anger cues like clenched fists, rigid posture, or shrugged shoulders are "natural" expressions, but I think that many of them are learned by watching others.

Let me pass along some key hints that can help make communication smoother and more effective. It's important to mention your name when starting a conversation with people who are blind: Don't assume they can figure out who you are from your voice. At the end of a conversation, please say that you're leaving. I often feel embarrassed when I'm talking to someone, only to find out that they walked away mid-sentence.

Most important: Clue in visually-impaired people when something is going on that they can't see. Often at my sorority meetings, something will happen that everyone is laughing about, but I'm left out of the loop because I can't see the nonverbal cues. Over the years my friends and family have learned that whispering a quick description of the events helps me feel more a part of the interaction.

contact with them,[62] and communicators who make direct eye contact are more likely to get others to comply with their requests.[63] This is why panhandlers, salespeople, and petitioners try to catch our eye.

The eyes can also communicate positive or negative attitudes,[64] like when someone is seeking to demonstrate interest; hence the expression "making eyes." When our long glances toward someone else are avoided, we get the idea that they are not interested. (Of course, there are all sorts of courtship games where the receiver of a glance pretends not to notice.) The eyes can also communicate both dominance and submission.[65] We've all played the game of trying to stare down somebody, and there are times when downcast eyes are a sign of giving in.

Even the pupils of our eyes communicate. Researchers measured the amount of pupil dilation while showing men and women various types of pictures.[66] Heterosexual men's pupils grew about 18 percent larger when looking at pictures of a naked woman, and women's pupils grew 20 percent when looking at pictures of a naked man. Interestingly, the greatest increase in pupil size occurred when women looked at a picture of a mother and an infant.

> It was terribly dangerous to let your thoughts wander when you were in any public place or within range of a telescreen. The smallest thing could give you away. A nervous tic, an unconscious look of anxiety, a habit of muttering to yourself—anything that carried with it the suggestion of abnormality, of having something to hide. In any case, to wear an improper expression on your face (to look incredulous when a victory was announced, for example) was itself a punishable offense. There was even a word for it in Newspeak: facecrime, it was called.
>
> —George Orwell,
> *1984*

way a message is spoken can give the same word or words many meanings. For example, note how many meanings come from a single sentence just by shifting the emphasis from one word to another:

This is a fantastic communication book. (Not just any book, but *this* one in particular.)

This is a *fantastic* communication book. (This book is superior, exciting.)

This is a fantastic *communication* book. (The book is good as far as communication goes; it may not be so great as literature or drama.)

This is a fantastic communication *book*. (It's not a play or album; it's a book.)

> A pause in the wrong place, an intonation misunderstood, and a whole conversation went awry.
>
> —E. M. Forster,
> *A Passage to India*

LO³
Individual Factors

In addition to the types of nonverbal communication, individual factors such as voice, touch, and physical attractiveness are also related to nonverbal communication.

Voice

People are often surprised to find voice included in a chapter on nonverbal communication, but social scientists use the term **paralanguage** to describe nonverbal vocal messages. The

Paralanguage
Nonlinguistic means of vocal expression: rate, pitch, tone, and so on.

By Rueben Bolling, from the weekly comic strip "Tom the Dancing Bug."

We communicate paralinguistically through tone, rate, pitch, volume—even through pauses. Two types of pauses can lead to communication snags. The first is the *unintentional pause*—when people collect their thoughts before deciding how best to proceed with their verbal message. Liars tend to have more unintentional pauses because they often make up stories on the fly.[67] A second type of pause is the *vocalized pause*, which includes the use of **disfluencies** such as "um," "er," and "uh" or vocal filler words such as "like," "okay," and "ya know." Research shows that vocalized pauses reduce a person's perceived credibility[68] and negatively affect perceptions of candidates in job interviews.[69]

Researchers have identified the power of paralanguage through the use of content-free speech—ordinary speech that has been electronically manipulated so that the words are unintelligible but the paralanguage remains unaffected. (Hearing a foreign language has the same effect.) Subjects who hear content-free speech can consistently recognize the emotion that's being expressed, and its strength.[70] Young children respond to the paralanguage of adults, warming up to those who speak warmly and shying away from those who speak in a less friendly manner.[71]

Paralanguage can affect behaviour in some surprising ways. For example, communicators are most likely to comply with requests that are delivered by speakers whose rate is similar to their own. One study showed that people who spoke rapidly responded most favourably to rapid talkers, whereas slow speakers preferred those whose rate was also slow.[72] Further, listeners feel more positively about people who speak at their own rate.

Sarcasm is created through the use of emphasis and tone of voice to change a statement's meaning to the opposite of its verbal message. Experience this reversal yourself with the following three statements. First say them literally, and then say them sarcastically.

> "Thanks a lot!"
> "I really had a wonderful time on my blind date."
> "There's nothing I like better than lima beans."

As they do with other nonverbal messages, people often ignore or misinterpret the vocal nuances of sarcasm. Children, people with weak intellectual skills, and poor listeners are more likely to misunderstand sarcastic messages,[73] and children under 10 lack the linguistic sophistication to tell when a message is sarcastic.[74]

Besides reinforcing or contradicting messages, some vocal factors influence the way speakers are perceived by others. For instance, communicators who speak loudly and without hesitations are viewed as more confident than those who pause and speak quietly.[75] People with more attractive voices are rated more highly than those with less attractive voices.[76] Further, there's a gender difference

when it comes to paralanguage. Women have a tendency to raise the pitch of their voices at the end of statements, thus turning them into questions. For example, "I can meet with you at three this afternoon?" or "I submitted the report on Tuesday?" These tonal patterns reduce credibility and make the women using them sound unsure of themselves.

> An artificially high-pitched tone universally suggests a disarming tentativeness in the speaker. Canadians are noticeably inclined to turn a statement into a question by means of a rising intonation: This expresses hope that there are no objections and simultaneously requests a sign from the listener that the statement has been understood. Corresponding politely hesitant questions might be "OK?" "You know?"
>
> —Margaret Visser,
> *The Way We Are*

Finally, vocal features can be used for fun. Inuit throat songs, for instance, are essentially vocal games with the low-pitched sounds representing birds and animals. Typically created by two females standing face to face, the goal of the exercise is for one person to set a pattern and for the other to imitate the sounds and rhythms. This creates a wonderfully odd sound, produced by inhaling in the throat and varying the pitch while exhaling. "Inuit throat singing is a skill that has to be taught and developed. Inuit throat singers try to show their vocal abilities in a fun competitive manner, and the first one to either run out of breath, stop, or laugh is declared the loser of the game."[77] You can check out Inuit throat singers on Internet sites such as YouTube.

Touch

Social scientists use the word **haptics** to describe the study of touching. Touch can

Disfluency
A nonlinguistic verbalization; for example, stammering or saying "um," "er," or "ah."

Haptics
The study of touching.

communicate many messages and signify a variety of relationships:[78]

- functional/professional (dental exam, haircut)
- social/polite (handshake)
- friendship/warmth (clap on back)
- sexual arousal (some kisses, strokes)
- aggression (shoves, slaps)

Because of the ambiguous nature of communication, however, touch is often misunderstood. Is a hug playful or suggestive of stronger feelings? Is a touch on the shoulder a friendly gesture or an attempt at domination? And a kiss can mean anything from a polite but superficial greeting to the most intense arousal. What makes touch more or less intense depends on a number of factors:

- the part of the body doing the touching
- the part of the body being touched
- the length of the touch
- the pressure of the touch
- whether there is movement after contact
- whether anyone else is present
- the situation in which the touch occurs
- the relationship between the persons involved[79]

Further, touch plays a powerful role in our responses to others. For instance, in a laboratory task, subjects evaluated partners more positively when they were touched (appropriately, of course) by them.[80] Besides increasing liking, touch also increases compliance. In one study, subjects were asked by a male and female confederate to sign a petition or complete a rating scale. Subjects were more likely to cooperate when they were touched lightly on the arm. In the rating-scale variation of the study, the results were especially dramatic: 70 percent of those who

were touched complied, whereas only 40 percent of the untouched subjects were willing to cooperate, indicating a predisposition not to comply.[81]

An additional power of touch is its on-the-job utility: A restaurant server's fleeting touches on the hand and shoulder result in larger tips,[82] as does squatting down to make eye contact with customers.[83] Both women and men in taverns increase their alcohol consumption when touched by a waitress.[84]

Touching is also essential for healthy development. During the 19th and early 20th centuries, a large percentage of children born every year died—especially those in orphanages—because they hadn't been touched enough. When institutions began "mothering" infants by picking them up, carrying them around, and handling them several times each day, the death rate fell dramatically. One hospital reported a drop from 30 to 35 percent to below 10 percent.[85]

Today we know that premature babies grow faster and gain more weight when massaged.[86] Massage also helps colicky children sleep better, improves the mood of depressed adolescents, and boosts the immune function of cancer and HIV patients. Research shows that touch between therapists and clients encourages self-disclosure, client self-acceptance, and more positive client–therapist relationships.[87]

© iStockphoto.com/Jacob Wackerhausen

Appearance

Whether or not we're aware of the fact, how we look sends messages to others. There are two dimensions to appearance: physical attractiveness and clothing.

Physical Attractiveness

The importance of physical attractiveness has been emphasized in the arts for centuries. More recently, social scientists have found that physical attractiveness affects interaction between people.[88] For example, women who are perceived as attractive have more dates, receive higher grades in university or college, persuade males with greater ease, and receive lighter court sentences. Both men and women whom others find attractive are rated as being more

sensitive, kind, strong, sociable, and interesting than their less fortunate brothers and sisters. Physical attractiveness is also an asset in the professional world, affecting hiring, promotion, and performance evaluation decisions.[89]

The influence of physical attractiveness begins early in life.[90] When preschoolers were shown photographs of children their own age and asked to choose potential friends and enemies, children as young as three agreed about who was attractive and unattractive. Furthermore, the children valued their attractive counterparts—of both the same and the opposite sex—more highly. Teachers also are affected by students' attractiveness. Physically attractive students are usually judged more favourably—as being more intelligent, friendly, and popular—than their less attractive counterparts.[91] And teacher–student assessments work in both directions—physically attractive professors receive higher evaluations from their students.[92]

Fortunately, attractiveness is controllable. Beauty isn't just based on the "original equipment." Evidence suggests that, as we get to know more about people and like them, we start to regard them as better-looking.[93] Further, posture, gestures, facial expressions, and other behaviours all add to our physical attractiveness.

Beauty is also culturally defined in that what may be considered beautiful in one country might not be so in another. Further, beauty is a product of what advertisers tell us is it. Today's culturally defined notion of beauty is a narrow one where women and men are supposed to be extremely thin and fit.

Clothing

Clothing is also a means of nonverbal communication that can convey 10 types of messages to others:[94]

- economic level
- economic background
- educational level
- social background
- trustworthiness
- educational background
- social position
- level of success
- level of sophistication
- moral character

Research shows that we do make assumptions about people based on their clothing. Uniforms and formal attire, for example, carry influence. Researchers dressed in uniforms resembling police officers were more successful than researchers dressed in civilian clothing in requesting pedestrians to pick up litter and persuading them to lend a dime to an overparked motorist.[95] Likewise, solicitors wearing sheriff's and nurse's uniforms increased the level of contributions to law enforcement and health care campaigns.[96] In another study, a male and a female were stationed in a hallway so that anyone who wished to go by had to avoid them or pass between them. When the male and female wore "formal daytime dress," passersby responded positively, but when the protagonists wore casual clothing, passersby responded negatively.[97]

> One of the most distinctively modern ideals in clothing is that we ought to avoid bright colours. "Smart" people respond by doggedly and deliberately dressing in grey, beige, black, and brown—perhaps to go with our concrete, tarred, and steel cityscapes. Or, so much colour now being so easily available, we enjoy fastidiously turning it all down for "classy" discretion. Blue is a compromise: a colour, but quiet. Never has it been as popular as it is now: A recent survey established that half of us choose blue as our favourite colour; and TV cameras endorse our preference by reproducing blue extraordinarily well. Even synthetic indigo fades—and we should hate it not to. As moderns, we are cool, moderate, and far more obedient than the myths about us pretend; we do not often seek to "put ourselves forward."
>
> —Margaret Visser,
> *The Way We Are*

We're also more likely to obey people dressed in a high-status manner. Pedestrians were more likely to return lost coins to well-dressed people than to more poorly dressed individuals.[98] Further, we follow the lead of high-status dressers, even when it violates social rules.

"Tell me about yourself, Kugelman—your hopes, dreams, career path, and what that damn earring means."

Harley Schwadron/Wall Street Journal/Cartoon Features Syndicate

In one study, 83 percent of the pedestrians followed a well-dressed jaywalker who violated a "wait" crossing signal, whereas only 48 percent followed a confederate dressed in lower-status clothing.[99] And women who wear a jacket are rated as more powerful than those wearing only a dress or skirt and blouse.[100]

Of course, our clothing-based assumptions aren't always accurate. The stranger wearing wrinkled, ill-fitting old clothes might be a manager on vacation, a normally stylish person on the way to clean a fireplace, or even an eccentric millionaire. As we get to know others better, the importance of clothing shrinks,[101] thus making clothing more important in the initial

CHAPTER 6 Nonverbal Communication: Messages beyond Words

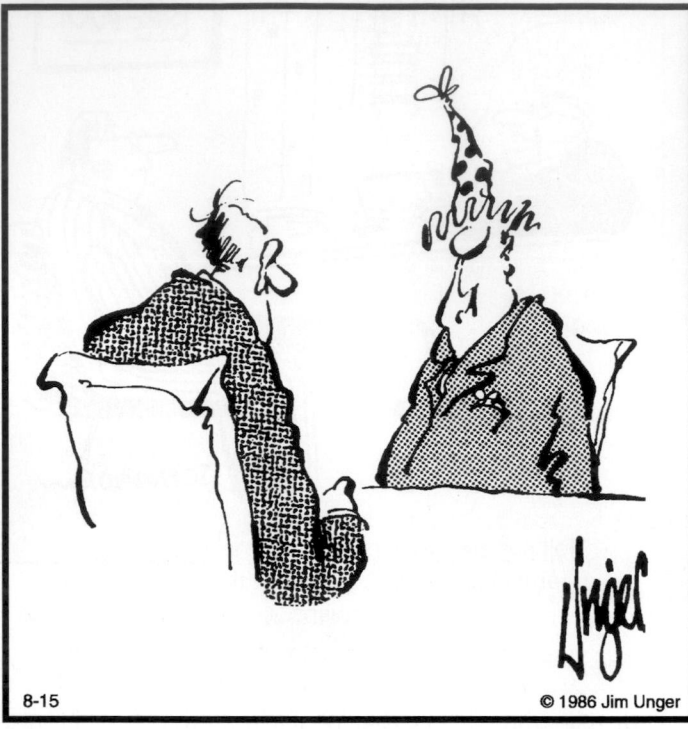

8-15 © 1986 Jim Unger

"I always wear my lucky hat for job interviews."

HERMAN: © Jim Unger/Dist. by Newspaper Enterprise Association, Inc.

stages of relationships. In an employment interview, for example, our style of dress (and personal grooming) can make all the difference between success and outright rejection.

LO⁴
External Factors

External factors such as distance, environment, and time are also related to nonverbal communication.

Physical Space

Proxemics is the study of how people and animals use space. There are at least two dimensions of proxemics: distance and territoriality.

Distance

You can often tell how people feel about one another by noting the distance between them.[102] This is because each of us carries around a sort of invisible bubble of personal space. We think of the areas inside this bubble as our private territory—almost as

Proxemics
The study of how people and animals use space.

much a part of us as our own bodies. When someone invades it, we feel uncomfortable—physically as well as emotionally. We then move or adjust ourselves according to the person we're with and the situation we're in. It is precisely the distance that we voluntarily put between ourselves and others that gives a nonverbal clue about our feelings and the nature of the relationship.

> Some thirty inches from my nose
> The frontier of my Person goes,
> And all the untilled air between
> Is private pagus or demesne.
> Stranger, unless with bedroom eyes
> I beckon you to fraternise,
> Beware of rudely crossing it:
> I have no gun, but I can spit.
>
> —W. H. Auden,
> "I Have No Gun, But I Can Spit"

As you read earlier in this chapter, appropriate proxemic distances differ from culture to culture. Anthropologist Edward T. Hall described four distances that we use in our everyday lives,[103] and we choose a particular distance depending on how we feel toward the other person according to the time, the context, and our interpersonal goals.

Neo vision/Getty Images

© iStockphoto.com/Nikolay Mamluke

- The first of Hall's four spatial zones begins with skin contact and ranges out to about 45 centimetres. We usually use **intimate distance** with people who are emotionally very close to us, and then mostly in private situations—making love, caressing, comforting, protecting.
- The second spatial zone, **personal distance**, ranges from 45 centimetres at its closest point to 1.2 metres at its farthest. Its closer range is the distance at which most couples stand in public. The far range runs from about 75 centimetres to 1.2 metres. As Hall puts it, at this distance we can keep someone "at arm's length." This choice of words suggests the type of communication that goes on at this range: The contacts are still reasonably close, but they're much less personal than the ones that occur a foot or so closer.
- The third spatial zone, **social distance**, ranges from 1.2 to 3.6 metres. Within it are the kinds of communication that usually occur in business. Its closer range, from 1.2 to 2.1 metres, is the distance at which conversations usually occur between salespeople and customers and between people who work together. We use the far range of social distance—2.1 to 3.6 metres—for more formal and impersonal situations. Sitting at this distance signals a far different and less relaxed type of conversation than would pulling a chair around to the boss's side of the desk and sitting 90 centimetres away.
- **Public distance** is Hall's term for the farthest zone, running outward from 3.6 metres. The closer range of public distance is the one that most teachers use in the classroom. In the farther ranges of public space—7.5 metres and beyond—two-way communication is almost impossible. In some cases, it's necessary for speakers to use public distance because of the size of their audience, but we can assume that anyone who voluntarily chooses to use it when he or she could be closer is not interested in communication.

Choosing the optimal distance can have a powerful effect on how we regard and respond to others. For example, students are more satisfied with teachers who reduce the distance between themselves and their classes. They are also more satisfied with the course itself, and they are more likely to follow a teacher's instructions.[104] Medical patients are more satisfied with physicians who operate at the closer end of the social distance zone.[105]

> **Intimate distance**
> One of anthropologist Edward Hall's four distance zones, ranging from skin contact to 45 centimetres.
>
> **Personal distance**
> One of Hall's four distance zones, ranging from 45 centimetres to 1.2 metres.
>
> **Social distance**
> One of Hall's four distance zones, ranging from 1.2 to 3.6 metres.
>
> **Public distance**
> One of Hall's four distance zones, extending outward from 3.6 metres.

Invitation TO INSIGHT

Distance Makes a Difference

1. Choose a partner and go to opposite sides of the room and face each other.
2. Very slowly begin walking toward each other while carrying on a conversation. You might simply talk about how you feel as you conduct the exercise. As you move closer, try to be aware of any change in your feelings. Continue moving slowly toward each other until you are only an inch or so apart. Remember how you feel at this point.
3. Now, while still facing each other, back up until you're at a comfortable distance for carrying on your conversation.
4. Share your feelings with each other and/or the whole group.

Territoriality

Whereas personal space is the invisible bubble we carry around as an extension of our physical being, territory remains stationary. Any geographical area, such as a work station, room, house, or other physical space, to which we assume some kind of "rights" is our territory. Even though there's no real basis for these proprietary rights, the feeling of "owning" exists nonetheless. You see this on the first day of class, when students select a seat that typically remains "theirs" for the duration of the course, or in different students groups' hanging out in particular areas of the university. This exemplifies the notion of **territoriality**.

How people use space communicates a good deal about power and status.[106] Generally, we grant people with higher status more personal territory and greater privacy.

Territoriality
The notion that an area is claimed by an individual or a group of individuals.

We knock before entering a boss's office, whereas the boss can usually walk into our workspace area without hesitating. In traditional colleges and universities, professors have offices and dining rooms that are private, whereas students, who are presumably less important, have no such sanctuaries.

Physical Environment

Physical settings, architecture, and interior design also affect our communication. For example, some homes are very warm and make you feel comfortable, while others have what Mark Knapp calls "unliving rooms." They essentially say not to touch anything, not to put your feet up, and not to be comfortable.

> Childhood homes stay with us. They lurk in the chaise lounge where your mother took naps or in the coffee grinder your grandfather laboured over at the kitchen table. They are in the colours we never want to see again—the ubiquitous turquoise—and in the flagstone path flanked by purple iris. Whether we know it or not, most of us decorate our adult homes with either a reverence or disdain for the past, and the choices we make add one more layer to a family story.
>
> —Dorothy Foltz-Gray, "Not Your Mother's Living Room"

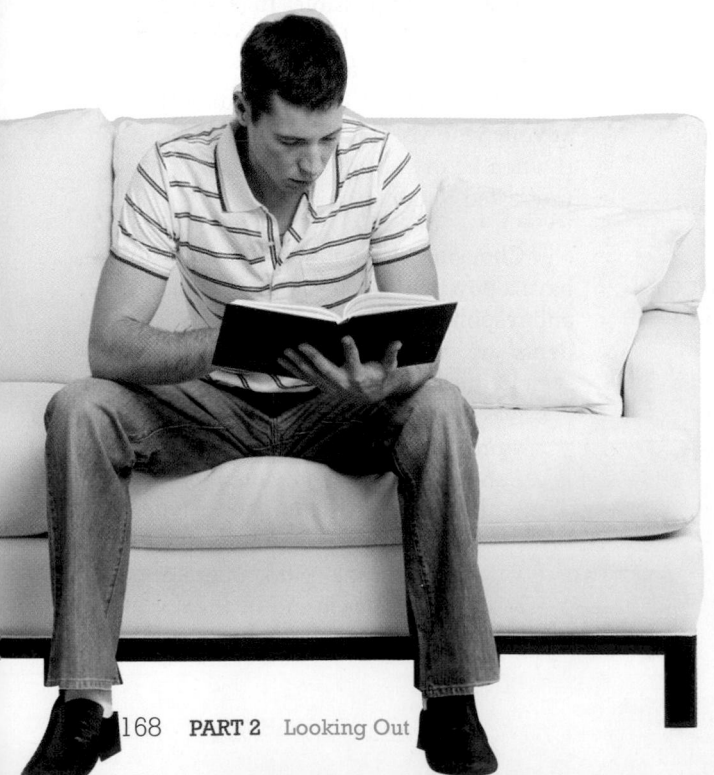

The impressions that home designs communicate can be remarkably accurate. Researchers showed 99 students exterior and interior slides of 12 upper-middle-class homes and then asked them to infer the owner's personality from their impressions.[107] The students were especially accurate after glancing at interior photos. The decorating schemes communicated homeowners' intellectualism, politeness, maturity, optimism, tenseness, willingness for adventures, and family orientations. The home exteriors also gave viewers accurate perceptions of the owners' artistic interests, graciousness, privacy, and quietness.

Environment can also shape the kind of interaction that takes place in it. In one experiment, subjects working in a "beautiful" room were more positive and energetic than those working in "average" or "ugly" spaces.[108] In another experiment, students perceived professors who occupied well-decorated offices as being more credible than those occupying less attractive offices,[109] and when doctors remove their desk, patients feel almost five times more at ease during office visits.[110] Further, when chairs were removed from the edge of a convalescence ward and placed around small tables, the number of conversations among patients doubled. In office cubicles, those occupants who face out rather than in send the message that they're open to communication—and it also allows them to better protect their work's confidentiality.[111]

> ## At the beginning of the long dash . . .
>
> —Phrase introducing national time signal since 1941, *Dominion Observatory*

Time

Chronemics is the study of how humans use and structure time. The way we handle time can express both intentional and unintentional messages.[112] For instance, waiting can be an indicator of status. "Important" people, whose time is supposedly more valuable than that of others, may be seen by appointment only, while it is acceptable to intrude without notice on lesser beings. A related rule is that low-status people must never make high-status people wait. It would be a serious mistake to show up late for a job interview, whereas the interviewer might keep you cooling your heels in the lobby. Important people are often whisked to the head of a restaurant or airport line, while presumably less exalted masses are forced to wait their turn.

> **Chronemics**
> The study of how humans use and structure time.

Time can be a marker not only of power and status but also of relationships. Research shows that the amount of time spent with a relational partner sends important messages about valuing that person.[113] In one study analyzing 20 nonverbal behaviours, "spending time together" was the most powerful predictor of both relational satisfaction and perceived interpersonal understanding.[114] Time is also measured and valued in mediated communication. Studies show that the length of time it takes for someone to respond to e-mail messages or to postings in virtual groups has a strong correlation with perceptions of that person.[115] As you

Invitation TO INSIGHT

Classroom Communication Climate

Teachers and professors have a lot of control over the type of communication climate that is created in their classrooms, and they generally do this by nonverbal means. For instance, the professor's influence becomes more evident in situations where you take two different courses in exactly the same classroom. If one follows the other, it can be amazing just how dissimilar the room, and the atmosphere, can feel.

Think about the types of classes that you find most conducive to learning. Which ones work better for you: large lecture halls where information is fed to students via PowerPoint presentations and "miked" professors, or smaller classes where seats can be arranged to suit a variety of activities, such as in a circle for class discussion, in small clumps for small-group discussions, or around tables that allow professors to visit student groups?

Become aware of the communication climate in your classes. Use the following nonverbal dimensions to analyze how nonverbal messages influence your classroom comfort level:

- lighting
- seating arrangements
- the professor's use of space
- the professor's use of facial expressions, gestures, and eye contact
- the professor's use of visual aids
- the professor's tone of voice
- the colour and temperature of the room
- the number of windows and other objects in the room
- the professor's attention to chronemics, or time
- the closeness of the other students
- the smells in the room
- the wall coverings and other decorating schemata
- the ventilation system
- the physical attractiveness of class members

might guess, quick responses get positive appraisals, while tardy or neglected replies can have an adverse effect on trust and effectiveness in virtual groups.[116]

LO[5]
Communication in the Workplace

Nonverbal Communication in the Workplace

To get a job, most people go through the interview process, and their success or failure depends largely on their nonverbal communication. For instance, one review of research concluded that successful candidates had good eye contact and communicated in a dynamic, enthusiastic, professional, and assertive manner. They also smiled and nodded more than unsuccessful interviewees.[117] See the box for some suggested nonverbal behaviours that can increase your chances of being hired.

Regardless of whether you work in education, health care, government, the service industry, or construction, you will be more effective at your job if you are skilled at sending (encoding) and receiving (decoding) nonverbal messages. Communicate in a professional manner by using eye contact to signal interest, attentiveness, and credibility. Move out from behind your desk and arrange meetings so participants are seated around a table, preferably a round one.[118] Be sensitive to your posture, facial expressions, and paralanguage. Increase your awareness of the nonverbal messages of others to get the entire message they are conveying. It's also important to watch for subtle nuances, those microexpressions that contain so much unspoken information. To widen your knowledge and tolerance of intercultural communication, associate with individuals from different cultures.[119]

"Say what's on your mind, Harris—the language of dance has always eluded me."

© Robert Mankoff / The New Yorker Collection / www.cartoonbank.com.

Tips for Using Nonverbal Cues to Land the Job

Dress appropriately.
Shake hands with the interviewer.
Sit after you have been invited to do so.
Lean forward.
Use your posture to indicate interest.
Mirror the interviewer's position.
Establish and maintain eye contact.
Use appropriate facial expressions.
Smile when appropriate.
Use appropriate gestures.
Avoid adaptors.
Show your enthusiasm through your body and voice.
Avoid the use of disfluencies.
Maintain a good rate.
Match your interviewer's volume.
Be attentive.

© OJO Images/Superstock

Consider your clothing. Since the late 1990s, employees are dressing more casually—*profession* casual is the term. At the same time, because image is so important in the business world, young professionals are seeking advice from image consultants to help them hone their look.[120] They're being directed to invest in good-quality, professional-looking clothing and to focus on grooming and projecting an air of confidence.[121] Related to this is etiquette, particularly during the business lunch. Adeodata Czink, founder of Business of Manners in Toronto, recommends that hosts arrive early, toast their guests, and arrange payment so the bill never reaches the table. She also recommends that you alert guests if there's spinach, a pepper grain, or broccoli lodged in their teeth. Make eye contact and gently touch your tooth to indicate where the food is lodged. Czink says that fellow diners will appreciate your concern—and discretion.[122]

Endnotes

1. Research summarized by J. K. Burgoon (1994). "Nonverbal Signals." In M. L. Knapp & G. R. Miller (Eds.). *Handbook of Interpersonal Communication* (p. 235). Newbury Park, CA: Sage.

2. For a review of the importance of nonverbal skills in interpersonal communication, see R. E. Riggio (2006). "Nonverbal Skills and Abilities." In V. Manusov & M. L. Patterson (Eds.). *The Sage Handbook of Nonverbal Communication* (pp. 79–86). Thousand Oaks, CA: Sage.

3. Research supporting these claims is cited in J. K. Burgoon & G. D. Hoobler (2002). "Nonverbal Signals." In M. L. Knapp & J. A. Daly (Eds.), *Handbook of Interpersonal Communication*, 3rd ed. Thousand Oaks, CA: Sage.

4. S. E. Jones & C. D. LeBaron (2002). "Research on the Relationship between Verbal and Nonverbal Communication: Emerging Interactions." *Journal of Communication, 52*, 499–521.

5. B. M. DePaulo (1994). "Spotting Lies: Can Humans Learn to Do Better?" *Current Directions in Psychological Science, 3*, 83–86.

6. Not all communication theorists agree with the claim that all nonverbal behaviour has communicative value. For a contrasting opinion, see Burgoon, "Nonverbal Signals," pp. 229–232.

7. F. Manusov (Summer 1991). "Perceiving Nonverbal Messages: Effects of Immediacy and Encoded Intent on Receiver Judgments." *Western Journal of Speech Communication, 55*, 235–253. See also R. Buck and C. A. VanLear (2002). "Verbal and Nonverbal Communication: Distinguishing Symbolic, Spontaneous, and Pseudo-Spontaneous Nonverbal Behaviour." *Journal of Communication, 52*, 522–541.

8. See, for example, T. Clevenger Jr. (1991). "Can One Not Communicate? A Conflict of Models." *Communication Studies, 42*, 340–353.

9. J. K. Burgoon & B. A. LePoire (1999). "Nonverbal Cues and Interpersonal Judgments: Participant and Observer Perceptions of Intimacy, Dominance, Composure, and Formality." *Communication Monographs, 66*, 105–124. See also Burgoon & Hoobler, op. cit.

10. C. F. Keating (2006). "Why and How the Silent Self Speaks Volumes: Functional Approaches to Nonverbal Impression Management." In V. Manusov & M. L. Patterson (Eds.). *The Sage Handbook of Nonverbal Communication* (pp. 321–340). Thousand Oaks, CA: Sage.

11. A. Ramirez & J. K. Burgoon (2004). "The Effect of Interactivity on Initial Interactions: The Influence of Information Valence and Modality and Information Richness on Computer-Mediated Interaction." *Communication Monographs, 71*, 442–447.

12. K. Byron & D. Baldridge, D. (2007). "E-Mail Recipients' Impressions of Senders' Likeability: The Interactive Effect of Nonverbal Cues and Recipients' Personality." *Journal of Business Communication, 44*, 137.

13. "Smile When You Write That." *Los Angeles Times,* March 18, 1999, p. C2.

14. E. S. Cross & E. A. Franz (April 2003). *Talking Hands: Observation of Bimanual Gestures as a Facilitative Working Memory Mechanism.* Cognitive Neuroscience Society 10th Annual Meeting, New York.

15. M. T. Motley (1993). "Facial Affect and Verbal Context in Conversation: Facial Expression as Interjection." *Human Communication Research, 20*, 3–40.

16. J. N. Capella & D. M. Schreiber (2006). "The Interaction Management Function of Nonverbal Cues." In V. Manusov & M. L. Patterson (Eds.). *The Sage Handbook of Nonverbal Communication* (pp. 361–379). Thousand Oaks, CA: Sage.

17. See, for example, K. Drummond and R. Hopper (1993). "Acknowledgment Tokens in Series," *Communication Reports, 6*, 47–53; and H. M. Rosenfeld (1987). "Conversational Control Functions of Nonverbal Behaviour." In A. W. Siegman and S. Feldstein (Eds.). *Nonverbal Behaviour and Communication*, 2nd ed. Hillsdale, NJ: Erlbaum.

18. H. Giles & B. A. LePoire (2006). "The Ubiquity of Social Meaningfulness of Nonverbal Communication." In V. Manusov & M. L. Patterson (Eds.). *The Sage Handbook of Nonverbal Communication* (pp. xv–xxvii). Thousand Oaks, CA: Sage.

19. J. Hale & J. B. Stiff (1990). "Nonverbal Primacy in Veracity Judgments." *Communication Reports, 3*, 75–83; and J. B. Stiff, J. L. Hale, R. Garlick, & R. G. Rogan (1990). "Effect of Individual Judgments of Honesty and Deceit." *Southern Speech Communication Journal, 55*, 206–229.

20. J. K. Burgoon, T. Birk, & M. Pfau (1990). "Nonverbal Behaviours, Persuasion, and Credibility." *Human Communication Research, 17*, 140–169.

21. P. Ekman (2003). *Emotions Revealed: Recognizing Faces and Feelings to Improve Communication and Emotional Life.* New York: Holt.

22. A. Vrig (2006). "Nonverbal Communication and Deception." In V. Manusov & M. L. Patterson (Eds.). *The Sage Handbook of Nonverbal Communication* (pp. 341–360). Thousand Oaks, CA: Sage.

23. Summarized in L. K. Guerrero and K. Floyd (2006). *Nonverbal Communication in Close Relationships.* Mahweh, NJ: Erlbaum. See also B. M. DePaulo (1980). "Detecting Deception Modality Effects." In L. Wheeler (Ed.). *Review of Personality and Social Psychology,* vol. 1. Beverly Hills, CA: Sage; and J. Greene, D. O'Hair, M. Cody, & C. Yen (1985). "Planning and Control of Behaviour during Deception." *Human Communication Research, 11*, 335–364.

24. J. K. Burgoon & T. R. Levine (2010). "Advances in Deception Detection." In S. W. Smith & S. R. Wilson (Eds.). *New Directions in Interpersonal Communication Research* (pp. 201–220). Thousand Oaks, CA: Sage.

25. C. Lock (2004). "Deception Detection: Psychologists Try to Learn How to Spot a Liar." *Science News Online, 166*, 72.

26. L. Caso, A. Vrij, S. Mann, & G. DeLeo (2006). "Deceptive Responses: The Impact of Verbal and Non-Verbal Countermeasures." *Legal and Criminological Psychology, 11*, 99–111; and A. Vrig (2004). "Why Professionals Fail to Catch Liars and How They Can Improve." *Legal and Criminological Psychology, 9*, 159–181.

27. T. Levine (2009). "To Catch a Liar." *Communication Currents, 4*, 1–2.

28. A. E. Lindsey & V. Vigil (1999). "The Interpretation and Evaluation of Winking in Stranger Dyads." *Communication Research Reports, 16*, 256–265.

29. S. Synmanovich (Sept. 11,1998). "Safeway's Perky Rules Yield Plastic Smiles." *San Francisco Business Times.*

30. J. Amos (Sept. 8. 2005). "How Boys Miss Teacher's Reprimand." BBC News, http://news.bbc.co.uk/1/hi/sci/tech/ 4227296.stm. Accessed September 11, 2006.

31. B. P. Rourke (1989). *Nonverbal Learning Disabilities: The Syndrome and the Model.* New York: Guilford. Also see E. S. Fudge (n.d.). "Nonverbal Learning Disorder Syndrome?" www.nldontheweb.org/fudge.htm. Accessed September 11, 2006.

32. J. C. Rosip & J. A. Hall (2004). "Knowledge of Nonverbal Cues, Gender, and Nonverbal Decoding Accuracy." *Journal of Nonverbal Behaviour, 28*, 267–286; and J. A. Hall (1985). "Male and Female Nonverbal Behaviour." In A. W. Siegman & S. Feldstein (Eds.). *Multichannel Integrations of Nonverbal Behaviour.* Hillsdale, NJ: Erlbaum.

33. J. A. Hall (2006). "Women and Men's Nonverbal Communication." In V. Manusov & M. L. Patterson (Eds.). *The Sage Handbook of Nonverbal Communication* (pp. 201–218). Thousand Oaks, CA: Sage.

34. For a comprehensive summary of female/male non-verbal communication differences and similarities, see P.A. Anderson (1999). *Nonverbal Communication: Forms and Functions.* Mountain View, CA: Mayfield; and D. J. Canary & T. M. Emmers-Sommer (1997). *Sex and Gender Differences in Personal Relationships.* New York: Guilford.

35. D. Matsumoto & S. H. Yoo (2005). "Culture and Applied Nonverbal Communication." In R. S. Feldman & R. E. Riggio (Eds.). *Applications of Nonverbal Communication* (pp. 255–277). Mahweh, NJ: Erlbaum.

36. J. M. Lacroix & Y. Rious. (1978). "La Communication Nonverbal Chez Bilingue." *Canadian Journal of Behavioural Science, 10*, 130–140.

37. For further discussion, see J. E. Alcock, D. W. Carmet, & W. W. Sadava (1996). *A Textbook of Social Psychology.* Scarborough, ON: Prentice-Hall.

38. P. Ekman, W. V. Friesen, & J. Baer (May 1984). "The International Language of Gestures." *Psychology Today, 18*, 64–69.

39. M. W. Lustig & J. Koester (1996). *Intercultural Competence:Interpersonal Communication across Cultures.* New York: HarperCollins College.

40. E. Hall (1969). *The Hidden Dimension.* Garden City, NY: Anchor Books.

41. D. Matsumoto (2006). "Culture and Nonverbal Behaviour." In V. Manusov & M. L. Patterson (Eds.). *The Sage Handbook of Nonverbal Communication* (pp. 219–235). Thousand Oaks, CA: Sage.

42. J. B. Bavelas, L. Coates, & T. Johnson (2002). "Listener Responses as a Collaborative Process: The Role of Gaze." *Journal of Communication, 52*, 566–579.

43. R. Levine (1988). "The Pace of Life across Cultures." In J. E. McGrath (Ed.). *The Social Psychology of Time.* Newbury Park, CA: Sage.

44. E. T. Hall & M. R. Hall (1987). *Hidden Differences: Doing Business with the Japanese.* Garden City, NY: Anchor Press.

45. R. Levine & E. Wolff (March 1985). "Social Time: The Heartbeat of Culture." *Psychology Today, 19*, 28–35.

46. P. Eckman (2003). *Emotions Revealed.* New York: Holt.

47. J. Eibl-Eibesfeldt (1972). "Universals and Cultural Differences in Facial Expressions of Emotions." In J. Cole (Ed.). *Nebraska Symposium on Motivation.* Lincoln: University of Nebraska Press.

48. M. Coulson (2004). "Attributing Emotion to Static Body Postures: Recognition Accuracy, Confusions, and Viewpoint Dependence." *Journal of Nonverbal Behaviour, 28*, 117–139.

49. A. Mehrabian (1981). *Silent Messages,* 2nd ed. Belmont, CA: Wadsworth. pp. 47–48, 61–62.

50. J. M. Iverson (1999). "How to Get to the Cafeteria: Gesture and Speech in Blind and Sighted Children's Spatial Descriptions." *Developmental Psychology, 35*, 1132–1142.

51. M. C. Corballis (2002). *From Hand to Mouth: The Origins of Language.* Princeton, NJ: Princeton University Press.

52. Baby Signs Canada (2006). "The Original Baby Sings Program,"www.babysigns.ca/information.htm#1_2. Accessed April 2, 2010.

53. P. A. Andersen (2008). *Nonverbal Communication: Forms and Functions,* 2nd ed. Long Grove, IL: Waveland Press, p. 37.

54. P. Ekman & W. V. Friesen (1969). "The Repertoire of Nonverbal Behaviour: Categories, Origins, Usage, and Coding." *Semiotica, 1*, 49–98.

55. A. Sueyoshi & D. M. Hardison (2005). "The Role of Gestures and Facial Cues in Second Language Listening Comprehension." *Language Learning, 55*, 661–699.

56. B. I. Koerner (March 28, 2003). "What Does a 'Thumbs Up' Mean in Iraq?" Slate, www.slate.com/id/2080812. Accesssed September 11, 2006.

57. P. Ekman & W. V. Friesen (1974). "Nonverbal Behaviour and Psychopathology." In R. J. Friedman & M. N. Katz (Eds.). *The Psychology of Depression: Contemporary Theory and Research.* Washington, DC: J. Winston.

58. Ekman, *Telling Lies,* p. 107.

59. P. Ekman & W. V. Friesen (1975). *Unmasking the Face: A Guide to Recognizing Emotions from Facial Clues.* Englewood Cliffs, NJ: Prentice-Hall.

60. Ibid., p. 150.

61. E. Krumhuber & A. Kappas (2005). "Moving Smiles: The Role of Dynamic Components for the Perception of the Genuineness of Smiles." *Journal of Nonverbal Behaviour, 29*, 3–24.

62. S. F. Davis & J. C. Kieffer (1998). "Restaurant Servers Influence Tipping Behaviour." *Psychological Reports, 83,* 223–226.

63. N. Gueguen & C. Jacob (2002). "Direct Look versus Evasive Glance and Compliance With a Request." *Journal of Social Psychology, 142,* 393–396.

64. P. A. Andersen, L. K. Guerrero, & S. M. Jones (2006). "Nonverbal Behaviour in Intimate Interactions and Intimate Relationships." In V. Manusov & M. L. Patterson (Eds.). *The Sage Handbook of Nonverbal Communication* (pp. 259–278). Thousand Oaks, CA: Sage.

65. J. K. Burgoon & N. E. Dunbar (2006). "Nonverbal Skills and Abilities." In V. Manusov & M. L. Patterson (Eds.). *The Sage Handbook of Nonverbal Communication* (pp. 279–298). Thousand Oaks, CA: Sage.

66. E. H. Hess & J. M. Polt (1960). "Pupil Size as Related to Interest Value of Visual Stimuli." *Science, 132,* 349–350.

67. L. K. Guerrero & K. Floyd (2006). *Nonverbal Communication in Close Relationships.* Mahweh, NJ: Erlbaum.

68. M. Davis, K. A. Markus, & S. B. Walters (2006). "Judging the Credibility of Criminal Suspect Statements: Does Mode of Presentation Matter?" *Journal of Nonverbal Behaviour, 30,* 181–198.

69. L. J. Einhorn (1981). "An Inner View of the Job Interview: An Investigation of Successful Communicative Behaviours. *Communication Education, 30,* 217–228.

70. For a summary, see M. L. Knapp & J. A. Hall (2010). *Nonverbal Communication in Human Interaction, 7th ed.* (pp.344–346). Boston: Cengage. and Hall, op. cit., pp. 344–346.

71. A. R. Trees (2000). "Nonverbal Communication and the Support Process: Interactional Sensitivity in Interactions between Mothers and Young Adult Children." *Communication Monographs, 67,* 239–261.

72. D. Buller & K. Aune (1992). "The Effects of Speech Rate Similarity on Compliance: Application of Communication Accommodation Theory." *Western Journal of Communication, 56,* 37–53. See also D. Buller, B. A. LePoire, K. Aune, & S. V. Eloy (1992). "Social Perceptions as Mediators of the Effect of Speech Rate Similarity on Compliance." *Human Communication Research, 19,* 286–311; and D. B. Buller & R. K. Aune (1988). "The Effects of Vocalics and Nonverbal Sensitivity on Compliance: A Speech Accommodation Theory Explanation." *Human Communication Research, 14,* 301–332.

73. P. A. Andersen (1984). "Nonverbal Communication in the Small Group." In R. S. Cathcart & L. A. Samovar (Eds.). *Small Group Communication: A Reader,* 4th ed. Dubuque, IA: W. C. Brown.

74. M. Harris, S. Ivanko, S. Jungen, S. Hala, & P. Pexman (Oct. 2001). *You're Really Nice: Children's Understanding of Sarcasm and Personality Traits.* Poster presented at the 2nd Biennial Meeting of the Cognitive Development Society, Virginia Beach, VA.

75. K. J. Tusing & J. P. Dillard (2000). "The Sounds of Dominance: Vocal Precursors of Perceived Dominance during Interpersonal Influence." *Human Communication Research, 26,* 148–171.

76. M. Zuckerman & R. E. Driver (1989). "What Sounds Beautiful Is Good: The Vocal Attractiveness Stereotype." *Journal of Nonverbal Behaviour, 13,* 67–82.

77. Free Spirit Gallery (2009). "Throat Singing Music in Inuit Culture," www.freespiritgallery.ca/inuitthroatsinging.htm. Accessed April 3, 2010.

78. R. Heslin & T. Alper (1983). "Touch: A Bonding Gesture." In J. M. Wiemann & R. P. Harrison (Eds.). *Nonverbal Interaction* (pp. 47–75). Beverly Hills, CA: Sage.

79. Ibid.

80. J. Burgoon, J. Walther, & E. Baesler (1992). "Interpretations, Evaluations, and Consequences of Interpersonal Touch." *Human Communication Research, 19,* 237–263.

81. F. N. Willis & H. K. Hamm (1980). "The Use of Interpersonal Touch in Securing Compliance." *Journal of Nonverbal Behaviour, 5,* 49–55.

82. A. H. Crusco & C. G. Wetzel (1984). "The Midas Touch: Effects of Interpersonal Touch on Restaurant Tipping." *Personality and Social Psychology Bulletin, 10,* 512–517.

83. M. Lynn & K. Mynier (1993). " Effect of Server Posture on Restaurant Tipping." *Journal of Applied Social Psychology, 23,* 678–685.

84. D. Kaufman & J. M. Mahoney (1999). "The Effect of Waitresses' Touch on Alcohol Consumption in Dyads." *Journal of Social Psychology, 139,* 261–267.

85. H. Bakwin (1949). "Emotional Deprivation in Infants." *Journal of Pediatrics, 35,* 512–521.

86. T. Adler (Feb. 1993). "Congressional Staffers Witness Miracle of Touch." *APA Monitor,* 12–13.

87. M. S. Driscoll, D. L. Newman, & J. M. Seal (1988). "The Effect of Touch on the Perception of Counsellors." *Counsellor Education and Supervision, 27,* 344–354; and J. M. Wilson (1982). "The Value of Touch in Psychotherapy." *American Journal of Orthopsychiatry, 52,* 65–72.

88. For a summary, see Knapp & Hall, *Nonverbal Communication in Human Interaction,* pp. 93–132.

89. M. Hosoda, E. F. Stone-Romero, & G. Coats (2003). "The Effects of Physical Attractiveness on Job-Related Outcomes: A Meta-Analysis of Experimental Studies." *Personnel Psychology, 56,* 431–462.

90. K. K. Dion (1973). "Young Children's Stereotyping of Facial Attractiveness." *Developmental Psychology, 9,* 183–188.

91. V. Ritts, M. L. Patterson, & M. E. Tubbs (1992). "Expectations, Impressions, and Judgments of Physically Attractive Students: A Review." *Review of Educational Research, 62,* 413–426.

92. T. C. Riniolo, K. C. Johnson, & T. R. Sherman (2006). "Hot or Not: Do Professors Perceived as Physically Attractive Receive Higher Student Evaluations?" *Journal of General Psychology, 133,* 19–35.

93. K. F. Albada, M. L. Knapp, & K. E. Theune (2002). "Interaction Appearance Theory: Changing Perceptions

of Physical Attractiveness Through Social Interaction." *Communication Theory, 12,* 8–40.

94. W. Thourlby (1978). *You Are What You Wear.* New York: New American Library, p. 1.

95. L. Bickman (1974). "The Social Power of a Uniform." *Journal of Applied Social Psychology, 4,* 47–61.

96. S. G. Lawrence & M. Watson (1991). "Getting Others to Help: The Effectiveness of Professional Uniforms in Charitable Fund Raising." *Journal of Applied Communication Research, 19,* 170–185.

97. H. Fortenberry, J. Maclean, P. Morris, & M. O'Connell (1978). "Mode of Dress as a Perceptual Cue to Deference." *Journal of Social Psychology, 104,* 139–150.

98. L. Bickman (April 1974). "Social Roles and Uniforms: Clothes Make the Person." *Psychology Today, 7,* 48–51.

99. M. Lefkowitz, R. R. Blake, & J. S. Mouton (1955). "Status of Actors in Pedestrian Violation of Traffic Signals." *Journal of Abnormal and Social Psychology, 51,* 704–706.

100. L. E. Temple & K. R. Loewen (1993). "Perceptions of Power: First Impressions of a Woman Wearing a Jacket." *Perceptual and Motor Skills, 76,* 339–348.

101. T. F. Hoult (1954). "Experimental Measurement of Clothing as a Factor in Some Social Ratings of Selected American Men." *American Sociological Review, 19,* 326–327.

102. P. A. Andersen, L. K. Guerrero, & S. M. Jones (2006). "Nonverbal Behaviour in Intimate Interactions and Intimate Relationships." In V. Manusov & M. L. Patterson (Eds.). *The Sage Handbook of Nonverbal Communication* (pp. 259–278). Thousand Oaks, CA: Sage.

103. Hall, *The Hidden Dimension.*

104. M. Hackman & K. Walker (1990). "Instructional Communication in the Televised Classroom: The Effects of System Design and Teacher Immediacy." *Communication Education, 39,* 196–206. See also J. C. McCroskey & V. P. Richmond (1992). "Increasing Teacher Influence through Immediacy." In V. P. Richmond & J. C. McCroskey (Eds.). *Power in the Classroom: Communication, Control, and Concern.* Hillsdale, NJ: Erlbaum.

105. C. Conlee, J. Olvera, & N. Vagim (1993). "The Relationships among Physician Nonverbal Immediacy and Measures of Patient Satisfaction with Physician Care." *Communication Reports, 6,* 25–33.

106. G. Brown, T. B. Lawrence, & S. L. Robinson, (2005). "Territoriality in Organizations." *Academy of Management Review, 30,* 577–594.

107. E. Sadalla (1987). "Identity and Symbolism in Housing." *Environment and Behaviour, 19,* 569–587.

108. A. Maslow & N. Mintz (1956). "Effects of Aesthetic Surroundings: Initial Effects of Those Aesthetic Surroundings upon Perceiving 'Energy' and 'Well-Being' in Faces." *Journal of Psychology, 41,* 247–254.

109. J. J. Teven & M. E. Comadena (1996). "The Effects of Office Aesthetic Quality on Students' Perceptions of Teacher Credibility and Communicator Style." *Communication Research Reports, 13,* 101–108.

110. R. Sommer (1969). *Personal Space: The Behavioural Basis of Design.* Englewood Cliffs, NJ: Prentice-Hall.

111. R. Sommer & S. Augustin (2007). "Spatial Orientation in the Cubicle." *Journal of Facilities Management, 5,* 205-214.

112. D. I. Ballard & D. R. Seibold (2000). "Time Orientation and Temporal Variation across Work Groups: Implications for Group and Organizational Communication." *Western Journal of Communication, 64,* 218–242.

113. P. A. Andersen, L. K. Guerrero, & S. M. Jones (2006). "Nonverbal Behaviour in Intimate Interactions and Intimate Relationships." In V. Manusov & M. L. Patterson (Eds.). *The Sage Handbook of Nonverbal Communication* (pp. 259–278). Thousand Oaks, CA: Sage.

114. K. I. Egland, M. A. Stelzner, P. A. Andersen, & B. S. Spitzberg (1997). "Perceived Understanding, Nonverbal Communication, and Relational Satisfaction." In J. E. Aitken & L. J. Shedletsky (Eds.). *Intrapersonal Communication Processes* (pp. 386–396). Annandale, VA: Speech Communication Association.

115. J. B. Walther (2006). "Nonverbal Dynamics in Computer-Mediated Communication." In V. Manusov & M. L. Patterson (Eds.). *The Sage Handbook of Nonverbal Communication* (pp. 461–479). Thousand Oaks, CA: Sage.

116. J. B. Walther & U. Bunz (2005). "The Rules of Virtual Groups: Trust, Liking, and Performance in Computer-Mediated Communication." *Journal of Communication, 55,* 828–846.

117. R. Anderson & G. Killenberg (1999). *Interviewing: Speaking, Listening, and Learning for Professional Life.* Mountain View, CA: Mayfield.

118. M. E. Guffey, K. Rhodes, & P. Rogin (2005). *Business Communication: Process and Product,* 4th Canadian ed. Toronto: Thomson Nelson, p. 88.

119. Ibid.

120. Ibid, p. 86.

121. Ibid.

122. "Let's Do Lunch." *Canadian Business, 78* (2005), 87.

CHAPTER

7

Listening

More than
Meets the Ear

What do you THINK?

I'd rather be the speaker than the listener.

1   2   3   4   5   6   7
strongly agree   strongly disagree

LEARNING OUTCOMES

LO¹ Identify the situations in which you listen mindfully and those when you listen mindlessly, and evaluate the appropriateness of each style in a given situation.

LO² Identify the circumstances in which you listen ineffectively and the poor listening habits you use in these circumstances.

LO³ Identify the response styles (listed on pages 188–198) that you commonly use when listening to others.

LO⁴ Demonstrate a combination of listening styles you could use to respond effectively in a given situation.

I have just wandered back into our conversation and find that you are still rattling on about something or other i think i must have been gone at least twenty minutes and you never missed me now this might say something about my acting ability or it might say something about your sensitivity one thing troubles me tho when it is my turn to rattle on for twenty minutes which I have been known to do have you been missing too.

—Ric Masten

Ric Masten's poem on this page shows that there's more to listening than nodding your head and gazing politely at a speaker. Listening is a demanding activity—and one that is just as important as speaking.

If frequency is a measure of importance, then listening easily qualifies as the most important kind of communication. We spend more time listening than in any other type of communication, including writing, speaking, and reading. One study, summarized in

Figure 7.1, revealed that post-secondary students spend about 11 percent of their communicating time writing, 16 percent speaking, 17 percent reading, but more than 55 percent listening.[1] On the job, studies show that most employees of major corporations in North America spend about 60 percent of each workday listening to others.[2]

FIGURE 7.1

Time Devoted to Communication Activities

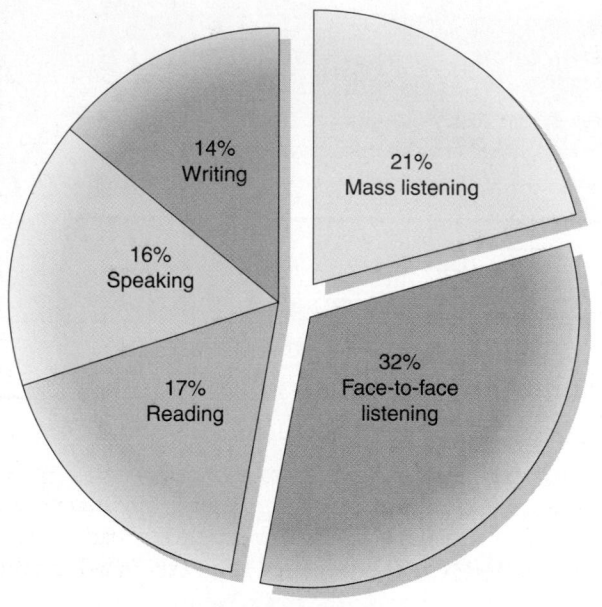

- 14% Writing
- 21% Mass listening
- 16% Speaking
- 17% Reading
- 32% Face-to-face listening

Source: R. Emanuel, J. Adams, K. Baker, E. K. Daufin, C. Ellington, E. Fitts, J. Himsel, L. Holladay, & D. Okewowo (2008). "How College Students Spend Their Time Communicating." *International Journal of Listening*, 22, 13–28.

Listening is also important in terms of making relationships work. In committed relationships, listening to personal information in everyday conversations is considered a vital ingredient of satisfaction.[3] Marital counsellors identified "failing to take the other's perspective when listening" as one of the most frequent communication problems in the couples they see.[4] When a group of adults was asked what communication skills were most important in family and social settings, listening was ranked first.[5] In fact, the *International Journal of Listening* devoted an entire issue to exploring various contexts in which listening skills are crucial. These included education,[6] health care,[7] religion,[8] and the business world.[9] The vital role that listening plays in the workplace is further discussed later in the chapter.

MANKOFF

"I'm sorry, dear. I wasn't listening. Could you repeat what you've said since we've been married?"

© Robert Mankoff/The New Yorker Collection/www.cartoonbank.com

> Listening, not imitation, may be the sincerest form of flattery.
>
> —Dr. Joyce Brothers

LO[1]
Listening Defined

So far we've used the term *listening* as if it needs no explanation. Actually, there's more to this concept than you might think. Interpersonal **listening** is defined as the process of making sense of others' spoken messages. Because listening is a response to speech, there's a nonverbal dimension as well, because the way a statement is expressed can affect its meaning. Good listeners pay attention to paralanguage, facial expression, and a host of other nonverbal cues.

> **Listening**
> Making sense of others' spoken messages.

Hearing versus Listening

People often think of hearing and listening as the same thing, but they are quite different. Hearing is the process in which sound waves strike the eardrum and cause vibrations that are transmitted to the brain. Listening occurs when the brain reconstructs these electrochemical impulses into a representation of the original sound and then gives them meaning. Barring illness, injury, or earplugs, you can't stop hearing.[10] Your ears will pick up sound waves and transmit them to your brain whether you want them to or not.

As the cartoon on this page shows, people hear all the time without listening. We automatically and unconsciously block out irritating sounds or stop listening when

EYES

UNDIVIDED ATTENTION

HEART

EAR

The Chinese characters that make up the verb *to listen* tell us something significant about this skill.

we find a subject unimportant or uninteresting. TV commercials and nagging complaints are common examples of messages we may tune out.

Mindless Listening

When we listen, we tend to process information in two ways, and this is referred to as the *dual-process theory*.[11] Social scientists use the terms *mindless* and *mindful* to describe these different ways of listening.[12] **Mindless listening** occurs when we react to others' messages automatically and routinely, without much mental investment. It's a kind of "superficial" listening.

While the term *mindless* may sound negative, this type of processing can be valuable in that it frees us to focus on messages that require careful attention.[13] Plus, it's impractical to listen carefully to the huge number of messages we're exposed to daily. The only realistic way to manage this onslaught of messages is to be "lazy" at times. If you think about the messages you heard today, you've probably processed most of them mindlessly.

Mindful Listening

By contrast, **mindful listening** involves giving careful and thoughtful attention and responses to the messages we receive. You tend to listen mindfully when a message is important to you or when people you care about speak about something that's important to them. Think of how your ears perk up when someone starts talking about your money ("The car insurance will cost how much?") or how you tune in when a close friend tells you about the loss of a loved one. In situations like these, you give the message sender your complete attention.

Sometimes we respond mindlessly to information that deserves mindful attention. For instance, Ellen Langer's determination to study mindfulness began when her grandmother complained about headaches coming from a "snake crawling around" beneath her skull. She was diagnosed with senility, but her grandmother actually had a brain tumor that eventually took her life. The event made a deep impression on Langer:

> For years afterward I kept thinking about the doctors' reactions to my grandmother's complaints,

Mindless listening
Reacting to others' messages automatically, without much mental investment.

Mindful listening
Giving careful and thoughtful attention and responses to the messages we receive.

ZITS © ZITS PARTNERSHIP, KING FEATURES SYNDICATE

and about our reactions to the doctors. They went through the motions of diagnosis, but were not open to what they were hearing. Mindsets about senility interfered. We did not question the doctors; mindsets about experts interfered.[14]

Clearly, there are times when we need to consciously and carefully listen to what others are telling us. That kind of mindful listening is the focus of the remainder of this chapter.

Teaching Doctors to Listen

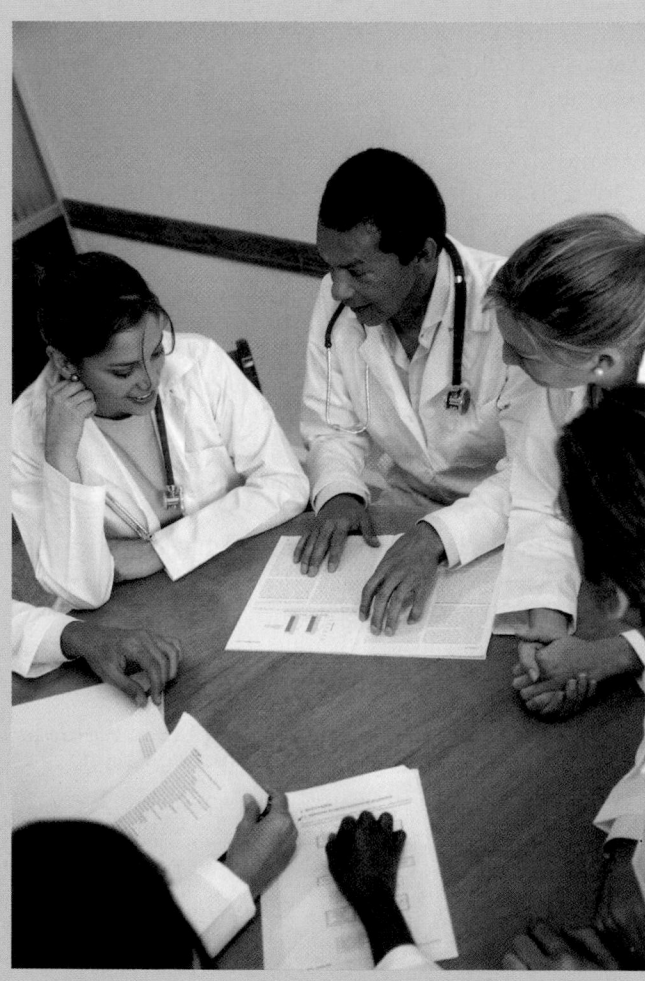

As she looks up at the young faces in the auditorium, Cathy Chovaz's voice wavers slightly. "I could be you," she tells the audience. "You could be me. I went through university like every other student, and when I graduated, the whole world was there waiting for me. Then, bang—that whole reality changed drastically for me and my family." Her hands never stop gesturing, a habit cultivated after losing her hearing nine years ago. Chovaz has RED-M syndrome, a rare condition associated with constrictions of the small arteries in the brain,

eyes, and ears that can result in small strokes, deafness, blindness, and brain dysfunction. "It wasn't just me lying there in the hospital," Chovaz tells the medical students. "With a patient come her dreams, hopes, and ambitions. When you admit a patient, you admit all of that."

Chovaz, 35, is telling her story to first-year medical students at the University of Western Ontario in a unique program where patients become teachers and medical students learn about the human side of medicine. Developed by Dr. John Howard, it was designed as part of a shift toward patient-centred medicine. "Sometimes doctors need to be encouraged to listen to what the patient wants, rather than simply dispensing treatment," says Dr. Howard.

Dr. Wayne Weston sees the need to create doctors who are good advocates, gatekeepers, collaborators, and, most importantly, communicators. Patients' number one beef about doctors is their poor listening skills, and according to Weston, "It's one of the most common complaints to the College of Physicians and Surgeons of Ontario and a leading cause of lawsuits." It's also one of the chief reasons why women switch doctors.

On the first day of UWO's clinical methods course, students listen to the stories of several patients and develop a mission statement that describes the qualities that make good physicians. That mission becomes a focal point of the class's undergraduate medical education for students and instructors alike and helps students determine the kind of doctors they want to become. The day is an invaluable one for students, and the first-year students really listen to the patients' stories.

For Chovaz, her experience with doctors ranged from those who truly acknowledged the power of her spirit to those who treated her as a fascinating collection of symptoms. Her advice to students: "Approach your patients as whole people. People who come to you need to be in partnership with you. Keep your minds and hearts open." An improved doctor-patient relationship is long overdue.

Dahlia Reich

Dahlia Reich, "Building Better Doctors: A Medical School Teaches Compassion to Future MDs (University of Western Ontario)", *Chatelaine*, v 69(4), April 1996, p. 190. Courtesy of *Chatelaine* Magazine © Rogers Publishing Ltd.

> Do not speak, my son, unless you can improve on silence.
>
> —Buddhist saying

Elements in the Listening Process

There's more to listening than passively absorbing a speaker's words. In reality, listening is a process that consists of five elements: hearing, attending, understanding, responding, and remembering.

Hearing

Hearing is the physiological dimension of listening when sound waves strike the ear at a certain frequency and loudness. Hearing can be influenced by background noises, especially if they are loud or at the same frequency. For many people, the challenge of hearing is even more difficult due to physiological problems. According to a survey conducted by the Canadian Hearing Society, some 23 percent of Canadians suffer from some degree of hearing loss.[15]

The major cause of hearing loss is exposure to noise. Marshall Chasin, an audiologist at the University of Toronto, notes that prolonged exposure to sounds above 85 decibels—equivalent of the sound of a dial tone—can cause permanent hearing loss. Little wonder individuals experience temporary hearing loss after attending a rock concert, which registers about 110 decibels. Chasin recommends that we preserve our hearing by reducing the volume of our MP3 players.[16]

Attending

Whereas hearing is a physiological process, **attending** is a psychological part of the selection process. We would go crazy if we attended to everything we hear, so we filter out some messages and focus on others. Needs, wants, desires, and interests determine what is attended to, and we attend most carefully to messages when there's a payoff for doing so.[17] If you want to get better acquainted with others, you'll pay careful attention to almost anything they say, in hopes of improving the relationship.

Surprisingly, attending also helps the message sender. Participants in one study viewed brief movie segments and then described them to listeners who varied in their degree of attentiveness to the speakers. Later, when researchers tested the speakers' long-term recall, speakers who had recounted the movie to attentive listeners remembered more details of the film.[18]

Understanding

Understanding occurs when we make sense of a message. But it is possible to hear and attend to a message without understanding it at all. And, of course, it's possible to misunderstand a message. Communication researchers use the term **listening fidelity** to describe the degree of congruence between what a listener understands and what the message sender attempted to communicate.[19]

Responding

Responding to a message consists of giving observable feedback to the speaker, and while we don't always respond visibly to a speaker, research suggests we should. One study of 195 critical incidents in banking and medical settings showed that a major difference between effective and ineffective listening was the type of feedback offered.[20] Good listeners kept eye contact and reacted with appropriate facial expressions—which was of particular importance to children in one study who were asked to evaluate "good" versus "bad" listeners.[21] Verbal feedback such as answering questions and exchanging ideas also demonstrate attentive behaviour. It's easy to imagine how a slumped posture, bored expression, and yawning can signal less effective listening.

Igor Kopelnitsky/Getty Images

Attending
The process of filtering out some messages and focusing on others.

Understanding
Occurs when sense is made of a message.

Listening fidelity
The degree of congruence between what a listener understands and what the message sender intended to convey.

Responding
Giving observable feedback to a speaker.

Monkey Business Images/Shutterstock

message (what we remember) is a small fraction of what we hear. You can begin to get a sense of how tough it is to listen effectively by trying this exercise.

LO²
The Challenge of Listening

One way to become a better listener is to recognize areas that need improvement.

Types of Ineffective Listening

Although a certain amount of ineffective listening is inevitable, and sometimes even understandable, there are several types of ineffective listening.

Pseudolistening

Pseudolistening is an imitation of the real thing. Pseudolisteners give the appearance of being attentive, but their thoughts are elsewhere. They look you in the eye, nod and smile at the right times, and occasionally they even respond with an "uh huh." Pseudolistening is like counterfeit communciation.

Stage-hogging

Stage-hogs (sometimes called "conversational narcissists") try to turn the topic of conversations to themselves instead of showing interest in the speaker.[23] One **stage-hogging** strategy is a "shift-response"—changing the focus of the conversation from the speaker to the narcissist: "You think *your* math class is tough? You ought to try my communication theory class!"

Interruptions are another hallmark of stage-hogging. Interrupting prevents listeners from learning potentially valuable information and can damage their

Because interpersonal communciation is *transactional* in nature, remember that as we are receiving messages, we are also responding.

Remembering

Remembering is the ability to recall information. Unfortunately, we remember only 50 percent of what we hear *immediately* after hearing it, even if we work hard to listen.[22] Within eight hours, that 50 percent drops to about 35 percent. After two months, the average recall is only about 25 percent of the original message. Given the amount of information we process daily—from teachers, friends, the radio, TV, and other sources—the *residual*

Invitation TO INSIGHT

Listening Breakdowns
You can overcome believing in some common myths about listening by recalling specific instances when

1. You heard another person's message but did not attend to it.
2. You attended to a message but forgot it almost immediately.
3. You attended to and remembered a message but did not understand it accurately.
4. You understood a message but did not respond sufficiently to convey your understanding to the sender.
5. You failed to remember some or all of an important message.

"Someday, you'll act like you understand."

© Bruce Eric Kaplan/The New Yorker Collection/www.cartoonbank.com

relationship with the speaker. Applicants who interrupt the questions in an employment interview, for example, are likely to be rated less favourably than job seekers who wait until the interviewer finishes speaking before they respond.[24]

> Listening ear pressed against stone it isn't quiet but silent so that the sounds I hear are not from outside me any longer but gyrating dancing thoughts or the small noise my body makes in its act of living.
>
> —Al Purdy,
> "Listening"

Selective Listening

Selective listeners respond only to the parts of your remarks that interest them and reject everything else. While **selective listening** can be legitimate (e.g., screening out commercials, background noises), it is less appropriate in personal settings where your inattention can be insulting and hurtful.

> You may as well tell people the truth because they don't listen anyway.
>
> —Earl Work, sales motivator,
> Quoting "a friend from Prince Albert"

Insulated Listening

Insulated listening is a style of listening in which the receiver ignores undesirable information. If a topic arises that the listener would rather not deal with, he or she simply fails to hear or acknowledge it. If reminded about an unfinished job or poor grades, she or he may nod and answer, but then promptly forget what you've just said.

Defensive Listening

Defensive listening means taking others' remarks as personal attacks. An example is when teenagers take their parents' questions about their friends and activities as distrustful snooping. Many defensive listeners suffer from shaky presenting images and avoid admitting it by projecting their own insecurities onto others.

Ambushing

Ambushers listen carefully to you, but only because they're collecting information to pounce on you. The cross-examining prosecution attorney is a good example of **ambushing**. Using this kind of strategy will justifiably initiate defensiveness in the other person.

Selective listening
A listening style in which receivers respond only to the messages that interest them.

Insulated listening
A style in which the receiver ignores undesirable information.

Defensive listening
A response style in which the receiver perceives a speaker's comments as an attack.

Ambushing
A style in which the receiver listens carefully to gather information to use in an attack on the speaker.

GoGo Images/Jupiter images

Bright-eyed college students in lecture halls aren't necessarily listening to the professor, the American Psychological Association was told yesterday.

If you shot off a gun at sporadic intervals and asked the students to encode their thoughts and moods at that moment, you would discover that

- About 20 percent of the students, men and women, are pursuing erotic thoughts.
- Another 20 percent are reminiscing about something.
- Only 20 percent are actually paying attention to the lecture, and 12 percent actively listen. The others are worrying, daydreaming, thinking about lunch or—surprise—religion (8 percent).

This confirmation of the lecturer's worst fears was reported by Paul Cameron, an assistant professor at Wayne State University in Detroit. Cameron's results were based on a nine-week course in introductory psychology that included 85 college sophomores. A gun was fired 21 times at random intervals, usually when Cameron was in the middle of a sentence.

Sunday edition, *San Francisco Examiner and Chronicle*

Insensitive Listening

Those who use **insensitive listening** respond to the superficial content in a message but miss the more important emotional information that may not be expressed directly. Insensitive listeners tend to ignore nonverbal cues and lack empathy.

> Most conversations are simply monologues delivered in the presence of a witness.
>
> —Margaret Millar,
> *The Weak-Eyed Bat*

Why We Don't Listen Better

In addition to the various types of ineffective listening, there are several other reasons that make it impossible for us to listen well *all* the time. We'll outline a few of them here.

Message Overload

Clearly, we live in a message overloaded society. We have face-to-face messages and personal media messages (text messages, phone calls, e-mails, and instant messages), all competing for our attention. This deluge of communication has made the challenge of attending tougher than at any time in human history,[25] and it's little wonder that listening can be difficult.

Preoccupation

Another reason we don't always listen carefully is that we're often preoccupied with personal concerns. It's hard to pay attention when you're worrying about an upcoming exam or thinking about what you're going to do with your life.

Rapid Thought

Listening carefully is also difficult for physiological reasons. The average person speaks between 100 and 150 words per minute,[26] but we can process information at rates up to 600 words per minute. Thus, we have "spare time" in our minds, which we ultimately fill by thinking about personal interests, daydreaming, planning a rebuttal, and so on. The trick is to use this spare time to understand the speaker's ideas.

Effort

Listening effectively is hard work—so hard that physical changes actually occur during careful listening: The heart rate quickens, respiration increases, and body temperature rises.[27] These changes are similar to the body's reaction to physical effort. This is no coincidence—listening carefully can be just as taxing as a workout.[28] If you've come home exhausted after an evening of listening intently to a friend in need, you know how draining the process can be.

In the movie **The Devil Wears Prada,** Miranda Priestly (Meryl Streep) is every employee's nightmare. She's a self-centered, domineering, hard-driven boss who treats the people who work for her like slaves. The domineering boss is a model of ineffective listening.

Insensitive listening
Failure to recognize the thoughts or feelings that are not directly expressed by a speaker.

20th Century Fox/The Kobal Collection/Lacombe, Brigitte

> I don't mind that you are talking so long as you don't mind that I'm not listening.
>
> —"Morning Smile"
> *Cape Breton Post*

External Noise

The physical world in which we live often presents distractions that make it hard to pay attention to others. Consider, for example, how the efficiency of your listening decreases when you are seated in a crowded, hot, stuffy room, surrounded by others talking next to you and traffic noises outside. Even the best intentions aren't enough to ensure clear understanding in such circumstances.

Faulty Assumptions

We often make faulty assumptions that lead us to believe we're listening attentively when quite the opposite is true. For instance, we are less likely to listen when the subject is a familiar one, when we assume the speaker's thoughts are too simple or too complex, or when we think the topic is unimportant. In such circumstances, we should try to pay close attention to compensate for our assumptions.

Lack of Apparent Advantages

It often seems that there's more to gain by speaking than by listening. When business consultant Nancy Kline asked some of her clients why they interrupted their colleagues, these are the reasons she heard:

My idea is better than theirs.

If I don't interrupt them, I'll never get to say my idea.

I know what they are about to say.

They don't need to finish their thoughts since mine are better.

Nothing about their idea will improve with further development.

It is more important for me to get recognized than it is to hear their idea.

I am more important than they are.[29]

Even if some of these thoughts are true, the egotism behind them is stunning. Furthermore, nonlisteners are likely to find that the people they cut off are less likely to treat their ideas with respect. Like defensiveness, listening is often reciprocal: You get what you give.

> I talk too much but the manner of your listening calls the words out of me. You say almost nothing. Yet there would be only silence if you were not here.
>
> —Alden Nowlan,
> "Apology"

Lack of Training

A common but mistaken belief is that listening, like breathing, is natural. In truth, listening is a skill that few people do well. Unfortunately, there is no connection between how competently most communicators *think* they listen and how competent they really are in their ability to understand others.[30] The good news is that listening can be improved through instruction and training.[31] Unfortunately, more time is spent teaching other types of communication than is spent teaching listening. Table 7.1 reflects this lopsided arrangement.

TABLE 7.1
Comparison of Communication Activities

	Listening	Speaking	Reading	Writing
Learned	First	Second	Third	Fourth
Used	Most	Next to most	Next to least	Least
Taught	Least	Next to least	Next to most	Most

CHAPTER 7 Listening: More than Meets the Ear

How to Communicate with Someone with a Hearing Disability

Bruce C. Anderson has some useful advice.

I grew up with a mild hearing disability. The word "mild" doesn't begin to describe how this affected my life. I couldn't hear many of the sounds or tones that are part of most people's voices. You can get an idea what this is like by imagining how hard it would be to listen to a muffled, quiet voice that is being drowned out by loud TV and radio playing at the same time, or trying to understand somebody whispering words while your ears are covered and your head is turned away.

If you're communicating with someone who has a hearing disability, here are a few tips. Have patience when asked to repeat something once, twice, or even three times. Remember, the deaf and hard of hearing are doing the best they can. Help is very hard to ask for, and it is very difficult to draw attention to yourself by asking others what was said. If this still has not solved the problem, try another avenue, such as using different words or moving to a more quiet location to talk. Even writing something down may be necessary. Hard of hearing and deaf people listen with our eyes, so make sure you're standing or sitting so that the other person can see your face and your gestures.

If you make efforts like these, you will help people with hearing disabilities. And you might also get a new appreciation and respect for their world.

Hearing Problems

Sometimes a person's listening ability suffers from a physiological hearing problem. In such cases, both the person with the problem and others can become frustrated at the ineffective communication that results. One survey explored the feelings of adults who have spouses with hearing loss. Nearly two-thirds of the respondents said they feel annoyed when their partner can't hear them clearly. Almost a quarter said that beyond just being annoyed, they felt ignored, hurt, or sad. Many of the respondents believe their spouses are in denial about their condition, which makes the problem even more frustrating.[32] If you suspect that you or someone you know suffers from a hearing loss, it's wise to consult a physician or audiologist.

Meeting the Challenge of Listening Better

After reading the preceeding few pages, you might decide that listening well is impossible. However, here are some simple ways to improve you listening.

> Learn to listen. Opportunity could be knocking at your door very softly.
>
> —Frank Tyger

Talk Less

Zeno of Citium put it most succinctly: "We have been given two ears and but a single mouth, in order that we may hear more and talk less." If you truly want to understand the speaker, don't stage-hog and shift the conversation to your ideas. Talking less doesn't mean you must remain completely silent. Using feedback to clarify your understanding and seeking new information promotes understanding. Nonetheless, most of us talk too much. Other cultures, including many First Nations people, value listening as much as talking.[33] You can appreciate the value of this approach by trying the exercise on the next page.

To be heard, there are times you must be silent.
—Chinese proverb

© iStockphoto.com/Jodi Matthews

Meetings Going "Topless"

As the capital of information technology, Silicon Valley may have more gadgets per capita than any other place on the planet. Yet even here, "always on" can be a real turnoff.

Frustrated by workers so plugged in that they tuned out in the middle of business meetings, a growing number of companies are going "topless," as in no laptops allowed. Also banned from some conference rooms: BlackBerrys, iPhones, and other devices on which so many people have come to depend.

Over the years, companies have come up with innovative ways to keep meetings from sucking up time. Some remove chairs and force people to stand. Others get everyone to drink a glass of water beforehand.

But as laptops got lighter and smart phones even smarter, people discovered a handy diversion—making more eye contact with their screens than one another. The practice became so pervasive that Todd Wilkens, who runs a San Francisco design firm, waged a "personal war against CrackBerry."

"In this age of wireless Internet and mobile e-mail devices, having an effective meeting or working session is becoming more and more difficult," he wrote on his company blog in November. "Laptops, BlackBerrys, Sidekicks, iPhones and the like keep people from being fully present. Aside from just being rude, partial attention generally leads to partial results."

Wilkens' firm, Adaptive Path, now encourages everyone to leave their laptops at their desks. His colleague Dan Saffer coined the term "topless," as in laptop-less. Mobile and smart phones must be stowed on a counter or in a box during meetings. "All of our meetings got a lot more productive," Wilkens said.

Jessica Guynn

Los Angeles Times, "Silicon Valley Meetings Go 'Topless,'" Business section, 3/31/08, http://articles.latimes.com/2008/mar/31/business/fi-nolaptops31

Invitation TO INSIGHT

Speaking and Listening with a "Talking Stick"

Explore the benefits of talking less and listening more by using a "talking stick." This exercise is based on the First Nations tradition of "council." Gather a group of people in a circle and designate a particular object as the talking stick. (Almost any manageable object will do.) Participants then pass the object around the circle. Each person may speak

a. when holding the stick,
b. for as long as he or she holds the stick, and
c. without interruption from anyone else in the circle.

When a member is through speaking, the stick passes to the left and the speaker surrendering the stick must wait until it has made its way around the circle before speaking again.

After each member of the group has had the chance to speak, discuss how this experience differed from more common approaches to listening. Decide how the desirable parts of this method could be introduced into everyday conversations.

Get Rid of Distractions

Some distractions are external: ringing telephones, radio or television programs, friends dropping in, and so on. Other distractions are internal: preoccupation with your problems, being hungry, etc. If the information you're seeking is important, do everything possible to eliminate the internal and external distractions. This means turning off the TV, shutting off your cellphone, or moving to a quiet place where you won't be bothered by the work on your desk or the food on the counter.

Don't Judge Prematurely

Most people agree that it's essential to understand ideas before judging them. However, we often make snap judgments before we hear the entire idea, especially when it conflicts with one of our own. Conversations meant to be exchanges of ideas turn into verbal battles. Not all premature judgments are negative, though. We sometimes jump to overly favourable conclusions. It's also tempting to counterattack when we're being criticized, even when those criticisms are true. The lesson contained in these negative examples is clear: Listen first. Make sure you understand. *Then* evaluate.

Look for Key Ideas

It's easy to lose patience with long-winded speakers who don't get to the point—or don't *have* a point, for that matter. Nonetheless, most people do have a central idea. Using your ability to think more quickly than the speaker can talk, you may be able to extract the central idea from the surrounding mass of words. If you can't figure out what the speaker is driving at, use some of the response skills examined in the next section.

LO³
Types of Listening Responses

Of the five components of listening, it's responding that lets us know how well others are tuned in to what we're saying. Think for a moment of someone you consider a good listener. Why did you choose that person? It's probably because of the way she or he responds while you're speaking: making eye contact and nodding when you're talking, staying attentive, reacting with an exclamation when you say something startling, expressing empathy and support when you're hurting, and offering another perspective or advice when you ask for it.[34]

The rest of this chapter will describe a variety of response styles.

> ## Listen or your tongue will keep you deaf.
>
> —Cree proverb

Prompting

Sometimes the best response a listener can give is a small nudge to keep the speaker talking. **Prompting** involves using silences and brief statements of encouragement to draw out others. Besides helping you to better understand the speaker, prompting can help listeners clarify their thoughts and feelings. Consider this example:

> **Katie:** Julie's dad is selling his complete computer system, everything, for $300! He only had it for less than a year, but if I want it I have to buy it now. Someone else is interested. It's a great deal, but it would wipe out my savings. At the rate I spend money, it would take me a year to save up this much again.

> **Logan:** Uh-huh.
>
> **Katie:** I wouldn't be able to take that ski trip over winter break . . . but I sure could save time with my schoolwork . . . and do a better job, too.
>
> **Logan:** That's true.
>
> **Katie:** Do you think I should buy it?
>
> **Logan:** I don't know. What do *you* think?
>
> **Katie:** I just can't decide.
>
> **Logan:** (*silence*)
>
> **Katie:** I'm going to do it. I'll never get a deal like this again.

In cases like this, prompting can be a catalyst to help others find their own answers. Prompting works best when it's sincere. Your eye contact, posture, facial expression, and tone of voice must show your concern as well. Mechanical prompting will just irritate the person.

Questioning

Questioning can help both the person doing the asking and the person answering the question. Questioning can help the asker fill in facts and details, learn what others are thinking and feeling, and find out what the other person may want. For the person answering the questions, they can serve as a tool for self-discovery. While

Prompting
Using silences and brief statements of encouragement to draw out a speaker.

Questioning
A style of helping in which the receiver seeks additional information from the sender to be sure the speaker's thoughts and feelings are being received accurately.

playing counsellor can be dangerous, some questions can encourage others to explore their thoughts and feelings.

Closed questions
Questions that call for a specific or yes/no response.

Open questions
Questions that allow the respondent to answer in a variety of ways and to include a great deal of description and detail.

Sincere questions
Questions aimed at soliciting information that enables the asker to understand the other person.

Counterfeit questions
Questions aimed at sending rather than receiving a message.

Questions are often described as open or closed. **Closed questions** seek a specific or short answer ("What is your name?" "Where do you live?") and are good for gathering facts, but not for drawing out individuals. **Open questions** allow speakers to respond in a variety of ways and to express how they think or feel about something ("Describe how you felt when Pat left you." "Explain your philosophical take on war."). While closed questions ask for specifics, open ones can actually be statements.

Despite their apparent benefits, not all questions are equally helpful. Whereas **sincere questions** are aimed at understanding others, **counterfeit questions** are aimed at sending a message, not receiving one. Counterfeit questions come in several varieties:

- *Questions that trap the speaker.* When your friend says, "You didn't like that movie, did you?" it's clear that your friend disapproves. The question leaves you with two choices: disagree and defend your position, or devalue your reaction by lying or equivocating—"I guess it wasn't perfect." It would be so much easier to respond to a sincere question, such as, "What did you think of the movie?"
- *A tag question.* Phrases like "did you?" or "isn't that right?" at the end of a question can be a tip-off that the asker is looking for agreement, not information. Although some tag questions are genuine requests for confirmation, counterfeit ones are used to coerce agreement: "Don't you think he would make a good boss?" directs you toward a desired response. As a simple solution, changing "Don't you?" to "Do you?" makes the question less leading.
- *Questions that make statements.* "Are you *finally* off the phone?" is more of a statement than a question, and emphasizing certain words can also turn a question into a statement: "You lent money to *Tony*?" We also use questions to offer advice. The person who asks, "Are you going to stand up to him and give him what he deserves?" clearly has stated an opinion about what should be done.

From Don Parker (1968). *Communication: The Transfer of Meaning.* Used by permission of Allyn and Bacon, Boston, MA.

- *Questions that carry hidden agendas.* "Are you busy Friday night?" is a dangerous question to answer. If you say no, you'll be hearing, "Good, because I need some help moving my piano." Obviously, such questions are not designed to enhance understanding; they're setups for the proposal that follows. Other examples include, "Will you do me a favour?" or "If I tell you what happened, will you promise not to get mad?" Wise communicators learn to answer such questions with responses like "It depends" or "Let me hear what you have in mind before I answer."

- *Questions that seek "correct" answers.* Most of us have been victims of a questioner who seeks a particular response. "Which shoes do you think I should wear?" can be a sincere question—unless the asker has a predetermined preference. When this happens, the asker isn't interested in listening to contrary opinions and "incorrect" responses get shot down. Some of these questions may venture into delicate territory: "Do these jeans make me look fat?"

- *Questions based on unchecked assumptions.* "Why aren't you listening to me?" assumes that the other person isn't paying attention. "What's the matter?" assumes that something is wrong. Perception checking is a better way to confirm your assumptions. A perception check offers a description and two interpretations, followed by a sincere request for clarification: "When you didn't show up for class today, I thought maybe you'd slept in or you were sick. What happened?"

Paraphrasing

However valuable, questioning won't always help you understand or help others, because questions can lead to even greater confusion. Therefore, you might want to consider anothe kind of feedback, one that tells you if you've understood what's been said before you ask more questions. This type of feedback, called **paraphrasing** or **active listening**, involves restating the message you thought you heard in your own words and without adding anything new. Sometimes a paraphrase will reflect the ideas you think a speaker has expressed:

> (*To a direction-giver*) "You're telling me to drive down to the traffic light by the high school and turn toward the mountains, is that it?"

> (*To the boss*) "So you need me both this Saturday *and* next Saturday—right?"

Paraphrasing
Repeating a speaker's thoughts and/or feelings in the listener's own words. Also known as *active listening*.

Active listening
Repeating a speaker's thoughts and/or feelings in the listener's own words. Also known as *paraphrasing*.

> The reality of the other person is not in what he reveals to you, but in what he cannot reveal to you. Therefore, if you would understand him, listen not to what he says but rather to what he does not say.
>
> —Kahlil Gibran

Although paraphrasing is typically used to clarify facts or information, it can also be used to learn whether your perception of a person's feelings is accurate:

> "I get the sense that you're in a hurry and would prefer to talk later on. Am I correct in my assumption?"

> "Although you said, 'Forget it,' I get the feeling you're angry. Is this right?"

The key to successful paraphrasing is to restate the other person's comments in your own words as a way of cross-checking the information. But don't simply repeat the person's comments verbatim—it will sound foolish, and you still might not understand what was actually said. Notice the difference between simply parroting a statement and true paraphrasing:

> **Speaker:** I'd like to go, but I can't afford it.
>
> **Parroting:** You'd like to go, but you can't afford it.
>
> **Paraphrasing:** So if we could find a way to cover your costs, you'd be willing to come? Is that right?

> **Speaker:** You look awful!
>
> **Parroting:** You think I look terrible.
>
> **Paraphrasing:** Sounds like you think I've putting on a little weight.

Jupiter images

This conversation between two co-workers shows how paraphrasing can help people solve their own problems. Notice how Jill comes to a conclusion without Mark's advice. Notice also how the paraphrasing sounds natural when combined with sincere questions and other helping styles.

Jill: I've had the strangest feeling about John *(their boss)* lately.

Mark: What's that? *(A simple question invites Jill to go on.)*

Jill: I'm starting to think maybe he has this thing about women—or maybe it's just about me.

Mark: You mean he's coming on to you? *(Mark paraphrases what he thinks Jill has said.)*

Jill: Oh, no, not at all! But it seems like he doesn't take women—or at least me—seriously. *(Jill corrects Mark's misunderstanding and explains herself.)*

Mark: What do you mean? *(Mark asks another simple question to get more information.)*

Jill: Well, whenever we're in a meeting or just talking around the office and he asks for ideas, he always seems to pick men. He gives orders to women—men, too—but he never asks the women to say what they think.

Mark: So you think maybe he doesn't take women seriously, is that it? *(Mark paraphrases Jill's last statement.)*

Jill: He sure doesn't seem interested in their ideas. But that doesn't mean he's a total woman-hater. I know he counts on some women in the office. Teresa has been here forever, and he's always saying he couldn't live without her. And when Brenda got the new computer system up and running last month, I know he appreciated that. He gave her a day off and told everybody how she saved our lives.

Mark: Now you sound confused. *(Reflects her apparent feeling.)*

Jill: I *am* confused. I don't think it's just my imagination. I mean, I'm a good producer, but he has never—not once—asked me for my ideas about how to improve sales or anything. And I can't remember a time when he's asked any other women. But maybe I'm overreacting.

Mark: You're not positive whether you're right, but I can tell that this has you concerned. *(Mark paraphrases both Jill's central theme and her feeling.)*

Jill: Yes. But I don't know what to do about it.

Mark: Maybe you should . . . *(Starts to offer advice but catches himself and decides to ask a question instead.)* So what are your choices?

Jill: Well, I could just ask him if he's aware that he never asks women's opinions. But that might sound too aggressive and angry.

Mark: And you're not angry? *(Tries to clarify how Jill is feeling.)*

Jill: Not really. I don't know whether I should be angry because he's not taking ideas seriously, or whether he just doesn't take my ideas seriously, or whether it's nothing at all.

Mark: So you're mostly confused. *(Reflects Jill's apparent feeling again.)*

Jill: Yes! I don't know where I stand with John, and not being sure is starting to get to me. I wish I knew what he thinks of me. Maybe I could just tell him I'm confused about what is going on here and ask him to clear it up. But what if it's nothing? Then I'll look insecure.

Mark: *(Mark thinks Jill should confront the boss, but he isn't positive that this is the best approach, so he paraphrases what Jill seems to be saying.)* And that would make you look bad.

Jill: I'm afraid maybe it would. I wonder if I could talk it over with anybody else in the office and get their ideas . . .

Mark: . . . see what they think . . .

Jill: Yeah. Maybe I could ask Brenna. She's easy to talk to, and I do respect her judgment. Maybe she could give me some ideas about how to handle this.

Mark: Sounds like you're comfortable with talking to Brenna first. *(Paraphrases.)*

Jill: *(Warming to the idea.)* Yes! Then if it's nothing, I can calm down. But if I do need to talk to John, I'll know I'm doing the right thing.

Mark: Great. Let me know how it goes.

SKILL BUILDER

Paraphrasing Practice

This exercise will help you see that it is possible to understand someone who disagrees with you, without arguing or sacrificing your point of view.

1. Find a partner. Designate one person as *A* and the other as *B*.

2. Find a subject on which you and your partner apparently disagree—a current events topic, a philosophical or moral issue, or perhaps simply a matter of personal taste.

3. Person *A* begins by making a statement on the subject. Person *B*'s job is then to paraphrase the statement. *B*'s job is simply to understand here, and doing so in no way should signify agreement or disagreement with *A*'s remarks.

4. *A* then responds by telling *B* whether her response was accurate. If there was some misunderstanding, *A* should make the correction and *B* should feed back her new understanding of the statement. Continue this process until you're both sure that *B* understands *A*'s statement.

5. Now it's *B*'s turn to respond to *A*'s statement and for *A* to help the process of understanding by correcting *B*.

6. Continue this process until each partner is satisfied that she has explained herself fully and has been understood by the other person.

7. Now discuss the following questions:
   a. How did your understanding of the speaker's statement change after you used active listening?
   b. Did you find that the gap between your position and that of your partner narrowed as a result of active listening?
   c. How did you feel at the end of your conversation? How does this feeling compare to your usual feeling after discussing controversial issues?
   d. How might your life change if you used paraphrasing at home? At work? With friends?

Paraphrasing personal information can also be a tool for helping others, as the "In Real Life" transcript on pages 191–192. shows.[35] Reflecting the speaker's thoughts and feelings (instead of judging or analyzing, for example) shows your involvement and concern. The nonevaluative nature of paraphrasing encourages the problem-holder to discuss the matter and unload some of the concerns he or she may have been carrying around. This catharsis often leads to relief. Finally, paraphrasing helps the problem-holder to sort through the problem and find solutions that weren't apparent before. Such features make paraphrasing a vital skill for those in human services professions, leadership training, and even hostage negotiation.[36]

Effective paraphrasing is a skill that takes time to develop. You can make your paraphrasing sound more natural by taking any of these three approaches, depending on the situation:

1. Change the speaker's wording.

   Speaker: "Social assistance is just another way for Canadians to freeload off the government."

   Paraphrase: "Let me see if I got this right. You're upset because you think social assistance recipients should have to work to receive money."

2. Offer an example of what you think the speaker is talking about.

   Speaker: "Lee is such a jerk. I can't believe the way he acted last night."

   Paraphrase: "You think those jokes were pretty offensive, huh?"

3. Reflect the underlying theme of the speaker's remarks.

   Paraphrase: "You keep reminding me to be careful. Sounds like you're worried that something might happen to me. Am I right?"

Paraphrasing won't always be accurate, but even if your restatement is off-base, your response gives the other person a chance to make a correction. (Note how the examples end with questions in an attempt to confirm if the paraphrase was accurate.)

Because it's an unfamiliar way of responding, paraphrasing may feel awkward at first, but if you start by paraphrasing occasionally and then gradually increase the frequency of such responses, you can begin to learn the benefits of this method.

There are several factors to consider before you decide to paraphrase:

1. *Is the issue complex enough?* If you're fixing dinner, and someone wants to know when it will be ready, it would be exasperating to hear, "You're interested in knowing when we'll be eating."

2. *Do you have the necessary time and concern?* Paraphrasing can take a good deal of time. Therefore,

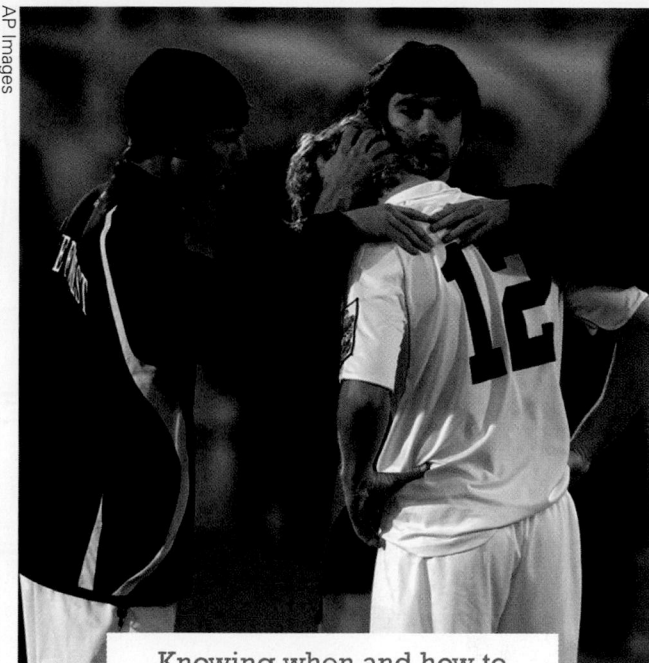

Knowing when and how to provide social support is an important dimension of communication competence.

if you're in a hurry, don't start a conversation you won't be able to finish. Even more important than time is concern: Paraphrasing that comes across as mechanical or as insincere reflecting can do more harm than good.[37]

3. *Can you withhold judgment?* Use paraphrasing only if you are willing to focus on the speaker's message without injecting your own judgments. It can be tempting to rephrase others' comments in a way that leads them toward the position you think is best without ever clearly stating your intentions.

4. *Is your paraphrasing in proportion to other responses?* Paraphrasing can become annoying when it's overused. This is especially true if you suddenly add this approach to your style. It's better to introduce paraphrasing gradually into your repertoire.

Supporting

There are times when people want to hear more than a reflection of how *they* feel— they want to know how *you* feel. **Supportive responses** reveal a listener's solidarity with the speaker's situation and come in the form of "expressions of care, concern, affection, and interest, especially during times of stress or upset."[38]

> **Supporting**
> A helping response that reveals a listener's solidarity with the speaker's situation.

There are several types of support:

Empathizing	"I can understand why you'd be upset about this"
	"Yeah, that class was tough for me, too."
Agreement	"You're right—the landlord is being unfair."
	"Sounds like the job is a perfect match for you."
Offers to help	"I'm here if you need me."
	"I'd be happy to study with you for the next test if you'd like."
Praise	"Wow—you did a fantastic job!"
	"You're a terrific person, and if she doesn't recognize it, that's her problem!"
Reassurance	"The worst part seems to be over. It will probably get easier from here."
	"I'm sure you'll do a great job."

Clearly, receiving comfort and support in the face of personal problems is very helpful. One survey showed that "comforting ability" was among the most important communication skills a friend could have.[39] Research shows that smaller, everyday distresses and upsets can actually take a bigger toll on mental health and physical well-being than major problems.[40] There's no doubt that receiving

"Listen, Mom, I'm not your little girl anymore."

© Bruce Eric Kaplan/The New Yorker Collection/www.cartoonbank.com

emotional support during times of stress is good for your health.[41] This contrasts sharply with nonsupportive messages, which some scholars have called "cold comfort."[42] See Table 7.2 for real cold-comfort messages found in an online discussion.

As these examples show, you're not being supportive if you:

- *Deny others the right to their feelings.* For example, when you say, "Don't worry about it," the underlying message is that you want the person to feel differently, but people cannot just stop worrying. According to the research, "Messages that explicitly acknowledge, elaborate, and legitimize the feelings

TABLE 7.2

Cold Comfort: Messages That Don't Help When You've Just Been Dumped

Don't take it so hard. S/he was a slut/prick anyway.

That's nothing! Want to hear how I got dumped?

I don't know what you ever saw in him/her anyway. S/he's ugly. You can do much better.

You know you had this coming—you were overdue for payback.

S/he was way too young (old) for you.

You can't have everything you want in this life.

Now that it's finally over, I can tell you s/he's been cheating on you.

S/he was just using you for sex.

S/he was always a jerk about you behind your back. Who needs that?

Now we'll have more time to hang out together, just like we used to!

and perspective of a distressed person are perceived as more helpful than messages which only implicitly recognize or deny the feelings and perspective of the other."[43]

- *Minimize the significance of the situation.* Consider the times you've been told, "Hey, it's only _____." Fill in the blank with words like "a job," "her opinion," "a test," "a party." To a victim of verbal abuse, the hurtful message isn't "just words," or to a child who didn't get an invitation, it isn't "just a party."

- *Focus on "then and there" rather than "here and now."* Although it is sometimes true that "you'll feel better tomorrow," sometimes you won't. Even if the prediction, "in 10 years you won't remember her/his name" proves correct, it provides little comfort today.

> # I won't leave you lonely tonight I want you to hold me all night It's gonna be alright won't leave you lonely tonight
>
> —Shania Twain,
> "I Won't Leave You Lonely"

- *Cast judgment.* "It's your own fault—you really shouldn't have done that" is not very encouraging to hear, and it can make people defensive.

- *Focus on yourself.* While it's tempting to share a similar experience you've encountered ("I know exactly how you feel. When something like that happened to me . . ."), such messages aren't perceived as helpful because they draw attention away from the distressed person. [44]

- *Defend yourself.* When your response to others' concerns is to defend yourself ("Don't blame me; I've done my part"), it's clear that you are more concerned with yourself than with supporting the other person.

People often fail to provide appropriate supportive responses. Mourners, for example, report that 80 percent of the statements made to bereaved individuals were unhelpful.[45] Statements such as, "You've got to get out more," "Don't question God's will," "She's out of pain now," were helpful only 3 percent of the time. More helpful were expressions that acknowledged the mourner's feelings. Guidelines for effective support include:

1. *Recognize that you can support another person's struggles without approving of his or her decisions.* Suppose, for instance, that a friend decides to quit a job and you disagree with the decision. You could still be supportive by saying, "I know you've given this a lot of thought and you're doing what you think is best." Responses like this can provide face-saving support without compromising your principles.[46]

2. *Monitor the other person's reaction to your support.* If it doesn't seem to help, consider other types of responses that let him or her explore the issue.

3. *Realize that support isn't always welcome.* In one survey, some people reported occasions when social support wasn't necessary because they felt they could handle the problem themselves.[47] Many regarded uninvited support as an intrusion, while others said it left them feeling more nervous. Most respondents preferred to control whether their distressing situations were discussed, even with the most helpful friend.

Let Mourners Grieve

After a recent death in my family, I received a number of condolence cards that tried to talk me out of my grief. "You should be happy you have your memories," wrote one friend. "You should feel lucky you got to be with your father in the hospital." Lucky? Happy? You've got to be kidding!

Condolences are some of the most difficult words to write or say. So it's natural that we freeze with writer's block when faced with such an immense task. Here are my basic guidelines for mastering the Art of the Condolence:

- Always begin directly and simply. "I am so sorry about your mother's death."
- It's better to ask, "How are you?" or "How are you feeling?" instead of telling someone how she should feel.

- Never give advice about how someone should get through the loss. Some mourners go to parties; others stay home with the shades drawn. Be open to the mourner's individual needs. Be open to the possibility that these needs will change day by day.
- If you want to offer something upbeat, share a funny anecdote or memory about the deceased that might bring a smile to the mourner's face.

Grieving is private, but it can be public, too. We need to stop being afraid of public mourning. We need to be open to mourners. We need to look each other in the eye, and say, "I am so sorry."

Jess Decourcy Hinds

Reprinted with permission from Jocelyn Laurence.

Rob Wilkinson / Alamy/ GetStock.com

Analyzing
A helping style in which the listener offers an interpretation of a speaker's message.

Advising
A helping response in which the receiver offers suggestions about how the speaker should deal with a problem.

Analyzing

In an **analyzing** response, listeners offer an interpretation of a speaker's message. Analyses like these are probably familiar to you:

"I think what's really bothering you is . . ."

"She's doing it because . . ."

"Maybe the problem started when he . . ."

Interpretations can help people consider alternative meanings—things they wouldn't have thought of without your help. Sometimes an analysis can clarify a confusing problem so that a solution emerges. In other cases, an analysis can create more problems than it solves.

There are two potential problems with analyzing. First, your interpretation may not be correct, in which case the speaker may become even more confused by accepting it. Second, even if your analysis is correct, telling it to the problem-holder might not be useful. It could arouse defensiveness, because analysis implies superiority. Even if it doesn't, the person may not be able to understand your view of the problem without working it out personally.

To know when it's helpful to offer an analysis, follow the guidelines below:

> Try to feel, in your heart's core, the reality of others. This is the most painful thing in the world, probably, and the most necessary. In times of personal adversity, know that you are not alone. Know that although in the eternal scheme of things you are small, you are also unique and irreplaceable, as are all your fellow humans everywhere in the world. Know that your commitment is above all to life itself.
>
> —Margaret Laurence, Trent University address

- *Offer your interpretation as tentative rather than as absolute fact.* There's a big difference between saying, "Maybe the reason is . . ." or "The way it looks to me . . ." and insisting, "This is the truth."
- *Make sure that the person is receptive to your analysis.* Even if you're completely accurate, your thoughts won't help if the problem-holder isn't ready to consider them.
- *Be sure that your motive for offering an analysis is truly to help the other person.* It can be tempting to offer an analysis to show how brilliant you are or even to make the other person feel bad for not having thought of the right answer in the first place. Needless to say, an analysis offered under such conditions isn't helpful.

Advising

When approached with another's problem, a common tendency is to give an **advising** response: to help by offering a solution.[48] Advice can be helpful if it's given in a respectful, caring way,[49] but research has shown that it is actually *unhelpful* at least as often as it's helpful.[50] Studies on advice-giving offer the following considerations when trying to help others:[51]

- *Is the advice needed?* If the person has already taken a course of action, advice is rarely appreciated.
- *Is the advice wanted?* People generally don't value unsolicited advice. It's better to ask if the person is interested in hearing your counsel. Sometimes people just want a listening ear, not solutions.
- *Is the advice given in the right sequence?* Advice will more likely be received if the listener first offers supporting, paraphrasing, and questioning responses to better understand the situation.

ZITS © ZITS PARTNERSHIP, KING FEATURES SYNDICATE

- *Is the advice coming from an expert?* It's important to have experience and success in the topic on which you are advising. If you *don't*, offer the speaker supportive responses, then encourage that person to seek expert counsel.
- *Is the advisor a close and trusted person?* In most cases, we value advice given within the context of a close and ongoing interpersonal relationship.
- *Is the advice offered in a sensitive, face-saving manner?* Remember that messages have both content and relational dimensions, and sometimes the unstated relational messages ("I'm smarter than you," or "You're not bright enough to figure this out yourself") will keep people from hearing your counsel.[52]

Rob Van Petten/JupiterImages

Judging

A **judging** response evaluates the sender's thoughts or behaviours in some way. The judgment may be favourable—"That's a good idea," or "You're on the right track now"—or unfavourable—"An attitude like that won't get you anywhere." But in either case, it implies that the person doing the judging is in some way qualified to pass judgment on the speaker's thoughts or actions.

> **Judging**
> A response in which the receiver evaluates the sender's message either favourably or unfavourably.

Invitation TO INSIGHT

When Advising Does—and Doesn't—Work

To see why advising can be tricky business, follow these steps:

1. Recall an instance when someone gave you advice that proved helpful. See how closely that advising communication followed the guidelines in the bulleted list on pages 196–197.

2. Now recall an instance when someone gave you advice that wasn't helpful. See whether that person violated any of the guidelines in the bulleted list on pages 196–197.

3. Based on your insights here, describe how you can advise (or not advise) others in a way that is truly helpful.

> But when the child asks me
> Because Why or Why Because I
> can only say Go outside and play.
>
> —Red Lane,
> "Margins IV"

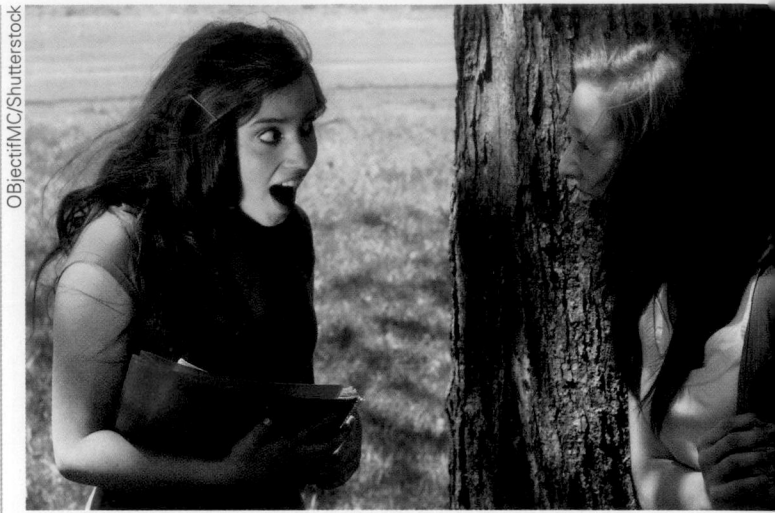

©BjectifMC/Shutterstock

Sometimes negative judgments are purely critical. How many times have you heard a response like "Well, you asked for it!" or "I *told* you so!" Although comments like these sometimes serve as a verbal slap that brings problem-holders to their senses, they usually make matters worse.

In other cases, negative judgments are less critical. These involve *constructive criticism* that is intended to help the person in the future. This is the sort of response given by friends about everything from the choice of clothing to jobs to friends. Constructive criticism occurs in school, where instructors evaluate students' work to help them master concepts and skills. Whether it's justified or not, constructive criticism can run the risk of arousing defensiveness because it may threaten the person's self-concept.

Judgments have the best chance of being received when two conditions exist:

1. *The person with the problem should have requested an evaluation from you.* Occasionally an unsolicited evaluation may bring someone to his or her senses, but more often unsolicited evaluation triggers a defensive response.

2. *The intent of your judgement should be genuinely constructive and not designed as a put-down.* If you are tempted to use judgments as a weapon, don't fool yourself into thinking that you're being helpful. Often the statement "I'm telling you this for your own good . . ." simply isn't true.

Now that you're aware of all the possible listening responses, try the exercise on this page to see how you might use them in everyday situations.

Invitation TO INSIGHT

What Would You Say?

1. In each situation below, describe what you would say in response to the problem being shared:
   a. My family doesn't understand me. Everything I like seems to go against their values, and they just won't accept my feelings as being right for me. It's not that they don't love me—they do. But they don't accept me.
   b. I've been pretty discouraged lately. I just can't get a good relationship going with any guys. I've got plenty of male friends, but that's always as far as it goes. I'm tired of being just a pal . . . I want to be more than that.
   c. *(Child to parents)* I hate you guys! You always go out and leave me with some stupid sitter. Why don't you like me?
   d. I don't know what I want to do with my life. I'm tired of school, but there aren't any good jobs around. I could just drop out for a while, but that doesn't really sound very good either.
   e. Things really seem to be kind of lousy in my marriage lately. It's not that we fight much, but all the excitement seems to be gone. We're in a rut, and it keeps getting worse . . .
   f. I keep getting the idea that my boss is angry at me. It seems as if lately he hasn't been joking around very much, and he hasn't said anything at all about my work for about three weeks now. I wonder what I should do.

2. After you've written your response to each of these messages, imagine the probable outcome of the conversation that would have followed. If you've tried this exercise in class, you might have two group members role-play each response. Based on your idea of how the conversation might have gone, decide which responses were productive and which were unproductive.

LO⁴
Choosing the Best Listening Response

As you can see, there are many ways to respond as a listener. In the right circumstances, *all* response styles can help others accept their situation, feel better, and have a sense of control over their problems.[53] But there is enormous variability in which style will work with a given person.[54] This explains why communicators who use a wide variety of response styles are usually more effective than those who use just one or two styles.[55] However, there are other factors to consider when choosing how to respond to a speaker.

dmitrieva/Shutterstock

Gender

Research shows that men and women differ in the way they listen and respond to others.[56] Women are more likely to give supportive responses,[57] are more skilful at composing such messages,[58] and are more likely to seek out such responses from listeners.[59] Men are less skilful at providing emotional support and tend to respond to others' problems by offering advice or diverting the topic.[60] In a study of helping styles in sororities and fraternities, researchers found that sorority women frequently respond with emotional support when asked to help. Sorority sisters were also rated better at listening nonjudgmentally, comforting, and showing concern. Fraternity men, on the other hand, fit the stereotypical pattern of offering help by challenging their brothers to evaluate their attitudes and values.[61]

Based on the previous facts, you might assume that women want support and men want advice at difficult times, but research doesn't bear that out. Numerous studies show that both men and women prefer and want supportive, endorsing messages in difficult situations.[62] The fact that women are more adept at creating and delivering such messages explains why both males and females tend to seek out women listeners when they want emotional support.

The Situation

Competent communicators need to analyze the situation and develop an appropriate response for the individual.[63] As a rule of thumb, begin by seeking an understanding of the situation by using prompting, questioning, paraphrasing, and supporting responses. Then the speaker will be more receptive to and perhaps even ask for your analyzing, advising, and evaluating responses.[64]

The Other Person

Besides the situation, sophisticated listeners choose a style that fits the person. Some people will consider advice thoughtfully, while others will use it to avoid making their own decisions. Some may become defensive or are not capable of receiving analysis or judgments without lashing out. Still others are not equipped to think through problems clearly enough to profit from paraphrasing and probing. One way to determine the appropriate response is to ask the speaker what she or he wants from you. A simple question such as, "Are you looking for my advice, or do you just want a listening ear right now?" can help you give others the kinds of responses they're looking for.

Your Personal Style

Most of us reflexively use one or two response styles. Perhaps you're best at listening quietly, offering a prompt from time to time. Or maybe you're especially insightful and can offer a truly useful analysis. Of course, it's also possible to rely on a response style that is *unhelpful*. You may be overly judgmental or too eager to advise, even when your suggestions aren't invited or productive. As you think about how to respond to another's messages, consider both your strengths and weaknesses and adapt accordingly.

CSI AND *LAW & ORDER* (TV SHOWS, 2000– AND 1990–, ALSO AVAILABLE ON DVD)

In the crime shows *CSI* and *Law and Order,* the main characters must engage in active listening to do their jobs effectively. Sometimes a lawyer uses prompting and support to draw out a difficult confession. Other times a private investigator asks probing questions and offers analyzing responses to arrive at important conclusions. In other instances, a police officer carefully attends to and remembers specific details during a testimony, which later helps solve a case. And in a variety of situations, the characters offer advising and judging responses to their clients, colleagues, and co-workers. Watch an episode of one of these programs and see how many of the listening responses you can observe. Chances are, you'll find quite a few.

Listening in the Workplace

Listening is just as important on the job as in personal relationships. A study examining the link between listening and career success revealed that better listeners rose to higher levels in their organizations.[65] When 1000 human resource executives were asked to identify skills of the ideal manager, the ability to listen effectively ranked at the top of the list.[66] In problem-solving groups, effective listeners are judged as having the most leadership skills.[67] When a diverse group of senior executives was asked what skills were most important on the job, listening was identified more often than any other skill, including technical competence, computer knowledge, creativity, and administrative talent.[68]

Poor listening also comes at a cost. A CEO of an information technology consulting firm estimated that the cost of application development increases by as much as 50 percent because of poor listening in the workplace.[69] John Joyner, in an article in *Computing Canada*, says, "Effective listening saves time and money, and people who listen well make fewer mistakes, create fewer interpersonal misunderstandings, and are more likely to make positive first impressions. Good listening skills result in happier customers and less employee turnover."[70]

Listening is particularly important in the helping professions. Vancouver researchers found that women living with breast cancer identified active listening as the most helpful characteristic their physicians displayed during diagnosis. They noted that the most important quality for their physicians to have was listening. They valued doctors who looked at them when speaking and who listened and acted on their concerns. They also valued doctors who avoided interruptions and paraphrased what they had said.[71]

To be successful in the workplace, effective listening is necessary. Here are some practical recommendations to keep your listening on track:

- *Eliminate your poor listening habits*, such as pseudolistening, insulated listening, insensitive listening, and so forth.
- *Take the basic steps* to effective listening by talking less and getting rid of distractions.
- *Send the right nonverbal cues* by leaning forward, making eye contact, nodding, and responding with appropriate facial expressions.
- *Be patient when listening to non-native-language speakers* by not judging accents, finishing sentences, correcting grammar and pronunciation, and pretending to understand when you don't.[72]
- *Paraphrase* whenever the opportunity presents itself.
- *Monitor your input and limit the length of your comments* at meetings by keeping them brief and not repeating what others have said.
- *Encourage quiet individuals to provide their input* by drawing out their thoughts.
- *Remember that listening is hard work* and takes effort.

Endnotes

1. R. Emanuel, J. Adams, K. Baker, E. K. Daufin, C. Ellington, E. Fitts, J. Himsel, L. Holladay, & D. Okeowo (2008). "How College Students Spend Their Time Communicating." *International Journal of Listening*, 22, 13–28. See also L. Barker, R. Edwards, C. Gaines, K. Gladney, & R. Holley (1981). "An Investigation of Proportional Time Spent in Various Communication Activities by College Students." *Journal of Applied Communication Research*, 8, 101–109.

2. Research summarized in A. D. Wolvin & C. G. Coakley (1981). "A Survey of the Status of Listening Training in Some Fortune 500 Corporations," *Communication Education*, 40, 152–164.

3. K. J. Prager & D. Buhrmester (1998). "Intimacy and Need Fulfillment in Couple Relationships." *Journal of Social and Personal Relationships*. 15, 435–469.

4. A. L. Vangelisti (1994). "Couples' Communication Problems: The Counsellor's Perspective." *Journal of Applied Communication Research*. 22, 106–126.

5. A. D. Wolvin (1984). "Meeting the Communication Needs of the Adult Learners." *Communication Education*, 33, 267–271.

6. M. L. Beall, J. Gill-Rosier, J. Tate, & A. Matten (2008). "State of the Context: Listening in Education." *International Journal of Listening*, 22, 123–132.

7. J. Davis, A. Foley, N. Crigger, & M. C. Brannigan (2008). "Healthcare and Listening: A Relationship for Caring." *International Journal of Listening*, 22, 168–175; and J. Davis, C. R. Thompson, A. Foley, C. D. Bond, & J. DeWitt (2008). "An Examination of Listening Concepts in the Healthcare Context: Differences Among Nurses, Physicians, and Administrators." *International Journal of Listening*, 22, 152–167.

8. D. C. Schnapp (2008). "Listening in Context: Religion and Spirituality." *International Journal of Listening*, 22, 133–140.

9. J. Flynn, T. Valikoski, J. Grau (2008). "Listening in the Business Context: Reviewing the State of Research." *International Journal of Listening*, 22, 141–151.

10. A. Fernald (2001). "Hearing, Listening, and Understanding: Auditory Development in Infancy." In G. Bemner & A. Fogel (Eds.). *Blackwell Handbook of Infant Development* (pp. 35–70). Malden, MA: Blackwell.

11. B. R. Burleson (2010). "Explaining Recipient Responses to Supportive Messages: Development and Tests of a Dual-Process Theory. In S. W. Smith & S. R. Wilson (Eds.). *New Directions in Interpersonal Communication Research* (pp. 159–179). Los Angeles: Sage. See also G. D. Bodie & B. R. Burleson (2008). "Explaining Variations in the Effects

of Supportive Messages: A Dual-Process Framework." In C. S. Beck (Ed.). *Communication Yearbook 32.* New York: Routledge.

12. E. Langer (1990). *Mindfulness.* Reading, MA: Addison-Wesley. See also J. K. Burgoon, C. R. Berger, & V. R. Waldron (2000). "Mindfulness and Interpersonal Communication." *Journal of Social Issues, 56,* 105–127.

13. Burgoon et al., op. cit.

14. Langer, op. cit., p. 90.

15. Canadian Hearing Society (April 30, 2002). *The Canadian Hearing Society Awareness Survey,* www.canadianhearingsociety.com/survey/deck20402.ppt.pdf. Accessed April 19, 2010.

16. M. Chasin (July 1997). "Fast Facts on Noise, Loud Music and Hearing Loss," www.chs.ca/resources/vibes/1997/july/noise.htm; and M. Chasin (Oct. 1995). "Musicians and Hearing Loss." Accessed July 12, 2006.

17. L. R. Smeltzer & K. W. Watson (1984). "Listening: An Empirical Comparison of Discussion Length and Level of Incentive." *Central States Speech Journal, 35,* 166–170.

18. M. Pasupathi, L. M. Stallworth, & K. Murdoch (1998). "How What We Tell Becomes What We Know: Listener Effects on Speakers' Long-Term Memory for Events." *Discourse Processes, 26,* 1–25.

19. W. G. Powers & P. L. Witt (2008). "Expanding the Theoretical Framework of Communication Fidelity." *Communication Quarterly, 56,* 247–267; M. Fitch-Hauser, W. G. Powers, K. O'Brien, & S. Hanson (2007). "Extending the Conceptualization of Listening Fidelity." *International Journal of Listening, 21,* 81–91; and W. G. Powers & G. D. Bodie (2003). "Listening Fidelity: Seeking Congruence Between Cognitions of the Listener and the Sender." *International Journal of Listening, 17,* 19–31.

20. M. H. Lewis & N. L. Reinsch Jr. (1988). "Listening in Organizational Environments." *Journal of Business Communication, 23,* 49–67.

21. M. Imhof (2002). "In The Eye of the Beholder: Children's Perception of Good and Poor Listening Behavior." *International Journal of Listening, 16,* 40–57.

22. L. L. Barker (1971). *Listening Behavior.* Englewood Cliffs, NJ: Prentice-Hall.

23. A. L. Vangelisti, M. L. Knapp, & J. A. Daly (1990). "Conversational Narcissism." *Communication Monographs, 57,* 251–274. See also J. C. McCroskey & V. P. Richmond (1993). "Identifying Compulsive Communicators: The Talkaholic Scale." *Communication Research Reports, 10,* 107–114.

24. K. B. McComb & F. M. Jablin (1984). "Verbal Correlates of Interviewer Empathic Listening and Employment Interview Outcomes." *Communication Monographs, 51,* 367.

25. J. Hansen (2007). *24/7: How Cell Phones and the Internet Change the Way We Live, Work, and Play.* New York: Praeger. See also J. W. Turner & N. L. Reinsch (2007). "The Business Communicator as Presence Allocator: Multicommunicating, Equivocality, and Status at Work." *Journal of Business Communication, 44,* 36–58.

26. A. Wolvin & C. G. Coakley (1988). *Listening,* 3rd ed. Dubuque, IA: W.C. Brown, p. 208.

27. R. Nichols (September 1987). "Listening Is a Ten-Part Skill." *Nation's Business, 75,* 40.

28. S. Golen (1990). "A Factor Analysis of Barriers to Effective Listening," *Journal of Business Communication, 27,* 25–36.

29. N. Kline (1999). *Time to Think: Listening to Ignite the Human Mind.* London: Ward Lock, p. 21.

30. L. J. Carrell & S. C. Willmington (1996). "A Comparison of Self-Report and Performance Data in Assessing Speaking and Listening Competence." *Communication Reports, 9,* 185–191.

31. R. G. Nichols, J. I. Brown, & R. J. Keller (2006). "Measurement of Communication Skills." *International Journal of Listening, 20,* 13–17; N. Spinks & B. Wells (1991). "Improving Listening Power: The Payoff." *Bulletin of the Association for Business Communication, 54,* 75–32.

32. "Listen to This: Hearing Problems Can Stress Relationships." (2008). Available at www.energizer.com/livehealthy/#listentothis. See also D. N. Shafer (2007). "Hearing Loss Hinders Relationships." *ASHA Leader, 12,* 5–7.

33. D. Carbaugh (1999). "'Just Listen': 'Listening' and Landscape among the Blackfeet." *Western Journal of Communication, 63,* 250–270.

34. A. M. Bippus (2001). "Recipients' Criteria for Evaluating the Skillfulness of Comforting Communication and the Outcomes of Comforting Interactions." *Communication Monographs, 68,* 301–313.

35. Adapted from B. R. Burleson (1994). "Comforting Messages: Features, Functions, and Outcomes." In J. A. Daly & J. M. Wiemann (Eds.). *Strategic Interpersonal Communication* (p. 140). Hillsdale, NJ: Erlbaum.

36. S. Myers (2000). "Empathic Listening: Reports on the Experience of Being Heard." *Journal of Humanistic Psychology, 40,* 148–173; S. G. Grant (1998). "A Principal's Active Listening Skills and Teachers' Perceptions of the Principal's Leader Behaviors." *Dissertation Abstracts International Section A: Humanities and Social Sciences, 58,* 2933; and V. B. Van Hasselt, M. T. Baker, & S. J. Romano (2006). "Crisis (Hostage) Negotiation Training: A Preliminary Evaluation of Program Efficacy." *Criminal Justice and Behavior, 33,* 56–69.

37. See J. Bruneau (1989). "Empathy and Listening: A Conceptual Review and Theoretical Directions," *Journal of the International Listening Association, 3,* 1–20; and K. N. Cissna & R. Anderson (1990). "The Contributions of Carl R. Rogers to a Philosophical Praxis of Dialogue." *Western Journal of Speech Communication, 54,* 137–147.

38. B. R. Burleson (2003). "Emotional Support Skills." In J. O. Greene and B. R. Burleson (Eds.). *Handbook of Communication and Social Interaction Skills* (p. 552). Mahwah, NJ: Erlbaum.

39. B. Burleson & W. Samter (Aug. 1987). *Cognitive Complexity, Communication Skills, and Friendship.* Paper presented at the 7th International Congress on Personal Construct Psychology, Memphis, TN.

40. See, for example, J. Ekenrode (1984). "Impact of Chronic and Acute Stressors on Daily Reports of Mood." *Journal of Personality and Social Psychology, 46,* 907–918; A. D. Kanner, J. C. Coyne, C. Schaefer, & R. S. Lazarus (1981). "Comparison of Two Modes of Stress Measurement: Daily Hassles and Uplifts versus Major Life Events." *Journal of Behavioural Medicine, 4,* 1–39; and A. DeLongis, J. C. Coyne, G. Dakof, S. Polkman, & R. S. Lazarus (1982). "Relation of Daily Hassles, Uplifts, and Major Life Events to Health Status." *Health Psychology, 1,* 119–136.

41. E. L. MacGeorge, W. Samter, & S. J. Gillihan (2005). "Academic Stress, Supportive Communication, and Health." *Communication Education, 54,* 365–372; B. R. Burleson 2003). "Emotional Support Skills." In J. O. Greene & B. R. Burleson (Eds.). *Handbook of Communication and Social Interaction Skills* (pp. 551–594). Mahwah, NJ: Erlbaum.

42. "D. Hample (2006). "Anti-Comforting Messages." In K. M. Galvin & P. J. Cooper (Eds.). *Making Connections: Readings in Relational Communication,* 4th ed. (pp. 222–227). Los Angeles: Roxbury. See also B. R. Burleson & E. L. MacGeorge (2002). "Supportive Communication." In M. L. Knapp & J. A. Daly (Eds.). *Handbook of Interpersonal Communication,* 3rd ed. Thousand Oaks, CA: Sage.

43. W. Samter, B. R. Burleson, & L. B. Murphy (1987). "Comforting Conversations: The Effects of Strategy Type on Evaluations of Messages and Message Producers." *Southern Speech Communication Journal, 52,* 263–284.

44. B. Burleson (2008). "What Counts as Effective Emotional Support?" In M. T. Motley (Ed.). *Studies in Applied Interpersonal Communication* (pp. 207–227). Thousand Oaks, CA: Sage.

45. M. Davidowitz & R. D. Myrick (1984). "Responding to the Bereaved: An Analysis of 'Helping' Statements." *Death Education, 8,* 1–10. See also H. L. Servaty-Seib & B. R. Burleson (2007). "Bereaved Adolescents Evaluations of the Helpfulness of Support-Intended Statements." *Journal of Social and Personal Relationships, 24,* 207–223.

46. N. Miczo & J. K. Burgoon (2008). "Facework and Nonverbal Behaviour in Social Support Interactions Within Romantic Dyads." In M. T. Motley (Ed.). *Studies in Applied Interpersonal Communication* (pp. 245–266). Thousand Oaks, CA: Sage.

47. R. A. Clark & J. G. Delia (1997). "Individuals' Preferences for Friends' Approaches to Providing Support in Distressing Situations." *Communication Reports, 10,* 115–121.

48. E. L. MacGeorge, B. Feng, & E. R. Thompson (2008). "'Good' and 'Bad' Advice: How to Advise More Effectively." In M. T. Motley (Ed.). *Studies in Applied Interpersonal Communication* (pp. 145–164). Thousand Oaks, CA: Sage. See also C. J. Notarius & L. R. Herrick (1988). "Listener Response Strategies to a Distressed Other." *Journal of Social and Personal Relationships, 5,* 97–108.

49. S. J. Messman, D. J. Canary, & K. S. Hause (2000). "Motives to Remain Platonic, Equity, and the Use of Maintenance Strategies in Opposite-Sex Friendships." *Journal of Social and Personal Relationships, 17,* 67–94.

50. D. J. Goldsmith & K. Fitch (1997). "The Normative Context of Advice as Social Support." *Human Communication Research, 23,* 454–476. See also D. J. Goldsmith & E. L. MacGeorge (2000). "The Impact of Politeness and Relationship on Perceived Quality of Advice about a Problem." *Human Communication Research, 26,* 234–263; and B. R. Burleson (1992). "Social Support." In M. L. Knapp & J. A. Daly (Eds.). *Handbook of Interpersonal Communication,* 3rd ed. Thousand Oaks, CA: Sage.

51. E. L. MacGeorge, B. Feng, & E. R. Thompson, op cit.

52. N. Miczo & J. K. Burgoon (2008). "Facework and Nonverbal Behaviour in Social Support Interactions within Romantic Dyads." In M. T. Motley (Ed.). *Studies in Applied Interpersonal Communication* (pp. 245–266). Thousand Oaks, CA: Sage.

53. See, for example, R. Silver & C. Wortman (1981). "Coping with Undesirable Life Events." In J. Garber & M. Seligman (Eds.). *Human Helplessness: Theory and Applications* (pp. 279–340). New York: Academic Press; and C. R. Young, D. E. Giles, & M. C. Plantz (1982). "Natural Networks: Help-Giving and Help-Seeking in Two Rural Communities." *American Journal of Community Psychology, 10,* 457–469.

54. Clark & Delia, op. cit.

55. See research cited in B. Burleson (1990). "Comforting Messages: Their Significance and Effects." In J. A. Daly & J. M. Wiemann (Eds.). *Communicating Strategically: Strategies in Interpersonal Communication.* Hillside, NJ: Erlbaum. See also J. L. Chesbro (1999). "The Relationship between Listening Styles and Conversational Sensitivity." *Communication Research Reports, 16,* 233–238.

56. S. L. Sargent & J. B. Weaver (2003). "Listening Styles: Sex Differences in Perceptions of Self and Others." *International Journal of Listening, 17,* 5–18. See also M. Johnston, M. Kirtley, J. B. Weaver, K. Watson, & L. Barker (2000). "Listening Styles: Biological or Psychological Differences?" *International Journal of Listening, 14,* 32–47.

57. W. Samter (2002). "How Gender and Cognitive Complexity Influence the Provision of Emotional Support: A Study of Indirect Effects." *Communication Reports, 15,* 5–17; and J. L. Hale, M. R. Tighe, & P. A. Mongeau (1997). "Effects of Event Type and Sex on Comforting Messages." *Communication Research Reports, 14,* 214–220.

58. B. R. Burleson (1982). "The Development of Comforting Communication Skills in Childhood and Adolescence." *Child Development, 53,* 1578–1588.

59. R. Lemieux & M. R. Tighe (2004). "Attachment Styles and the Evaluation of Comforting Responses: A Receiver Perspective." *Communication Research Reports, 21,* 144–153.

60. B. R. Burleson, A. J. Holmstrom, & C. M. Gilstrap (2005). "'Guys Can't Say That to Guys: Four Experiments Assessing the Normative Motivation Account for Deficiencies in the Emotional Support Provided by Men." *Communication Monographs, 72,* 468–501.

61. M. S. Woodward, L. B. Rosenfeld, & S. K. May (1996). "Sex Differences in Social Support in Sororities and Fraternities." *Journal of Applied Communication Research, 24,* 260–272.

62. B. R. Burleson & A. Kunkel (2006). "Revisiting the Different Cultures Thesis: An Assessment of Sex Differences and Similarities in Supportive Communication." In K. Dindia & D. J. Canary (Eds.). *Sex Differences and Similarities in Communication*, 2nd ed. (pp. 137–159). Mawah, NJ: Erlbaum.

63. L. M. Horowitz, E. N. Krasnoperova, & D. G. Tatar (2001). "The Way to Console May Depend on the Goal: Experimental Studies of Social Support." *Journal of Experimental Social Psychology, 37,* 49–61.

64. E. L. MacGeorge, B. Feng, & E. R. Thompson (2008), op cit. See also R. W. Young & C. M. Cates (2004). "Emotional and Directive Listening in Peer Mentoring." *International Journal of Listening, 18,* 21–33.

65. B. D. Sypher, R. N. Bostrom, & J. H. Seibert (1989). "Listening Communication Abilities and Success at Work." *Journal of Business Communication, 26,* 293–303. See also E. R. Alexander, L. E. Penley, & I. E. Jernigan (1992). "The Relationship of Basic Decoding Skills to Managerial Effectiveness." *Management Communication Quarterly, 6,* 58–73.

66. J. L. Winsor, D. B. Curtis, & R. D. Stephens (1999). "National Preferences in Business and Communication Education: An Update." *Journal of the Association for Communication Administration, 3,* 170–179.

67. S. Johnson & C. Bechler (1998). "Examining the Relationship between Listening Effectiveness and Leadership Emergence: Perceptions, Behaviours, and Recall." *Small Group Research, 29,* 452–471.

68. V. Marchant (June 28, 1999). "Listen Up!" *Time, 153,* 74. See also M. Stern (2004). "The Right Stuff." *Canadian Business, 77,* 95–102.

69. A. S. Horowitz (1996). "Hey! Listen Up!" *Computerworld, 30,* 63–65.

70. J. Joyner (2001). "Listening Increases Support from Co-Workers." *Computing Canada, 27,* 31.

71. S. R. Harris & E. Templeton (2001). "Who's Listening: Experiences of Women with Breast Cancer in Communicating with Physicians." *Breast Journal, 7,* 444–449.

72. M. E. Guffey, K. Rhodes, and P. Rogin (2005). *Business Communication: Process and Product,* 4th Canadian ed. Toronto: Thomson Nelson, p. 79.

CHAPTER

8 Communication and Relational DYNAMICS

What do you
THINK?

Real lovers share all their thoughts
and feelings with each other.

1 2 3 4 5 6 7
strongly agree   strongly disagree

LEARNING OUTCOMES

LO¹ Identify factors that have influenced your choice of relational partners.

LO² Use Knapp's model to describe the nature of communication in the various stages of a relationship.

LO³ Describe the dialectical tensions in a given relationship, how they influence communication, and the most effective strategies for managing them.

LO⁴ Describe the possible strategies for repairing a given relational transgression.

LO⁵ Identify the content and relational dimensions of communication in a given transaction.

LO⁶ Describe how metacommunication can be used to improve the quality of a given relationship.

LO⁷ Identify the dimensions of intimacy and how they are expressed in a specific relationship.

LO⁸ Use the social penetration and Johari Window models to identify the nature of self-disclosing communication in one of your relationships.

LO⁹ Outline the potential benefits and risks of disclosing in a selected situation.

LO¹⁰ Assess the most competent mixture of candour and equivocation in a given situation.

When we think of relationships, we tend to think in romantic terms. But we also have relationships with friends, family members, acquaintances, co-workers, and, in some cases, with people merely because we have to. **Interpersonal relationships** involve the way people deal with one another socially. This chapter will offer some insights into this process, beginning with why we form relationships.

> **Interpersonal relationship**
> An association in which the parties meet each other's social needs to a greater or lesser degree.

LO¹
Why We Form Relationships

The large body of research on interpersonal attraction suggests that we form relationships with others for a variety of reasons that include appearance, similarity and complementarity, reciprocal attraction, competence, disclosure, and proximity.[1]

Appearance

While most people know that we shouldn't judge others by their appearance, the reality is quite the opposite.[2] In one study, more than 700 men and women were matched as blind dates for a "computer dance." Afterwards, they were asked whether they would like to date their partners again. The

© Steve Prezant/Masterfile Corporation

result? The more physically attractive the person, as judged in advance by independent raters, the more likely that person was seen as desirable. Factors like social skills or intelligence didn't seem to affect the decision.[3]

However, after initial impressions pass, ordinary-looking people with pleasing personalities are likely to be judged as attractive,[4] and physical factors become less important as a relationship progresses.[5] Interestingly, as romantic relationships develop, partners view one another as more attractive with time.[6] As one social scientist put it, "Attractive features may open doors, but apparently it takes more than physical beauty to keep them open."[7]

Similarity

We generally like people who are similar to us.[8] For example, the more similar a married couple's personalities are, the more likely that they will be happy and satisfied in the marriage.[9] Junior and high school friends also report being similar in terms of mutual friends, enjoying the same sports, liking similar social activities, and using (or not using) alcohol and cigarettes to the same degree.[10] Friendships can last decades when the friends are similar to one another,[11] regardless of whether or not they have high or low levels of communication skills.[12]

Accounting for this attraction might be the fact that if we find people like ourselves attractive, then we too must be attractive. In fact, the results of one study showed that people are disproportionately likely to marry others whose first or last names resemble their own, and they are also attracted to those with similar birthdays or even jersey numbers![13]

When we're similar to others in a high percentage of important areas such as career goals, friends, and beliefs about human rights, attraction is greatest. With enough similarity in key areas, couples can survive disputes in a number of areas, but if the number and content of disagreements become too great, the relationship may be threatened.

Attraction turns to dislike, however, when the other person behaves in a strange or socially offensive manner.[14] In such cases, these individuals threaten our self-esteem in that we fear that we may be as unappealing as they are. When that happens, we'll distance ourselves from them to protect our ideal self-image.

Complementarity

The familiar saying that "opposites attract" is also valid. Differences strengthen a relationship when they are complementary—when each partner's characteristics satisfy the other's needs. Research suggests that attraction to partners who have complementary temperaments might be rooted in

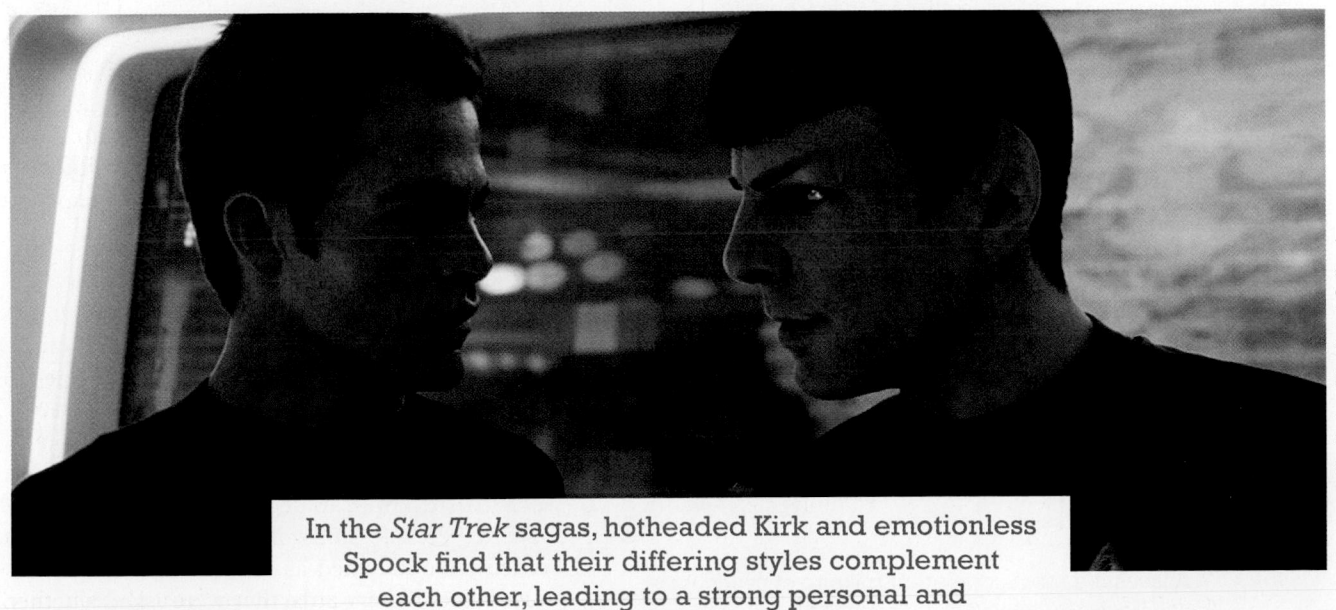

Paramount/BadRobot/The Kobal Collection

In the *Star Trek* sagas, hotheaded Kirk and emotionless Spock find that their differing styles complement each other, leading to a strong personal and professional friendship.

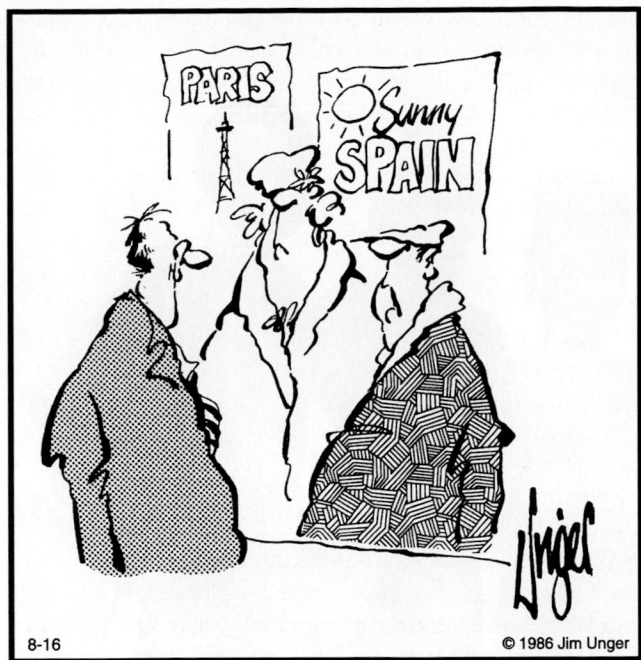

"Two round-the-world cruises in opposite directions."

HERMAN © Jim Unger/Dist. by Newspaper Enterprise Association, Inc.

biology.[15] For instance, a dominant person may be attracted to a passive one.[16] Relationships also work well when the partners agree that one will exercise control in certain areas ("You make financial decisions") and the other will exercise control in different areas ("I'll decide how to decorate the place"). Strains occur when control issues are disputed.

When successful and unsuccessful couples are compared over a 20-year period, partners in successful marriages tend to be similar enough to satisfy each other physically and mentally but different enough to keep the relationship interesting. Successful couples find ways to balance their similarities and differences by adjusting to the changes that occur over the years.

> I believe that for friendship there should be similarity; but for love there must be dissimilarity.
>
> —Lucy Maud Montgomery,
> *My Dear Mr. M.: Letters to G. B. MacMillan*

Reciprocal Attraction

We usually like people who like us, and conversely, we don't care much for people who seem indifferent or attack us in some way.[17]

It's no mystery why reciprocal liking builds attractiveness—people who approve of us bolster our feelings of self-esteem. But we don't like people when we think the other person's supposed liking is counterfeit—an insincere device to get something from us. Or the liking may not fit with our own self-concept. For example, if someone says you're good-looking and intelligent but you think you're ugly and stupid, then you may disregard the flattery. Groucho Marx summarized this attitude when he said he would never join any club that would consider having him as a member.

Competence

We also like talented, competent people, but not if they're too competent—this makes us look bad by comparison. People are generally attracted to those who are talented but flawed in some way because it shows that they are human, like us.[18] There are some qualifications to this principle. People with especially high or low self-esteem find "perfect" people more attractive than those who are competent but flawed, and some studies suggest that women are more impressed by uniformly superior people of both sexes. Men, on the other hand, tend to be more impressed by desirable but "human" subjects.

Self-Disclosure

Revealing important information about yourself can also build liking.[19] Sometimes the basis of this liking comes from learning about how we are similar, either in experiences ("I broke off an engagement myself") or in attitudes ("I feel nervous with strangers, too"). Self-disclosure is also a sign of regard. When people share private information, it suggests that they respect and trust you.

But not all disclosure leads to liking. The key to satisfying self-disclosure is reciprocity: getting back the amount and kind of information equivalent to that which you reveal.[20] Further, the timing must be right, and it's important not to disclose intimate information when you first meet someone. Finally, only reveal personal information to people you know are trustworthy.[21]

Proximity

We are likely to develop relationships with people with whom we interact with frequently.[22] For instance, we develop friendships with neighbours, classmates, co-workers, members of organizations we belong to, and so forth. Proximity allows us to get more information about other people and benefit from a relationship with them. The Internet provides a new means for creating closeness, as users are able to experience "virtual proximity" in cyberspace.[23]

Monkey Business Images/Shutterstock

Familiarity can also breed contempt. For example, most aggravated assaults occur within the family or among close neighbours, and thieves frequently prey on nearby victims, even though the risk of being recognized is greater.

Rewards

Some social scientists say that relationships—both impersonal and personal—are based on a socioeconomic model called **social exchange theory**.[24] This model suggests that we seek out people who can give us tangible or emotional rewards that are greater than or equal to the costs we encounter in dealing with them. According to social exchange theory, relationships suffer when one partner feels "underbenefited."[25]

Tangible rewards might be a nice place to live or a high-paying job, while intangible ones might include prestige, emotional support, or companionship. Costs refer to undesirable outcomes: unpleasant work, emotional pain, and so on. A simple formula captures the social exchange theory of why we form and maintain relationships:

"I'd like to buy everyone a drink. All I ask in return is that you listen patiently to my shallow and simplistic views on a broad range of social and political issues."

> **Social exchange theory**
> A socioeconomic theory of relational development that suggests people seek relationships in which the rewards they receive from others are equal to or greater than the costs they encounter.

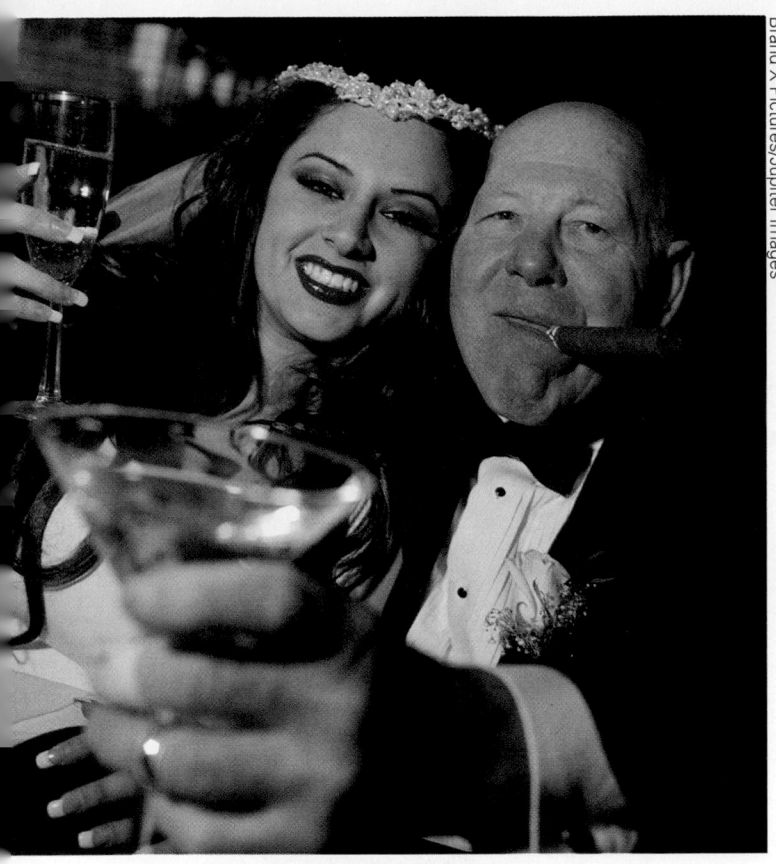

Rewards − Costs = Outcome

While exchange theory seems cold and calculating, it seems quite appropriate in business relationships and in some friendships: "I don't mind listening to the ups and

AT THE MOVIES

Waitress (2007), Rated 13+

Jenna (Keri Russell) is a small-town waitress who creates delicious pies for the customers at Joe's Diner. Unfortunately, she feels stuck in an unhappy marriage to a controlling and abusive husband. Social exchange theory explains why Jenna stays in the relationship—and it also describes why she wants to get out. She isn't alone: Virtually every character in the film makes relational choices based on rewards, costs, and comparisons with alternatives. For the folks who frequent Joe's Diner, social exchange is as much a part of their everyday lives as Jenna's scrumptious pies.

downs of your love life because you rescue me when the house needs repairs." Even close relationships have an element of exchange. Friends and lovers tolerate each other's quirks because the comfort they get overrides them. When the costs outweigh the rewards, some people feel that the relationship is not worth the effort. Others choose to be in a bad relationship as opposed to no relationship at all.

Models of Relational Development and Maintenance

So far we have looked at some factors that influence why we are attracted to certain people. In the following pages we'll examine the kinds of communication that we use to start, maintain, and end relationships.

LO^2
Developmental Models

One well-known model of relational stages was developed by Mark Knapp. He divided the rise and fall of relationships into 10 stages consisting of two broad phases: "coming together" and "coming apart."[26] Other researchers suggest that models of relational communication should have a third area—**relational maintenance**—communication aimed at keeping relationships operating smoothly and satisfactorily.[27] Figure 8.1 (p. 210) shows how Knapp's 10 stages fit this three-phase view of relational communication.

This model seems most appropriate for romantic relationships, but it also works well for other types of close relationships.[28] As you read the following section, consider how the stages could describe a long-term friendship, a couple in love, or business partners.

Initiating

In the **initiating** stage, we make contact. Communication is usually brief and follows conventional formulas: handshakes, innocuous remarks about the weather, and friendly expressions. These seemingly superficial and meaningless behaviours signal interest in building a relationship. They allow us to say—without saying—"I'm friendly and I'd like to get to know you."

Initiating relationships—especially romantic ones—can be hard for shy people, and here's where the Internet comes into play. One study of an online dating service found that participants who identified themselves as shy expressed a greater appreciation for the

> **Relational maintenance**
> Communication aimed at keeping relationships operating smoothly and satisfactorily.
>
> **Initiating**
> The first stage in relational development, in which the parties express interest in one another.

FIGURE 8.1
Stages of Relational Development

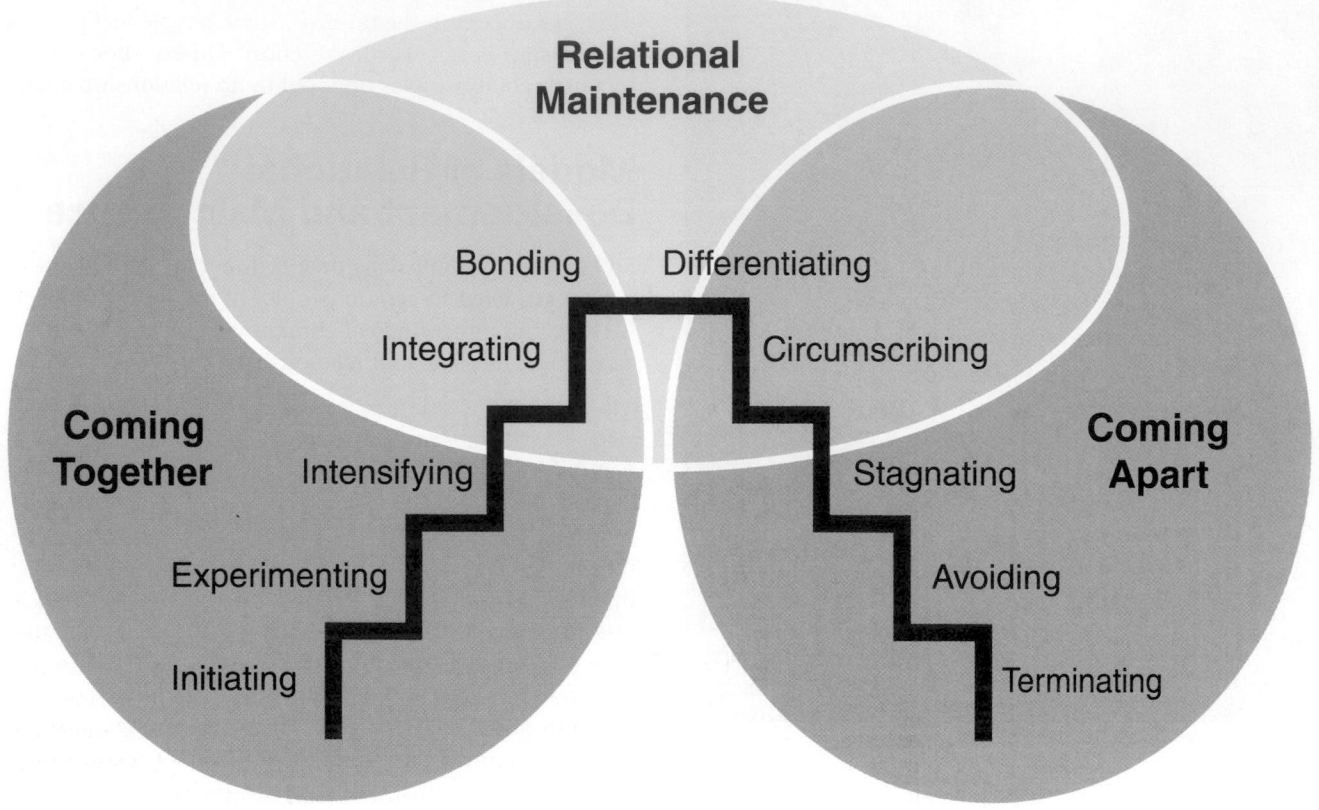

Relational Maintenance

Bonding · Differentiating

Integrating · Circumscribing

Coming Together · Intensifying · Stagnating · **Coming Apart**

Experimenting · Avoiding

Initiating · Terminating

Adapted from Mark L. Knapp & Anita L. Vangelisti (1992). *Interpersonal Communication and Human Relationships*, 2nd ed. (Boston, MA: Allyn and Bacon). Copyright © 1992 by Pearson Education. Adapted by permission of the publisher.

system's anonymous, nonthreatening environment than did non-shy users.[29] Shy people used the service to help overcome their inhibitions about initiating relationships in face-to-face settings.

As the old saying goes, you never get a second chance to make a first impression.

Getty Images

Experimenting

Once we've made contact, the next step is deciding whether we're interested in pursuing the relationship. This involves **uncertainty reduction**—the process of getting to know others by gaining more information about them.[30] Typically, people search for common ground with conversational basics such as, "Where are you from?" or "What's your major?" and then move on to similarities: "You're a runner, too? How many klicks do you do a week?"

The hallmark of the **experimenting** stage is small talk. It enables us to learn what interests we have in common and to "audition" the other person—to help us decide whether a relationship is worth pursuing. Small talk is also a safe way to ease into a relationship.

The move from initiating to experimenting seems to occur even more rapidly in cyberspace. One study found

> **Uncertainty reduction**
> The process of getting to know others by gaining more information about them.
>
> **Experimenting**
> An early stage in relational development, consisting of a search for common ground. If the experimentation is successful, the relationship will progress to *intensifying*. If not, it may go no further.

"Good game." "Good game." "Nice game." "Good game." "I'm in love with you." "Good game." "Nice game."

© Harry Bliss/The New Yorker Collection/www.cartoonbank.com

that people who develop relationships via e-mail begin asking questions about attitudes, opinions, and preferences more quickly than those in face-to-face contact.[31] It probably helps that e-mailers don't have to worry about their nonverbal behaviour (blushing, stammering, or looking away if they realize that they asked for too much information too quickly).

Intensifying

A stage of relational development, preceding *integrating*, in which the parties move toward integration by increasing the amount of contact and the breadth and depth of self-disclosure.

Intensifying

In the **intensifying** stage, the parties increase contact time as well as the breadth and depth of their self-disclosure. Dating couples use a wide range of communication strategies to describe their feelings of attraction.[32] About a quarter of the time they express feelings directly, using metacommunication to openly discuss the state of the relationship. More often they use less direct methods of communication: spending an increasing amount of time together, asking for support from one another, doing favours for each other, giving tokens of affection, hinting and flirting, expressing feelings nonverbally, getting to know the partner's friends and family, and trying to look more physically attractive. In developing friendships, partners might share activities, hang out with mutual friends, or take trips together.[33]

The intensifying stage is the most exciting and even euphoric stage. For romantic partners, it's often filled with starstruck gazes, goosebumps, and daydreaming. It's the stage most often depicted in movies and romance novels. But, as you know, this stage doesn't last, and when romantic partners stop feeling those goosebumps, they question whether they're still in love. But they've simply moved into the next stage of their relationship—integrating.

> "Love passes" . . . men say (and women sigh), but it isn't true. Infatuation passes, but not a love that has become one's life!
>
> —Henriette Dessaulles,
> *Hopes and Dreams: The Diary of Henriette Dessaulles, 1874–1881*

ZITS © ZITS PARTNERSHIP KING FEATURES SYNDICATE

Integrating

At the **integrating** stage, the parties take on an identity as a social unit—invitations come addressed to the couple. Partners also begin to take on each other's commitments: "Sure, we'll spend Christmas with your family." Common property may begin to be designated our apartment, our car, our song.[34] Partners develop unique, ritualistic ways of behaving[35] and begin to speak alike.[36] In the integrating stage, individuals give up some characteristics of their old selves and develop shared identities. As we become more integrated with others, our sense of obligation to them grows.[37]

> **Integrating**
> A stage of relational development in which the parties begin to take on a single identity.
>
> **Bonding**
> A stage of relational development in which the parties make symbolic public gestures to show that their relationship exists.
>
> **Differentiating**
> A stage of relational development in which the parties reestablish their individual identities after having bonded together.

Bonding

During the **bonding** stage, parties make symbolic public gestures to show the world that their relationship exists. Bonding is the peak of what Knapp calls the "coming together" phase of relational development. What constitutes a bonded, committed relationship isn't easily defined.[38] "Common-law," "cohabitation," and "life partners" are all used to describe such relationships.

For our purposes, we'll define bonded relationships as those involving a significant measure to "officialize" the integration—marriage, sharing a residence, a public ceremony, or a written or verbal pledge.

Relationships don't have to be romantic to achieve bonding. We see it with contracts that formalize a business partnership or initiation ceremonies into a fraternity or sorority.

Differentiating

In the **differentiating** stage, couples assert their individual identities. The "we" orientation shifts to more "me" messages. Previously agreed upon issues ("You work and I'll look after the children") now become points of contention: "Why am I stuck at home when I have better career potential?"

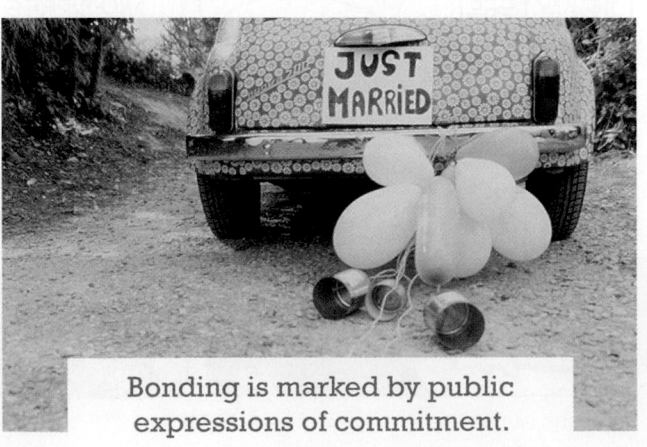

Bonding is marked by public expressions of commitment.

unopix/Shutterstock

But the need for autonomy needn't be a negative experience. For instance, young adults forge their own unique lives and identity, even while maintaining their relationships with their parents.[39] The key to successful differentiating is maintaining a commitment to the relationship while you create your individual "spaces."

Circumscribing

While most long-term relationships reach a plateau of development, others pass through several stages of decline and dissolution. In the **circumscribing** stage, communication between members decreases in quantity and quality, and the stage is characterized by restrictions and restraints. Rather than discuss a disagreement, members withdraw mentally or physically. Circumscribing doesn't involve total avoidance, but there's a definite shrinking of interest and commitment.

Stagnating

If circumscribing continues, the relationship enters the **stagnating** stage, where there's not much feeling and no growth. We see stagnation in workers who have lost enthusiasm for their job and end up just going through the motions. The same thing happens when couples unenthusiastically have the same conversations, see the same people, and follow the same routines without any sense of joy or novelty.

Avoiding

In the **avoiding** stage, partners create physical distance between each other, either indirectly by using a guise of excuses ("I've been sick lately") or directly ("Don't call me; I don't want to see you now"). The prognosis for the relationship is not good at this stage.

But deterioration is not inevitable. A key difference between marriages that end in separation and those that are restored is the type of communication that occurs when partners are unsatisfied.[40] Unsuccessful couples deal with problems by avoidance, indirectness, and less involvement with each other. Couples who "repair" their relationship confront each other with their concerns and negotiate solutions to their problems.

Circumscribing
A stage of relational development in which parties begin to reduce the scope of their contact and commitment to one another.

Stagnating
A stage of relational development characterized by declining enthusiasm and standardized forms of behaviour.

Avoiding
A stage of relational development, immediately prior to *terminating,* in which the parties minimize contact with one another.

Terminating
The concluding stage of relational development, characterized by the acknowledgment of one or both parties that the relationship is over.

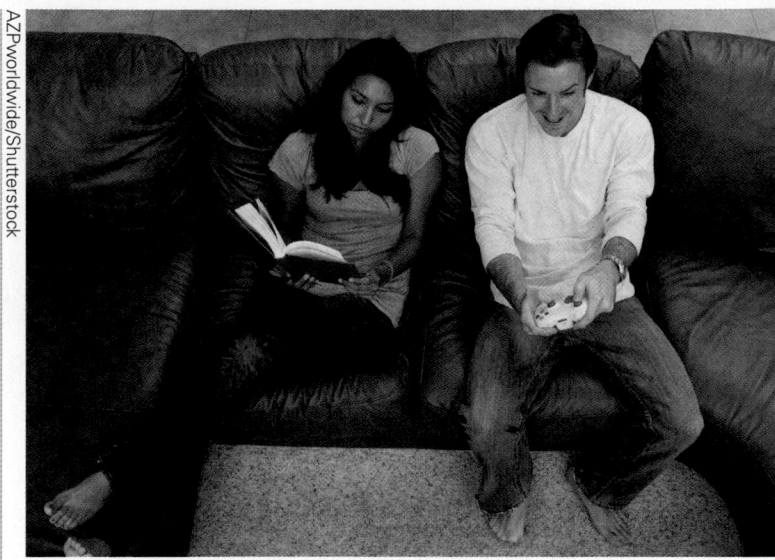

AZPworldwide/Shutterstock

Terminating

At the **terminating** stage, couples engage in summary dialogues of where the relationship has gone and the desire to dissociate. The relationship may end with a cordial dinner, a note left on the kitchen table, an e-mail, or a legal document. This stage can be short or drawn out. Not all relationships move toward termination in a straight line. Some go back and forth toward dissolution.[41] Nor does termination have to be negative. Understanding each other's needs for personal growth may dilute hard feelings. The best predictor of whether romantic parties will remain friends is whether they were friends beforehand.[42] But how a couple splits up also influences the outcome. Obviously, friendships are most possible when the breakup is amicable.

"We'll always have Facebook"

© 2008 Harry Bliss distributed by Tribune Media Services Inc.

Love can knock you to your knees
It can have you beggin' please
And even if you don't believe
It can have you prayin' to the
heavens above
Lord please help me ease the pain
That's the price you can pay
for love

Love can take you up so high
You think you could reach out and
touch the sky
But boy you better learn
how to fly
Cause when the push comes
down to the shove
You'll be falling from above
That's the price you can pay
for love

—Matt Minglewood,
"The Price of Love"

FIGURE 8.2

Patterns of Relational Development and Deterioration

Pattern One

Pattern Two

Pattern Three

Pattern Four

Pattern Five

Adapted from A. Johnson, E. Wittenberg, M. Haigh, S. Wigley, J. Becker, K. Brown, & E. Craig (2004). "The Process of Relationship Development and Deterioration: Turning Points in Friendships that Have Terminated." *Communication Quarterly, 52,* 54–67.

While Knapp's model offers insights into relational stages, it doesn't describe the ebb and flow of communication in every relationship. And while many relationships follow this predictable pattern, several other patterns of development and deterioration have been identified.[43] Not all relationships begin, progress, decline, and end in the same linear fashion.

Finally, Knapp's model suggests that partners go through one stage at a time, but in real life elements of other stages are usually present. For example, two lovers deep in the throes of integrating may still do their share of experimenting ("Wow, I never knew that about you!") or differentiating ("Nothing personal, but I need a weekend to myself").

LO[3]
Dialectical Perspectives

Not everyone agrees with a stage-related explanation of relationships. Some suggest that communicators have inherently incompatible goals throughout their entire relationship. The struggle to achieve these goals creates **dialectical tensions**: conflicts that arise when two opposing or incompatible forces exist simultaneously. Dialectical tensions make successful communication challenging, and the struggle to manage them creates the most powerful dynamics in relational communication.[44]

Connection versus Autonomy

Needing both connection and independence within relationships results in the **connection–autonomy dialectic**, and research shows that relational partners who can't find ways to manage these personal needs break up.[45] Comments like "We barely spent any time together," "We had different needs," or "I felt trapped" are often cited as reasons to end a relationship. Some research suggests that men value autonomy in relationships more than women, while women tend to value connection and commitment.[46]

The levels of connection and autonomy that are needed within a relationship change over time. In *Intimate Behaviour*, Desmond Morris suggests that we repeatedly go through three stages: "Hold me tight," "Put me down," and "Leave me alone."[47] We see the "hold me tight" stage in infancy, the "put me down" stage in three-year-olds, who what to explore the world, and the "leave me alone" orientation in teenagers. As adolescents move into adulthood, they typically grow closer to their families again.[48]

In marriages, the "hold me tight" bonds of the first year are often followed by a need for autonomy. This desire can manifest itself in wanting to make new friends, engage

> **Dialectical tensions**
> Inherent conflicts that arise when two opposing or incompatible forces exist simultaneously.
>
> **Connection–autonomy dialectic**
> The dialectical tension between a desire for connection and a need for independence in a relationship.

© iStockphoto.com/Gary Ferguson

in activities without the spouse, or to make a career move that might disrupt the relationship. This movement from connection to autonomy may lead to the breakup of a relationship—but it can also be part of a cycle that redefines it in new and interesting ways.

Both men and women in heterosexual relationships cite the connection–autonomy dialectic as one of the most significant factors affecting their relationship as they learn to negotiate commitment, conflict, disengagement, and reconciliation.[49] Managing the connection–autonomy dialectic also occurs at the end of a relationship. Partners seek ways to salvage parts of their relationship and take steps toward independence.[50] Even at the end of life, the connection–autonomy dialectic comes into play. Couples grapple with the desire to stay close and the need to let go, especially in cases where one partner suffers from Alzheimer disease and has been mentally "absent" while physically present.[51]

> Events happen every day and in quick succession. We stop talking to our partner about our day-to-day experiences, telling ourselves we do not want to burden them or that it would take too much time to get them up to the point where the information would make sense or be compelling. But the truth is that we have gotten out of the habit—or maybe never really developed the skill—of sharing our lives in the first place. The process of allowing for separate lives starts innocently enough, but ultimately our lack of communication so radically reduces interest in each other that respect, the bedrock of any relationship, suffers.
>
> —Pepper Schwartz,
> *Peer Marriage*

Invitation TO INSIGHT

Your Relational Stage

You can gain a clearer appreciation of the accuracy and value of relational stages by answering the following questions:

1. Describe the present stage of your relationship and the behaviours that characterize your communication at this stage. Give specific examples to support your assessment.

2. Discuss the trend of the communication in terms of the stages described on pages 209–214. Are you likely to remain in the present stage, or do you anticipate movement to another stage? Which one? Explain your answer.

3. Describe your level of satisfaction with the answer to question 2. If you are satisfied, describe what you can do to increase the likelihood that the relationship will operate at the stage you described. If you are not satisfied, discuss what you can do to move the relationship toward a more satisfying stage.

4. Because both parties define a relationship, define your partner's perspective. Would she or he say the relationship is at the same stage as you describe it? If not, explain how your partner would describe it. What does your partner do to determine the stage at which your relationship operates? (Give specific examples.) How would you like your partner to behave in order to move the relationship to or maintain it at the stage you desire? What can you do to encourage your partner to behave in the way you desire?

5. Now consider a relationship (friendship or romance) you have been in that has terminated. Which of the five graphs on page 214 best describes the development and decline of that relationship? If none of the graphs matches your experience, develop a new graph to illustrate your relationship's pattern.

For instance, deciding how much to disclose can be tricky. Low-context cultures such as Canada's value directness, while high-context ones like Japan's consider tact far more important. The titles of two self-help books reveal the mindset of these approaches. An American self-help book is titled *How to Say No Without Feeling Guilty*,[64] while its Japanese counterpart is called *16 Ways to Avoid Saying No*.[65] You can see how these differences can lead to interpersonal challenges. Possessing a level of intercultural competence is useful when couples from different cultures come together.

Relationships Require Maintenance

Just as gardens need tending, so too do relationships need maintenance to keep them successful and satisfying.[66] Given that communication accounts for about 80 percent of what's satisfying and unsatisfying in relationships, it's important to explore maintenance-related interaction.[67]

Researchers have identified five strategies that couples use to keep their interaction satisfying:[68]

- *Positivity*. Keeping the relational climate polite and upbeat, and avoiding criticism.
- *Openness*. Talking directly about the nature of the relationship and disclosing personal needs and concerns.
- *Assurances*. Letting the other person know that he or she matters to you.
- *Social networks*. Having communication with friends, family, co-workers to provide companionship to take pressure off the relationship to satisfy all the partners' needs.
- *Sharing tasks*. Helping one another take care of life's chores and obligations.

These maintenance strategies are useful for other relationships as well.[69] One study found that college students depended on two strategies with family and friends: openness ("Things have been a little crazy for me lately") and social networks ("How are you and Sam?

liubomir/Shutterstock

Hopefully good"). With romantic partners, however, assurances ("This is just a little e-mail to say I love you") were used most.

Some communicators are more likely to use maintenance strategies than others. One study found that gay and lesbian partners seem to be better at maintaining a positive tone by using some of the maintenance strategies outlined above.[70] Compared to straight couples, gay and lesbian partners are more upbeat in the face of conflict. They tend to take disagreements less personally; use fewer controlling, hostile tactics; and get less emotionally aroused when problems arise.

Technology and Indian Marriage: A Match Made in Heaven

Ken Street/CORBIS

Some 18 months ago in southern India, the parents of a software engineer working in Chennai began to despair of finding him a suitable bride. They were, truth to tell, rather picky: "Our requirement is a suitable Hindu Nadar girl of Sivakasi/Madurai side origin, preferably employed as a software engineer in Chennai, age between 21 to 24, height 5 feet 2 inches to 5 feet 6 inches and sufficiently good-looking." She also had to speak Tamil.

There was, however, a happy ending. They ventured online, to a website called Bharatmatrimony.com, which now flaunts their story. They identified a girl, received a message from her father, matched horoscopes, and having introduced the happy couple to each other, will celebrate the wedding next month.

Online marriage-broking is one of the successes of Indian e-business, used by the single looking for "love matches" as well as by their parents and siblings. So complex are the requirements of Indians seeking a partner that the Internet might have been designed to meet their needs. Bharatmatrimony's boss, Janakiram Murugavel, says that language is the biggest criterion. His site is divided into 15 linguistic sections. Then comes status and caste, which divides Indians at birth into thousands of groups. About 70% of his customers want to marry within their caste. Most still also use astrology. Bharatmatrimony offers an online horoscope service.

The Economist, Oct. 22, 2005, p. 70.

Relationships Require Commitment

Commitment is important in every type of interpersonal relationship—friendship, ("Friends for life!"), family ("We're always here for you"), a work team ("I've got you covered"), or a romantic relationship ("Till death do us part"). **Relational commitment** involves a promise—sometimes implied and sometimes explicit—to remain and make a relationship successful. Further, behaviours such as providing support and affection, and maintaining integrity are some of the things that successful couples do. See Table 8.1 (p. 220) for others.

LO^4
Repairing Damaged Relationships

Sooner or later, all relationships hit bumpy patches. Problems arise from outside forces (work, finances), differences and disagreements within your relationship, and from relational transgressions, when one partner violates the explicit or implicit terms of the relationship.[71] There are several types of **relational transgressions**.[72]

Minor versus Significant

A little distance can make the heart grow fonder and a little jealousy can be a sign of affection. But in large and regular doses, they will seriously damage personal relationships.

Relational commitment
An implied or explicit promise to remain and make a relationship successful.

Photodisc/Getty Images

TABLE 8.1

Major Indicators of a Committed Romantic Relationship

Providing affection
Providing support
Maintaining integrity
Sharing companionship
Making an effort to communicate regularly
Showing respect
Creating a relational future
Creating a positive relational atmosphere
Working on relationship problems together
Reassuring one's commitment

Weigel, D. J. (2008). Mutuality and the communication of commitment in romantic relationships. Southern Communication Journal, 73, 24–41.

Social versus Relational

Some transgressions violate social rules shared by society at large. For example, most people agree that ridiculing or humiliating a friend in public is rude. Other rules are uniquely constructed by the parties involved. For instance, some families have a rule stating, "If you're going to be late, call so we won't worry." Failure to honour this accepted procedure then feels like a violation.

Deliberate versus Unintentional

An unintentional transgression would be inadvertently revealing something about a friend's past. An intentional transgression might be purposely making a cruel comment because you know it will hurt the person's feelings.

One-time versus Incremental

The most obvious transgressions occur in a single episode: an act of betrayal, a verbal assault, or stalking out in anger. But subtle transgressions, such as emotional withdrawal, can occur over time. If the withdrawal is pervasive, however, it violates the fundamental nature of relationships in that partners are unavailable to one another.

Strategies for Relational Repair

The first step in repairing a transgression is to talk about the violation.[73] In cases where you're responsible for the transgression, raise the issue by asking, in an appropriate tone of voice, "What did I do that you found so hurtful?" "Why was my behaviour a problem for you?"

The best way to right a wrong is to take responsibility for your transgression.[74] Even though apologizing doesn't come easy in Western cultures,[75] not offering an apology can be worse. Participants in one study reported that they felt more remorse over apologies they didn't offer than those they did.[76] Further, transgressors who have been forgiven are less likely to repeat their offences.[77]

To repair damaged relationships, your apology requires three elements:

1. An explicit acknowledgment that the transgression was wrong: "I acted like a selfish jerk."

2. A sincere apology: "I'm really sorry. I feel awful for letting you down."

3. Some type of compensation: "If I act that way again, you can call me on it."[78]

Again, make sure your nonverbal behaviours match your words when you apologize. Even then, it may be unrealistic to expect immediate forgiveness. With severe transgressions, expressions of regret and promises of new behaviour need to be acted on before the aggrieved party accepts them as genuine.[79]

Forgiving Transgressions

Forgiveness has both personal and relational benefits. On a personal level, forgiveness can reduce emotional distress and aggression[80] and improve cardiovascular functioning.[81] Interpersonally, it can restore damaged relationships.[82] In a study of how women recover from romantic relationships, forgiving their former partner was a turning point in their recovery process.[83]

While an apology should contain certain elements, so too must forgiveness:

1. An explicit statement: "I can't forget what you did, but I believe your apology and I accept it."

2. A discussion of the implications of the transgression and the future of the relationship: "I have to be honest. It's going to take time before I can trust you again."[84]

Of course, some transgressions are harder to forgive than others—sexual infidelity and breaking up with the partner are the two least forgivable offences,[85] but being emotionally unfaithful can be as distressing as sexual infidelity.[86]

TABLE 8.2
Some Types of Relational Transgressions

Lack of commitment	Failure to honor important obligations (e.g., financial, emotional, task-related)
	Self-serving dishonesty
	Unfaithfulness
Distance	Physical separation (beyond what is necessary)
	Psychological separation (avoidance, ignoring)
Disrespect	Criticism (especially in front of third parties)
Problematic emotions	Jealousy
	Unjustified suspicion
	Rage
Aggression	Verbal hostility
	Physical violence

"I said I'm sorry."

© Mick Stevens/The New Yorker Collection/www.cartoonbank.com.

Even when a sincere apology is offered, forgiving others can be difficult. To improve your ability to forgive, recall times when you have hurt others and needed their forgiveness.[87] Douglas Kelley encourages us to remember these words from R. P. Walters: "When we have been hurt we have two alternatives: be destroyed by resentment, or forgive. Resentment is death; forgiving leads to healing and life."[88]

LO[5]
Communicating about Relationships

Clearly, relationships are complex, dynamic, and important. But what kinds of messages do we exchange as we communicate in those relationships?

Content and Relational Messages

Recall from Chapter 1 that every message has a content and a relational dimension. The **content**, the most obvious component, is the subject being discussed: "It's your turn to do the dishes." **Relational messages**, on the other hand, make statements about how the parties feel toward one another.[89] Imagine two ways of saying, "It's your turn to do the dishes," one that is demanding and another that is matter-of-fact. The nonverbal messages also make statements about how the sender views control. A demanding tone says, in effect, "I have a right to tell you what to do around the house," whereas the matter-of-fact tone suggests, "I'm just reminding you of something you might have overlooked."

The relational dimension isn't discussed, and often

Content message
A message that communicates information about the subject being discussed.

Relational message
A message that essentially makes statements about how the parties feel toward one another.

Invitation TO INSIGHT

Your Relational Transgressions

1. Identify transgressions you have made in one important relationship. Describe whether these transgressions were minor or significant, social or relational, deliberate or unintentional, and one-time or incremental. (If you think the relationship can handle it, consider asking the "victim" of your transgression to describe your behaviour and its effects.)

2. Consider (or ask the other person) whether it's necessary to repair your transgression. Examine the strategies described above and decide how you could put them into action.

we're not conscious of it. Sometimes we're unaware of relational messages because they match our beliefs about the amount of respect, control, and affection that is appropriate. For example, you probably wouldn't be offended if your boss told you to do a certain job, because you agree that supervisors have the right to direct employees. But if the message was delivered in a condescending or sarcastic tone, you would probably be offended. Your complaint wouldn't be with the order but with how it was delivered.

Types of Relational Messages

There are four categories or relational messages: affinity, immediacy, respect, and control.

Affinity

Affinity refers to the degree to which people like or appreciate one another.[90] Not surprisingly, affection is the most important ingredient in romantic relationships.[91] But not all affinity messages are positive: A glare or an angry word shows the level of liking just as clearly as a smile or profession of love.

Immediacy

Immediacy refers to the degree of interest and attention that we feel toward and communicate to others. Not surprisingly, immediacy is an important element of relationships.[92] A great deal of immediacy comes from nonverbal behaviours such as eye contact, facial expression, tone of voice, or the distance we put between ourselves and others.[93] Immediacy is expressed through language when we say things like, "We have a problem," instead of "You have a problem."

Immediacy is different from affinity in that it's possible to like someone without really showing it—being

You say, 'Off with her head,' but what I'm hearing is, 'I feel neglected.'

Drawing by Mike Ewers. Reprinted by permission

immediate—with them. While highly immediate communication, such as greeting someone with a big hug and a kiss, has its value, there are also times when a low degree of immediacy is desirable in relationships.

It is also inappropriate to communicate with high immediacy in cultures that frown upon such behaviours, particularly in public settings. The key to relational satisfaction is to create a level of immediacy that works for you and the other person.

Respect

While respect might seem identical to affinity, the two attitudes differ.[94] Whereas affinity involves liking, **respect** involves esteem. It's possible to like others without respecting them. You might have a good deal of affection for some friends, yet not respect the way they behave. Or, conversely, it's possible to respect someone you don't like. You might hold an acquaintance in high esteem for being hardworking and honest but not enjoy that person's company.

Respect is an extremely important ingredient in relationships, and it's a better predictor of relational satisfaction than liking or loving.[95] Sometimes, being respected is more important than being liked. Being taken seriously is a vital ingredient of self-esteem.

Control

A final dimension of relational communication involves **control**—the degree to which the parties in a relationship have the power to influence one another. Some types of control involve conversation—who talks, interrupts, or changes the topic most often.[96] Another dimension involves decisions: who determines what will happen in the relationship.

Relational problems arise when the people concerned have different ideas about the distribution of control. If you and a friend each push for your own idea, problems are likely to arise. Of course, it can be just as difficult when neither person wants to make a decision: "What do you want to do tonight?" "I don't know . . . why don't you decide." "No, you decide."

People in healthy relationships handle the distribution of control in a flexible way. They shift between one-up, one-down, and straight-across roles. For instance, Kyle may handle decisions about car repairs and menu planning while Ashley manages the finances and child care. When a decision is important to one partner, the other willingly gives in,

> **Affinity**
> The degree to which people like or appreciate one another.
>
> **Immediacy**
> The degree of interest and attention that we feel toward and communicate to others.
>
> **Respect**
> The social need to be held in esteem by others.
>
> **Control**
> The degree to which the parties in a relationship have the power to influence one another.

knowing that the favour will be returned. When issues are important to both partners, they try to share power equally. But when an impasse occurs, each will make concessions in a way that keeps the overall balance of power equal.

LO[6]
Metacommunication

Social scientists use the term **metacommunication** to describe messages that people exchange, verbally or nonverbally, about their relationship.[97] In other words, metacommunication is communication about communication—"I wish we could stop arguing so much." Metacommunication is essential in successful relationships, and sooner or later you'll have to talk about what is going on between you.

Metacommunication is useful for solving conflicts because it enables you to shift discussion from the content level to relational questions, where most interpersonal problems lie. Further, metacommunication can reinforce the satisfying aspects of a relationship: "I really appreciate it when you compliment my work in front of the boss." Such comments let others know that their behaviour is appreciated and boost the odds that the behaviour will be continued.

Intimacy in Relationships

People who have satisfying intimate relationships have higher self-esteem, a stronger sense of identity, and greater feelings of control over their lives.[98] When researchers interviewed dying people, 90 percent said that what mattered most in life was having relationships. One mother of three who was dying of cancer said, "You need not wait until you are in my condition to know that nothing in life is as important as loving relationships."[99] Another researcher concluded that close relationships "may be the single most important source of life satisfaction and emotional well-being, across different ages and cultures."[100] With this in mind, let's take a closer look at intimate relationships.

LO[7]
Dimensions of Intimacy

Intimacy, that state of close contact with another, occurs in a variety of relationships. Forty-seven percent of college students reported that they had their "closest, deepest" intimate relationship with a romantic partner, 36 percent said it was with a close friend, and 14 percent cited a family member.[101] There are several dimensions of intimacy: physical, intellectual, emotional, and shared activities.

Physical intimacy begins before birth, when the fetus experiences a physical closeness with its mother that will never happen again.[102] Some physical intimacy is sexual, but sex is not always connected with a close relationship. One study of sexually active teens reported that half of them were not dating, nor did they want to date their sexual partner.[103]

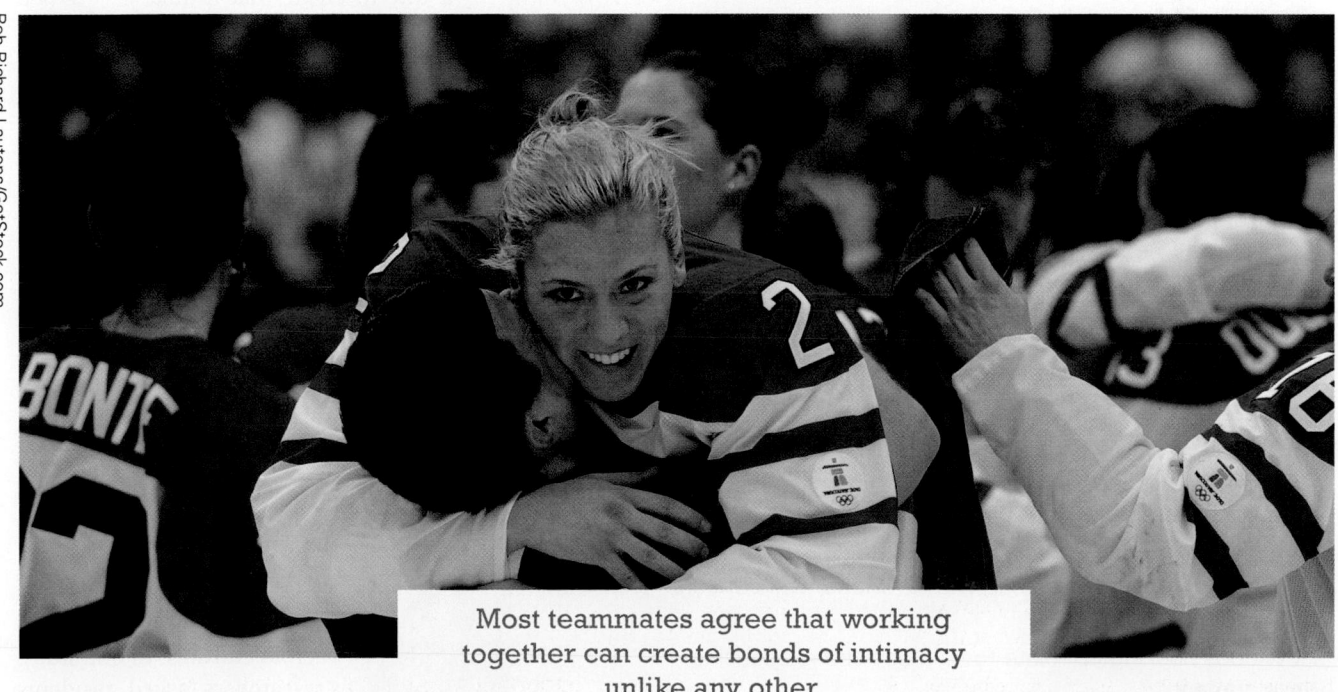

Rob Richard Lautens/GetStock.com

Most teammates agree that working together can create bonds of intimacy unlike any other.

Intellectual intimacy occurs when we share important ideas. This can result in an exciting closeness. Emotional intimacy comes from exchanging important feelings in both face-to-face and Internet interactions. Two-thirds of e-mail users reported forming a personal relationship with someone they met through an Internet newsgroup,[104] and interdependence, breadth, depth, and commitment were demonstrated in both face-to-face and online relationships.

Shared activities is the fourth dimension. When partners do things together, they develop in ways that can transform the relationship. For example, couples "play" by inventing private codes, acting like other people, teasing one another, and so forth.[105] Companions who have endured physical challenges together—in athletics or emergencies, for example—also form lifetime bonds.

Some intimate relationships exhibit all four dimensions, while others display only one or two. Of course, not even the closest relationships always operate at the highest level of intimacy, but despite this, living without any sort of intimacy is hardly desirable.

Masculine and Feminine Intimacy Styles

Because of the link between self-disclosure and intimacy, plus women's propensity to disclose information disclosure,[106] it was believed that they were better than men at developing and maintaining intimate relationships.[107] Men's lack of self-disclosure was seen as a sign of unwillingness or inability to develop close relationships. But

LeilaCutler/Alamy/GetStock.com

emotional expression isn't the only way to develop close relationships. Men develop meaningful relationships through shared activities.[108] By doing things together, they "grow on one another," develop feelings of interdependence, show appreciation for one another, and demonstrate mutual liking. Men also think of help as a measure of caring; a friend does things for you and with you.

Because women and men express caring differently,[109] this can lead to misunderstandings. Women who look for emotional disclosure as a measure of affection may overlook an "inexpressive" man's efforts to show he cares by helping her. A man who fixes a leaky faucet may do so as a bid for intimacy. Further, while women think of sex as a way to express intimacy that has already developed, men see it as a way to create that intimacy.[110] When men want sex early in a relationship or after a fight, they see it as a way to build closeness. By contrast, women may resist physical closeness until the emotional side of the relationship is resolved.

However, what constitutes appropriate male behaviour is changing.[111] Male characters who disclose personal information receive favourable responses from other characters on prime-time sitcoms,[112] and fathers are becoming more affectionate with their sons, although some love is still expressed through shared activities.[113]

Cultural Influences on Intimacy

The notion of intimacy varies across cultures. In one study, researchers asked residents of Britain, Japan, Hong Kong, and Italy to describe their use of 33 rules that governed interaction in social relationships.[114] These included everything from using humour to shaking hands to managing money. The results showed that the greatest differences between Asian and European cultures had to do with intimacy: showing emotions, expressing affection in public, conducting sexual activity, respecting privacy, and so on.

While people from the United States disclose most, intimacy varies across groups.[115] For example, working-class African American men disclose more than their white counterparts, but upwardly mobile black men communicate more like white men.[116] In collectivistic cultures such as Taiwan and Japan, people communicate very differently with members of their "in-groups" (family, close friends) than with their "out-groups."[117] They don't reach out to strangers and wait to be introduced before joining in a conversation. Outsiders are addressed formally, and unfavourable information about in-group members is hidden—you don't air dirty laundry in public in collectivistic cultures. In individualistic cultures (Canada, United States, Australia), there is less distinction between personal and casual relationships. People are "familiar" with strangers and readily disclose information. But the large differences that once existed between Western and Eastern cultures is fast disappearing.[118]

Intimacy in Mediated Communication

In today's world, intimacy is common in mediated contexts, and it develops more quickly through mediated channels than in face-to-face communication.[119] Further, IMing, blogging, Facebooking, etc., enhance verbal, emotional, and social intimacy in interpersonal relationships.[120] The relative anonymity of chat rooms, blogs, and online dating services provides a freedom of expression that might not occur in face-to-face meetings.[121] In addition, instant messaging, e-mailing, and text messaging offer more constant contact with people than might otherwise be possible.[122] As one Internet punster put it, "I've never clicked this much with anyone in my life."[123] As in face-to-face relationships, communicators choose varying

SALLY FORTH © KING FEATURES SYNDICATE

DEBBIE, I HAVE A PROBLEM WITH INTIMACY — TONY

© Bruce Eric Kaplan/ The New Yorker Collection/www.cartoonbank.com.

corepics/Shutterstock

levels of self-disclosure with their cyberpartners, including the way they manage their privacy settings.[124] Mediated communication is an important component in creating and maintaining intimacy in contemporary relationships.

The Limits of Intimacy

It's impossible to have a close relationship with everyone you know—nor is that necessarily desirable. Most people want four to six close relationships in their lives at any given time.[125] Scholars have pointed out that an obsession with intimacy actually leads to less satisfying relationships.[126] When you consider the pleasure that comes from polite but distant communication, the limitations of intimacy become clear. Intimacy is rewarding, but it's not the only way to relate to others.

Self-Disclosure in Relationships

Self-disclosure is the process of deliberately revealing significant information about oneself that is not normally known by others. In self-disclosure, the sharing is deliberate, significant, and previously unknown to the listener. If you accidentally tell a friend something, that information wouldn't qualify because it isn't deliberate. Other characteristics of self-disclosure are outlined in Table 8.3.

> **Self-disclosure**
> The process of deliberately revealing information about oneself that is significant and not normally known by others.

Invitation TO INSIGHT

Your IQ (Intimacy Quotient)

What is the level of intimacy in your important relationships? Find out by following these directions.

1. Identify the point on each scale below that best describes one of your important relationships.
   a. Your level of physical intimacy

   | 1 | 2 | 3 | 4 | 5 |
   low ——————————————— high

   b. Your amount of emotional intimacy

   | 1 | 2 | 3 | 4 | 5 |
   low ——————————————— high

   c. The extent of your intellectual intimacy

   | 1 | 2 | 3 | 4 | 5 |
   low ——————————————— high

   d. The degree of shared activities in your relationship

   | 1 | 2 | 3 | 4 | 5 |
   low ——————————————— high

2. Now answer the following questions:
   a. What responses to each dimension of intimacy seem most significant to you?
   b. Are you satisfied with the intimacy profile outlined by your responses?
   c. If you are not satisfied, what steps can you take to change your degree of intimacy?

TABLE 8.3

Characteristics of Self-Disclosure

Characteristic	Comments
Usually occurs in dyads	One-on-one disclosures are usually more comfortable than more public revelations.
Incremental	Small disclosures build confidence to reveal more important information later.
Relatively scarce	Most common early in relationships and at crucial times later. Not frequent in mature relationships (where partners know each other well).
Best in context of positive relationships	Most productive when delivered in a constructive manner, even if the information is difficult. Positive relationships have the strength to handle such revelations.

LO^8
Degrees of Self-Disclosure

Irwin Altman and Dalmas Taylor, in their model of **social penetration** (pictured in Figure 8.4), suggest that there are two dimensions of self-disclosure: depth and breadth.[127] **Breadth** refers to the range of subjects discussed. For example, the breadth of disclosure in your relationship with a fellow worker will expand as you reveal things about your life away from the job. **Depth** refers to the shift from impersonal topics to more personal ones.

Depending on the breadth and depth of information shared, a relationship will be casual or intimate. In casual relationships, the breadth may be great but not the depth. In intimate relationships, there's probably high depth in at least one area. The most intimate relationships are those in which disclosure is great in both breadth and depth. Altman and Taylor see the development of a relationship as a progression from the periphery of their model to its centre, a process that typically occurs over time. Each of your personal relationships probably has a different combination of breadth of subjects and depth of disclosure. Figure 8.5 (p. 228) pictures a student's self-disclosure in one relationship.

What makes the disclosure in some messages deeper than others depends on its significance or its privacy level. You can also measure the depth of disclosure by looking at the levels of information below.

Social penetration
A model that describes relationships in terms of their breadth and depth.

Breadth
The first dimension of self-disclosure, involving the range of subjects being discussed.

Depth
A dimension of self-disclosure involving a shift from relatively nonrevealing messages to more personal ones.

Cliché
A ritualized, stock statement delivered in response to a social situation.

Clichés

Clichés are ritualized, stock responses—the complete opposite of self-disclosure: "How are you doing?" "Fine!" Although they sound superficial, clichés serve to acknowledge a person's presence and to engage in the social graces.

Facts

To qualify as self-disclosure, facts must be intentional, significant, and not otherwise known:

> "This isn't my first try at college. I dropped out a year ago with terrible grades."

FIGURE 8.4

Social Penetration Model

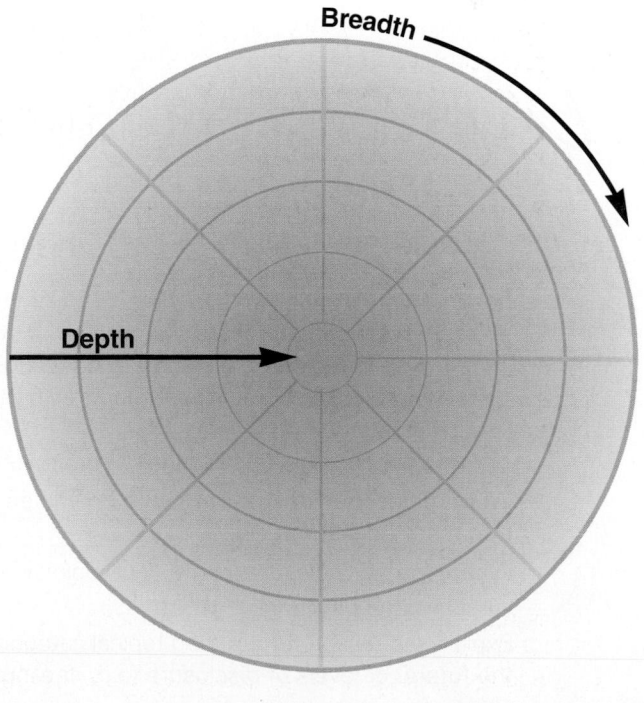

FIGURE 8.5

Sample Model of Social Penetration

Disclosing important information suggests a level of trust and commitment that signals a desire to move the relationship to a new level.

Opinions

Sharing opinions is more revealing:

> "I really like Karen."
> "I don't think the government is doing what it can to protect the environment."

Opinions like these reveal more about a person in that if you know where the speaker stands on a subject, you have more insight into their character and approach to life.

Feelings

Expressing your feelings is the highest level of self-disclosure. While feelings may seem the same as opinions, feelings refer to your emotions. For example:

> "I really like Karen because I feel I can trust her."
> "I don't think the government is doing what it can to protect the environment, and that makes me feel angry and frustrated."

The differences among the levels suggest why relationships can be frustrating. Some communicators never get to the opinions or feelings levels, while others spend too much time there. Just as a steady diet of rich foods can become unappealing, so too can too much personal information. Other problems occur when communicators disclose at different levels, making it uncomfortable for both of them.

A Model of Self-Disclosure

One way to look at the role of self-disclosure in interpersonal communication is by means of the **Johari Window**, created by Joseph Luft and Harry Ingham.[128] Imagine a frame like Figure 8.6 (p. 229) that contains everything about you: your likes, dislikes, goals, secrets, needs—everything.

Of course, even you don't know everything about yourself; you're probably discovering new things all the time. To represent this, the frame can be divided into two parts: the part you know about and the part not yet

---

Invitation TO INSIGHT

EXAMINING YOUR SELF-DISCLOSURE

Here's a chance to explore the levels of self-disclosure you use with some important people in your life.

Choose a "significant other" as the subject of this exercise.

Over a three-day period, record the number of statements you make in each category: clichés, facts, opinions, and feelings. Try to be aware of the topics you discuss on each level, along with the number of statements in each category.

Based on your findings, answer these questions:

a. Which categories of self-disclosure do you engage in most frequently? Least often?

b. What type of disclosure (cliché, fact, opinion, or feeling) do you use in each topic area?

c. Explain the reason for omitting topical categories (e.g., conflicts, the future) or levels of disclosure (e.g., feelings), or both.

d. Explain the consequences of any omissions described in part c.

FIGURE 8.6

The frame containing everything about you can also be divided into the things about you that others know and the things you keep hidden. Figure 8.8 represents this view.

When we impose these two divided frames one atop the other, we have a Johari Window. By looking at Figure 8.9, you can see everything about you divided into four parts.

FIGURE 8.7

FIGURE 8.8

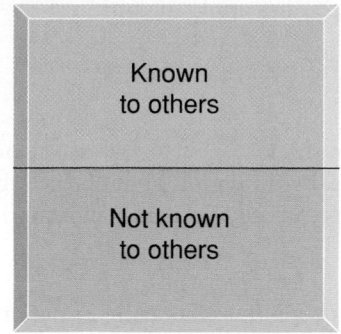

known, as in Figure 8.7. For instance, you may not know that your instructors think highly of you or that you have a particular talent, because you haven't had the opportunity to demonstrate it.

FIGURE 8.9

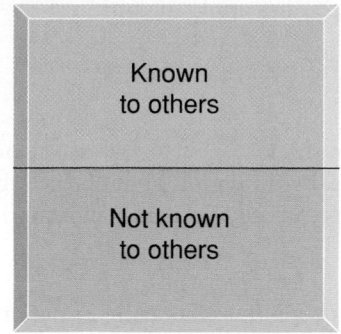

- Part 1, the open area, represents the information that you and others know about you.
- Part 2, the blind area, represents information that you are unaware of but others know.
- Part 3, your hidden area, represents information that you don't share with others.
- Part 4, the unknown area, represents information unknown to both you and others. This would include future honours or awards or your "hidden" talents that have yet to emerge.

Invitation TO INSIGHT

Building a Johari Window

You can use the Johari Window model to examine the level of self-disclosure in your own relationships.

1. Use the format described in the preceding section to draw two Johari Windows representing the relationship between you and one other person. Remember to reverse one of the windows so that your open area and that of the other person face each other.

2. Describe which parts of yourself you keep in the hidden area. Explain your reasons for doing so. Describe the advantages or disadvantages or both of not disclosing these parts of yourself.

3. Look at the blind area of your model. Is this area large or small because of the amount of feedback (much or little) that you get from your partner or because of your willingness to receive the feedback that is offered?

4. Explain whether you are satisfied with the results illustrated by your answers. If you are not satisfied, explain what you can do to remedy the problem.

LO⁹
Benefits and Risks of Self-Disclosure

Like most things in life, there are benefits and risks of self-disclosing. The choices people make to reveal or conceal information about themselves is referred to as **privacy management**.[129] People disclose for a variety of reasons—which ones apply to you?

Benefits of Self-Disclosure

Catharsis

Sometimes we disclose just to "get it off our chest," As when you reveal your regrets about behaving badly in the past. Cartharsis can provide mental and emotional relief.[130]

Reciprocity

Self-disclosure usually begets more of the same.[131] While your own self-disclosures won't guarantee self-disclosure by others, your honesty will create a climate that makes others feel safe or even obligated to reciprocate. Sometimes reciprocity occurs later; you tell a friend something today, and she or he opens up at a later date.

Self-Clarification

Sometimes we clarify our beliefs, opinions, thoughts, attitudes, and feelings merely by talking about them out loud. This "talking the problem out" occurs with psychotherapists, but also good friends, bartenders, and hairdressers.

Self-Validation

When you disclose with the hope of obtaining a listener's agreement ("I think I did the right thing when . . ."), you are disclosing for self-validation, a confirmation of something about you. This occurs, for example, in the "coming out" process when gay individuals choose to integrate their sexual preference into their personal, family, and social lives.[132]

Identity Management

Sometimes information is revealed as a sort of marketing of ourselves.[133] For instance, couples on first dates may share information that makes them appear more sincere, interesting, sensitive, or interested in the other person.

Relationship Maintenance and Enhancement

Self-disclosure also plays a role in relational success.[134] For example, there's a strong relationship between the quality of self-disclosure and marital satisfaction,[135] and the bond between grandparents and grandchildren grows stronger when honesty and depth of sharing are high.[136]

Social Influence

Revealing personal information can sometimes increase your control over a person and the situation. An

"Bob, as a token of my appreciation for this wonderful lunch I would like to disclose to you my income-tax returns for the past four years."

© Jack Ziegler/The New Yorker Collection/www.cartoonbank.com.

employee who tells the boss that another firm is making overtures will likely have a greater chance of getting a raise or other perks. This only works if the disclosure is not premeditated; otherwise, it can have negative results.

Of the many reasons for self-disclosure, how well we know the listener is the strongest.[137] People disclose most to friends for relationship maintenance and enhancement. In other words, we disclose to strengthen our relationships. The second most important reason is self-clarification—to understand ourselves better.

Risks of Self-Disclosure

Disclosing can be risky when topics are difficult or painful,[138] but there are several categories of risks.[139] These include rejection, negative impressions, a decrease in relational satisfaction, loss of influence, and hurting the

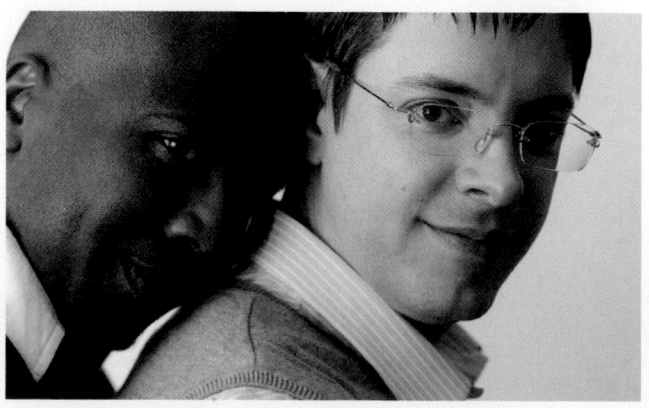

© iStockphoto.com/Eduardo Jose Bernardino

Secrets Website Gets a Million Hits a Week

When Tina Malament was 17, she felt isolated and alone. Suffering from anorexia, depression, and suicidal thoughts, she lashed out at everyone close to her.

It took an intervention from family and friends for her to realize starving herself to be thin wasn't worth it. Over the next few years, she became serious about her recovery, and she took heart from a blog called PostSecret, where strangers mail in postcards to be posted online every Sunday. On the postcards, people anonymously share their secrets—funny secrets, happy secrets, and secrets filled with anguish, remorse, and pain. It is a place where people can release the secrets that suffocate them. About 1 million people visit the site each week.

The secrets posted on the site vary widely. One reads, "My mom won't tell me who my real father is. I wonder if she told him about me." Another reads, "I am so much bigger than the life I am leading."

Malament, now 21 and living in Colorado, sent in her own secret as well. She took a picture of herself standing in front of another postcard, which had a cupcake crossed out on it. She put her hands across the postcard and wrote across the picture that she was going to win her fight with anorexia. Although her secret wasn't posted, she found the process of making and sending it therapeutic, and the idea that someone else might read it and get something out of it encouraging.

PostSecret's ability to help people inspired Malament to start her own project. When she was a freshman at American University she made a T-shirt with a message about anorexia. On the front was a statistic about anorexics who die from the disorder. The back read: "I refuse to become a statistic." She wore the shirt around campus and eventually to a PostSecret event. At the end she stood up and told her story. Afterward six girls approached her crying and told her how much her story had affected them. They also asked her to make them T-shirts.

Courtney R. Brooks

other person. Deciding when and how much information to disclose can be complicated. Therefore, the following guidelines can help match the level to the situation.

Guidelines for Self-Disclosure

A few guidelines can help you choose an appropriate level of self-disclosure in a given situation.

Do You Have a Moral Obligation to Disclose?

Sometimes we are morally obliged to disclose. Most HIV-positive patients believe it's their "duty" to reveal their status to healthcare providers and partners.[140] Yet 40 percent didn't reveal this information to their sexual partners.[141]

Is the Other Person Important to You?

If the person is important enough, disclosure is a way to grow and develop your relationship. It is also important to maintain relationships.

Are the Amount and Types of Disclosure Appropriate?

In most relationships, disclosure occurs gradually, beginning with relatively superficial information.[142] Having someone you've just met disclose personal information can be embarrassing. As the relationship grows, so too might the disclosure. In most everyday conversations,

"Since we're both being honest, I should tell you I have fleas."

there is little or no disclosure.[143] Even partners in intimate relationships rarely talk about personal information.[144]

Aside from moderation, self-disclosure should not always be negative and the timing needs to be right. Making sure a person isn't tired or preoccupied is important when sharing important information.

Is the Risk of Disclosing Reasonable?

There is always risk involved in disclosure, especially on the job.[145] However, if your partner is trustworthy and supportive, the prospect of disclosing may be more reasonable. And some relationships are well worth the risk.

Is the Disclosure Relevant to the Situation at Hand?

Highly personal information should be disclosed in personal settings. For instance, too much classroom disclosure can result in less cohesiveness than a "relatively" honest climate in which pleasant but superficial relationships were the norm.[146]

Will the Effect Be Constructive?

Self-disclosure can be a vicious tool if it's not used carefully, so consider the effects of your candour before opening up. Comments such as, "Last year I slept with your partner," may resolve your guilt but devastate the listener.

Is the Self-Disclosure Clear and Understandable?

It's important to be clear when you reveal information, and it's better to describe another's behaviour by saying, "When you don't answer my phone calls . . ." than it is to complain vaguely: "When you avoid me . . ."

Is the Self-Disclosure Reciprocated?

The amount of personal information you share usually depends on how much the other person reveals. Typically, disclosure is a two-way street and couples are happiest when their levels of openness are roughly equal.[147] One-way disclosure does have a role in therapeutic relationships, like when clients disclose to a trained professional. But you wouldn't expect or be receptive to your doctor's disclosing personal problems or ailments.[148]

LO[10]
Alternatives to Self-Disclosure

Although self-disclosure plays an important role in interpersonal relationships, complete honesty isn't always an easy or ideal choice. Consider the following:

"I'm a very sensual person. How about you, Mr. Gellerman?"

© Stan Hunt/The New Yorker Collection/www.cartoonbank.com.

You're attracted to your best friend's mate, who has confessed that s/he is attracted to you. You agreed not to act on your feelings but now your friend asks if you're attracted to his or her mate. Would you tell the truth?

A relative who visits often gives you a large, ugly painting and asks, "Where will you put it?" What do you say?

These situations highlight some issues surrounding deceptive communication. On one hand, you believe in honestly and hold that the very existence of a society seems based on a foundation of truthfulness.[149] On the other, honesty can have potentially unpleasant consequences. In such situations, communicators aren't always honest[150] and resort to four alternatives: silence, lying, equivocating, and hinting.

Silence

Silence—withholding thoughts and feelings—need not be dishonourable, especially when total candour is likely to cause pain. People make distinctions between "lies of omission" and "lies of commission"—and saying nothing (omission) is usually judged less harshly than telling an outright lie (commission).[151]

> I want the man in my life to love me enough to lie to me a little—or at least to be selective about the truth he tells me. As Emerson said, "God offers to every mind its choice between truth and repose." When it comes to love, I'll take repose.
>
> —Joan Sutton, *Lovers and Others*

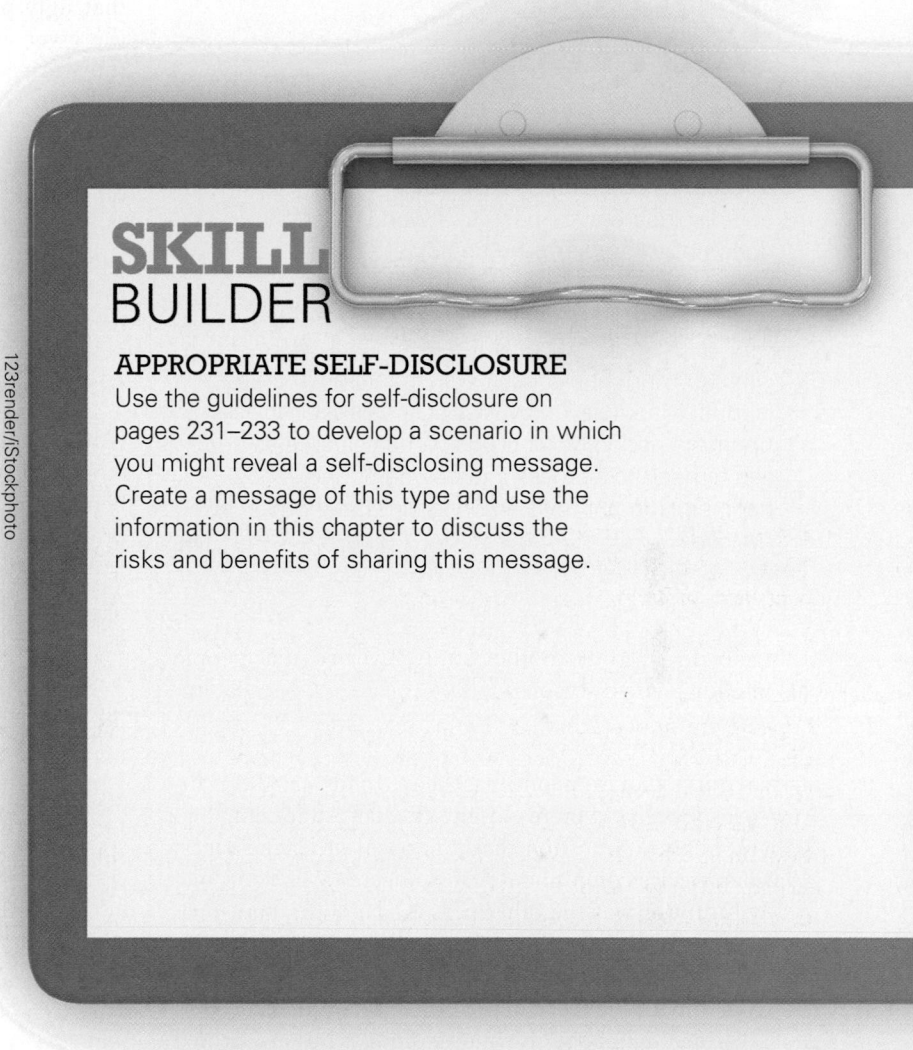

123render/iStockphoto

SKILL BUILDER

APPROPRIATE SELF-DISCLOSURE
Use the guidelines for self-disclosure on pages 231–233 to develop a scenario in which you might reveal a self-disclosing message. Create a message of this type and use the information in this chapter to discuss the risks and benefits of sharing this message.

Lying

Although lying to gain unfair advantage is wrong, the "benevolent lie" isn't so easy to dismiss. A **benevolent lie** is defined as unmalicious or even helpful to the person to whom it is told, and they are quite common in face-to-face and mediated relationships.[152] Most people believe that there are times when lying is justified,[153] and one study found that only 38.5 percent of the subjects' statements were totally honest.[154] Another showed that people lie at a rate of three fibs per 10 minutes of conversation![155] Apparently our world is not such an honest one.

Reasons for Lying

Subjects in one study revealed that people lie for five major reasons: to save face, to avoid tension or conflict, to guide social interaction, to expand or reduce relationships, and to gain power.[156] Another study reported that people exaggerated to make their stories more interesting or because it was the "right

Benevolent lie
A lie defined by the teller as unmalicious or even helpful to the person to whom it is told.

© Boden/Ledingham/Masterfile Corporation

thing to do."[157] But another study revealed that people also lie for "selfish reasons."[158]

Effects of Lies

Discovering that someone has lied to you can be traumatic, especially if you're close to the liar. After being lied to, you begin to question the honesty of other messages: Was last week's compliment really sincere? Was your joke really funny, or was the other person's laughter a put-on?

Research shows that deception threatens relationships,[159] but not all lies are equally devastating. The liar's motives can influence whether the deception is acceptable or not.[160] Self-serving and exploitive lies are treated as a relational transgression, while lies aimed at sparing another's feelings are generally forgiven. But lying about major parts of your relationship can have the gravest consequences.

> I am in that state of mind where even a lie is a comfort, providing it is a cheerful lie.
>
> —Lucy Maud Montgomery,
> *Rilla of Ingleside*

Equivocating

When faced with the choice of telling an unpleasant truth, communicators often equivocate—responding in language that has two plausible meanings. If a friend asks what you think of an awful outfit, you could say, "It's really unusual—one of a kind!" The value of equivocation becomes clear when you consider the dilemma of what

to say when you've been given an unwanted present— that ugly painting mentioned earlier, for example—and the giver asks what you think of it. Do you lie or tell the truth? You could choose to give a vague response, but equivocating is positive in that it spares the receiver embarrassment, it can save face for both the sender and the receiver,[161] and it provides a viable alternative to lying.[162]

Given these advantages, it's not surprising that people equivocate. They say they prefer truth-telling to equivocating, but given the choice, people prefer to finesse the truth.[163]

Hinting

Hints are more direct than equivocal statements. Whereas equivocal statements aren't aimed at changing others' behaviour, hints seek to get a desired response from others.[164]

Direct Statement	Face-Saving Hint
I'm too busy to continue with this conversation.	I know you're busy; I better let you go.

The face-saving value of hints explains why communicators are more likely to be indirect than fully disclosing when they deliver a potentially embarrassing message.[165] Hints are only as successful as the other person's ability to pick up on them. Subtle remarks might go right over the head of insensitive receivers, or they may chose not to respond.

> We are hard on each other and call it honesty, choosing our jagged truths with care and aiming them across the neutral table.
>
> The things we say are true; it is our crooked aims, our choices turn them criminal.
>
> —Margaret Atwood,
> *Power Politics*

The Ethics of Evasion

People use hints, equivocations, and benevolent lies because they help manage difficult situations. But are they ethical? Most people accept lies when the speaker's motives and the effects of the lie are positive. In some circumstances, lies are judged as more appropriate than the undiluted truth.[166] Further, we're not likely to

Dilbert © Scott Adams/Dist. by United Feature Syndicate, Inc.

challenge untruthful statements under the following circumstances:[167]

- We expect others to fib. (You listen to a friend's tall tales, knowing they're exaggerating.)
- The lie is mutually advantageous. (A co-worker's account of a job mix-up gets you off the hook.)
- A lie helps us avoid embarrassment. (You compliment your host, even though the meal tasted awful.)
- The lie helps us avoid confronting an unpleasant truth. (A family ignores that fact that a member is an alcoholic.)
- We asked the other person to lie. (One partner tells the other, "If you're ever unfaithful to me, I don't want to know about it.")

In light of these facts, perhaps it's better to ask whether an indirect message is truly in the interests of the receiver and whether this sort of evasion is the only, or the best, way to behave in a given situation.

Communication in the Workplace

Given the amount of time we spend in the workplace, developing and maintaining both interpersonal and professional relationships is very important. This can indeed be challenging. First, we can expect to work with three generations other than our own, and each one communicates and learns differently than we do. Then we're forced to interact with a variety of individuals—co-workers, bosses, mentors, customers or clients, and other professionals related to our work—all of whom communicate differently according to their role. On top of that, we do not get to select any of these individuals, yet we are expected to work well with them.

As a result, getting off to a good start is just as important on the job as it is in romances or friendships. Scholars use the terms *assimilation* and *socialization* to describe how employees are integrated into their organizations. Not surprisingly, communication plays a major role in the socialization process. When helpful information is plentiful, new employees grow more satisfied with and committed to their jobs in the long run.[168]

In one study, researchers explored the nature of socialization messages.[169] While orientation sessions, handbooks, e-mails, and memos were useful, new employees reported that the most valuable messages often come via informal conversations—over 90 percent of which took place in face-to-face settings.

Many of the helpful messages were about professional behaviour and office rules ("It's crucial to be punctual," "Be careful when you challenge the boss"). Office politics also came into play ("Always be nice to the administrative assistant, Nadine, because she's the gateway to the supervisor"). Not all the messages were warnings; some were warm and welcoming ("It's one big family here," "We're glad they hired you"). Regardless of the specific content, virtually all of the messages were perceived as positive, supportive, and designed to help the recipient, the company, or both.

It's important to remember the importance of messages—both large and small, deliberate and offhand—in building a happy, effective work team. As a newcomer, it's wise to seek the counsel and support of your colleagues. As a veteran, it's important to help rookies get off to a good start.

Endnotes

1. D. Byrne (1997). "An Overview (and Underview) of Research and Theory within the Attraction Paradigm." *Journal of Social and Personal Relationships, 17,* 417–431.

2. E. Hatfield & S. Sprecher (1986). *Mirror, Mirror: The Importance of Looks in Everyday Life.* Albany: State University of New York Press.

3. E. Walster, E. Aronson, D. Abrahams, & L. Rottmann (1966). "Importance of Physical Attractiveness in Dating Behaviour." *Journal of Personality and Social Psychology, 4,* 508–516.

4. G . W. Lewandowski, A. Aron, & J. Gee (2007). "Personality Goes a Long Way: The Malleability of Opposite-Sex Physical Attractiveness." *Personal Relationships, 14,* 571–585.

5. K. F. Albada (2002). "Interaction Appearance Theory: Changing Perceptions of Physical Attractiveness through Social Interaction." *Communication Theory, 12,* 8–41.

6. D. Barelds & P. Dijkstra (2009). "Positive Illusions about a Partner's Physical Attractiveness and Relationship Quality." *Personal Relationships, 16,* 263–283.

7. D. Hamachek (1982). *Encounters with Others: Interpersonal Relationships and You.* New York: Holt, Rinehart and Winston.

8. K.A.Yun (2002). "Similarity and Attraction." In M. Allen, N. Burrell, B. M. Eayle, & R. W. Preiss (Eds.). *Interpersonal Communication Research: Advances Through Meta-analysis* (pp. 145–168). Mahwah, NJ: Erlbaum.

9. S. Luo & E. Klohnen (2005). "Assortative Mating and Marital Quality in Newlyweds: A Couple-Centered Approach," *Journal of Personality and Social Psychology, 88,* 304–326. See also D. M. Amodio & C. J. Showers (2005). "Similarity Breeds Liking Revisited: The Moderating Role of Commitment." *Journal of Social and Personal Relationships, 22,* 817–836.

10. F. E. Aboud & M. J. Mendelson (1998). "Determinants of Friendship Selection and Quality: Developmental Perspectives." In W. M. Bukowski & A. F. Newcomb (Eds.). *The Company They Keep: Friendship in Childhood and Adolescence.* New York: Cambridge University Press.

11. A. M. Ledbetter, E. Griffin, & G. G. Sparks (2007). "Forecasting Friends Forever: A Longitudinal Investigation of Sustained Closeness Between Best Friends." *Personal Relationships, 14,* 343–350.

12. B. R. Burleson & W. Samter (1996). "Similarity in the Communication Skills of Young Adults: Foundations of Attraction, Friendship, and Relationship Satisfaction." *Communication Reports, 9,* 127–139.

13. J. T. Jones, B. W. Pelham, & M. Carvallo (2004) "How Do I Love Thee? Let Me Count the J's: Implicit Egotism and Interpersonal Attraction." *Journal of Personality and Social Psychology, 87,* 665–683.

14. D. Mette & S. Taylor (1971). "When Similarity Breeds Contempt." *Journal of Personality and Social Psychology, 20,* 75–81.

15. H. Fisher (May/June 2007). "The Laws of Chemistry." *Psychology Today, 40,* 76–81.

16. L. Heatherington, V. Escudero, & M. L. Friedlander (2005). "Couple Interaction During Problem Discussions: Toward an Integrative Methodology." *Journal of Family Communication, 5,* 191–207.

17. S. Specher (1998). "Insiders' Perspectives on Reasons for Attraction to a Close Other." *Social Psychology Quarterly, 61,* 287–300.

18. E. Aronson (2004). *The Social Animal,* 9th ed. New York: Bedford, Freeman, & Worth. See Chapter 9.

19. K. Dindia (2002). "Self-Disclosure Research: Knowledge Through Meta-Analysis." In M. Allen & R. W. Preiss (Eds.). *Interpersonal Communication Research: Advances Through Meta-Analysis* (pp. 169–185). Mahwah, NJ: Erlbaum.

20. Ibid.

21. J. A. Shirley, W. G. Powers, and C. R. Sawyer (2007). "Psychologically Abusive Relationships and Self-Disclosure Orientations." *Human Communication, 10,* 289–301.

22. C. Flora (Jan/Feb 2004). "Close Quarters." *Psychology Today, 37,* 15–16.

23. C. Haythornthwaite, M. M. Kazmer, & J. Robbins (2000). "Community Development Among Distance Learners: Temporal and Technological Dimensions." *Journal of Computer- Mediated Communication, 6(1),* article 2, http://jcmc.indiana.edu/vol6/ issue1/haythornthwaite.html. Accessed September 11, 2006.

24. See, for example, M. E. Roloff (1981). *Interpersonal Communication: The Social Exchange Approach.* Beverly Hills, CA: Sage.

25. A. DeMaris, (2007). "The Role Of Relationship Inequity in Marital Disruption." *Journal of Social and Personal Relationships, 24,* 177–195.

26. M. L. Knapp & A. L. Vangelisti (2006). *Interpersonal Communication and Human Relationships,* 6th ed. Boston: Allyn and Bacon. See also T. A. Avtgis, D. V. West, & T. L. Anderson (1998) Relationship Stages: An Inductive Analysis Identifying Cognitive, Affective, and Behavioural Dimensions of Knapp fs Relational Stages Model." *Communication Research Reports 15,* 280–287; and S. A. Welch & R. B. Rubin (2002) Development of Relationship Stage Measures." *Communication Quarterly, 50,* 34–40.

27. K. Dindia (2003). "Definitions and Perspectives on Relational Maintenance Communication." In D. J. Canary and M. Dainton, (Eds.). *Maintaining Relationships through Communication.* Mahwah, NJ: Erlbaum.

28. A. J. Johnson, E. Wittenberg, M. Haigh, S. Wigley, J. Becker, K. Brown, & E. Craig (2004). "The Process of Relationship Development and Deterioration: Turning Points in Friendships That Have Terminated." *Communication Quarterly, 52,* 54–67.

29. B. W. Scharlott & W. G. Christ (1995). "Overcoming Relationship-Initiation Barriers: The Impact of a Computer-Dating System on Sex Role, Shyness, and

Appearance Inhibitions." *Computers in Human Behaviour,* *11*, 191–204.

30. C. R. Berger (1987). "Communicating under Uncertainty." In M. E. Roloff & G. R. Miller (Eds.). *Interpersonal Processes: New Directions in Communication Research.* Newbury Park, CA: Sage. See also C. R. Berger & R. J. Calabrese (1975). "Some Explorations in Initial Interaction and Beyond: Toward a Developmental Theory of Interpersonal Communication." *Human Communication Research, 1,* 99–112.

31. L. Pratt, R. L. Wiseman, M. J. Cody, & P. F. Wendt (1999). "Interrogative Strategies and Information Exchange in Computer-Mediated Communication." *Communication Quarterly, 47,* 46–66.

32. J. H. Tolhuizen (1989). "Communication Strategies for Intensifying Dating Relationships: Identification, Use and Structure." *Journal of Social and Personal Relationships, 6,* 413–434.

33. Johnson et al., op. cit.

34. L. A. Baxter (1987). "Symbols of Relationship Identity in Relationship Culture." *Journal of Social and Personal Relationships, 4,* 261–280.

35. C. J. S. Buress & J. C. Pearson (1997). "Interpersonal Rituals in Marriage and Adult Friendship," *Communication Monographs, 64,* 25–46.

36. R. A. Bell & J. G. Healey (1992) "Idiomatic Communication and Interpersonal Solidarity in Friends' Relational Cultures." *Human Communication Research, 18,* 307–335.

37. M. Roloff, C. A. Janiszewski, M. A. McGrath, C. S. Burns, & L. A. Manrai (1988). "Acquiring Resources from Intimates: When Obligation Substitutes for Persuasion." *Human Communication Research 14,* 364–396.

38. E. Foster (2008). 'Commitment, Communication, and Contending with Heteronormativity: An Invitation to Greater Reflexivity in Interpersonal Research." *Southern Communication Journal, 73,* 84–101.

39. L. G. Ferdinand (2005). "The Influence of Differentiation of Self and Family of Origin on Individual and Relationship Functioning in Young Adults." *Dissertation Abstracts International: Section B: The Sciences and Engineering, 66,* 1715.

40. J. A. Courtright, F. E. Miller, L. E. Rogers, & D. Bagarozzi (1990). "Interaction Dynamics of Relational Negotiation: Reconciliation versus Termination of Distressed Relationships." *Western Journal of Speech Communication, 54,* 429–453.

41. D. M. Battaglia, F. D. Richard, D. L. Datteri, & C. G. Lord (1998). "Breaking Up Is (Relatively) Easy to Do: A Script for the Dissolution of Close Relationships." *Journal of Social and Personal Relationships, 15,* 829–845.

42. S. Metts, W. R. Cupach, & R. A. Bejllovec (1989). "'I Love You Too Much to Ever Start Liking You': Redefining Romantic Relationships." *Journal of Social and Personal Relationships, 6,* 259–274.

43. A. Johnson, E. Wittenberg, M. Haigh, S. Wigley, J. Becker., K. Brown, & E. Craig (2004). "The Process of Relationship Development and Deterioration: Turning Points in Friendships That Have Terminated." *Communication Quarterly, 52,* 54–67.

44. See, for example, L. A. Baxter & B. M. Montgomery (1992). *Relation: Dialogues and Dialectics.* New York: Guilford; and W. K. Rawlins (1996). *Friendship Matters: Communication Dialectics, and the Life Course.* New York: Aldine de Gruyter.

45. Summarized by L. A. Baxter (1994). "A Dialogic Approach to Relationship Maintenance." In D. J. Canary & L. Stafford (Eds.). *Communication and Relational Maintenance.* San Diego, CA: Academic Press. See also E. Sahlstein & T. Dun (2008). "'I Wanted Time to Myself and He Wanted to be Together All the Time': Constructing Breakups and Managing Autonomy-Connection," *Qualitative Research Reports in Communication, 9,* 37–45.

46. A. P. Buunk (2005). "How Do People Respond to Others with High Commitment or Autonomy in their Relationships?" *Journal of Social and Personal Relationships, 22,* 653–672. See also E. Sahlstein & T. Dun (2008), op cit.

47. D. Morris (1997) *Intimate Behaviour.* New York: Kodansha International, pp. 21–29.

48. T. D. Golish (2000). "Changes in Closeness between Adult Children and Their Parents: A Turning Point Analysis." *Communication Reports, 13,* 78–97.

49. L. A. Baxter & L. A. Erbert (1999). "Perceptions of Dialectical Contradictions in Turning Points of Development in Heterosexual Romantic Relationships." *Journal of Social and Personal Relationships, 16,* 547–569.

50. E. E. Graham (2003). "Dialectic Contradictions in Post-Marital Relationships." *Journal of Family Communication, 3,* 193–215.

51. L. A. Baxter, D. O. Braithwaite, T. D. Golish, & L. N. Olson (2002). "Contradictions of Interaction for Wives of Elderly Husbands with Adult Dementia." *Journal of Applied Communication Research, 30,* 1–20.

52. S. Petronio (2000). "The Boundaries of Privacy: Praxis of Everyday Life." In S. Petronio (Ed.). *Balancing the Secrets of Private Disclosures* (pp. 37–49). Mahwah, NJ: Erlbaum.

53. D. R. Pawlowski (1998). "Dialectical Tensions in Marital Partners' Accounts of Their Relationships," *Communication Quarterly, 46,* 396–416.

54. E. M. Griffin (2000). *A First Look at Communication Theory,* 4th ed. New York: McGraw-Hill.

55. D. O. Braithwaite & L. Baxter (2006). "'You're My Parent But You're Not': Dialectical Tensions in Stepchildren's Perceptions About Communicating with the Nonresident Parent." *Journal of Applied Communication Research, 34,* 30–48.

56. B. M. Montgomery (1993). "Relationship Maintenance versus Relationship Change: A Dialectical Dilemma." *Journal of Social and Personal Relationships, 10,* 205–223.

57. D. O. Braithwaite, L. A. Baxter, & A. M. Harper (1998). "The Role of Rituals in the Management of the Dialectical Tension of 'Old' and 'New' in Blended Families." *Communication Studies, 49,* 101–120.

58. See A. Christensen & J. Jacobson (2000). *Reconcilable Differences*. New York: Guilford.

59. R. L. Conville (1991). *Relational Transitions: The Evolution of Personal Relationships*. New York: Praeger, p. 80.

60. For a discussion of similarities across cultures, see D. E. Brown (1991). *Human Universals*. New York: McGraw-Hill.

61. R. R. Hamon & B. B. Ingoldsby (Eds.) (2003). *Mate Selection Across Cultures*. Thousand Oaks, CA: Sage.

62. J. E. Myers, J. Madathil, & L. R. Tingle (2005). "Marriage Satisfaction and Wellness in India and the United States: A Preliminary Comparison of Arranged Marriages and Marriages of Choice." *Journal of Counselling & Development, 83,* 183–190; and P. Yelsma & K. Athappilly (1988). "Marriage Satisfaction and Communication Practices: Comparisons Among Indian and American Couples." *Journal of Comparative Family Studies, 19,* 37–54.

63. For a detailed discussion of cultural differences that affect relationships, see M. Sun Kim (2002). *Non-Western Perspectives on Human Communication: Implications for Theory and Practice*. Thousand Oaks, CA: Sage.

64. P. Breitman & C. Hatch (2000). *How To Say No Without Feeling Guilty*. New York: Broadway Books.

65. M. Imami (1981). *16 Ways to Avoid Saying No*. Tokyo: The Nihon Keizai Shimbun.

66. D. J. Canary & L. Stafford (1992). "Relational Maintenance Strategies and Equity in Marriage." *Communication Monographs. 59,* 243–267.

67. D. J. Weigel & D. S. Ballard-Reisch (1999). "Using Paired Data to Test Models of Relational Maintenance and Marital Quality." *Journal of Social and Personal Relationships, 16,* 175–191.

68. L. Stafford & D. J. Canary (1991). "Maintenance Strategies and Romantic Relationship Type, Gender, and Relational Characteristics." *Journal of Personality and Social Psychology, 7,* 217–242.

69. A. J. Johnson, M. M. Haigh, J. A. H. Becker, E. A. Craig, & S. Wigley (2008). "College Students' Use of Relational Management Strategies in Email in Long-Distance and Geographically Close Relationships." *Journal of Computer-Mediated Communication, 13,* 381–404.

70. For a description of this ongoing research program, see The Gottman Institute. "Twelve-Year Study of Gay and Lesbian Couples," *www.gottman.com/research*. Accessed July 28, 2006.

71. For an overview of this topic, see C. E. Rusbult, P. A. Hannon, S .L. Stocker, & E.J. Finkel (2005). "Forgiveness and Relational Repair." In E.L. Worthington (Ed.). *Handbook of Forgiveness* (pp. 185–206). New York: Routledge.

72. T. M. Emmers-Sommer (2003). "When Partners Falter: Repair After a Transgression." In D. J. Canary & M. Dainton (Eds.). *Maintaining Relationships through Communication* (pp. 185–205). Mahwah, NJ: Erlbaum.

73. K. Dindia & L. A. Baxter (1987). "Strategies for Maintaining and Repairing Marital Relationships." *Journal of Social and Personal Relationships, 4,* 143–158.

74. V. R. Waldron, D. L. Kelley, & J. Harvey (2008). "Forgiving Communication and Relational Consequence." In M. T. Motley (Ed.). *Studies in Applied Interpersonal Communication* (pp. 165–184). Thousand Oaks, CA: Sage.

75. H. S. Park (2009). "Cross-Cultural Comparison of Verbal and Nonverbal Strategies of Apologizing." *Journal of International and Intercultural Communication, 2,* 66–87. See also H. S. Park and X. Guan (2006). "Effects of National Culture and Face Concerns on Intention to Apologize: A Comparison of U.S. and China." *Journal of Intercultural Communication Research, 35,* 183–204.

76. J. J. Exline, L. Deshea, & V. T. Holeman (2007). "Is Apology Worth the Risk? Predictors, Outcomes, and Ways to Avoid Regret." *Journal of Social & Clinical Psychology, 26,* 479–504.

77. H. M. Wallace, J. J. Exline, & R. F. Baumeister (2008). "Interpersonal Consequences of Forgiveness: Does Forgiveness Deter or Encourage Repeat Offenses?" *Journal of Experimental Social Psychology, 44,* 453–460.

78. D. L. Kelley & V. R. Waldron (2005). "An Investigation of Forgiveness-Seeking Communication and Relational Outcomes." *Communication Quarterly, 53,* 339–358.

79. A. J. Merolla (2008). "Communicating Forgiveness in Friendships and Dating Relationships." *Communication Studies, 59,* 114–131.

80. H. K. Orcutt (2006). "The Prospective Relationship of Interpersonal Forgiveness and Psychological Distress Symptoms Among College Women." *Journal of Counselling Psychology, 53,* 350–361; and J. Eaton & C. W. Struthers (2006). "The Reduction of Psychological Aggression Across Varied Interpersonal Contexts Through Repentance and Forgiveness." *Aggressive Behaviour, 32,* 195–206.

81. K. A. Lawler, J. W. Younger, R. L. Piferi, et al. (2003). "A Change of Heart: Cardiovascular Correlates of Forgiveness in Response to Interpersonal Conflict." *Journal of Behavioural Medicine, 26,* 373–393.

82. V. R. Waldron & D. L. Kelley (2005). "Forgiving Communication as a Response to Relational Transgressions." *Journal of Social and Personal Relationships, 22,* 723–742.

83. J. A. Rolls (2010). "Tales from Broken Hearts: Women and Recovery from Romantic Relationships." *Storytelling, Self, Society: An Interdisciplinary Journal of Storytelling Studies, 6,* 107–121.

84. V. R. Waldron & D. L. Kelley (2008). *Communicating Forgiveness*. Thousand Oaks, CA: Sage.

85. F. Bachman & L. K. Guerrero (2006). "Forgiveness, Apology, and Communicative Responses to Hurtful Events." *Communication Reports, 19,* 45–56.

86. Henline, B. H., L. K. Lamke, & M. D. Howard (2007). "Exploring Perceptions of Online Infidelity." *Personal Relationships, 14,* 113–128.

87. S. Takaku, B. Weiner, & K. Ohbuchi (2001) A Cross-Cultural Examination of the Effects of Apology and Perspective-Taking on Forgiveness." *Journal of Language & Social Psychology, 20,* 144–167.

88. D. L. Kelley (1998). "The Communication of Forgiveness." *Communication Studies, 49,* 255–272.

89. See P. Watzlawick, J. H. Beavin, & D. D. Jackson (1967). *Pragmatics of Human Communication.* New York: Norton; and W. J. Lederer & D. D. Jackson (1968). *The Mirages of Marriage.* New York: Norton.

90. See, for example, R. A. Bell & J. A. Daly (1995). "The Affinity-Seeking Function of Communication." In M. V. Redmond (Ed.). *Interpersonal Communication: Readings in Theory and Research.* Fort Worth, TX: Harcourt Brace.

91. M. Dainton (1998). "Everyday Interaction in Marital Relationships: Variations in Relative Importance and Event Duration." *Communication Reports, 11,* 101–143.

92. S. A. Myers & T. A. Avtgis (1997). "The Association of Socio-Communicative Style and Relational Types on Perceptions of Nonverbal Immediacy." *Communication Research Reports, 14,* 339–349.

93. For a thorough examination of this topic, see Chapter 11, "Nonverbal Immediacy," in V. P. Richmond & J. C. McCroskey (2004). *Nonverbal Behaviour in Interpersonal Relationships,* 5th ed. Boston: Allyn and Bacon.

94. T. S. Lim & J. W. Bowers (1991). "Facework: Solidarity, Approbation, and Tact." *Human Communication Research, 17,* 415–450.

95. J. R. Frei & P. R. Shaver (2002). "Respect in Close Relationships: Prototype, Definition, Self-Report Assessment, and Initial Correlates." *Personal Relationships, 9,* 121–139.

96. M. T. Palmer (1989). "Controlling Conversations: Turns, Topics, and Interpersonal Control." *Communication Monographs, 56,* 1–18.

97. Watzlawick et al., op. cit.

98. K. J. Prager & D. Buhrmester (1998). "Intimacy and Need Fulfillment in Couple Relationships." *Journal of Social and Personal Relationships, 15,* 435–469.

99. C. E. Crowther & G. Stone (1986). *Intimacy: Strategies for Successful Relationships.* Santa Barbara, CA: Capra Press, p. 13.

100. C. Peterson (2006). *A Primer in Positive Psychology.* New York: Oxford.

101. E. Berscheid, M. Schneider, & A. M. Omoto (1989). "Issues in Studying Close Relationships: Conceptualizing and Measuring Closeness." In C. Hendrick (Ed.). *Close Relationships* (pp. 63–91).Newbury Park, CA: Sage.

102. D. Morris (1973). *Intimate Behaviour.* New York: Bantam, p. 7.

103. W. D. Manning, P. C. Giordano, & M. A. Longmore (2006). "Hooking Up: The Relationship Contexts of 'Nonrelationship' Sex." *Journal of Adolescent Research, 21,* 459–483.

104. M. R. Parks & K. Floyd (1996). "Making Friends in Cyberspace." *Journal of Communication, 46,* 80–97.

105. L. A. Baxter (1994). "A Dialogic Approach to Relationship Maintenance." In D. Canary & L. Stafford (Eds.). *Communication and Relational Maintenance.* San Diego, CA: Academic Press.

106. See, for example, K. Dindia (2000). "Sex Differences in Self-Disclosure, Reciprocity of Self-Disclosure, and Self-Disclosure and Liking: Three Meta-Analyses Reviewed." In S. Petronio (Ed.). *Balancing Disclosure, Privacy and Secrecy.* Mahwah, NJ: Erlbaum.

107. J. T. Wood & C. C. Inman (1993). "In a Different Mode: Masculine Styles of Communicating Closeness." *Applied Communication Research, 21,* 279–295; and K. Floyd (1995). "Gender and Closeness among Friends and Siblings." *Journal of Psychology, 129,* 193–202.

108. S. Swain (1989). "Covert Intimacy in Men's Friendships: Closeness in Men's Friendships." In B. J. Risman & P. Schwartz (Eds.). *Gender in Intimate Relationships: A Microstructural Approach.* Belmont, CA: Wadsworth.

109. L. Stafford, M. Dainton, & S. Haas (2000). "Measuring Routine and Strategic Relational Maintenance: Scale Revision, Sex versus Gender Roles, and the Prediction of Relational Characteristics." *Communication Monographs, 67,* 306–323.

110. C. K. Reissman (1990). *Divorce Talk: Women and Men Make Sense of Personal Relationships.* New Brunswick, NJ: Rutgers University Press.

111. J. M. Bowman (2008). "Gender Role Orientation and Relational Closeness: Self-Disclosive Behaviour in Same-Sex Male Friendships." *Journal of Men's Studies, 16,* 316–330.

112. G. E. Good, M. J. Porter, & M. G. Dillon (2002). "When Men Divulge: Men's Self-Disclosure on Prime Time Situation Comedies." *Sex Roles, 46,* 419–427.

113. M. T. Morman & K. Floyd (2002). "A 'Changing Culture of Fatherhood': Effects of Affectionate Communication, Closeness, and Satisfaction in Men's Relationships With Their Fathers and Their Sons." *Western Journal of Communication, 66,* 395–411.

114. M. Argyle & M. Henderson (1985). "The Rules of Relationships." In S. Duck & D. Perlman (Eds.). *Understanding Personal Relationships.* Beverly Hills, CA: Sage.

115. W. B. Gudykunst & S. Ting-Toomey (1988). *Culture and Interpersonal Communication.* Newbury Park, CA: Sage, pp. 197–198.

116. C. W. Franklin (1992). "'Hey Home—Yo Bro': Friendship among Black Men." In P. M. Nardi (Ed.). *Men's Friendships.* Newbury Park, CA: Sage.

117. H. C. Triandis (1994). *Culture and Social Behaviour.* New York: McGraw-Hill, p. 230.

118. E. Hatfield & R. L. Rapson (2006). "Passionate Love, Sexual Desire, and Mate Selection: Cross-Cultural and Historical Perspectives." In P. Noller & J. A. Feeney (Eds.). *Close Relationships: Functions, Forms and Processes* (pp. 227–243). Hove, England: Psychology Press/Taylor & Francis.

119. L. B. Hian, S. L. Chuan, T. M. K. Trevor, & B. H. Detenber (2004). "Getting to Know You: Exploring the Development of Relational Intimacy in Computer-Mediated Communication." *Journal of Computer-Mediated Communication, 9,* Issue 3.

120. P. Valkenberg & J. Peter (2009). "The Effects of Instant Messaging on the Quality of Adolescents' Existing Friendships: A Longitudinal Study." *Journal of Communication, 59*, 79–97; H. Ko & F. Kuo (2009). "Can Blogging Enhance Subjective Well-Being Through Self-Disclosure?" *CyberPsychology & Behaviour, 12*, 75–79; J. P. Mazer, R. E. Murphy, & C. J. Simonds (2008). "The Effects of Teacher Self-Disclosure via 'Facebook' on Teacher Credibility." RCA Vestnik (*Russian Communication Association*), 30–37; and Y. Hu, J. F. Wood, V. Smith, & N. Westbrook (2004) Friendships Through IM: Examining the Relationship Between Instant Messaging and Intimacy." *Journal of Computer-Mediated Communication, 10*, Issue 1.

121. L. D. Rosen et al. (2008). "The Impact of Emotionality and Self-Disclosure on Online Dating versus Traditional Dating." *Computers in Human Behaviour, 24*, 2124–2157; and A. Ben-Ze fev (2003) Privacy, Emotional Closeness, and Openness in Cyberspace." *Computers in Human Behaviour, 19*, 451–467.

122. J. Boase, J. B. Horrigan, B. Wellman, & L Rainie (2006). *The Strength of Internet Ties.* Pew Internet & American Life Project, *www.pewinternet.org/pdfs/PIP_Internet_ties.pdf*. Accessed September 11, 2006.

123. S. Henderson & M. Gilding (2004). "I've Never Clicked This Much with Anyone in My Life': Trust and Hyperpersonal Communication in Online Friendships." *New Media & Society, 6*, 487–506.

124. K. Lewis, J. Kaufman, & N. Christakis (2008). "The Taste for Privacy: An Analysis of College Student Privacy Settings in an Online Social Network." *Journal of Computer-Mediated Communication, 14*, 79–100; and Z. Tufekei (2008) "Can You See Me Now? Audience and Disclosure Regulation in Online Social Network Sites." *Bulletin of Science, Technology & Society, 28*, 20–36.

125. R. F. Baumeister (2005). *The Cultural Animal: Human Nature, Meaning, and Social Life.* New York: Oxford.

126. See, for example, R. Bellah, W. M. Madsen, A. Sullivan, & S. M. Tipton (1985). *Habits of the Heart: Individualism and Commitment in American Life.* Berkeley: University of California Press; R. Sennett (1974). *The Fall of Public Man: On the Social Psychology of Capitalism.* New York: Random House; and S. Trenholm & A. Jensen (1990). *The Guarded Self: Toward a Social History of Interpersonal Styles.* Paper presented at the Speech Communication Association meeting, San Juan, PR.

127. I. Altman & D. A. Taylor (1973). *Social Penetration: The Development of Interpersonal Relationships* New York: Holt, Rinehart and Winston. See also D. A. Taylor & I. Altman (1987). "Communication in Interpersonal Relationships: Social Penetration Processes." In M. E. Roloff & G. R. Miller (Eds.). *Interpersonal Processes: New Directions in Communication Research.* Newbury Park, CA: Sage.

128. J. Luft (1969). *Of Human Interaction.* Palo Alto, CA: National Press Books.

129. S. Petronio (2007). "Translational Research Endeavors and the Practices of Communication Privacy Management." *Journal of Applied Communication Research, 35*, 218–22.

130. T. D. Affifi & K. Steuber (2009). "The Revelation Risk Model (RRM): Factors that Predict the Revelation of Secrets and the Strategies Used to Reveal Them." *Communication Monographs, 76*, 144–176. See also T. D. Affifi & K. Steuber (2009) Keeping and Revealing Secrets." *Communication Currents, 4*, 1–2.

131. K. Dindia (2002). "Self-Disclosure Research: Advances Through Meta-Analysis." In M. Allen & R. W. Preiss (Eds.). *Interpersonal Communication Research: Advances Through Meta-Analysis* (pp. 169–185). Mahwah, NJ: Erlbaum; and V. J. Derlega & A. L. Chaikin (1975). *Sharing Intimacy: What We Reveal to Others and Why.* Englewood Cliffs, NJ: Prentice-Hall.

132. R. C. Savin-Williams (2001). *Mom, Dad. I'm Gay: How Families Negotiate Coming Out.* Washington, DC: American Psychological Association.

133. H. L. Wintrob (1987). "Self-Disclosure as a Marketable Commodity." *Journal of Social Behaviour and Personality, 2*, 77–88.

134. J. A. Hess, A. D. Fannin, & L. H. Pollom (2007). "Creating Closeness: Discerning and Measuring Strategies for Fostering Closer Relationships. *Personal Relationships, 14*, 25–44; and A. E. Mitchell et al. (2008). "Predictors of Intimacy in Couples' Discussions of Relationship Injuries: An Observational Study." *Journal of Family Psychology, 22*, 21–29.

135. S. MacNeil & E. S. Byers (2009). "Role of Sexual Self-Disclosure in the Sexual Satisfaction of Long-Term Heterosexual Couples." *Journal of Sex Research, 46*, 3–14; and F. D. Fincham & T. N. Bradbury (1989) The Impact of Attributions in Marriage: An Individual Difference Analysis." *Journal of Social and Personal Relationships, 6*, 69–85.

136. V. G. Downs (1988). "Grandparents and Grandchildren: The Relationship between Self-Disclosure and Solidarity in an Intergenerational Relationship." *Communication Research Reports, 5*, 173–179.

137. L. B. Rosenfeld & W. L. Kendrick (Fall 1984). "Choosing to Be Open: Subjective Reasons for Self-Disclosing." *Western Journal of Speech Communication, 48*, 326–343.

138. V. Derlega, B. A. Winstead, A. Mathews, & A. L. Braitman (2008). "Why Does Someone Reveal Highly Personal Information? Attributions for and against Self-Disclosure in Close Relationships." *Communication Research Reports, 25*, 115–130; K. G. Niederhoffer & J. W. Pennebaker (2002). "Sharing One fs Story: On the Benefits of Writing or Talking About Emotional Experience." In C. R. Snyder & S. J. Lopez (Eds.). *Handbook of Positive Psychology* (pp. 573–583). London: Oxford University Press.

139. K. Greene, V. J. Derlega, & A. Mathews (2006). "Self-Disclosure in Personal Relationships." In A. Vangelisti & D. Perlman (Eds.). *The Cambridge Handbook of Personal Relationships.* New York: Cambridge University Press; and L. B. Rosenfeld (2000). "Overview of the Ways Privacy, Secrecy, and Disclosure are Balanced in Today's Society." In S. Petronio (Ed.). *Balancing the Secrets of Private Disclosures* (pp. 3–17). Mahweh, NJ: Erlbaum.

140. R. Agne, T. L. Thompson, & L. P. Cusella (2000). "Stigma in the Line of Face: Self-Disclosure of Patients' HIV Status to Health Care Providers." *Journal of Applied Communication Research, 28,* 235–261; and V. J. Derlega, B. A. Winstead, & L. Folk-Barron (2000). "Reasons For and Against Disclosing HIV-Seropositive Test Results to an Intimate Partner: A Functional Perspective." In S. Petronio (Ed.). *Balancing the Secrets of Private Disclosures* (pp. 71–82). Mahwah, NJ: Erlbaum. See also J P. Caughlin et al. 2009). "Do Message Features Influence Reactions to HIV Disclosures? A Multiple-Goals Perspective." *Health Communication, 24,* 270–283.

141. M. Allen et al (2008). "Persons Living with HIV: Disclosure to Sexual Partners." *Communication Research Reports, 25,* 192–199.

142. K. Dindia, M. A. Fitzpatrick, & D. A. Kenny (1988). *Self-Disclosure in Spouse and Stranger Interaction: A Social Relations Analysis.* Paper presented at the annual meeting of the International Communication Association, New Orleans, LA; and S. W. Duck & D. E. Miell (1991). "Charting the Development of Personal Relationships." In R. Gilmour & S. W. Duck (Eds.). *Studying Interpersonal Interaction* (pp. 133–144). New York: Guilford.

143. S. Duck (1991). "Some Evident Truths about Conversations in Everyday Relationships: All Communications Are Not Created Equal." *Human Communication Research, 18,* 228–267.

144. C. L. Kleinke (1979). "Effects of Personal Evaluations." In *Self-Disclosure.* San Francisco: Jossey-Bass.

145. E. M. Eisenbery & M. B. Witten (1987) "Reconsidering Openess in Organizational Communication." *Academy of Management Review, 12,* 418–428.

146. L. B. Rosenfeld & J. R. Gilbert (1989). "The Measurement of Cohesion and Its Relationship to Dimensions of Self-Disclosure in Classroom Settings." *Small Group Behaviour, 20,* 291–301.

147. L. B. Rosenfeld & G. I. Bowen (1991). "Marital Disclosure and Marital Satisfaction: Direct-Effect versus Interaction-Effect Models." *Western Journal of Speech Communication, 55,* 69–84.

148. S. H. McDaniel et al. (2007). "Physician Self-Disclosure in Primary Care Visits: Enough About You, What About Me?" *Archives of Internal Medicine, 167,* 1321–1326.

149. A. Jaksa & M. Pritchard (1993). *Communication Ethics: Methods of Analysis,* 2nd ed. Belmont, CA: Wadsworth, pp. 65–66.

150. D. O'Hair & M. J. Cody (1993). "Interpersonal Deception: The Dark Side of Interpersonal Communication?" In B. H. Spitzberg & W. R. Cupach (Eds.). *The Dark Side of Interpersonal Communication.* Hillsdale, NJ: Erlbaum.

151. M. Spranca, E. Minsk, & J. Baron (1991). "Omission and Commission in Judgement and Choice." *Journal of Experimental Social Psychology, 27,* 76–105.

152. J. F. George and A. Robb (2008). "Deception and Computer-Mediated Communication in Daily Life." *Communication Reports, http://mail.cbu.ca/Owner/Local Settings/Temporary Internet Files/OLK1B/title~content=t7145 92826~db=all~tab=issueslist~branches=21 - v2121,* 92–103. Accesssed July 13, 2008.

153. M. L. Knapp (2006). "Lying and Deception in Close Relationships." In A. Vangelisti & D. Perlman (Eds.). *The Cambridge Handbook of Personal Relationships.* New York: Cambridge University Press.

154. R. E. Turner, C. Edgely, & G. Olmstead (1975). "Information Control in Conversation: Honesty Is Not Always the Best Policy." *Kansas Journal of Sociology, 11,* 69–89.

155. R. S. Feldman, J. A. Forrest, & B. R. Happ (2002). "Self-Presentation and Verbal Deception: Do Self-Presenters Lie More?" *Basic and Applied Social Psychology, 24,* 163–170.

156. B. M. DePaulo, D. A. Kashy, S. E. Kirkendol, & M. M. Wyer (1996). "Lying in Everyday Life." *Journal of Personality and Social Psychology, 70,* 779–795.

157. J. Bavelas (1983). "Situations that Lead to Disqualification." *Human Communication Research, 9,* 130–145.

158. D. Hample (1980). "Purposes and Effects of Lying." *Southern Speech Communication Journal, 46,* 33–47.

159. S. A. McCornack & T. R. Levine (1990). "When Lies Are Uncovered: Emotional and Relational Outcomes of Discovered Deception." *Communication Monographs, 57,* 119–138.

160. J. S. Seiter, J. Bruschke, & C. Bai (2002). "The Acceptability of Deception as a Function of Perceivers' Culture, Deceiver's Intention, and Deceiver-Deceived Relationship." *Western Journal of Communication, 66,* 158–181.

161. S. Metts, W. R. Cupach, & T. T. Imahori (1992). "Perceptions of Sexual Compliance-Resisting Messages in Three Types of Cross-Sex Relationships." *Western Journal of Communication, 56,* 1–17.

162. J. B. Bavelas, A. Black, N. Chovil, & J. Mullett (1990). *Equivocal Communication.* Newbury Park, CA: Sage, p. 171.

163. W. P. Robinson, A. Shepherd, & J. Heywood (1998). "Truth, Equivocation/Concealment, & Lies in Job Applications & Doctor-Patient Communication." *Journal of Language & Social Psychology, 17,* 149–164.

164. M. T. Motley (1992). "Mindfulness in Solving Communicators' Dilemmas." *Communication Monographs, 59,* 306–314.

165. S. B. Shimanoff (1988). "Degree of Emotional Expressiveness as a Function of Face-Needs, Gender, & Interpersonal Relationship." *Communication Reports, 1,* 43–53.

166. A. P. Hubbell (May 1999). *"I Love Your Family—They Are Just Like You": Lies We Tell to Lovers and Perceptions of Their Honesty and Appropriateness.* Paper presented at the annual meeting of the International Communication Association, San Francisco. See also S. A. McCornack (1992). "Information Manipulation Theory." *Communication Monographs, 59,* 1–16.

167. P. Andersen (1999). *Nonverbal Communication: Forms & Functions.* Mountain View, CA: Mayfield, pp. 297–298.

168. J. H. Waldeck & K. K. Myers (2007). "Organizational Assimilation Theory, Research, and Implications for

GET ONLINE

The easy-to-navigate website for **LOOK** offers guidance on key topics in **Interpersonal Communications** in a variety of engaging formats. You have the opportunity to refine and check your understanding via interactive quizzes and flashcards. Videos and podcasts provide inspiration for your own further exploration. And, in order to make **LOOK** an even better learning tool, we invite you to speak up about your experience with **LOOK** by completing a survey form and sending us your comments.

Get online and discover the following resources:

- Printable and Interactive Flashcards
- Interactive Quizzing
- Crossword Puzzles
- Discipline-Specific Activities

"I think this book is awesome for students of all ages. It is a much simpler way to study."

—Yasmine Al-Hashimi, Fanshawe College

Visit **www.icanlookinout.com** to find the resources you need today!

CHAPTER

9 Improving Communication Climates

What do you THINK?

I become defensive when I think I am being attacked.

1 2 3 4 5 6 7
strongly agree   strongly disagree

LEARNING OUTCOMES

LO¹ Identify confirming, disagreeing, and disconfirming messages and patterns in your own important relationships and describe their consequences.

LO² Describe how communication climates develop through positive or negative reciprocal communication patterns.

LO³ Use Gibb's categories and the assertive message format to create messages that are likely to build supportive rather than defensive communication climates.

LO⁴ Create appropriate nondefensive responses to real or hypothetical criticisms.

Personal relationships are a lot like the weather. Some are cool and formal, some are hot and steamy, some are polluted, and so forth. Some relationships have stable climates, whereas others change dramatically—calm one moment and turbulent the next. Every relationship has a feeling, a pervasive mood that colours the interactions of the participants.

Although we can't change the external weather, we *can* improve our interpersonal climate. This chapter explains the forces that make some relationships pleasant and others unpleasant.

Communication Climate: The Key to Positive Relationships

Communication climate refers to the emotional tone of a relationship—the way people feel about each other. The role of climate in families and friendships is obvious. So is the impact of climate in the workplace. Have you ever worked in a climate where backbiting, criticism, and suspicion were the norm? Or have you been lucky enough to be employed at a place where the atmosphere was positive and supportive? If you've experienced both, you know what a difference the climate makes.

The importance of climate cannot be overstated. For example, climate is the best predictor of marital satisfaction.[1] Contented couples have a 5 to 1 ratio of positive to negative statements, whereas the ratio for dissatisfied couples is 1 to 1.[2] Positive, confirming messages are just as

> **Communication climate**
> The emotional tone of a relationship between two or more individuals.

important in families, and the climate parents create affect how their children interact.[3] Children who feel confirmed have more open communication with parents, higher self-esteem, and lower stress levels, while unconfirmed children suffer a broad range of emotional and behavioural problems.[4] The satisfaction that siblings feel with one another drops sharply as aggressive, disconfirming messages increase.[5]

Communication climates are shared climates, and it's rare to find one person describing a relationship as open and positive while another characterizes it as cold and hostile. But climates can change over time, and people can greatly influence that change.

> First we'd climb a tree and maybe then we'd talk
> Or sit silently and listen to our thoughts
> With illusions of someday casting a golden light
> No dress rehearsal, this is our life
>
> —*The Tragically Hip,*
> *"Ahead by a Century"*

LO[1]
Levels of Message Confirmation

What makes a communication climate positive or negative is surprisingly simple. It's basically the degree to which the people believe themselves to be valued by one another. Social scientists use the term **confirming communication** to describe messages that convey value and contribute to supportive communication climates. On the other hand, **disconfirming communication** describes behaviours that show a lack of regard and make listeners feel defensive. It is obvious that confirming messages are more desirable than disconfirming ones. But what characteristics or behaviours distinguish the two types?

Like beauty, whether a message is confirming or disconfirming is up to the beholder.[6] Consider times when you used a comment as a sign of affection, but to an outsider it sounded like insulting or disconfirming ("You turkey!"). Likewise, a comment that the sender

Confirming communication
A message that expresses caring or respect for another person.

Disconfirming communication
A message that expresses a lack of caring or respect for another person.

might have meant to be helpful ("I'm telling you this for your own good…") could easily disconfirm and put the receiver on the defensive.

What makes some messages more confirming than others? Table 9.1 outlines the levels of message confirmation that are described in the following pages.

TABLE 9.1
Levels of Message Confirmation and Disconfirmation

Disconfirming	Disagreeing Confirming
Impervious	Aggressiveness
Interrupting	Complaining
Irrelevant	Argumentativeness
Tangential	Recognition
Impersonal	Acknowledgement
Ambiguous	Endorsement
Incongruous	
Least Valuing	**Most Valuing**

Disconfirming Messages

Disconfirming communication shows a lack of regard for the other person, either by disputing or ignoring some important part of that person's message.[7] Communication researchers have identified seven types of disconfirming messages.[8]

Impervious Responses

An *impervious response* doesn't acknowledge the other person's message. It is very disconcerting when there's no reaction from a person with whom you're attempting to communicate. It can be even more disconfirming than being dismissed or attacked. Research shows that employees sometimes nudge unwanted co-workers toward

In the TV show *Everybody Loves Raymond*, the Barone family exchanged messages ranging from highly confirming to highly disconfirming.

quitting by not interacting with them.[9] And stonewalling in marriage is a strong predictor of divorce.[10]

Interrupting

While an occasional *interrupting response* is not likely to be taken as a disconfirmation, repeatedly interrupting a speaker can be both discouraging and irritating.

Irrelevant Responses

A comment unrelated to what the other person has just said is an *irrelevant response*:

A: What a day! The car overheated, I had to call a tow truck, and the computer at work broke down.

B: Listen, we have to talk about Ami's birthday present. I only have tomorrow to shop for it.

A: I'm beat. Let's talk later. This day was something else.

B: I can't figure out what to get. She's got everything...

Tangential Responses

Conversational "take-aways," where listeners don't entirely ignore the speaker's remarks but use them as a starting point for a shift to a different topic, are called *tangential responses*:

A: I'd like to know soon if you're interested in a skiing vacation. Otherwise, it'll be impossible to get reservations anywhere.

B: Yeah. And if I don't finish this sociology paper, I won't want to go anywhere. Could you proofread this for me?

Impersonal Responses

Impersonal responses refer to clichés and other statements that don't truly respond to the speaker:

A: I'm having some personal problems, and I need to leave early a couple of afternoons this week.

B: Ah, yes. We've all got problems, Jane.

Ambiguous Responses

Ambiguous responses have more than one meaning and leave the other party unsure of the responder's position:

A: I'd like to get together soon. How about Tuesday?

B: Uh, maybe.

A: Well, how about it? Can we talk Tuesday?

B: Probably.

Incongruous Responses

An *incongruous response* contains two contradictory messages, one of which is nonverbal:

A: Darling, I love you.

B: I love you, too. *(said in a monotone while watching TV)*

ANGEL

"Angel" by Sarah McLachlan, taken from the album *Surfacing* © 1997 by Tyde Music.

You spend all your time waiting for that second chance
For a break that would make it OK
There's always some reason to feel not good enough
And it's hard at the end of the day

I need some distraction, oh, beautiful release
Memory seep from my veins
Let me be empty, oh, and weightless
And maybe I'll find some peace tonight

In the arms of the angel
Fly away from here
From this dark cold hotel room
And the endlessness that you fear

You are pulled from the wreckage
Of your silent reverie
You're in the arms of the angel
May you find some comfort here

In the arms of the angel
May you find some comfort here

Sarah McLachlan

Disconfirming messages can pollute a communication climate. Read on to learn ways to disagree without being disagreeable.

Disagreeing Messages

Between disconfirming and confirming communication lie **disagreeing messages**—messages that say "you're wrong" in one way or another. Some disagreements are quite hostile, but others aren't as disconfirming as they may first seem. There are three types of disagreeing messages: aggressiveness, complaining, and argumentativeness.

> **Disagreeing messages**
> Messages that say "you're wrong" in one way or another.

Aggressiveness

Aggressiveness is the most destructive way to disagree because it attacks the self-concepts of other people to inflict psychological pain.[11] Aggressiveness demeans the worth of others through the use of name calling, putdowns, sarcasm, taunting, yelling, and badgering.

Complaining

When communicators aren't prepared to argue but want to register dissatisfaction, they *complain*. Some ways of complaining are better than others. Satisfied couples tend to offer behavioural complaints ("You always throw your socks on the floor"), while unsatisfied couples make personal attacks ("You're a slob").[12] Personal complaints are more likely to result in an episode of escalated conflict because they attack a more fundamental part of the presenting self.[13] Talking about socks deals with a change of habits; calling someone a slob is a character assault that is unlikely to be forgotten. While complaining isn't necessarily a sign of a troubled relationship, the complaint should be coached in behavioural language rather than as a personal criticism.[14]

Argumentativeness

Calling someone *argumentative* is an unfavourable evaluation, yet we value the ability to create and deliver a sound argument in lawyers, talk-show participants, letters to the editor, and political debates. Communication researchers define argumentativeness as presenting and defending positions on issues while attacking positions taken by others.[15] Argumentativeness is associated with positive attributes such as an enhanced self-concept and communicative competence.

To maintain a positive climate while arguing, make sure to attack issues, not people. Also, arguments are better received when they're delivered in a supportive, affirming manner.[16]

Confirming Messages

Research shows that three increasingly positive types of messages have the best chance of being confirming: recognition, acknowledgment, and endorsement.[17]

Recognition

The most fundamental way to confirm someone is to *recognize* the other person. Recognition seems easy, yet there are times when we don't even respond to others on this basic level. Failing to return an e-mail or phone message are common examples. Even if it's an oversight, the message has a disconfirming effect.

Acknowledgment

Acknowledging another's ideas and feelings is a stronger form of confirmation. Listening is probably the most common form of acknowledgment, but counterfeit listening—stage-hogging, pseudolistening, and so on—has the opposite effect. Acknowledgment includes asking questions, paraphrasing, and reflecting. Managers who solicit opinions—even when they're not accepted—are rated highly by employees.[18]

Endorsement

Endorsement means that you agree with another's ideas or find them important. Endorsement is the strongest type of confirming message because it communicates valuing.

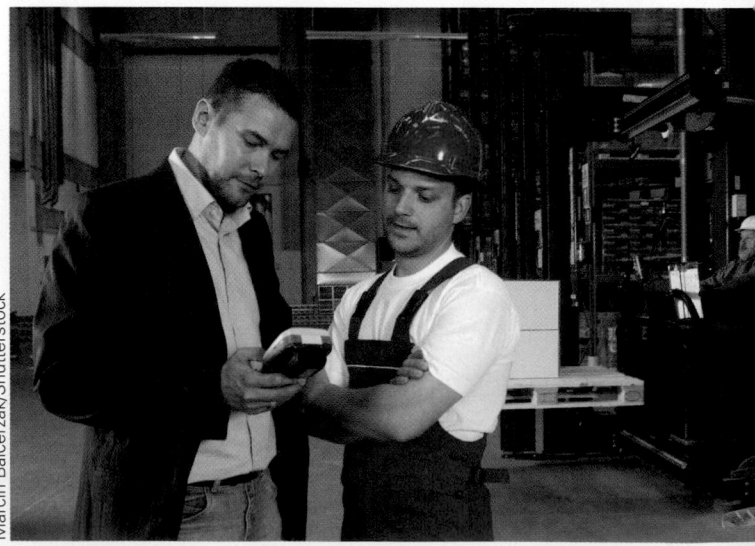

But you don't have to agree completely with another person to endorse a message; you just need to find something that you endorse. "I can see why you were so angry," you might say, even if you don't approve of the outburst. Outright praise is a strong form of endorsement, and one that can be used surprisingly often.

LO^2
How Communication Climates Develop

Relational climates begin to develop as soon as two people start to communicate. If the messages are confirming, the climate will be positive. If not, it will be hostile or defensive. Many climate-shaping messages are nonverbal[19]—smiles or frowns, the presence or absence of eye contact, tone of voice, or the use of personal space all send messages about how the parties feel about one another.

Once climates are formed, they take on lives their own and grow in self-perpetuating **spirals**: reciprocating communication patterns in which each person's message reinforces the other's.[20] In positive spirals, one partner's confirming message leads to a similar message from the other, which leads the first person to be even more confirming. Negative spirals are just as powerful, though they leave the partners feeling worse about themselves and each other. See Table 9.2 for examples of how reciprocal communication patterns occur.

Escalatory conflict spirals are the most visible way that disconfirming messages reinforce one another.[21] One attack leads to another until a skirmish escalates into a full-fledged battle:

> **Spiral**
> A reciprocal communication pattern in which each person's message reinforces the other's.
>
> **Escalatory conflict spiral**
> A communication spiral in which one attack leads to another until the initial skirmish escalates into a full-fledged battle.

TABLE 9.2
Positive and Negative Reciprocal Communication Patterns

Negative Reciprocal Patterns	
Pattern	*Example*
Complaint—counter complaint	A: I wish you weren't so self-centered. B: Well, I wish you weren't so critical.
Disagreement—disagreement	A: Why are you so hard on Marta? She's a great boss. B: Are you kidding? She's the biggest phony I've ever seen. A: You wouldn't know a good boss if you saw one. B: Neither would you.
Mutual indifference	A: I don't care if you want to stay. I'm exhausted, and I'm getting out of here. B: Go ahead if you want, but find your own way home.
Arguments involving punctuation	A: How can I talk when you won't listen? B: How can I listen when you won't talk?
Positive Reciprocal Patterns	
Pattern	*Example*
Validation of other's perspective	A: This assignment is really confusing. Nobody can figure out what we're supposed to do. B: I can understand how it might be unclear. Let me try to explain…
Recognizing similarities	A: I can't believe you want to take an expensive vacation! We should be saving money, not spending more! B: I agree we should be saving. But I think we can take this trip and still save some money. Let me show you what I've figured out…
Supportiveness	A: I'm going crazy with this job. It was supposed to be temporary. I have to do something different, and soon. B: I can see how much you hate it. Let's figure out how we can get the project finished soon, so you can get back to your regular work.

Adapted from *Competence and Interpersonal Conflict* by W. Cupach and D. Canary, p. 51–52. Copyright © 1997.

Sugar Gold Images/Jupiter Images

A: (*mildly irritated*) Where were you? We were supposed to meet a half-hour ago.

B: (*defensively*) I'm sorry. I got hung up at the library. I don't have as much free time as you do, you know.

A: I wasn't *blaming* you, so don't be so touchy. I do resent what you just said, though. I'm plenty busy. And I've got lots of better things to do than wait around for you!

B: Who's getting touchy? I just made a simple comment. You've sure been defensive lately. What's the matter with you?

Although they are less obvious, **de-escalatory conflict spirals** can also be destructive.[22] Rather than fighting, parties decrease their dependence on each other, withdraw, and become less invested in the relationship. But spirals can also be positive. A word of praise can lead to a returned compliment, which can lead to an act of kindness, which can result in an improved relational climate.

> **De-escalatory conflict spiral**
> A communication spiral in which the parties slowly lessen their dependence on one another, withdraw, and become less invested in the relationship.
>
> **Defensiveness**
> The attempt to protect a presenting image a person believes is being attacked.

Defensiveness: Causes and Remedies

No type of communication pollutes an interpersonal climate more than **defensiveness**. The word suggests protecting oneself from physical harm. In this case, however, we are most likely protecting our presenting self—our face.

Face-Threatening Acts

Recall that a person's face consists of the physical traits, personality characteristics, attitudes, aptitudes, and all the other parts of the image that he or she wants to present to the world. But it's a mistake to talk about a single face, because we try to project different faces to different people. You might, for example, want an employer to see you as serious but your friends to see you as witty and outrageous.

We don't feel defensive when others accept and acknowledge important parts of our presenting image. But when confronted with **face-threatening acts**—messages that challenge the image we want to project—we are likely to resist.[23] Defensiveness, then, is the process of protecting our presenting self, our face.

For example, we may feel threatened and act defensively if a boss criticizes a job we have done, especially if the supervisor was correct! In fact, we tend to feel most defensive when criticism is on target.[24] The drive to defend a presenting image—even when it is false—leads some people to act in destructive ways, such as being sarcastic or verbally abusive.[25]

Defensiveness is not only the responsibility of the person who feels threatened. If that were so, all you would need to do is grow a thick skin. There is also the role played by those who send face-threatening messages.

LO³
Preventing Defensiveness in Others

Researcher Jack Gibb offers some useful tools for reducing defensiveness.[26] He isolated six types of defence-arousing communication and six contrasting behaviours that reduce the level of threat and defensiveness by conveying face-honouring relational messages of respect (see Table 9.3)

Evaluation versus Description

The first type of defence-arousing behaviour is **evaluation**. Most people become irritated at judgmental statements,

TABLE 9.3

The Gibb Categories of Defensive and Supportive Behaviours

Defensive Behaviours	Supportive Behaviours
1. Evaluation	1. Description
2. Control	2. Problem orientation
3. Strategy	3. Spontaneity
4. Neutrality	4. Empathy
5. Superiority	5. Equality
6. Certainty	6. Provisionalism

"The Gibb Catefories of Defensive and Supportive Behaviours" from "Defensive Communications" by Jack R. Gibb © 1961 in *The Journal of Communication*, Vol. 11:3. Used with permission of Jack Gibb.

Even if you're justified, it's easy to become defensive when someone threatens your presenting self.

Photodisc collection/Getty Images

which they are likely to interpret as a lack of regard. One form of evaluation is "you" language.

Unlike evaluative "you" language, which judges a person, **description** focuses on the *speaker's* thoughts and feelings. Descriptive messages are often expressed in "I" language, which provokes less defensiveness.[27] Contrast the following evaluative "you" claims with their descriptive "I" counterparts:

Evaluation:	"This place is a *#$%&*@ mess!"
Description:	"When you don't clean up, I have to either do it or live in squalor. That's why I'm mad!"
Evaluation:	"Those jokes are sick and depraved!"

© iStockphoto.com/Cliff Parnell

Description:	"When you tell off-color jokes, I get embarrassed."

Note how the descriptive statements focus on the speaker's thoughts and feelings without judging the person. But effectiveness also depends on when, where, and how the language is used. If the preceding descriptive statements were delivered in front of a room full of bystanders or in a whining tone of voice, they wouldn't work. Then there are people who will react defensively to anything you say or do. Nonetheless, describing how the other person's behaviour affects you is likely to produce better results than judgmentally attacking the person.

Control versus Problem Orientation

Controlling communication occurs when senders impose solutions on receivers with little regard for the receivers' needs or interests. Control can involve almost anything: where to eat dinner, what TV program to watch, or how to spend a large sum of money. When people act in controlling ways, it creates a defensive climate. No one likes to feel that their ideas are worthless or that nothing they say will change other people's determination to have their way—yet this is precisely the attitude a controller communicates. Whether with words, gestures, tone of voice, or status, the controller generates hostility wherever he or she goes. The unspoken message is, "I know what's best for you, and we'll get along if you do as I say."

In **problem orientation**, communicators seek a solution that satisfies everyone's needs. The goal is to work out an arrangement where everybody wins.

Here are some examples of how some controlling and problem-orientation messages might sound:

Controlling:	"You need to stay off the phone for the next two hours."
Problem orientation:	"I'm expecting some important calls. Can we work out a way to keep the line open?"
Controlling:	"There's only one way to handle this problem…"

Descriptive communication
Messages that describe the speaker's position without evaluating others. Synonymous with *"I" language.*

Controlling communication
Messages in which the sender tries to impose some sort of outcome on the receiver, usually resulting in a defensive reaction.

Problem orientation
A supportive style of communication described by Jack Gibb in which the communicators focus on working together to solve their problems instead of trying to impose their own solutions on one another.

Problem orientation:	"Looks like we have a problem. Let's work out a solution we can both live with."

Strategy versus Spontaneity

Gibb uses the word **strategy** to characterize defence-arousing messages where speakers hide their ulterior motives. *Dishonesty* and *manipulation* characterize this strategy. Even if the intentions of strategic communication are honourable, victims feel defensive when they discover they were played for a naive sucker.

In contrast to this behaviour is **spontaneity**, which simply means being honest with others. It doesn't mean blurting out every idea that comes into your head, though. You would undoubtedly threaten others' presenting selves if you were "spontaneous" about every opinion that crossed your mind. Gibb's notion of spontaneity involves setting aside hidden agendas that others both sense and resist. These examples illustrate the difference:

Strategy:	"What are you doing Friday after work?"
Spontaneity:	"I have a piano I need to move Friday after work. Can you give me a hand?"
Strategy:	"Pat and Jen go out to dinner every week."
Spontaneity:	"I'd like to go out to dinner more often."

Neutrality versus Empathy

Gibb uses the term **neutrality** to describe *indifference*— a lack of concern for the welfare of another that implies that the person isn't important to you. Such perceived indifference promotes defensiveness because people don't like to think of themselves as worthless and they'll fight a self-concept that portrays them as such. Notice the difference between neutral and empathetic statements:

Neutral:	"That's what happens when you don't plan properly."
Empathetic:	"Ouch—looks like this didn't turn out the way you expected."
Neutral:	"Sometimes things just don't work out. That's the way it goes."
Empathetic:	"I know you put a lot of time and effort into this project."

Gibb found that *empathy* helps rid communication of the quality of indifference. **Empathy** means accepting another's feelings by putting yourself in another's place. This doesn't mean that you need to agree with that person—you simply convey your care and respect in a supportive way. Gibb also noted the nonverbal expressions of concern were just as if not more important to the receiver than the words used.

Superiority versus Equality

The fifth defence-creating behaviour is **superiority**. Any message that suggests, "I'm better than you," is likely to arouse feelings of defensiveness in the recipients. At least in Western cultures, both young people and senior citizens are irritated when people patronize them.[28] Consider, for example, how using simplified grammar and vocabulary, talking loudly and slowly, not listening, and varying speaking pitch convey a patronizing attitude.

Here are two examples of the difference between superiority and equality:

Superior:	"You don't know what you're talking about."
Equal:	"I see it a different way."
Superior:	"No, that's not the right way to do it!"
Equal:	"If you want, I can show you a way that has worked for me."

Gibb found ample evidence that many people who have superior skills and talents are capable of projecting

Strategy
A defence-arousing style of communication described by Jack Gibb in which the sender tries to manipulate or deceive a receiver.

Spontaneity
A supportive communication behaviour described by Jack Gibb in which the sender expresses a message without any attempt to manipulate the receiver.

Neutrality
A defence-arousing behaviour described by Jack Gibb in which the sender expresses indifference toward a receiver.

Empathy
The ability to project oneself onto another person's point of view so as to experience the other's thoughts and feelings.

Superiority
A defence-arousing style of communication described by Jack Gibb in which the sender states or implies that the receiver is not worthy of respect.

© iStockphoto.com/Elena Elisseeva

"I understand completely. I like good movies,
and you like bad movies."

Equality

A type of supportive communication described by Jack Gibb suggesting that the sender regards the receiver as worthy of respect.

Certainty

An attitude behind messages that dogmatically implies that the speaker's position is correct and the other person's ideas are not worth considering. Likely to generate a defensive response.

Provisionalism

A supportive style of communication described by Jack Gibb in which the sender expresses a willingness to consider the other person's position.

feelings of **equality** rather than superiority. Such people convey that, although they may have greater talent in certain areas, they see others as having just as much worth as human beings.

Certainty versus Provisionalism

People who are positive they're right, who think theirs is the only way of doing something, or who insist that they have all the facts project the defence-arousing behaviour that Gibb calls **certainty**. Communicators who regard their own opinions with sureness while disregarding those of others demonstrate a lack of regard for what others hold to be important. It's likely that the receiver will take the certainty as a personal affront and react defensively.

In contrast, there is **provisionalism**. This occurs when people with strong opinions are willing to acknowledge that they don't have a corner on the truth and will change their stand if another position seems more reasonable. Consider the contrasting examples below:

Certain:	"That won't work!"
Provisional:	"I think you'll run into problems with that approach."
Certain:	"You don't know what you're talking about!"

Provisional: "I've never heard anything like that before. Where did you hear it?"

> # The need to be right—the sign of a vulgar mind.
>
> —Albert Camus

There is no guarantee that using Gibb's supportive, confirming approach to communication will build a positive climate. However, the chances for a constructive relationship will be greatest when communication consists of the supportive approach described here. Besides boosting the odds of getting a positive response from others, supportive communication can leave you feeling more comfortable and more positive toward others.

Saving Face

Gibb's categories of supportive communication offer useful guidelines for reducing defensiveness. In the following pages, you will learn some specific ways to use these approaches when you need to deliver challenging messages.

Cathy by Cathy Guisewite; ©1983. Reprinted by permission of Universal Press Syndicte. All rights reserved.

The Assertive Message Format

As you've already seen, building a supportive climate requires that you avoid attacking others so as to preserve their face. However, there are times when you need to share your legitimate concerns. The assertive format is a method that allows you to speak your mind in a clear yet nonthreatening assertive way without judging or dictating to others. It can be used on a variety of messages: your hopes, problems, complaints, and appreciations.[29] A complete assertive message has five parts: behaviour, interpretation, feeling, consequences, and intent.

Behaviour

As you read in Chapter 5, a **behavioural description** is objective and only describes the raw material to which you react. It does not involve interpreting it.

Two examples of behavioural descriptions might look like this:

Example 1

"A week ago John promised me that he would ask my permission to smoke if I was in the room. Just a moment ago, he lit a cigarette without asking."

Example 2

"Chris has acted differently this week. I don't recall her laughing, she didn't drop by like she usually does, and she didn't return my phone calls."

Notice that, in both cases, the descriptive statement included only data that are available through the senses. The observer hasn't attached any judgment or evaluation.

> **Behavioural description**
> An account that refers only to observable phenomena.
>
> **Interpretation statement**
> A statement that describes a speaker's interpretation of the meaning of another person's behaviour.

Interpretation

An **interpretation statement** describes the meaning you've attached to the other person's behaviour. The important thing to realize is that interpretations are *subjective* and that we can attach more than one interpretation to any behaviour. For example, look at these two different interpretations of each of the preceding descriptions:

Example 1

Interpretation A: "John must have forgotten that he wouldn't smoke without asking me first. I'm sure he's too considerate to go back on his word."

Interpretation B: "John is rude and inconsiderate. After promising not to smoke around me without asking, he's just deliberately done so. He's just doing this to drive me crazy!"

Example 2

Interpretation A: "Chris must be worried about her family. She'll probably just feel worse if I keep pestering her."

Interpretation B: "Chris is probably mad at me because I gave her a hard time about the tennis match. I'd better leave her alone until she cools off."

CHAPTER 9 Improving Communication Climates

© iStockphoto.com/Timur Nisametdinov

Feeling

While reporting behaviour and sharing your interpretations are important, **feeling statements** add a new dimension to a message. For example, consider the difference between saying, "When you laugh at me (*behaviour*), I think you find my comments foolish (*interpretation*)," versus, "When you laugh at me, I think you find my comments foolish, and *I feel angry*."

It's important to recognize that some statements *seem* as if they're expressing feelings but are actually interpretations or statements of intention. For instance, it's not accurate to say, "I feel like leaving," (really an intention) or "I feel you're wrong," (an interpretation). Statements like these obscure the true expression of feelings.

Feeling statement
An expression of a sender's emotions that results from interpretation of sense data.

Once you're aware of the difference between observable behaviour and interpretation, you'll see how many communication problems occur when senders fail to describe the behaviour on which an interpretation is based. For instance, imagine the difference between hearing a friend say, "You're a tightwad!" (*no behavioural description*) versus explaining, "When you never offer to pay me back for the coffee and snacks I often buy you, I think you're a tightwad" (*behaviour plus interpretation*). The first speaker's failure to specify behaviour would probably confuse the receiver, who has no way of knowing what prompted the remarks. This failure to describe behaviour also reduces any chance that the receiver will change the offensive behaviour, which, after all, is unknown to that person.

Just as important as specifying behaviour is the need to label an interpretation as such instead of presenting it as a matter of fact. Consider the difference between saying, "It's obvious that if you cared for me you'd write more often," (*interpretation presented as fact*) versus, "When I didn't get a letter or even a postcard from you, I thought that you didn't care for me" (*interpretation made clear*).

123render/iStockphoto

SKILL BUILDER

Behaviours and Interpretations

1. Select a partner and share several interpretations that you have recently made about other people in your life. For each interpretation, describe the behaviour on which you based your interpretations.

2. With your partners' help, consider some alternate interpretations of the behaviour that might be as plausible as your original one.

3. After considering the alternate interpretations, decide
   a. which one was most reasonable
   b. how you might share that interpretation (along with the behaviour) with the other person involved in a tentative, provisional way

Todd Bigelow/Aurora Photos/Getstock.ca

Consequence

A **consequence statement** explains the results of the situation you've described so far. There are three types of consequences:

- What happens to you, the speaker "When I didn't get the phone message yesterday (*behaviour*) that my doctor's appointment was delayed, I ended up waiting for an hour when I could have been studying (*consequences*). It seems to me that you don't care how busy I am, not even to write a simple note (*interpretation*), and that's why I'm so mad (*feeling*)."

- What happens to the person you're addressing "When you have seven or eight beers at a party (*behaviour*), you change. You make crude jokes that offend everybody and you become argumentative (*consequences*). For instance, last night you almost got into a fight (*more behaviour*). I don't think you realize how differently you act (*interpretation*), and I'm worried (*feeling*) about what will happen if you keep drinking like this.

- What happens to others "You probably don't know because you couldn't hear her cry (*interpretation*), but when you rehearse your lines for the play without closing the doors (*behaviour*), the baby can't sleep

123render/iStockphoto

(*consequence*). I'm worried (*feeling*) about her because she's had a cold lately."

Consequence statements are valuable because they help you understand why you are bothered or pleased by another's behaviour. Also, telling others about the consequences of their actions clarifies the results of their behaviour. As with interpretations, we often think that others *should* be aware of consequences without being told, but that's not necessarily the case. Explicitly stating consequences can ensure that you—or your message—leave nothing to the listener's imagination.

> **Consequence statement**
> An explanation of the results that follow either from the behaviour of the person to whom the message is addressed or from the speaker's interpretation of and feelings about the addressee's behaviour. Consequence statements can describe what happens to the speaker, the addressee, or others.

SKILL BUILDER

Name the Feeling
Add a feeling that you would be likely to have to each of the following messages:

1. I felt _____ when I found out you didn't invite me on the camping trip. You said you thought I wouldn't want to go, but I have a hard time accepting that.

2. I felt _____ when you offered to help me move. I know how busy you are.

3. When you tell me you still want to be a friend but you want to "lighten up a little," I get the idea you're tired of me and I feel _____.

4. You told me you wanted my honest opinion about your paintings, and then when I tell you what I think, you say I don't understand them. I'm _____.
How would the impact of each message be different if it didn't include a feeling statement?

When you are stating consequences, it's important to describe what happens without moralizing. For instance, it's one thing to say, "When you didn't call to say you'd be late, I stayed up worrying," and another to rant on, "How can I ever trust you? You're going to drive me crazy!"

Intention

Intention statements make up the final element of the assertive message format. They can communicate three kinds of messages:

- Where you stand on an issue
  "When you call us 'girls' after I've told you we want to be called 'women' (*behaviour*), I get the idea you don't appreciate how important the difference is to us (*interpretation*) and how demeaning it feels (*feeling*). Now I'm in an awkward spot: Either I have to keep bringing up the subject or else drop it and feel bad (*consequence*). I want you to know how much this bothers me (*intention*)."

- Requests of others
  "When I didn't hear from you last night (*behaviour*), I thought you were mad at me (*interpretation*). I've been thinking about it ever since (*consequence*), and I'm still worried (*feeling*). I'd like to know if you're angry (*intention*)."

- *Descriptions of how you plan to act in the future*
  "I've asked you to repay the $25 you owe me (*behaviour*). I'm getting the idea that you're avoiding me (*interpretation*), and I'm pretty angry (*feeling*). Unless we clear this up now, don't expect me to lend you anything ever again (*intention*)."

(In Real Life) The Assertive Message Format

consequence for other

© Cengage Learning

While the elements of the assertive message format don't vary, the way they sound depends on the situation and your personal style. Here are some examples to show how this approach can operate in real life.

To a neighbour

I had an awful scare just now *(feeling)*. I was backing out of the driveway, and Angela *(neighbour's toddler)* wandered right behind my car *(behaviour)*. Thank God I saw her, but she's so small that it would have been easy to miss her. I can't bear to think what might have happened if I hadn't seen her *(consequences for others)*. I know how toddlers can run off *(interpretation)*, but I really hope you can keep the door locked so she won't get outside without you knowing it *(intention)*.

To a friend

I just checked my Facebook account and saw that you tagged me in your photos from the party last weekend *(behaviour)*. I'm afraid those kinds of pictures could blow my chance of getting a good job *(consequence for you)*. You may think that I'm over-reacting *(interpretation)*, but this is a big deal for me, so I need you to remember not to post any embarrassing pictures of me. If you aren't sure about a photo, just ask me *(intention)*.

To a boss

I've got a favour to ask *(intention)*. Last month I told you I wanted to work extra hours, and I know you're doing me a favour by giving me more shifts *(interpretation)*. But it would really help if you could give me a couple of days' advance notice instead of telling me the night before you want me to work *(clarifies intention)*. That way I can say yes to the extra shifts *(consequence for boss)*. It would also cause a lot less stress for me *(feeling)*.

To an auto mechanic

I need to tell you that I'm pretty unhappy *(feeling)*. When I dropped the car off yesterday, you told me it would definitely be ready today by noon. Now it's 12:30 and it isn't ready *(behaviour)*. I'm going to be late for an important meeting *(consequence for you)*. I know you aim to please *(interpretation)*, but you have to understand that I can't bring my car to you unless I can count on it being ready when you promise *(consequence for other)*.

As in the preceding cases, we're often motivated by a single intention. Sometimes, however, we act from a combination of intentions, which may even be in conflict with each other. When this happens, our conflicting intentions often make it difficult for us to reach decisions:

> "I want to be truthful with you, but I don't want to violate my friend's privacy."
>
> "I want to continue to enjoy your friendship and company, but I don't want to get too attached right now."
>
> "I want to have time to study and get good grades, but I also want to have a job with some money coming in."

Using the Assertive Message Format

Before you try to deliver messages by using the assertive message format, there are a few points to remember:

1. *The elements may be delivered in mixed order.* As the examples on the preceding pages show, sometimes it's best to begin by stating your feelings, and at other times sharing your intentions or interpretations or describing consequences works better.

2. *Word the message to suit your personal style.* Instead of saying, "I interpret your behaviour to mean…" you might want to say, "I think…" or "It seems to me…" or perhaps "I get the idea…" In the same way, you can express your intentions by saying, "I hope you'll understand (or do)…" or perhaps "I wish you would…" The words that you choose should sound authentic in order to reinforce the genuineness of your statement.

3. *When appropriate, combine two elements in a single phrase.* The statement ". . . and ever since then I've been wanting to talk to you" expresses both a consequence and an intention. In the same way, saying, ". . . and after you said that, I felt confused" expresses a consequence and a feeling. Whether you combine elements or state them separately, the important point is to be sure that each one is present in your statement.

4. *Take your time delivering the message.* It isn't always possible to deliver messages such as the ones here all at

one time, wrapped up in neat paragraphs. Most likely you have to repeat or restate one part before the other person understands what you're saying. As you've already read, there are many types of psychological and physical noise that make it difficult for us to understand each other. In communication, as in many other activities, patience and persistence are essential.

Now try your hand at combining all these elements in the exercise below.

LO⁴
Responding Nondefensively to Criticism

You can see how easy it might be to respond to a thoughtful, assertive message, but how can you respond nondefensively when you receive an aggressive messages that doesn't match the prescriptions outlined in

SKILL BUILDER

Putting Your Message Together

1. Join with two other class members. Each person in turn should share a message that he or she might want to send to another person, being sure to include behaviour, interpretation, feeling, consequence, and intention statements in the message.

2. The others in the group should help the speaker by offering feedback about how the message could be made clearer if there is any question about the meaning.

3. After the speaker has composed a satisfactory message, he or she should practise actually delivering it by having another group member play the role of the intended receiver. Continue this practice until the speaker is confident that he or she can deliver the message effectively.

4. Repeat this process until each group member has had a chance to practise delivering a message.

this chapter? Despite your best intentions, it's hard to be reasonable when you're being attacked, and even harder when the criticism is on target. There's a tendency either to counterattack or to withdraw nonassertively.

Because neither of these is likely to resolve a dispute, we need alternative ways of behaving. There are two such ways. Despite their apparent simplicity, they have proven to be among the most valuable skills many communicators have learned.[30]

Seek More Information

Seeking more information makes sense when you realize that it's foolish to respond to a critical attack until you understand what the other person has said. Even attacks that appear unjustified or foolish at first often contain some truth, if not much more.

Many readers object to asking for details, and their resistance stems from confusing the act of *listening open-mindedly* with *accepting* the comments. You can listen to, understand, and even acknowledge the most hostile comments without necessarily accepting them. If you disagree with a person's criticism, you'll be able to explain yourself better after you

understand the criticism. On the other hand, you might see that it's valid, in which case you have learned some valuable information about yourself. In either case, you have everything to gain and nothing to lose by listening to the critic.

After spending years of instinctively resisting criticism, learning to listen to the other person will take some practice. Here are several ways to seek additional information from your critics.

> Nothing is weaker than water;
> Yet, for attacking what is hard and tough,
> Nothing surpasses it,
> nothing equals it.
> The principle, that what is weak overcomes what is strong,
> And what is yielding conquers what is resistant, is known to everyone.
> Yet few utilize it profitably in practice...
>
> —Lao Tzu,
> *Tao Te Ching*

Ask for Specifics

Vague attacks, such as, "You're being unfair," or "You never help out," can be difficult to understand, even if you sincerely want to change. In such cases, ask the critic for specific information. "What do I *do* that's unfair?" is an important question to ask before you can judge whether the attack is correct. You might ask, "When haven't I helped out?" before agreeing with or disagreeing with the attack.

If you are still accused of reacting defensively after you've asked for specifics, the problem may be in the *way* you ask. Your tone of voice and other nonverbal clues can give the same words radically different connotations. For example, think of how the words "Exactly what are you talking about?" can communicate a genuine desire to know or your belief that the speaker is crazy. Only request specific information if you genuinely want to learn more from the speaker; otherwise, it will only make matters worse.

Guess about Specifics

When your sincere and well-phrased requests for specific information aren't successful because your critics aren't able to define precisely the behaviour they find offensive, offer a guess! In a sense, you become both detective and suspect, the goal being to figure out exactly what

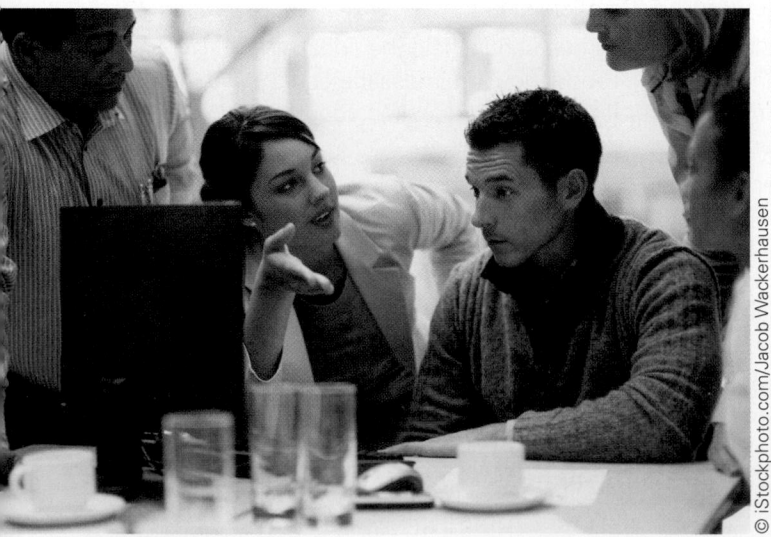

"crime" you've committed. Like the technique of asking for specifics, guessing must be done with goodwill and the appropriate nonverbal cues if it's to produce satisfying results. You need to convey to the critic that for both of your sakes, you're truly interested in finding out what is the matter. Here are some typical questions you might hear from someone guessing about the specifics of another's criticism:

> "So you object to the language I used in writing the paper. Was my language too formal?"
>
> "OK, I understand that you think the outfit looks funny. What's so bad about it? The colour? Does it have something to do with the fit? The fabric?"

Paraphrase the Speaker's Ideas

Paraphrasing, which involves active listening skills, is another strategy to understand a critic. It is especially important when critics think your behaviour has created a problem for them. By clarifying or amplifying what you understand critics to be saying, you'll learn more about their objections. A brief dialogue between a disgruntled customer and an especially talented store manager using paraphrasing might sound like this:

Customer: The way you people run this store is disgusting! I just want to tell you that I'll never shop here again.

Manager: (*reflecting the customer's feeling*) You seem to be upset. Can you tell me your problem?

Customer: It isn't *my* problem; it's the problem your salespeople have. They seem to think it's an inconvenience to help a customer find something.

Manager: So you didn't get enough help locating the items you were looking for, is that it?

Customer: Help? I spent 20 minutes looking around before I even talked to someone. It's a hell of a way to run a store.

Manager: So what you're saying is that the clerks seemed to be ignoring the customers?

Customer: No. They were all busy with other people. It just seems to me that you ought to have enough staff to handle the crowds that come in at this time of day.

Manager: I understand now. What frustrated you most was the fact that we didn't have enough staff to serve you promptly.

Customer: That's right. I have no complaint with the service I get after I'm waited on, and I've always thought you had a good selection here. It's just that I'm too busy to wait so long for help.

Manager: Well, I'm glad you brought this to my attention. We certainly don't want loyal customers going away mad. I'll try to see that it doesn't happen again.

This conversation illustrates two advantages of paraphrasing. First, the critic often reduces the intensity of the attack after he or she realizes that the complaint is being heard. Criticism generally grows from the frustration of unmet needs—which in this case was partly a lack of attention. Once the manager showed an interest in the customer, the customer began to feel better and was able to leave the store relatively calm. Of course, this sort of reflective listening won't always mollify a critic, but even when it doesn't, there's still another benefit that makes the strategy worthwhile. For example, the manager learned some valuable information by taking time to understand the customer—that a lack of staff might lose the store business. Had the manager reacted defensively to the customer, this information wouldn't have emerged.

> Placing the blame is a bad habit, but taking the blame is a sure builder of character.
>
> —O. A. Battista

Ask What the Critic Wants

Sometimes your critic's demand will be obvious: "Turn down that music!" or "I wish you'd remember to tell me

"We really need to talk about our relationship, so I've booked us on a TV show."

© Alex Gregory/The New Yorker Collection/www.cartoonbank.com.

about phone messages." In other cases, some investigation will be needed to learn what the critic wants:

Anna: I can't believe you invited all those people over without asking me first!

Dejun: Are you saying you want me to cancel the party?

Anna: No, I just wish you'd ask me before you make plans.

Erica: You're so critical! It sounds like you don't like anything about this paper.

Maria: But you asked for my opinion. What do you expect me to do when you ask?

Erica: I want to know what's wrong, but I don't *just* want to hear criticisms. If you think there's anything good about my work, I wish you'd tell me that, too.

This last example illustrates the importance of accompanying your questions with the right nonverbal behaviour. It's easy to imagine two ways in which Maria could have nonverbally supported her response "What do you expect me to do when you ask?" One tone of voice would show a genuine desire to clarify what Erica wanted, whereas the other would be clearly hostile and defensive. As with all the styles in this section, your responses to criticism must be sincere to work.

Ask about the Consequences of Your Behaviour

Generally, people criticize when some need is not being met. You can respond to this kind of criticism by learning what consequences your behaviour has for them. Actions that seem perfectly legitimate to you may cause difficulties for your critics. Once you understood this, criticisms that previously sounded foolish take on new meanings:

Worker A: Why do you care whether I'm late to work?

Worker B: Because when the boss asks, I feel obligated to make up some story so you won't get in trouble, and I don't like to lie.

Husband: Why does it bother you when I lose money at poker? You know I never gamble more than I can afford.

Wife: It's not the cash itself. It's that when you lose, you're cranky for two or three days, and that's no fun for me or the children.

Ask What Else Is Wrong

It might seem crazy to invite more criticism, but sometimes asking about other complaints can uncover the real problem:

Raul: Are you mad at me?

Tina: No. Why are you asking?

Raul: Because you hardly spent any time talking to me at the picnic. In fact, it seemed like whenever I came over to talk, you went somewhere else.

Tina: Is anything else wrong?

Raul: Well, I've been wondering lately if you're tired of me.

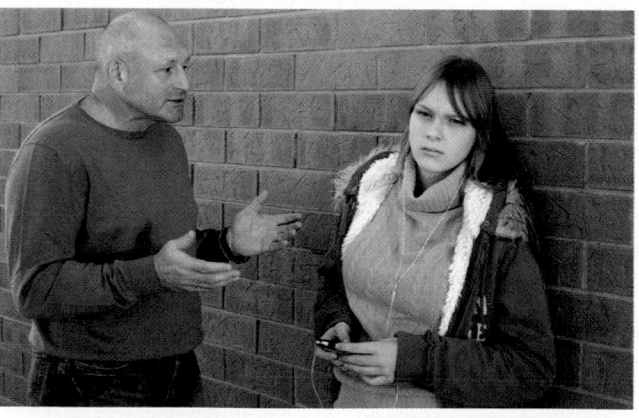

Alon Brik/Shutterstock

Asking if anything else bothers your critic isn't just an exercise in masochism. If you keep your defensiveness in check, further probing can lead to the real source of the critic's dissatisfaction.

Before soliciting more information from a critic, you may wish to role-play the scenario with someone. Not only will you gain another perspective, but you'll be able to practise and hone your nondefensive response skills.

Sometimes, however, soliciting more information isn't enough. What if you fully understand the other person's criticism and still feel defensive? You know that if you try to defend yourself, you'll get into an argument; on the other hand, you simply can't accept what the other person is saying about you. The solution to such a dilemma is outrageously simple: Agree with the critic!

Agree with the Critic

While you can't honestly agree with criticisms that you don't believe are true, you can agree with either the facts or the critic's perception of the problem. Here's how you do it.

Agree with the Facts

Agreeing with the critic restores the critic's damaged reputation.[31] Agree with your critic when the accusation is factually correct:

> "You're right, I am angry."
> "I suppose I was being defensive."
> "Now that you mention it, I did get pretty sarcastic."

Agreeing with the facts seems sensible when you realize that certain facts are indisputable. If you agree to meet at four and don't show up until five, there's no question, you're late. If you've broken a borrowed object, run out of gas, or failed to finish a job you started, there's no point in denying it. In the same way, if you're honest, you may have to agree with many interpretations of your behaviour even when they're not flattering. You do get angry, act foolishly, fail to listen, and behave inconsiderately. But once you rid yourself of the myth of perfection, it's much easier to acknowledge these truths.

> ## Love your enemies, for they tell you your faults.
>
> —Benjamin Franklin

But why is it so difficult to accept these accurate criticisms without getting defensive? The answer lies in the confusion between agreeing with the *facts* and accepting the *judgment* that so often accompanies them. Most critics don't merely describe the action that offends them; they also evaluate it, and it's this evaluation that we resist:

> "It's silly to be angry."
> "You have no reason for being defensive."
> "You were wrong to be so sarcastic."

It's judgments like these that we resent. By realizing that you can agree with—and even learn from—the descriptive part of many criticisms and still not accept the accompanying evaluations, you'll find that you'll have a response that is both honest and nondefensive.

Of course, to reduce defensiveness, you must honestly agree with the facts. It's humiliating to accept descriptions that aren't accurate, and pretending to agree leads to trouble. You can imagine how unproductive the conversation on page 261 would have been if the manager had spoken the same words in a sarcastic tone. Only agree with the facts when you can do so sincerely. Though this won't always be possible, you'll be surprised at how often you can use this simple response.

Chris Rout / Alamy / GetStock.com

Agree with the Critic's Perception

Agreeing with your critics may be fine when you think the criticisms are justified, but how can you confess when they are completely unjustified? You've listened and asked questions to understand the criticisms, but the more you listen, the more positive you are that the critic is totally out of line. Even in these cases, there is a way of agreeing—this time with the critic's right to see things a particular way.

Co-worker A: I want to let you know right from the start that I was against hiring you for the job. I think you got it because you're a woman.

Co-worker B: I can understand why you'd believe that, with the equal opportunities laws. I hope that after I've been here for a while, you'll change your mind.

"When will he be able to sit up and take criticism?"

Roommate A: I don't think you're being totally honest about your reason for wanting to stay home. You say it's because you have a headache, but I think you're avoiding Mary.

Roommate B: I can see why that would make sense to you, because Mary and I got into an argument the last time we were together. All I can say is that I do have a headache.

You may feel more comfortable agreeing with and acknowledging accurate criticism when you understand that you're not necessarily obliged to *apologize*. If you're not responsible for the behaviour that your critic finds objectionable, an explanation might be more appropriate than an apology:

"I know I'm late. There was an accident downtown, and the streets are jammed." (*spoken in an explanatory, nondefensive tone*)

In other cases, your behaviour might be understandable, if not perfect. When this happens, you can acknowledge the validity of the criticism without apologizing:

"You're right. I *did* lose my temper. I've had to remind you three or four times, and I guess I finally used up all my patience." (*again, delivered as an explanation, not a defence or counterattack*)

In still other cases, you can acknowledge your critic's right to see things differently than you without backing off from your position:

"I can understand why you think I'm overreacting. I know this doesn't seem as important to you as it does to me. I hope you can understand why I think this is such a big deal."

Farcus

by David Waisglass
Gordon Coulthart

© 1996 Farcus Cartoons

WAISGLASS/COULTHART

"We need to improve morale… any of you boneheads have a good idea?"

Apologizing is fine if you can do so sincerely; but you will be able to agree with critics more often if you understand that doing so doesn't require you to grovel. Some critics don't seem to deserve the kinds of respectful responses outlined here. They seem more interested in attacking you than explaining themselves. Before you counterattack these hostile critics, ask yourself whether a defensive response will be worth the consequences.

Communication in the Workplace

During your career, you are likely to spend more waking hours on the job than in any other setting. This means the emotional climate of the workplace can be just as important as salary or working conditions in shaping the quality of your life.

Research confirms that positive communication climates lead to increased job satisfaction.[32] And two factors are consistently connected to supportive workplace environments.[33]

The first is *praise and encouragement*. Employees feel valued when their work is recognized. Acknowledgment doesn't require promotions, raises, or awards, although those are always welcome. As researcher Daniel Goleman notes, "Small exchanges—a compliment on work well done, a word of support after a setback—add up to how we feel on the job.[34]

The second climate-boosting practice is *open communication*. Employees appreciate managers and co-workers with "open-door policies" allowing them opportunities to get and give feedback, make suggestions, and voice concerns.

Some Canadian companies send confirming messages in practical ways. One company offers on-site spring break and summer camps for employees' children. Another provides a month-long paid sabbatical leave after four years with the company. Other perks include lifetime health benefits, 12 personal days per year (on top of regular vacation time), and monthly draws for car rentals and weekend getaways.[35]

Trainers and managers also set affirming climates when they sensitize themselves to the cross-cultural needs of employees. They are aware that the practices that work well in domestic headquarters must be adapted if they're to be embraced by employees across the globe.[36] What is acceptable, confirming, and appropriate in one culture may not be in another. For example, individual awards and tributes for employees may embarrass workers in a collectivistic society where teamwork and group harmony are emphasized.[37]

Climate is just as important in virtual organizations as in face-to-face communication.[38] When most contact is text-based, taking time to treat co-workers cordially can make a real difference. One study revealed that morale and trust were higher in companies where e-mail correspondence opened with friendly greetings (even a simple "Hi") and closed with a friendly farewell ("Thanks" "Have a nice day") than in messages that lacked these elements.[39]

SKILL BUILDER

Coping with Criticism

Take turns practising nondefensive responses with a partner.

1. Choose one of the following criticisms and brief your partner on how it might be directed at you:
    a. You're so selfish sometimes. You think only of yourself.
    b. Don't be so touchy!
    c. You say you understand me, but you don't really.
    d. I wish you'd do your share around here.
    e. You're so critical!

2. As your partner criticizes you, answer with an appropriate response from the preceding pages. As you do so, try to adopt an attitude of genuinely wanting to understand the criticism and finding parts that you can sincerely agree with.

3. Ask your partner to evaluate your response. Does it follow the forms described in the previous pages? Does it sound sincere?

4. Replay the same scene, trying to improve your response.

(In Real Life) Communication Transcript

Responding Nondefensively to Criticism

Defending yourself—even when you're right—isn't always the best approach. The following dialogue shows the importance of self-control and thinking before responding when you're being criticized. The employee realizes that arguing won't change his boss's mind, so he decides to reply as honestly as he can without becoming defensive.

Boss: How'd things go while I was out?

Employee: Pretty well, except for one thing. Mr. Macintosh—he said you knew him—came in and wanted to buy about $200 worth of stuff. He wanted me to charge him wholesale, and I asked him for his tax number, just like you told me. He said he didn't have it, so I told him he'd have to pay retail. He got pretty mad.

Boss: He's a good customer. I hope you gave him the discount.

Employee: (*beginning to sound defensive*) Well, I didn't. You told me last week that the law said we had to charge full price unless the customer had a tax number.

Boss: Oh my God! Didn't Macintosh tell you he had a number?

Employee: (*becoming more defensive*) He did, but he didn't have it with him. I didn't want to get you mad at me for breaking the law.

Boss: (*barely concealing his exasperation*) Well, customers don't always have their tax numbers memorized. Macintosh has been coming here for years, and we just fill in his number on the records later.

Employee: (*deciding to respond nondefensively instead of getting into an argument he knows he can't win*) I can see why it looks like I gave Mr. Macintosh a hard time. You don't ask him for the number, and I insisted on having it. (*agrees with the boss's perception*)

Boss: Yes! There's a lot of competition in this business, and we have to keep our customers happy—especially the good ones—or we'll lose them. Macintosh drives across town to do business with us. There are places right near him. If we jerk him around, he'll go there and we'll lose a good customer.

Employee: That's true. (*agrees with the fact that it is important to keep customers happy*) And I want to know how to treat customers right. But I'm confused about how to handle people who want a discount and don't have tax numbers. What should I do? (*asks what the boss wants*)

Boss: Well, you need to be a little flexible with good customers.

Employee: How should I do that? (*asks for specifics*)

Boss: Well, it's OK to trust people who are regulars.

Employee: So I don't need to ask regular customers for their tax numbers. I should look them up later? (*paraphrases to clarify boss's ambiguous directions to "trust" regular customers*)

Boss: That's right. You've got to use your head in business!

Employee: (*ignores the indirect accusation about not "using his head," recognizing that there's no point in defending himself*) OK, so when regular customers come in, I won't even ask them for their tax numbers… right? (*paraphrases again, to be sure he has the message correct; the employee has no desire to get criticized again about this matter*)

Boss: No, go ahead and ask for the number. If they have it, we won't have to look it up later. But if they don't have the number, just say OK and give them the discount.

Employee: Got it. I only have one question: How can I know who the regular customers are? Should I take their word for it? (*asks for specifics*)

Boss: Well, you'll get to know most of them after you've been here a while. But it's OK to trust them until then. If they say they're regulars, just take their word for it. You've got to trust people sometimes, you know!

Employee: (*ignores the fact that the boss originally told him not to trust people but to insist on getting their number; decides instead to agree with the boss*) I can see how important it is to trust good customers.

Boss: Right.

Employee: Thanks for clearing up how to handle the tax numbers. Is there anything else I ought to know so things will run smoothly when you're not in the store? (*asks if anything else is wrong*)

Boss: I don't think so. (*patronizingly*) Don't get discouraged; you'll catch on. It took me 20 years to build this business. Stick with it and someday you could be running a place like this.

Employee: (*trying to agree with his boss without sounding sarcastic*) I guess I could.

Endnotes

1. J. Veroff, E. Douvan, T. L. Orbuch, & L. K. Acitelli (1998). "Happiness in Stable Marriages: The Early Years." In T. N. Bradbury (Ed.), *The Developmental Course of Marital Dysfunction*. New York: Cambridge University Press.

2. J. Gottman (2006). "Why Marriages Fail." In K. M. Galvin & P. J. Cooper (Eds.), *Making Connections: Readings in Relational Communication*, 4th ed. (pp. 228–236). Los Angeles: Roxbury. See also A. M. Hicks and L. M. Diamond (2008). "How Was Your Day? Couples' Affect When Telling and Hearing Daily Events." *Personal Relationships, 15,* 205–228.

3. C. A. Barbato, E. E. Graham, & E. E. Perse (2003). "Communicating in the Family: An Examination of the Relationship of Family Communication Climate & Interpersonal Communication Motives." *Journal of Family Communication, 3,* 123–148.

4. R. M. Dailey (2006). "Confirmation in Parent-Adolescent Relationships and Adolescent Openness: Toward Extending Confirmation Theory. *Communication Monographs, 73,* 434–458.

5. J. J. Teven, M. M. Martin, & N. C. Neupauer (1998). "Sibling Relationships: Verbally Aggressive Messages & Their Effect on Relational Satisfaction." *Communication Reports, 11,* 179–186.

6. A. L. Vangelisti & S. L. Young (2000). "When Words Hurt: The Effects of Perceived Intentionality on Interpersonal Relationships." *Journal of Social & Personal Relationship, 17,* 393–424.

7. E. Seiberg (1976). "Confirming & Disconfirming Communication in an Organizational Setting." In J. Owen, P. Page, & G. Zimmerman (Eds.), *Communication in Organizations* (pp. 129–149). St. Paul, MN: West.

8. E. Sieberg & C. Larson (1971). *Dimensions of Interpersonal Response*. Paper presented at the meeting of the International Communication Association, Phoenix, AZ.

9. S. A. Cox (1999). "Group Communication & Employee Turnover: How Coworkers Encourage Peers to Voluntarily Exit." *Southern Communication Journal, 64,* 181–192.

10. J. M. Gottman and R. W. Levenson (2000). "The Timing of Divorce: Predicting When a Couple Will Divorce over a 14-Year Period." *Journal of Marriage and the Family, 62,* 737–745.

11. A. S. Rancer & T. A. Avtgis (2006). *Argumentative and Aggressive Communication: Theory, Research, and Application.* Thousand Oaks, CA: Sage.

12. J. K. Alberts (1988). "An Analysis of Couples' Conversational Complaints." *Communication Monographs, 55,* 184–197.

13. J. K. Alberts & G. Driscoll (1992). "Containment versus Escalation: The Trajectory of Couples' Conversational Complaints." *Western Journal of Communication, 56,* 394–412.

14. J. M. Gottman & N. Silver (1999). *The Seven Principles for Making Marriage Work.* New York: Random House.

15. A. S. Rancer & T. A. Avtgis (2006). *Argumentative and Aggressive Communication: Theory, Research, and Application.* Thousand Oaks, CA: Sage.

16. F. F. Jordan-Jackson, Y. Lin, A. S. Rancer, & D. A. Infante (2008). "Perceptions of Males and Females' Use of Aggressive Affirming and Nonaffirming Messages in an Interpersonal Dispute: You've Come a Long Way Baby?? *Western Journal of Communication, 72,* 239–258.

17. K. Cissna & E. Seiberg (1995). "Patterns of Interactional Confirmation & Disconfirmation." In M. V. Redmond (Ed.), *Interpersonal Communication: Readings in Theory & Research.* Fort Worth: Harcourt Brace.

18. M. W. Allen (1995). "Communication Concepts Related to Perceived Organizational Support." *Western Journal of Communication, 59,* 326–346.

19. See, for example, R. M. Dailey (2008). "Assessing the Contribution of Nonverbal Behaviours in Displays of Confirmation During Parent-Adolescent Interactions: An Actor-Partner Interdependence Model." *Journal of Family Communication, 8,* 62–91.

20. W. W. Wilmot, *Dyadic Communication* (New York: R&om House, 1987), pp. 149–158.

21. J. L. Hocker & W. W. Wilmot (1995). *Interpersonal Conflict,* 4th ed. (p. 34). Dubuque, IA: Brown & Benchmark.

22. Ibid., p. 36.

23. K. Domenici & S. Littlejohn (2006): *Facework: Bridging Theory and Practice.* Thousand Oaks, CA: Sage; M. K. Lapinski & F. J. Boster (2001). "Modeling the Ego-Defensive Function of Attitudes." *Communication Monographs, 68,* 314–324.

24. J. A. H. Becker, B. Ellevold, & G. H. Stamp (2008). "The Creation of Defensiveness in Social Interaction II: A Model of Defensive Communication Among Romantic Couples." *Communication Monographs, 75,* 86–110; G. H. Stamp, A. L. Vangelisti, & J. A. Daly (1992). "The Creation of Defensiveness in Social Interaction." *Communication Quarterly, 40,* 177–190.

25. D. R. Turk & J. L. Monahan (1999). "'Here I Go Again': An Examination of Repetitive Behaviours during Interpersonal Conflicts." *Southern Communication Journal, 64,* 232–244.

26. J. Gibb (September 1961). "Defensive Communication." *Journal of Communication, 11,* 141–148. See also E. Robertson (2005). "Placing Leaders at the Heart of Organizational Communication." *Communication Management, 9,* 34–37.

27. R. F. Proctor & J. R. Wilcox (1993). "An Exploratory Analysis of Responses to Owned Messages in Interpersonal Communication." *ETC: A Review of General Semantics, 50,* 201–220.

28. Research summarized in J. Harwood, E. B. Ryan, H. Giles, & S. Tysoski (1997). "Evaluations of Patronizing Speech & Three Response Styles in a Non-Service-Providing Context." *Journal of Applied Communication Research, 25,* 170–195.

29. Adapted from S. Miller, E. W. Nunnally, & D. B. Wackman (1975). *Alive & Aware: How to Improve Your Relationships through Better Communication.* Minneapolis, MN: International Communication Programs. See also R. Remer & P. deMesquita (1990). "Teaching & Learning the Skills of Interpersonal Confrontation." In D. D. Cahn (Ed.), *Intimates in Conflict: A Communication Perspective.* Hillsdale, NJ: Erlbaum.

30. Adapted from M. Smith 1975). *When I Say No, I Feel Guilty* (pp. 93–110). New York: Dial Press.

31. W. L. Benoit & S. Drew (1997). "Appropriateness & Effectiveness of Image Repair Strategies." *Communication Reports, 10,* 153–163. See also Stamp et al., "Creation of Defensiveness."

32. B. Cooil, L. Aksoy, T. L. Keiningham, & K. M. Maryott (2009). "The Relationship of Employee Perceptions of Organizational Climate to Business-Unit Outcomes: An MPLS Approach." *Journal of Service Research, 11,* 277–294; D. Pincus (1986). "Communication Satisfaction, Job Satisfaction, & Job Performance." *Human Communication Research, 12,* 395–419.

33. E. Sopow (2008). "The Communication Climate Change at RCMP." *Strategic Communication Management, 12,* 20–23. J. W. Kassing (2008). "Consider This: A Comparison of Factors Contributing to Employees' Expressions of Dissent." *Communication Quarterly, 56,* 342–355; D. Saunders (2008). "Create an Open Climate for Communication." *Supervision, 69,* 6–8; C. E. Beck & E. A. Beck (1996). "The Manager's Open Door and the Communication Climate." In K. M. Galving & P Cooper (Eds.), *Making Connections: Readings in Relational Communication* (pp. 286–290). Los Angeles: Roxbury.

34. D. Goleman (2006). *Social Intelligence.* New York: Random House, p. 279.

35. J. Intini & M. Snider (2005). "It's All in The Perks," *MacLean's, 118,* 34–39.

36. J. A. Rolls (1998). *Training Corporate Outsiders: Doing it the Cape Breton Way.* Paper presented at the Joint Conference of the National Communication Association and the International Communication Association, Rome, Italy.

37. T. Sonja (2003). "International Training: The Training of Managers for Assignment Abroad," *Education + Training, 45,* 550–557.

38. A. D. Akkirman & D. L. Harris (2005). "Organizational Communication Satisfaction in the Virtual Workplace." *Journal of Management Development, 24,* 397–409.

39. J. Waldvogel (2007). "Greetings and Closings in Workplace Email." *Journal of Computer-Mediated Communication, 12,* 456–477.

CHAPTER **10**

MANAGING INTERPERSONAL
CONFLICTS

What do you
THINK?
Conflict should be avoided
at all costs.

1 2 3 4 5 6 7

strongly agree   strongly disagree

LEARNING OUTCOMES

LO¹ Identify the conflicts in your important relationships and how satisfied you are with the way they have been handled.

LO² Describe your personal conflict styles, evaluate their effectiveness, and suggest alternatives as appropriate.

LO³ Identify the relational conflict styles, patterns of behaviour, and conflict rituals that define a given relationship.

LO⁴ Demonstrate how you could use the win–win approach in a given conflict.

For most people, conflict has about the same appeal as a trip to the dentist; it is something to be avoided.[1] However, conflict *can* be constructive. With the right set of communication skills, conflict can be less like a struggle and more like a kind of dance in which partners work together to create something that would be impossible without their cooperation. One study revealed that college students in close romantic relationships who believed that conflicts were destructive were most likely to neglect or quit the relationship and less likely to seek a solution than couples who had less negative attitudes.[2] The kinds of skills outlined in this chapter can help well-intentioned partners handle their disagreements constructively.

LO¹
The Nature of Conflict

Before focusing on how to solve interpersonal problems constructively, we need to take a brief look at the nature of conflict.

Conflict Defined

Whatever form they may take, all interpersonal conflicts share certain characteristics. William Wilmot and Joyce Hocker provide a thorough definition when they define **conflict** as "an

Conflict
An expressed struggle between at least two interdependent parties who perceive incompatible goals, scarce resources, and interference from the other party in achieving their goals.

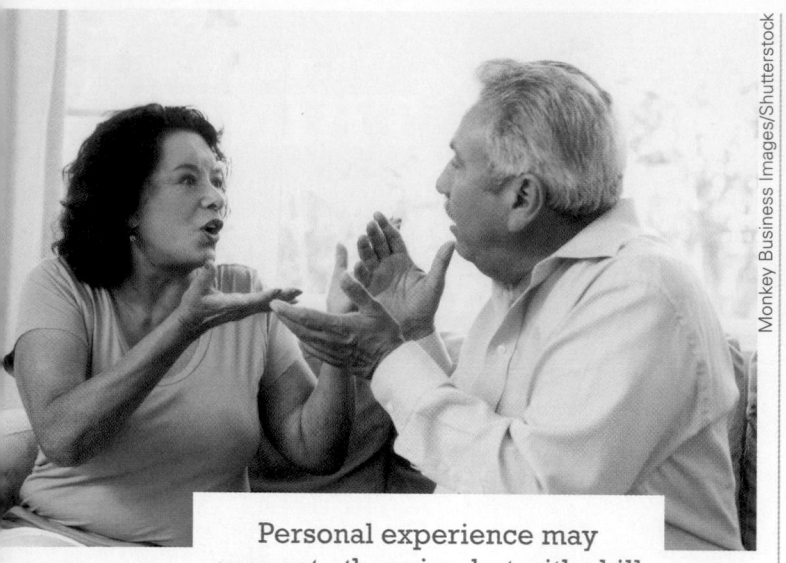

Monkey Business Images/Shutterstock

Personal experience may suggest otherwise, but with skill and the right attitude, conflicts can be constructive.

expressed struggle between at least two interdependent parties who perceive incompatible goals, scarce resources, and interference from the other party in achieving their goals."[3] A closer look at this definition will help you recognize how conflict operates in your life.

Expressed Struggle

Conflict can exist only when both parties are aware of a disagreement. You may be upset for months about a neighbour's noisy music, but no conflict exists until the neighbour learns about the problem. You can show your displeasure nonverbally through a dirty look or the silent treatment. One way or another, however, both parties must know that a problem exists before they're in conflict.

Perceived Incompatible Goals

All conflicts appear as if one party's gain is another's loss. If the neighbour turns down the music, she loses the enjoyment of hearing it at full volume, but if she keeps the volume up, you're subjected to unwanted music.

The goals in this situation really aren't completely incompatible—there are solutions that allow both parties to get what they want. For instance, you could close your windows or the neighbour could close hers. You might use earplugs and she could use earphones. If these solutions prove workable, the conflict disappears. Unfortunately, people often fail to see mutually satisfying solutions to their problems. As long as they *perceive* their goals to be mutually exclusive, a conflict exists.

Perceived Scarce Resources

Conflicts also exist when people believe there isn't enough of something to go around. Money is an obvious example. If a worker asks for a raise and the boss prefers to use extra profit to expand the business, the two parties are in conflict.

Time is another scarce commodity. For example, the authors of this textbook constantly face struggles about how to use the limited time we have at home. The book, spouses, children, editors, students, and friends all want more time than we have to give.

Interdependence

Parties in conflict are usually interdependent: The welfare and satisfaction of one depends on the actions of the other. Interdependence exists between conflicting nations, social groups, organizations, friends, and lovers. If the parties didn't need each other to solve the problem, they would go their separate ways. The first step toward resolving a conflict is taking the attitude that "we're all in this together."

> When a conflict between Inuit tribes is about to start up, a poetry contest is held between the two best poets of each tribe. The jury comprises equal numbers from each tribe. The winning poet wins the war with the winner decided by both sides. They have thus shifted from fighting physically to competing with words.
>
> —John Oliver

Interference from the Other Party

No matter how much one person's position may differ from another's, a full-fledged conflict won't occur until the participants act in ways that prevent one another from reaching their goals. For example, you might let some friends know that you object to their driving after drinking, but the conflict won't escalate until you try to take away their keys.

Conflict Is Natural

Every relationship of any depth at all has conflict.[4] No matter how close, how understanding, and how compatible you are, there will be times when your ideas or actions or needs or goals won't match. You want to see other people, but your partner wants to keep the relationship exclusive; you think a paper you've written is fine, but your instructor wants it changed. There's no end to the number and kinds of disagreements possible.

University students have an average of seven arguments per week, and most have argued with the other person before, often about the same topic.[5] In another survey, 81 percent of the respondents acknowledged that they had conflicts with friends.[6] Conflict can be even more frequent in families. Researchers recorded dinner conversations for 52 families and found an average of 3.3 "conflict episodes" per meal.[7]

At first this might seem depressing. But it's not the conflict that's bad, it's how the conflict is handled. Conflict is a natural part of meaningful relationships, and you can change the way you approach it.

Conflict Can Be Beneficial

Because we can't avoid conflicts, the challenge is to handle them well. Effective communication during conflicts can actually keep good relationships strong. People who use constructive problem-solving strategies are more satisfied with their relationships[8] and with the outcomes of their conflicts.[9]

The best evidence of how constructive conflict skills can benefit a relationship focuses on spousal communication. More than 20 years of research shows that both happy and unhappy marriages have conflicts, but they manage it differently.[10] Another study revealed that unhappy couples argue in ways that are considered destructive.[11] They focus on defending themselves rather than being problem-oriented, they don't listen to each other, they don't empathize with each other, they use evaluative "you" language, and they ignore each other's nonverbal messages.

Satisfied couples see disagreement as healthy and recognize that conflicts need to be faced.[12] Although they may argue vigorously, they use perception checking and

Monkey Business Images/Shutterstock

let each other know that they understand the other side of the dispute.[13] They willingly admit mistakes and try to solve the problem at hand.

Before reviewing the communication skills that make conflicts constructive, we need to examine how individuals handle conflict.

> We're so much alike that we can't discuss. We can only fight.
>
> —Stephen Leacock,
> "Rebuilding the Cities," *Journal*, Royal Architectural Institute of Canada

LO[2]
Conflict Styles

Most people have "default" styles—their typical approach to conflict—but these won't work in all situations. For example, check out how Paul and Lucia manage a problem.

For more than a year, running partners Paul and Lucia have run three times a week and spent an hour working out. Equally matched, they challenge one another to cover longer distances at quicker rates. Over the year, their friendship has grown to include personal matters that they don't share with anyone else.

Recently Lucia has invited less athletic friends to join them and Paul finds the outings a much less satisfying workout. He also fears losing his one-on-one time with Lucia. When

"There's no point in our being friends if you won't let me fix you."

he shared his concerns with her, she said, "I don't see the problem. We still get plenty of time on the road, and you said you like my friends." "But it isn't the same," replied Paul.

This situation has all the elements of a conflict: expressed struggle, perceived incompatible goals, apparently scarce resources (they only have so much time for running), and interdependence.

They would approach the conflict in one of five ways:

1. They could say, "Let's forget it," and stop running together.

2. Paul could give in, sacrificing his desire for one-on-one conversations and challenging runs. Or Lucia could give in, sacrificing her friendships to maintain her friendship with Paul.

3. One or the other could issue an ultimatum: "Either we do it my way, or we stop running together."

4. They could compromise, inviting friends along on some runs but excluding them on other days.

5. Lucia and Paul could brainstorm ways they could run with her friends and still get their workouts and one-on-one time with each other.

These approaches represent the five styles depicted in Figure 10.1, each of which is described in the following paragraphs.

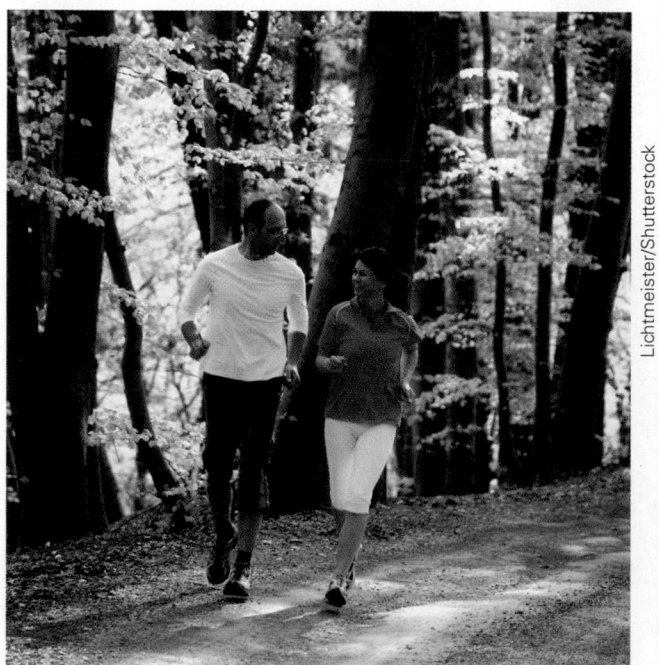

Lichtmeister/Shutterstock

FIGURE 10.1
Conflict Styles

HIGH

Competing
(Win/Lose)
"My Way"

Collaborating
(Win/Win)
"Our Way"

CONCERN FOR SELF

Compromising
(Partial Lose/Lose)
"Half Way"

Avoiding
(Lose/Lose)
"No Way"

Accommodating
(Lose/Win)
"Your Way"

LOW   CONCERN FOR OTHERS   HIGH

Adapted from W. W. Wilmot & J. L. Hocker (2010). *Interpersonal Conflict,* 8th ed. New York: McGraw-Hill.

Avoiding (Lose–Lose)

Avoiding occurs when people nonassertively stay away from conflict. You can avoid someone physically or conversationally (changing the topic, joking, denying that a problem exists), but this approach has its costs. It is much more difficult for partners of "self-silencers" to deal with conflict construcively.[14]

> **Avoiding**
> A lose–lose conflict style in which the parties ignore the problem at hand.

Avoidance reflects the attitude that there's no good way to resolve an issue, and some avoiders figure that it's just easier to put up with the problem. In all, avoiding generally results in *lose–lose* outcomes where neither party gets what it wants.

In Paul and Lucia's case, avoiding means that, rather than struggling with their disagreement, they would stop running together. Although it wouldn't seem like fighting, they would lose their running partner and good friend. This "solution" shows how avoidance can produce lose–lose results.

Although avoiding may keep the peace, it typically leads to unsatisfying relationships.[15] As misunderstandings, resentments, and disappointments pile up, the communication climate becomes contaminated. It seems that avoiders have a low concern both for their own needs as well as the other person's needs (see Figure 10.1).

© iStockphoto.com/Cliff Parnell

But avoiding isn't always a bad idea.[16] You might avoid certain topics or situations when the risk of speaking up is too great or if the relationship isn't worth the effort. In close relationships, avoidance is logical if the issue is temporary or minor. This explains why communication between happily married couples is characterized by "selectively ignoring" the other person's minor flaws.[17] This doesn't mean that you should avoid *all* conflicts, but rather that you should conserve energy for the important ones.

Accommodating (Lose–Win)

Accommodating occurs when you give in to others rather than asserting your own point of view. Figure 10.1 depicts accommodators as having low concern for themselves and high concern for others, resulting in *lose–win*, "we'll do it your way" outcomes. For example, Paul could accommodate Lucia by letting her friends join their runs, even though it reduced the physical challenge and the quality

---

On TV

Conflict Styles

30 Rock (TV show, 2006–)

TV comedy producer Liz Lemon (Tina Fey) and her boss, Jack Donaghy (Alec Baldwin), are "frenemies." They obviously value their relationship, yet they constantly struggle over both work-related issues and personal matters. Jack clearly enjoys provoking Liz—not out of malice, but because he relishes conflict. By contrast, Liz is an accommodator. Keeping everyone around her happy is her goal, and she'll punish herself to keep the peace. Many episodes of this popular series revolve around the complications that arise from Jack's confrontational style and Liz's obsession with harmony. The results are amusing, but in real life each character would profit from adopting some of the other's approach.

---

time with Lucia—or Lucia could accommodate Paul by running with just him.

The accommodator's motive plays a significant role in this style's effectiveness. If accommodation is genuine, then chances are it will enhance the relationship. Most people appreciate those who "take one for the team" or "lose the battle to win the war." However, people are less appreciative of those who habitually play the "martyr."[18]

> ## Isn't it queer that only sensible people agree with you?
>
> —Robert C. (Bob) Edwards, publisher, *Calgary Eye Opener*

It's important to mention that culture can affect perceptions of conflict styles. People from high-context, collectivistic backgrounds, such as many Asian cultures, are likely to regard avoidance and accommodation as face-saving and noble ways to handle conflict.[19] In low-context, individualistic cultures, such as Canada, avoidance and accommodation are perceived less positively and people who give up or give in during conflicts are considered "pushovers" or "doormats." The point is that all conflict styles have value in certain situations and culture influences how each style is valued.

Competing (Win–Lose)

The flip side of accommodating is **competing**. This *win–lose* approach involves high concern for self and low concern for others. As Figure 10.1 shows, competition seeks to resolve conflicts "my way." If Lucia and Paul tried to force the other to concede, one would prevail—but at the other's expense.

Accommodating
A win–lose conflict style in which the communicator submits to a situation rather than attempting to have his or her needs met.

Competing
A win–lose approach to conflicts that seeks to resolve them in one's own way.

> ## There are two kinds of problems. Those that get better and almost solve themselves and those that get worse. You can afford to let the first type ride, but you better get the second fast.
>
> —John Turner, quoted in *Maclean's*

"Well, if it doesn't matter who's right and who's wrong, why don't I be right and you be wrong?"

© David Sipress/ The New Yorker Collection/www.cartoonbank.com.

People compete when they see a situation as an "either-or" one: Either I get what I want or you get what you want. You see this in most conflicts that require a winner and a loser. Some interpersonal issues also fit into this win–lose framework, such as two co-workers seeking a promotion to the same job. Only one can be promoted.

Sometimes competition can enhance relationships. For example, men and women in satisfying dating relationships use competition to enrich their interaction.[20] They compete in play (who's the better racquetball player?), in achievement (who gets the better job offer?), and in altruism (who's more romantic?). They develop a shared narrative that defines competition in altruistic terms. But these arrangements can backfire if one partner becomes a gloating winner or a sore loser. If one person tries to get even, it can create a downward competitive spiral that turns into a *lose–lose* relationship.[21]

Power is the distinguishing characteristic in win–lose problem solving because it is necessary to defeat an opponent. There are different types of power, the most obvious of which is physical. There is also real and enforced power. For example, parents threaten children, adults threaten each other, and the legal system threatens those who use physical power: "Follow the rules, or we'll lock you up."

Then there are people who rely on authority of various types to engage in win–lose methods without ever threatening physical coercion. For example, supervisors have authority over assigned working hours, job promotions, and distribution of desirable or undesirable tasks. Teachers can use the power of grades to coerce students to act in desired ways.

The dark side of competition is that it often breeds aggression.[22] Sometimes aggression is obvious, but at other times it can be more subtle. To understand how, read on.

Direct Aggression

Direct aggression occurs when a communicator expresses a criticism or demand that threatens the face of the person at whom it is directed. There are several types of direct aggression: character attacks, competence attacks, physical appearance attacks, maledictions (wishing the other ill fortune), teasing, ridicule, threats, swearing, and nonverbal emblems.[23]

Direct aggression can have a severe impact on the target, making a recipient feel embarrassed, inadequate, humiliated, hopeless, desperate, or depressed.[24] This can result in decreased effectiveness in personal relationships, on the job, and in families.[25] There is also a significant connection between verbal aggression and physical aggression,[26] but even if the attacks never lead to blows, the psychological effects can be devastating. For example, siblings who were teased by a sibling report less satisfaction and trust than those whose relationships are free of such aggression.[27] And high school teams with aggressive coaches lose more games than teams with less aggressive coaches.[28]

> **Direct aggression**
> A criticism or demand that threatens the face of the person at whom it is directed.
>
> **Passive aggression**
> An indirect expression of aggression that occurs when a communicator expresses hostility in an obscure or manipulative way.

Passive Aggression

Passive aggression occurs when a communicator expresses hostility in an obscure or manipulative way. This behaviour has been termed "crazymaking," and it occurs when people have feelings of resentment, anger, or rage that they are unable or unwilling to express directly. Instead of keeping them to themselves, crazymakers send aggressive messages in subtle, indirect ways, thus maintaining the

Inc./Alamy/GetStock.com

front of kindness. But the façade eventually crumbles, and crazymaker's victims feel confused and angry for having been fooled. In response, they either react with aggressive behaviour or retreat to nurse their hurt feelings.

Passive aggression seldom has anything but harmful effects on a relationship.[29] If Lucia took a passive-aggressive approach toward Paul, she might show up late to run just to annoy him. Paul could become passive-aggressive by agreeing to include Lucia's friends, then pouring on the speed and leaving them behind.

Aggressive behaviour can be bad for the attacker as well. Men who view conversations as contests and partners as opponents are 60 percent more likely to die early than less aggressive men.[30] Partners in newly married couples who use sarcasm, interruptions, and criticism in disagreements suffer a drop in their immune system's effectiveness.[31]

Dirty Fighting with Crazymakers

Psychologist George Bach uses the term *crazymakers* to describe passive-aggressive behaviour. His term reflects the insidious nature of indirect aggression, which can confuse and anger a victim who may not even be aware of being victimized. Although a case can be made for using all the other approaches to conflict described in this chapter, it is difficult to find a justification for passive-aggressive crazymaking.

The following categories represent a nonexhaustive list of crazymaking. They are presented here as a warning for potential victims, who might choose to use perception checking, "I" language, assertion, or other communication strategies to explore whether the user has a complaint that can be addressed in a more constructive manner.

The Avoider Avoiders refuse to fight. When a conflict arises, they leave, fall asleep, pretend to be busy at work, or keep from facing the problem in some other way. Because avoiders won't fight back, this strategy can frustrate the person who wants to address an issue.

The Pseudoaccommodator Pseudoaccommodators pretend to give in and then continue to act in the same way.

The Guiltmaker Instead of expressing dissatisfaction directly, guiltmakers try to make others feel responsible for causing pain. A guiltmaker's favourite line is, "It's OK; don't worry about me . . ." accompanied by a big sigh.

The Mind Reader Instead of allowing their partners to express feelings honestly, mind readers go into character analysis, explaining what the partner really means or what's wrong with the partner. By behaving this way, mind readers refuse to handle their own feelings and leave no room for their partners to express themselves.

The Trapper Trappers play an especially dirty trick by setting up a desired behaviour for their partners and then, when it's met, attacking the very behaviour they requested. An example of this technique is for the trapper to say, "Let's be totally honest with each other," and then attack the partner's self-disclosure.

The Crisis Tickler Crisis ticklers almost bring what's bothering them to the surface but never quite come out and express themselves. Instead of admitting concern about finances, they innocently ask, "Gee, how much did that cost?" dropping a rather obvious hint but never really dealing with the crisis.

The Gunnysacker These people don't share complaints as they arise. Instead, they put their resentments into a psychological gunnysack, which after a while begins to bulge with both large and small gripes. Then, when the sack is about to burst, the gunnysacker pours out all the pent-up aggressions on the overwhelmed and unsuspecting victim.

The Trivial Tyrannizer Instead of honestly sharing their resentments, trivial tyrannizers do things they know will get their partners' goat—leaving dirty dishes in the sink, clipping fingernails in bed, belching out loud, turning up the television too loud, and so on.

The Beltliner Everyone has a psychological "belt-line," and below it are subjects too sensitive to be approached without damaging the relationship. Beltlines may have to do with physical characteristics, intelligence, past behaviour, or deeply ingrained personality traits that a person is trying to overcome. In an attempt to "get even" or hurt their partners, beltliners will use intimate knowledge to hit below the belt, where they know it will hurt.

The Joker Because they are afraid to face conflicts squarely, jokers kid around when their partners want to be serious, thus blocking the expression of important feelings.

The Withholder Instead of expressing their anger honestly and directly, withholders punish their partners by keeping back something—courtesy, affection, good cooking, humour, sex. As you can imagine, this is likely to build up even greater resentments in the relationship.

The Benedict Arnold These characters get back at their partners by sabotage, by failing to defend them from attackers, and even by encouraging ridicule or disregard from outside the relationship.

For more information about crazymaking, see G. Bach & Peter Wyden (1968). *The Intimate Enemy.* New York: Avon; and G. Bach (1971). *Aggression Lab: The Fair Fight Manual.* Dubuque, IA: Kendall-Hunt.

Compromising (Partial Lose–Lose)

A **compromise** gives both people some of what they want, although both sacrifice part of their goals. Compromise is used when it seems that partial satisfaction is the best they can hope for. For example, Paul and Lucia could strike a "halfway" deal to alternate workouts with and without her friends. Unlike avoidance, where both parties lose because they don't address their problem, in a compromise "you win some, you lose some" in the negotiation.

Compromising is sometimes touted as an effective way to handle conflicts because it's better than losing everything. Although compromises may be the best obtainable result in some conflicts, it's important to realize that both people in a conflict can often work together to find much better solutions.

Some compromises are bad. Consider the conflict between one person's desire to smoke and another's need for clean air. The win–lose outcomes of this issue are obvious: Either the smoker abstains or the nonsmoker gets polluted lungs. But a compromise in which the smoker gets to enjoy a rare cigarette and the non-smoker must inhale some fumes is hardly better. The costs involved in other compromises are even greater. If a divorced couple compromise on child care by haggling over custody and then grudgingly agree to split the time with their children, it's hard to say that anybody has won.

> ## Cooperation is not a one-way street.
>
> —Maurice Duplessis,
> favourite phrase used in speeches as
> premier of Quebec, 1936–39, 1944–59

Collaborating (Win–Win)

Compromising
An approach to conflict resolution in which both parties attain at least part of what they wanted through self-sacrifice.

Collaborating
A conflict management style that seeks win–win solutions.

Collaborating seeks win–win solutions to conflict, and collaborators demonstrate a high degree of concern for themselves and others. They try to find solutions that meet everyone's needs. If Lucia and Paul collaborate, they might come around to seeing that they can continue their one-on-one workouts but invite Lucia's friends to join at the end of each run. They might have some less challenging workouts that include the friends, or they could to get together with Lucia's friends at other times.

iofoto/Shutterstock

Not only do the partners avoid trying to win at the other's expense, but they also try to find solutions that go beyond a mere compromise. Here are some examples:

- Jason and Jennifer of Barrie, Ontario, were planning their first vacation. Jason, a golf enthusiast, wanted to head for Banff, while Jennifer, who had never seen the ocean, was thinking of Vancouver. Neither was interested in the other's vacation plans. After checking the Internet together, they realized that both of their needs could be met on Prince Edward Island. With several golf courses and plenty of warm, sandy beaches, they opted for Cavendish Beach. And, as a bonus, they would be within walking distance of the popular Anne of Green Gables site.
- Celine, a store manager, hated rescheduling employee work shifts to accommodate their social and family needs. She and her staff developed an arrangement where employees organized schedule swaps on their own and then notified her in writing.

> ## As a country, we are in the incredibly fortunate position of having no problems which cannot be substantially resolved by an act of our own national will. Therefore, let us will once again to live together in peace and equality, respecting each other's rights and freedoms, sharing fairly the rich opportunities of this great land.
>
> —Pierre Elliott Trudeau,
> New Year's message, published in the
> *Toronto Star*

TABLE 10.1

Factors to Consider When Choosing the Most Appropriate Conflict Style

Avoiding (lose–lose)	Accommodating (lose–win)	Competing (win–lose)	Compromising (partial lose–lose)	Collaborating (win–win)
When the issue is of little importance	When you discover you are wrong	When there is not enough time to seek a win–win outcome	To achieve quick, temporary solutions to complex problems	When the issue is too important for a compromise
When the costs of confrontation outweigh the benefits	When the issue is more important to the other person than it is to you	When the issue is not important enough to negotiate at length	When opponents are strongly committed to mutually exclusive goals	When a long-term relationship between you and the other person is important
To cool down and gain perspective	When the long-term cost of winning isn't worth the short-term gain	When the other person is not willing to cooperate	When the issues are moderately important but not enough for a stalemate	To merge insights with someone who has a different perspective on the problem
	To build up credits for later conflicts	When you are convinced that your position is right and necessary	As a backup mode when collaboration doesn't work	To develop a relationship by showing commitment to the concerns of both parties
	To let others learn by making their own mistakes	To protect yourself against a person who takes advantage of noncompetitive people		To come up with creative and unique solutions to problems

Adapted from W. W. Wilmot & J. L. Hocker (2010). *Interpersonal Conflict,* 8th ed. New York: McGraw-Hill.

The point is not that these solutions are the correct ones for everybody with similar problems. The win–win method is an approach to help you find just the right answer for your unique problem. By generating win–win solutions, you can tailor-make a way of resolving your conflicts that everyone can live with comfortably.

Which Style to Use?

Collaborating might seem like the ideal approach to solving problems, but it's an oversimplification to imagine that there is a single "best" way.[32] Generally speaking, win–win approaches are preferable to win–lose and lose–lose solutions, but there are times when avoiding, accommodating, and so forth are appropriate (see Table 10.1). To decide which approach to use, consider several factors:

1. *The relationship.* Accommodation is the best approach when someone else has more power than you. If the boss tells you to fill that order "*Now!*" a more assertive response ("I'm still tied up with yesterday's work.") might be reasonable but may cost you your job.

2. *The situation.* Different situations call for different conflict styles. After haggling over the price of a car for hours, it might be best to compromise and split the difference. In other cases, it may be a matter of sticking to your principle and attempting to get what you believe is right.

3. *The other person.* In some cases, the other person is unwilling or can't collaborate. Some people are so competitive that they put winning ahead of everything else. In such cases, your efforts to collaborate may have little chance of success.

4. *Your goals.* Sometimes your concern may be to calm an enraged or upset person. Accommodating an outburst from your crotchety sick neighbour, for example, is probably better than shouting back and triggering a stroke. In still other cases, your moral principles might compel an aggressive statement even though it might not get you what you originally sought: "I've had enough of your racist jokes. I've tried to explain why they're so offensive, but you obviously haven't listened. I'm leaving!"

LO³
Conflict in Relational Systems

The style you choose isn't the only factor that determines how conflicts unfold. In reality, conflict is relational: Its character is usually determined by the way the parties interact with each other.[33] You may, for example, plan to hint to a professor that you are bothered by her apparent indifference but wind up discussing the matter in an open, assertive way in reaction to her constructive response. This example suggests that conflict also depends on how the partners interact.

When two or more people are in a long-term relationship they develop a **relational conflict style**—a pattern of managing disagreements that repeats itself over time. The mutual influence that parties have on one another is so powerful that it can overcome a disposition to handle conflicts in a particular way.[34] Some relational conflict styles are constructive, while others can make life miserable.

> To ensure survival in an often hostile environment, Native societies found it essential to maintain group unity and cohesiveness. Hence, every effort was made to avoid interpersonal conflict among members of the group, a tendency that has persisted even into modern times. Behavioural norms designed to suppress conflict and promote group unity and survival are encouraged and reinforced by child rearing practices.
>
> —Clare Brant,
> "Native Ethics and Rules of Behaviour"

Complementary, Symmetrical, and Parallel Styles

Partners in interpersonal and impersonal relationships can use one of three styles to manage their conflicts. In a **complementary conflict style**, partners use different but mutually reinforcing behaviours. In a **symmetrical conflict style**, both partners use the same tactics. In a **parallel conflict style**, the style shifts between complementary and symmetrical. Table 10.2 (p. 281) illustrates how the same conflict could unfold in very different ways, depending on the style used to deal with it.

ejwhite/Shutterstock

Research shows that a complementary "fight–flight" style is common in many unhappy marriages. One partner—most commonly the wife—addresses the conflict directly, whereas the other—usually the husband—withdraws.[35] This pattern can lead to a cycle of increasing hostility and isolation because each partner punctuates the conflict differently. "I withdraw because she's so critical," a husband might say, while the wife organizes see it as "I criticize because he withdraws."

Complementary styles aren't the only ones that can lead to problems. Some distressed marriages suffer from destructively symmetrical communication. If both partners treat each other with matching hostility, one threat or insult leads to another in an escalatory spiral. If the partners withdraw instead of facing their problems, a de-escalatory spiral results, leaving neither partner satisfied with the relationship.

As Table 10.2 shows, both complementary and symmetrical behaviours can produce "good" results as well as "bad" results. If the complementary behaviours are positive, then a positive spiral results and the conflict stands a good chance of being resolved. This is the case in Example 2 in Table 10.2, where the boss is open to hearing the employee's concerns. Here, a complementary talk–listen pattern works well.

Symmetrical styles can also be beneficial. The clearest example of constructive symmetry occurs when both parties communicate assertively, listening to each other's

Relational conflict style
A pattern of managing disagreements that repeats itself over time in a relationship.

Complementary conflict style
A relational conflict style in which partners use different but mutually reinforcing behaviours.

Symmetrical conflict style
A relational conflict style in which both partners use the same tactics.

Parallel conflict style
A relational conflict style in which the approach of the partners varies from one situation to another.

TABLE 10.2
Complementary and Symmetrical Conflict Styles

Situation	Complementary Styles	Symmetrical Styles
Example 1 Wife upset because husband is spending little time at home.	Wife complains; husband withdraws, spending even less time at home. (Destructive)	Wife complains. Husband responds angrily and defensively. (Destructive)
Example 2 Female employee offended when male boss calls her "sweetie."	Employee objects to boss, explaining her reasons for being offended. Boss apologizes for his unintentional insult. (Constructive)	Employee maliciously "jokes" about boss at company party. (Destructive)
Example 3 Parents uncomfortable with teenager's new friends.	Parents express concerns. Teen dismisses them, saying, "There's nothing to worry about." (Destructive)	Teen expresses discomfort with parents' protectiveness. Parents and teen negotiate a mutually agreeable solution. (Constructive)

concerns and working together to resolve them. The potential for this sort of solution occurs in Example 3, in the parent–teenager conflict. With enough mutual respect and careful listening, both the parents and their teenager can understand one another's concerns and very possibly find a way to give both parties what they want.

Intimate and Aggressive Styles

Another way to look at conflict styles is to examine the interaction between intimacy and aggression. Originally used to describe communication between couples, the scheme also works well for other types of relationships.

- *Nonintimate-aggressive.* These partners fight unsuccessfully to satisfy important content and relational goals. In some relationships, aggression is expressed directly: "Forget it. I'm not going to another stupid party with your friends. All they do is talk shop." In other relationships, indirect aggression is the norm: (Sarcastically) "Sure, I'd *love* to go to another party with your friends." Neither approach is satisfying because there are few rewards to justify the costs of the unpleasantness.
- *Nonintimate-nonaggressive.* The parties avoid conflicts—and each other—instead of facing issues head-on: "You won't be coming home for the holidays? Oh, well, I guess that's OK . . ." Relationships of this sort can be quite stable, but not confronting and resolving problems can cause it to lose its vitality.
- *Intimate-aggressive.* This pattern combines aggression and intimacy in a manner that might seem upsetting to outsiders but works well in some

---

Invitation TO INSIGHT

Understanding Conflict Styles

You can gain a clearer idea of how conflict styles differ by completing the following exercise:

1. Join a partner and choose one of the following conflicts to work on or substitute a conflict of your own.
   a. Roommates disagree about the noise level in their apartment.
   b. Parents want their college sophomore son or daughter to stay home for the winter vacation. The son or daughter wants to travel with friends.
   c. One person in a couple wants to spend free time socializing with friends. The other wants to stay at home together.
2. Role-play the conflict four times, reflecting each of the following styles:

   Nonintimate-aggressive   Intimate-aggressive
   Nonintimate-nonaggressive   Intimate-nonaggressive

3. After experiencing each of these styles, determine which of them characterizes the way conflict is managed in one of your interpersonal relationships. Are you satisfied with this approach? If not, describe what style would be more appropriate.

John Lund/Nevada Wier/Blend/GetStock.com

relationships. Lovers may argue like cats and dogs but then make up just as intensely. Co-workers might argue heatedly but cherish their association.

- *Intimate-nonaggressive.* There's not much attacking or blaming in this sort of relationship. Partners may confront each other directly or indirectly, but one way or another they manage to prevent issues from interfering with their relationship.

The pattern that partners use reveals a lot about their relationship. Mary Ann Fitzpatrick identified three types of couples: separates, independents, and traditionals.[36] Partners in each type of relationship approached conflict differently.[37] Separates and independents avoid conflict. Traditionals, by contrast, focus on their interaction. They also felt most secure about their relationships. They express negative emotions frequently but seek and reveal large amounts of personal information. Satisfied traditional couples fit the intimate-nonaggressive pattern, communicating more positive and less negative information than independents.

These findings suggest that there's no single "best" relational conflict style.[38] Some families or couples may fight intensely but love one another just as strongly. Others handle issues more rationally and calmly. Even a nonintimate-nonaggressive style can work when there's no desire to have an interpersonal relationship. You might, for example, accommodate the demands of an eccentric professor in order to get credit for a course.

Conflict Rituals

When people have been in a relationship for some time, their communication often develops into **conflict rituals**—usually unacknowledged but very real patterns of interlocking behaviour.[39] Consider a few common rituals:

- A young child interrupts her parents, demanding to be included in their conversation. The parents tell the child to wait, but she whines and cries so much that they listen rather than ignore the fussing.

- A couple fights. One partner leaves. The other accepts the blame for the problem and begs forgiveness. When the partner returns, they have a happy reunion. Soon they fight again.

- A boss flies into rage when the pressure builds at work. Recognizing this, employees avoid him as much as possible. When the crisis is over, the boss compensates by being especially receptive to employee requests.

> **Conflict ritual**
> An unacknowledged repeating pattern of interlocking behaviour used by participants in a conflict.

There's nothing inherently wrong with the interaction in many rituals, especially when those involved accept them as ways of managing conflict.[40] Consider the preceding examples. The little girl's whining may be the only way to get the parents' attention. In the second, both partners might use fighting to blow off steam, viewing the grief of separation as worth the joy of a reunion. The third ritual might help the boss release pressure and the employees to get their requests met.

Rituals cause problems when they are the *only* means used to handle conflicts. Competent communicators have a large repertoire of behaviours and select the most effective response for a given situation. Relying on one ritual pattern to handle all conflicts is no more effective than putting the same seasoning in every dish you cook. Although some rituals may be familiar and comfortable, they're not likely to resolve the various conflicts you encounter in relationships.

Variables in Conflict Styles

Along with the differences that arise in individual relationships, there are two powerful variables that affect the way people manage conflict: gender and culture.

Cheryl Casey/Shutterstock

Gender

Men and women often approach conflicts differently. Even in childhood, males are more likely to be aggressive, demanding, and competitive, whereas females are more cooperative. Studies of children from preschool to early adolescence show that boys try to get their way by ordering one another around ("Gimme your arm"), while girls will begin proposals with the word *let's* ("Let's go find some").[41] Whereas boys tell each other what role to take in pretend play ("Come on, be a doctor"), girls either ask what one each person wants or make a joint proposal ("We can both be doctors"). Furthermore, boys often make demands without offering an explanation, whereas girls provide reasons for their suggestions ("We gotta clean 'em first . . . 'cause they got germs.").

Adolescent girls use aggression in conflicts, but their methods are less direct. While verbal showdowns and physical fights are common in teenage boys, girls resort to gossip, backbiting, and social exclusion,[42] which can be just as destructive as the tactics boys use. The film *Mean Girls,* based on the book *Queen Bees and Wannabes,*[43] offers a vivid depiction of just how injurious these indirect assaults can be on the self-concept and relationships of young women.

Differences like these persist into adulthood, and female and male college students view conflicts in contrasting ways.[44] Regardless of their cultural background, female students saw men as more concerned with power and content than relational issues. By contrast, women were described as more concerned with maintaining the relationship during a conflict. When the conflict behaviours of both sexes are observed, women are more assertive about expressing their ideas and feelings, and men are more likely to withdraw from discussing issues.[45]

These sorts of differences don't preclude men from forming good relationships, but their notions of a good relationship are different. For some men, friendship and aggression aren't mutually exclusive. In fact, many strong male relationships are built around competition. Women can be competitive too, but they are more likely to use logical reasoning and bargaining as opposed to aggression.[46] Men are less aggressive and more cooperative when they communicate with women than they are in all-male groups.

A look at the entire body of research on gender and conflict suggests that the differences in how the two sexes handle conflict are relatively small, and sometimes different from the stereotypical picture of aggressive men and passive women.[47] People *think* there are more differences

"I'm not yelling at you, I'm yelling with you."

© David Sipress/ The New Yorker Collection/www.cartoonbank.com.

> Men and women are supposed to argue, and one of the reasons why they get married is so they won't have to argue with strangers.
>
> —H. Gordon Green,
> *Professor Go Home*

Invitation TO INSIGHT

Your Conflict Rituals

Describe two conflict rituals in one of your important relationships. One of your examples should consist of a positive ritual and the other of a negative ritual. For each example, explain

1. A subject that is likely to trigger the conflict (money, leisure time, affection)

2. The behaviour of one partner that initiates the ritual

3. The series of responses by both partners that follow the initiating event

4. How the ritual ends

Based on your description, explain an alternative to the unsatifying ritual and describe how you could change the way you manage the conflict to a more satisfying way.

Credit: Jules Feiffer

in male and female ways of handling conflicts than there actually are.[48] People who assume that men are aggressive and women accommodating may notice behaviour that fits these stereotypes and overlook those that do not.

Although men and women may have characteristically different conflict styles, the individual style of each communicator—regardless of gender—and the nature of the relationship are more important than gender in shaping the way he or she handles conflict.

Culture

The way people manage conflict also depends on their cultural background. For instance, the straight-talking, assertive approach that is common across North America is not the universal norm.[49]

An orientation toward individualism or collectivism is the most important cultural influence on conflict.[50] In individualistic cultures like Canada's, the goals, rights, and needs of each person are considered important and individuals have the right to stand up for themselves. In collectivistic cultures— more common in Latin America and Asia—the group's concerns are more important than the individual's needs. The assertive behaviour that might seem perfectly appropriate in North America would be considered rude and insensitive in collectivistic cultures.

Another factor is the difference between high- and low-context cultural styles.[51] Low-context cultures like Canada's place a premium on being direct and literal. By contrast, high-context cultures like Japan's avoid confrontation and value self-restraint. Communicators in these cultures derive meaning from the context, social conventions, and hints. Preserving

The film character Borat Sagdiyev claimed to visit the United States to bring "cultural learnings" back to his own country. But his colossal insensitivity created conflict wherever he travelled.

and honouring the other's person's face is a prime goal, and communicators go to great lengths to avoid embarrassing a conversational partner. In Japan, for example, even a simple request like "Close the door" would be too straightforward.[52] Instead, an indirect statement like "It is somewhat cold today" would be used. People in Japan are also reluctant to say no to a request. They would be likely to say, "Let me think about it for a while," which would be recognized as a refusal in Japan.

When people from different cultures face a conflict, their habitual communication patterns may not mesh smoothly. The challenge faced by a Canadian husband and his Taiwanese wife illustrates this sort of problem:

> The husband would try to confront his wife verbally and directly (as is typical in the Canada), leading her to either become defensive or withdraw completely from the discussion. She, on the other hand, would attempt to indicate her displeasure by changes in mood and eye contact (typical of Chinese culture) that were either not noticed (or uninterpretable) by her husband. Thus, neither "his way" nor "her way" was working and they could not see any realistic way to "compromise."[53]

Other cultural differences also influence conflict. Canadians visiting Greece, for example, often think they are witnessing an argument when they're overhearing a friendly conversation.[54] A comparative study of North American and Italian nursery school children showed that one of the Italian children's favourite pastimes was a kind of heated debating that Italians call *discussione* but that we would regard as arguing. Within Canada, the ethnic background of communicators also plays a role. Dolores Francis, a Mi'kmaq student, explained how there was really no need to adopt the communication patterns offered in this text because conflict is rare in her culture. When children say or do inappropriate things, for example, adults don't reprimand them because it would shame them. Instead, parents talk alone to the child about appropriate behaviour. Out of respect for their parents, the children wouldn't engage in the disorderly behaviour again. When Delores has a conflict with a First Nations person, she would describe the problem using one word, but she would have to use several with a non-Aboriginal person. In her words, "They would go on and

(Looking at Diversity)

An Alternative to Divorce: One Couple's Solution

In an article in *Maclean's* magazine, **Nora Underwood** looks at an unusual living arrangement.

Martin and Deborah (unless full names are given, people cited have been given pseudonyms on request) met when they were 12, got married eight years later, started a retail business together, and raised two children. But 10 years ago, after two decades of marriage, each became involved with someone else. For the sake of the kids (now grown and away from home), as much as for their own, the Ontario couple decided to continue cohabiting—they have never divorced. "I think it's possible that people can go in different directions sometimes without losing the love for the person," explains Martin, who still lives with Deborah and the man Deborah fell in love with a decade ago. "The fact that it hasn't worked out exactly right doesn't mean you should lose sight of what brought you together in the first place."

There are usually other casualties when a long-term relationship breaks up, but Martin and Deborah have managed to maintain positive con-nections with each other's families as well as with all their friends. And while the community has never fully adjusted to the couple's decision to continue living together, it was best for the kids. "For them it was better than living separately," says Deborah. "They found it difficult to explain to their friends, but their friends all grew to really care about us and all of the weird stuff that people thought was going on was forgotten. Our daughter told us she's really proud of us."

While Martin knew rationally the new arrange-ment was for the best, it still took him about five years to feel completely comfortable with it emo-tionally. "But I was lucky that her partner was a person I found to be a very good man, who under-stood how it would be difficult for me for the love of my life to be with a different person." Martin, meanwhile, has had relationships; one girlfriend even joined the family for a while, but there was friction with Deborah over parenting issues. Overall, says Martin, the struggle was worth it. "Continuity is really important," adds Martin, who still runs a busi-ness with Deborah. "For me, a journey through life is far more interesting if you don't force dislocations into it that aren't necessary."

Nora Underwood "An alternative to divorce: One couple's solution", *Maclean's Magazine*, 21 June 2002. Reprinted by permission of the author.

---

on." To adapt to the non-Aboriginal approach, she must exaggerate, which runs contrary to her cultural norms. It's easy to imagine how two friends, lovers, or co-workers from different cultural backgrounds might have trouble finding a compatible conflict style.

Despite cultural differences, it's important to realize that our approach to conflict may be biological.[55] Furthermore, scholarship suggests that the self-concept is more powerful than culture in determining conflict style.[56] For example, assertive individuals raised in environments that downplay conflict are likely to be more aggressive than unassertive persons growing up in cultures where conflict is common. You might handle conflicts calmly at work, where civility is the norm, but shriek like a banshee at home if that's how you and your partner handle conflict.

LO⁴
Constructive Conflict Skills

Although the win–win conflict style described earlier has many advantages over win–lose and lose–lose approaches, it is rarely used. There are three reasons for this. The first is lack of awareness. Some people are so used to competition that they mistakenly think that they have to win at all costs. Second, because conflict is accompanied by emotion, people don't stop to think of better alterna-tives. Therefore, it's often necessary to stop yourself from speaking out aggressively and starting an escalating spiral of defensiveness. The time-honoured advice of "counting to 10" applies here. This provides time to *act* construc-tively instead of *reacting* in a way that's likely to produce a lose–lose outcome.

> Your climate is the mood
> Of living, the hinge of now,
> In time the present tense.
>
> —Al Purdy,
> "Where the Moment Is"

A third reason win–win solutions are rare is that they require the other person's cooperation. It's difficult to negotiate constructively when someone insists on defeating you. In this case, use your best persuasive skills to explain that by working together you can find a solu-tion that satisfies both of you.

Excerpt from "Where the Moment Is" by Al Purdy, *Beyond Remembering: The Collected Poems of Al Purdy*, edited and selected by Al Purdy and Sam Solecki; Harbour Publishing, 2000.

Despite these challenges, you can get better at resolving conflicts by trying the method below. It will increase your chances of being able to handle your conflicts in a collaborative, win–win manner.

1. Identify Your Problem and Unmet Needs

The first part of this step is to recognize that *you* have the problem because you are the one who is dissatisfied. Whether you want to return an unsatisfactory piece of merchandise or request a change in working conditions, the problem is yours because you paid for the defective article while the merchant has had the use of your good money, or you are the one who is unhappy with your working conditions, not your employer.*

Realizing that the problem is yours will make a big difference when the time comes to approach the other party. Instead of feeling and acting in an evaluative way, you'll be more likely to state your problem in a descriptive way. This will be more accurate and reduce the chance of a defensive reaction.

After you realize that the problem is yours, the next step is to identify the unmet needs that make you dissatisfied. This isn't as simple as it seems. Behind the apparent content of an issue is often a relational need. Consider this example:

> A friend hasn't returned some money you lent long ago. Your apparent need is to get the cash back, but even if you were rolling in money, your important need might be *to avoid feeling victimized by your friend's taking advantage of you.*

As you'll soon see, the ability to identify your real needs plays a key role in resolving interpersonal problems. The point to remember is that before you voice your problem to your partner, you ought to be clear about which of your needs aren't being met.

2. Make a Date

Destructive fights often start because the initiator confronts a partner who isn't ready. The person might be fatigued, in a hurry, upset over another problem, or not feeling well. At such times, it's unfair to "jump" a person

SIPRESS

"Is this a good time to have a big fight?"

© David Sipress/The New Yorker Collection/www.cartoonbank.com.

without notice and expect to get their full attention. Instead, you'll probably have a row.

After you clarify the problem, approach your partner with a request to try to solve it. For example, "Something's been bothering me. Can we talk?" If the answer is yes, you're ready to go further. If it isn't the right time to confront your partner, find a time that's agreeable to both of you.

3. Describe Your Problem and Needs

Your partner can't possibly meet your needs without knowing why you're upset or what you want. Therefore, describe your problem as specifically as possible. The best way to deliver a complete, accurate message is to use the assertive message format discussed in Chapter 9. Notice how well this approach works in the following example:

> "I have a problem. It's about you leaving dirty clothes around the house after I've told you how much it bothers me (*behaviour*). It's a problem because I have to run around like crazy and pick things up whenever guests come (*consequence*). I'm starting to think that either you're not paying attention to my requests or you're trying to drive me crazy (*thoughts*), and either way I'm getting more and more resentful (*feeling*). I'd like to find some way to have a neat place without my having to be a maid or a nag."

After stating your problem and describing what you need, it's important to make sure that your partner has

---

* Of course, others involved in the conflict may have problems of their own. For instance, the merchant and your boss may be bothered by your requests. However, the fact remains that the reason you are speaking up about these matters is because you are dissatisfied. Thus, the problem is at least initially yours.

Negotiating a solution usually lacks the fireworks of more volatile approaches—and can produce more satisfying results.

1. *Identify and define the conflict*. This consists of discovering each person's problem and needs, thus setting the stage for meeting all of them.

2. *Generate a number of possible solutions*. You and your partner generate but do not evaluate a list of possible solutions (the key is quantity). Nothing is too crazy or stupid. Sometimes a far-fetched idea will lead to a more workable one.

3. *Evaluate the alternative solutions*. Talk about which solutions will work and which ones won't—and be honest. If a solution is going to work, everyone involved has to support it.

4. *Decide on the best solution*. Select the solution that looks the best to everyone. Your decision doesn't have to be final, but it should look potentially successful.

understood what you've said. As you can remember from the discussion of listening in Chapter 7, there's a good chance—especially in a stressful conflict—that your words will be misinterpreted. Therefore, you might try saying, "I'm not sure I expressed myself very well just now. Maybe you should tell what you heard me say so I can be sure I got it right." In any case, be sure that your partner understands your whole message before going any further. Legitimate arguments are tough enough without getting upset about a conflict that doesn't even exist.

4. Consider Your Partner's Point of View

The next step is to find out what your partner needs to feel satisfied. This is important because the other person has just as much right as you to feel satisfied. If you expect help in meeting your needs, it's reasonable that you behave in the same way. But in addition to fairness, an unhappy partner will make it hard for you to become satisfied and a happy partner will be more likely to cooperate in letting you reach your goals. Thus, it's in your own self-interest to discover and meet your partner's needs.

You can learn your partner's needs simply by asking: "Now I've told you what I want and why. Tell me what you need to feel OK about this." Once your partner begins to talk, use your listening skills to make sure that you understand.

5. Negotiate a Solution

The next step is to negotiate a solution by using a modification of Thomas Gordon's approach as outlined in *Parent Effectiveness Training*.[57]

FIGURE 10.2

Flow Chart of the Win–Win Negotiation Process

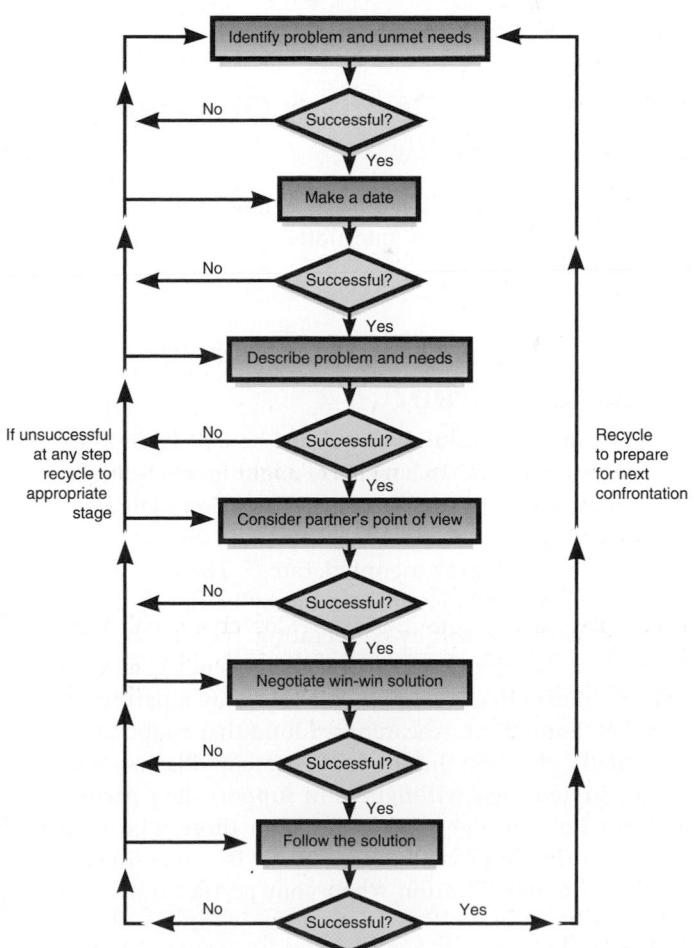

Adapted from Rory Remer and Paul deMesquita (1990). "Teaching and Learning Skills of Interpersonal Confrontation." In Dudley D. Cahn (Ed). *Intimates in Conflict: A Communication Perspective*. Mahweh, NJ: Erlbaum, p. 227.

6. Follow Up the Solution

After you've tested the solution for a while, take time to discuss its progress. It may need some adjustments, or you may need to rethink the whole problem. The idea is to keep on top of the problem, to keep using creativity to solve it.

To apply this method properly, it's important to follow every step. This prevents misunderstandings and the possibility of degenerating into a negative spiral. Second, realize that in real life this method is not likely to flow smoothly from one step to another. Expect and prepare for a certain amount of resistance from the other person. When a step doesn't meet with success, simply move back and repeat the preceding ones as necessary. See Figure 10.2 (p. 287).

Win–win solutions aren't always possible. There will be times when even the best-intentioned people simply won't be able to find a way of meeting all their needs. In times like these, the process of negotiation has to include some compromises.

Constructive Conflict: Questions and Answers

People often express doubts about how well win–win negotiating works. Four questions typically arise, and they deserve an answer.

Isn't the Win–Win Approach Too Good to Be True?

Research shows that seeking mutual benefit is not only desirable—it works. In a series of experiments, subjects were presented with a bargaining situation called the "prisoner's dilemma" in which they could choose either to cooperate or betray a confederate.[58] There are three outcomes: One partner can win big by betraying a confederate, both can win by cooperating, or both can lose by betraying each other. Although cynics might assume that the most effective strategy is to betray a partner (a win–lose approach), researchers found that cooperation is actually the best hard-nosed strategy. Players who demonstrated their willingness to support their partner and not hold grudges did better than those who took a competitive approach. However, it is impossible to reach a win–win solution when your partner refuses to cooperate.

Isn't the Win–Win Approach Too Elaborate?

Not really. Once you are familiar with and skilled at using the steps, you can select what you need in a given

"Listen, I've decided to go back to being selfish."

situation. For important issues, you'll find that every step of the win–win approach is important. If this process seems time-consuming, consider the time and energy that not solving the issue will take.

Isn't Win–Win Negotiating Too Rational?

Some *Looking Out/Looking In* readers complain that they get so angry they just want to explode. When this occurs, remove yourself from the scene, confide in a third party, or blow off steam through physical exercise. An understanding partner may even allow you to have a "Vesuvius"—an uncontrollable outburst. Let your partner know that you want to find a solution but that you might behave emotionally on occasion.

Is It Possible to Change Others?

Although you won't always be able to gain your partner's cooperation, a good attempt can do the trick most of the time. Showing that it's in the individual's self-interest to work together is key. You can boost the odds of getting your partner's cooperation by modelling the communication skills described in this book. And even if this doesn't succeed, you'll gain self-respect by knowing that you behaved honourably and constructively.

Communication in the Workplace

Today's workplace is team-oriented, which means that we encounter conflict. Conflict can be dysfunctional or functional. **Dysfunctional conflict** creates animosity

> **Dysfunctional conflict**
> Conflict that creates animosity, causes interpersonal stress, and hinders a group's progress.

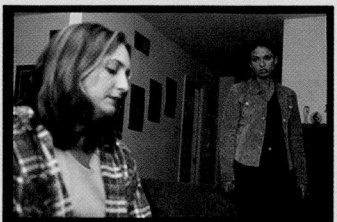

Jason Harris/Cengage Learning

It is 7:15 a.m. on a typical school day. Chris enters the kitchen and finds the sink full of dirty dishes. It was her roommate Terry's turn to do them. She sighs in disgust and begins to clean up, slamming pots and pans.

Terry Can't you be a little more quiet? I don't have a class till 10:00, and I want to catch up on sleep.

Chris (*Expressing her aggression indirectly in a sarcastic tone of voice*) Sorry to bother you. I was cleaning up last night's dinner dishes.

Terry (*Misses the message*) Well, I wish you'd do it a little more quietly. I was up late studying last night, and I'm beat.

Chris (*Decides to communicate her irritation more directly, if aggressively*) Well, if you'd done the dishes last night, I wouldn't have had to wash them now.

Terry (*Finally realizes that Chris is mad at her, responds defensively*) I was going to do them when I got up. I've got two midterms this week, and I was studying until two last night. What's more important, grades or a spotless kitchen?

Chris (*Perpetuating the growing defensive spiral*) I've got classes too, you know. But that doesn't mean we have to live like pigs!

Terry (*Angrily*) Forget it. If it's such a big deal, I'll never leave another dirty dish!

> Chris and Terry avoid each other as they get ready for school. During the day, Chris realizes that attacking Terry will only make matters worse. She decides on a more constructive approach that evening.

Chris That wasn't much fun this morning. Want to talk about it?

Terry I suppose so. But I'm going out to study with Kim and Alisa in a few minutes.

Chris (*Realizing that it's important to talk at a good time*) If you have to leave soon, let's not get into it now. How about talking when you get back?

Terry OK, if I'm not too tired.

Chris Or we could talk tomorrow before class.

Terry OK.

> Later that evening, Terry and Chris continue their conversation.

Chris (*Defines the issue as her problem by using the assertive clear message format*) I hated to start the day with a fight. But I also hate having to do the dishes when it's not my turn (*behaviour*). It doesn't seem fair for me to do my job and yours (*interpretation*), and that's why I got so mad (*feeling*) and nagged at you (*consequence*).

Terry But I was studying! You know how much I have to do. It's not like I was partying.

Chris (*Avoids attacking Terry by sincerely agreeing with the facts and explaining further why she was upset*) I know. It wasn't just doing the dishes that got me upset. It seems like there have been a lot of times when I've done your jobs and mine too.

Terry (*Defensively*) Like when?

Chris (*Gives specific descriptions of Terry's behaviour*) Well, this was the third time this week that I've done the dishes when it's your turn, and I can think of a couple of times lately when I've had to clean up your stuff before people came over.

Terry I don't see why it's such a big deal. If you just leave the stuff there, I'll clean it up.

Chris (*Still trying to explain herself, she continues to use "I" language*) I know you would. I guess it's harder for me to put up with a messy place than it is for you.

Terry Yeah. If you'd just relax, living together would be a lot easier!

Chris (*Resenting Terry's judgmental accusation that the problem is all hers*) Hey, wait a second! Don't blame the whole thing on me. It's just that we have different standards. It looks to you like I'm too hung up on keeping the place clean . . .

Terry Right.

Chris . . . and if we do it your way, then I'd be giving up. I'd have to either live with the place messier than I like it or clean everything up myself. Then I'd get mad at you, and things would be pretty tense around here. (*Describes the unpleasant consequences of not solving the problem in a mutually satisfactory way*)

Terry I suppose so.

Chris We need to figure out how to take care of the apartment in a way we can both live with. (*Describes the broad outline of a win–win solution*)

Terry Yeah.

Chris So what could we do?

Terry (*Sounding resigned*) Look, from now on I'll just do the dishes right away. It isn't worth arguing about.

Chris Sure it is. If you're sore, the apartment may be clean, but it won't be worth it.

Terry (*Skeptically*) OK; what do you suggest?

Chris Well, I'm not sure. You don't want the pressure of having to clean up right away, and I don't want to have to do my jobs and yours, too. Right?

Terry Yeah. *(Still sounding skeptical)* So what are we going to do—hire a housekeeper to clean up?

Chris *(Refusing to let Terry sidetrack the discussion)* That would be great if we could afford it. How about using paper plates? That would make cleaning up from meals easier.

Terry Yeah, but there would still be pots and pans.

Chris Well, it's not a perfect fix, but it might help a little. *(Goes on to suggest other ideas)* How about cooking meals that don't take a lot of work to clean up—maybe more salads and less fried stuff that sticks to pans. That would be a better diet too.

Terry Yeah. I do hate to scrub crusty frying pans. But that doesn't do anything about your wanting the living room picked up all the time, and I bet I still wouldn't keep the kitchen as clean as you like it. Keeping the place super clean just isn't as big a deal to me as it is for you.

Chris That's true, and I don't want to have to nag you! *(Clarifies the end she's seeking)* You know, it's not really cleaning up that bothers me. It's doing more than my share of work. I wonder if there's a way I could be responsible for keeping the kitchen clean and picking up if you could do something else to keep the workload even.

Terry Are you serious? I'd love to get out of doing the dishes! You mean you'd do them . . . and keep the place picked up . . . if I did something else?

Chris As long as the work was equal and you really did your jobs without me having to remind you.

Terry What kind of work would you want me to do?

Chris How about cleaning up the bathroom?

Terry Forget it. That's worse than doing the dishes.

Chris OK. How about cooking?

Terry That might work, but then we'd have to eat together all the time. It's nice to do our own cooking when we want to. It's more flexible that way.

Chris OK. But what about shopping? I hate the time it takes, and you don't mind it that much, do you?

Terry You mean shop for groceries? You'd trade that for cleaning the kitchen?

Chris Sure. And picking up the living room. It takes an hour every time we shop, and we make two trips a week. Doing the dishes would be much quicker.

Terry All right!

The plan didn't work perfectly: At first Terry put off shopping until all the food was gone and Chris took advantage by asking Terry to run other errands during her shopping trips. But their new arrangement proved much more successful than the old arrangement. The apartment was cleaner and the workload more even, which satisfied Chris. Terry was less the object of Chris's nagging and she had no kitchen chores, which made her happier. Just as important, the relationship between Chris and Terry was more comfortable—thanks to win–win problem solving.

---

among group members and hinders a group's progress—and it can result in sleep loss. Stephen Mill suggests that if information technology professionals could address interpersonal conflict in the workplace, it would reduce their likelihood of burnout.[59] **Functional conflict**, however, is positive and focuses on issues rather than personalities. For example, a group in charge of developing a workplace behaviour policy might argue over content, implementation, or how to govern it. The more argument there is, the better their final decisions will be, because they will have considered a variety of ideas and potential paths.[60]

To create work environments where functional arguments are encouraged and dysfunctional arguments frowned upon, be mindful of group norms—those unwritten expectations that we have of one another. Negative norms might be using put-down humour or accepting rudeness. Both can have a negative effect. In fact, one study on rudeness in the workplace concluded that it reduced the quality of work, people lost work time trying to avoid people, some people considered leaving, and others actually left their jobs because of rudeness.[61]

Knowing how different cultures handle conflict can help us avoid dysfunctional conflict. For instance, when individuals from individualistic and collectivistic cultures have a sense of where each is coming from, they might develop alternative ways to resolve conflict. The same is true with the notion of saving face. Further, some dysfunctional conflicts can be reduced by recognizing *immigrant syndrome*, caused by struggles with a different language, customs, the adaptations of family members, changes in cultural values, and loss of identity.[62]

Finally, people in different professions deal with conflict differently, and this presents a challenge for multiprofessional teams, especially those working in health care contexts. A researcher from the Faculty of Medicine at the University of Ottawa suggests that by better understanding educational, systemic, and personal factors that

Functional conflict
Positive conflict that focuses on issues rather than personalities.

inform the culture of a profession, we will be more likely to create better collaborative health practices.[63]

In an ideal world, employees would love their jobs and stay happily employed forever. In reality, that rarely happens. Some people leave for positive reasons, such as career advancement or new opportunities. Many, however, quit because of workplace conflicts.[64] Some conflicts arise when workers don't get enough information to do their jobs, and others come from conflicting demands (e.g., "Work faster, but don't make any mistakes.").[65] Sometimes the reasons for leaving are darker, such as bullying by co-workers or bosses.[66] Whatever the reasons for quitting, these strategies will help you leave on the best possible terms.[67]

Leave Before You Lose Your Cool

Waiting until your situation is intolerable may cause you to blow up and say things you'll regret later. Once the writing is on the wall, it's smart to move on.

Tell Your Boss First

Management will be insulted if they hear about your departure plans through the grapevine. When you explain your reasons directly to the boss, you can control the information he or she hears, rather than risking misunderstandings and misinformation.

Don't Trash the Company

Even if you have been treated poorly, be careful about criticizing the organization or its personnel. It's a small world, and you may need the goodwill of these people in the future.

Finish on a Strong Note

Make sure to do an exemplary job during your final days and weeks. The impression you leave can influence the references you get later, as well as the attitudes of supervisors and colleagues you may encounter again during your career.

Endnotes

1. W. Wilmot & J. L. Hocker (2010). *Interpersonal Conflict*, 8th ed. (pp. 44–56). New York: McGraw-Hill. See also P. M. Buzzanell & N. A. Burrell (1997). "Family & Workplace Conflict: Examining Metaphorical Conflict Schemas & Expressions across Context & Sex." *Human Communication Research, 24*, 109–146.

2. S. Metts & W. Cupach (1990). "The Influence of Relationship Beliefs & Problem-Solving Responses on Satisfaction in Romantic Relationships." *Human Communication Research, 17*, 170–185.

3. Wilmot & Hocker, op cit.. 11–19.

4. For a summary of research detailing the prevalence of conflict in relationships, see W. R. Cupach & D. J. Canary (1997). *Competence in Interpersonal Conflict* (pp. 5–6). New York: McGraw-Hill.

5. W. L. Benoit & P. J. Benoit (1987). "Everyday Argument Practices of Naive Social Actors." In J. Wenzel (Ed.). *Argument and Critical Practices*. Annandale, VA: Speech Communication Association.

6. W. Samter & W. R. Cupach (1998). "Friendly Fire: Topical Variations in Conflict among Same- & Cross-Sex Friends." *Communication Studies, 49*, 121–138.

7. S. Vuchinich (1987). "Starting & Stopping Spontaneous Family Conflicts." *Journal of Marriage and the Family 49*, 591–601.

8. J. M. Gottman (1982). "Emotional Responsiveness in Marital Conversations." *Journal of Communication, 32*, 108–120. See also W. R. Cupach (1982, May). *Communication Satisfaction and Interpersonal Solidarity as Outcomes of Conflict Message Strategy Use*. Paper presented at the International Communication Association conference, Boston.

9. P. Koren, K. Carlton, & D. Shaw (1980). "Marital Conflict: Relations among Behaviours, Outcomes, and Distress." *Journal of Consulting and Clinical Psychology, 48*, 460–468.

10. Hocker & Wilmot, op cit., p. 37.

11. J. M. Gottman (1979). *Marital Interaction: Experimental Investigations*. New York: Academic Press. See also D. A. Infante, S. A. Myers, & R. A. Buerkel (1994). "Argument and Verbal Aggression in Constructive and Destructive Family and Organizational Disagreements." *Western Journal of Communication, 58*, 73–84.

12. S. E. Crohan (1992). "Marital Happiness & Spousal Consensus on Beliefs about Marital Conflict: A Longitudinal Investigation." *Journal of Science and Personal Relationships, 9*, 89–102.

13. D. J. Canary, H. Weger, Jr., & L. Stafford (1991). "Couples' Argument Sequences and Their Associations with Relational Characteristics." *Western Journal of Speech Communication, 55*, 159–179.

14. M. S. Harper and D.P. Welsh (2007). "Keeping Quiet: Self-Silencing and Its Association with Relational and Individual Functioning among Adolescent Romantic Couples." *Journal of Social & Personal Relationships, 24*, 99–116.

15. J. P. Caughlin & T. D. Golish (2002). "An Analysis of the Association between Topic Avoidance and Dissatisfcation: Comparing Perceptual and Interpersonal Explanations." *Communication Monographs, 69*, 275–295.

16. J. P. Caughlin & T. D. Arr (2004). "When is Topic Avoidance Unsatisfying? Examining Moderators of the Association between Avoidance and Dissatisfaction." *Human Communication Research, 30*, 479–513.

17. D. D. Cahn (1992). *Conflict in Intimate Relationships*. New York: Guilford, p. 100.

18. Wilmot & Hocker, op cit., p. 159.

19. J. G. Oetzel & S. Ting-Toomey (2003). "Face Concerns in Interpersonal Conflict: A Cross-Cultural Empirical Test of the Face Negotiation Theory." *Communication Research, 30*, 599–625; and M. U. Dsilva & L. O. Whyte (1998). "Cultural Differences in Conflict Styles: Vietnamese Refugees and Established Residents." *Howard Journal of Communication, 9*, 57–68.

20. S. J. Messman & R. L. Mikesell (2000). "Competition and Interpersonal Conflict in Dating Relationships." *Communication Reports, 13*, 21–34.

21. L. N. Olson & D. O. Braithwaite (2004). "'If You Hit Me Again, I'll Hit You Back': Conflict Management Strategies of Individuals Experiencing Aggression During Conflicts." *Communication Studies, 55*, 271–285.

22. K. Warren, S. Schoppelrey, & D. Moberg (2005). "'A Model of Contagion Through Competition in the Aggressive Behaviours of Elementary School Students." *Journal of Abnormal Child Psychology, 33*, 283–292.

23. D. A. Infante (1987). "Aggressiveness." In J. C. McCroskey & J. A. Daly (Eds.). *Personality & Interpersonal Communication*. Newbury Park, CA: Sage.

24. M. E. Roloff & R. M. Reznick (2008). "Communication During Serial Arguments: Connections with Individuals' Mental and Physical Well-Being." In M. T. Motley (Ed.). *Studies in Applied Interpersonal Communication* (pp. 97–120). Thousand Oaks, CA: Sage.

25. D. A. Infante, A. S. Rancer, & F. F. Jordan (1996). "Affirming & Nonaffirming Style, Dyad Sex, and the Perception of Argumentation andVerbal Aggression in an Interpersonal Dispute." *Human Communication Research, 22*, 315–334.

26. D. A. Infante, T. A. Chandler, & J. E. Rudd (1989). "Test of an Argumentative Skill Deficiency Model of Interspousal Violence." *Communication Monographs, 56*, 163–177.

27. M. M. Martin, C. M. Anderson, P. A. Burant, & K. Weber (1997). "Verbal Aggression in Sibling Relationships." *Communication Quarterly, 45*, 304–317.

28. J. W. Kassing & D. A. Infante (1999). "Aggressive Communication in the Coach-Athlete Relationship." *Communication Research Reports, 16*, 110–120.

29. M. J. Beatty, K. M. Valencic, J. E. Rudd, & J. A. Dobos (1999). "A 'Dark Side' of Communication Avoidance: Indirect Interpersonal Aggressiveness." *Communication Research Reports, 16*, 103–109.

30. B. K. Houston, M. A. Babyak, M. A. Chesney, & G. Black (1997). "Social Dominance and 22-Year All-Cause Mortality in Men." *Psychosomatic Medicine, 59*, 5–12.

31. "Marital Tiffs Spark Immune Swoon." *Science News* (September 4, 1993), 153.

32. D. Canary (2003). "Managing Interpersonal Conflict: A Model of Events Related to Strategic Choices." In J. O. Greene & B. R. Burleson (Eds.). *Handbook of Communication and Social Interaction Skills* (pp. 515–549). Mahwah, NJ: Erlbaum.

33. Hocker & Wilmot, *Interpersonal Conflict*; also, M. L. Knapp, L. L. Putnam, & L. J. Davis (1988). "Measuring Interpersonal Conflict in Organizations: Where Do We Go from Here?" *Management Communication Quarterly, 1*, 414–429.

34. C. S. Burggraf & A. L. Sillars (1987). "A Critical Examination of Sex Differences in Marital Communication." *Communication Monographs, 53*, 276–294.

35. J. Gottman & L. J. Krofoff (1989). "Marital Interaction and Satisfaction: A Longitudinal View." *Journal of Consulting and Clinical Psychology, 67*, 47–52; G. R. Pike & A. L. Sillars (1985). "Reciprocity of Marital Communication." *Journal of Social and Personal Relationships, 2*, 303–324.

36. M. A. Fitzpatrick (1977). "A Typological Approach to Communication in Relationships." In B. Rubin (Ed.). *Communication Yearbook 1*. New Brunswick, NJ: Transaction Books.

37. M. A. Fitzpatrick, J. Fey, C. Segrin, & J. L. Schiff (1993). "Internal Working Models of Relationships and Marital Communication." *Journal of Language and Social Psychology, 12*, 103–131. See also M. A. Fitzpatrick, S. Fallis, & L. Vance (1982). "Multifunctional Coding of Conflict Resolution Strategies in Marital Dyads." *Family Relations, 21*, 61–70.

38. J. Gottman (2006). "Why Marriages Fail." In K. M. Galvin & P. J. Cooper, *Making Connections: Readings in Relational Communication*, 4th ed. Los Angeles: Roxbury.

39. Wilmot & Hocker, op cit.

40. Cupach & Canary, op cit. p. 109.

41. Research summarized by D. Tannen (1989). *You Just Don't Understand: Women and Men in Conversation*. New York: William Morrow, pp. 152–157, 162–165.

42. N. H. Hess & E. H. Hagen (2006). *Evolution and Human Behaviour, 27*, 231–245; and M. K. Underwood (2003). *Social Aggression Among Girls*. New York: Guilford.

43. R. Wiseman (2003). *Queen Bees & Wannabes: Helping Your Daughter Survive Cliques, Gossip, Boyfriends, and Other Realities of Adolescence*. New York: Three Rivers Press.

44. M. J. Collier (1991). "Conflict Competence within African, Mexican, and Anglo-American Friendships." In S. Ting-Toomey & F. Korzenny (Eds.). *Cross-Cultural Interpersonal Communication*. Newbury Park, CA: Sage.

45. D. J. Canary, W. R. Cupach, & S. J. Messman (1995). *Relationship Conflict*. Newbury Park, CA: Sage.

46. See M. J. Papa & E. J. Natalle (1989). "Gender, Strategy Selection, and Discussion Satisfaction in Interpersonal Conflict." *Western Journal of Speech Communication, 52*, 260–272.

47. B. M. Gayle, R. W. Preiss, & M. A. Allen (2001). "A Meta-Analytic Interpretation of Intimate and Non-Intimate Interpersonal Conflict." In M. A. Allen, R. W. Preiss, B. M. Gayle, & N. Burrell (Eds.). *Interpersonal Communication: Advances through Meta-Analysis*. New York: Erlbaum.

48. M. Allen (1998). "Methodological Considerations When Examining a Gendered World." In D. Canary & K. Dindia (Eds.). *Handbook of Sex Differences and Similarities in Communication*. Mahwah, NJ: Erlbaum.

49. For a more detailed discussion of culture, conflict, and context, see W. B. Gudykunst & S. Ting-Toomey (1988). *Culture and Interpersonal Communication*. Newbury Park, CA: Sage, pp. 153–160.

50. See, for example, J. L. Holt & C. J. DeVore (2005). "Culture, Gender, Organizational Role, and Styles of Conflict Resolution: A Meta-Analysis." *International Journal of Intercultural Relations, 29,* 165–196.

51. See, for example, S. Ting-Toomey (1988). "Rhetorical Sensitivity Style in Three Cultures: France, Japan, and the United States." *Central States Speech Journal, 39,* 28–36.

52. K. Okabe (1987). "Indirect Speech Acts of the Japanese." In L. Kincaid (Ed.), *Communication Theory: Eastern and Western Perspectives* (pp. 127–136). San Diego, CA: Academic Press.

53. G. Fontaine (1991). "Cultural Diversity in Intimate Intercultural Relationships." In D. D. Cahn, *Intimates in Conflict: A Communication Perspective*. Hillsdale, NJ: Erlbaum.

54. Summarized in Tannen, *You Just Don't Understand,* p. 160.

55. See, for example, K. J. Beatty & J. C. McCroskey (1997). "It's in Our Nature: Verbal Aggressiveness as Temperamental Expression." *Communication Quarterly, 45,* 466–460.

56. J. G. Oetzel (1998). "Explaining Individual Communication Processes in Homogeneous and Heterogeneous Groups through Individualism-Collectivism and Self-Construal." *Human Communication Research, 25,* 202–224.

57. T. Gordon (1970). *Parent Effectiveness Training*. New York: Wyden, pp. 236–264.

58. R. Axelrod (1984). *The Evolution of Cooperation*. New York: Basic Books.

59. S. Mill (2004). "Addressing Stress Helps Minimize Potential of Burnout." *Computing Canada, 30,* 27.

60. S. M. Heathfield. "Personal Courage and Conflict Resolution at Work," http://humanresources.about.com/cs/conflictresolves/a/conflictcourage.htm. Accessed July 10, 2007.

61. See "The Cost of Rudeness," *Motivational Manager* (Nov. 1998), p. 9, as cited in P. H. Andrews and J. E. Baird Jr. (2000). *Communication for Business and the Professions,* Boston: McGraw-Hill, p. 230.

62. J. Suderman (2007). *Understanding Intercultural Communication*. Toronto, ON: Thomson Nelson, p. 288.

63. P. Hall (2005). "Interprofessional Teamwork: Professional Cultures as Barriers." *Journal of Professional Care, 19,* 188–196.

64. Smith, S. (2006). "Quitting Time: "Top 10 Reasons People Leave Their Jobs." *Training, 43,* 8.

65. Anton, C. (2009). "The Impact of Role Stress on Workers' Behaviour through Job Satisfaction and Organizational Commitment." *International Journal of Psychology, 44,* 187–194.

66. Lutgen-Sandvik, P. (2006). "Take This Job and…: Quitting and Other Forms of Resistance to Workplace Bullying." *Communication Monographs, 73,* 406–433.

67. P. Trunk (2006). "9 Tips for Quitting a Job Gracefully," http://blog.penelopetrunk.com/2006/08/20/9-tips-for-quitting-a-job-gracefully.Accessed August 3, 2009.

Index

control, 69, 105, 207, 222–23. *See also*
  power; self-control
controlling communication, 251*t*,
  252–53
convergence, 124
conversational narcissist, 131, 182
conversational style, 124, 134–35
coordination, 122
counterfeit communication, 97, 182,
  189, 207, 248
courtship behaviour, 47, 151, 158, 160
crazymaking, 276–77
criticism
  agreeing with critic, 263–64
  constructive, 198
  responding nondefensively to,
    259–64, 266
  seeking more information, 260–62
culture. *See also* diversity; ethnicity
  conflict style and, 284–85
  emotional expression influenced by, 91
  high-context, 78, 136–37, 137*t*
  intimacy influenced by, 224–25
  language and, 135–39
  low-context, 78, 136–37, 137*t*
  nonverbal communication influenced
    by, 153–56, 154*t*
  perception influenced by, 68–71
  relationships affected by, 217–18
  self-concept as reflection of, 40–41

D

debilitative emotions, 100–108
  fallacies, 102–6
  irrational thinking and, 102–8
  minimizing, 106–8
  sources of, 101–2
deception cues, 150, 151. *See also* lying
decode, 7, 10, 64, 152. *See also*
  interpretation
de-escalatory conflict spiral, 250, 280
defensive listening, 183
defensiveness, 250–54
  causes, 250–51
  certainty *versus* provisionalism, 254
  control *versus* problem orientation,
    252–53
  evaluation *versus* description, 252
  Gibb behaviour categories, 251*t*
  nondefensive response to criticism,
    259–64

preventing, 251–54
  strategy *versus* spontaneity, 253
  superiority *versus* equality, 253–54
deferential language, 125–26, 125*t*
denial, 216
denotative meaning, 121
depth, 211, 224, 227, 227*f*, 228*f*
descriptive communication, 251–52,
  251*t*, 255, 286–87
dharma, 139
dialectical tensions, 214–17
  managing, 216–17
  types, 214–16
differentiating stage, 210*f*, 212–13, 214
direct aggression, 276
disconfirming message, 246–47, 246*t*,
  248, 249
  ambiguous response, 247
  impersonal response, 247
  impervious responses, 246–47
  incongruous response, 247
  interrupting, 247
  irrelevant responses, 247
  tangential response, 247
disfluency, 162
dishonesty, 221, 253. *See also* lying
disinhibition, 16
disruptive language, 126–28
distance, 148*t*, 153, 166–67, 213, 221*t*
divergence, 124
diversity. *See also* culture
  listening, 186
  perception, 69, 82
  relationship building, 212
  self-concept, 39–40, 48
divorce alternative, 285
dual-process theory, 179–80
dyadic communication, 11, 227*t*
dysfunctional conflict, 288, 290

E

ego booster, 33–34
ego buster, 33–34
e-mail, 13
  acronyms used in, 124
  asynchronous nature of, 15
  convergence, 124
  emotional expression and, 94–95, 99
  flaming, 16, 94–95, 122
  identity management and, 52
  intimacy in, 225

1 Chapter in Review

LO¹ Assess the needs (physical, identity, social, and practical) that communicators are attempting to satisfy in a given situation or relationship.

It turns out that interpersonal communication is more than haphazard interaction. We communicate to satisfy physical needs (e.g., touch is therapeutic and comforting). Communication also helps us to discover what we're like as individuals (our identity needs) and to attain the pleasure, affection, and relaxation that come when our social needs are met. Finally, communication is practical: It helps us get a deal, meet a special someone, or find out where the nearest Tim Hortons is located.

LO² Apply the transactional communication model to a specific situation.

Before reading this chapter, you might have thought of interpersonal communication as two people sending messages back and forth (the linear model). But communication is more complicated than that. In transactional communication, communicators send and receive messages simultaneously, and their individual interpretations of messages are influenced by the degree to which they share an *environment* or by the external, physiological, or psychological noise they are experiencing.

LO³ Describe how the communication principles on pages 9–10 and misconceptions on pages 10–11 are evident in a specific situation.

Regardless of our situation, several communication principles hold true: Communication can be intentional or unintentional; it is both irreversible and unrepeatable; we cannot stop communicating because we continually send nonverbal cues; finally, all communication events have content and relational dimensions. Communication misconceptions are rampant: We tend to think that more communication is always better, that meanings are in words, that successful communication involves shared understanding, that people or events cause our reactions, or that communication solves all problems.

LO⁴ Describe the degree to which communication is qualitatively impersonal or interpersonal, as well as the consequences of these levels of interaction.

You can look at interpersonal communication from both a quantitative and a qualitative perspective. A quantitative definition involves two individuals (a dyad) in impersonal communication, like that between a clerk

LO¹

Instrumental goals Goals aimed at getting others to behave in desired ways.

LO²

Linear communication model A characterization of communication as a one-way event in which a message flows from sender to receiver.
Sender The creator of a message.
Encode The process of putting thoughts into symbols, most commonly words.
Message Information sent from a sender to a receiver.
Channel The medium through which a message passes from sender to receiver.
Receiver One who notices and attends to a message.
Decode The process in which a receiver attaches meaning to a message. Synonymous with *interpretation*.
Noise External, physiological, or psychological distractions that interfere with the accurate transmission and reception of a message.
Transactional communication model A characterization of communication as the simultaneous sending and receiving of messages in an ongoing, irreversible process.
Environment The field of experiences that lead a person to make sense of another's behaviour.
Interpersonal communication A continuous transactional process involving participants who occupy different but overlapping environments and create relationships through the exchange of messages, many of which are affected by external, physiological, and psychological noise.

LO³

Content message A message that communicates information about the subject being discussed.
Relational message A message that expresses the social relationship between two or more individuals.

LO⁴

Quantitative definition of interpersonal communication Impersonal communication, usually face to face, between two individuals.
Dyad Two people interacting.
Impersonal communication Behaviour that treats others as objects rather than as individuals.

and a customer. A qualitative view entails much more. Communication is more personal, with the people involved treating one another as unique and irreplaceable. This view of communication is also characterized by interdependence (the other's joy is our joy) and the disclosure of thoughts and feelings. Finally, individuals in qualitatively interpersonal relationships communicate for intrinsic rewards—that is, for the joy of it.

LO^5 Diagnose the effectiveness of various communication channels in a specific situation.

Communicating through text messages, e-mails, or tweets or by using social networking sites such as Facebook can be as effective as face-to-face communication. Electronic devices allow us to connect with people with similar interests or to interact with individuals anywhere in the world. They also help us to enhance our present relationships and to make new friends. But there are challenges: These messages are generally leaner than face-to-face communication in that they lack nonverbal cues, often making them difficult to interpret. We also tend to send messages without considering the consequences (disinhibition) and to forget about the permanent nature of the Internet. Those weekend photos might not appeal to a potential employer.

LO^6 Use the criteria on pages 17–20 to determine the level of communication competence in a specific instance or relationship.

Just as you learn new computer applications, so too can you learn new communication skills. For instance, communication competence depends on the situation and your relationship with the other person; thus, there's no "proper" way to communicate. But competent communicators do share some similarities. They possess a wide range of behaviours and choose the most appropriate depending on the context, the goal, and the other person. They also demonstrate empathy, cognitive complexity, and self-monitoring and have an understanding of intercultural communication. These strengths allow them to fare well in the workplace.

Chapter 1 Quiz Questions

1. A view of communication that suggests that communicators simultaneously send and receive messages best describes the _____ view of communication.
   a. linear
   b. transactional
   c. qualitative
   d. quantitative

2. You explain something to your friend and find out later that she completely misinterpreted your meaning. This example suggests that
   a. meaning is not in words
   b. communication is unrepeatable
   c. communication is unintentional
   d. more communication is not always better

3. Suggesting that interpersonal communication is defined by the worth, value, and uniqueness of the individuals best describes a _____ view of communication.
   a. linear
   b. transactional
   c. qualitative
   d. quantitative

4. Decoding is the same as
   a. cognitive complexity
   b. commitment
   c. interpretation
   d. encoding

5. Caitlyn always seems to know what to say and how to act. She can walk into a room, and within minutes she knows how to behave. It is obvious to you that Caitlyn
   a. is a high self-monitor
   b. has the ability to choose the most appropriate behaviour
   c. demonstrates cognitive complexity
   d. demonstrates empathy

6. You were checking out a classmate's Facebook page, and she posts more information about herself than anyone you know. She talks about her sex life, her arguments with parents and co-workers, even how she shortchanges people at work. This example could best be described as
   a. mediated communication
   b. content messages
   c. transactional communication
   d. disinhibition

7. Kristen enjoys meeting and interacting with people from other cultures. She finds it entertaining when she does something "wrong" because the gesture, norm, or behaviour tends to mean something very different than it does in her culture. Which attribute of intercultural communication competence does this example best demonstrate?
   a. motivation
   b. tolerance for ambiguity
   c. open-mindedness
   d. knowledge and skill

8. Maslow's hierarchy of needs is important to the study of interpersonal communication because
   a. we all have needs
   b. we can't understand our needs without communication
   c. communication can help us meet each need
   d. the need for communication is the sixth, "hidden" need

9. Integrated communicators express themselves in skilful ways because
   a. their communication is a self-conscious act
   b. they have more experience
   c. skills are basic to communication
   d. they have internalized effective behaviour

10. According to the chapter,
    a. while effective communication can help you get a job, it's not so important afterward
    b. there's no relationship between communication and employee satisfaction
    c. engineers don't have a need for effective communication because of the nature of their work
    d. communicating on the job can be challenging these days because four generations with four different value systems work side by side

Chapter 1 Questions for Thought and Discussion

1. Provide examples from your own life that explain how communication was used to satisfy your physical, identity, and social needs and to meet an instrumental goal.
2. Explain why the transactional model of interpersonal communication more accurately explains what happens when individuals communicate than does the linear model.
3. "Mediated communication is great for developing and maintaining relationships, but it is not so effective for communication." Do you agree or disagree with this statement? Provide support for your answer.
4. Your two friends will be teaching English as a second language in Japan next semester. What advice would you give them about intercultural communication?

Answers

1. b; 2. a; 3. c; 4. c; 5. a; 6. d; 7. c; 8. c; 9. d; 10. d

2 Communication and Identity: Creating and Presenting the Self

Chapter in Review

LO¹ Describe the relationship between self-concept, self-esteem, and communication.

Communication, self-concept, and self-esteem are interrelated in that self-concept is formed from the comments and evaluations that others make about you (reflected appraisal) and also from the comparisons you make between yourself and others (social comparison). Further, diversity, culture, and gender affect your identity. Once you have a sense of your basic characteristics, they, in turn, influence your self-esteem. Evaluating your qualities positively results in high self-esteem while negative evaluations result in low self-esteem. Self-esteem, regardless of its level, affects how you communicate with others.

LO² Explain how self-fulfilling prophecies shape the self-concept and influence communication.

Self-imposed and other-imposed self-fulfilling prophecies greatly influence self-concept and, hence, communication. It works like this: Once you have an expectation of yourself ("I'm not smart enough to get this job"), you behave accordingly (you act uninterested and timid during the interview), which makes that expectation come to pass (you don't get the job). When the expected event occurs, it not only influences your self-concept but reinforces the original notion ("I knew I couldn't do it—I'm such a loser").

LO³ Demonstrate how the principles on pages 44–45 can be used to change the self-concept and, hence, communication.

You're not stuck with your self-concept, and changing it could help you feel better. But you'll need the will to change (the self-concept resists change, so it's going to require work), and you'll need to have realistic expectations of yourself. You'll also need to develop the skills to change, which you can learn by understanding how communication works and by watching how competent communicators act. It's worth the effort. Changing your self-concept can make you feel more positive about yourself, which will affect your communication with others and also make them feel more positively about you.

LO⁴ Compare and contrast the perceived self and the presenting self as they relate to identity management.

We typically show others a public self in order to enhance relationships, gain compliance, save face, or explore new areas of ourselves. We do this by creating multiple identities (e.g., student, worker, sibling, musician) and managing those identities. Identity management can be deliberate or unconscious, but it must also be collaborative in that we

LO¹

Self-concept The relatively stable set of perceptions individuals hold about themselves.

Self-esteem The part of the self-concept that involves evaluations of self-worth.

Personality Characteristic ways that you think and behave across a variety of situations.

Reflected appraisal The theory that a person's self-concept matches the way the person believes others regard him or her.

Significant other A person whose opinion is important enough to affect one's self-concept strongly.

Social comparison Evaluation of oneself in terms of or by comparison to others.

Reference groups Groups against which we compare ourselves, thereby influencing our self-concept and self-esteem.

Cognitive conservatism The tendency to seek and attend to information that conforms to an existing self-concept.

LO²

Self-fulfilling prophecy A prediction or expectation of an event that makes the outcome more likely to occur than would otherwise have been the case.

Self-imposed prophecy Occurs when your own expectations influence your behaviour.

Other-imposed prophecy Occurs when your actions may be governed by the expectations that others have of you.

LO⁴

Identity management The communication strategies people use to influence how others view them.

Perceived self The person you believe yourself to be in moments of honest self-examination. It may be identical with or different from the presenting and ideal selves.

Presenting self The image a person presents to others. It may be identical with or different from the perceived and ideal selves.

need others to support us in it. It also varies according to the situation. However, not everyone manages identity to the same degree. High self-monitors engage in identity management more often than do low self-monitors.

LO⁵ Describe the role that identity management plays in both face-to-face and mediated relationships.

In face-to-face communication, you manage your identity through your manner, nonverbal gestures, and appearance (e.g., clothing, hairstyle, body art). Even the car you drive or how your room or office cubicle looks influences your identity. Identity management is even more prominent on the Internet. Many people change their appearance, personality, age, or interests, and some take on entirely new personas. It is important to be aware of what your social networking sites convey about you.

Chapter 2 Quiz Questions

1. Basing our self-concept on messages that significant others may have given us is what occurs in
   a. social comparison
   b. self-matching
   c. reflected appraisal
   d. distorted feedback

2. A person who is always putting you down is referred to in your text as
   a. a psychological influence
   b. an ego buster
   c. a high self-monitor
   d. an ego booster

3. Tingting is a woman in good physical shape. She sees herself as unfit, but she hangs out with university athletes. This is an example of
   a. social comparison
   b. self-matching
   c. reflected appraisal
   d. distorted feedback

4. "Cipher in the Snow" is included in your text to illustrate
   a. the importance of self-appraisal
   b. the impact of dishonest self-identity
   c. the way people construct multiple identities
   d. the impact of significant others on self-concept

5. In North American society, we are generally taught to be successful at all costs, to stand out from the crowd, and to make our "mark." This is typical of which type of culture?
   a. collectivistic
   b. high context
   c. low context
   d. individualistic

6. The relatively stable set of perceptions you hold about yourself, or how you see yourself, is referred to as
   a. reflected appraisal
   b. cognitive complexity
   c. self-concept
   d. subjectivity

7. All of the following are methods you could use to make your self-concept more realistic except
   a. sharing your perception of yourself with a friend
   b. trying to engage in more accurate self-talk
   c. making an effort to recognize more "ego-buster" messages
   d. paying less attention to your past and more attention to your present behaviours

8. When you pay attention to your behaviour in relationships, you are
   a. unlikely to pay attention to others
   b. too uptight
   c. probably ego-driven
   d. self-monitoring

9. What is the relationship between identity management and self-monitoring?
   a. Identity management makes people more aware of themselves so that they can be more effective self-monitors.
   b. Self-monitoring makes people more aware of their identity management.
   c. Identity management reduces the need for self-monitoring.
   d. Identity management and self-monitoring are not connected.

10. Many students travelling abroad display the Canadian maple leaf on their backpacks or jackets. This is an example of identity management by
    a. appearance
    b. manner
    c. setting
    d. symbol

Chapter 2 Questions for Thought and Discussion

1. Describe two recent changes that took place in your self-concept and explain the role that communication played in these changes.
2. Explain the obvious and more subtle ways in which you manage your identity on social networking sites. Why do you do this?
3. Provide examples of how a person's private and public selves become blended on the Internet and discuss how mediated communication in general can violate a person's privacy.
4. Explain the role that identity management plays in today's politicians. Provide lots of examples.
5. Describe how identity management could be an effective tool in the workplace. Offer several examples.

Answers

1. c; 2. b; 3. a; 4. d; 5. d; 6. c; 7. c; 8. d; 9. b; 10. a

Notes

3 Perception: What You See Is What You Get

Chapter in Review

LO¹ Describe how the processes of selection, organization, interpretation, and negotiation shape communication in a given situation.

Your communication depends on how you "size up" a situation, or what you perceive. First, you select or tune in to something, typically things that are intense, repetitious, or related to your motives (I'm late, so I notice a cab on a crowded, busy city street). Then the stimuli are organized based on perceptual schemata such as physical, role, interaction, psychological, or membership constructs. This brings you to interpretation, and finally, you negotiate your story with others so that your narrative jives with theirs.

LO² Explain how the influences on perception affect communication in a specific situation.

Several factors influence how any situation is perceived. Physiological influences include the senses, age, health, fatigue, and hunger. Any one of these can greatly affect how you "see" a situation. So too can psychological challenges such as having ADHD. Perception and communication are also affected by culture, diversity, and social roles. For instance, gender, occupation, and your relational roles all shape your interpretation of any event. It's not hard to see how and why two individuals might see a situation differently.

LO³ Analyze how the common tendencies in perception distort your perceptions of another person and, hence, your communication. Use this information to present a more accurate alternative set of perceptions.

While we perceive the world differently, we share some common perceptual tendencies. For instance, we tend to judge ourselves more charitably than we judge others (self-serving bias). We also cling to first impressions and assume that others are similar to us. Finally, we are influenced by the obvious: If it's not right in front of us, we tend to overlook it. Once we are aware of these tendencies, we can rethink any situation to uncover a more realistic sense of what's really happening. This can only enhance our communication with others.

LO¹

Perception The process whereby we assign meaning to the world around us.

Selection The first stage in the perception process, in which some data are chosen to attend to and others to ignore.

Organization The stage in the perception process that involves arranging data in a meaningful way.

Perceptual schemata Cognitive frameworks that allow individuals to organize perceptual data that they have selected from the environment. These include physical, role, interaction, psychological, and membership constructs.

Stereotyping Categorizing individuals according to a set of characteristics assumed to belong to all members of a group.

Punctuation The process of determining the causal order of events.

Interpretation The process of attaching meaning to sense data; synonymous with *decode*.

Negotiation What occurs between and among people as they influence one another's perceptions and try to achieve a shared perspective.

Narratives The stories we use to describe our personal worlds.

LO²

Ethnocentrism The attitude that one's own culture is superior to others.

Androgynous Possessing both feminine and masculine traits.

LO³

Attribution The process of attaching meaning to behaviour.

Self-serving bias The tendency to interpret and explain information in a way that casts the perceiver in the most favourable manner.

Halo effect The tendency to form an overall positive impression on the basis of one positive characteristic.

LO⁴

Perception checking A three-part method for verifying the accuracy of interpretations, including a description of the behaviour, two possible interpretations, and a request for clarification of the interpretation.
Empathy The ability to project oneself into another person's point of view so as to experience the other's thoughts and feelings.
Sympathy Compassion for another's situation.

LO⁵

Pillow method A way of understanding an issue from several perspectives, rather than with an egocentric "I'm right and you're wrong" attitude.

LO⁴ Demonstrate how you might use the skill of perception checking in a significant relationship.

Perception checking allows you to check interpretations. It has three phases: State the other person's behaviour, offer two possible interpretations, and ask for clarification. If a good friend rushes out of the room, later on you could say, "When you left the room this afternoon (state behaviour), I didn't know if you were sick or if I had said something that bothered you (offer two possible interpretations). What happened (request clarification)?" Offered with the appropriate nonverbal communication and sensitivity to cultural rules, the other person won't get defensive, and you'll learn what's going on.

LO⁵ Enhance your cognitive complexity by applying the "pillow method" in a significant disagreement. Explain how your expanded view of this situation might affect your communication with the other(s) involved.

The pillow method can foster empathy when we disagree with someone. Using a real-life disagreement with a roommate, review the problem from the following five positions: position 1: "I'm right and my roommate is wrong"; position 2: "My roommate's right and I'm wrong"; position 3: "We are both right and both wrong"; position 4: "The issue isn't important"; and position 5: "There is truth in all perspectives." Expanding your view of the problem will positively affect your communication with your roommate.

Chapter 3 Quiz Questions

1. The stages of the perception process are
   a. selection, organization, interpretation, and negotiation
   b. stereotyping, punctuation, perceptual schemata
   c. selection, punctuation, organization, interpretation
   d. physical, role, interaction

2. The recognition of a *"figure"* as standing out from a *"ground"* of other stimuli takes place during what phase of the perception process?
   a. ideation
   b. selection
   c. verification
   d. organization

3. Kristen found that her social worker was compassionate and caring. What type of construct is Kristen using?
   a. interaction
   b. membership
   c. psychological
   d. role

4. Nonverbal congruency is extremely important in which of the following?
   a. the perception process
   b. perception checking
   c. the pillow method
   d. all of the above

5. All of the following are attribution errors except
   a. we tend to judge others more charitably than we judge ourselves
   b. we tend to assume others are similar to us
   c. we cling to first impressions
   d. all of the above are perceptual errors described in Chapter 3

6. When someone botches a job, you think that she or he was not listening or trying hard enough to get it right. When you botch a job, you think the directions were not clear or there was not enough time to do it. This type of attitude exemplifies
   a. that we are influenced by the obvious
   b. the halo effect
   c. the self-serving bias
   d. that we tend to assume others are similar to us

7. How could you improve this perception checking statement: "When you gave me an F on my essay, I figured you hated me. Right?"
   a. describe behaviour
   b. give another interpretation
   c. request clarification
   d. the perception checking statement is fine the way it is

8. Individuals with _____ are able to describe situations more thoroughly, have better communication within their marriages, and are more persuasive.
   a. empathy
   b. sympathy
   c. self-serving bias
   d. cognitive complexity

9. Communicating to a friend how sorry you are about the breakup of his or her romance is an example of
   a. sympathy
   b. empathy
   c. role taking
   d. perception checking

10. When you can't find any reason to accept the behaviour of another person, it can be helpful to
    a. use perception checking
    b. examine your own self-concept
    c. use a different communication channel
    d. use the pillow method

Chapter 3 Questions for Thought and Discussion

1. Provide examples of how culture and diversity affect the perception process.
2. Describe a subculture to which you belong. Give examples of and explain several misunderstandings you have had with members of another subculture. How do these misunderstandings reflect your view of that subculture?
3. Develop a situation in which one person is confused about another's behaviour, and then explain what the person could do to implement the perception checking process. Write out the things the person should say and indicate the part of the perception checking process that goes with each statement.
4. Select a conflict you have with another person and apply the pillow method.

Answers

1. a; 2. d; 3. c; 4. b; 5. a; 6. c; 7. b; 8. d; 9. a; 10. d

Notes

4 Emotions: Feeling, Thinking, and Communicating

Chapter in Review

LO¹ Describe how the four components listed on pages 88–89 affect your emotions and, hence, your communication.

Emotions and communication have several components. Physiological factors (e.g., increased heart rate, increased adrenaline secretions, pupil dilation) alert us that we're having an emotional moment. Nonverbal factors (e.g., changes in gestures, vocal tone, trembling) can be either a reaction to an emotion or a cause of an emotional state. But it's the cognitive interpretations and how symptoms are labelled that affect our emotions. Trembling hands could be viewed as fear or excitement. In some cases, however, the only way to express deep, complex feelings is through verbal expression.

LO² Describe how the influences on emotional expression listed on pages 90–94 have affected your communication in an important relationship.

Several influences affect emotional expression. In terms of personality, extroverts report more positive emotions than do people with neurotic personalities. Expressing negative emotions is discouraged in collectivistic cultures. Even gender has an impact, supporting the unexpressive male and more expressive female stereotypes. Men express emotions with women, married individuals recognize the emotions of their partners, and women are better than men at interpreting emotions. Social conventions discourage emotional expression, and hence, fear of self-disclosure is common. Finally, emotions are transferred from one person to another—known as emotional contagion.

LO³ Apply the guidelines for effectively communicating emotions (pages 95–100) in an important situation.

Constructive emotional expression can be learned. Being able to identify and label your emotions and recognizing the differences between feeling, talking, and acting are helpful. But you don't have to act on every feeling. Expand your emotional vocabulary and recognize that if you have multiple and/or conflicting emotions at the same time, you'll need to express each one. You'll also have to select the proper time to express feelings and to take responsibility for your feelings and be mindful of the communication channel you select.

LO¹

Emotional intelligence The ability to understand and manage one's own emotions and be sensitive to others' feelings.

Reappraisal Rethinking the meaning of emotionally charged events in ways that alter their emotional impact.

Primary emotions Basic emotions such as anger, joy, fear, and sadness.

Mixed emotions Feeling two or more conflicting emotions at the same time.

LO²

Emotion labour The notion that managing and even suppressing emotions is both appropriate and necessary.

Emotional contagion The process by which emotions are transferred from one person to another

LO⁴

Facilitative emotions Emotions that contribute to effective functioning.

Debilitative emotions Emotions that prevent a person from functioning effectively.

Rumination Dwelling persistently on negative thoughts that, in turn, intensify negative feelings.

Self-talk The process of thinking. On some level, self-talk occurs as a person interprets another's behaviour.

Fallacies Debilitative feelings that come from accepting irrational thoughts.

Fallacy of perfection The irrational belief that a worthwhile communicator should be able to handle every situation with complete confidence and skill.

Fallacy of approval The irrational belief that it is vital to win the approval of virtually every person a communicator deals with.

Fallacy of shoulds The inability to distinguish between what is and what should be.

Fallacy of overgeneralization Irrational beliefs in which conclusions (usually negative) are based on limited evidence or communicators exaggerate their shortcomings.

Fallacy of causation The irrational belief that emotions are caused by others and not by the person who experiences them.

Fallacy of helplessness The irrational belief that satisfaction in life is determined by forces beyond one's control.

Fallacy of catastrophic expectations The irrational belief that the worst possible outcome will probably occur.

LO⁴ Identify and dispute the fallacies (pages 100–108) that are creating debilitative emotions in an important situation. Explain how more rational thinking can lead to more constructive communication.

Debilitative emotions emerge from irrational thoughts, referred to as fallacies. The fallacy of perfection holds that you communicate perfectly in every situation, a feat that is humanly impossible. The fallacy of approval is based on the idea of seeking the approval of everyone, but this too is not achievable. The fallacy of shoulds focuses on how things "should" be, yet it is unreasonable to expect that the world operate according to your whims. With overgeneralization, conclusions are based on limited information, or shortcomings are exaggerated. Either way, positive attributes are ignored or minimized. Causation occurs when you believe that others cause emotions, but emotions are based on individual interpretations. Helplessness is the irrational belief that satisfaction in life is determined by forces beyond your control. But looking more closely, many "can't" statements are actually "won't" statements. Those believing in the fallacy of catastrophic expectations assume that the worst possible outcome will occur. In many cases, self-fulfilling prophecy drives outcomes. Irrational thinking is minimized when you monitor your emotional reactions, note the activating event, record your self-talk, and reappraise your irrational beliefs.

Chapter 4 Quiz Questions

1. The mood of the party was pleasant but subdued. Then Roddy arrived. He was animated, upbeat and outgoing; before long, most of the people at the party were laughing and joking. Roddy's impact on the party is an example of
   a. emotional contagion
   b. empathy
   c. presenting self
   d. social values

2. Your text tells you that you should
   a. express all your emotions to your friends
   b. try to recognize your emotions
   c. be glad you have debilitative emotions
   d. express only positive emotions

3. Two things that distinguish facilitative feelings from debilitative ones are
   a. emotions and behaviour
   b. longevity and interpretation
   c. intention and intensity
   d. intensity and duration

4. Subscribing to the fallacy of catastrophic expectations can lead to
   a. self-fulfilling prophecies
   b. erroneous perception checking
   c. reflected appraisals
   d. physical noise

5. The statement "Bob never has a good word to say about anyone" is an example of the fallacy of
   a. shoulds
   b. approval
   c. overgeneralization
   d. causation

6. In individualistic cultures, people are more likely to
   a. keep their emotions to themselves
   b. share emotions only with those they are especially close to
   c. feel it is their right to tell others how they feel about things
   d. express emotions such as dislike

7. Debilitative feelings that come from irrational thoughts are referred to as
   a. perceptual difficulties
   b. cognitive interpretations
   c. fallacies
   d. impression management

8. Which of the following is not a step used to minimize debilitative emotions?
   a. note the activating event
   b. engage in identity management
   c. monitor your emotional responses
   d. dispute your irrational beliefs

9. You attend a work social function, and after interacting with your boss, you have changed your interpretations of her. At work she is rushed, unfriendly, and demanding, but in a social setting, she is funny, pleasant, and good natured. This exemplifies
   a. mixed emotions
   b. emotional contagion
   c. social conventions
   d. reappraisal

10. Which of the following does the text offer as a guideline for expressing your emotions?
    a. the sooner a feeling is shared, the better
    b. try to avoid sharing negative feelings whenever possible
    c. let others know that they have caused you to feel a certain way
    d. share mixed feelings when appropriate

Know Your Fallacies

Insert the fallacy that best fits the following statements:
a. Basing a belief on a limited amount of evidence or exaggerating shortcomings: fallacy of _____
b. Working under the assumption that if something bad can possibly happen, it will: fallacy of _____
c. The inability to distinguish between what is and what should be: fallacy of _____
d. The notion that a worthwhile communicator can handle every situation with complete confidence and skill: fallacy of _____
e. A belief that emotions are caused by others, not by our own self-talk: fallacy of _____
f. The idea that satisfaction in life is determined by forces beyond our control: fallacy of _____
g. Feeling a need for the approval of everyone: fallacy of h. Believing that you have to handle every situation with complete confidence and skill _____

Chapter 4 Questions for Thought and Discussion

1. How successful are you at recognizing the emotional messages that are communicated via e-mail, instant messaging, social media sites, and so forth? How can this chapter help you to become more insightful when reading or responding to messages?

2. Read the case study below and then answer the questions provided.

> Matt and Sarah have been dating for over a year. They love each other and are considering marriage, but each person has at least one big reservation about the other. Matt thinks Sarah is moody. It seems that one minute she's "up" and happy, and the next she's criticizing everything about him. Sarah finds Matt difficult because he seems to keep everything inside. She wants him to tell her in detail when he feels good and bad, but he either says nothing or responds in a few words.

   a. What do you think is the appropriate level of emotional expression between committed partners? Do you think either Matt or Sarah should change the way they express their emotions? Why or why not?

   b. Do you think that Matt and Sarah accurately perceive each other's emotional state? What influences—culture, gender, social conventions, social roles, emotional contagion, fear of self-disclosure—might be affecting their emotional expression?

   c. Explain any irrational fallacies that might be operating within this relationship.

   d. What would you recommend that Sarah and Matt do about their emotional expressions to improve the quality of their relationship?

3. Identify and provide examples of the three fallacies that are most prevalent in your life. What harm can each one cause if you fail to dispute it?

4. Explain and provide examples of how you use the guidelines for expressing feelings in your life. Which ones do you do well and/or often? Where do you need further work? Give examples.

Answers

1. a; 2. b; 3. d; 4. a; 5. c; 6. c; 7. c; 8. b; 9. d; 10. d

Fallacies

a. overgeneralization; b. catastrophic expectations; c. shoulds; d. causation; e. helplessness; f. approval; g. affection

5 Language: Barrier and Bridge

Chapter in Review

LO¹ Analyze a real or potential misunderstanding in terms of semantic or pragmatic rules.

Semantics often cause misunderstandings. For instance, equivocal misunderstandings occur because many words have more than one meaning, and relative language gets its meaning only through comparison. With static evaluation, the verb *is* suggests absolute truth and unchangeability. And then there's abstract language, which is vague at best, while behavioural language is very specific. Pragmatic rules suggest that language is interpreted depending on context. Clearly, with so many semantic variables coupled with the pragmatic rules, it's easy to see how even simple statements can be misunderstood.

LO² Describe how principles in the section titled "The Impact of Language" operate in your life.

Language affects perception. For instance, people make judgments about others based on whether their name is trendy or old-fashioned. Whether a professor is referred to as Miss, Ms., or Dr. affects how others perceive her credibility. Some individuals establish affiliation with groups by engaging in convergence—that is, using similar vocabulary or slang. Avoiding the use of deferential language markers such as hedges, tag questions, hesitations, or intensifiers can make a person seem more powerful.

LO³ Rephrase disruptive statements in less inflammatory terms.

Fact–opinion confusion occurs when opinions and assumptions (inferences) are treated as facts. Instead, you should use perception checking or disclaimers such as "In my opinion..." Rather than using emotive language that announces your opinion, use descriptive statements. Because "it" statements distance you from your opinions, take responsibility by using "I" statements. "But" statements cancel preceding messages, so it's better to state the central idea without the "but." While using questions may be a way to be tactful or to hide something, speaking up for yourself is also important.

LO⁴ Recast "you" statements into "I" or "we" statements to reflect your responsibility for the message content.

While "you" statements express judgment of others, "I" statements demonstrate responsibility. "I" statements have four elements that can be stated in any order: (1) the other person's behaviour; (2) your interpretations; (3) your feelings; and (4) the consequences that the other person's behaviour has for you. To avoid overusing "I" statements, make "we" statements that suggest concern and responsibility for both parties. Communicators generally receive I/we combinations (e.g., "I think that we...") more favourably.

LO¹

Semantic rules Rules that govern the meaning of language, as opposed to its structure.
Equivocal language Words, word orders, phrases, or expressions that have more than one commonly accepted definition.
Relative words Words that gain their meaning through comparison.
Static evaluation The tendency to view people or relationships as unchanging.
Abstract language Language that is vague and unclear.
Behavioural language Language that refers to specific things that people do or say.
Abstraction ladder A range of more to less abstract terms describing an event or object.
Syntactic rules Rules that govern the way symbols can be arranged, as opposed to the meanings of those symbols.
Pragmatic rules Linguistic rules that help communicators understand how messages may be used and interpreted in a given context.

LO²

Convergence The process of adapting one's speech style to match that of others with whom the communicator wants to identify.
Divergence Speech mannerisms that emphasize a communicator's differences from others.
Deferential language A language style in which speakers defer to listeners by using hedges, hesitations, intensifiers, polite forms, tag questions, and disclaimers.

LO³

Inference A conclusion that is arrived at from an interpretation of evidence.
Emotive language Language that conveys the speaker's attitude rather than simply offering an objective description.
"It" statements Statements that replace the personal pronoun *I* with the less immediate word *it*, often with the effect of reducing the speaker's acceptance of responsibility for the statements.

"I" language A statement that describes the speaker's reaction to another person's behaviour without making judgments about the behaviour's worth.
"But" statements Statements in which the word *but* cancels out the expression that preceded it.

LO⁴

"You" language A statement that expresses or implies a judgment of the other person.
"We" statement A statement that implies that the issue is the concern and responsibility of both the sender and receiver of a message.

LO⁵

Low-context cultures Cultures that use language primarily to express thoughts, feelings, and ideas as clearly and logically as possible.
High-context cultures Cultures that avoid direct use of language, relying instead on the context of a message to convey meaning.
Linguistic relativism The notion that the worldview of a culture is shaped and reflected by the language its members speak.
Sapir–Whorf hypothesis This hypothesis suggests that the language we speak affects how we interact with the world around us.

LO⁵ Analyze how gender and/or cultural differences may affect the quality of interaction.

Women discuss relationships, family, health, food, clothing, men, and women. Men discuss music, current events, sports, business, and other men. Men find same-sex talk enjoyable; women see same-sex talk as the essence of the relationship. Men in mixed-sex groups interrupt more and use a direct, non-deferential style while women are supportive, ask more questions, show empathy, and use a deferential style. Culture also affects interaction. For example, in high-context cultures, language is indirect, and in low-context cultures like Canada, language is direct. When translated into different languages, words can have different connotations.

Chapter 5 Quiz Questions

1. "I have to powder my nose," "I'm going to the little girls' room," and "Kevin has gone to the great beyond" are all examples of
   a. equivocation
   b. high-level abstraction language
   c. relative language
   d. euphemisms

2. In a low-context language culture, you will notice
   a. indirect expression of opinions
   b. that the use of silence is admired
   c. less reliance on explicit verbal messages
   d. that self-expression is valued

3. Terms like *mailman, fireman, businessman,* and *chairman* are known as
   a. inclusive language
   b. man-linked terminology
   c. heterosexist language
   d. disruptive language

4. Which of the following is the highest-level abstraction?
   a. complaining
   b. complaining about chores
   c. complaining about my housework
   d. reminding me about chores I haven't done

5. When we use the verb is in describing a person, we are engaging in
   a. euphemisms
   b. static evaluation
   c. equivocation
   d. deferential language

6. When you use a deferential language style, you
   a. use hedges, hesitations, intensifiers, and tag questions
   b. avoid hedges, hesitations, intensifiers, and tag questions
   c. are thought to be more competent, intelligent, and dynamic
   d. usually show sympathy and empathy for the listener

7. The Sapir–Whorf hypothesis postulates that
   a. all languages share the same pragmatic rules
   b. language operates as a perceptual schema
   c. language patterns reflect and shape an individual's power
   d. men and women use language for different purposes

8. When it comes to language and gender, which of the following is <u>not</u> true?
   a. men use language to get the job done while women use language to develop and maintain relationships
   b. some scholars say gender differences are highly significant while others say they are not
   c. males make an effort to keep conversations going
   d. female and male supervisors pretty much act the same when they're on the job

9. If you take an "easy" class your friend recommended and find it "hard," you have had semantic problems due to
   a. euphemistic language
   b. relative words
   c. equivocal words
   d. high-level abstraction

10. When we treat something as a fact when it is not, we are using
    a. emotive language
    b. relative language
    c. an inference
    d. low-level abstraction

Know Your Terms

Match the following definitions with the terms below.
1. Way in which languages differ from culture to culture. _____
2. Altering your speech to match that of someone with whom you wish to identify. _____
3. Language that conveys a speaker's judgment of another. _____
4. Rules that help us understand how messages may be interpreted. _____
5. Rules that govern the way symbols can be arranged. _____
6. Female equivalent of Mr. _____
7. Using pauses, tag questions, polite forms. _____
8. Speaking in a way that emphasizes differences. _____
9. Where language is used to express thoughts clearly. _____
10. Rules that govern the meaning of language, as opposed to its structure. _____
11. Language that conveys a person's reaction to another. _____

Mrs.	inference	euphemism
secondary emotions	linguistic relativism	convergence
syntactic rules	emotive language	"I" language
low-context culture	deferential language	semantic rules
Miss	Ms.	high-context cultures
deferential language	linguistic relativism	Sapir–Whorf hypothesis
pragmatic rules	divergence	succinctness and formality
"you" language	"it" statements	

Chapter 5 Questions for Thought and Discussion

1. Make a list of the words associated with technology (iPod, Skype, Twitter, blog, etc.) that did not exist when you were a child. Find other examples of how your language differs from your parents' and then explain how misunderstandings occur as a result of such differences. Finally, develop a list of some words or language that your grandparents use and indicate what they mean.
2. Should married women retain their last names or change their names to their husband's? How does this concept apply to gay and lesbian couples? Share your answers with the class.

3. How do the user names you've selected for various online sites reflect your identity?
4. Describe what abstract language is and how you use unnecessarily abstract language that causes communication problems. Give at least five examples. Tell how you could lower the level of abstraction in each of the examples you have given or explain why the higher-level abstraction is justified and relationally beneficial.
5. Describe why and how a person might make his or her language style more "powerful." What are the pros and cons of using this type of language? Explain any gender differences that may be evident in relation to the use of powerful and powerless (deferential) language.
6. Your friend will soon be going to Korea to teach English as a second language. What information would you provide about the use of language in general in countries such as Japan, China, and Korea? Make sure to use the terminology presented in the chapter.

Answers

1. d; 2. d; 3. b; 4. a; 5. b; 6. a; 7. b; 8. c; 9. b; 10. c

Matching

1. succinctness and formality; 2. convergence; 3. "you" language; 4. pragmatic rules; 5. syntactic rules; 6. Ms.; 7. deferential language; 8. divergence; 9. low-context culture; 10. semantic rules; 11. "I" language

6 Nonverbal Communication: Messages beyond Words

Chapter in Review

LO¹ Explain the defining characteristics of nonverbal communication as described on pages 146–156.

Good nonverbal communicators are thought to possess emotional intelligence and socioemotional well-being. They're considered popular, persuasive, attractive, and successful in careers and romance. All non-verbal behaviour has communicative value and conveys emotions and relational messages well. Nonverbal communication is used to repeat, complement, substitute, accent, and regulate verbal messages as well as contradict them. Nonverbal indicators of lying are called deception cues, but we're not good at picking up on them. Finally, nonverbal com-munication is ambiguous and can have several meanings.

LO² List and offer examples of each type of nonverbal message introduced in this chapter.

Facing someone directly or being at a right angle to another are examples of body orientation, while slumping or sitting up straight are examples of posture. Gestures include illustrators (e.g., making move-ments to signify a ball or an airplane), emblems (e.g., okay or thumbs-up signs) and adaptors or manipulators (e.g., touching hair, tapping a pen). Many adaptors are similar to courtship gestures—those indicators sug-gesting an interest in someone. Facial expressions include pouting lips or an open mouth. The eyes are also expressive and send a variety of messages.

LO³ Recognize how individual factors such as voice, touch, and physical attractiveness are related to nonverbal communication.

Emphasis can change a sentence's meaning, tone of voice can create sarcasm, and using disfluencies (e.g., "um" or "ah") can reduce cred-ibility. People are more comfortable with and more likely to comply with speakers who speak at a similar pace as they do. Women tend to raise their pitch at the end of sentences. Touch can signify a variety of rela-tionships, and its intensity depends on what's being touched, the length and pressure of the touch, movement after contact, and so on. Touch is related positively to power, persuasion, and health. Physical attractive-ness is positively related to popularity, higher grades, hiring, promotion, performance evaluation, intelligence, and so forth. Clothing conveys economic level, education level, social background, trustworthiness, moral character, and status.

LO¹

Nonverbal communication Messages expressed by other than linguistic means.
Repeating Nonverbal behaviours that duplicate the content of a verbal message.
Complementing Nonverbal behaviour that reinforces a verbal message.
Substituting Nonverbal behaviour that takes the place of a verbal message.
Accenting Nonverbal behaviours that emphasize part of a verbal message.
Regulating A function of nonverbal communication in which nonverbal cues control the flow of verbal communication between and among individuals.
Contradicting Nonverbal behaviour that is inconsistent with a verbal message.
Mixed messages Situations in which a person's words are incongruent with his or her nonverbal behaviour.
Leakage Nonverbal behaviours that reveal information a communicator does not disclose verbally.
Deception cues Nonverbal behaviours that signal the untruthfulness of a verbal message.

LO²

Kinesics The study of body position and motion.
Body orientation The degree to which we face toward or away from someone with our body, feet, and head.
Gestures Motions of the body, usually hands or arms, that have communicative value.
Illustrators Nonverbal behaviours that accompany and support verbal messages.
Emblems Deliberate nonverbal behaviours with precise meanings known to virtually all members of a cultural group.
Adaptors Movements in which one part of the body grooms, massages, rubs, holds, fidgets, pinches, picks, or otherwise manipulates another part. Also known as *manipulators*.
Microexpression Brief facial expression.

LO³

Paralanguage Nonlinguistic means of vocal expression: rate, pitch, tone, and so on.
Disfluency A nonlinguistic verbalization; for example, stammering or saying "um," "er," or "ah."
Haptics The study of touching.

LO⁴

Proxemics The study of how people and animals use space.
Intimate distance One of anthropologist Edward Hall's four distance zones, ranging from skin contact to 45 centimetres.
Personal distance One of Hall's four distance zones, ranging from 45 centimetres to 1.2 metres.
Social distance One of Hall's four distance zones, ranging from 1.2 to 3.6 metres.
Public distance One of Hall's four distance zones, extending outward from 3.6 metres.
Territoriality The notion that an area is claimed by an individual or a group of individuals.
Chronemics The study of how humans use and structure time.

LO⁴ Become more aware of how external factors such as distance, environment, and time are related to nonverbal communication.

You can tell how people feel about one another by noting the distance between them. Edward T. Hall describes four spatial zones: intimate, personal, social, and public. Territoriality refers to the area claimed by an individual or a group of people, and those with more status have more territory. Physical environment both sends messages and influences communication (workers are more positive and energetic in beautiful rooms). Even chronemics sends messages. Lower-status people often must wait for higher-status individuals, and the amount of time a person spends with another relates to the importance of the relationship.

LO⁵ Improve your nonverbal communication in the workplace.

Just landing a job requires certain nonverbal communication (e.g., dressing appropriately, shaking hands, leaning forward, using appropriate facial expressions, mirroring the interviewer's posture). To be successful on the job, use eye contact to signal interest, move out from behind your desk to interact with others, try to be aware of your facial expressions and how your paralanguage might be interpreted by others, increase your awareness of the nonverbal messages of others, and broaden your intercultural skills.

Chapter 6 Quiz Questions

1. Which of the following is not related to nonverbal communication?
   a. your paralanguage
   b. your gender
   c. the language you speak
   d. the rate and speed of your voice

2. When you become aware of nonverbal messages in your everyday life, you should interpret them as
   a. reliable facts
   b. clues that need to be verified
   c. ways of knowing what a person is thinking
   d. ways to understand meanings

3. The nonverbal function equivalent to telling the person that it's his or her turn to speak is called
   a. an adaptor
   b. a regulator
   c. a microexpression
   d. an illustrator

4. Body orientation, posture, gestures, facial expressions, and eye movements fit under the term
   a. kinesics
   b. external factors
   c. the relational dimension of nonverbal communication
   d. a function of nonverbal communication

5. You make an appointment for 3:30 to see your doctor. You arrive on time but find yourself sitting in the waiting room for 45 minutes before you're finally called in. This falls under the nonverbal notion of
   a. public distance
   b. status
   c. regulating
   d. chronemics

6. How a touch to the shoulder can be interpreted depends on
   a. the pressure of the touch
   b. whether or not the person is touching both shoulders
   c. whether the touch is intentional or unintentional
   d. what the "toucher" meant by it

7. According to your text,
   a. if we watch people very carefully, we can detect their deception cues
   b. our ability to pick up deception cues is only a little better than leaving it to chance
   c. people avoid eye contact when they are lying
   d. people with nonverbal learning disorders are better detectors of deception

8. Even the distance we place between ourselves and others is a form of nonverbal communication. This is known as
   a. social distance
   b. territoriality
   c. kinesics
   d. proxemics

9. You can learn about a person's economic level, educational level, social position, or trustworthiness from
   a. their clothing
   b. their nonverbal communication
   c. by watching for leakage
   d. their paralanguage

10. You hear two individuals speaking a language you don't recognize, yet you understand that they're both very sad or distraught about something. You could be correct because
    a. paralanguage is an excellent indicator of a person's emotional state
    b. nonverbal cues can give words a particular meaning
    c. even if we don't understand a language, we can identify the emotion and its strength
    d. emblems have the same meanings in every culture

Know Your Terms

Match the following statements with the terms below.
1. Movements of the arms are called _____.
2. Movements in which one part of the body grooms, rubs, holds, or fidgets are called

   _____.
3. The way in which individuals carry themselves is called _____.
4. Nonverbal behaviours that regulate the flow of verbal communication are called

   _____.
5. Nonverbal behaviours that accompany or support verbal messages are called

   _____.
6. A quick flash that crosses a person's face is called a _____.
7. People's words' being incongruent with their nonverbal behaviour is called

   a _____.
8. The degree to which we face toward or away from someone is called _____.
9. Nonverbal behaviours that have a precise meaning within a culture are called

   _____.

10. The ways in which physical setting, architecture, and interior design affect our communication are called _____.
11. Hall's distance zone that ranges from skin contact to about 45 centimetres is called _____.
12. The term used to describe nonverbal vocal messages is _____.
13. The study of the way in which people and animals use space is called _____.
14. Hall's distance zone that is used in conversations and in business is called _____.
15. The study of how humans use and structure time is called _____.
16. A geographical area such as a room, seat, or even a section of the university to which we have made a claim is called _____.
17. The term used to describe the use of stammering or saying "uh," "um," "er," and so on is _____.
18. Nonverbal behaviours that signal an interest in another person are called _____.
19. Signals of deception are called _____.
20. A handshake, a clap on the back, a shove, or a kiss are manifestations of _____.

adaptors	courtship gestures	
body orientation	chronemics	disfluencies
emblems	gestures	illustrators
intimate distance	leakage	microexpression
mixed message	nonverbal communication	paralanguage
personal distance	physical attractiveness	physical environment
posture	proxemics	social distance
public distance	regulators	
territoriality	touch	

Chapter 6 Questions for Thought and Discussion

1. How can you detect deception in computer-mediated communication?
2. In these days of instant messaging, we expect instant responses. Describe how the intentional and unintentional use of time (that is, the length it takes someone to respond to your messages, etc.) affects your relationships.
3. What misunderstandings have occurred in your electronic communication because of nonverbal communication? because of a lack of nonverbal communication?
4. What significance might the quotation from George Orwell's *1984* on page 161 have in today's technological world?
5. Describe how the knowledge you gained by reading this chapter can influence your life in a positive way in terms of the following:
   - family
   - friends
   - your professional life
   - your student life
   - your ability to find and maintain a romantic relationship

Answers

1. c; 2. b; 3. c; 4. a; 5. d; 6. d; 7. b; 8. d; 9. a; 10. c

Matching

1. gestures; 2. adaptors; 3. posture; 4. regulators; 5. illustrators; 6. microexpression; 7. mixed message; 8. body orientation; 9. emblems; 10. physical environment; 11. intimate distance; 12. paralanguage; 13. proxemics; 14. social distance; 15. chronemics; 16. territoriality; 17. disfluencies; 18. courtship gestures; 19. leakage; 20. touch

Chapter in Review

LO¹ Identify the situations in which you listen mindfully and those in which you listen mindlessly, and evaluate the appropriateness of each style in a given situation.

Mindless listening is superficial and involves giving automatic, routine responses. Because it is impossible to listen to everything we hear, mindless listening frees us up to focus on messages that require careful attention. You might listen mindlessly to someone describing a movie that doesn't interest you. Mindful listening involves careful, thoughtful attention and responses. People listen mindfully to issues regarding their money or to a difficulty a friend is experiencing. Because of stereotypes and mindsets, we sometimes listen mindlessly when we should be listening mindfully.

LO² Identify the circumstances in which you listen ineffectively and the poor listening habits you use in these circumstances.

Certain circumstances can make listening easier. Nevertheless, many people have bad listening habits. There are several types of ineffective listening: pseudolistening (pretending), stage-hogging (interrupting to make your point), selective listening (listening only to the good parts), insulated listening (ignoring undesirable topics), defensive listening (taking things personally), ambushing (gathering information to attack the speaker), and insensitive listening (ignoring nonverbal cues that convey feelings). To improve your listening skills, eliminate these habits, talk less, get rid of distractions, don't judge prematurely, and listen for key information.

LO³ Identify the response styles (listed on pages 188–198) that you commonly use when listening to others.

There are several different types of response styles: prompting (using silence to prompt the speaker), questioning (seeking additional informa-tion about the speaker's thoughts and feelings), paraphrasing (repeating the message in your own words), supporting (showing solidarity), analyzing (offering an interpretation of the message), advising (offering helpful suggestions), and judging (evaluating the message as positive or negative). Being able to offer all the response styles will make you a better listener and a more competent communicator.

LO¹

Listening Making sense of others' spoken messages.
Mindless listening Reacting to others' messages automatically, without much mental investment.
Mindful listening Giving careful and thoughtful attention and responses to the messages we receive.
Attending The process of filtering out some messages and focusing on others.
Understanding Occurs when sense is made of a message.
Listening fidelity The degree of congruence between what a listener understands and what the message sender intended to convey.
Responding Giving observable feedback to a speaker.
Remembering The ability to recall information.

LO²

Pseudolistening An imitation of true listening in which the receiver's mind is elsewhere.
Stage-hogging A listening style in which the receiver is more concerned with making a point than with understanding the speaker.
Selective listening A listening style in which receivers respond only to the messages that interest them.
Insulated listening A style in which the receiver ignores undesirable information.
Defensive listening A response style in which the receiver perceives a speaker's comments as an attack.
Ambushing A style in which the receiver listens carefully to gather information to use in an attack on the speaker.
Insensitive listening Failure to recognize the thoughts or feelings that are not directly expressed by a speaker.

LO³

Prompting Using silences and brief statements of encouragement to draw out a speaker.
Questioning A style of helping in which the receiver seeks additional information from the sender to be sure the speaker's thoughts and feelings are being received accurately.
Closed questions Questions that call for a specific or yes/no response.

Open questions Questions that allow the respondent to answer in a variety of ways and to include a great deal of description and detail.

Sincere questions Questions aimed at soliciting information that enables the asker to understand the other person.

Counterfeit questions Questions aimed at sending rather than receiving a message.

Paraphrasing Repeating a speaker's thoughts and/or feelings in the listener's own words. Also known as *active listening*.

Active listening Repeating a speaker's thoughts and/or feelings in the listener's own words. Also known as *paraphrasing*.

Supporting A helping response that reveals a listener's solidarity with the speaker's situation.

Analyzing A helping style in which the listener offers an interpretation of a speaker's message.

Advising A helping response in which the receiver offers suggestions about how the speaker should deal with a problem.

Judging A response in which the receiver evaluates the sender's message either favourably or unfavourably.

LO⁴ Demonstrate a combination of listening styles you could use to respond effectively in a given situation.

The suitability of a listening style depends on the situation. Begin with prompting, questioning, paraphrasing, and supporting to learn more about what's happening. Move on to analyzing, advising, and judging at the individual's request. The best listening style(s) for the circumstance also depends on the other person. Asking how you can help provides insight into which style(s) to use. We generally have one or two default listening styles. Women are good at supporting while men give advice well. You'll be most helpful by excelling at each style.

Chapter 7 Quiz Questions

1. Which statement about gender and communication is not true?
   a. Men tend to offer more advice.
   b. Women are more likely to give supportive responses.
   c. Men are more skilled at composing supportive messages.
   d. Fraternity men challenge their brothers in order to evaluate their attitudes and values.

2. Which of the following is not suggested in the text as a way of listening to help?
   a. analyzing
   b. questioning
   c. prompting
   d. repeating

3. When all your friends tell you something about the person you're seeing that you just don't want to hear, you'll most likely engage in which type of listening?
   a. pseudolistening
   b. selective listening
   c. insulated listening
   d. empathic listening

4. Getting rid of distractions, asking questions, and speaking less are
   a. ways to get others to use the correct type of listening response
   b. some of the methods suggested in the text for offering confirming messages
   c. dimensions of supportive listening
   d. ways to help improve your listening

5. Listening is particularly important in the helping professions. One study indicated that patients liked doctors who
   a. avoided interruptions
   b. paraphrased what the patient said
   c. looked at the patient when speaking
   d. all of the above

6. When lawyers are cross-examining someone, they are most likely engaging in which type of listening?
   a. defensive listening
   b. selective listening
   c. stage-hogging
   d. ambushing

7. Questions that disguise a speaker's true motives are called
   a. counterfeit questions
   b. closed questions
   c. sincere questions
   d. open questions

8. These two terms describe the process in which you repeat a speaker's thoughts and/or feelings in your own words:
   a. paraphrasing and supporting responses
   b. active listening and paraphrasing
   c. advising and paraphrasing responses
   d. supporting responses and active listening

9. According to your text, you'll most likely forget about _____ percent of the original message after two months.
   a. 50
   b. 35
   c. 25
   d. 75

10. Giving the appearance of being attentive while listening to someone is referred to as
    a. pseudolistening
    b. selective listening
    c. insulated listening
    d. empathic listening

Chapter 7 Questions for Thought and Discussion

1. Answer the following questions and then compare your results with others in the class.
   a. We live in a world where the media present information in brief segments. What effect will this have on our ability to listen to complex ideas that take time to explain?
   b. Describe ineffective listening styles that your group thinks are more predominant in electronic contexts.
   c. What types of listening may be done more effectively through computer-mediated and electronic channels (e.g., informational listening versus listening to help)?
   d. How might you be a more effective listener when you use various channels (e.g., telephone, voice mail, e-mail, chat groups) to receive and respond to others' messages?

2. Read the case below and then answer the following questions. Afterward, share your response with others in the class.

   Jen and Sook-yin have been friends since elementary school and are now in their early 30s. Sook-yin has been happily married for 10 years. Jen has been engaged four times and each time has broken it off as the marriage date has approached. Sook-yin has listened, mainly questioning, supporting, and para-phrasing. Jen has just announced another engagement.

   a. Sook-yin wants to give Jen advice this time. Should she? If she does, what would she say? Evaluate the possible effects on their relationship.
   b. Because Sook-yin has known Jen for such a long time, do you think she should use an analyzing style? If she does, what would she say?
   c. What listening styles do you think would be the most helpful to Jen? What would Sook-yin say in the listening style(s) you have chosen?
   d. Pretend you are Sook-yin. Consider the situation, the other person, and yourself. Given these considerations, how would you listen? Give examples.
   e. Suppose the two friends described here were men. Would your answers to any of the preceding questions change?

3. Review the poor listening behaviours below and identify the ones in which you typically engage. Provide an example of each problem behaviour and then indicate how you can eliminate or minimize your use of these poor listening behaviours.
   a. pseudolistening
   b. stage-hogging
   c. selective listening
   d. insulated listening
   e. defensive listening
   f. ambushing
   g. insensitive listening

4. Which of the listening responses do you most often use when helping someone—paraphrasing, questioning, advising, judging, analyzing, supporting, or prompting? Describe a situation in which you felt that you used the wrong helping style. What happened, and how would you correct the situation if given the opportunity?
5. List your overall strengths and weaknesses as a listener and develop a plan to help yourself become a better listener in the future.

Answers

1. c; 2. d; 3. c; 4. d; 5. d; 6. d; 7. a; 8. b; 9. d; 10. a

8 Communication and Relational Dynamics

Chapter in Review

LO¹ Identify factors that have influenced your choice of relational partners.

Appearance gets a relationship started; other characteristics keep it alive. People like those who share similar values and outlooks. Some relationships are complementary—a dominant person and a passive one make a good team. People also like competent and talented individuals as well as anyone who likes them (reciprocal attraction). Disclosure builds liking, and relationships develop as people learn about each other. With proximity, relationships form because of continued exposure. Finally, relationships offer physical, mental, and social rewards. Therefore, some relationships are based on social exchange theory.

LO² Use Knapp's model to describe the nature of communication in the various stages of a relationship.

Divided into the broad phases of "coming together" and "breaking apart," Knapp's model consists of initiating (making contact), experimenting (expressing interest), intensifying (having more contact and disclosure), integrating (taking on a single identity), and bonding (denoting the relationship through a symbolic public gesture). In breaking apart, the stages are differentiating (asserting individual values), circumscribing (reducing contact and commitment), stagnating (losing enthusiasm), avoiding (minimizing contact), and terminating (acknowledging the end of the relationship). Of course, not all relationships terminate.

LO³ Describe the dialectical tensions in a given relationship, how they influence communication, and the most effective strategies for managing them.

Some hold that relationships may continue because individuals deal with the dialectical tensions (opposing forces) that exist naturally in relationships. The connection–autonomy dialectic can be managed by spending enough time together to maintain and nurture the relationship but allowing time apart to develop independent interests. The openness–privacy dialectic (needing both communication and privacy) is managed by disclosing information about daily affairs but keeping some things private. The predictability–novelty dialectic is managed by have some routines but also allowing for novelty in terms of social life, vacations, and so forth.

LO⁴ Describe the possible strategies for repairing a given relational transgression.

Relational transgressions can be minor or significant, social or relational, deliberate or unintentional, or one-time or incremental. Repairing them calls for a discussion of the transgression and an acceptance of

LO¹

Interpersonal relationship An association in which the parties meet each other's social needs to a greater or lesser degree.

Social exchange theory A socioeconomic theory of relational development that suggests people seek relationships in which the rewards they receive from others are equal to or greater than the costs they encounter.

LO²

Relational maintenance Communication aimed at keeping relationships operating smoothly and satisfactorily.

Initiating The first stage in relational development, in which the parties express interest in one another.

Uncertainty reduction The process of getting to know others by gaining more information about them.

Experimenting An early stage in relational development, consisting of a search for common ground. If the experimentation is successful, the relationship will progress to *intensifying*. If not, it may go no further.

Intensifying A stage of relational development, preceding *integrating*, in which the parties move toward integration by increasing the amount of contact and the breadth and depth of self-disclosure.

Integrating A stage of relational development in which the parties begin to take on a single identity.

Bonding A stage of relational development in which the parties make symbolic public gestures to show that their relationship exists.

Differentiating A stage of relational development in which the parties reestablish their individual identities after having bonded together.

Circumscribing A stage of relational development in which parties begin to reduce the scope of their contact and commitment to one another.

Stagnating A stage of relational development characterized by declining enthusiasm and standardized forms of behaviour.

Avoiding A stage of relational development, immediately prior to *terminating*, in which the parties minimize contact with one another.

Terminating The concluding stage of relational development, characterized by the acknowledgment of one or both parties that the relationship is over.

LO³

Dialectical tensions Inherent conflicts that arise when two opposing or incompatible forces exist simultaneously.

Connection–autonomy dialectic The dialectical tension between a desire for connection and a need for independence in a relationship.

Openness–privacy dialectic The dialectical tension between a desire for open communication and the need for privacy in a relationship.

Predictability–novelty dialectic The dialectical tension between a desire for stability and the need for novelty in a relationship.

Relational commitment An implied or explicit promise to remain and make a relationship successful.

LO⁵

Content message A message that communicates information about the subject being discussed.

Relational message A message that essentially makes statements about how the parties feel toward one another.

LO⁶

Affinity The degree to which people like or appreciate one another.

Immediacy The degree of interest and attention that we feel toward and communicate to others.

Respect The social need to be held in esteem by others.

Control The degree to which the parties in a relationship have the power to influence one another.

Metacommunication Messages that people exchange, verbally or nonverbally, about their relationship—communication about communication.

LO⁷

Intimacy A state of personal sharing arising from physical, intellectual, and/or emotional contact.

LO⁸

Self-disclosure The process of deliberately revealing information about oneself that is significant and not normally known by others.

Social penetration A model that describes relationships in terms of their breadth and depth.

Breadth The first dimension of self-disclosure, involving the range of subjects being discussed.

Depth A dimension of self-disclosure involving a shift from relatively nonrevealing messages to more personal ones.

Cliché A ritualized, stock statement delivered in response to a social situation.

---

responsibility for the transgression. To apologize, acknowledge that the transgression was wrong, offer a sincere apology, and offer some kind of compensation. You must be genuine, and your nonverbal and verbal communication must be congruent. To forgive a transgressor, offer an explicit acceptance of the apology and indicate the implications that the transgression has for the relationship.

LO⁵ Identify the content and relational dimensions of communication in a given transaction.

The content dimension refers to the information you wish to convey (e.g., why you selected a particular holiday destination). The relational dimension refers to your feelings about the individual, commonly expressed nonverbally. Four categories of relational messages are affinity (the degree to which individuals like or appreciate one another), immediacy (the amount of attention given to one another), respect (the esteem felt for one another), and power (the degree to which the parties have control over one another).

LO⁶ Describe how metacommunication can be used to improve the quality of a given relationship.

Metacommunication is communication about communication, and using it can improve the quality of relationships. It can be used to resolve conflict because it shifts emphasis from the content to the relational dimension of the relationship. It can also be used to reinforce the satisfying aspects of a relationship and boosts the odds that positive behaviour will continue.

LO⁷ Identify the dimensions of intimacy and how they are expressed in a specific relationship.

Intimacy has several dimensions: Physical intimacy involves sexual expression; intellectual intimacy refers to the closeness of sharing thoughts and ideas; emotional intimacy occurs when we share feelings. Sharing activities also provides avenues of intimacy. Women self-disclose for intimacy while men prefer to engage in shared activities, thus causing misunderstandings in heterosexual couples. Intimacy also varies across cultures. In collectivistic cultures, people communicate differently with "in-group" members than they do with "out-groups," whereas in individualistic cultures, the distinctions between personal and casual relationships are blurred. Mediated communication promotes and maintains intimacy in contemporary relationships.

LO⁸ Use the social penetration and Johari Window models to identify the nature of self-disclosing communication in one of your relationships.

The social penetration model explains self-disclosure in terms of breadth (range of topics covered) and depth (from clichés and facts to opinions and feelings). Greater depth and breadth result in greater intimacy. The Johari Window model examines self-disclosure from four perspectives: information known to you and others (open area); information unknown to you but known to others (blind area); information known to you but unknown to others (hidden area); information unknown to you and others (unknown area). The model allows you to examine the self-disclosure in your relationships.

LO⁹ Outline the potential benefits and risks of disclosing in a selected situation.

Benefits of self-disclosure include catharsis, reciprocity, self-clarification, self-validation, identity management, relationship maintenance and enhancement, and social influence. The risks are rejection, negative impressions, decrease in relational satisfaction, loss of influence, and hurting the other person. To minimize risks, determine if you must disclose, if the relationship is important, if the risk of disclosing is reasonable, and if the disclosure is relevant. You might also determine if it will be constructive, understood by the listener, and reciprocated.

LO¹⁰ Assess the most competent mixture of candour and equivocation in a given situation.

While malicious lying is frowned upon, benevolent lies (ones that may help an individual) are more acceptable. Equivocating is also a viable option as it spares embarrassment and hurt and saves face for both parties ("You're right. That's some outfit!"). Hinting is more direct than equivocating but depends on the listener's ability to pick up on the hint. Lies aren't challenged when we expect someone to lie, when the lie is mutually advantageous, when lying means avoiding embarrassment and confrontation, or when we asked the person to lie.

Chapter 8 Quiz Questions

1. Couples who say that their relationship broke up either because they didn't spend enough time together or because they were feeling trapped by the relationship were most likely
   a. experiencing a lot of relational trangressions
   b. dealing with a predictability–novelty dialectic
   c. experiencing a lot of unintentional transgressions
   d. dealing with a connection–autonomy dialectic

2. The openness–privacy dialectic refers to
   a. the notion that as we form relationships we become more open with that individual and thus experience less privacy
   b. the notion of having a relationship with a very private individual
   c. relationships in which both partners are free to come and go as they please, as long as they respect one another's privacy
   d. a time in a relationship when one partner wants or needs more privacy and the other expects that person to be much more open than he or she currently is

3. How Jack feels about Lucy comes through in his tone of voice and his nonverbal communication. This type of message is referred to as
   a. a content message
   b. an interpersonal transgression
   c. a relational message
   d. catharsis

4. Kyle and Matthew are associates who support one another's businesses. This type of relationship could be described as
   a. managing dialectical tensions
   b. bonding
   c. differentiating
   d. social exchange theory

5. It's odd that Ella and Hanna are friends because Ella is very tidy, conservative, and reserved. Hanna is messy, creative, open-minded, and outgoing. Their continued friendship exemplifies
   a. reciprocal attraction
   b. complementarity
   c. relational transgressions
   d. metacommunication

6. An association in which the parties meet each other's social needs to a greater or lesser degree refers to
   a. integrating
   b. a relational commitment
   c. the connection–autonomy dialectic
   d. an interpersonal relationship

7. Integration, reaffirmation, and balance are
   a. ways to balance dialectical tensions
   b. stages in the development and decline model of relationships
   c. ways to manage dialectical tensions
   d. strategies to repair relational transgressions

8. Conflicts that arise when two opposing or incompatible forces exist simultaneously are known as
   a. the predictability–novelty dialectic
   b. recalibration
   c. the openness–privacy dialectic
   d. dialectical tension

9. According to Richard Conville, you can expect that your relationships
   a. will change constantly throughout the process
   b. will basically remain the same
   c. will stay at the same level
   d. will not continually move through the stages outlined by Knapp

10. Jill finds that every once in a while, her partner will get extremely violent and hit things in the house. This is an example of
    a. an unintentional transgression
    b. a significant transgression
    c. violating a social transgression
    d. a one-time transgression

Know Your Knapp

Match the following with Knapp's developmental stages.
1. A stage of relational development characterized by declining enthusiasm and standardized forms of behaviour. _____
2. A stage of relational development in which the parties make symbolic public gestures to show that their relationship exists. _____
3. A stage of relational development in which parties begin to reduce the scope of their contact and commitment to one another. _____

4. The concluding stage of relational development, characterized by the acknowledgment of one or both parties that the relationship is over. _____
5. The first stage in relational development, in which the parties express interest in one another. _____
6. A stage of relational development in which the parties begin to take on a single identity. _____
7. An early stage in relational development, consisting of a search for common ground. If this stage is successful, the relationship will progress to intensifying. If not, it may go no further. _____
8. A stage of relational development in which the parties reestablish their individual identities after having bonded together. _____
9. A stage of relational development, preceding integrating, in which the parties move toward integration by increasing the amount of contact and the breadth and depth of self-disclosure. _____
10. A stage of relational development, immediately prior to terminating, in which the parties minimize contact with one another. _____

Stages

avoiding	initiating
bonding	integrating
circumscribing	intensifying
differentiating	stagnating
experimenting	terminating

Chapter 8 Questions for Thought and Discussion

1. Using Mark Knapp's model of relationship development and decline, analyze a romantic relationship you once had. Would a knowledge of the dialectical tensions and how to reduce them have "saved" your relationship? Explain your response.
2. We form relationships for a variety of reasons: appearance, similarity, complementarity, reciprocal attraction, competence, disclosure, proximity, and rewards. Match a relationship you've had in your life with each of these rationales for a relationship. Do you recognize any patterns?
3. Think back to some of the relational transgressions that you have experienced. Indicate which category they fell into and examine them in terms of repair. Explain the role that forgiveness played in these transgressions.
4. Draw your Johari Window for each of the following and explain how the differences in the windows compare to the differences in how the relationships affect your life.
   a. a sibling or cousin
   b. a close friend
   c. a boss or supervisor
   d. a romantic partner

Answers

1. d; 2. d; 3. c; 4. d; 5. b; 6. d; 7. c; 8. d; 9. a; 10. b

Matching

1. stagnating; 2. bonding; 3. circumscribing; 4. terminating; 5. initiating; 6. integrating; 7. experimenting; 8. differentiating; 9. intensifying; 10. avoiding

To help you succeed, we have designed a review card for each chapter.

9 Improving Communication Climates

Chapter in Review

LO¹ Identify confirming, disagreeing, and disconfirming messages and patterns in your own important relationships and describe their consequences.

Confirming messages convey value and come in the form of recognition, acknowledgment, and endorsement. Disconfirming messages convey a lack of value and come in the form of interruptions or responses that are impervious, irrelevant, tangential, impersonal, ambiguous, or incongruous. Disagreeing messages that say the other is wrong are conveyed through aggressiveness, complaining, and argumentativeness.

LO² Describe how communication climates develop through positive or negative reciprocal communication patterns.

Communication climates develop through reciprocating communication patterns that reinforce the other's messages (spirals). Escalatory conflict spirals build on one another to create negative climates while positive spirals lead to positive communication climates. De-escalatory spirals can also be destructive in that parties slowly lessen their dependence on one another, withdraw, and become less interested in the relationship.

LO³ Use Gibb's categories to create messages that are likely to build supportive rather than defensive communication climates.

To develop supportive climates, use description (focus on speaker's thoughts and feelings) rather than evaluation; take a problem orientation (find solution together) rather than controlling the situation (imposing solution); be spontaneous (honest) instead of strategic (hiding ulterior motives); demonstrate empathy instead of neutrality or indifference; recognize equality rather than acting superior; and exercise provisionalism (acknowledging opposing opinions) instead of certainty.

LO⁴ Create appropriate nondefensive responses to real or hypothetical criticisms.

To respond nondefensively, seek more information so you'll understand the critic better. You can do this by asking for specifics and/or making guesses about the specifics, paraphrasing the critic's remarks to help defuse the intensity of the attack, asking what the critic wants, asking about the consequences of your behaviour, or asking if anything else is

LO¹

Communication climate The emotional tone of a relationship between two or more individuals.
Confirming communication A message that expresses caring or respect for another person.
Disconfirming communication A message that expresses a lack of caring or respect for another person.
Disagreeing messages Messages that say "you're wrong" in one way or another.

LO²

Spiral A reciprocal communication pattern in which each person's message reinforces the other's.
Escalatory conflict spiral A communication spiral in which one attack leads to another until the initial skirmish escalates into a full-fledged battle.
De-escalatory conflict spiral A communication spiral in which the parties slowly lessen their dependence on one another, withdraw, and become less invested in the relationship.
Defensiveness The attempt to protect a presenting image a person believes is being attacked.
Face-threatening act Behaviour by another that is perceived as attacking an individual's presenting image, or face.

LO³

Evaluative communication Messages in which the sender judges the receiver in some way, usually resulting in a defensive response.
Descriptive communication Messages that describe the speaker's position without evaluating others. Synonymous with "I" language.
Controlling communication Messages in which the sender tries to impose some sort of outcome on the receiver, usually resulting in a defensive reaction.
Problem orientation A supportive style of communication described by Jack Gibb in which the communicators focus on working together to solve their problems instead of trying to impose their own solutions on one another.
Strategy A defence-arousing style of communication described by Jack Gibb in which the sender tries to manipulate or deceive a receiver.

Spontaneity A supportive communication behaviour described by Jack Gibb in which the sender expresses a message without any attempt to manipulate the receiver.

Neutrality A defence-arousing behaviour described by Jack Gibb in which the sender expresses indifference.

Empathy The ability to project oneself onto another person's point of view so as to experience the other's thoughts and feelings.

Superiority A defence-arousing style of communication described by Jack Gibb in which the sender states or implies that the receiver is not worthy of respect.

Equality A type of supportive communication described by Jack Gibb suggesting that the sender regards the receiver as worthy of respect.

Certainty An attitude behind messages that dogmatically implies that the speaker's position is correct and the other person's ideas are not worth considering. Likely to generate a defensive response.

Provisionalism A supportive style of communication described by Jack Gibb in which the sender expresses a willingness to consider the other person's position.

Behavioural description An account that refers only to observable phenomena.

Interpretation statement A statement that describes a speaker's interpretation of the meaning of another person's behaviour.

Feeling statement An expression of a sender's emotions that results from interpretation of sense data.

Consequence statement An explanation of the results that follow either from the behaviour of the person to whom the message is addressed or from the speaker's interpretation of and feelings about the addressee's behaviour. Consequence statements can describe what happens to the speaker, the addressee, or others.

Intention statement A description of where the speaker stands on an issue, what he or she wants, or how he or she plans to act in the future.

bothering the other person. You can also agree with the critic even if you disagree with the criticism. For instance, you could agree with some of the facts or with how the critic perceived the situation.

Chapter 9 Quiz Questions

1. A disagreeing message
   a. is a confirming message
   b. consists of evaluation, strategy, and neutrality
   c. consists of complaining, aggressiveness, and argumentativeness
   d. is a nonconfirming message

2. When you decide to agree with your critic, you
   a. have to agree with the facts
   b. can agree with the critic's perceptions but not the facts
   c. have to agree with the facts and the critic's perceptions
   d. have to be prepared to offer an apology

3. When you want to respond nondefensively to criticism, the text recommends that you
   a. basically seek more information and agree with the critic
   b. ask for specifics, guess about specifics, and paraphrase the speaker's ideas
   c. make sure to use tangential, impersonal, and incongruous responses
   d. be extra aware of escalatory conflict spirals

4. A new boss arrives at the office and tells the staff that changes are going into effect immediately. The strategy worked at other places and it will work here as well. A couple of employees offer some suggestions, but their ideas are dismissed. Which of Jack Gibb's categories is the boss demonstrating?
   a. evaluation
   b. problem orientation
   c. provisionalism
   d. certainty

5. Which aspect of responding nondefensively does the following example represent?

   Person A: I can't believe you said we'd pick up Sam on the way to the concert.
   Person B: Are you saying that I should call him and tell him he has to get there himself?
   Person A: No, I just wish you'd asked me first.

   a. asking about specifics
   b. paraphrasing the speaker's ideas
   c. asking what the critic wants
   d. asking about the consequences of your behaviour

6. When you try to protect your presenting self as a person attacks your behaviour, you are most likely
   a. engaging in escalatory communication
   b. being defensive
   c. to offer consequence statements
   d. paraphrasing the speaker's ideas

7. Jane always feels good after she speaks with Professor MacLean. He listens intently to her ideas and speaks in a very respectful manner. Based on these statements, which of the following best describes Professor MacLean's communication?
   a. He is engaging in what Jack Gibb calls problem orientation.
   b. He is using confirming communication.
   c. He is using intentional statements.
   d. He is sending face-saving messages.

8. Which of the following is a consequence statement?
   a. When you don't pick up the groceries like you said you would, I feel frustrated.
   b. You didn't pick up the groceries like you said you would, you lazy jerk.
   c. You didn't pick up the groceries like you said you would. Were you working late?
   d. You didn't pick up the groceries like you said you would, and now we don't have bread or milk for tomorrow's breakfast.

9. When you use the assertive message format,
   a. the elements must be delivered in a specific manner
   b. make sure to keep the elements separate and clear for the listener
   c. seek more information before you begin
   d. word the messages to fit your personal communication style

10. The most visible way that disconfirming messages reinforce one another is through
    a. de-escalatory conflict spirals
    b. aggressiveness
    c. escalatory conflict spirals
    d. complaining and argumentativeness

Know Your Terms

Match the statements with the terms below.
1. A disagreeing message. _____
2. Acknowledgment. _____
3. Final element in the assertive message format. _____
4. A way to respond nondefensively. _____
5. Being completely indifferent to someone. _____
6. Finding a solution that satisfies both parties. _____
7. A message that challenges the image we want to project. _____
8. Providing an objective description of an event without interpreting it. _____
9. A factor that is consistently connected to a positive workplace. _____
10. Messages that show a lack of regard for the other person. _____

argumentativeness
behavioural description
confirming message
disagreeing message
disconfirming messages
encouragement
escalatory spiral
face-threatening act
guess about specifics
intention
interpretation
neutrality
spiral
strategy
problem orientation

Chapter 9 Questions for Thought and Discussion

1. Begin by reflecting on the various types of disconfirming messages: verbal abuse, complaining, impervious responses, interrupting, irrelevant responses, tangential responses, impersonal responses, ambiguous responses, and incongruous responses. Then answer the following questions:
   a. Which types of disconfirming messages do you find the most hurtful or frustrating when they are directed at you?
   b. Are there particular people in your life who give you disconfirming messages? If so, describe how they make you feel and how you tend to react.
   c. Which disconfirming messages are you most likely to use?
   d. To whom are you most likely to direct your disconfirming messages, and how do they respond?
   e. How can you reduce the number of disconfirming messages you send and receive?

2. Think of a time when someone criticized you and it left you feeling bad. Contrast that experience with a time when someone criticized in a way that did not have a negative outcome. What accounted for the differences between the two experiences?
3. How do you respond when someone directs criticism toward you? Is there room for improvement on your part? If so, explain how you will change in future interactions.
4. Print the messages you and a friend or partner exchanged over a week-long period. With the printouts in front of you, engage in a face-to-face conversation to explore variations in the intended and received messages. For each message sent, explain how you felt at the time and what your intent was. For each message received, explain your interpretation and how it made you feel. Continue back and forth until every message is reviewed. What did you learn from this exercise?

Answers

1. c; 2. b; 3. a; 4. d; 5. c; 6. b; 7. b; 8. d; 9. d; 10. c

Matching

1. argumentativeness; 2. confirming message; 3. intention; 4. guess about specifics; 5. neutrality; 6. problem orientation; 7. face-threatening act; 8. behavioural description; 9. encouragement; 10. disconfirming messages

10 Managing Interpersonal Conflicts
Chapter in Review

LO¹ Identify the conflicts in your important relationships and how satisfied you are with the way they have been handled.

Conflict, an expressed struggle, is an inevitable part of any relationship and comes about as a result of perceived incompatible goals (e.g., wanting different things out of a vacation), perceived scarce resources (e.g., how extra money will be spent), interdependence (we're in this together), or interference from another party. Whatever the cause, conflict is natural and can actually be healthy in a relationship.

LO² Describe your personal conflict styles, evaluate their effectiveness, and suggest alternatives as appropriate.

When engaging in avoidance (lose–lose), the involved parties ignore the problem. When accommodating (lose–win), one party gives in. These styles are more positively regarded in high-context, collectivistic cultures. When competing (win–lose), parties try to resolve the issue to their own advantage, which can involve direct or passive aggression. When compromising (partial lose–lose), both parties sacrifice to gain a little of what they want. Accommodating (win–win) seeks a solution that meets everyone's needs. Which style to use depends on the relationship, the situation, the other person, and your goals.

LO³ Identify the relational conflict styles, patterns of behaviour, and conflict rituals that define a given relationship.

Relational conflict styles are patterns of disagreement that repeat themselves. In the complementary conflict style, partners use different but mutually reinforcing behaviours. In the symmetrical conflict style, both partners use the same tactics. In the parallel conflict style, the approach varies according to the situation. In addition, there are several patterns of behaviour: nonintimate-aggressive, nonintimate-nonaggressive, intimate-aggressive, and intimate-nonaggressive. A conflict ritual is an unacknowledged repeating pattern of interlocking behaviours used by participants in a conflict.

LO⁴ Demonstrate how you could use the win–win approach in a given conflict.

To use the win–win approach, (1) identify your problem and unmet needs; (2) make a date to discuss the problem; (3) describe your problem and needs by using the assertive message format; (4) consider your partner's point of view; (5) negotiate a solution by identifying and defining the conflict, generating a number of possible solutions, evaluating the alternative solutions, and deciding on the best solution; and (6) follow up the solution. After a "test run," you may decide to alter the solution.

LO¹

Conflict An expressed struggle between at least two interdependent parties who perceive incompatible goals, scarce resources, and interference from the other party in achieving their goals.

LO²

Avoiding A lose–lose conflict style in which the parties ignore the problem at hand.
Accommodating A win–lose conflict style in which the communicator submits to a situation rather than attempting to have his or her needs met.
Competing A win–lose approach to conflicts that seeks to resolve them in one's own way.
Direct aggression A criticism or demand that threatens the face of the person at whom it is directed.
Passive aggression An indirect expression of aggression that occurs when a communicator expresses hostility in an obscure or manipulative way.
Compromising An approach to conflict resolution in which both parties attain at least part of what they wanted through self-sacrifice.
Collaborating A conflict management style that seeks win–win solutions.

LO³

Relational conflict style A pattern of managing disagreements that repeats itself over time in a relationship.
Complementary conflict style A relational conflict style in which partners use different but mutually reinforcing behaviours.
Symmetrical conflict style A relational conflict style in which both partners use the same tactics.
Parallel conflict style A relational conflict style in which the approach of the partners varies from one situation to another.
Conflict ritual An unacknowledged repeating pattern of interlocking behaviour used by participants in a conflict.

LO⁴

Dysfunctional conflict Conflict that creates animosity, causes interpersonal stress, and hinders a group's progress.

Functional conflict Positive conflict that focuses on issues rather than personalities.

Chapter 10 Quiz Questions

1. When Charley and Allen have a problem about something, they use the same old behaviours every time to deal with it. Clearly, they have
   a. a compromising conflict style
   b. constructive conflict skills
   c. a complementary conflict style
   d. a symmetrical conflict style

2. Work teams that have a lot of functional conflict
   a. cause people to suffer undue stress
   b. make better final decisions
   c. tend to use parallel conflict styles
   d. are common in high-context cultures

3. In terms of culture,
   a. people tend to be more assertive in low-context cultures
   b. people tend to be more nonassertive in low-context cultures
   c. there is no relationship between assertiveness and the high- or low-context cultures
   d. assertiveness is common in collectivistic cultures

4. Describing your problems and needs
   a. is part and parcel of an assertive communication style
   b. is considered a positive conflict skill
   c. is a conflict ritual
   d. is common in a parallel conflict style

5. To determine which conflict style is best for a situation, you should
   a. ask the person what works best for him or her
   b. put your goals aside and let the relationship unfold
   c. consider the particular situation
   d. use the style that has worked best for you in the past

6. Considering the relationship, your goals, and the other person are ways to
   a. determine which conflict style to use
   b. engage in a win–win conflict style
   c. become more sensitive to the gender dimension of conflict
   d. look at the elements in the complementary relational conflict style

7. Direct aggression and passive aggression are common in which conflict style?
   a. compromise
   b. avoiding
   c. accommodating
   d. competing

8. Which of the following is not a characteristic of conflict?
   a. dependence
   b. perceived scarce resources
   c. expressed struggle
   d. perceived incompatible goals

9. Although Jill and Kim have worked together for years, they don't get along. Therefore, they do their best to avoid one another. Their conflict style is best described as
   a. nonintimate–aggressive
   b. nonintimate–nonaggressive
   c. intimate–aggressive
   d. intimate–nonaggressive

10. Character attacks, appearance attacks, and competence attacks are all examples of
    a. a lose–lose conflict style
    b. passive aggression
    c. direct aggression
    d. a symmetrical conflict style

Know Your Terms

Match the following with the terms below.

1. Make a date. _____
2. Conflict that focuses on the issues rather than personalities. _____
3. A low amount of attacking or blaming in the relationship. _____
4. Repeating patterns of interlocking behaviours by participants in conflict. _____
5. The style used by the couple who decided to vacation in PEI. _____
6. A crazymaker's approach. _____
7. When both parties get at least part of what they wanted. _____

accommodating
collaborating
compromise
constructive conflict skill
conflict ritual
dysfunctional conflict
functional conflict
intimate-nonaggressive
nonintimate-nonaggressive
relational conflict style
the pseudoaccommodator

Answers

1. d; 2. b; 3. a; 4. b; 5. c; 6. a; 7. d; 8. a; 9. b; 10. c

Matching

a. constructive conflict skill; b. functional conflict; c. intimate-nonaggressive; d. conflict ritual; e. collaborating; f. the pseudoaccommodator; g. compromise

We know that no two students are alike. **LOOK** was developed to help you learn **Interpersonal Communications** in a way that works for you.

Not only is the format fresh and contemporary, it's also concise and focused. And **LOOK** is loaded with a variety of supplements, like chapter review cards, printable flashcards, and more!

At www.icanlookinout.com, you will find interactive flashcards, crossword puzzles, discipline-specific activities, a glossary of terms, and more. To test your knowledge of key concepts. It includes plenty of resources to help you study, no matter what learning style you like best!

"I enjoy the cards in the back of the book and the fact that it partners with the website."

—Cassandra Jewell, Sir Sandford Fleming College

Visit **www.icanlookinout.com** to find the resources you need today!